D0536728

Fix Your Own PC

Eighth Edition

Fix Your Own PC

Eighth Edition

by Corey Sandler

Wiley Publishing, Inc.

Fix Your Own PC, Eighth Edition

Published by
Wiley Publishing, Inc.
111 River Street
Hoboken, NJ 07030-5774
www.wiley.com

Copyright © 2007 by Wiley Publishing, Inc., Indianapolis, Indiana

Published by Wiley Publishing, Inc., Indianapolis, Indiana

Published simultaneously in Canada

For general information on our other products and services, please contact our Customer Care Department within the U.S. at 800-762-2974, outside the U.S. at 317-572-3993, or fax 317-572-4002.

For technical support, please visit www.wiley.com/techsupport.

Wiley also publishes its books in a variety of electronic formats. Some content that appears in print may not be available in electronic books.

Library of Congress Control Number: 2007920004

ISBN: 978-0-470-10787-4

Manufactured in the United States of America

10 9 8 7 6 5 4 3 2 1

WILEY

About the Author

Corey Sandler is one of the pioneers of computer journalism. After covering IBM for Gannett Newspapers and the Associated Press, he became the first executive editor of *PC Magazine*. He was later the founding editor of *Digital News*. Sandler has written more than 180 books on computer, business, video game, and travel topics. Recent bestsellers include *Fix Your Own PC,* Seventh Edition (Wiley), the *Econoguide Travel Book* series (Globe Pequot), *Upgrading & Fixing Laptops For Dummies* (Wiley), and *Laptops For Dummies Quick Reference* (Wiley).

*To my father, who showed me the way things work.
Ask me how to drive to the post office, and I explain
how a carburetor works.*

Author's Acknowledgments

Let's take a look behind the scenes of this book:

At the Word Association offices, Janice Keefe managed operations and the author with good cheer and professionalism. Tom Badgett, regular squadron leader of my high-tech flying circus, worried the bits and bytes as technical editor for this edition.

Thanks to Pat O'Brien, Kevin Kent, and Greg Croy of Wiley Publishing, Inc. for their capable stewardship of the manuscript.

They follow in the capable footsteps of old friends Tracy Brown, Sharon Eames, Ed Adams, Martine Edwards, Juliana Aldous, Terry Somerson, Brenda McLaughlin, Paul Farrell, Jono Hardjowirigo, and Michael Sprague, champions of the book in its earlier editions.

Thanks, too, to editor Tonya Cupp, a worthy and professional partner, as well as the entire production and art team at Wiley Publishing, Inc.

Preface

What? You want me to take off the covers of my PC and poke around inside?

Yes, actually. That's the reason you bought this book, right?

But wait: I'll be very gentle. And all the work will be very basic. You are *not* going to be building a PC from nuts and bolts; there will be no wiring and soldering involved. And, to tell the truth . . . as I promise I will . . . the majority of upgrades and workarounds for a modern machine now occur outside of the case; today's computers are designed to work with an almost unlimited supply of devices that attach to external ports and connectors.

This is the eighth time that we have come together in these pages. The first edition of this book was published all the way back in 1990, when the PC was still a slow and clumsy toddler. I had been present at the birth, in 1981, becoming the first Executive Editor of *PC Magazine* soon after IBM changed an enthusiasts' hobby into a multi-billion-dollar business.

In some ways, the original IBM PC (like the one I still have in a closet of my office) bears the same relation to a modern personal computer that a Ford Model T does to a 2007 Lamborghini Murcielago. The first widely sold automobile and today's most expensive luxury roadster each have four wheels, an engine, a steering mechanism, and a set of brakes; the first PC and the latest Windows Vista Pentium duo-core computer each have a processor, memory, video adapter, keyboard, and monitor. Although the original PC was slow and limited in its capabilities, today's machines have many more similarities than differences.

And even as the pace of change moves faster than ever before and the underlying technology of personal computers is more and more complex, the process of making repairs and upgrades has become more and more simple.

Modern computers are well made, but they are still not capable of eternal life. According to a survey by the Gartner consulting group in 2006, a desktop system purchased in 2005-2006 has about a 5 percent chance of failure in its first year of life and about a 12 percent chance of serious problems by its fourth year of use; both of these figures represent an improvement of several percent over estimates done two years before.

More so than ever, computers are a mix-and-match product. Think about it: You don't throw away your car when the battery fails or a tire goes flat; you can even consider major changes, such as replacing an engine with a more powerful or updated model. So, too, you can update your computer and its memory, drives, and adapters.

And as computers and software become smarter, they are capable of assisting you in their own upkeep. Modern motherboards, controller chips, and adapters can report on the health of a system, working closely with the Windows operating systems.

All that said, I will be the first to admit that I once trembled at the thought of applying a screwdriver to a brand-spanking-new PC. But I can assure you that after the first time you add more memory, plug in a video card, and install a replacement or second hard drive, you'll find yourself prowling the corridors of your office or the streets of your town in search of more challenging electronic territory to conquer.

Why Fix Your Own PC?

First of all, you should consider fixing your own PC *because you can*.

PCs are constructed with a modular design — a sort of high-tech Lego set — that lets even nontechnical types unplug one module and replace it with another quite easily. The biggest challenge is not the actual repair or upgrade process but figuring out which modules to change and whether to do so makes economic sense.

And although computers have become incredibly more complex over their short history, the number of modules within them has actually decreased. Memory is now installed in huge blocks instead of bit by bit, and motherboards are now highly integrated, meaning that they include many functions that used to be handled by accessories.

The advent of the Universal Serial Bus (USB) has moved many of the expansions and extensions of the computer out of the box. (The same is true of the less-used FireWire port and the developing External SATA system.) If you need another hard disk drive or a DVD-RW drive or a Voice Over Internet Protocol adapter, you just plug a cable into a port on the back (or front) of the computer and let the machine's intelligence and the operating system's instructions figure out how to make them work. *Fix Your Own PC* will give you a road map to working inside and outside of the box. I'll help you do it yourself so that you can save time and money, customize your system in every way, and give yourself the sense of pride that comes with accomplishing work on your own.

This book is your personal guide to diagnosing, fixing, and understanding your PC. I direct you in words, with tons of photos and illustrations, as well as troubleshooting flowcharts through all the nooks and crannies of your personal computer.

Who Should Read This Book?

Repairing a PC is much less physically challenging than fixing a toaster, a bicycle, or an automobile. It does, though, require quite a bit more expenditure of logical energy. In other words, this is a job that exercises the muscle between your ears.

This book is not for the PC technician, the microelectronics designer, or the neighborhood propeller-head who wants to build a PC from a box of resistors, transistors, copper wire, and chewing gum. Not that there's anything wrong with that. . . .

Instead, this book is for the intelligent, adventurous, nontechnical PC user. You are someone who's not afraid to take a screwdriver to a PC (or if you are, you soon won't be anymore), and you want to know how to change a hard drive, replace balky memory or add more, or figure out why your monitor has gone black.

This book presents news that you can use. Just like you don't have to know how a carburetor works in order to drive to the post office, you don't have to know the coercivity levels of the read-write head in order to install a hard drive.

The Tools You Need

Repair jobs on PCs require few specialized tools. You can purchase a simple computer tool kit from mail-order houses or computer superstores. Here's a basic kit for all the projects in this book:

1. **A set of good-quality Phillips-head screwdrivers.** These are the screwdrivers with the X-shaped head. You want small-, medium-, and large-diameter heads.
2. **A set of standard flat-blade screwdrivers.** You should have screwdrivers in small, medium, and large sizes.
3. **An antistatic strap or grounding pad.** These inexpensive devices are available at most computer stores or through mail-order outfits.

I'd also suggest that you have at hand a vacuum cleaner with a soft bristle brush end and a strong pinpoint light source. You also need a clean and sturdy work surface; I recommend a desk or table with a white or light-colored surface.

Another nicety: a claw part holder to grab onto tiny screws and start them into a hole. Oh, and an empty egg carton or a compartmented plastic jewelry box to hold parts when they're temporarily out of their assigned place. That's all you need to make nearly any repair or upgrade to a PC. If you choose to get into some advanced projects, you'll want to beg, steal, or borrow a multifunction voltmeter.

What's in This Book?

Through the years, this book has helped hundreds of thousands of readers understand how their PCs work — and to solve the knotty modern-day problems that sooner or later afflict your electronic desktop companion.

These pages cover PCs from the first IBM right through to the latest Intel Core 2 Duo, Intel Pentium D, Intel Pentium 4 Extreme Edition, Intel Pentium 4, Intel Celeron, Intel Itanium, AMD Athlon 64 X2, AMD Athlon, and AMD Duron screamers. This book's newest edition has been completely updated and expanded, and it includes details on new and enhanced technologies including PCI Express slots in 1X, 4X, and 16X variations, the accelerated graphics port (AGP); the Universal Serial Bus (USB), including version 2.0; Serial ATA hard drives and External SATA devices; enhanced IDE (now also known as Parallel ATA) controllers and hard drives; new memory technologies; CD-Rs and CD-RWs, DVDs; and much more.

How This Book Is Organized

This book consists of 24 chapters, a special section of troubleshooting flowcharts that guide you to the sections of the book that will best help you diagnose and fix your PC's problems, a glossary of technical terms, an encyclopedia of cables and connectors, and a suggested hardware and software tool kit for readers.

On the CD-ROM that is included with the book you'll find further resources, including step-by-step video demonstrations of some of the most common PC repair and upgrade projects.

In this book, I begin with an exploration of the modular design of the computer, move on to a discussion of the family tree of CPUs (the microprocessor brain of the PC), delve into BIOS chips (the set of basic instructions for the hardware), and then look at the bus (the superhighway that interconnects the parts). Next, I discuss some basic hardware skills, including a tour of the motherboard. And then I take apart a brand-new machine. From there, it's on to detailed chapters covering major components of the machine — from memory to floppy and hard drives, monitors, serial and parallel ports, modems, printers, mice, and scanners.

A synopsis of each chapter

Chapter 1: Looking Under the Hood. Start with this chapter to take a look under the hoods of personal computers — whether dinosaurs, senior citizens, or modern machines. We'll examine motherboard types, cooling techniques, and explore the modular design of a modern PC.

Chapter 2: The Microprocessor. Here you perform a bit of PC psychiatry, examining the brain of your computer's CPU. We'll explain the history of the PC's microprocessor from its (now apparent) humble beginnings to the latest and greatest, including new dual-core processors from Intel and AMD.

Chapter 3: BIOS. Here you learn the importance of the BIOS of your machine, and why it may make sense to update it on some machines.

Chapter 4: The Computer Bus. This chapter explores the march of PC buses up to and including the most modern of current buses, the PCI Express and its immediate predecessor the PCI bus. We'll also consider the special-purpose AGP graphics slot that was part of older modern machines, and look backwards at older industry standard architecture (ISA) or AT-bus, PC cards, and senior-citizen and dinosaur buses.

Chapter 5: Basic Hardware Skills. You learn the tools of the trade while investigating the basic components of the computer in detail, from the case and cover to the motherboard and expansion cards, the CPU and BIOS, system memory, and more.

Chapter 6: Step-by-Step through a Modern PC. In the service of the reader, I take apart a brand-new modern machine, based on a dual-core processor and an advanced BTX motherboard and prepare the way for repairs and upgrades to any machine. We'll also examine other modern machines and older machines.

Chapter 7: Shopping for PC Parts. This chapter explores the minimum configuration for current versions of Windows including Vista and XP, as well as older editions including Windows 2000, Windows 95/98, and the senior-citizen Windows 3.1 operating system.

Chapter 8: Memory. Computer memory is the essential thinking space for your machine. In this chapter, you learn about types of memory and as much technical background as you need to understand how they work.

Chapter 9: Floppy Drives. A once-marvelous technology no longer standard on the most current of modern machines, floppy drives played a very important role in the early history of the PC. There are millions of them still in use. This chapter introduces you to floppies and related storage technologies as well as troubleshooting and repair strategies.

Chapter 10: Media Hard Drives. Faster, larger, cheaper . . . what more could you want? How about a user's guide to understanding and troubleshooting hard drive types, interfaces, and cabling.

Chapter 11: Removable Media Hard Drives. Here I discuss removable storage devices, from high-capacity floppies, such as Rev and Zip drives and the SuperDisk, to the gigabyte-sized cartridge systems. I also introduce the CD-recordable device.

Chapter 12: CD and DVD Drives. This chapter is where you learn about the hardware side of optical drives, which have moved from an aficionado's fancy to a modern user's necessity. We'll explore CD and DVD drives in their player, recorder, and rewriteable versions.

Chapter 13: Video Display Adapters and Standards. In this chapter, you learn about the history and technology of video adapters, from dinosaur CGA, MDA, EGA, and other ancient systems to modern VGA and SVGA controllers. You'll also learn about digital interfaces for LCD screens.

Chapter 14: Monitors and LCD Displays. And, of course, you need to have a screen to view your computer's work in progress. Here I explore the types of monitors available for your PC and then explain the essential components of a high-quality display. LCD screens have already taken over a significant portion of the market, and we'll look at how they work.

Chapter 15: Working Outside the Box: External Serial, USB, eSATA, and FireWire Connections. How a serial port works and how to troubleshoot it when it doesn't — that's what you learn in this chapter. You also learn about Universal Serial Bus (USB) technology and about the FireWire protocol for high-speed serial communication.

Chapter 16: Modem Telecommunications. Without a modem, you'd have no Internet, no online chats, and no easy way to play Super Space Creature Massacre with your cousin in Columbus. In this chapter, you learn about how to choose and troubleshoot a high-speed broadband cable or DSL modem or a basic dial-up modem.

Chapter 17: The Parallel Interface. This chapter delves into the original parallel port (sometimes referred to as unidirectional), as well as more recent bidirectional, enhanced parallel port, and enhanced capabilities port designs.

Chapter 18: Hard Copy. Put your words and pictures on paper with a printer. This is the place to learn about types of printers, from dinosaur daisywheels to state-of-the-art ink jet and laser devices.

Chapter 19: Your Computer's Hands, Eyes, and Ears. Reach in and control your PC through the keyboard or with a mouse or give it a view with a scanner or a digital camera. And lend an ear to a guide to sound cards and game ports. You learn about the hardware and the repair strategies for each within these pages.

Chapter 20: Networks, Gateways, Routers, and WiFi Wireless. Get connected: setting up a small office or home network to share computers, printers, and modems.

Chapter 21: Backup Strategies. Before you have to deal with the hardware side of a system failure, read this chapter to learn about strategies and methods for making back-up copies of your work in a safe place — on a removable disk, on another PC, or in other ways.

Chapter 22: Antivirus, Utility, and Diagnostic Programs. Utilities are power tools for savvy PC users; they extend the operating system and your applications in ways that make your machine adapt to you instead of the other way around. One specialized, essential utility is a capable diagnostic program to give your PC a health check. And I begin with a discussion of a must for any computer user: an antivirus program.

Chapter 23: Windows Troubleshooting and Repairs. Current versions of the Microsoft operating system offer some powerful utilities for configuring and troubleshooting your PC, including Device Manager, the Maintenance Wizard, and the System Information Utility.

Chapter 24: Common-Sense Solutions to Hardware Headaches. You are not alone: Here are some sensible solutions to knotty problems that the gurus of hardware and software have revealed.

Glossary: PCs are covered here from A (accelerated graphics port) to Z (Zip Drive) and everything in between, with nearly 500 definitions of terms used in this book and in the instruction manuals for your system and software.

Appendixes and bonus chapters on the CD

The appendixes contain references to some of the essential — and arcane — communications that you receive from a PC in distress, a listing of hardware and software suppliers and manufacturers, and an encyclopedia of cable connectors.

Also, let your fingers do the walking through 11 flowcharts that help you figure out the source of problems in your system.

The charts begin with diagnosing a dead machine and move on to specific problems with floppy disks, hard disk drives, parallel ports, serial ports, multimedia devices, and video quality. And finally, there's a guide to decision-making after an electrical disaster.

Each of the charts includes a cross-reference to the appropriate chapter of this book for details on troubleshooting, repair, and replacement.

Appendixes on the CD-ROM:

- Appendix A: Troubleshooting Charts
- Appendix B: Encyclopedia of Cables and Connectors
- Appendix C: Hardware and Software Toolkit
- Appendix D: Modern Machine Diagnostic Codes and Messages
- Appendix E: Dinosaur and Senior-Citizen Numeric Codes, Text Messages, and Beep Codes
- Appendix F: IRQ, DMA, and Memory Assignments

Bonus Chapters on the CD-ROM:

- Chapter 5
- Chapter 6
- Chapter 8
- Chapter 8
- Chapter 9
- Chapter 10
- Chapter 11
- Chapter 12
- Chapter 13
- Chapter 14
- Chapter 15
- Chapter 18
- Chapter 19
- Chapter 20

Icons

To help you identify important points, I use several icons throughout the book.

CROSS-REFERENCE

Follow the link to more details elsewhere in the book.

WARNING

Here be dragons — don't say you weren't warned.

NOTE

Here's more than you ever thought to ask about the subject.

Modern Machines, Senior Citizens, and Dinosaurs

Almost every PC ever made can be used for basic functions such as word processing and spreadsheets. In fact, some of the original machines are still plugging away here and there.

That said, software has become the tail that wags the computer dog. Nearly every computer user wants to get on the Internet and connect to a wireless network in the home or the office and play the latest games or download and edit video and pictures. In order to perform these modern tasks, you'll need a modern machine.

Throughout this book, I make an important distinction between what I call modern machines, senior citizens, and dinosaurs.

- **Modern machines** are those that can work with current operating systems (Windows Vista, Windows XP, Windows 2000, and Windows NT) and can use current hardware peripherals. (Although no longer a current operating system, I also include Windows 98SE at the ragged edge of modernity.) On the hardware side of the equation, with this eighth edition, modern machines begin with Intel's Celeron and Pentium 4 microprocessors and also include the latest Pentium D and Celeron D dual-core chips. Also included are the AMD Athlon 64 X2, Athlon, Opteron, and Sempron microprocessors. In this edition, the Intel Pentium III and Pentium II processors and the AMD Duron and K6 move to the senior citizen endangered species list.

- **Senior citizens** include machines that are still capable of productive work and deserving of our respect, even though they have lost more than a few steps to the new chips on the block. You may be able to get on the Internet with these machines, but they're not going to be able to keep up with the latest video and audio tricks you'll find there. This group includes Pentium III processors, Pentium II chips, the original Intel Pentium series as well as the Intel 486 family, in DX, DX-2, and DX-4 versions. Basically, the decision on whether to perform life-prolonging surgery on a senior-citizen machine or to pull the plug is a close call. If they are still capable of running the software you need, I would be willing to invest a small amount of money — less than

$150 — on replacing a failed fan, power supply, or hard disk. But it no longer makes sense to resuscitate a failed motherboard or memory. The cost of replacement parts — if they are available — does not compare well against the low price for an entry-level modern machine.

■ **Dinosaurs** are based on the obsolete 8088, 8086, 80286, 386, and 486SX microprocessors — including IBM PCs, PC-XTs, and PC-ATs, as well as dozens of clone machines using the same chips. They're interesting to historians and collectors, but not well adapted to the modern era. But if you want to keep one alive or if it is essential to resuscitate a dinosaur in order to retrieve data, I instruct you on how to make repairs to these devices, too. Modern machines generally use advanced bus designs, including the current PCI Express as well as PCI and PCI/ISA mixes along with specialized graphic buses such as AGP. Senior citizens usually employ ISA, EISA, or VL designs. By definition, dinosaurs limp along with the outmoded PC or AT bus.

Don't let your eyes glaze over with this sudden introduction to the alphabet soup of the PC world. I translate most technical terms as I introduce them; you can also turn to the Glossary at the end of this book for more help.

If you're truly starting from scratch, I also help you figure out exactly what type of machine lies beneath the covers.

And don't feel that all is lost if you happen to be the somewhat proud owner of a senior citizen. It is still possible to get a reasonable amount of work from an older machine, and it is also possible in some cases to upgrade a senior citizen to near-modern capabilities in a cost-effective manner. I discuss your options in this book.

How to Reach Me

If you want to contact the author, you can send me an e-mail; I can't promise to diagnose your machine from 10,000 miles away, but I might be able to point you in the right direction if you think you have stumbled across a problem not directly addressed in this book.

You can send me e-mail at fixyourownpc@econoguide.com.

My web page is at www.econoguide.com.

—Corey Sandler

Publisher's Acknowledgments

We're proud of this book; please send us your comments through our online registration form located at www.dummies.com/register/.

Some of the people who helped bring this book to market include the following:

Acquisitions, Editorial, and Media Development

Project Editor: Tonya Cupp
Executive Editor: Greg Croy
Technical Editor: Tom Badgett
Editorial Manager: Jodi Jensen
Media Development and Quality Assurance: Angela Denny, Kate Jenkins, Steven Kudirka, Kit Malone
Media Development Coordinator: Jenny Swisher
Media Project Supervisor: Laura Moss-Hollister
Editorial Assistant: Amanda Foxworth
Sr. Editorial Assistant: Cherie Case

Composition Services

Project Coordinator: Adrienne Martinez
Layout and Graphics: Denny Hager, Joyce Haughey, Shane Johnson, Jennifer Mayberry, Melanee, Prendergast, Brent Savage
Proofreaders: Dwight Ramsey, Shannon Ramsey, Mildred Rosenzweig
Indexer: Joan Griffitts
Anniversary Logo Design: Richard Pacifico

Publishing and Editorial for Technology Dummies

Richard Swadley, Vice President and Executive Group Publisher
Andy Cummings, Vice President and Publisher
Mary Bednarek, Executive Acquisitions Director
Mary C. Corder, Editorial Director

Publishing for Consumer Dummies

Diane Graves Steele, Vice President and Publisher
Joyce Pepple, Acquisitions Director

Composition Services

Gerry Fahey, Vice President of Production Services
Debbie Stailey, Director of Composition Services

Contents at a Glance

Contents

Fix Your Own PC
Eighth Edition

Chapter 1

Tools Needed:

- Phillips screwdriver
- Antistatic strip, wrist strap, or grounding pad

Looking Under the Hood

Welcome to anatomy class. It's time to prepare for open-case exploratory surgery on your computer.

You may or may not ever have to add, remove, or repair a component that exists under your machine's hood. But as a savvy computer owner you should have some idea of what lies beneath; in this chapter I tell you what you can expect to see inside a range of modern machines, as well as some older, still-useful senior citizens of PC society. Later on in the book, I explore individual components in much greater detail. But the first step in understanding the way your machine works is to expose its innards.

Before you remove the cover, turn off the computer and unplug it. Why do both? This is a great habit to get into. It helps protect you from mental lapses — sort of a belt-and-suspenders kind of thing.

NOTE

Some advice-givers suggest that you turn off the computer but leave it plugged into the wall outlet. In that way, they reason, the computer is grounded and there's less chance of damage from static electricity. This reasoning is true enough, but I don't like that procedure. For example, although the power switch may be off, the switch itself and in some instances the power supply may contain line voltage and a dropped screw or tool can cause major damage. Additionally, the power cord from the computer to the wall socket is an attractive nuisance; sooner or later you're going to trip over it and the machine will crash to the floor. Instead of taking chances, unplug your PC before removing the cover. And invest in a grounding strap and use it religiously.

No electricity circulates in the computer when it's off and unplugged. Actually, very little shock hazard exists when the computer is on — as long as you never disassemble the sealed power supply or a CRT monitor. The computer bus runs on the 3.3-, 5-, or 12-volt DC current that comes out of a properly functioning power supply.

However, you face the potential danger of short-circuiting components of an electrified system if you touch a screwdriver across the traces of the motherboard or drop a bracket into the works. Also, plugging a card into the powered-up bus or plugging a cable into a connector can momentarily short some of the electrical lines and destroy the motherboard or a peripheral.

- And so, *Fix Your Own PC* **basic repair rule number one** is this: Avoid touching the interior of a powered-on computer with any metallic tool, adapter card, screw, or cable. One more note about electricity: Whether your computer is powered-on or not, you can very easily damage the microprocessor, memory chips, and other components if you stroll across the carpeted floor of your office or den and deliver from your fingertips a static electricity shock of a few thousand volts.

- Therefore, *Fix Your Own PC* **basic repair rule number two** is this: Ground yourself before you lay hands on the innards of a PC, an adapter, a memory module, or any other exposed electronic device. If you're going to be doing repair work regularly, you should make the worthwhile investment of a few dollars in an antistatic strip, wrist strap, or grounding pad with a wire that is connected to an electrical ground. The straps cost just a few dollars and are an inexpensive solution to a potentially dangerous and costly problem. Figure 1-1 shows an example of an antistatic strap in use.

NOTE

One easy way to ground yourself is to touch the unpainted center screw that holds the plastic cover over the nearest electric outlet. Don't stick your finger in the outlet; just touch the screw. (If the screw is painted, scrape off a spot to make a better electrical contact.) This technique works well for most buildings and wiring schemes. Remember, however, that older buildings may not fully adhere to modern electrical codes and outlet boxes may be floating without a good ground connection. For purposes of discharging any static electricity in your body, this metallic contact may still be sufficient; however, don't depend on older house or office wiring to offer a real ground through the outlet box.

- Next, prepare your operating room. You don't want to add to your troubles by crashing your system to the floor. That leads to *Fix Your Own PC* **basic repair rule number three**: Place the computer on a sturdy surface under a strong light.
- You have to remove screws and most or all of the cables that attach to the computer to remove the cover. Therefore, *Fix Your Own PC* **basic repair rule number four** is this: Remember, you've got to put this thing back together.

Keep a small, compartmentalized box at hand to hold screws and other parts; an empty egg carton, or a plastic jewelry box works well. You should also have a notepad, a roll of masking tape, and a marker pen. Keep notes on any unusual steps in disassembling the case and use the tape and pen to mark cables with their intended destination. (You could even color-code parts that go together.)

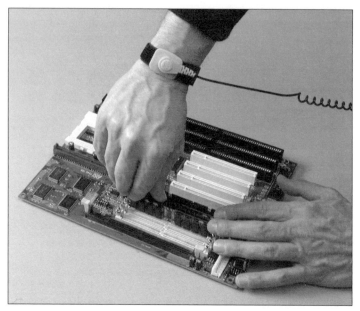

FIGURE 1-1: *A good way to protect the electronics of your PC from static electricity is to wear an antistatic wrist strap that attaches to an electrical ground, such as a cold water pipe or the center screw on a power outlet.*

The Case for Computer Cases

The computer case has two important purposes:

- To hold the contents in a safe, cool, and relatively clean environment
- To keep radio frequency radiation within

A properly designed case supports the motherboard mechanically and electrically and gives you all the room that you need for internal hard drives, floppy drives, and adapter cards, along with providing easily accessible input-output ports for keyboards, a mouse, and external peripherals, such as a monitor and printer.

NOTE

Electromagnetic shielding is increasingly important as modern machines move data at faster and faster speeds. To pass Federal

Communications Commission (FCC) regulations, when the PC is sold, the case must present an essentially unbroken wall with all openings filled to keep electromagnetic waves generated by the computer inside the case.

Radio station PC

PC cases are available in dozens of types, but nearly all follow one of two basic designs:

- A heavy metal shell that slides tightly into place over a metal frame that holds the computer's motherboard and all the internal devices attached to it
- A metal-backed clamshell that closes in place over the internal parts, locking shut with a latch

Why all this heavy metal? Blame it on or credit it to the government — the Federal Communications Commission to be exact. All electronic devices, including microprocessors, generate electrical signals that can become interference; they become, in effect, tiny local radio transmitters. As long as the signals are bouncing around within a closed metal box, that's where they will stay.

The problems of radio frequency (RF) interference became worse as PCs began to operate faster and faster. Currently, the fastest microcomputer chips commercially available have reached more than 3.5 GHz, with plans for 5 GHz and faster designs.

Consider for a moment that the clock speed of the original IBM PC was an anemic 4.77 MHz (MHz stands for megahertz, meaning one million cycles per second), and you can gain some perspective on just how fast processors are running today. A 2-GHz CPU operates about 420 times faster than an original 4.77 MHz microprocessor; advances in bus speeds and memory technologies push the differential to the equivalent of thousands of times faster.

Therefore, to avoid interference with your neighbor's garage door opener, your kids' television set, or the PC in the next cubicle, the FCC requires that all computers be tested for RF leakage. The solution to passing the test generally involves heavy metal cases, internal shielding, and less obvious solutions, including little copper fingers that help extend an electronic girdle around your interfering PC. Figure 1-2 shows an example of a basic desktop PC that includes a copper protective shield.

FIGURE 1-2: *Slide the cover back away from the flange at the front of the case and then lift the cover up and away. On some machines, copper fingers are part of the system's defense against release of RF radiation.*

CROSS-REFERENCE

You can find more detail on current microprocessors in Chapter 2.

WARNING

When the computer is in your hands, however, nothing prevents you from leaving slot covers off or even running the PC without its cover. Neither is a good idea because you end up endangering the life of your PC and the quality of radio signals in your home or office. In addition to permitting broadcast of stray radio signals, operating the computer without covers may introduce dirt into the disk drives and onto the electrical contacts, and allow metal objects like paper clips or staples or a cup of coffee to fall in and short the wires, and interfere with the cooling air flow of the PC's fan.

Though stray electromagnetic radiation won't harm the computer or cause it to malfunction, it may cause interference with televisions, FM radios, portable and cellular telephones, and other devices whenever the computer is on. And although prevailing wisdom is that electromagnetic radiation is not a threat to human beings — at least at the levels present in a PC — it is good practice to stay an arm's length away from your computer and the video monitor and to keep slot covers and cases on.

NOTE

Lightweight laptop or portable computers have electromagnetic shielding, too — even those with plastic cases. Some portables, for example, have aluminum plates embedded in the plastic. Another solution that laptops employ is to apply a layer of aluminum paint over the plastic parts.

Keeping things cool

The first PCs generated only a small amount of heat; the biggest source was the puny power supply. On most early machines, the case was cooled with an exhaust fan on the power supply that pulled a small amount of air into the case through a few holes here and there.

In the quarter-century that has followed, almost everything has gotten much, much hotter. Without proper cooling, a 3-GHz CPU gets hot enough to fry a tiny egg . . . that is, it would before it fried itself. So, too, the banks of high-speed memory in a modern machine — typically more than a thousand times larger and hundreds of times faster than the original PC RAM chips. And it goes on: Advanced graphics cards today have their own very high-speed processors and memory. A modern power supply typically uses 300 to 400 watts of power. And finally, a modern machine typically has motors spinning at least one hard drive and optical disc drive and sometimes multiple devices.

Let me back up for a minute for a quick lesson in physics. I promise I'll keep it simple.

Nearly all computers perform their work by moving electricity from one place to another — from the wall socket to the power supply to the motherboard and CPU to the memory to storage devices and out to external devices through ports and sockets. Electricity is a physical thing, a stream of electrons, and in a computer (and most other modern devices) it moves along wires. A motherboard contains thousands of tiny *traces,* which are wires that are painted in place. Within a microprocessor are even tinier connections that are etched into place with a photographic or other process.

The movement of electricity across a wire is not perfect. The flow always experiences some *resistance.* And the resistance tends to increase as the flow increases and also as the size of the wire (think of it as a pipe) gets smaller.

So, back to our modern computer. It is no longer sufficient to have just a simple exhaust fan on the power supply. Unless the fan is huge (and noisy), it will not draw enough air through the case to cool all the components. And then there are the internal roadblocks — upright adapter cards, fat data cables, and other impediments — that block the flow of air.

Over the years there have been many solutions:

- Small fans that sit directly atop the microprocessor, lifting heat off them and (in theory) pushing the heat into the stream of air that exits the machine
- Extra fans that draw room air through vents in the front of the computer, increasing the flow to the exit at the rear
- Heat sinks that draw heat to themselves, dissipating the elevated temperature into the flow of air
- Specially designed tunnels that channel the flow of fans on the microprocessor directly to an exit from the case

All of these solutions were basically workarounds for inherited problems that have built up over the years. Each new and hotter CPU or chipset had to find its place somewhere on a motherboard with a basic design — the location of ports, power inputs, and slots — had been set as much as a decade ago, which in computer terms is almost prehistoric. The most common "form factor" for modern motherboards was called ATX, based on a specification that was developed in 1995 by Intel and its partners.

NOTE

As this edition goes to press, manufacturers building motherboards for Intel processors and chipsets began to offer a new design, called BTX. That design, laid out in 2003 and 2004, received its first wide use in mid-2006. At the heart of that design was specific planning for evacuation of heat from the system through natural and powered exhaust. (I discuss form factors including ATX and BTX in more detail in Chapter 5.)

PCs by the case

Cases are available in either desktop (full, low-profile, or baby sizes) or tower (full and mid-size) models.

A *baby case* is a tightly packed, slimmed-down box with limited options for expansion; two variants of the baby case put the motherboard in a slightly oversized keyboard or in the body of a monitor or LCD. A *low-profile* case, just as the name implies, is designed to squeeze the equivalent of ten pounds of computer into a five-pound case.

My strong preference is for *tower cases*, in either full-size or mid-size designs, like the one shown in Figure 1-3 and, undressed, in Figure 1-4. Towers usually offer considerably more room for additional internal hard drives, CD-ROM and DVD drives, and other storage devices such as Zip drives. And they usually include larger power supplies to support those extra devices. In general, a larger power supply is a good thing to have because it allows a healthy margin for those times when the CD-ROM drive is loading to the hard drive while the network card is pumping data across the Ethernet and the high-end video card is displaying a complex graphic; modern switching power supplies adjust their output to the need.

As more and more external USB devices are used in computing (and with external SATA devices becoming more common for add-on or backup storage), it will be harder to find a full-size tower case with four internal bays for expansion. Mid-sized towers with two internal bays are becoming more common. Full-sized towers will likely continue to be offered for machines intended as servers in a network.

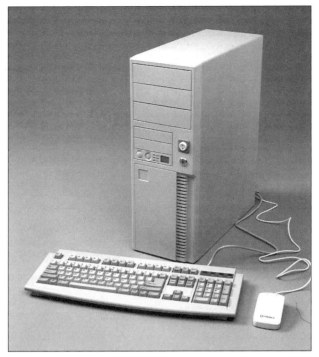

FIGURE 1-3: *Vertical or tower cases offer maximum expandability. This sturdy case has a pair of drive cages that can hold three 5.25-inch devices and four 3.5-inch drives.*

Another advantage of a tower unit is that it is designed to sit on the floor, so it does not take up precious desk space. However, almost any computer can be mounted on its side; just take care to support it properly so that it does not tip over. If the case maker does not provide it, one way to add this support is with a snap-on unit that adds a wider base to the desktop case. Such units are available from office supply stores and computer stores.

If you have a dinosaur CD-ROM that uses a caddy to hold the disc, the device may only work in a horizontal position.

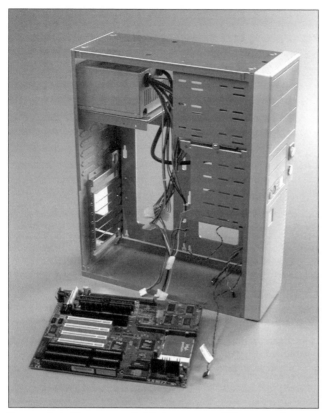

FIGURE 1-4: *The cover of this tower case lifts up and away to expose both sides of the internal frame within. A new motherboard is shown here connected to electrical and data cables before installation in the case.*

Opening the case

Consult your instruction manual to see whether your computer's case uses any unusual fasteners or means of closing.

Begin by unplugging the power cord. It is a good practice also to unplug all cables leading into the PC — video, printer, modem, keyboard, and mouse. If the connectors on the PC are not labeled, tape small paper tags on the back panel to identify the ports; add corresponding identification labels to the cables.

A standard Phillips screwdriver will remove the screws on a PC case; you may also be able to use a socket wrench or nut driver. Some older computers used special screws that required a hex driver for removal; when I find a machine like that, one of the first things I do is rummage through my toolbox for a set of standard replacement screws. The same applies to some older Compaq models that use Torx screws; you need to obtain a star-shaped Torx screwdriver to remove the fasteners.

NOTE

Many systems have a few smaller screws around the air exhaust from the power supply fan; you don't want to remove them to get to the innards of the case. Consult the instruction manual for your PC if you have any doubts about the location of the screws.

Some manufacturers have introduced screwless cases that substitute simple latches or thumbscrews. You can also purchase large plastic screws and substitute them for the original metal screws to make it a bit easier to remove a standard cover. Figure 1-5 shows an example of a state-of-the-art case opening with the push of a pair of latches at each end, like a clamshell, to reveal an easy-to-work-on interior.

Remove the cover screws and then pull the cover forward and up, or backward and up, depending on the design. The tower case sometimes has a full-length plastic faceplate with lights and cutouts for the floppy drives. Some older models won't let you remove the floppy or hard disk drives until you snap this plastic cover off. Other tower models mount this faceplate semipermanently with screws and let you slip the drives out from the back. Examine your computer's manual and use your own judgment.

A desktop computer case, like the one shown in Figure 1-6, usually has four or five screws on the back panel to hold its cover in place. A tower case may have four to six screws.

Another case design has panels on each of the vertical sides of the tower case. Each panel is held in place with just two screws, and after you remove them, you'll find very easy access to the motherboard and devices within. This design is represented in a bare-bones system examined in more detail in Chapter 7.

FIGURE 1-5: *This ultramodern case opens with the push of two buttons. In this photo, the motherboard sits on the desktop while the upright half of the case holds the drive cage with a CD-R, hard drive, and floppy disk drive.*

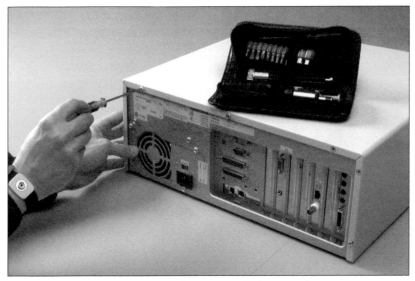

FIGURE 1-6: *To remove the cover from most desktop and tower cases, remove the screws around the perimeter of the back panel. On some ultra-compact desktop cases, the screws may attach along the sides. Be careful not to remove the group of screws that surround the power supply and hold it in place.*

Now comes the time to slide off the cover on a standard case. Some cases pull back toward the rear of the PC, others lift straight up, and with some designs, you must pull them back slightly before lifting them straight up. Additionally, some cases include plastic or metal compression fittings that you must hold to keep them unlatched while you pull off the cover; consult your instruction manual for the details of your particular system. The cover may be a bit sticky until it breaks loose, but once it starts sliding, it should move smoothly.

Remove the case slowly and evenly. You want to avoid pinching or cutting any misbehaving wires that may have crept up near the top of the case, and you want to avoid tumbling the whole assemblage onto the floor with a misguided yank.

Some cases include decorative front panels (sometimes referred to as *bezels*) that hide some of the access points; an example is shown in Figure 1-7. This sort of design adds a touch of class to an office or home installation, but the panels can also stand in the way of a power user with a wide range of devices. The best compromise is a case that allows you to remove or reposition the front panel cover to match your needs. In Figure 1-8, you can see the interior construction of this sort of case.

 WARNING

It's easy to catch the power supply wires or the floppy drive ribbon cable on the sharp edges of the case cover. Be gentle and use good sense when removing or reinstalling the cover. Ripping these wires loose increases the diagnostic challenge. One way to reduce the chances of catching the wires: Before replacing the case, attach any loose wires to internal supports using non-conductive tape such as masking tape or plastic wire ties.

Here's another reason to do your work in a well-lit and comfortable environment: If the case seems to catch on something in removal or reinstallation, examine the situation with a powerful lamp or flashlight before you force the cover on or off.

FIGURE 1-7: *The panel on this earlier generation of a modern case sits in front of four device bays. The panel includes an opening for a CD-ROM. If you install another 5.25-inch device, such as a DVD-ROM or tape backup system, you have to open the panel for access.*

FIGURE 1-8: *To open the side panels on this case, pop off the front bezel and then slide the panels off.*

Taking a good look

Now take a close look at the innards of a typical modern computer. The large circuit board is filled with components, slots, and devices in the motherboard. Near the center (on an ATX motherboard) or at one of the corners (on a BTX design) you'll see a large vertical or horizontal microprocessor topped by a fan or heat sink. On some ATX designs and most BTX boards the microprocessor lives within a plastic tunnel that directs the output of the fan to an opening at the back of the case.

You'll also see one or more rows of memory modules, several plug-in circuit boards, a metal box holding the power supply, a hard drive, a CD-ROM, and a floppy drive.

On earlier-generation modern machines, you'll see a spaghetti bowl of two-inch-wide gray ribbon cables that connect the computer's hard disk drives, CD or DVD, and floppy disk drive to ports on the motherboard. The most modern of machines have embraced a changeover from IDE/ATA drive technology to SATA (Serial ATA) controllers and wiring. The beauty of SATA is that simple two-wire cables have replaced the wide ribbon cables so difficult to route neatly through the interior of the machine.

One thing I know for sure: There is no way to predict exactly what you'll find when you open a PC. There are hundreds of thousands of combinations of add-in cards, drives, memory modules, and other devices. Even an office full of the same brand of PCs is likely to have very different combinations of parts under the hood. Users may have had different requirements when the machines were purchased, technologies may have changed over the course of a series of orders, or the manufacturer may have had a mix-and-match assembly line where Brand X disk drives were installed on Mondays and Wednesdays, Brand Y on Tuesdays and Thursdays, and whatever was on sale was stuck in boxes put together on Fridays.

But as I have already observed, most computers—from the very first IBM PC to the latest state-of-the-art Pentium 4 or AMD Athlon—are more alike than they are different.

By the way, if the inside of the case looks like the back of your shoe closet—full of dust balls, cat hair, and spider webs—go get your vacuum cleaner. Working very carefully, hover the suction hose an inch or so above the electronics and let it suck out the dirt. Pay special attention to the air holes on the front or back of the machine; if these holes are clogged, the PC's fan will be much less effective in bringing cooling air through the case.

The Modular Design of a PC

One of the most important features of the PC is its modular design. Nearly every PC is made up of the same basic building blocks: motherboard, expansion cards, power supply, drives connected by cables to internal controllers, and external keyboard and monitor. You can insert or remove these pieces relatively easily to let make many types of repairs and to upgrade your system.

The biggest circuit board in your computer is the *motherboard*, sometimes called the *mainboard*. The motherboard is the home of the *CPU* (central processing unit), also called the *microprocessor*. The CPU is the brain of the computer, where the bulk of the actual manipulation of data and instructions takes place. In modern machines (as defined in this book), the CPU uses one of the younger members of the Pentium family, including the Pentium D, Pentium 4, and Celeron, or equivalent chips, including AMD's Athlon and Duron and K6 chips. Senior-citizen machines use an original Pentium, Pentium II, Pentium III, or one of the later 486 chips. And dinosaurs were based on early 486s and older 386, 80286, 8088, or similar CPUs.

Expansion cards or *adapters* are smaller, special-purpose circuit boards that plug into sockets on the motherboard. These sockets are called *bus slots* or *expansion slots*. The computer bus is functionally an extension of the address lines of the microprocessor. The particular kind of bus slot on your motherboard tells a lot about the motherboard and your computer's capabilities. With this edition, the speediest and most flexible example of a bus slot is the PCI Express. Half a step behind is the *accelerated graphics port (AGP),* a special pathway to the microprocessor intended for use by a particular class of high-speed graphics adapters.

Your computer also has a *power supply,* a transformer that converts AC current into low-voltage DC current to run the computer. The power supply is easy to identify on the inside of the case; it's usually a large shiny or black metal box, sprouting many wires and connectors that spread out like spaghetti to all corners of the case. You can also spot the power supply from the back panel of the case; look for the AC power cord from a wall outlet.

Floppy drives and hard drives are electromechanical boxes usually connected to the rest of the computer with gray, flat-ribbon cables and four-wire power connectors from the power supply box. Floppy disk drives need to have an opening for the insertion of disks; hard drives may be mounted just behind the front panel of the computer, but also can be hung anywhere there is space and connecting cables. More modern PCs no longer automatically come with a floppy disk drive; you can add an internal floppy if you need one or attach an external drive to the USB port. (In many homes and offices the floppy disk drive has been supplanted by the tiny and extremely portable USB memory key that can transport hundreds of megabytes of data or more from one machine to another. I discuss the memory key in Chapter 9.)

NOTE

Some older IBM PS/2 machines and a handful of current machines use fixed plug-in connectors for power and data, thus allowing easy swap of devices; the downside is that standard drives can't be used in such systems without adaptation. Consult your PC's instruction manual for details.

Most modern machines also include a CD-ROM or CD-RW or an even more capable DVD-ROM or DVD-RW. You also find advanced storage devices, such as Zip drives, SuperDisks, tape backups, and the like. When mounted internally, each of these devices connects to your computer in two ways: with a data cable (usually to the internal IDE connector on the motherboard) and with a cable from the power supply. Each of these devices needs an access slot on the outside of the machine for insertion of disks or tapes.

Some thin wires lead to the drive indicator light, the speaker, the power-on indicator, and other lamps and switches on the front panel. Other wires can include connectors from the CD-ROM or DVD-ROM to a sound card, from the motherboard to front-panel displays, and specialized environment-friendly (or green) functions, including sleep mode, temperature monitors, and variable fan-speed controls.

If your PC is a dinosaur, the memory chips — marked with identifying numbers — are probably arranged in rows of nine and reside in a segregated section of the motherboard.

Whether your computer is a modern machine or senior citizen, it uses one or another variant of a memory module that holds a large block of RAM that plugs into a location close to the CPU.

Single in-line memory modules (SIMMs) or *dual in-line memory modules (DIMMs)* are strips of circuit board — typically about two to three inches long — that plug into special connectors on the motherboard or occasionally into a plug-in board that attaches to the motherboard. Depending on the design and the type and capacity of memory chip used, the SIMMs or DIMMs may have just a few or as many as 16 or 18 RAM (random access memory) chips installed. SIMM boards have 72 pins or edge connectors that attach them to the motherboard, while DIMMs use a 168-pin circuit board configuration.

SIMMs typically hold from 1MB to 64MB of memory and DIMMs from 8MB to 2GB of RAM. The highest-capacity, fastest chips usually sell at a premium. When you examine a price list for memory, you should see a logical progression for most sizes: A 256MB DIMM should be about twice the price of a 128MB module, a 512MB DIMM about double the cost of a 256MB, and so on. But the largest sizes are sometimes a bit pricier because they often represent new technology or a smaller market. Unless you absolutely need the latest and greatest, you're always better off waiting for prices to fall more into line.

When the seventh edition of *Fix Your Own PC* came out in 2003, 1GB DIMMs were at the top of the chart, and their price had already dropped from a scary price of about $1,800 to about $200. By 2006, prices for 1GB SIMMs had dropped by 50 percent, to less than $100. And the premium price was commanded by 2GB memory, which sold for about $360 per module.

In 2001, the advanced RIMM (Rambus in-line memory module) technology began a short but ultimately unsuccessful competition for a share of the market. RIMMs use a special 184-pin connector. Another advanced memory design, double data-rate DIMMs (DDR DIMMs), use similar but incompatible 184-pin sockets.

A near-cousin to the SIMM and DIMM memory configuration is the single in-line package (SIP), an earlier version that uses tiny pins instead of edge connectors to connect to the motherboard. SIPs were used only for a short period and were supplanted by SIMMs, but you may still see SIP devices that do other things inside your computer, such as hold terminating resistors or other components.

CROSS-REFERENCE

Chapter 8 examines memory types and configuration in much greater detail.

After you've grounded yourself, it is okay to press down on the chips or strips to make sure that they're seated firmly, but don't blindly poke around inside the computer with a screwdriver. Take special care not to scratch or push down on any of the metal traces of the circuit board that serve as the wiring between elements of the computer; it is relatively easy to introduce a tiny crack across the traces, thus disrupting the flow of power or data.

Notice the expansion cards lined up in neat rows and plugged into a set of plastic and metal slots on the motherboard. In most designs, the cards are held in place by the clamping action of the metal fingers within the slot and are locked down with a single screw that connects through a bracket into a support frame of the computer case. (Some modern case designs use a plastic lockdown lever that holds expansion cards in place without the need for screws.)

To remove a card, you need to disconnect any external cables attached to the card, unscrew the bracket screw, and carefully work the card out of the slot in the motherboard. Installing a card is just as simple; just be careful to ensure that the card is fully inserted into the slot.

NOTE

Some baby and other mini- and low-profile case designs use a riser card that installs into a single slot on the small motherboard; add-on cards plug into slots on the riser.

And finally, take a look at the motherboard. In most designs, the board floats above the bottom or side of the case on plastic standoffs with a handful of screws holding it in place. Somewhere near the center you should be able to spot the CPU; it's usually the largest chip on the board and generally installed in an oversized holder with a heat sink, fan, or both. On dinosaurs and most senior citizens, you should be able to read the inscription on the chip; on most modern machines, the high-speed CPU is usually covered with a heat sink or fan and stands up vertically like a black monolith.

Located at the back of the machine are ports for serial and parallel cables to external devices, a video port to connect to the monitor, and connectors for a keyboard and mouse, as shown in Figure 1-9. On some systems, you may find other connectors, including ports for SCSI devices, joysticks, speakers, microphones, and more. The newest machines include two or four universal serial bus (USB) ports, and the most modern of multimedia devices may include a FireWire port for connecting digital camcorders and other devices.

Through mid-2006, most modern machines used motherboards that followed a specification called ATX or microATX, which places most input-output connectors directly on the board, matching up with an opening in the case. You can see an example of an ATX motherboard, with a Pentium II CPU in place, in Figure 1-10.

The BTX form factor motherboard began arriving in mass quantities in 2006, in BTX, microBTX, and picoBTX sizes. (Think of them as small, even smaller, and very small if you'd like.) BTX motherboards will be used in most tower and desktop computers. The microBTX and picoBTX sizes are expected to be employed in all-in-one systems and when a computer is embedded within another device. You can see the back of a BTX board in Figure 1-11.

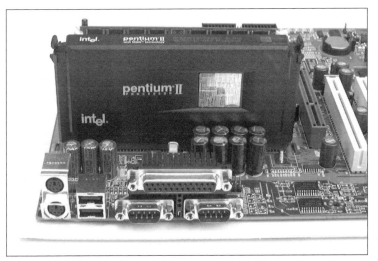

FIGURE 1-10: *The ATX-form factor motherboard brings together a bank of connectors directly on the motherboard, thus eliminating most cable connections. And most ATX-design systems also include a pair of USB ports (shown next to the keyboard and mouse ports in this design).*

A typical BTX motherboard may offer six USB ports on the rear for devices that typically remain connected (such as a keyboard, mouse, and external hard drive); an additional set of USB ports on the front of the machine is available for devices that are temporarily connected (such as cameras and portable audio devices). Microsoft and Intel helped simplify the process of connecting cables to adapters on a modern PC with the introduction of the PC99 specification, which has been updated over the years. Most motherboard and adapter makers have subscribed to the specification's recommendations for color-coding connectors and the ends of appropriate cables. Table 1-1 lists the major connectors. Colors marked with an asterisk (*) represent unofficial extensions to the PC99 color coding table. Colors marked with a asterisk are not used on many of the most modern of PCs, replaced instead by the multipurpose USB port.

FIGURE 1-9: *The back panel of a basic AT-form Pentium machine has serial, parallel, video, mouse, keyboard, and Ethernet connections. Many of the connectors are attached by specialized cables to points on the motherboard.*

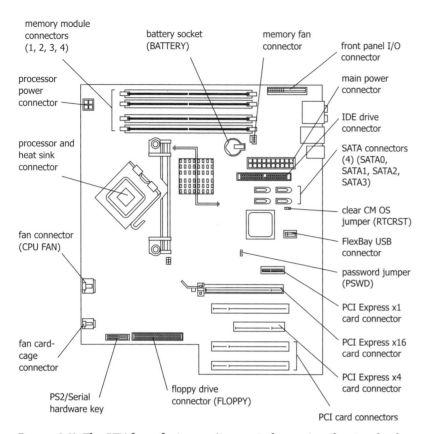

memory module
connectors
(1, 2, 3, 4)

battery socket
(BATTERY)

memory fan
connector

front panel I/O
connector

processor
power
connector

main power
connector

IDE drive
connector

processor and
heat sink
connector

SATA connectors
(4) (SATA0,
SATA1, SATA2,
SATA3)

clear CM OS
jumper (RTCRST)

fan connector
(CPU FAN)

FlexBay USB
connector

password jumper
(PSWD)

fan card-
cage
connector

PCI Express x1
card connector

PCI Express x16
card connector

PS2/Serial
hardware key

floppy drive
connector (FLOPPY)

PCI Express x4
card connector

PCI card connectors

FIGURE 1-11: *The BTX form factor, on its way to becoming the standard
design for current machines, adjusts the mix of connectors to
emphasize multipurpose ports such as the USB.*

Table 1-1: PC Port Color Coding		
Connector	Color	Port
Analog VGA	Blue	15-pin VGA D
Audio line in	Light blue	3.5mm jack
Audio line out (main speakers)	Lime	3.5mm jack
Audio line out (rear or surround speakers)	Black*	3.5mm jack
Audio line out (R to L speakers)	Brown*	3.5mm jack
Audio line out (center or subwoofer)	Yellow or orange*	3.5mm jack

Connector	Color	Port
Audio line out (S/PDIF digital audio)	Orange	3.5mm jack
Digital monitor	White	DVI
IEEE 1394 FireWire	Gray	6-pin FireWire 400
Microphone analog input	Pink	3.5mm jack
MIDI/Gameport	Gold	15-pin D
Parallel	Burgundy	25-pin D
PS/2-compatible keyboard	Purple	6-pin mini-DIN
PS/2-compatible mouse	Green	6-pin mini-DIN
Serial	Teal or turquoise	9-pin D
USB	Black	USB Type A
Video composite out	Yellow	RCA jack
Video S-Video	Yellow*	6-pin mini-DIN

PCs by Numbers: Basic Parts

Just how modular is a PC? The following are the basic parts for most
systems; I've indicated where you can find more details about each
particular part in this book:

- **Case.** The box that holds the internal parts of the computer and,
  almost as important, serves as a critical element of the cooling
  system for the electronic parts within. See Chapter 1.
- **Motherboard.** This is the heart of the computer and is home to
  the CPU, its supporting logic chips, and system memory. See
  Chapter 5.
- **CPU.** The microprocessor brain of the computer. See Chapter 2.
- **BIOS.** The basic set of instructions used by the computer to
  bring itself to life and to control input and output of data. See
  Chapter 3.
- **RAM.** The thinking space for the computer, used to hold
  programs and data under the control of the CPU. See Chapter 8.
- **Video adapter.** Responsible for converting the 0s and 1s of a
  computer's digital data into an image that can be displayed on a
  television-like screen. See Chapter 13.
- **Keyboard.** The primary means of communication between a
  human user and the machine. See Chapter 5.
- **Monitor.** The video display device that provides a window into
  the operations and results of a computer's work. See Chapter 13.

- **Power supply.** The source of carefully regulated voltage for all of the computer's internal parts. See Chapter 5.
- **Floppy and hard drive controllers.** The taskmasters for a computer's primary storage devices. See Chapters 9 and 10.
- **Floppy disk drive.** A simple, removable mechanism for storing data and programs. See Chapter 9.
- **Hard disk drive.** A high-capacity, high-speed storage system usually mounted within the case of the computer. See Chapter 10.
- **High-capacity removable drive.** A variant of the hard drive used for archiving data and for transporting large amounts of data or large programs from one machine to another. See Chapter 11.
- **Serial port.** A basic means of communication from your computer to external devices such as modems, certain printers, and other peripherals. See Chapter 15.
- **Parallel port.** A communication route generally used for printers. See Chapter 17.
- **Internal or external modem.** A hardware device that converts a computer's digital signals into an analog equivalent, used to transmit data over a telephone connection. See Chapter 16.
- **Printer.** A hard-copy output device. See Chapter 18.

Multimedia-capable systems may include a few additional modular parts:

- **Sound card.** A device that gives your computer a voice and an orchestra; basic sound facilities are offered as part of the motherboard chipset but serious audiophiles and gamers may want to extend the capabilities by adding a sound card in an available internal slot. A handful of external audio adapters connect to the USB port. See Chapter 12.
- **Internal or external CD-ROM drive.** A form of removable storage primarily used to install programs or as a source of video or audio. See Chapter 12.
- **CD Recordable, CD Read/Write, or DVD drive.** A variant of the CD-ROM that can be used to play and record discs. DVD is a developing protocol that packs huge amounts of data onto a disc and can be used to hold entire movies or other large multimedia files. See Chapter 12.
- **Network adapter.** The concept of connecting two or more computers together for the exchange of data and the sharing of certain software applications began in businesses and other large organizations. Machines required an adapter that plugged into an available slot (and had to be carefully configured to avoid conflict with other components making demands on system resources). Today, though, nearly every modern machine includes built-in Ethernet circuitry as part of the motherboard; the port is used for home or office wired or WiFi (wireless) networks and, through a router, allows multiple computers to share a single cable or DSL modem for high-speed Internet access. Plug-in adapters, like the one shown in Figure 1-12, still are available to upgrade an older machine that needs them.

- **Video devices.** Mostly external graphic devices including scanners, video-capture cards, and video-editing cards bring a bit of Hollywood — or at least an advanced hobbyist's editing capabilities — to the desktop.
- **Game controller.** A hardware interface for joysticks and other devices used with games. On older machines, the controller was added as an adapter card. By the dawn of the modern machine, most joysticks employed the PS/2 keyboard or mouse port. And now, the most modern of machines have dispensed with the controller and PS/2 ports; instead, the game controller has joined the list of devices that attach to the computer through a USB port. See Chapter 12.

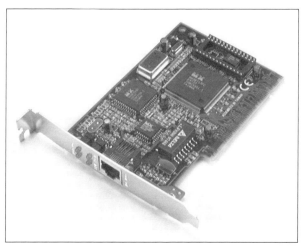

FIGURE 1-12: *A basic Ethernet card intended for installation in a modern machine; most current modern machines now offer high-speed Ethernet adapters as part of the motherboard instead of requiring installation of an adapter. All current versions of Windows include basic networking software for setting up a small office or home installation.*

Ch
1

What Kind of PC Do You Have?

The first step in analyzing a PC is to understand what type of system it is: Is it a modern machine, a senior citizen, or a dinosaur? Does it have a state-of-the-art PCI Express bus, or an older PCI? Does the graphics card sit in a standard slot , or is it attached through a special-purpose AGP path or a fast and versatile PCI Express slot? Is the machine based around a dinosaur skeleton that uses an ISA or EISA or VL bus? Does it possess a poky 8-MHz CPU, a capable but outmoded 300-MHz processor, or a current 2.8 GHz or faster scorcher? Is the hard disk an old ST506, an obsolete ESDI, or a modern IDE? Is the IDE (like most made in the past 15 years) attached to a standard parallel ATA port, or is it among the most modern that use the simple and speedy *Serial ATA (SATA)* system?

NOTE

Don't worry about the jargon yet. I define the terms later in the explanations of repairs and upgrades. If you need an immediate explanation, however, check the glossary at the back of this book.

On many older machines, the front *bezel* — the plastic faceplate where the computer manufacturer used to proudly hang an advertising sign — is the first place to learn about the machine's innards. This is much less the case today. For example, Dell's popular Dimension series carries a number (E510, 8200, 9200, and the like) that gives you information only when you look up the specifications in the technical manual or consult system information utility reports. The same sort of labeling is used by HP for its Compaq desktops (2000, 5000, 7000) and by Gateway (E-1500, E-2600, and E-4500). The only thing you can learn from this sort of a labeling scheme is the *relative* positioning of the model in a company's hierarchy of speed or capability and sometimes the model's *relative* age. But, as I said, things used to be different. For example, the following sections give a few sample names from machines I have used over the years.

Senior-citizen machines based on Intel processors

The collection of machines in my office includes PCs from a variety of makers, including Dell, Gateway, Hewlett Packard, IBM, and from defunct makers including Austin and CompuAdd, as well as units put together using parts sold by companies including Dalco Electronics and TigerDirect. A quick survey of model names turned up the following alphanumeric soup for PCs built around processors from Intel and AMD:

- **P4-1800.** A modern machine but a few steps behind the state-of-the-art, this machine mates a 1.8 GHz Pentium 4 CPU with 256MB of high-speed RDRAM, an ATA/100 40GB hard drive, a 4X AGP video slot, and four USB ports.

- **PIII-800.** A Pentium III running at 800 MHz made for a pretty speedy computer for its time, able to work with Windows versions through Windows 98SE. Standard equipment on this level of machine includes AGP video and USB ports. With this edition of the book, this model moved from the bottom of the modern computer list to the top of the Senior Citizen rolls.

- **PII-300.** PII indicates a Pentium II CPU, running in this example at a brisk 300 MHz. As a Pentium-based computer, it uses a combination of PCI and ISA buses to interconnect various elements. Later-model Pentium II machines based on ATX form motherboards introduced AGP video and USB ports.

- **P6-200.** P6 was an unofficial industry label for Intel's Pentium Pro, in this case running at what was once considered a zippy 200 MHz clock speed. The Pentium Pro had its short moment in the sun and was primarily used in servers and very demanding business applications. It quickly gave way to the more capable Pentium II processor, which was eventually supplanted by the Pentium III.

- **P5-100-PCI.** A P or P5 in a product name generally indicates that the computer uses a Pentium processor, in this case running at 100 MHz. The letters after the number indicate that the motherboard includes a PCI bus, which was introduced about the same time as the arrival of the Pentium.

- **P5-200 with MMX.** This Intel 200 MHz Pentium processor uses MMX technology; a set of extensions that delivers improved graphics and multimedia functions. This particular model includes 512K of pipeline burst SRAM cache, 32MB of SDRAM DIMM memory, and a PCI local-bus 3-D graphics accelerator with 2MB SGRAM video memory.

- **Pentium 100ES.** The Pentium part is easy, and the 100 indicates a 100-MHz chip. The meaning of ES, however, is less obvious but is an important distinction. This model, intended for use as a high-performance file server, uses an EISA bus, a relatively uncommon design that was also supplanted by PCI. If you have one of these, your upgrade and repair path is sharply limited.

- **4DX2-66V.** The processor in this venerable senior citizen is a 486DX2 running at 66 MHz. The V at the end means that this particular motherboard uses a VL or local bus, a popular design of several years ago that PCI bus models pushed aside.
- **486DX4-100.** Are you getting the clues here? A top-end 486 system in the senior citizen class, this system uses an Intel DX4 chip that, despite its enumeration, is actually clock-tripled rather than quadrupled. It runs at 100 MHz internally.
- **4SX-33.** This is a 486SX model running at 33 MHz. With this edition of *Fix Your Own PC*, this class of machines marks the line between senior citizen and dinosaur. You have to poke around under the covers or in the instruction manual to determine the type of bus it uses. This somewhat underpowered chip came out near the end of the VL bus era and the dawn of the PCI age; some motherboards included slots to serve both designs.
- **216.** Another dinosaur, this is an 80286 running at an anemic 16 MHz. The motherboard almost certainly uses a very basic AT (also called ISA) 16-bit bus. I keep this one around as a museum piece; it's like a sled without wheels among racing cars.
- **IBM Personal Computer.** Even deeper in the closet is an original IBM PC, the classic dinosaur that started the PC revolution. It uses an 8088 processor running at 4.77 MHz, a pair of gigantic (in size, not capacity) 5.25-inch 360K floppy drives, 64K of memory chips on the motherboard, and a crude CGA video adapter. I haven't fired it up in years, but I can't quite bring myself to deliver it to the dump. It cost almost $5,000 when I bought it.

AMD processors

What remains is the rest of the world: machines that use CPUs other than Intel chips. I have worked with machines built around AMD, Cyrix, SGS, and NexGen microprocessors. Of that group, only AMD is still a significant player in the PC marketplace; in fact, for the last part of 2005 and early 2006, AMD reached parity with Intel in shipments of new processors led by its successful Athlon, Opteron, and Sempron chips. By mid-2006, though, aggressive price-cutting and marketing by Intel returned it to the leading position in sales to PC end users. National Semiconductor bought Cyrix in 1997, and has dropped from sight, replaced on a tiny percentage of machines by VIA processors

from NS. VIA, in turn, settled a long-standing patent-infringement case with Intel in 2003, and by 2006 was concentrating on chipsets and special-purpose CPUs for notebooks and other small, mobile systems.

The following is a tour of some of these models:

- **AMD Athlon 64 X2.** As this edition goes to press, AMD was in something close to a lockstep with Intel in the developing market for multi-core processors. The Athlon 64 X2 is close to the Intel Core 2 Duo in performance in certain models, and generally offers the advantage of lower power consumption.
- **AMD Athlon, Athlon XP.** Athlon is AMD's answer to Intel's Pentium 4, and in some ways — including power consumption — it equaled or surpassed it in some models. An AMD Athlon can't be substituted in a motherboard designed for an Intel Pentium 4, or the other way around.
- **AMD K6-III 450.** Systems based on AMD's K6-III offer similar, or even better, performance compared with similarly equipped Intel PIII systems, at a lower initial cost.
- **AMD K6-266 MMX.** AMD's K6 modern machine processor delivers full compatibility with — and some superiority over — similar Pentium CPUs from Intel at a significant cost saving.

Dinosaur CPU makers

- **Cyrix 6x86-P166 + , IBM 6x86-P200 + , Cyrix 6x86-P200 + .** The Cyrix series of modern machine processors are functionally equivalent to Intel Pentium designs. The company used some special tricks to eke more speed out of their designs while maintaining near-perfect compatibility with Intel equivalents. They do make things a bit difficult with their naming scheme, however. The Cyrix 6x86-P166 + actually runs at 133 MHz, but claims to outperform an Intel Pentium 166 MHz chip. Isn't marketing fun? Now, one more issue: IBM manufactured chips for Cyrix for some time, and some machines may have chips with the IBM name instead of Cyrix. An IBM 6x86-P200 + runs at 166 MHz, acts like a 200 MHz Intel CPU, and is the same as a Cyrix 6x86-P200 + . Similarly, SGS-Thomson also made chips for Cyrix, and some systems may have an SGS logo.
- **AMD K5 PR100 MHz.** AMD's K5 is roughly equivalent to a Pentium P5.
- **Nx586 P100.** This system uses the NexGen Nx586 processor, a now-discontinued competitor to Intel's Pentium chip. The Nx586 was not pin-compatible with the Pentium and therefore required special motherboards and chip sets. It also lacked an on-chip

floating point unit (FPU). The chip model here is the P100, which actually runs at 93 MHz but claimed to rival a Pentium at 100 MHz. NexGen was bought out by AMD, and although that company may be able to support the chip, serious problems with a NexGen-based machine may require a change of motherboard and CPU.

The next place to look is the instruction manual that comes with the system. If you don't have the manual, there's a quick and easy way to check most of the elements of a PC if you have a copy of MSD (Microsoft Diagnostics), a capable utility that was supplied as part of MS-DOS 6.x and Windows 3.1. If you're running one of these out-dated operating systems, boot up the system and go to the DOS prompt. Microsoft warns that not all of MSD's readings are accurate if you run it from within Windows or from a DOS window opened under Windows, so exit Windows if it's running and execute MSD from the DOS prompt.

If your machine is running a current version of Windows and a basic Microsoft application, there's a quick and easy way to check most of a PC's elements. Under Windows XP, Windows Me, Windows 2000, Windows 98, or Windows 95, a built-in system information screen is available from within Microsoft applications, such as Word, Excel, and other Office programs. Just click Help, About Microsoft Word (or the name of the application running), System Info. You receive a full report like the one shown in Figure 1-13.

In those same operating systems, you can display this information directly by choosing System Information in the System Tools dialog box (Start ➪ Programs ➪ Accessories ➪ System Tools).

The final way to determine the nature of your machine is to look for yourself, although this is more difficult on modern machines because of the use of heat sinks, fans, and cooling tunnels that sit atop the processor. On an older machine, open the case and locate the CPU chip on the motherboard. The processor's manufacturer and number are printed on the chip. Although some computers tuck the CPU chip and part of the motherboard under the drives to save space, the CPU itself is still pretty easy to find; it's usually the largest single chip on the motherboard.

Most Pentium II and early Pentium III and AMD Athlon chips reside in carriers that stand up vertically from the motherboard. Later versions of Pentium III and Athlon CPUs, and current Pentium 4 microprocessors, have returned to a horizontal surface socket on the motherboard.

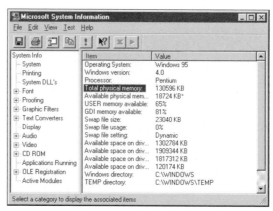

FIGURE 1-13: *A System Information report from within Microsoft Word from an older machine. Similar displays are available under Windows 98, Windows Me, Windows 2000, and Windows XP.*

The 8088 CPUs of a dinosaur are rectangular, about two inches long and half an inch wide. The 80286 chip is roughly one inch square. Senior citizen 80386, 486, and Pentium CPUs are big square chips that are hard to miss. Some 486 and Pentium chips are mounted in large chip carriers that make them easy to remove for upgrades; you may also see aluminum heat sinks atop some of the advanced chips.

The CPU may be labeled 8088, 80286, 80386, 80486, Pentium, or Pentium Pro; some dinosaur XT-style clones used an NEC V20 or V30 chip, and some modern machines use chips from manufacturers including AMD, NexGen, and Cyrix. And TI (Texas Instruments) and IBM also have variants of the Intel CPU with their names on them.

 CROSS-REFERENCE

See Chapter 2 for a more thorough discussion of the CPU march of time from the dawn of computer dinosaurs to the arrival of the modern machine.

Reinstalling the Cover

After you've looked around inside the machine, put the cover back on the computer, tucking in the cables.

Before you reinstall the cover, look down inside it and check to see whether there are any pegs or other protrusions on the inside front surface. If there aren't any pegs, simply tip the cover up extra high in front as you slide it onto the chassis, and then slide it straight back into place. Tighten the machine screws gently; force is neither necessary nor helpful. If there is a peg or two on the inside of the cover, installing the cover is a bit trickier; you must wiggle the cover up and down a bit to make it slide that last half-inch into position. You may have a wraparound cover that takes a little adjustment to get in place, or you may have just one side to snap back on.

If you have one of the newer cover designs that opens like a clamshell, simply reverse the process that you used to take the cover off in the first place.

As with any repair procedure, you might want to make notes (or use a digital camera to make a few visual reminders) as you take things apart. It helps greatly when you have to put your PC back together again.

After you get the cover in place, install the screws, reattach the power cable and other connecting cables (video, mouse, keyboard, and other external devices), and flip on the power switch.

If the computer doesn't boot up, don't panic. If the machine worked before you took off the cover, the problem almost certainly is an accidentally dislodged, misconnected, or pinched cable. You did plug it back into the power outlet, right?

SUMMARY

Now that you've completed a basic tour of the PC, you can move on to a more detailed examination of the brain of the computer — its microprocessor. The information in the next chapter prepares you to learn about the CPU inside your own machine and also prepares you for fixing and upgrading your machine to some of the latest technology.

Chapter 2

The Microprocessor

Intel has owned the heart of the PC market from its birth, when IBM chose Intel's 8088 microprocessor as the brains of the first PC. Today, Intel is still inside most PCs (called *x86* machines in the industry), although *Advanced Micro Devices (AMD)* has mounted a serious challenge in recent years. In 2006, Intel shipped about 75 percent of all processors for servers, workstations, and laptops; AMD had risen to about 24 percent of the overall market. But in certain segments, including low-cost consumer PCs sold at retail in the United States, Intel and AMD were nearly even. (A tiny sliver of the market is held by several special-purpose x86 processor makers, including Transmeta and Via. Longtime chip-maker Motorola and its partner IBM lost the PowerPC account with Apple in 2006 as that computer maker made the switch to Intel chips.)

The emergence of AMD as a serious competitor to Intel is good news for PC users. It brings competition on three very important levels: speed, quality, and price. Although some techies express very strong preferences for one design over the other, the fact is that chips from either company in the same class — high-performance, midrange, or budget — are very close in performance for most users. And Microsoft Windows and nearly every current piece of software do not care whether there's an Intel or an AMD chip inside.

When the IBM PC was born in 1981, Intel's 8088 was not the fastest processor available, but designers felt that the chip offered the best combination of speed, price, and availability of peripherals; and perhaps most important, the 8088 did not seem to present much of a threat to "real" computers, such as the massive mainframes and mini-computer that were IBM's bread and butter.

IBM's choice actually hobbled the expansion capabilities of PCs for many years and is still a residual factor in today's backward-compatible hardware and operating systems. Backward compatibility is an essential part of high-tech; it means that the latest, greatest hardware is still able to work with software developed for previous generations of machines. This is mostly true, assuming that everyone — from software designers to hardware makers — follows the rules at every step.

Software developed for dinosaurs and senior citizens should be able to run in some fashion on modern machines, although advances in the Windows operating system and hardware may make it difficult. For example, older programs may make assumptions about graphics modes or memory configurations that are no longer offered on highly integrated motherboards. Or, how do you install an old program that requires loading from a floppy disk drive?

Another change in recent years is the relative rarity of brain transplant surgery. At the height of what is now the senior citizen era, it was not uncommon for a computer user to remove the socketed Intel 486 or Intel Pentium chip from the motherboard and replace it with a faster or otherwise more advanced model.

It is important to note that, in general, you can't change your computer's CPU from one family to another because they involve different supporting chipsets, sockets, bus designs, and sometimes changes in electrical voltages. In most cases, however, you can replace a slower processor with a faster version within the same family.

It is possible to remove and upgrade a processor, but the economics may not make sense. Purchasing an upgraded processor for an existing machine may cost several hundred dollars; it might make more sense to sell or give away your older machine and buy a new one. The best time to spend a bit of extra money on a PC is when you first buy it; computer makers pay wholesale for their processors, motherboards, and other basic system components.

As you've already learned, in this book I segregate computers into modern machines, senior citizens, and dinosaurs. Modern PCs work with nearly all current software and hardware; senior citizens may be a few steps behind the younger competition but are still capable, and dinosaurs are mostly valuable for curiosity's sake.

In this chapter, you take a tour of all of the major processors used in PCs, working backward from the state-of-the-art to the day of the dinosaur. An artist's peek beneath the covers of a state-of-the-art Intel Core 2 Quad Extreme Edition processor is shown in Figure 2-1.

NOTE

Before this discussion of CPUs begins in earnest, here's an interesting perspective on the speed of today's CPUs. Intel's first microprocessor, the 4004, ran at 108 KHz (108,000 cycles per second). The fastest clock speeds for modern processors is in the range of about 3.8 GHz. If automobile speed had increased similarly over the same period, you could now drive from San Francisco to New York in about 5 seconds.

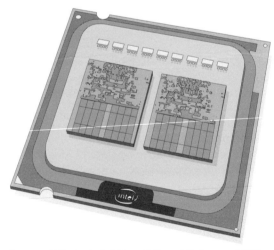

FIGURE 2-1: *An Intel Core 2 Quad Extreme Edition processor with two of its four cores exposed.*

Photo illustration courtesy of Intel Corporation.

The Amazing Arc of Moore's Law

An interesting perspective on computer history comes from Moore's Law, one of the underlying unofficial basic tenets of microprocessor development. Gordon Moore, one of the founders of Intel, predicted in 1965 that the number of transistors per integrated circuit would double every 18 months. Moore's original horizon was just ten years, but his forecast has proven to be uncannily accurate.

The curve has held up pretty well for more than 40 years, although other factors have come into play in recent years when it comes to processor design. The advent of the multicore processor from Intel and AMD has merged together two or four central processing spaces onto a single die. Design emphasis has shifted away from the sheer number of transistors in a processor, and away from raw clock speed, to appraisals of the actual amount of work that can be accomplished. The move toward multicore processors and other technologies including HyperThreading and large L2 caches often means that sets of smaller, leaner chips can work together to produce greater productivity.

Intel's first commercially used microprocessor, predating the personal computer, was the 4004, which had 2,250 transistors when it was introduced in 1971. By early 2006, the last of the single-core Pentium 4 processors managed to cram as many as 125 million transistors onto its tiny surface. As this book goes to press, the extreme edition of the Intel Core 2 Quad chip had 582 million transistors split amongst its four engines. The details of the most important members of the Intel family and their relation to Moore's Law are shown in Table 2-1. The same information is presented as a graph in Figure 2-2.

Table 2-1: The Numbers behind Moore's Law

Processor	Introduction Year	Transistors
4004	1971	2,300
8008	1972	3,500
8080	1974	4,500
8086	1978	29,000
8088	1979	29,000
286	1982	134,000
386	1985–1989	275,000
486 DX	1989–1994	1,180,000 to 1,600,000
Pentium	1993–1997	3,100,000 to 4,500,000
Pentium Pro	1995–1997	5,500,000

Processor	Introduction Year	Transistors
Pentium II	1997–1998	7,500,000
Pentium III	1999–2000	24,000,000
Celeron	1998–2003	28,000,000
Pentium 4	2000–2006	42,000,000 to 125,000,000
Pentium D	2005	230,000,000 to 376,000,000
Intel Core 2 Duo	2006	167,000,000 (2MB cache) or 291,000,000 (4MB cache)
Intel Core 2 Quad	2007	582,000,000 (QX6700, QX6800)

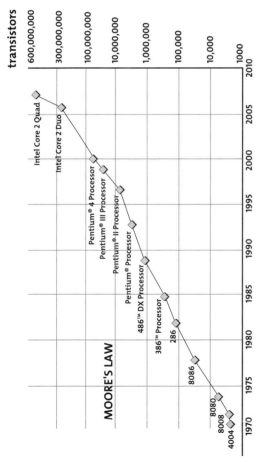

FIGURE 2-2: *Moore's Law.*

How a CPU Works

The tiny CPU microprocessor — which over the history of the PC has ranged in size from a sugar cube to a cell phone and now back to a matchbook — is the locomotive of the computer and is often its single most expensive internal component. The basic assignment of the CPU is to read data from storage, manipulate that information, and then move the data back to storage or to video circuitry for display. It can also output information to an Ethernet subsystem for transfer over a local area network or the Internet, and send data through a port to printers or external storage devices.

CPUs are measured by the number of cycles per second used by the processor; think of cycles as clicks on the ratchet wheel of a machine pushing something forward. The cycles are measured in megahertz and gigahertz, meaning millions or billions of cycles per second.

The CPU's clock speed, however, is not the only determinant of the ultimate speed of the computer. The processor must be wedded to a fast bus — an electronic superhighway — for the interchange of information and connection to memory and peripherals that can keep up with its speed. In general, speed is limited by the slowest element in the data stream.

The heart of the CPU is a dime-sized piece of silicon. Etched onto the silicon are tens or hundreds of millions of tiny transistors that operate as voltage-controlled switches, turning current flow off and on. CPUs are manufactured in high-tech clean rooms; depending on the maker and technology, the transistors are etched by chemicals or by exposure to intense light (photolithographic processes). As I have noted, in the most current modern processors, Intel and AMD have begun offering single chips that have two or four (with eight on the horizon) cores, mating the processing power of multiple CPUs with a single set of support chips, connectors, and buses.

A computer is a binary device, meaning that all information is stored and manipulated as a series of 0s or 1s, or Offs and Ons. The transistors are grouped to create computer words that represent letters, numbers, or individual elements of a complex picture or sound.

Another type of information manipulated by the CPU is an *instruction,* a code that tells the system what to do with a particular piece or group of data: move it from one location to another or apply a mathematical operation to it. Think of instructions as verbs. Some of the transistors of the CPU hold *instruction pointers* that tell the CPU the location in memory for an instruction. *Registers* hold data waiting to be processed, or data that has been processed and is waiting to be moved or stored. A specialized section of the CPU is the *arithmetic logic unit (ALU)*, which acts as a calculator to perform math and logic functions.

Here's an example of a sequence that may take place in a CPU:

1. The CPU comes to an instruction pointer; this triggers an *instruction fetch* to bring the instruction from memory within the CPU, in RAM, or elsewhere in the system. (The further the fetch has to go to retrieve the instruction, the slower the process.)
2. Then the *instruction decoder* accepts the instruction from the fetch and translates it for the use of the CPU.
3. The entire operation is coordinated by the *control unit*. This specialized area issues the commands for action by the fetch and decoder.
4. Once the ALU performs the instruction or series of instructions, the control unit moves on to the next fetch.

Sometimes what seems like a very simple instruction can actually involve dozens, hundreds, or thousands of steps. In fact, most computers are capable of just one operation: addition. Through manipulation, addition can be used to solve multiplication, division, and subtraction problems.

This points up the basic truth of computers: They are very stupid but extremely fast. Though a human may intuitively know that 25×25 equals 625, a computer has to work it out step by step, starting with summing 00011001 25 times to come up with the binary answer of 00000010 01110001.

Some instructions take more time than others to execute, and some data or instructions are closer at hand than others. And so, to keep everything moving along in a coordinated fashion, the microprocessor creates a regularly beating heartbeat. The system's clock or clock generator sends out precisely spaced pulses that push along instructions and data.

The original IBM PC, with the Intel 8088 as its CPU, had a clock speed of 4.77 MHz or just under 5 million cycles per second. Today, modern machines have moved into gigahertz territory, with CPUs capable of speeds of more than 3 billion cycles per second.

But as I have mentioned, the number of cycles per second is just one element of a CPU's speed. Another is the architecture of the chip and the system itself. One important improvement in recent years has been the addition of *cache* memory within the CPU or located nearby on the CPU carrier. Either design allows the microprocessor to store instructions or data close at hand; sophisticated algorithms anticipate the need for information before the CPU calls for it and pre-fetches it. When the information is needed, the CPU doesn't have to waste cycles waiting for a fetch instruction to be issued, move across the system bus to memory, and then return across the bus. Advanced processors, including nearly all modern CPUs, add a second level of high-speed memory called *L2 cache* (level 2 cache) between the CPU's cache and the system RAM.

Key to getting the most out of cache is a sophisticated algorithm to manage its use. *Branch prediction* makes an intelligent guess at the next direction for the processor to fetch the instruction before it is called. *Speculative execution* goes one step beyond to execute the predicted branch before the CPU even asks for it. And *out-of-order completion* works on instructions in an illogical but more efficient manner.

Other improvements on the hardware side in recent years include *multiple ALUs* to allow subdivision of complex mathematical problems into multiple concurrent processes. A specialized *floating point arithmetic unit* offloads some of the ALU's work, concentrating on very large and small numbers with many integers on either side of the decimal point. And *pipelining* works with the CPU to divide instructions into small pieces that can piggyback one on the other, moving along on nearly parallel tracks.

Taking the Measure of a CPU

Microprocessors have three important measures of their speed and capability: the data bus, the address bus, and the processor clock speed. The following is an essential guide to these key measures:

Data bus

The more bits of information that can be moved in and out of the chip at a time, the better the flow of data. The computer moves information in the form of bytes, which are made up of eight bits (individual 0s or 1s) of the binary code. Depending on the microprocessor's ability to manipulate and store blocks of data, computer words can be made up of 8, 16, 32, or more bits (or 1, 2, 3, or more bytes).

All information within the computer is represented by numbers, and for simplicity's sake, the PC uses binary math — just 0s and 1s, on and off, yes and no. And so the letter *W* is represented by the ASCII code 87, which is represented in binary math as 1 0 1 0 1 1 1 (from right to left, one 1, one 2, one 4, no 8s, one 16, no 32s, one 64 — for a grand total of 87 in decimal notation).

The original PC could work on just one computer word at a time. Modern machines can chomp on four or eight words with each cycle. Put another way, an eight-word machine is a 64-bit processor.

Think of the data bus as the highway the CPU uses to move information: A two-lane (16-bit) highway is twice as good as a one-lane (8-bit) road, and a four- or eight-lane superhighway is that much better. The original 8088 CPU has an 8-bit data bus. The 286 and 386SX microprocessors have a 16-bit data bus. The 386DX CPUs, as well as the 486 series, have 32-bit data buses, while modern processors from the Pentium onward pump data through a 64-bit external data bus.

Address bus

These are the wires the CPU uses to describe the location in memory where data is retrieved or sent. The more bits in the address bus, the more memory locations are possible. Remember that the computer calculates numbers using a binary system: A 4-bit number, for example, can hold values from 0 to 15.

An original 8088 and 8086 processor had a 20-bit address bus, meaning it could work with up to 1,048,576 bytes of memory, which translates in computer shorthand to 1,024K or 1MB. The 286 and 386SX families used a 24-bit bus, which expanded the memory capacity of the system to 16MB. The 386DX, 486, Pentium, and Pentium Pro chips offered a 32-bit address bus, which zoomed memory capacity to 4,096MB, or 4GB. And the Pentium II chip went up a notch to a 36-bit bus, permitting memory addresses corresponding to 64GB of memory. (Some of the last models in the Pentium Pro series also used a 36-bit bus.) The current generation of chips, from Pentium 4 and AMD Athlon onward, have 64-bit address buses and support tens of gigabytes of memory (1.84×1019 bytes, theoretically).

Processor clock speed

The clock is the CPU's metronome. Each beat of the clock — actually a crystal oscillator or an electronic equivalent that vibrates a fixed number of times per second when electricity is applied — is a signal to the CPU to perform an action or move data. The clock speed is measured in cycles per second, which are reported in hertz. A 700 MHz (megahertz) clock operates at 700 million cycles per second; a 1.7 GHz clock pulses at 1.7 billion cycles per second.

Obviously, the faster the clock speed, the faster the CPU can move data. However, each CPU has its own speed limit, based on such issues as heat buildup caused by high-frequency operations and the electrical characteristics of each actual product. Furthermore, a CPU's performance depends not only on its clock speed but also on its processing capability (including the number of internal cycles necessary to execute an instruction), how fast the bus can move data to and from the chip, and other factors, such as internal and external cache sizes, pipelining, and superscalar architecture.

The 8088 and 8086 processors needed about 12 cycles to complete a basic instruction. Improvements in the internal instructions enabled a drop to about five cycles for the 286 and 386 class, and two cycles for a 486 chip. The Pentium chip can generally operate at one cycle per instruction.

And then there are *wait cycles,* which are wasted clock ticks while the CPU pauses until the rest of the system catches up with it. Old, slow 8086 systems needed four cycles plus several wait cycles to transfer data to and from memory.

Finally, just to make things more difficult, modern CPUs are capable of running at multiples of the motherboard's speed. The original Pentiums, running at 60 MHz and 66 MHz, matched the speed of the motherboard at a 1:1 ratio. But every Pentium-class microprocessor since then runs faster than the motherboard.

Chip makers have pushed to change the fabrication process to allow transistors to be even tinier and closer together; it's all in the service of speed, energy consumption, and heat reduction. Several years ago it was big news when processors were being produced at 0.18 or 0.13 micron separations. As this edition goes to press, Intel has crunched its products down by another 50 percent, to 0.065 microns. The sizes have become so small that makers have shifted from measurements in microns to the smaller nanometer. (One nanometer is equal to 1,000 microns. Today's 0.065 micron process is expressed as 65 nanometers.)

The problem engineers face is one of physics: As wiring and components get closer, they approach the limits (at least as we currently understand them) of manufacturing processes and problems related to interference between closely packed electrical devices. There has to be a limit; wires cannot be placed 0 nanometers apart, because that would put them one atop the other. But meanwhile, companies are experimenting with 45 nanometer processes using technology similar to today's chips, and IBM is working on a new technology using deep-ultraviolet optical lithography that may permit creating chips with circuitry only 29.9 nanometers apart.

HyperThreading or Multi-Core Technologies

The quest to create microprocessors that do two things at the same time is as old as the personal computer. There have been a number of solutions, most of which have involved electronic trickery: essentially harnessing the great speed of the CPU to rapidly switch back and forth amongst multiple assignments. That's not quite the same as simultaneity, but it works reasonably well in certain combinations of hardware, software, and tasks.

In more recent years, chipmakers introduced a pair of technologies that allow today's processors (with huge numbers of transistors and blazing speed) to adapt themselves to tasks by dividing themselves (either logically or physically) to take on multiple tasks.

HyperThreading (HT) is an Intel technology that allows one physical processor to operate as two logical processors. To benefit from this design you'll need

- A CPU with HT technology
- A current version of Windows (Windows XP Service Pack 1 or later)
- One or more software applications optimized to work with HT

The final piece of the puzzle is to turn on HyperThreading. You can enable or disable HT through your computer's system setup screen. To check if your computer is making use of this facility, do the following:

1. Click Start, then right-click My Computer. Click Properties.
2. Click Hardware ⇨ Device Manager.
3. Locate the plus (+) sign next to Processors. If HyperThreading is enabled, you see the processor listed twice.

Multi-core is a current trend in microprocessor design introduced by Intel, with an equivalent technology from AMD. First out the door were dual-core processors, including the Pentium D and Intel Core 2 Duo; in early 2007 Intel delivered the first quad-core processors for desktop machines. AMD has kept pace, and both makers are also planning processors with eight or more cores.

Under this scheme there is a physical separation between two or more cores on a single processor chip (or *die* as designers call it). The cores, which run at the same frequency, can handle different tasks, or take parts of the same task and tackle them separately.

In the initial release of Dual Core processors from Intel, the low end of the family offered 2MB of L2 cache while the more advanced CPUs came with 4MB of cache. That memory — dedicated to holding anticipated instructions and data — can be split evenly between the cores or dynamically adjusted to benefit one or the other core if needed.

Among the bonus benefits of multicore processors are a reduction in power consumption and heat generation.

Overall, Intel claimed as much as a 40-percent increase in performance and a 40-percent decrease in power consumption for its Intel Core 2 Duo processors compared to its own single-core CPUs. And initial tests of quad core processors showed a 70-percent performance improvement over dual core models.

The Intel Family Tree

For purposes of this book (concentrating on PCs and excluding laptops, handheld computers, and special-purpose devices) the Intel family of processors has gone through nine major generations. The first four generations used the number 8 as a first name, beginning with the 8088/8086/80186 family and running through the 80286, 80386, and 80486 series. Over the years, Intel dropped the 80 prefix from the names of the chips for marketing purposes, calling them 386 and 486 processors. Within the 80386 and 80486 families, some chips were subdivided into SX and DX, DX2, and DX4 groups.

NOTE

The Intel 8088 was closely related to its successor in the marketplace, the 8086. And all subsequent chips used in PCs have kept compatibility with the basic instruction set of the original design. For that reason, processors for use in machines in the PC family are sometimes referred to as *x86* processors even though they have moved well beyond their ancestors in capabilities and names.

The fifth family was the Pentium. With its introduction, Intel changed its naming convention by inventing a label that has a connection to the Greek word *pente*, meaning five. On the legal side, choosing an invented name gave Intel something it could use as a brand name; numbers can't be easily registered as trademarks. Some technical types maintained a link to the family by calling the Pentium the P5, a reference to its once-intended 80586 name. Next came the Pentium Pro (the P6 to some), used almost exclusively in servers and other special-purpose machines. Intel later added the MMX multimedia extensions to the Pentium family, creating a subgroup of CPUs.

The sixth generation was the Pentium II, a completely new chip architecture. These chips were initially expensive, physically huge by existing standards, and required relatively high power. Within a relatively short time, however, the PII became a popular, high-speed alternative for the Pentium and Pentium Pro.

Seventh in line was the Pentium III, an enhanced and expanded Pentium II architecture. The Pentium III was the last in Intel's line of 32-bit processors, available in a wide range of speeds and socket arrangements.

The Celeron chip was originally introduced as a subset of the Pentium II, a slower and less-expensive cousin intended for use in low-priced but still-capable new systems. Later and more advanced versions of the Celeron were based on the Pentium III design.

Though they were not used in PCs, but instead in high-end servers and workstations, it is worth noting Intel's Pentium Xeon II processors. The Xeon and the 350 MHz and 400 MHz Pentium IIs were the first Intel chips to run on a system bus of 100 MHz, offering up to a 50-percent increase in bus performance over the common 66 MHz speed of most machines current at the time. Later, Intel introduced the Pentium III Xeon chip, a natural follow-on to the Pentium III in much the same way as the PII Xeon followed the Pentium II chip.

The Xeon chip family began at 400 MHz and included as much as 2MB of high-speed cache memory to increase chip performance. Xeon chips are more expensive to manufacture because the processors come in a Slot 2 (SC330) package, which is larger (330 pins as opposed to 242 pins) than the current Slot 1 (SC242) package used for desktops. The custom-made cache memory also adds to the price.

The eighth family from Intel was the Pentium 4, a 64-bit microprocessor introduced in 2000 at 1.4 GHz and eventually reaching to 3 GHz or more even as Intel and its competitor AMD switched their design philosophy (and their marketing) away from sheer clock speed in favor of chips that get more done per clock cycle. The ninth generation of Intel microprocessors, then, are the multicores. The current leaders are the Intel Core 2 Quad and the Intel Core 2 Duo, with the Intel Pentium D serving as a lesser, entry-level version.

Table 2-2 shows the progression of CPUs from Intel.

Upping the ante: AMD

As this book goes to press, AMD was prepared to launch its 4×4 technology, which is built around a motherboard and chipset that can tie together a pair of dual-core CPUs. And in 2007, AMD was set to introduce the AMD Quad FX technology, which allows manufacturers or users to attach two dual-core AMD Athlon FX processors into separate sockets on a motherboard, giving four physical cores. Since the two multi-core processors are not on the same connector, AMD gives each CPU its own cache and its own dedicated memory. As with the Intel design, AMD allows the multi-core processors to work separately or together, as needed.

And further along in the pipeline is an AMD plan to expand its existing HyperTransport bus, the high-speed connection between AMD microprocessors, memory, graphics adapters, and other devices, to allow design of specialized coprocessors and accelerators.

Ch
2

Table 2-2: Intel CPUs by Family

Intel Core 2 Quad Processor Extreme Edition

Intel Core 2 Extreme Quad Processor. *QX6800* 2.93 GHz. *QX6700* 2.667 GHz.	**Processor Package:** FC-LGA. 775-land socket. Front-side bus speed: 1066 MHz. Introduced 2006. 65 nanometer process technology. Two integrated 4MB L2 caches.

Intel Core 2 Quad Processor

Intel Core 2 Quad Processor. *Q6600* 2.4 GHz.	**Processor Package:** FC-LGA. 775-land socket. Front-side bus speed: 1066 MHz. Introduced 2006. 65 nanometer process technology. Two integrated 4MB L2 caches.

Intel Core 2 Duo Processor Extreme Edition

Intel Core 2 Duo Processor. *X6800* 2.93 GHz.	**Processor Package:** FC-LGA. 775-land socket. Front-side bus speed: 1066 MHz. Introduced 2006. 65 nanometer process technology. Integrated 4MB L2 cache.

Intel Core 2 Duo

Intel Core 2 Duo Processor. *E6700* 2.66 GHz, *E6600* 2.4 GHz.	**Processor Package:** FC-LGA. 775-land socket. Front-side bus speed: 1066 MHz. Introduced 2006. 65 nanometer process technology. Integrated 4MB L2 cache.
Intel Core 2 Duo Processor. *E6400* 2.13 GHz, *E6300* 1.86 GHz.	**Processor Package:** FC-LGA. 775-land socket. Front-side bus speed: 1066 MHz. Introduced 2006. 65 nanometer process technology. Integrated 2MB L2 cache.

Pentium 4 Processor Supporting HyperThreading Technology

Pentium 4 Processor Supporting HyperThreading Technology.	Processors have numbers independent of clock speed. *672* 3.8 GHz. *670* 3.8 GHz. *662* 3.6 GHz. *660* 3.6 GHz. *650* 3.4 GHz. *640* 3.2 GHz. *630* 3.0 GHz. **Processor Package:** FC-LGA. 775-land socket. Front-side bus speed: 800 MHz. 90 nanometer process technology. Integrated 2MB L2 cache.
Pentium 4 Processor Supporting HyperThreading Technology.	Processors have numbers independent of clock speed. *661* 3.6 GHz. *651* 3.4 GHz. *641* 3.2 GHz. *631* 3.0 GHz. **Processor Package:** FC-LGA. 775-land socket. **Front-side Bus Speed:** 800 MHz. 65 nanometer process technology. Integrated 2MB L2 cache.
Pentium 4 Processor Supporting HyperThreading Technology.	Processors have numbers independent of clock speed. *571* 3.8 GHz. *570J* 3.8 GHz. *561* 3.6 GHz. *560* 3.6 GHz. *551* 3.4 GHz. *550* 3.4 GHz. *541* 3.2 GHz. *540* 3.2 GHz. *531* 3.0 GHz. *530* 3.0 GHz. *521* 2.8 GHz. *520* 2.8 GHz. **Processor Package:** FC-LGA. 775-land socket. **Front-side Bus Speed:** 800 MHz. 90 nanometer process technology. Integrated 1MB L2 cache.
Pentium 4 Processor Supporting HyperThreading Technology.	Processors have numbers independent of clock speed. *524* 3.06 GHz. **Processor package:** FC-LGA. 775-land socket. Front-side bus speed: 533 MHz. 90 nanometer process technology. Integrated 1MB L2 cache.
Pentium 4 Processor Supporting HyperThreading Technology. 3.4, 3.2, 3.0, 2.8 GHz.	**Processor Package:** FC-PGA4. 478-pin land socket. **Front-side Bus Speed:** 800 MHz. 90 nanometer process technology. Integrated 1MB L2 cache.

Pentium 4 Processor Supporting HyperThreading Technology

Pentium 4 Processor Supporting HyperThreading Technology. 3.4, 3.2, 3.0, 2.8, 2.6, 2.4 GHz.	**Processor Package:** FC-PGA2. 478-pin socket. **Front-side Bus Speed:** 800 MHz. 90 nanometer process technology. Integrated 512KB L2 cache.

Pentium 4 Processor Extreme Edition Supporting HyperThreading Technology

Pentium 4 Processor Extreme Edition Supporting HyperThreading Technology. 3.73 GHz.	**Processor Package:** FC-LGA. 775-land socket. Front-side bus speed: 1066 MHz. 90 nanometer process technology. Integrated 2MB L2 cache.
Pentium 4 Processor Supporting HyperThreading Technology. 3.73 GHz.	**Processor Package:** FC-LGA. 775-land socket. Front-side bus speed: 1066 MHz. 90 nanometer process technology. Integrated 2MB L2 cache.
Pentium 4 Processor Extreme Edition Supporting HyperThreading Technology. 3.4 GHz.	**Processor Package:** FC-LGA. 775-land socket. Front-side bus speed: 800 MHz. 0.13 micron process technology. Integrated 512KB L2 cache, 2MB L3 cache.
Pentium 4 Processor Extreme Edition Supporting HyperThreading Technology. 3.4 GHz.	**Processor Package:** mPGA478. 478-pin socket. Front-side bus speed: 800 MHz. 0.13 micron process technology. Integrated 512KB L2 cache, 2MB L3 cache.
Pentium 4 Processor Extreme Edition Supporting HyperThreading Technology. 3.2 GHz.	**Processor Package:** FC-PGA2. 478-pin socket. Front-side bus speed: 800 MHz. 0.13 micron process technology. Integrated 2MB L2 cache.

Pentium D Processor

Pentium D Processor.	Processors have numbers independent of clock speed. 950 3.40 GHz. 940 3.2 GHz. 930 3.0 GHz. 920 2.8 GHz. **Processor Package:** FC-LGA. 775-land socket. Front-side bus speed: 800 MHz. 65 nanometer process technology. Integrated 2MBx2 L2 cache.
Pentium D Processor.	Processors have numbers independent of clock speed. 840 3.2 GHz. 830 3.0 GHz. 820 2.8 GHz. **Processor package:** FC-LGA. 775-land socket. Front-side bus speed: 800 MHz. 90 nanometer process technology. Integrated 1MBx2 L2 cache.
Pentium D Processor.	Processors have numbers independent of clock speed. 805 2.66 GHz. **Processor Package:** FC-LGA. 775-land socket. Front-side bus speed: 533 MHz. 90 nanometer process technology. Integrated 1MBx2 L2 cache.
Pentium D Processor.	Processors have numbers independent of clock speed. 960 3.6 GHz. **Processor Package:** LGA775. 775-land socket. Front-side bus speed: 800 MHz. 65 nanometer process technology. Integrated 2MBx2 L2 cache.
Pentium D Processor.	Processors have numbers independent of clock speed. 915 2.8 GHz. 945 3.4. **Processor Package:** FC-LGA. 775-land socket. Front-side bus speed: 800 MHz. 65 nanometer process technology. Integrated 2MBx2 L2 cache.

Continued

Table 2-2: *Continued*

Pentium Processor Extreme Edition

Pentium Processor Extreme Edition.	Processors have numbers independent of clock speed. 965 3.73 GHz. 955 3.46 GHz. **Processor Package:** FC-LGA. 775-land socket. Front-side bus speed: 1066 MHz. 65 nanometer process technology. Integrated 2MBx2 L2 cache.
Pentium Processor Extreme Edition.	Processors have numbers independent of clock speed. 840 3.2 GHz. **Processor Package:** FC-LGA. 775-land socket. Front-side bus speed: 800 MHz. 90 nanometer process technology. Integrated 1MBx2 L2 cache.

Pentium 4

Pentium 4. 2.8 GHz.	Processor package: FC-PGA4. 478-pin socket. Front-side bus speed: 533 MHz. Introduced 2003. 55 million transistors. 90 nanometer process technology. Integrated 1MB L2 cache.
Pentium. 2.4 GHz.	**Processor Package:** mPGA478. 478-pin socket. Front-side bus speed: 533 MHz. Introduced 2003. 55 million transistors. 90 nanometer process technology. Integrated 1MB L2 cache.
Pentium 4. 3.06, 2.8, 2.66, 2.53, 2.4, 2.26 GHz.	**Processor Package:** FC-PGA2. 478-pin socket. System bus speed: 533 MHz. Introduced 2002. 55 million transistors. 0.13 micron process technology. Integrated 512K L2 cache.
Pentium 4. 2.6, 2.5, 2.4, 2.2, 2.0, 1.9, 1.8 GHz.	**Processor Package:** FC-PGA2. 478-pin socket. System bus speed: 400 MHz. Introduced 2002. 55 million transistors. 0.18 micron process technology. Integrated 512K L2 cache.
Pentium 4. 2.0, 1.9, 1.8, 1.7, 1.6, 1.5 GHz.	**Processor Package:** FC-PGA2. 478-pin socket. System bus speed: 400 MHz. Introduced 2002. 55 million transistors. 0.18 micron process technology. Integrated 256K L2 cache.
Pentium 4. 2.0, 1.9, 1.8, 1.7, 1.6, 1.5 GHz.	**Processor Package:** PPGA INT3. 423-pin socket. System bus speed: 400 MHz. Introduced 2002. 55 million transistors. 0.18 micron process technology. Integrated 256K L2 cache.
Pentium 4. 1.4, 1.3 GHz.	**Processor Package:** PPGA INT2. 423-pin socket. System bus speed: 400 MHz. Introduced 2002. 55 million transistors. 0.18 micron process technology. Integrated 256K L2 cache.
Pentium 4. 2.0, 1.9, 1.8, 1.7, 1.6 GHz.	**Processor Package:** PGA423 and PGA478. 423 or 478 pin socket. System bus speed: 400 MHz. Introduced July and August 2001. 42 million transistors. 0.18 micron process technology. Integrated 256K L2 advanced transfer cache.
Pentium 4. 1.4 and 1.5 GHz.	**Processor Package:** PGA423. System bus speed: 400 MHz. Introduced: November 2000. 0.18 micron process. 256K L2 integrated advanced transfer cache.

Celeron

Intel Celeron. 2.4, 2.3, 2.2, 2.1, 2.0, 1.8, 1.7 MHz.	**Processor Package:** Flip-Chip Pin Grid Array (FC-PGA). System bus speed: 400 MHz. Introduced mid-2002 through mid-2003. 128K cache on-die. 0.13 micron technology. Used in value PCs.
Intel Celeron. 1.4, 1.3, 1.2 MHz.	**Processor Package:** Flip-Chip Pin Grid Array (FC-PGA). System bus speed: 100 MHz. Introduced late 2001 through mid-2002. 256K cache on-die. 0.13 micron technology. Used in value PCs.
Intel Celeron. 1.0–1.1 MHz.	**Processor Package:** Flip-Chip Pin Grid Array (FC-PGA). System bus speed: 100 MHz. 128K cache on-die. 0.18 micron process. Used in value PCs.

Celeron

Intel Celeron. 800–950 MHz.	**Processor Package:** Flip-Chip Pin Grid Array (FC-PGA). System bus speed: 100 MHz. Introduced: July 2001. 128K cache on-die. 0.18 micron process. Used in value PCs.
Intel Celeron. 850 MHz.	**Processor Package:** Flip-Chip Pin Grid Array (FC-PGA). System bus speed: 100 MHz. Introduced: May 2001. 0.18 micron process. Designed for value PCs.
Intel Celeron. 800 MHz.	**Processor Package:** Flip-Chip Pin Grid Array (FC-PGA). System bus speed: 100 MHz. Introduced: January 2001. 128K on-die L2 cache. 0.18 micron process. Designed for value PCs.
Intel Celeron. 733 and 766 MHz.	**Processor Package:** Flip-Chip Pin Grid Array (FC-PGA). System bus speed: 66 MHz. Introduced: November 2000. 128K on-die L2 cache. 0.18 micron process. Designed for value PCs.
Intel Celeron. 633, 667, and 700 MHz.	**Processor Package:** Flip-Chip Pin Grid Array (FC-PGA). System bus speed: 66 MHz. Introduced: June 2000. 128K on-die L2 cache. 0.18 micron process. Designed for value PCs.
Intel Celeron. 566 and 600 MHz.	**Processor Package:** Flip-Chip Pin Grid Array (FC-PGA). System bus speed: 66 MHz. Introduced: March 2000. 128K on-die cache. 0.18 micron process. Designed for value PCs.
Intel Celeron. 533 MHz.	**Processor Package:** Plastic Pin Grid Array (PPGA), 370 pins. System bus speed: 66 MHz. Introduced: January 2000. 19 million transistors. 0.25 micron process. 128K on-die cache. Designed for value PCs.
Intel Celeron. 466 and 500 MHz.	**Processor Package:** Plastic Pin Grid Array (PPGA), 370 pins. System bus speed: 66 MHz. Introduced: April 1999 and August 1999. 19 million transistors. 0.25 micron process. 128K on-die cache.
Intel Celeron. 433 MHz.	**Processor Package:** Single Edge Processor Package (SEPP), 242 pins. System bus speed: 66 MHz. Introduced: March 1999. 19 million transistors. 0.25 micron process. 128K on-die cache.
Intel Celeron. 400, 366 MHz.	**Processor Package:** Single Edge Processor Package (SEPP), 242 pins; or Plastic Pin Grid Array (PPGA), 370 pins. System bus speed: 66 MHz. Introduced: January 1999. 19 million transistors. 0.25 micron process. Designed for value PCs.
Intel Celeron. 333 MHz.	**Processor Package:** Single Edge Processor Package (SEPP), 242 pins. System bus speed: 66 MHz. Introduced: August 1998. 19 million transistors. 0.25 micron process. Designed for value PCs.
Intel Celeron. 300 MHz.	**Processor Package:** Single Edge Processor Package (SEPP), 242 pins. System bus speed: 66 MHz. Introduced: August 1998. The Intel Celeron processor was designed for use in economy PCs, optimized for uses including gaming and educational software. 19 million transistors. 0.25 micron process.
Intel Celeron. 300 MHz.	**Processor Package:** Single Edge Processor Package (SEPP), 242 pins. System bus speed: 66 MHz. Introduced: June 1998. 7.5 million transistors. 0.25 micron process. Designed for value PCs.
Intel Celeron. 266 MHz.	**Processor Package:** Single Edge Processor Package (SEPP), 242 pins. System bus speed: 66 MHz. Introduced: 7.5 million transistors. 0.25 micron process. Designed for value PCs.

Continued

Table 2-2: *Continued*

Xeon

Intel Xeon. 2.0, 1.7, 1.5, and 1.4 GHz.	**Processor Package:** Organic Lan Grid Array 603 (OLGA 603). System bus speed: 400 MHz. Introduced: September 25, 2001 (2.0 processor), May 2001. 256K integrated L2 advanced transfer cache. 0.18 micron process. Designed for high-performance and mid-range dual processor workstations.
Intel Xeon. 3.06, 2.80 GHz.	**Processor Package:** Organic Lan Grid Array 603 (OLGA 603). System bus speed: 533 MHz. Introduced: March 2003, November 2002. 108 million transistors. 512K integrated L2 advanced transfer cache. 0.13 micron process. Designed for workstations and servers.
Intel Xeon MP. 2.0, 1.90, 1.50 GHz.	**Processor Package:** Organic Lan Grid Array 603 (OLGA 603). System bus speed: 400 MHz. Introduced: November 2002. 108 million transistors. 2MB, 1 MB integrated L3 cache. 0.13 micron process. Designed for multiprocessing mid-tier and back-end servers.
Intel Xeon MP. 1.60, 1.50, 1.40 GHz.	**Processor Package:** Organic Lan Grid Array 603 (OLGA 603). System bus speed: 400 MHz. Introduced: March 2002. 108 million transistors. 256K integrated L2 advanced transfer cache. 0.13 micron process. Designed for workstations and servers.
Intel Xeon. 2.80, 2.60, 2.40, 2.20. 2.0, 1.80, GHz.	**Processor Package:** Organic Lan Grid Array 603 (OLGA 603). System bus speed: 400 MHz. Introduced: April and September 2002. 55 million transistors. 512K integrated L2 advanced transfer cache. 0.13 micron process. Designed for workstations and servers.
Intel Xeon. 2.0, 1.70, 1.50, 1.40.	**Processor Package:** Organic Lan Grid Array 603 (OLGA 603). System bus speed: 400 MHz. Introduced: May 2001. 42 million transistors. 256K integrated L2 advanced transfer cache. 0.13 micron process. Designed for high-performance and mid-range dual processor-enabled workstations and servers.

Pentium III

Pentium III Xeon. 933 MHz.	**Processor Package:** SC330. System bus speed: 133 MHz. Addressable memory: 64GB. Introduced: May 2001. Integrated 2MB advanced transfer cache. System bus width 64 bits; addressable memory 64GB. 0.18 micron process. Designed for high-end servers and multiprocessing systems.
Pentium III Xeon. 900 MHz.	**Processor Package:** SC330. System bus speed: 100 MHz. Addressable memory: 64GB. Introduced: March 2001. Integrated 2MB advanced transfer cache. System bus width 64 bits; addressable memory 64GB. 0.18 micron process. Designed for high-end servers and multiprocessing systems.
Pentium III and Pentium III Xeon. 933 MHz.	**Processor Package:** Single Edge Contact Cartridge (SECC2), Flip-Chip Pin Grid Array (FC-PGA), and SC330. System bus speed: 133 MHz. Addressable memory: 64GB. Introduced: May 2000. 256K L2 integrated advanced transfer cache. 0.18 micron process. Designed for servers and workstations.
Pentium III. 700 MHz.	**Processor Package:** SC330. System bus speed: 100 MHz. Addressable memory: 64GB. Introduced: May 2000. 1MB and 2MB integrated L2 advanced transfer cache. 0.18 micron process. Designed for four- and eight-way servers.

Pentium III Xeon. 866 MHz.

Processor Package: Single Edge Contact Cartridge (SECC2). System bus speed: 133 MHz. Addressable memory: 64GB. Introduced: April 2000. 28 million transistors. 0.18 micron process. 256K integrated L2 advanced transfer cache. Designed for servers and workstations.

Pentium III. 850 and 866 MHz, 1.0 GHz.

Processor Package: Single Edge Contact Cartridge (SECC and SECC2). System bus speed: 100 and 133 MHz. Addressable memory: 64GB. Introduced: March 2000. 0.18 micron process. 256K integrated L2 advanced transfer cache.

Pentium III Xeon. 800 MHz.

Processor Package: Single Edge Contact Cartridge (SECC2). System bus speed: 133 MHz. Addressable memory: 64GB. Introduced: January 2000. 256K integrated L2 advanced transfer cache. 0.18 micron process. Designed for servers and workstations.

Pentium III Xeon. 600, 667, and 733 MHz.

Processor Package: Single Edge Contact Cartridge (SECC2). System bus speed: 133 MHz. Addressable memory: 64GB. Introduced: October 1999. 28 million transistors. 0.18 micron process. 256K integrated L2 advanced transfer cache. Designed for servers and workstations.

Pentium III. 500, 533, 550, 600, 650, 667, 700, and 733MHz.

Processor Package: Single Edge Contact Cartridge (SECC2) and Flip-Chip Pin Grid Array (FC-PGA). System bus speed: 100 and 133 MHz. Introduced: October 1999. 28 million transistors. 0.18 micron process. 256K integrated L2 advanced transfer cache.

Pentium III Xeon. 500 and 550 MHz.

Processor Package: Single Edge Contact Cartridge (SECC2). System bus speed: 100 MHz. Addressable memory: 64GB. Introduced: March 1999. The Pentium III Xeon extended the Pentium III's instruction set to add advanced cache technology. It was designed for systems with multiprocessor configurations. 9.5 million transistors. 0.25 micron process. L2 cache: 512K, 1MB, or 2MB. Designed for servers and workstations.

Pentium III. 450, 500, 550, and 600 MHz.

Processor Package: Single Edge Contrast Cartridge (SECC2). System bus speed: 100 MHz. Addressable memory: 64GB. Introduced: February, May, and August 1999. The Pentium III processor featured 70 new instructions including many aimed at use with Internet applications including streaming audio, video, and speech recognition. 9.5 million transistors. 0.25 micron process. 512K L2 cache.

Pentium II

Pentium II Xeon. 450 MHz.

Processor Package: Single Edge Contact Cartridge (SECC). System bus speed: 100 MHz. Addressable memory: 64GB. Introduced: January 1999. L2 cache: 512K, 1MB, or 2MB. 7.5 million transistors. Designed for servers and workstations.

Pentium II Xeon. 450 MHz.

Processor Package: Single Edge Contact Cartridge (SECC). System bus speed: 100 MHz. Addressable memory: 64GB. Introduced: October 1998. 512K L2 cache. 7.5 million transistors. Designed for dual-processor workstations and servers.

Pentium II. 450 MHz.

Processor Package: Single Edge Contact Cartridge (SECC), 242 pins. System bus speed: 100 MHz. Addressable memory: 64GB. Introduced: August 1998. 7.5 million transistors. 0.25 micron process.

Continued

Table 2-2: *Continued*

Pentium II

Pentium II Xeon. 400 MHz.	**Processor Package:** Single Edge Contact Cartridge (SECC). System bus speed: 100 MHz. Addressable memory: 64GB. Introduced: June 1998. The Pentium II Xeon was intended for mid-range and high-end servers and workstations and included facilities that make it easier to perform advanced data warehousing, digital content creation, and electronic and mechanical design automation. Systems can be configured to scale to four or eight Xeon processors, with extensions for even larger banks of CPUs. L2 cache 512K or 1MB. 7.5 million transistors. 0.25 micron process.
Pentium II. 350 and 400 MHz.	**Processor Package:** Single Edge Contact Cartridge (SECC), 242 pins. System bus speed: 100 MHz. Addressable memory: 64GB. Introduced: April 1998. 7.5 million transistors. 0.25 micron process. 512K L2 cache.

Pentium II

Pentium II. 333 MHz.	**Processor Package:** Single Edge Contact Cartridge (SECC), 242 pins. System bus speed: 66 MHz. Addressable memory: 64GB. Introduced: 7.5 million transistors. 0.25 micron process. 512K L2 cache.
Pentium II. 300, 266, 233 MHz.	**Processor Package:** Single Edge Contact Cartridge (SECC), 242 pins. System bus speed: 66 MHz. Bus width: 64 bits. Addressable memory: 64GB. Introduced: May 1997. The Pentium II processor added Intel MMX technology, designed to process video, audio, and graphics data efficiently. It was introduced in the upright Single Edge Contact (SEC) cartridge that also incorporated a high-speed cache memory chip. 7.5 million transistors. 0.35 micron process. 512K L2 cache.

Pentium Pro

Pentium Pro. 200 MHz.	**Processor Package:** Dual Cavity Pin Grid Array Package, 387 pins. System bus speed: 66 MHz. Addressable memory: 4GB. Introduced: August 1997. 5.5 million transistors. 0.35 micron process. 1MB integrated L2 cache. Internal bus width 300 bits. Designed for workstations and servers.
Pentium Pro. 200, 180, 166, 150 MHz.	**Processor Package:** Dual Cavity Pin Grid Array Package, 387 pins. System bus speed: 66 and 60 MHz. Addressable memory: 4GB. Introduced: November 1995. The Pentium Pro was intended as the engine for 32-bit server and workstation applications, and was used widely for computer-aided design, mechanical engineering, and scientific computation. The CPU included a cache memory chip. 5.5 million transistors. 0.35 micron. 256K or 512K L2 cache.

Pentium

Pentium with MMX. 233 MHz.	**Processor Package:** Plastic Pin Grid Array Package, 296 pins. System bus speed: 66 MHz. Addressable memory: 4GB. Introduced: June 1997. 4.5 million transistors. 0.35 micron CMOS. 32-bit microprocessor with 64-bit external bus.

Pentium

Pentium with MMX. 200, 166 MHz.	**Processor Package:** Plastic Pin Grid Array Package, 296 pins. System bus speed: 66 MHz. Addressable memory: 4GB. Introduced: January 1997. 4.5 million transistors. 0.35 micron CMOS. 32-bit microprocessor with 64-bit external bus.
Pentium. 200 MHz.	**Processor Package:** Plastic Pin Grid Array Package, 296 pins. System bus speed: 66 MHz. Addressable memory: 4GB. Introduced: June 1996. 3.3 million transistors. 0.35 micron BiCMOS. 32-bit microprocessor with 64-bit external data bus.
Pentium. 166, 150 MHz.	**Processor Package:** Pin Grid Array Package, 296 pins. System bus speed: 66, 60, and 50 MHz. Addressable memory: 4GB. Introduced: January 1996. 3.3 million transistors. 0.35 micron BiCMOS. 32-bit microprocessor with 64-bit external data bus.
Pentium. 133 MHz.	**Processor Package:** Pin Grid Array Package, 296 pins. System bus speed: 66 MHz. Addressable memory: 4GB. Introduced: June 1995. 3.3 million transistors. 0.35 micron BiCMOS. 32-bit microprocessor with 64-bit external bus.
Pentium. 120 MHz.	**Processor Package:** Pin Grid Array Package, 296 pins. System bus speed: 66 MHz. Addressable memory: 4GB. Introduced: March 1995. 3.2 million transistors (0.6 and .35 micron processes). BiCMOS. 32-bit microprocessor with 64-bit external bus.
Pentium. 75 MHz.	**Processor Package:** Lead Tape Carrier Package (TCP), 320 pins; or Staggered Pin Grid Array (SPGA), 296 pins. System bus speed: 50 MHz. Addressable memory: 4GB. Introduced: October 1994. 3.2 million transistors. 0.6 micron, BiCMOS. 32-bit microprocessor with 64-bit external bus.
Pentium. 90, 100 MHz.	**Processor Package:** Pin Grid Array Package, 296 pins. System bus speed: 60 and 66 MHz. Addressable memory: 4GB. Introduced: March 1994. 3.2 million transistors. 0.6 micron, BiCMOS. 32-bit microprocessor with 64-bit external bus.
Pentium. 60, 66 MHz.	**Processor Package:** Pin Grid Array Package, 273 pins. System bus speed: 60 or 66 MHz. Addressable memory: 4GB. Introduced: March 1993. The advanced Pentium, the fifth major generation of Intel processors, included features that permitted multimedia audio and video. 3.1 million transistors. 0.8 micron, BiCMOS. 32-bit microprocessor with 64-bit external bus.

Intel 486

IntelDX4. 75 MHz.	**Processor Package:** Pin Grid Array Package, 168 pins; or SQFP Package, 208 pins. System bus speed: 50 MHz. Addressable memory: 4GB. Introduced: March 1994. 1.6 million transistors. 0.6 micron.
Intel486 SL. 20, 25, 33 MHz.	**System Bus Speed:** 33 or 55 MHz. Addressable memory: 4GB. Introduced: November 1992. 1.5 million transistors. 0.8 micron. First CPU specifically designed for notebook PCs.
IntelDX2. 50, 66 MHz.	**System Bus Speed:** 33 or 50 MHz. Addressable memory: 4GB. Introduced: March 1992. 1.2 million transistors. 0.8 micron. Introduced speed-doubling technology permitting microprocessor to run at twice the speed of the bus.

Continued

Table 2-2: *Continued*	
Intel 486	
Intel486 SX. 16, 20, 25, 33 MHz.	**System Bus Speed:** 33 or 50 MHz. Addressable memory: 4GB. Bus width: 32 bits. Addressable memory: 4GB. Introduced: April 1991 and September 1991. 1.2 million transistors at 1 micron process or 0.9 million at 0.8 process. Same as Intel486 DX without a math coprocessor on chip. Upgradeable with the Intel OverDrive processor.
Intel486. 25, 33, 60 MHz.	**System Bus Speed:** 33 or 50 MHz. Addressable memory: 4GB. Bus width: 32 bits. Addressable memory: 4GB. Introduced: April 1989. The first Intel processor to include a built-in math coprocessor, which sped computing by offloading complex math functions from the central processor. 1.2 million transistors at 0.8 micron.
Intel 386	
Intel386 SL. 20, 25 MHz.	**System Bus Speed:** 25 or 33 MHz. Addressable memory: 4GB. Introduced: October 1990, September 1991. 885,000 transistors at 1 micron process. 32-bit microprocessor with 16-bit external bus. First CPU made specifically for portable PCs.
Intel386 SX. 16, 20, 25, 33 MHz.	**System Bus Speed:** 25 or 33 MHz. Bus width: 16 bits. Addressable memory: 16MB. Introduced: June 1988. 275,000 transistors. Originally 1.5 micron process, then 1 micron. 32-bit microprocessor with 16-bit external bus.
Intel 386	
Intel386 DX. 20, 25, 33 MHz.	**System Bus Speed:** 25 or 33 MHz. bus width: 32 bits. Addressable memory: 4GB. Possessing more than 100 times as many transistors as the original 4004, the 32-bit chip was capable of multitasking, meaning it could run multiple programs at the same time. October 1985, February 1987, April 1988, April 1989. 275,000 transistors. Originally 1.5 micron process, then 1 micron.
Intel 80286	
80286. 6, 10, 12 MHz.	**System Bus Speed:** 6, 8, 8.33 MHz. Bus width: 16 bits. Addressable memory: 16MB. Introduced: February 1982. The first new generation of processor from Intel, it launched the PC AT clone industry and introduced the concept of downward compatibility with all of its predecessors, allowing nearly all earlier software to run on later chips. Within six years of release, an estimated 15 million personal computers were based on the 80286. 134,000 transistors. 1.5 micron process.
Intel 808X family	
8088. 4.77, 8 MHz.	**System Bus Speed:** 4.77 MHz. Bus width: 8 bits. Addressable memory: 1MB. Introduced: June 1979. The original chip for the IBM PC, identical to the 8086 except for its 8-bit external bus. 29,000 transistors. 3 micron process. 16-bit internal, 8-bit external.

Intel 808X family

8086. 8, 10 MHz.	**Bus Width:** 16 bits. Addressable memory: 1MB. Introduced: June 1978. 29,000 transistors. 3 micron process. Used in early portables.
8085. 5 MHz.	Introduced: March 1976. 6,500 transistors. 3 micron process. Used in scales and simple calculators.
8080. 2 MHz.	**Bus Width:** 8 bits. Addressable memory: 64K. Introduced: April 1974. Used as the brains of one of the first personal computers offered to the public, the Altair (named after a world visited by the Starship Enterprise in the original *Star Trek*). 6,000 transistors. 6 micron process.
8008. 200 KHz.	**Bus Width:** 8 bits. Addressable memory: 16K. Introduced: April 1972. Twice as powerful as the 4004, it was used in homemade and hobbyist computers, including the Mark-8, and in dumb terminals and simple calculators. 3,500 transistors. 10 micron process.
4004. 108 KHz.	**Bus Width:** 4 bits. Addressable memory: 640 bytes. Introduced: November 1971. Intel's first microprocessor was the engine behind the Busicom calculator. 2,300 transistors. 10 micron process.

Table 2-3 examines in greater detail the capabilities of Intel processors, from the dinosaur 8086 to modern CPUs.

Table 2-3: Intel Processors

	8086	8088	80286
Address bus	16 bit	16 bit	24 bit
Data bus	16 bit	8 bit	16 bit
FPU?	No	No	No
Memory management?	No	No	No
Internal cache?	No	No	No
Clock speed (MHz)	5, 8, 10	5, 8, 10	6, 8, 10, 12
Average cycles/ instruction	12	12	4.9
Frequency of FPU	=CPU	=CPU	2/3 CPU

	8086	8088	80286
Address range	1MB	1MB	16MB
Frequency scalability?	No	No	No
Voltage	5 volts	5 volts	5 volts
Number of transistors	29,000	29,000	134,000
Year of introduction	1978	1979	1982

	i386 SX	i386 DX	i386 SL
Address bus	24 bit	32 bit	24 bit
Data bus	16 bit	32 bit	16 bit

Continued

Ch
2

Table 2-3: *Continued*

	i386 SX	i386 DX	i386 SL
FPU?	n/a	n/a	n/a
Memory management?	Yes	Yes	Yes
Internal cache?	No	No	Control
Clock speed (MHz)	16, 20, 25, 33	16, 20, 25, 33	16, 20, 25
Average cycles/instruction	4.9	4.9	<4.9
Frequency of FPU	=CPU	=CPU	=CPU
Address range	16MB	4GB	16MB
Voltage	5 volts	5 volts	3 or 5 volts
Number of transistors	275,000	275,000	855,000
Year of introduction	1988	1985	1990

	i486 SX	i486 DX	i486 SL	i486 DX2	i486DX4
Internal bus	32 bits	.32 bits	32 bits	32 bits	32 bits
External bus	32 bits	32 bits	32 bits	32 bits	32 bits
Virtual address space	64TB	64TB	64TB	64TB	64TB
Physical address space	4GB	4GB	4GB	4GB	4GB
Clock speed (MHz)	16, 20, 25, 33	25, 33, 50	25, 33	50, 66	75, 100
Math coprocessor	Available	Built in	Built in	Built in	Built in
Cache control	Built in	Built in	Built in	Built in	Built in
Level 1 cache	Built in	Built in	Built in	Built in	Built in
OverDrive support?	Yes	Yes	No	Yes	Yes
Number of transistors	1.2 million	1.2 million	1.4 million	1.2 million	1.6 million
Year of introduction	1991	1989	1992	1992	1994

	Pentium	Pentium with MMX	Pentium Pro	Pentium II
Internal bus	32 bits	32 bits	32 bits	32 bits
External bus	64 bits	64 bits	64 bits to front, 64 bits to L2 cache	64 bits
Virtual address space	64TB	64TB	64TB	64TB
Physical address space	4GB	4GB	64GB	64GB
Clock speed (MHz)	60–165	150–200	150–200	233–400
Math coprocessor	Built in	Built in	Built in	Built in
Cache control	Built in	Built in	Built in	Built in
Level 1 cache	Built in	Built in	Built in	Built in

	Pentium	Pentium with MMX	Pentium Pro	Pentium II
OverDrive support?	Yes	Yes	Yes	Yes
Number of transistors	3.1–3.3 million	4.5 million	5.5 million	7.5 million
Year of introduction	1993	1997	1995	1997

	Celeron	Pentium III	Pentium 4
Internal bus	32 bits	32 bits	32 bits
External bus	64 bits	64 bits	64 bits
Virtual address space	64TB	64TB	64TB
Physical address space	64GB	64GB	64GB
Clock speed (MHz)	400–1100	450–1300	1300–3060
Math coprocessor	Built in	Built in	Built in
Cache control	Built in	Built in	Built in
1st-level cache	Built in	Built in	Built in
OverDrive support?	No	No	No
Number of transistors	19 million (includes L2 cache)	9.5 million	42 million to 55 million
Year of introduction	1998	1999	2000

	Pentium D	Pentium 4 HT	Intel Core 2 Duo	Intel Core 2 Quad
Internal bus	32 bits	32 bits	32 bits	32 bits
External bus	64 bits	64 bits	64 bits	64 bits
Virtual address space	64TB	64TB	64TB	64TB
Physical address space	64GB	64GB	64GB	64GB
Clock speed (MHz)	2660–3400	2400–3800	1860–2930	2400–2930
Math coprocessor	Built in	Built in	Built in	Built-in
Cache control	Built in	Built in	Built in	Built-in
1st-level cache	Built in	Built in	Built in	Built-in
OverDrive support?	No	No	No	No
Number of transistors	230 million	55–125 million	167–291 million	582 million
Year of introduction	2005	2002, 2004	2006	2006

The Much-Overlooked Chipset

No matter how great a superstar a modern CPU is, it still needs to be surrounded by the appropriate supporting cast. The most important such element is the motherboard's chipset, which serves as the traffic cop amongst and between the CPU, the BIOS, the data bus, and the memory bus.

Most Intel CPUs are mated to a particular Intel-manufactured chipset, although on some older or budget motherboard you'll also see supporting chips from third-party manufacturers such as nVIDIA, SiS, and VIA. It has been my experience that Intel chipsets offer the most stable support for Intel CPUs; clone chipsets are generally marketed to manufacturers on the basis of price rather than features.

Similarly, AMD processors are supported by AMD chipsets as well as circuitry produced by third parties, including nVIDIA. And AMD's purchase of ATI in 2006 is expected to result in tighter integration between those two sets of designs in years to come; it is reasonable to expect integrated ATI video to become common on AMD motherboards as well as support for linked ATI video adapters using the CrossFire technology. It remains to be seen what will be the future role of nVIDIA, which also manufactures video processors that are competitive with ATI.

The time to shop for a chipset is at the moment you purchase your system (or motherboard, if you are building or rebuilding a system). In most cases, the bus, system clock, BIOS, and motherboard are optimized for a particular chipset, and the support chips are likely to be soldered into place and not changeable.

Chipset failures are relatively rare; the gravest threat they face is from an electrical surge that would likely fry many of the components on the motherboard. In other words, if your chipset has died, chances are you've got more major problems with the motherboard.

Modern Intel chipsets

As this book goes to press, the most advanced chipsets produced by Intel include the Intel 975X Express. These circuits were released together with the most current families of Intel processors, including the Intel Pentium Extreme Edition and multi-core CPUs including the Pentium D, Intel Core 2 Duo, and Intel Core 2 Quad.

Among the features of the 975X are support HyperThreading, for multiple graphics cards linked together to provide extreme performance in certain systems, and 8GB of addressable memory to enable 64-bit computing. Motherboards based on the chipset can provide a 1066 MHz front side bus. Other supported features include:

- PCI Express bus slots
- Serial ATA (SATA) at transfer rates of as much as 3Gbps
- Integrated audio
- Dual-Channel DDR2 memory support

The 16 lanes of PCI Express in the Memory Controller Hub that is part of the chipset can deliver more than 3.5 times the performance over the traditional AGP 8X interface for video cards. The MCH also provides six PCI x1 lanes for basic adapters, and two PCI Express controllers that can work with a pair of 8-lane adapters. Other chipsets in the 900 Express series intended for use with high-performance motherboards include the 955 and 925, which offer many of the same features with some differences in configuration or setting options. Current chipsets aimed at mainstream computing include 965, 945, and 915 families.

Older modern Intel chipsets

A few steps behind current chipsets, but still in the modern computer class, are Intel's 800-series chipsets, which were the basis for support of the Pentium 4 and Pentium III processors.

Introduced in 2003, the 875P and 865 chipset families introduced important features including Serial ATA and the AGP8X graphics slot. They do not support the PCI Express slot now commonly used for graphics adapters on current machines.

Both families brought support for an 800 MHz Front-Side Bus, Serial ATA, AGP 8X, USB 2.0, and Intel Performance Acceleration Technology. Each was optimized to work with Pentium 4 processors with HyperThreading Technology to help manage and prioritize multiple threads received from the microprocessor.

The 865G chipset included an integrated graphics controller, while the 865PE and 865P chipsets do not; the P version will work with buses as fast as 533 MHz rather than the 800 MHz of its cousins.

The 860 chipset was designed for high-performance multiprocessor systems, generally those using Intel Xeon processors, and includes the following features:

- The 82860 Memory Controller Hub (MCH) is the main interface to the processor host bus, the memory, and graphics interfaces. The chip offers a 400 MHz system bus and the capability to add as many as two additional high-performance 64-bit 66 MHz PCI segments. And the set supports 1.5V AGP4X technology for graphics, allowing 1 GBps of graphics bandwidth.
- The dual RDRAM memory channels can together deliver 3.2 GBps of memory bandwidth to the processor.
- The enhanced 82801BA I/O Controller Hub (ICH2) delivers twice the I/O bandwidth over traditional bridge architecture. Included is a direct connection from the graphics and memory for faster access to peripherals, including support for 32-bit PCI, Ultra ATA/100, and an integrated LAN controller. Dual USB controllers can be used to configure four full-bandwidth USB ports.

- The set supports six channels of digital audio.
- The 82806AA 64-bit PCI Controller Hub (P64H) supports 64-bit PCI slots at 33 MHz or 66 MHz.

The Intel 850 chipset was designed in tandem with the Intel Pentium 4 processor and the Intel NetBurst micro-architecture, which doubles the length of the pipeline between the processor and the chipset for higher performance. (Although a longer pipeline does have some disadvantages, including an effective reduction in the number of instructions executed per cycle at a particular clock speed, the higher number of *stages,* or segments, in the pipeline permits the CPU to run at a higher clock speed.) The chipset permitted a system bus of 400 MHz, mating the Pentium 4's 3.2 GBps bus to 3.2 GBps of memory bandwidth using high-speed Dual RDRAM memory.

Some of this chipset's key features include the following:

- The 82850 Memory Controller Hub (MCH) delivers dual RDRAM memory channels, a 400 MHz system bus, and AGP4X technology for graphics.
- The 400 MHz system bus is balanced with dual RDRAM channels at 3.2 GBps, triple the potential bandwidth of systems based on Intel Pentium III processors.
- Included in the set is an 82801BA I/O Controller Hub (ICH2), like the Intel 860, providing a direct connection from the graphics and memory for faster access to peripherals.
- Two USB controllers double the bandwidth available for USB peripherals to 24 MBps over four ports.
- AC'97 audio delivers six channels of digital audio, including full surround-sound capability.
- The *LAN Connect Interface (LCI)* includes networking facilities such as home phone line and 10/100 MBps Ethernet.
- Dual Ultra ATA/100 controllers support the fastest IDE interface for transfers to storage devices.
- The set supports use of a Communication and Networking Riser (CNR), allowing the upgrade to include an integrated audio card, modem card, or network card.

Intel also offered the 845 chipset, similar to the 850 but allowing use of the Pentium 4 with slightly slower but less-expensive SDRAM memory. An earlier high-end chipset was Intel's 840, which supports dual Pentium III or Pentium III Xeon CPUs, dual RDRAM channels, up to 8GB of RAM with combined transfer speeds up to 3.2 GBps, and AGP graphics with up to 1 GBps data transfer speeds. It also enables bridging multiple PCI buses to expand the number of PCI slots available to the system and supports 100 MHz or 133 MHz system buses.

A notch below the 840 is the 820 chipset, which supports two CPUs and 1GB of RAM. The 820 also supports the Universal Serial Bus, bus mastering, IDE, AGP, and more. The 820 chipset was the first Intel chipset to support RDRAM and the first to support a 133 MHz system bus.

CROSS-REFERENCE

For more information on RDRAM, see Chapter 8.

AC'97 (Audio Codec 97) components are part of all current chipsets. AC'97 allows the processor to emulate an audio card or modem in software. In a way, this is both a step forward and backward. The idea is to use the system's CPU and memory instead of more expensive specialized controllers and RAM on a modem or audio card; the high-speed and abundant memory of modern machines make this possible and lower the system's overall cost. You still get better performance by using a dedicated modem or sound card, but many users will not notice the difference.

Modern AMD chipsets

AMD processors are not compatible with chipsets specifically designed for Intel CPUs. However, AMD's acquisition of specialty chipmaker ATI in 2006 resulted in some overlap in chipsets in 2006, as well as several series that were capable of supporting processors from AMD or Intel.

As this book goes to press, the flashiest member of the AMD product line was the AMD580X CrossFire chipset, which supports motherboards with two PCI Express x16 slots that can be used with a pair of ATI Radeon CrossFire-compatible graphics cards chained together for very high-performance video processing. It is compatible with AMD CPUs, including the Athlon 64, Athlon 64 FX, Athlon 64 X2 Dual-Core, and Sempron processors. A slightly less capable product is the AMD480X CrossFire Chipset, which supports two PCI Express x8 slots, a solution expected to be less commonly adopted.

The ATI Radeon Xpress 1100 Series for AMD Processors includes a Radeon video processor as part of the chipset as well as support for a PCI Express x16 slot that could be used for a second or replacement video card. The ATI Radeon Xpress 200 Series for AMD Processors is a scaled-down version of the same set. The ATI SB600 Series supported both AMD and older Intel processors.

Previous chipsets included the AMD-8000 series. They include support for 32- and 64-bit computing; Direct Connect Architecture, which links a high-bandwidth integrated memory controller and I/O to the microprocessor core; and a scalable system bus using HyperTransport technology with support for single- and multi-processor configurations.

Older modern AMD chipsets

Designed for the AMD Athlon processor, the AMD-760 set includes two chips: the AMD-761 system bus controller, or northbridge, and the AMD-766 peripheral bus controller, or southbridge. The chipset's principal advance is support for PC2100 DDR memory and PC1600 DDR memory. The AMD-760 chipset supports up to a 266 MHz front side bus and 266 MHz high-performance *Double Data Rate (DDR)* memory as well as AGP-4X graphics adapters.

The AMD-760MP chipset is aimed at use with AMD Athlon MP processors, and consists of the AMD-762 system bus controller, or northbridge, and the AMD-766 peripheral bus controller, or southbridge. The chipset can work with one or two AMD Athlon MP processors, a 266 MHz front side bus, PC2100 DDR memory, and AGP-4X graphics, and incorporates 33 MHz/32-bit/64-bit PCI support.

Identifying Your CPU

If you're not sure about the type and speed of CPU within your machine, you can, of course, take off the cover and examine the microprocessor installed on the motherboard; that's not so easy anymore on current modern machines, which cover the processor with heat sinks, fans, or elaborate wind tunnels to take away heat. You can also try to read the text on your monitor as the system BIOS goes through its bootup tests.

More realistically, the best way to determine the CPU inside a machine that is running under Windows is to go to the Control Panel and double-click the System icon. Choose the General tab to read a report on your processor's name and rated speed. You can also check System Information, a screen available from within Windows Accessories/System Tools. You can display similar screens from the Help tabs of Microsoft applications, and as part of diagnostic and repair utilities.

The only way to be absolutely certain that the 2.4 GHz chip you purchased really delivers that speed is to use a utility program that queries the internal identification of the CPU and tests its operation.

Intel offers a pair of utilities that check your processor's frequency or identity. Go to the company's main web site at www.intel.com and search for **Frequency ID** for processors through the Pentium 4, or for **Processor Identification** for more current CPUs.

The Processor Identification Utility delivers a report that reports your current CPU's expected (the specified speed) and the reported (the actual speed). On a multi-core processor you receive reports on each core. Two other tabs in the report show which advanced Intel technologies, such as HyperThreading and Extended Memory 64, the processor supports. And the CPUID tab digs deeper into the processor to tell you which stepping and revision were used in fabricating your processor; Intel makes minor changes to its products over their shelf lives and in very rare situations particular errors are associated with particular steppings. An image from the frequency test of a Core 2 Duo processor is shown in Figure 2-3.

Intel's older Frequency ID utility queries the microprocessor on your system and comes back with one or two status reports, depending on the age of your system. The utility will display a dialog box with the Frequency Test tab and the CPU ID data tab for the following processors: Pentium 4, Intel Xeon, Pentium III, Pentium III Xeon, and Intel Celerons with a 0.18 micron core. You'll see only the CPU ID data tab for Pentium II, Intel Celerons with a 0.25 micron core, Pentium Pro, Pentium, and Pentium MMX processors.

The CPU ID data tab reports the Intel processor name, family, type, and the *stepping* of the processor—the usually minor revisions to an existing product over the course of its life. Also on the page is information about the L1 and L2 memory caches in the processor, and the cartridge or packaging type for the CPU. Some of the information you find on this tab includes the following:

- The CPU Type number indicates whether the Intel processor was intended for installation by a consumer (indicated by a 1) or by a professional PC system manufacturer (0).
- The CPU Family number indicates the Intel processor generation and brand; for example, a Pentium III processor is considered a sixth-generation processor. The sixth generation extends through

all of the Pentium chips and into current Intel Core 2 Duo and Intel Core 2 Quad designs, which are advanced derivations of the same essential concepts.

- The CPU Model number identifies to Intel the processor's manufacturing technology and design generation within the family.

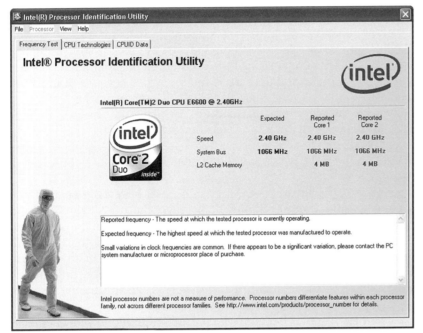

FIGURE 2-3: *The frequency report of the Intel Processor Identification Utility.*

The Frequency Test Tab provides information on the expected and actual operating status of the tested processor and system bus. If all is well, both sets of numbers will be the same. You can see an example of one report in Figure 2-4.

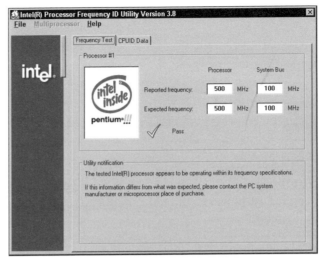

FIGURE 2-4: *The Frequency Test tab of Intel's Frequency ID utility reports on the expected and actual speed of this senior-citizen Pentium III processor and the system bus of the PC in which it is installed.*

Benchmark Index of Intel Processors

Over the years, Intel has introduced, updated, and then abandoned a number of different suites of benchmark tests to compare the relative speed of microprocessors; the benchmarks have changed as new microprocessors were optimized for new tasks, including graphics, video, and the Internet. In Table 2-4, I've listed seven different scales used by Intel over the years, but enough of an overlap exists to show the steady onward march of speed and capability.

The first suite was the *Intel Comparative Microprocessor Performance (iCOMP)* index, which tracked the relative performance of various Intel chips from early 386 chips through the Pentium III. It was primarily based on the PCBench 7.0 test, with lesser weight going to SPECint92, and a small component of the total score based on SPECfp92 and Whetstone tests.

In 1996, Intel updated and recalculated the iCOMP index to better reflect modern 32-bit software and multimedia applications, releasing the iCOMP Index 2.0. This result is a weighted average based on five industry-standard benchmarks: CPUmark32, Norton SI-32, SPECint95, SPECfp95, and the Intel Media Benchmark. The base processor for the iCOMP 2.0 was a Pentium 120 MHz processor, rated at 100 on the scale.

iCOMP 3.0 compares the performance of later CPUs in the Intel family. As with previous iCOMP comparisons, Index 3.0 is not a benchmark; rather, it is a collection of benchmarks that attempts to produce a meaningful index of relative performance based on a variety of criteria. For example, Index 3.0 takes into account the increasing importance of multimedia, 3-D technologies, and the Internet.

It's not easy to directly compare the various iCOMP benchmarks, or iCOMP and other tests, because each index compares different criteria. Within a given index, however, different numbers can help you evaluate relative CPU performance.

*SPECint_base*2000* is part of SPEC CPU*2000, a software benchmark produced by the Standard Performance Evaluation Corporation (SPEC), a group of computer vendors and researchers. Elements of the benchmark are SPECint_base*2000, which measures computer-intensive integer performance, and SPECfp_base*2000, which measures floating-point performance. SPEC benchmarks are selected from existing application and benchmark source code running across multiple platforms.

SYSmark2001 is a suite of software tests and benchmarks developed by the Business Applications Performance Corporation (BAPCO), a consortium of computer industry publications, independent testing labs, and manufacturers. It measures system performance on popular business-oriented applications in the Windows operating environment. Among the elements of the test are Microsoft Excel, Microsoft PowerPoint, Microsoft Word, Adobe Photoshop, Adobe Premiere, Macromedia Dreamweaver, and Macromedia Flash. *SYSmark 2000* was an earlier suite of tests based on older applications.

Although later indexes do not exactly track backward into older Intel processors, it is fair to say that an Intel Pentium 120 MHz operates about 30 times faster than an i386 SX-20 CPU, and about three times as fast as a 486DX-22 66 MHz workhorse. By a rough conversion of one index into another, a current Pentium 4 2-GHz (2000 MHz) could be considered as much as 12,000 times faster than an original 8088 chip at 4.77 MHz.

In Table 2-4, MIPS stands for millions of instructions per second and is a measure of a chip's raw horsepower; it doesn't take into account actual work performed by a machine and input-output log-jams. By the way, the original Cray 1 supercomputer, once considered the *sine qua non* of big iron machines, ran at 125 MIPS. Today's Pentium 4 machines are capable of speeds approaching 2,000 MIPS.

The real value of Table 2-4 is that it can help buyers evaluate the relative bang for the buck they will receive by specifying a particular CPU speed. For example, going from a Pentium 4 1.4 GHz to a 2.0 GHz model brings a theoretical processing increase of 30 percent; you have to decide how much that is worth to you in comparing models. Finally, Intel and AMD have backed away from claims directly related to chips' processor speeds. Although a 3.0 GHz chip is something like 640 times faster in operations than an original 8088 chip that worked at 4.77 MHz, the true difference is much greater because of improvements in things like the logic used by the processor, the amount of cache and the algorithm that controls its use, and physical changes such as the size of the tiny transistors etched into the chip. And in recent years processors' clock speed has come to a plateau somewhere around 3.0 GHz, even though actual performance continues to improve.

As you have already seen, Intel and AMD have each begun moving away from putting all the horsepower into a single CPU and instead are developing ways to install multiple cores on the same processor or to improve means of chaining together more than one processor. With that sort of design, many of the industry-standard benchmarks no longer provide meaningful information unless they are applied to actual computing tasks such as specific graphics, video, or database operations.

The best use of a benchmark chart like the one in this chapter is to compare the *relative* difference on various benchmarks. Look at CPUs in the same family and see how they differ on whichever benchmark they are tested against.

Table 2-4 has information for nearly every microprocessor produced by Intel, from the dawn of the dinosaur through a current Intel Core 2 Quad Extreme Edition processor. Over time, different benchmarks have been developed to test different functions; the way to look at the progress of the numbers is to think of them in relative terms; higher is always better than lower but as each benchmark changes, the units of measurement change.

Table 2-4: Benchmark Index of Intel Processors

Processor Type and Speed in MHz	Intel iCOMP	Intel iCOMP 2.0	MIPS	Intel iCOMP 3.0	SPECint base2000 Windows 2000	SYSmark 2000 under Windows 2000	Sysmark	Sysmark 2001 under Windows Me	Me
8088 4.77			0.33						
8088 8			0.75						
80286 8			1.2						
80286 10			1.5						
80286 12			2.66						
i386 DX-16			5.0–6.0						
i386 DX-20			6.0–7.0						
i386 SX-16			2.5						
i386 SX-20	32		4.2						
i386 SL-20			4.21						
i386 SL-25	41		5.3						
i386 SX-25	39								
i386 DX-25	49		8.5						
i386 SX-33	56								
i386 DX-33	68		11.4						
i486 SX-16	67		13.0						
i486 SX-20	78		16.5						
i486 SX-25	100		25.0						
i486 SL-25	122								
486 DX-25	122		20.0						
i486 SX-33	136		27.0						
i486 DX-33	166		27.0						
i486 SL-33	166								
i486 DX2-40	182								
i486 DX2-50	231		41.0						
i486 DX-50	249		41.0						
i486 DX2-66	297		54.0						
i486 DX4-75	319		53.0						
i486 DX4-100	435		70.7						
Pentium 60	510		100.0						
Pentium 66	567		112.0						
Pentium 75	610	67	126.5						
Pentium 90	735		149.8						
Pentium 100	870	90	166.3						

Continued

Ch 2

Table 2-4: *Continued*

Processor Type and Speed in MHz	Intel iCOMP	Intel iCOMP 2.0	MIPS	Intel iCOMP 3.0	SPECint base2000 Windows 2000	SYSmark 2000 under Windows 2000	Sysmark	Sysmark 2001 under Windows Me	Me
Pentium 120	1000	100	203.0						
Pentium 133	1110	111	218.9						
Pentium 150		114							
Pentium 166		127							
Pentium 166 with MMX		160							
Pentium 200		142							
Pentium 200 with MMX		182							
Pentium 233 with MMX		203							
Pentium Pro 150		168							
Pentium Pro 180		197							
Pentium Pro 200		220							
Pentium II 233		267							
Pentium II 266		303							
Pentium II 300		332		860					
Pentium II 333		366		940					
Pentium II 350		386		1000					
Pentium II 400		440		1130					
Pentium II 450				1240					
Pentium III 450		510		1500					
Pentium III 500				1650					
Pentium III 550				1780					
Pentium III 600				1930					
Celeron 566						96			
Celeron 600						100			
Celeron 633						106			
Celeron 667						109			
Celeron 700						111		55	
Celeron 733						114		57	
Celeron 766						115		58	
Celeron 800						126		66	
Celeron 850						130		68	
Celeron 900								71	
Celeron 950								73	

Processor Type and Speed in MHz	Intel iCOMP	Intel iCOMP 2.0	MIPS	Intel iCOMP 3.0	SPECint base2000 Windows 2000	SYSmark 2000 under Windows 2000	Sysmark	Sysmark 2001 under Windows Me	Me
Celeron 1000 (1 GHz)								75	
Celeron 1100 (1.1 GHz)								79	
Pentium III 600E				2110		139			
Pentium III 600EB						146			
Pentium III 650				2270		147			
Pentium III 667				2320		158			
Pentium III 700				2420		154			
Pentium III 733				2510		168			
Pentium III 750				2540		161			
Pentium III 800				2690		167			
Pentium III 800EB						178	96		
Pentium III 850						173			
Pentium III 866				2890	411	183			
Pentium III 933				3100	421	190			
Pentium III 1000 (1 GHz)				3280	402	200			
Pentium III 1300 (1.3 GHz)					421	212			
Pentium 4 1300 (1.3 GHz)		1,700			475		134		
Pentium 4 1400 (1.4 GHz)					498		143		
Pentium 4 1500 (1.5 GHz)					526		151		
Pentium 4 1600 (1.6 GHz)					551		160		
Pentium 4 1700 (1.7 GHz)					573		166		
Pentium 4 1800 (1.8 GHz)					598		174		
Pentium 4 1900 (1.9 GHz)					619		180		

Continued

Ch 2

Table 2-4: *Continued*

Processor Type and Speed in MHz	Intel iCOMP	Intel iCOMP 2.0	MIPS	Intel iCOMP 3.0	SPECint base2000 under Windows 2000	SYSmark 2000 under Windows 2000	Sysmark 2001 under Windows 2001	Sysmark 2002 under Windows 2000	Sysmark
Pentium 4 2000 (2 GHz)					640		187	219	
Pentium 4 2400 (2.4 GHz)					929			260	
Pentium 4 2400 (2.4 GHz) with Intel 875 chipset			984			278			
Pentium 4 2600 (2.6 GHz)					1047			295	
Pentium 4 2800 (2.8 GHz)					1107			312	125
Pentium Celeron D 340 (2.93 GHz)									126
Pentium 4 3000 (3.0 GHz)					1164			328	
Pentium 4 3060 (3.06 GHz)					1109			324	
Pentium 4 Processor 520 with HT Technology								149	
Pentium 4 Processor with HT Technology Extreme Edition (3.73 GHz)		1865				231			
Pentium D Processor 960									254
Pentium Processor Extreme Edition 965				1870					285
Intel Core 2 Duo Processor E6700									378
Intel Core 2 Quad Extreme Processor QX6700								378	
Intel Core 2 Duo Extreme Processor X6800				3099					404

Intel Core 2 Quad Extreme Processor X6800 397CPU Sockets and Slots

As chips have become more and more complex, they have made increasingly greater demands on the motherboard circuitry — more data lines, more power, and faster interconnections with the computer's various elements.

Since the arrival of the 486 CPU, Intel has produced its microprocessors with connectors for 15 different sockets or slots; one other socket was announced but never used in commercial products. Most of the sockets held the processor flat on the motherboard. Intel changed over to an upright package for the CPU with the arrival of the Pentium II; that design continued through most of the lifetime of the Pentium III. The upright slot allowed for better cooling of the increasingly hot CPU and took up a bit less space on the motherboard. Modern Pentium 4 chips — more densely integrated and thus smaller — have returned to a horizontal socket on the motherboard. Early AMD chips used industry-standard sockets, changing over to a proprietary slot with the arrival of the first Athlons and then back to a socket.

Why the change back to sockets? High-speed CPUs require shorter electrical connections, called *traces*; sockets sit directly on the motherboard, while cards plugged into slots sit relatively farther away. Another reason for a return to sockets is the integration of cache memory directly into the CPU carrier itself instead of on an attached circuit board.

Table 2-5 is a roadmap to the motherboard-microprocessor connection.

Table 2-5: Modern Machine CPU Sockets and Slots

Socket Name	Carrier Design	Processors
486 Socket	168-pin LIF	486 DX, DX2, DX4. Am5x86. Cyrix.
Socket 1	169-pin LIF or ZIF	486 SX/SX2, DX/DX2, DX4 with adapter, DX4 OverDrive, Cyrix 5x86.
Socket 2	238-pin LIF or ZIF	486 SX/SX2, DX/DX2, DX4 with adapter, DX4 OverDrive, Pentium OverDrive, Am5x86, Cyrix 5x86.
Socket 3	237-pin PGA	SX/SX2, DX/DX2, DX4 with adapter, LIF or ZIF DX4 OverDrive, 486 Pentium OverDrive, Pentium 60/66, Pentium 60/66 OverDrive.
Socket 4	273-pin PGA	Pentium 60/66, Pentium 60/66 LIF or ZIF OverDrive.
Socket 5	296-pin LIF or ZIF,	Pentium 75 through Pentium 133, or 320-pin SPGA Pentium 75+ OverDrive. LIF or ZIF AMD K5, AMD 6x86L. WinChip.
Socket 6	235-pin PGA ZIF	Designed for 486DX4, but not used in commercial products.
Socket 7/	296-pin LIF or	Pentium 75 through Pentium 200, Super 7 321-pin SPGA ZIF Pentium 75+ OverDrive, AMD K5, AMD K6, Cyrix 6x86, Cyrix 6x86MX, Cyrix M II, IDT WinChip 180-240. Super 7 supports AMD K6-2, AMD K6-3.
Socket 8	387-pin SPGA	Pentium Pro, Pentium II OverDrives. LIF or ZIF.
Socket 9/	370-pin PPGA ZIF	Celeron in PPGA, Pentium III, VIA Socket 370 C3.
Socket A	462-pin ZIF	AMD Duron, AMD Thunderbird.
Socket 423	423-pin ZIF	Pentium 4 1.3–2.0 GHz.
Socket 478	478-pin ZIF	Pentium 4 1.8 GHz and faster.
Socket 603	603-pin ZIF	Pentium Xeon 1.4 and faster.
PAC 418	418-pin VLIF	Itanium 733-800 MHz.
PAC 611	611-pin VLIF	Itanium 2 900 MHz-1.0 GHz.

Continued

Table 2-5: *Continued*

Socket Name	Carrier Design	Processors
Socket 754	754-pin ZIF	AMD K8 1.802.0 GHz.
PPGA INT2	423-pin	Pentium 4.
mPGA478	478-pin	Pentium 4 with HyperThreading, Pentium 4.
FC-PGA2	478-pin	Pentium 4 with HyperThreading, Pentium 4.
FC-PGA4	478-pin	Pentium 4 with HyperThreading, Pentium 4.
FC-LGA	775-land	Intel Core 2 Duo, Pentium 3 with HyperThreading, Pentium 4 Extreme Edition with HyperThreading, Pentium D, Pentium Extreme Edition.
Slot 1 (SC242)	242-pin SEPP	Pentium II, Pentium III, Celeron Slot A/B blocks, 121 pins each, or 242-pin SEPP.
Slot 2 (SC330)	330-pin SECC	Pentium II Xeon, Pentium III Xeon. A/B blocks, 165 pins each.
Slot A	242-pin SECC	AMD Athlon, AMD Thunderbird 750 MHz–1 GHz.
Slot M	418-pin SECC	Itanium. Not in wide use.

Key to Carrier Design:

Carriers — LIF: Low-Insertion Force, without handle; PGA: Pin Grid Array; PPGA: Plastic Pin Grid Array; SECC: Single Edge Contact Cartridge; SEPP: Single Edge Processor Package; SPGA: Staggered Pin Grid Array; VLIF: Very Low Insertion Force socket; ZIF: Zero-Insertion Force, with handle

Modern Intel CPUs

A modern machine requires a modern CPU, defined in this eighth edition as those that can work with current operating systems (Windows Vista, Windows XP, Windows 2000, and Windows NT and, though not current, I also include Windows 98SE) and can use current hardware peripherals. On the hardware side, modern machines begin with Intel's Celeron and Pentium 4 chips and also include the latest Pentium D and Celeron D dual-core chips. Also included are the AMD Opteron, Sempron, and Athlon microprocessors.

Intel (like AMD) has gone away from naming its processors based on clock speeds. Instead, CPUs are given processor numbers within each processor family. In general, a higher number within a family means a more capable processor.

Intel Core 2: A fully split personality

In late summer of 2006, Intel released a major extension of a new family of microprocessors that represent a major divergence in the way microprocessors are logically laid out and designed, and a further step away from reliance just on clock speed as a measure of the potential or actual speed of a CPU. The first processors were dual-core, followed a few months later by quad-core versions. At the top end of each family is a set of Extreme Edition chips, which are versions of the processors that Intel certifies for *overclocking*, running at faster clock speeds than their very close cousins.

The first group of processors in the family were:

- E6300 Intel Core 2 Duo. Two cores running at 1.86 GHz, 2MB of L2 cache, and a 1066 MHz front-side bus.
- E6400 Intel Core 2 Duo. Two cores running at 2.13 GHz, 2MB of L2 cache, and a 1066 MHz front-side bus.
- E6600 Intel Core 2 Duo. Two cores running at 2.4 GHz, 4MB of L2 cache, and a 1066 MHz front-side bus.
- E6700 Intel Core 2 Duo. Two cores running at 2.66GHz, 4MB of L2 cache, and a 1066 MHz front-side bus.
- X6800 Intel Core 2 Extreme Duo. Two cores running at 2.93 GHz, 4MB of L2 cache, and a 1066 MHz front-side bus.
- QX6700 Intel Core 2 Extreme Quad. Four cores running at 2.66 GHz, 8MB of L2 cache, and a 1066 MHz front-side bus.

When these chips were introduced, their pricing followed the same pattern I've identified for years in the computer industry. Unless you absolutely need to possess the latest and fastest chip — regardless of price — the best bang for the buck comes from buying a processor that is one step below the top of the line. In this instance, I set aside the Extreme versions of the Core 2 processors and selected the E6600 model. It offers a generous 4MB cache, which separates it from the lowest two rungs on the ladder (and most previous Intel processors) and it is only slightly slower at 2.4 GHz (for each of the cores) than the E6700 at 2.66 GHz. Thus, the E6600 powers the example machine examined in Chapter 6.

Intel's art of minimalism

The Core 2 chips use the same Socket 775 connector interface used by the later generations of motherboards built to work with Pentium 4 and Pentium D chips. However, they cannot be swapped; the new CPUs require a different chipset and there are other electrical differences. Only a motherboard designed for use with Core 2 microprocessors will work with them.

Among the key advantages of the new design is its greatly reduced power requirement. The basic Core 2 Duo chips draw only 64 watts, which is a lot of power but less than half the 135-watt draw of the previous top of the consumer line, the Pentium 4 Extreme Edition. Even the Core 2 Extreme X6800 draws just 75 watts. Less power means less heat generation and a generally more stable system.

Other advanced features include the ability of the CPU to slow down or shut off parts of its processor when they are not needed. This is a technology that was given wide use in the Pentium M processor series developed for laptops, where extended battery life is a great benefit; in a desktop machine, an adjustable power demand helps reduce heat buildup.

Intel Core 2 processors are also equipped with a new Digital Thermal Sensor (DTS) that enables efficient processor and platform thermal control. Thermal sensors within the microprocessor measure the maximum temperature on the die. Intel Quiet System Technology, included in the Intel 965 Express Chipset and later chipsets uses the DTS to regulate the system and processor fan speeds. The acoustic benefit of temperature monitoring is that system fans spin only as fast as needed to cool the system, and slower-spinning fans generate less noise.

On the processing side, the Core 2 series makes the most of its split design by adding an extra execution unit to each of its cores,

bringing the total to four units per CPU core. (The Pentium D, which fills a lower-price and lower-performance niche to the Core 2 Duo just as the Celeron did for the Pentium, has three units per core.)

Another logical trick performed by the new chip is the ability to recognize and act upon a series of common instructions as if it were just one command. (Think of the difference between saying to your significant other, "While you're out, please pick up a quart of milk" rather than having to say, "While you're out, make a right turn onto Pleasant Street and a left into the supermarket lot, park the car, go inside, find the milk aisle, take a quart, bring it to the checkout, pay for it, go out to the car . . .." You get the short and simple idea, right?)

And another boost to the chip's efficiency is the installation of as much as 8MB of L2 cache on the first quad-core processor, 4MB of L2 cache on the high-end dual-core chips (the 2.4 GHz E6600 and the 2.66 GHz E6700 chips) and 2MB of L2 cache on the 1.86 Ghz E6300 and the 2.13 GHz E6400. Cache helps keep the bucket of data and instructions full for high-speed processors, and advanced algorithms in the chipset attempt to anticipate needs before they are even called for.

Another technical advance is a design that allows the multiple cores on the CPU to share the full measure of cache, dividing it as needed and in the most effective manner. Earlier CPU designs for multi-core chips divided the cache evenly, with no opportunity to dynamically adjust its use. Cache sharing is managed by an Intel algorithm called Smart Cache, which can adjust the use of the memory as needed. (Compare this to the Pentium D, which is a dual-core processor where the two cores split the cache memory evenly between them without the ability to adjust use.)

There are two advantages of a dynamically adjusted memory cache. First of all, the processor runs more efficiently if it can devote more cache to the core that needs it most at the moment. Secondly, this sort of adjustment reduces — depending on the sort of tasks being performed — the chances that one or the other core will have to use slower (and more distant) RAM as the storage place for the data it needs immediately.

The managed cache also permits either core to reach in and grab data or instructions, whether or not it was the core that requested it. In other words, if the first core has a set of instructions in cache that can also be used by the second core, there is no need for the second core to make a separate request.

Core Duo

Core Duo is the mobile processor equivalent of the Core 2 Duo. The Core Duo was adapted from the successful Pentium M processor that was widely used in laptop and other mobile devices. Intel designers took a pair of Pentium M chips (manufactured using 90-nanometer technology) and squeezed them using 65-nanometer fabrication. The result is a chip with two cores at about the same manufacturing cost of a single processor.

The Core Duo was the first Intel processor used as the engine for an Apple computer. Apple has moved on to the Core 2 Duo in its current line of computers; the Apple machines can run Microsoft Windows as well as Apple's own operating systems. And current versions of Apple machines also share many hardware components, including USB, SATA, and FireWire devices.

Like the Core 2 Duo, it has Smart Cache management that allows sharing of the cache between the two cores as needed.

Pentium D with Dual-Core technology

Intel's first dual-core processor for desktops, the Pentium D blazed the path for the low-end of the multiple core market. It includes a pair of execution cores in one physical processor. It was accompanied by the Intel 945 Express chipset.

As this book went to press, the Pentium D was offered in two families: the 900 series with two 2MB L2 cache memory chips and the 800 series with two 1MB L2 cache memory chips. The 900 series (built with 65-nanometer dies) can work with a front-side bus of 800 MHz; the 800 series (built with 90-nanometer dies) is designed for front-side buses of 800 or 533 MHz. Clock speeds range from 2.66 GHz to 3.4 GHz.

The manager for the multiple cores is Intel Virtualization Technology, which enables one hardware platform to function as multiple virtual platforms. One possible use for this function is to isolate computing activities into separate partitions. Intel Extended Memory 64 Technology allows systems to access larger amounts of memory and supports 64-bit extended operating systems.

The Intel Designed Thermal Solution includes a four-pin connector allowing adjustment of fan speed to meet cooling needs, with the added benefit of quieter operation.

Pentium 4

The Pentium 4 processor arrived in November of 2000, delivering new levels of performance for processing video and audio, 3-D graphics, and advanced Internet technologies. First introduced at 1.3 GHz, the clock speed of the Pentium 4 reached the 2.0 GHz milestone in August of 2001, and topped out at a blazing 3.8 GHz HyperThreading Extreme Edition in 2006.

A key element of the Pentium 4 was NetBurst technology, which permits certain actions to be anticipated and pushed through quickly. Other highlights included Hyper Pipelined Technology, which enables the Pentium 4 processor to execute software instructions in a 20-stage pipeline, as compared to the 10-stage pipeline of the Pentium III processor. For higher performance, the Rapid Execution Engine allows frequently used Arithmetic Logic Unit instructions to be executed at double the core clock. Later versions of the Pentium 4 included a performance-enhancing secondary cache with 512KB of memory, double the size of the first chips in the series, and the HyperThreading version offered 2MB of cache.

Intel was a big supporter of the Rambus memory architecture, although that technology never grabbed hold of a majority of the market. In fact, acceptance of the Pentium 4 was held back somewhat by economic conditions and by the reluctance of some buyers to change to the more expensive Rambus memory. The second wave of Pentium 4 processors — by far the vast majority of CPUs in this family — were used on motherboards with conventional SDRAM.

A 400 MHz system bus speeds the transfer of data between the processor and main memory. In addition, 144 new instructions have been added to further speed the processing of video, audio, and 3-D applications.

The Pentium 4 was first introduced with a companion chipset, the Intel 850, which is designed to use RDRAM. In 2001, the company delivered the Intel 845 chipset, which mates the Pentium 4 to conventional and less-expensive SDRAM.

 CROSS-REFERENCE

See Chapter 8 for more detail on Rambus and other memory technologies.

Itanium and Itanium 2

Itanium, Intel's first 64-bit processor, is not the fastest when it comes to megahertz — operating in the range of 833 MHz to 1.0 GHz — but its wide data path made it very appropriate for scalable networks. Scalability is a computer buzzword that refers to a system's ability to expand to accommodate more users or more networked machines.

Many motherboards based around the Itanium — and its successor Itanium 2 — have slots for as many as four or eight processors and massive amounts of memory. The Itanium is designed to run existing IA-32 (32-bit Pentium) software, as well as new IA-64 (64-bit Itanium) software. The Itanium isn't the first workstation or desktop-class 64-bit CPU architecture. Hewlett-Packard, IBM, Sun, and others have had RISC (Reduced Instruction Set Computer) chips with 64-bit internal addressing for some time. However, Intel claims Itanium is different because it is more than just a 64-bit chip; it is an architecture that includes support for Internet server tasks, higher-end multimedia, and other jobs that users are demanding now and likely will demand in the near future. New and powerful multimedia instructions — similar to and compatible with MMX — help Itanium provide support for these future tasks.

One facet of Intel's IA-64 architecture is Explicitly Parallel Instruction Computing (EPIC), a technique that helps maximize CPU performance, throughput, and efficiency by supporting instruction level parallelism (ILP) as well as a high level of synergy between the compiler and the processor. Itanium's ILP supports multiple independent instruction bundles (three instructions per bundle). In addition to this parallel processing, Itanium is designed with sophisticated speculative or predictive features. Like a data cache in a hard disk controller that guesses what data will be required next based on previous data access, Itanium's speculative features help the processor look ahead to future instructions based on what has gone before. Properly executed, speculation obviously can improve CPU throughput because applications don't have to wait for an instruction fetch and execution. In other words, processing latency is reduced.

NOTE

A Level 1, or L1, cache is a special block of internal memory within the processor. It is used by the CPU to store instructions or data that the machine believes it will have to access again soon. Writing to or reading from that L1 cache is much faster than going out of the CPU and down the bus to the memory SIMMs or DIMMs. A Level 2, or L2, cache is a secondary external cache. If the CPU cannot find the data or instructions it wants in the internal cache, it looks in the Level 2 cache. If it still cannot find what it is looking for, the cache controller finds the data or instruction in system memory and copies it into one of the caches. Some motherboards offer a third level of cache, called L3, located between the processor and system memory.

Celeron

The Celeron processor is Intel's line of "value" CPUs, allowing manufacturers to use lower-price motherboards, chipsets, and components while still delivering systems that by most measures are quite capable for many users. When these processors were first introduced, they offered a way for users to buy a capable system for several hundred dollars less than a Pentium II or Pentium III system. Today, though, the drop in the cost of memory and other components has resulted in a small differential between Celerons and full-featured Pentium III and Pentium 4 systems.

The first generation of Celerons, based on the Pentium II and using a 66 MHz system bus, were introduced in 1998 in 333, 366, 400, 433, 466, 500, and 533 versions. The second generation, based on the Pentium III, included processors from 533 through 766 MHz, still wedded to a 66 MHz system bus. In 2000 and 2001, the Celeron gained access to a 100 MHz system bus as it was extended from 800 MHz to 1.2 GHz.

In October of 2001, Intel introduced a 1.2 GHz processor based on 0.13 micron process technology and including additional design features such as 256K of on-chip, L2 cache. Earlier Celerons offered just 128K of L2 cache.

Early Celeron systems used the Intel 440BX chipset; current Celeron systems use the Intel 810E2 chipset that includes an advanced I/O controller, support for ATA-100 Ultra DMA hard drives, and a USB controller that supports four ports.

The Celeron processor was introduced to provide Pentium II-level performance for most business applications at a lower cost than the full-featured Pentium II on which it was originally based. In fact, the original Celeron, for all practical purposes, was a Pentium II with a smaller amount of Level 2 cache, 128K compared to the PII's 512K.

Ch **2**

Under Windows 98, when you look at the computer information on the General tab of the System Properties dialog box, you may find that the operating system reports the presence of a Pentium II when you perfectly well know that you have an Intel Celeron inside. This is an error without any consequence. The original series of Celeron chips was derived from a Pentium II base, and some of the code may fool system utilities.

Depending on your motherboard and the socket design, you may be able to install a Celeron in a board designed for use with a Pentium II or III. This is one way for some users to ease into a Pentium III system. Some boards include both a Socket 370 and a Slot 1; if you can find one, another way to accomplish this is to use an adapter, like the one shown in Figure 2-5.

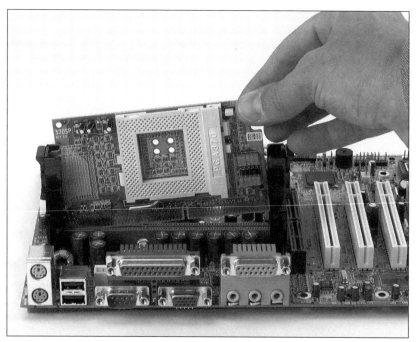

FIGURE 2-5: *This workaround adapter holds a Celeron processor in a socket that installs into Slot 1 on a senior citizen motherboard.*

Modern AMD CPUs

Although Intel is inside most PCs, it is not completely alone. In 2006, AMD held about a 20-percent share of sales of CPUs for desktops and laptops around the world; in certain segments, including low-price systems and specialized servers, AMD chips powered as much as half of the machines manufactured. Today there is no significant competition from other companies; over the years processors have come from IBM, Cyrix, IDT, and other makers. For more than 20 years, Apple Computer based nearly all of its machines around Motorola CPUs, but in 2006 began a migration to Intel dual-core processors.

AMD's Athlon processor, introduced in 1999 as a near-equivalent to the Intel Pentium 4, was at the heart of that company's growth. It also offered the lower-cost, simpler Duron as a competitor to Intel's Celeron. Today, the company's leading technology for desktop machines is found in the Athlon XP and the Athlon 64. AMD's processors run Microsoft Windows in all of its flavors, and nearly every current application works without problem. The only oddity some users may find are unusual or erroneous reports generated by some troubleshooting utilities expecting to find Intel ID codes in the processor.

AMD Opteron Processors

AMD's Opteron processors are intended for use in high-volume servers; the chips have successfully competed against Intel's Xeon and Itanium CPUs. The company has managed to make the processor scalable, moving from 32- to 64-bit computing and taking advantage of improved memory designs as they became available.

In addition to high speed and efficient processing, they continue AMD's push toward lower power demand for processors; the company touts their "performance-per-watt" capabilities.

In 2006, the company introduced the AMD Opteron Processor with DDR2 and AMD Virtualization, CPUs that match or exceed Intel's capabilities in a number of areas. The family features the Direct Connect Architecture, quad-core upgradeability, and AMD Virtualization (AMD-V). The processors are intended to work with energy-efficient DDR2 memory.

The 1000 series can include as many as two cores; it is intended to be installed in AMD's new Socket AM2. The 2000 series (which can combine as many as two processors and four cores) and the 8000 series (with four processors and eight cores, or eight processors and 16 cores) are designed for the new Socket F.

AMD64 Multi-core Processors

The company's leading desktop processor family runs the existing installed base of 32-bit applications and operating systems at peak performance, while allowing for a migration to 64-bit software. Because of that compatibility, it permits designers to come up with a single architecture across both 32- and 64-bit environments, reducing the cost of PCs based on the chip.

The initial release of dual-core processors in late 2006 was followed by quad-core chips in 2007; a properly designed system can easily be upgraded from the earlier double CPU to a later quad version.

The Direct Connect Architecture links the processors, integrated memory controller, and I/O directly to the CPU and communicates at CPU speed; this offers a potential improvement in throughput compared to front-side bus architectures used on motherboards designed for Intel processors. Another technology, HyperTransport, provides a scalable bandwidth interconnect between processors, I/O subsystems, and other chipsets. The Integrated Memory Controller resides on the CPU itself, offering a DDR2 DRAM memory controller that permits memory bandwidth of as much as 10.7 GBps (using DDR2-667 RAM) per processor. The processor can work with as much as 256 TB of memory address space, especially valuable for applications that hold large (or multiple) sets of data in memory.

The HE series of processors draws 55 watts, while the EE versions just 33 watts. This helps reduce heat buildup, especially when multiple processors are used in a system. AMD has its own version of power management technology built into its CPU and associated chipset. AMD PowerNow! can scale the speed of the processor to provide greater performance or reduced power consumption as required for particular tasks.

AMD Athlon 64 Processors

When introduced, these were the first Windows-compatible 64-bit processors. AMD64 technology allows the processor to run 32-bit applications at full speed while enabling a new generation of powerful 64-bit software applications. The chip is intended to work with current versions of Windows as well as 64-bit versions of Windows and operating systems from Red Hat, SuSE, and TurboLinux.

HyperTransport technology can increase overall system performance by removing I/O bottlenecks, increasing system bandwidth, and reducing system latency. As with other current AMD processors, the memory controller (compatible with DDR memory) is integrated into the processor. For use with advanced multimedia applications including audio, video, and digital graphics software, the AMD Athlon 64 includes 3DNow! Professional technology.

AMD Athlon 64 FX Processor

The FX version of the Athlon 64 processor is aimed at enthusiasts looking for that extra bit of SFX — special effects — in their games and other audio and video applications.

The AMD Athlon 64 FX processor runs on AMD64 Technology, a design that allows the processor to run 32-bit applications at full speed while still capable of running new 64-bit software. Enhanced Virus Protection, tied into Windows XP Service Pack 2 and Windows XP 64-bit Edition, is a feature of AMD64 technology; this facility is designed to trap a certain type of malicious activity known as *buffer overrun* or *buffer overflow.*

Other elements include HyperTransport technology and a 128-bit DDR memory controller integrated into the processor; this allows extreme bandwidth of as much as 6.4GB per second with significantly reduced memory latency.

AMD Sempron

A worthy compromise between performance and price, similar to the placement of the Celeron D in Intel's ladder of products, the AMD Sempron's upper end can include AMD64 Technology, HyperTransport technology, as much as 256KB of memory cache, and an integrated DDR memory controller. The Sempron replaced AMD's Duron, which was targeted against Intel's Celeron.

Athlon XP

At the time of its introduction in late 2001, AMD's new Athlon XP processor claimed to be the world's highest-performance processor for desktop PCs. The company also put forth a marketing and industry-standard proposal to develop a reliable measurement of processor performance that goes beyond mere measurement of a CPU's clock speed. The concept has stuck, and today Intel has also gone away from rating processors solely on the basis of clock speed.

AMD's True Performance Initiative is based on the company's position that the true indicator of performance is how fast applications run, not the megahertz of their processor. Megahertz measures only how many cycles per second the engine spins, not how much torque it delivers, the company says.

The initial Athlon XP processor contained about 37.5 million transistors and 384K of on-chip, full-speed cache while reducing power consumption by 20 percent over previous generations of the Athlon. The CPU, built with 0.18 micron technology and installed in a Pin Grid Array carrier, is compatible with AMD's Socket A infrastructure. The CPU supported a 266 MHz front-side bus. The chip is intended for use with DDR memory.

AMD compares its Athlon XP to the Pentium 4, and claims superiority. According to the company, the XP conducts nine operations per clock cycle, compared to six for the Pentium 4. The XP has 384K of on-chip cache (128K of L1 and 256K of L2) versus 264K for the Pentium 4 (8K of L1 and 256K of L2). The new processor also includes 3DNow! Professional technology, which adds 52 new instructions, accelerating 3-D performance for digital media applications such as photo, video, and audio editing.

AMD identifies the AMD Athlon XP processor using model numbers, as opposed to clock speed in megahertz. The numbers are supposed to indicate AMD's comparison to an Intel Pentium 4 CPU. The AMD Athlon XP processor 1800+ operates at a frequency of 1.53 GHz; AMD claims this model will outperform an Intel Pentium 4 processor operating at 1.8 GHz on a broad array of end-user applications.

AMD's conversion from the Thoroughbred to the Barton core for its processors resulted in a slight decline in clock speed and an increase in benchmark results among the latest CPUs in the series.

Although the Athlon XP processor is physically compatible with older Socket A motherboards intended for the original Athlon CPU, most systems will require an update to the BIOS to properly identify the processor and take advantage of the enhanced performance features. New motherboards will be certified by AMD to indicate their appropriateness for use with the Athlon XP.

AMD Athlon

AMD made its first serious foray against Intel at the low end with its K6 series. Intel countered with the Celeron chips, designed for medium- to low-priced personal and business systems. Then late in 1999, the two companies raised the stakes and started competing at the high end of the scale. AMD's Athlon chip series, designed to compete with the high end of Intel's Pentium III series and the full range of Pentium 4s, was first with a CPU that ran at 750 MHz, barely besting Intel's 733 MHz PIII.

The Athlon series performed well, and AMD priced it at a significant discount from Intel's price; at various times in 2000, AMD also took advantage of production difficulties at Intel to increase its market share. Many mainstream computer manufacturers promoted Athlon chips over Pentium 4s in that year. By 2001, though, aggressive cuts in prices by Intel and great leaps in technology began to push AMD aside.

AMD's Athlon series uses 0.18 micron technology, the same as the later series of Intel's Pentium III and most Pentium 4s, and the 200 MHz Athlon system bus is designed for scalable multiprocessing, using Digital Equipment Corporation's high-performance Alpha EV6 bus technology. Later Athlons advanced to use a 266 MHz system bus.

As with the Athlon XP, AMD compares its Athlon XP to the Pentium 4. According to the company, the XP conducts nine operations per clock cycle, compared to six for the Pentium 4. The later versions of the Athlon have 384K of on-chip cache (128K of L1 and 256K of L2) versus 264K for the Pentium 4 (8K of L1 and 256K of L2).

And just like Intel, AMD promotes the multimedia power of the Athlon design. The company says that Athlon, with its enhanced 3DNow! technology, includes 24 new instructions; of those, 19 are designed to improve MMX integer math calculations and enhance data movement for Internet streaming applications and five provide digital signal processing (DSP) extensions for soft modem, soft ADSL, Dolby Digital, and MP3 applications.

Another strong point of the Athlon is its cache design: the most current Athlons (as fast as 1.4 GHz) offer a total of 384K of cache (128K of L1 and 256K of on-chip L2), significantly more than the 264K on a Pentium 4. Early Athlons did not include L2 cache on the chip.

The original Athlons linked to the motherboard through AMD's Slot A. Intel kept some of the design elements of its Slot 1 (SC242) a trade secret, blocking use of the connector by its competitors — principally AMD. Slot A, AMD's equivalent connector, is mechanically all but identical to Intel's design, but its electrical design is based on the bus for the Alpha microprocessor originally developed by Digital Equipment Corporation. You cannot use an AMD Athlon in an Intel

Slot 1, or a Pentium III in a Slot A. Just like Intel, though, AMD changed back to a motherboard-mounted receptacle (Socket A) a few models into the production of the Athlon. You'll find Slot A versions of the Athlon from 600 MHz through 950 MHz. Socket A versions arrived with the 700 MHz version and continued through 1.4 GHz.

You may find adaptors that allow the use of a Socket A CPU in a Slot A, or the other way around. Although these may work, AMD does not support their use because of concerns about heat dissipation and possible electrical irregularities.

As you work to repair or upgrade your computer, remember that AMD does not sell directly to consumers. You have to go through an authorized reseller who, in most cases, will supply a total solution: motherboard, CPU, and support chips.

AMD made a midcourse change in the construction of Athlon chips in 2000, introducing an advanced version based on a project known as "Thunderbird." (Outsiders had at first expected Thunderbird to be released as a new product line.)

The main difference between the two chips is the location of L2 cache. The original Athlon had 512K of cache external to the processor, mounted within a cartridge that plugged into AMD's Slot A and communicating at 33, 40, or 50 percent of the core clock speed. Newer Athlons have 256K of L2 cache on the microprocessor die itself and communicates at 100 percent of the core clock speed; these CPUs are mostly offered in a version that plugs into a small Socket A on the motherboard, although some versions sold to system manufacturers were packaged in a Slot A carrier.

AMD Athlon MP

The AMD Athlon MP is a derivative of the Athlon designed for use in high-performance multiprocessing servers and workstations. A key element of the chip is Smart MP technology, which greatly enhances overall platform performance by increasing data movement between two or more CPUs, the chipset, and the memory system.

Smart MP technology features dual point-to-point, high-speed 266 MHz system buses with error correcting code support designed to provide up to 2.1 GBps of bus bandwidth per CPU in a dual-processor system.

Like other Athlons, the MP attaches through Socket A and supports DDR memory technology. Other features include a high-performance, full-speed cache with hardware data pre-fetch, a fully

pipelined superscalar floating point engine, and an L2 Translation Look-aside Buffer (TLB). The MP also incorporates 3DNow! Professional technology, which has 52 instructions that extend AMD's 3DNow! technology; the company claims this results in smoother, richer, and more lifelike images, more precise digital audio, and an enriched Internet experience.

SUMMARY

In this chapter, you've looked at the grand march of processor history. In the next chapter, you examine the system BIOS, the most basic level of instructions for the PC.

Ch
2

Chapter 3

Tools Needed:

- Internet connection for down-loading upgrade code on "flashable" BIOS

- Chip-removal tool for changing chips on an older motherboard

BIOS

The basic input/output system, or BIOS, is the lowest-level set of instructions for your computer, defining your PC's personality and handling essential tasks. The microprocessor uses the BIOS to bring the machine to life when you first turn the power on. The process is called booting the computer; the term comes from the old phrase "pulling yourself up by your bootstraps."

The BIOS also runs startup diagnostics on the system. After your PC is up and running, it oversees the basic functions of interpreting signals from the keyboard and the interchange of information through ports.

The BIOS exists as a ROM (read-only memory) chip or set of chips on your motherboard, together with additional ROM BIOS chips that may be present on some adapter cards. In logical terms, the BIOS sits between the hardware and the operating system.

The BIOS also ties into the set of device drivers added to your Windows operating system through the installation of various pieces of hardware within or attached to the computer. *Device drivers* are small pieces of software coding that help a generic system work with the specialized functions of these computer adaptations.

Device drivers, then, occupy a logical layer between the BIOS and the operating system. Figure 3.1 shows one way to envision the way BIOS works with your system.

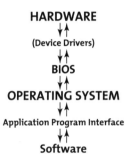

FIGURE 3-1: *Understanding the logical placement of device drivers.*

The purpose of this layered structure is to permit the operating system to do its thing without having to be adapted for any of a nearly unlimited number of combinations of motherboards, microprocessors, and hardware. The BIOS and associated drivers interpret commands for the needs of the specific mix of hardware in your system.

At the lower half of this stack of layers, the operating system does not have to deal directly with the specific set of software applications (such as word processors, browsers, databases, and the like). Instead, the Application Program Interface (API) stands between the operating system and applications; therefore, applications don't need to know much about the structure of the operating system and can just send a command that says "print this" or "save this to disk."

Some elements of the BIOS need to be available at the time of bootup (for example, basic functionality for the display of video as the machine goes through its startup, the keyboard, mouse, and a hard drive), whereas other elements (such as advanced graphics, a sound card, a printer, or scanner) can wait for the operating system to be fully loaded before they become fully functional. That's why certain devices have their instructions resident in the BIOS on the motherboard or in ROMs on adapter cards; these are scanned and loaded first and are usually indicated on your monitor during bootup. Device drivers are stored on the hard drive and are loaded a bit later along with the operating system.

Because ROM chips are relatively slow to disgorge their information (typically with access times of 150 nanoseconds versus as little as 6 nanoseconds for modern RAM), most systems pick up a bit of speed by "shadowing" the contents of ROM to system RAM as part of the bootup process. The information is copied to memory and made available there for use *after* the system is up and running. Shadowing is more useful in 16-bit operating systems including DOS and Windows 3.1; modern 32-bit operating systems generally use a different set of BIOS instructions after they are running, using the 16-bit code only for bootup. Consult the instruction manual for your motherboard and BIOS before making any changes to the shadowing settings.

Another important part of the BIOS is the POST (power-on self test) that checks for the presence and functionality of essential pieces of the system at bootup, and then gives a numeric or text report of any problems it has found.

As important as all of these functions are, most PC users don't know the maker and version of the BIOS in their machine, and few have ever explored the settings on the CMOS configuration screen that is a part of nearly every modern machine.

If you never add memory, drives, or other internal devices, have no interest in adjusting the personality of your machine to suit your needs, and never experience a problem with the basic functions of your PC, then you probably never need to visit the configuration settings of your BIOS. That is, of course, if you are satisfied that the manufacturer of your machine did the job correctly in the first place.

For the rest of us, it's important to know the identity and version of the BIOS in our PCs. We need to know how to display the configuration setup screen, how to make changes, and what broad range of available capabilities it offers.

Most users don't need to upgrade their PC's BIOS chips during the typical three-to-five years of usable life in a PC. Most modern machines can work with most current hardware or can be updated with device drivers; similarly, most existing BIOS chips can work with versions of operating systems that are introduced after the system has shipped from the factory.

In some situations, however, major alterations — usually improvements — lie beyond the predictions made by BIOS designers. In the early days of personal computers, the original PCs were quickly locked out of using higher-capacity floppy and hard disk drives and were unable to keep pace with advances in video standards. In more modern machines, some early BIOS chips had difficulties working with SCSI controllers and CD-ROMs. That is much less common today with the advent of USB, which allows external devices to identify themselves to the system when they are attached and even work with the computer to retrieve device drivers that may be on the hard drive or to go out on the Internet and obtain them when necessary. If your BIOS does fall behind the times, the good news is that in most cases the instructions it holds can be upgraded or replaced. Nearly all modern machines use a form of chip called a *Programmable ROM (PROM)*, sometimes referred to as an *EPROM* (erasable programmable ROM) or *flash memory*.

Elements of a Modern BIOS

What should you expect from a thoroughly modern BIOS? To begin with, you want a system that is capable of working with all of the most current hardware options, including high-speed hard drive interfaces, USB 2.0, FireWire, and more. These are the obvious needs. But one step beyond them are many niceties that have been added to BIOS systems in recent years.

An example of a modern machine BIOS is shown in Figure 3-2. This early screen, from a Dell Dimension PC, shows IRQ assignments.

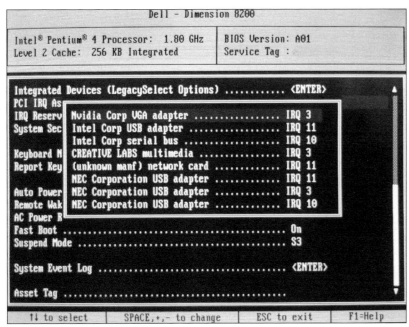

```
                    Dell - Dimension 8200

Intel® Pentium® 4 Processor:  1.80 GHz    BIOS Version: A01
Level 2 Cache:  256 KB Integrated         Service Tag :


Integrated Devices (LegacySelect Options) ........... <ENTER>  ▲
PCI IRQ As
IRQ Reserv  Nvidia Corp VGA adapter ................. IRQ 3
System Sec  Intel Corp USB adapter .................. IRQ 11
            Intel Corp serial bus .................. IRQ 10
Keyboard N  CREATIVE LABS multimedia ................ IRQ 3
Report Key  (unknown manf) network card ............ IRQ 11
            NEC Corporation USB adapter ............ IRQ 11
Auto Power  NEC Corporation USB adapter ............ IRQ 3
Remote Wak  NEC Corporation USB adapter ............ IRQ 10
AC Power R
Fast Boot ........................................ On
Suspend Mode ..................................... S3

System Event Log ................................. <ENTER>

Asset Tag ........................................              ▼

  ↑↓ to select  │  SPACE,+,- to change  │  ESC to exit  │  F1=Help
```

FIGURE 3-2: *One of the screens in the BIOS setup system for a Dell Dimension 8200, a capable modern machine produced before the introduction of SATA. The machine offers USB ports but still makes heavy use of legacy serial and parallel ports for external devices.*

In 2007, advanced features of a typical BIOS — as delivered or as upgraded after installation — included the following features:

- Full support for Windows XP, 2000, Me, and earlier operating systems including Windows 95/98. The most modern of machines, released in the second half of 2006 and later, are capable of working with the newest Microsoft operating system, Windows Vista.

- Full support for current CPUs including the Intel Core Quad, Intel Core 2 Duo, Intel Pentium D, Pentium 4, AMD Athlon, AMD Athlon XP, AMD Sempron, and AMD Opteron.
- Support for current chipsets. (I've included information about many modern chipsets in Chapter 2.)
- Provision for simple, high-speed Serial ATA connection for disk drives as well as older IDE (now known as Parallel ATA) devices
- The ability to choose to boot from a wide variety of drives, including a wide range of internal hard drives, the floppy disk drive (if one is installed), over a network, or from an internal CD-ROM, DVD-ROM, or other storage media, including Zip and Superdisk drives
- USB 2.0 and FireWire support
- The ability to work with large hard drives of up to 137GB in size and drives with more than 1,024 cylinders (and to work with adaptations that go well beyond that)
- HDD S.M.A.R.T. (Self Monitoring, Analysis and Reporting Technology) support for drive monitoring
- Facilities to assign IRQs to devices
- Support for Plug and Play under Windows
- Specialized high-speed bus slots including PCI Express and AGP allowing full support of advanced graphics functions
- Boot sector antivirus protection
- Multiple modes of password security
- Flash BIOS upgrades

Table 3-1 contains an example of the typical information that might be included in the system setup screen for a current modern machine such as a Dell Dimension machine based on an Intel Core 2 Duo CPU. Table 3-2 shows the actual contents of an older and less sophisticated machine, a Dell Dimension 8200 based on a Pentium 4 CPU from about 2003. This type of BIOS display contains system information data that you can't change as well as menu-like displays that let you configure many system features.

Ch 3

Ch 3

TABLE 3-1: A Modern BIOS Screen

SYSTEM

System Info	Details including the computer name, the version number, and BIOS creation date, and a system tag or other identification applied to the computer by the manufacturer.
CPU Info	The processor type and ID, processor bus speed, clock speed, L2 cache, and other details about the CPU. Intel and AMD no longer identify their processors based on their internal speed, but instead give them a series name or number.
Memory Info	The type and amount of installed memory, memory speed, and the configuration of its data channel (single or dual).
Date/Time	Current date and time settings for the computer, as maintained by the system's internal battery.
Boot Sequence	The list of devices the system can use to boot from, with the sequence selected by the user. Most machines boot from the primary hard drive; if that fails, the secondary device is typically a floppy disk drive (if installed) or a CD or DVD drive. Other options include booting from a network device, or on the most current of machines, booting from a device attached to a USB port.

DRIVES

Diskette Drive	The identity and specifications of a floppy disk drive that may be attached to the Floppy connector on the motherboard, or on certain current machines the details of a floppy disk drive that may be attached to a USB port. A modern BIOS permits selection between internal and external devices here.
SATA 0 through 5	The identity and specifications of one or more devices attached to SATA (Serial ATA) connectors on the motherboard, including the capacity and setup details.
SATA Operation	Details and setting for SATA controllers capable of working with RAID configurations that permit data to be mirrored (duplicated across multiple drives) or striped (split among multiple drives). Typical settings include **RAID Autodetect/ATA** or **RAID On.**
PATA Drives 0 through 1	Some machines sold from 2005 to 2007 included facilities to support older ATA drives, now renamed as PATA (Parallel ATA) devices. This setting allows enabling or disabling CD or DVD drives that use a PATA controller. Information displayed includes the controller type, the port number each device uses, the Drive ID number, capacity, and other information including whether the device is under control of the BIOS or other chips in the system.

ONBOARD DEVICES

Integrated NIC	Specifications and settings for the built-in Network Interface Card on the motherboard (not a card, but retaining the acronym used when adding network facilities required installation of an adapter card). Typical settings include **On** (default), **Off,** or specialized settings such as **On w/PXE** (Pre-Boot Execution Environment) that permit booting from a network device.
Integrated Audio	Enables or disables onboard audio circuitry. This can be used to turn off a balky or inadequate sound system; replacement cards can be installed in a bus slot or (on certain motherboards) as a specialized daughtercard or riser.

USB Controller	Enables or disables the USB system that extends the facilities of the motherboard outside of the case. The default setting is **On.**
USB for FlexBay	Enables or disables a proprietary Dell design called FlexBay that permits certain types of devices, such as floppy disk drives or hard disk drives, to be slid into an available bay and plug into customized connector for immediate use; power and data are transferred using internal USB ports. The default is **No Boot,** which enables an internal USB connection but does not make the device bootable. Other typical settings are **On** and **Off.**
Rear Quad USB	Enables or disables the stack of four USB ports on the backplane of the computer.
Rear Dual USB	Enables or disables the stack of two additional USB ports on the backplane of the computer.
Front USB	Enables or disables the stack of two USB ports on the front of the computer.
PS/2 mouse port	Enables or disables a legacy PS/2 mouse port if one is installed on the computer.

VIDEO

Primary Video	If two or more video controllers are installed in the computer (on the motherboard or in a bus adapter), this option allows specification of which controller is in charge of the primary screen.

PERFORMANCE

Multiple CPU Core	Details and settings related to a processor that offers multiple cores. As this book goes to press, these include the Intel Core 2 Duo and the Pentium D series.
Virtualization	Details and settings related to processors that permit virtual technology.
SpeedStep	If the installed processor offers Intel's SpeedStep technology, this feature can be enabled or disabled with settings offered here.
HyperThreading	If the installed processor offers Intel's HyperThreading technology, this feature can be enabled or disabled with settings offered here.
HDD Acoustic Mode	Depending on the BIOS, hard disk drive, and other computer components, you may be able to adjust settings for the hard disk drive to make it operate at its highest performance (highest speed at all times) or in a quieter mode that produces less noise and heat. Typical options include **Bypass** (default) which does not alter the predefined settings for the hard disk drive; **Quiet**, which operates the drive at its least-noisy setting; **Suggested**, which uses the recommended settings from the hard drive manufacturer; and **Performance**, which operates the drive at its fastest speed.

SECURITY

Admin Password	An option to limit access to the computer's system setup program to a designated system administrator.
System Password	An option to turn on or off the requirement for entry of a password to access the system, or to assign a password. Unless the password is locked (see Password Status) on some modern BIOS designs you can disable password security during bootup by pressing Ctrl+Enter while the computer starts.
Password Status	An option to lock the system password field with the setup password selected under System Password.

Continued

Ch 3

TABLE 3-1: *(Continued)*

POWER MANAGEMENT

AC Recovery	Offers a set of options to instruct the computer on what to do when AC power is restored to the computer after an outage.
Auto Power On	An option to set a time to automatically turn on the computer at a specified time (every day, or Monday through Friday). The default setting is Off.
Auto Power Time	If the computer is set for Auto Power On, you can set the time for power-up in this field.
Remote Wake Up	An option to allow the computer to power up when a NIC (network interface) or Remote Wakeup-capable modem receives a wake-up signal. The default setting is On. An additional setting is On w/Boot to NIC, which instructs the computer to boot from a network source.
Quick Resume	Enables or disables Intel's Viiv Quick Resume Technology if that facility is supported by the motherboard and chipset. The default setting is Off.

MAINTENANCE

Service Tag	Displays the system service tag that many manufacturers assign to a particular computer; the tag corresponds to information held in a manufacturer's database that can help technicians recommend repairs or upgrades.
SERR Message	Enables or disables the System Error message mechanism used in certain combinations of motherboards and adapter cards.
Load Defaults	Permits the user to reset all options in the setup menu back to the factory default.
Event Log	Displays the system event log, a record of messages and activities including the date and time for system startup and any crashes or errors.

POST BEHAVIOR

Fastboot	Enables or disables an option to skip some of the tests and configurations of the standard boot sequence. The default setting is On.
Numlock Key	Sets the condition for the Numlock key at bootup; if it is On (default), the numeric and mathematical characters indicated on the top of keys in the rightmost bank of keys is activated. If it is Off, the cursor-control functions indicated on the bottom of each key are active. The effect of this option depends on the motherboard and keyboard in use, and once the system starts you can override the current setting by pressing the Numlock key on the keyboard.
POST Hotkeys	Allows the selection of function keys that are displayed on the screen when the computer starts.
Keyboard Errors	Disables or enables keyboard error reporting at startup.

TABLE 3-2: A BIOS Screen from an Older Modern Machine

Intel Pentium 4 Processor:	1.80 GHz
BIOS Version:	A01
Level 2 Cache:	256K Integrated
Service Tag:	xxx

System Time	00:00:00
System Date	DY/MO/DATE/YR
Diskette Drive A:	3.5 inch, 1.44MB
Primary Drive 0:	Hard Drive
Primary Drive 1:	Off
Secondary Drive 0:	CD-R
Secondary Drive 1:	Off
Boot Sequence	<Enter>
System Memory	256 SDRAM
AGP Aperture	128MB
CPU Information	<Enter>
Integrated Devices (Legacy Select Options)	<Enter>
PCI IRQ Assignments	<Enter>
IRQ Reservations	<Enter>
System Security	<Enter>
Keyboard Numlock	On
Report Keyboard Errors	Report
Auto Power On	Disabled
Remote Wake Up	Off
AC Power Recovery	Last
Fast Boot	On
Suspend Mode	S3
System Event Log	<Enter>
Asset Tag	Xxxxxxxx

Legacy Select Options

Option	Function
Sound	Turns integrated sound (if present on the motherboard) off and on. The default is On.
Mouse Port	Turns the mouse port off and on. The default is On.
USB Emulation	Turns USB emulation off and on. The default is On.
USB Controller	Turns the USB controller off and on. The default is On.
Serial Port 1	Sets serial port options and turns the port off and on. The default is Auto.
Parallel Port	Displays parallel port settings when <Enter> is pressed. The default mode is PS/2 and the I/O address default is 378h.
IDE Drive Interface	Sets the IDE drive interface options. The default is Auto.
Diskette Interface	Sets diskette interface options. The default is Auto.
PC Speaker	Turns the PC speaker off and on. The default is On.
Primary Video	Sets the primary video controller.
Controller	The default is AGP.
Video DAC Snoop	Turns the video DAC Snoop off and on. The default is Off.

Boot options

In ordinary operation, you want to boot your PC from its primary hard drive. In case of trouble or certain types of maintenance operations, however, a flexible BIOS should allow you to choose another source for bootup files.

A capable modern BIOS should permit you to specify several startup devices and permit you to choose the order in which the system searches for a bootup disk. Typical options include a floppy disk drive (if installed, and only capable of the most basic level of bootup), a CD or DVD disc, a ZIP or other removable disk, and other hard disks in the system.

NOTE

It's a good idea to set your BIOS so that it searches first on the hard drive, rather than looking to a floppy disk (if one is installed in the computer). This action decreases the risk of loading a virus from a floppy disk inadvertently left in the drive. It also speeds up the booting process. If you need to boot from a floppy disk or any other device other than the hard disk drive, go to the BIOS screen and change the order of boot devices.

Most modern BIOS chips can boot from an alternate hard drive, either a secondary SATA or Parallel ATA or IDE drive. You can use this feature to choose from different hard drives loaded with different operating systems, for example.

The most capable of current machines can also boot from another device that is up and running on a network, or from an attached and powered-on USB device. One interesting option — not much used yet — involves the placement of some or all of the boot tracks on a USB memory key that can be removed from the system and locked away to prevent some attempts at unauthorized startup of an unattended machine.

Multiple video cards

Windows 98 and later versions of operating systems, including Windows XP and Vista, allow you to install two or more graphics cards to power multiple displays; or you can use the feature of many current video adapters that permit operation with two displays. Having two or more monitors is especially valuable to graphic artists and other users working with very complex applications such as financial analysts or brokers who may want to devote one screen to a constantly updated data stream and a second screen to an order-management system.

On my main computer, the one I am using to write these words, I have a large monitor directly in front of me and I choose to display my word processing screen there; a slight shift of my eyes brings me to a second screen to my right and there — depending on what I am working on — I can display a Web browser, my e-mail inbox, or a second word-processing document. I have at times worked with a third screen, this one to the left of center, which gives me all of the options I need to oversee the components of my work.

When I am working on graphics, I use the monitors in this way: The main screen holds the photograph or image, and the secondary screen holds all of the program's valuable but sometimes intrusive menus, palettes, and history screens.

Any current BIOS permits the use of multiple graphics cards or a single card with multiple outputs with a current version of Windows, and from within the operating system you can make a number of decisions about how the card or cards are used and how the displays appear.

Older modern machines, though, may have a bus structure and a BIOS that works against the best use of multiple graphics cards. Here's the combination: a BIOS that was written in 2002 or earlier and a motherboard with an AGP slot. On some, but not all, machines of that sort, if the system detected two graphics cards, the adapter in a PCI slot was recognized as the main card and a card in an AGP slot was secondary — despite the fact that AGP is usually faster and more capable than PCI. That's a good reason to look for an updated BIOS.

A thoroughly modern BIOS allows you to specify which card will be treated as the primary card, regardless of how it attaches to the bus.

Disabling ports

As PC designers found more and more uses for legacy input and output subsystems including serial, parallel, and PS/2 ports, a significant problem arose: The devices have available to them a limited number of interrupts, or IRQs, to signal to the CPU when they need attention.

That problem was mostly solved by three technologies that have had a major impact on PC design in the past few years:

- The PCI bus (and the successor PCI Express) is intelligently managed and allows some devices to share the same IRQ.
- The USB and the FireWire bus permit multiple devices to use a single port.

If you are working with an older modern machine, or a senior citizen, you may need to find a workaround. One solution is a feature on the BIOS that permits you to disable ports that are not in use and reclaim IRQ and DMA resources that the system would otherwise demand. For example, if you are working with a machine on a network, you may not need to use your parallel port to connect with a printer. Similarly, many systems use Ethernet cards to attach to networks and cable or DSL modems and therefore don't need serial ports; many current mouse or trackball devices connect to a USB port rather than to a serial port or PS/2 port. (In fact, many modern machines no longer offer parallel or serial ports; they've been replaced with more versatile USB ports.) Be aware that merely freeing up an IRQ or DMA resource does not necessarily mean that another device will automatically use the facility; you may have to make manual reassignments for resources.

BIOS Failure

BIOS chips are fairly reliable. Nevertheless, because of the importance of the bootup information included within them, the first task that the BIOS chip performs when it is turned on is to check its own validity by examining every single bit. In some designs, this can amount to a million bits or more.

In one commonly used scheme, the chip calculates a checksum — a mathematical summation of the value of the bits — and compares it with the official checksum stored in the BIOS ROM. If the numbers don't agree, the BIOS stops the boot and displays a BIOS Checksum Error message. If you receive this message, try turning off the machine and then starting over again. If the error does not recur, you can (nervously) hope that the problem was a once-in-a-very-blue-moon occurrence.

If you get past the BIOS self-check, chances are very strong that any problems you encounter don't lie within the BIOS. If you cannot get past the BIOS self-check, the only cure for a failed BIOS chip or chips is replacement.

Sources for BIOS chips

To replace a BIOS chip, begin by contacting a distributor that works with the existing code within your system. Although it is theoretically possible to upgrade a motherboard with a different brand of BIOS than it originally held, you may run into compatibility problems with some custom chipsets on the motherboard.

There are just a handful of significant manufacturers of BIOS chips for modern motherboards; they include Intel, Phoenix, and VIA. Former competitors Phoenix and Award (which between them owned a large market share) merged in 1998, now operating as Phoenix Technologies. You can obtain some information about legacy BIOS chips at www.phoenix.com.

A number of sources provide replacement and upgrade chips. You may have to go no further than the original supplier of your PC or the motherboard, or you may need to go to a specialized supplier. A set of chips typically sells for about $50 to $100, plus the cost of shipping.

Start by consulting the support department for your machine's maker. To begin with, the maker may have customized the BIOS code and they may only be available from the *original equipment manufacturer (OEM)*. And the maker may offer some support over the phone or in an Internet chat that you may not get from a third-party reseller.

If you have an older machine or one made by a defunct company, one particularly good reference and supply source for replacement BIOS chips is Unicore Software, Inc. (www.unicore.com). This company supplies a number of software utilities to help with BIOS problem diagnosis and sells upgrade BIOS chips. You can find out a lot about your system's BIOS with its online utilities, but some manufacturers may not display standard BIOS messages, which means you may need to call Unicore and discuss your particular BIOS issues.

Determining your system's BIOS

The first step is to determine the type of BIOS in your system, the number of chips, and their sizes. Modern machines typically use one or more 256K, 512K, or 1MB chips; BIOS systems for a state-of-the-art modern machines typically have chips as large as 4MB. And some motherboards come equipped with one or more redundant BIOS chips to guard against the possibility of a failure or scrambling bringing down your system.

Nearly every modern machine uses a form of flash memory, or electrically erasable programmable read-only memory (EEPROM), which is also known an non-volatile RAM (NVRAM). These chips allow the user or technician to load a new set of instructions from a CD-ROM, diskette, or over the Internet. Check your machine's instruction manual for details.

On the other hand, dinosaurs and some older senior citizens may use one or more BIOS chips that may have to be physically removed to be replaced or reprogrammed. Some of these chips are *EPROMs (erasable programmable read-only memory)* that can accept new instructions, which are burned into place by intensive ultraviolet light in a special device; they are recognizable because they have a clear window above the code on the chip.

Modern machines generally use just a single high-capacity chip. In the oldest of machines, the 128K BIOS may have been made up of eight 16K chips. Figure 3-3 shows an example of a modern machine's BIOS chip; Figure 3-4 shows an older version.

Your computer's instruction manual may not be all that helpful in disclosing the exact BIOS model in your system; manufacturers may change or update the BIOS over the course of the life of a particular model.

One way to be certain of the identity of your BIOS is to take off the covers and do some exploration. Follow the standard precautions, please: Turn off and unplug the system before removing the covers and ground yourself before touching the motherboard.

The chips may be clearly labeled on top, or you may need to carefully peel away a covering label. The chips are usually labeled with the name of the BIOS maker. Look for a number marked on the chip, usually located on the end opposite the notch. On many older machines, chips labeled with a number beginning with 27 are standard EPROMs, while those labeled with a number beginning with 28 or 29 are flash chips that you can upgrade in place.

Depending on how your motherboard manufacturer has configured its particular form of BIOS you may be able to learn a lot about what's inside your machine by reading BIOS messages during bootup. Look for the BIOS manufacturer, BIOS revision number, date, and other information. On some systems, you can pause the bootup process by pressing the Pause button on the keyboard.

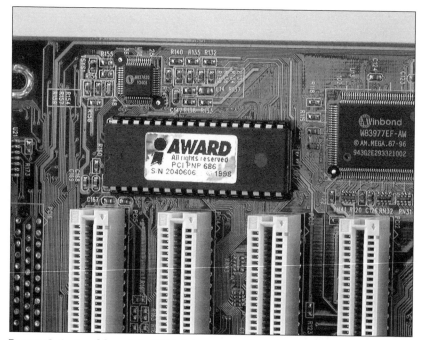

FIGURE 3-4: *An older-style BIOS chip on a senior-citizen motherboard.*

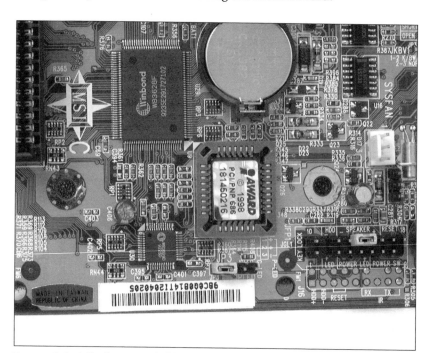

FIGURE 3-3: *A flash-upgradable Award BIOS in a chip carrier of an older but still capable motherboard.*

The Unicore Software Web site offers a free BIOS wizard that may be able to display key information from your system BIOS. Go to the web site at www.unicore.com to download a small program that queries the BIOS in your system and produces a report that you can use to shop for an upgrade on your own, or submit directly to Unicore for a quote. An example of a program report is shown in Figure 3-5.

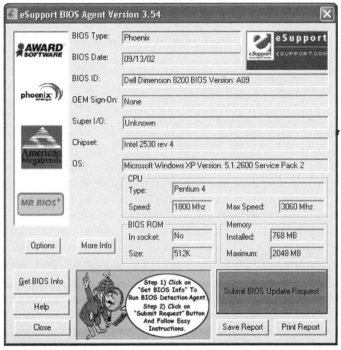

FIGURE 3-5: *The Unicore Software BIOS wizard.*

Installing a New BIOS

If necessary, it's relatively easy to upgrade the BIOS chips on your motherboard to add new capabilities. You can upgrade your BIOS by using one of the following two methods:

■ Most modern machines use a special type of ROM chip called *flash memory* that you can upgrade by running a software program from a CD, a diskette, or from a file downloaded from the Internet. The contents of the new BIOS are recorded electrically into the nonvolatile memory of the chips.

■ The other way to upgrade BIOS chips involves a bit of careful work with a chip-extraction tool.

Both of these methods are explored in the next two sections.

Flash updates for BIOS chips

As I've noted, nearly all current modern machines and many late-model senior citizens use a form of BIOS chip that can be upgraded in place by reading a new set of instructions from a floppy disk, a CD, or from your hard drive after you've downloaded the upgrade over the Internet. Point your browser to the web site of your motherboard's manufacturer and follow support or download links to get the upgrade software.

Contact the maker of your system or a distributor of BIOS upgrades for instructions. Be sure to correctly identify the brand and model number of the BIOS in your present system. Follow the instructions provided for the flash upgrade carefully; in most instances, the upgrade is done from the DOS prompt or from a special boot disk that takes control of the system independent of the BIOS.

I would never install a new BIOS without having in hand a full set of detailed instructions about the various settings or having a knowledgeable technician available by telephone.

Before you update any BIOS chips, make a copy of all of the entries on your system's CMOS Setup screen; in most cases, you'll have to resort to a pen and notepad, although a handful of BIOS designs allow you to print their settings or save them to a file.

For senior citizens and some dinosaurs, a route to upgrading the capabilities of an old system works around an outmoded BIOS by adding a specialized adapter card that expands or extends your motherboard BIOS. Some cards are BIOS upgrade specific; in other cases, BIOS extensions may be part of a card designed for another purpose. For example, I upgraded a senior-citizen machine that had a BIOS that would not recognize hard drives larger than 18GB. The solution was to install a new disk controller into the PCI bus and then disable the drive controller built into the motherboard.

I used an UltraATA 66 PCI controller card that added two high-speed IDE controllers and BIOS extensions to support drives up to 128GB. The card had its own BIOS code onboard specifically to support larger hard drive, and it also was capable of operating faster than the old machine's built-in IDE controller. With the machine turned off and unplugged, I installed the new card and moved the hard disk drive data cables from the motherboard to the PCI bus adapter card. Then during bootup, I went to the BIOS setup screen and disabled the motherboard's IDE controller. Presto, chango: The old BIOS had new life.

Changing the chips

If you have to physically remove and replace BIOS chips, it would be very helpful if you had a copy of all of the entries on your system's CMOS Setup screen. That's easy to do if you take the time to record entries in a notebook or on the corresponding page in the instruction manual that deals with BIOS settings. Of course, you're not going to be able to read the settings if the BIOS has given up the ghost; think ahead and make notes on the settings while your machine is in its prime.

Manufacturers of BIOS chips have come up with various different ways to call for the display of the CMOS Setup screen. On many systems, you have to press the Delete or F2 key at a particular moment during the bootup process; other systems use a Ctrl + Alt + Esc keyboard combination. Check the instruction manual that came with your computer or read the onscreen messages that appear during the bootup process.

To install the chips, turn off your machine and remove the power cord. Ground yourself before touching the innards of the PC. You may need to remove hard drives and adapter cards that block access to the BIOS chips. Use a chip-removal tool to gently and evenly pry the chips from their sockets.

 NOTE

Most dinosaur BIOS sets consist of one or more pairs of chips, referred to as the *odd* and *even* chips. You must replace both at the same time and install them in the proper sockets.

The BIOS vendor may supply a simple tweezers-like device with U-shaped hooks on the ends — or you can purchase fancier and better models from a tool catalog or store — that you can use to carefully remove the chips one at a time. Be sure to work the chips out of their sockets evenly; try to avoid bending the pins so that you can reinstall the chips if necessary. Install the new chips in their place. Follow any special instructions from the maker for setup routines.

As with most other electronic circuit and memory devices, the chips are marked at one end with a dot or a notch to indicate the end that matches a corresponding dot or notch on the socket. Spend a few moments making certain that you have the chips oriented properly and that they are intended for the specific socket.

On some new chips, the pins are set a bit wider than the corresponding holes on the socket. Before installation, gently rock the chips on a firm surface to push the pins inward a tiny amount. Be sure that you don't twist any of the pins.

Gently insert the chips into the sockets; be sure to apply pressure evenly so the pins are not bent or misaligned. When the chip is about halfway into the socket, stop your work and examine the socket from all four sides. Look for any pin that may be bent under or outside its intended hole. If you find any wrongly positioned pins, use your extractor and remove the chip and carefully straighten the pin or pins. Be careful not to bend a pin back and forth too much or it will break off. If a pin breaks, the chip is ruined.

After the new BIOS chips are in place, reinstall any components that you removed and power up the system. You will have to run a new setup program and inform the system of memory, drives, and other elements of your PC.

SUMMARY

You've now explored the BIOS instructions. The next chapter moves along to the system bus, which is the superhighway that interconnects most of the elements of the computer.

Notes

Chapter 4

The Computer Bus

The electrical bus that interconnects the microprocessor, system memory, and peripherals is a high-speed superhighway. But, as any commuter knows, even an expressway can suffer from slowdowns and bottlenecks.

Many PC system devices don't require blazing speed — for example, the keyboard and mouse demand very little from the system. However, in the modern era, the increasing demands from devices such as advanced video cards, sound cards, and network interfaces required the design of faster buses.

One of the downsides of the standard bus design, however, is that fast devices can become jammed behind slower ones. For example, think of a superhighway where speedy sports cars get stuck behind lumbering trucks. The solution was to take the higher-speed devices off the original I/O buses and give them an express lane — their own set of communication lines to the processor. This design was called a *local bus*.

Throughout the history of the PCs covered in this book, the user has had six routes to choose from; in other words, six standard bus designs have been available: PC, ISA, EISA, MCA, VL, and PCI. The newest of modern machines now rely principally on a seventh roadway: the PCI Express bus, which is logically similar to PCI but uses a new hardware scheme to deliver blazing speed and almost seamless flexibility.

It is also worth noting that over time designers came up with a few outrigger buses that they hung onto the main road like high-speed rush-hour lanes: AGP for internal video adapters, SCSI for internal or external high-bandwidth storage devices and scanners, and USB for an almost limitless array of fast and easy-to-configure external devices. Laptops and a small number of desktop machines also offered ports for PC Cards for communication and storage.

These buses fall into the modern machine category today:

- Current machines use motherboards based around the very fast, very flexible PCI Express specification. The most modern motherboards typically offer from one to three PCI Express slots plus several standard PCI slots. Initially, the PCI Express slots were used for video adapters; other uses of the slots include adding SATA and eSATA connectivity to an older modern machine.
- The vast majority of very capable modern machines manufactured from late 1994 through late 2005 were based on the PCI bus, usually with a single AGP slot dedicated to the needs of the graphics adapter. Many of these systems also offered several ISA bus slots, a means to allow use of older legacy add-in devices that required that form of attachment.
- The oldest group of modern machines, just barely able to keep up with the demands of current operating systems and Internet features, offered PCI and legacy ISA slots without special accommodation for the needs of an advanced graphics card.

In this chapter, I look at the various buses for modern machines and give a backwards glance at older buses. I also explore the black art of IRQs (interrupt requests) and DMA (direct memory access). These two features of all PCs are the doorbells (IRQs) and back alleys (DMA) of the bus; one rings the CPU's chimes to tell it that a piece of hardware is seeking its attention, and the other opens a channel for quick delivery of a message between a device and system memory without involving the CPU.

Modern Machine Bus Designs

A modern motherboard uses a hierarchy of several buses to connect the microprocessor to the system and memory and to interlink various devices. The processor bus is at the top of the hierarchy; below the processor bus is a typical motherboard that includes several subsidiary buses, such as an I/O or peripheral bus and a memory bus.

A bus, in electrical terms, is a set of parallel conductors that connects one element of the system to another, with all of the devices on the bus sharing the same data lines. Within a computer, a bus includes the following three principal lines of communication:

- **Control lines.** These wires or traces allow the microprocessor to direct devices to perform particular operations.
- **Address lines.** The microprocessor connects to specific memory locations within attached devices using this pathway.
- **Data lines.** Data that is transmitted or retrieved from a device travels on these lines.

Be sure to read the section in this chapter about the PCI Express design, the latest major change to PC motherboard design, which does not quite fit the preceding description.

Processor bus (front-side bus)

The processor bus (also known as the front-side bus or FSB) is the main highway of the computer, and, in most cases, the highest-speed route. It runs at the full motherboard speed, originally 66 MHz and reaching to as much as 266 MHz as this edition goes to press.

Essential elements of modern chipsets are the north and south bridges — Intel refers to them as the GMCH (Graphics and Memory Controller Hub) and the ICH (I/O Controller Hub), respectively.

In a modern system, the CPU uses the processor bus to communicate through the north bridge of the chipset to close-in cache memory and main memory. From there, the processor connects to the peripheral bus (including PCI on a modern machine) and special-purpose buses, such as AGP for a modern class of graphics cards. Some north bridge chipsets also include some integrated functions, such as video and audio controllers. On the most modern of Intel chipsets, the north bridge is part of a multifunction circuit called the Memory Controller Hub.

The processor bus also connects through the PCI bus to a slower south bridge, which controls the IDE bus that transports data to and from storage devices. Other elements of the south bridge include the USB serial subsystem; a bridge from PCI to the older ISA bus still used by some devices; the keyboard/mouse controller; power management; and various other features, including support for Plug-and-Play technology.

CROSS-REFERENCE

I discuss CPUs that support these high-speed system buses in Chapter 2.

In addition to the raw speed of the processor bus, two other elements determine the actual potential throughput of data in the system: the bus width and the number of data cycles per clock tick. All modern processor buses in consumer-level PCs work with 64-bit (8 byte) computer words; most also move data once in each clock cycle. However, the latest designs move as many as four blocks of data per clock cycle instead of just one, thus greatly increasing throughput.

The move to 100 MHz was not a huge one for motherboard makers. In many cases, existing 66-MHz board designs were easily adapted to a 100-MHz bus. The move to a 133-MHz system bus, however, required a redesign of the motherboard and supporting chips. The step to 266 was based on the 133-MHz design, as were the next two doublings, to 533 MHz and 1066 MHz.

NOTE

The electrical frequency of these high-speed buses is right in the middle of the FM radio band. You have to be especially careful to select and maintain the integrity of your computer case to prevent the speedy bus from shutting down a good portion of your radio and television reception with its own signal.

I/O or peripheral bus

One of the reasons behind the runaway success story of the PC has been the ability of owners to customize their machines in almost infinite ways through the use of devices that plug into the machine — under the covers by plugging into an internal bus connector or outside by attaching to a port. The computer communicates with add-on or peripheral devices through one of its I/O (input/output) buses.

As I've indicated, the largest block of modern machines still in use is based around the *PCI bus*, which evolved directly out of the original ISA design used in the second-generation PCs. The newest of modern machines have changed over to PCI Express, which marks a major improvement in speed and flexibility.

In its original basic version, PCI is a 32-bit bus that operates at 33 MHz, moving 32 bits with each clock cycle and yielding a maximum transfer rate of 133MB per second. In recent years, some manufacturers have doubled the clock speed for PCI to 66 MHz, yielding a maximum transfer rate of 266 MBps. (There have also been hybrid versions of PCI, used mostly in specialized servers, that offered clock speeds of as much as 133 MHz and moved as many as four blocks of data per clock cycle.)

The *AGP bus* was developed as a means to give the video adapter a more direct route to the microprocessor, working around the PCI bus and devices attached to it. AGP slots were offered in an original version capable of transfers of 266 MB/second and quickly improved upon with AGP 2X, AGP 4X, and AGP 8X designs.

The current *PCI Express* design entered the world of computers with a top transfer speed of 250 MBps and almost immediately became available in x4 and x16 versions with x32 capability designed into the standard.

The oldest group of still-modern machines offered PCI slots as well as a group of *ISA bus* slots to accommodate older legacy devices. At the time of this writing, though, motherboards with an independent ISA bus are trundling off to dinosaur land.

Antique buses, now formally living in the realm of the dinosaur, include *MCA*, an IBM advancement that never moved beyond that company's brand of machines. Also outdated is *EISA*, an extension to ISA with its own incompatible design.

Because ISA, MCA, and EISA came out of the original PC bus design, they all share some significant limitations on speed. The original I/O bus for the PC was essentially a direct expansion of the processor bus and devices communicated at the same speed as the processor bus. As new designs permitted the processor bus to operate faster and faster, the original I/O bus designs had to hold to their older, slower speeds to maintain compatibility with devices already on the market.

In Table 4-1 you can see the progression in data transfer rates from the original PCI specification to its doubling at a clock speed of 66 MHz and how it doubled again in systems that could work with 64-bit computer words. In the same table are the specs for the specialized AGP bus for video adapters.

Since the PCI Express bus operates in a different fashion, less dependent on clock cycles and clock speed, I've presented its speed progression in its own chart, Table 4-2. For comparison purposes I include the original PCI bus and the highest-speed AGP slot. PCI Express x2 and x8 are not in common use; most motherboards offer some combination of x1, x4, and x16 slots. As this book goes to press, the PCI Express x32 specification has not yet shown up on motherboards or adapter cards.

PCI Express: Getting off the bus

Up to this point, I have tried to keep things relatively simple by referring to the PCI Express as the latest and greatest in a series of ever-improving designs for a personal computer bus. And as far as a user is concerned, that's exactly the way it seems to work.

However, to be technically accurate, PCI Express is not a bus.

Earlier in this section, I defined a bus like this: in electrical terms, a set of parallel conductors that connects one element of the system to another, with all of the devices on the bus sharing the same data lines. That shoe does not fit PCI Express.

First of all, and most significantly, the PCI Express is the latest component of the most modern of PCs to make the switch from parallel to serial communication. As I discuss in later chapters about hard disk drives and controllers, advances in technology have allowed designers to push more and more data along a single wire than ever before. Even though parallel communication, with eight separate wires to carry each of the eight bits of information in a computer word, would seem to be eight times as fast as serial technology, in practice that has proven false. The faster you pump data along a parallel circuit, the greater the chances that not all eight (or 16, or 32 in some designs) bits will arrive at the other end at exactly the same moment. Any slowdown because of electrical interference or wire resistance results in discarded blocks of data that have to be re-sent.

Another difference between parallel and serial communication is that a parallel path runs only one direction at a time; once the device has finished sending information, or at an appropriate pause, the chipset or the CPU can use the same wires to respond. In the much simpler serial scheme used by PCI Express, a pair of wires runs in each direction — from the device to the chipset, and from the chipset to the device. (With just four wires, PCI Express achieves and then surpasses the equivalent throughput of 16 wires on the predecessor PCI.)

Secondly, PCI Express slots each have their own data path to the motherboard chipset. If you have three PCI Express slots and devices, there are three non-conflicting paths.

Data is sent in packets, similar to the way communication is conducted on an Ethernet or across the Internet. A burst of information is enclosed within a code that indicates the sender and recipient and includes a means to check the validity of the data.

On the technical side, each pair of wires that runs from a PCI Express slot to the chipset is called a *lane,* and each lane is capable of transferring as much as 250 MBps in one direction. The primary difference between PCI Express in its 1X, 2X, 4X, 8X, and 16X versions are the number of lanes each slot brings together; a 4X has four pairs of lanes, for example, which brings its possible maximum data transfer rate to 1000 MBps (which could also be expressed as 1 GBps).

The 16X PCI Express slot (and 32X when it becomes available) is best suited to the high demands of an advanced video card. In fact, the arrival of PCI Express x16 essentially spelled the end of the line for the AGP 8X slot on motherboards; AGP offers no advantage over PCI Express and requires more system resources and space on the surface of and within the motherboard. (If you've got an older modern machine with an AGP slot you will find replacement or upgrade adapters to fill the slot for years to come, although manufacturers are not likely to devote resources to improving performance of those devices.)

Although specifications exist for a 2X and an 8X PCI Express slot, those designs have not seen wide use in current machines. The most common setups offer 1X, 4X, and 16X slots, with some boards offering just 1X and 16X slots.

In any case, one of the great beauties of the PCI Express is that all of its advantages have been brought to the market without making new motherboards incompatible with existing operating systems, device drivers, and other modern machine elements. The chipset handles any necessary adjustments; if a device worked (on a logical level) with PCI, it will work with PCI Express.

On the physical level, though, a PCI Express slot will only work with an adapter designed to plug into its redesigned slot. And the various flavors of PCI Express, including x1, x4, and x16, each have their own connector design although slots are "downwardly compatible" within the specification: An x1 or x4 card, for example, will fit into and work with an x16 slot, but not the other way around.

The 1X slot is short and sweet, about an inch long; the 16X slot is about the same size as an older PCI slot, although it adds a positioning notch and hook to prevent accidental use of the wrong adapter design. Although each lane requires only a pair of wires for each direction, cards that plug into the slots also receive power and other information on other connectors. The PCI 1X connector has a total of 36 signal pins, the 4X has 64, the 8X has 98 pins, and the 16X has 164 pins.

And speaking of power, another of the advantages of the PCI Express specification is the amount of power it can deliver; the PCI Express x16 slot can deliver as much as 75 watts to a video card, a significant improvement over the 25- to 42-watt limit of the AGP design it replaces. More power supports higher-speed, more capable microprocessors and memory on the video card.

Again, none of this matters to you except for the advantages you receive: high speed, great flexibility, and little chance of conflict between devices on the bus. Oops . . . I called it a "bus" . . . actually, for your purposes in this book I continue that little charade all the way to the end.

Let's agree amongst ourselves on the following: PCI Express looks like a bus and acts like a bus, even though it is technically just a group of dedicated point-to-point data paths. So I call it a *bus.*

AMD's HyperTransport bus

Motherboards built to support current microprocessors from AMD offer a mix of buses that take advantages of that company's particular chips but also maintain compatibility with the large base of adapter cards and devices developed to work with Intel CPUs.

The current front-side bus for AMD microprocessors is the HyperTransport, a bidirectional system with serial and parallel circuits. The three versions of HT (not to be confused with Intel's HyperThreading technology, which is a feature of some of its processors) range in speed from 200 MHz to 2.6 GHz. The bus is a *double data rate (DDR)* system, meaning it sends data on both the rising and falling edges of a clock signal.

Most current motherboards for AMD also offer PCI Express and PCI slots for adapters; older modern motherboards offered PCI and AGP slots.

Although it is very difficult to compare bus designs when you are mixing in different designs for the CPU and chipset, Intel and AMD have differing amounts of overhead that result in adjustments to the true net bandwidth (raw bandwidth minus overhead). The latest definition for HyperTransport, version 3.0, is based on a 2.6-GHz clock rate; add to that the DDR scheme and the raw potential for transfer is 5.2 GHz, which places it well above PCI and just above PCI Express 16X.

You can't change the design of a bus already in place on your motherboard. Your alternative is a major construction project: installation of a new motherboard.

Many modern-machine motherboards are combinations of more than one type of bus, allowing a mix and match of expansion cards. The most common combo is a PCI motherboard that includes an AGP video slot as well as one or more ISA slots to allow use of older legacy cards. Most modern machines are based around the PCI Express specification, offering several slots of that design; to maintain compatibility with existing adapter designs, most motherboards also offer several standard PCI slots.

If you are working with a combination board, the issue often comes down to making decisions about which cards are worth holding on to, and which ones you should discard and replace with more modern versions. No method exists for converting an ISA card to plug into a PCI slot or vice versa; similarly, PCI Express cards are not intended to be used in a standard PCI slot and cannot be installed in one without the use of a pricey and inefficient converter, which I cannot recommend.

In any case, when you run out of parking spaces for cards, you have to go outside the box to external devices. In the early days of PCs, one large, cumbersome, and expensive solution was to purchase an expansion chassis, which was a PC-sized box with a whole set of PC slots and a connecting cable that hooked the box into a slot on the original PC.

Today, ISA cards are becoming increasingly difficult to find; you may have to try to find them at online auction sites such as eBay or browse the shelves of used computer stores.

The good news is that most modern machines offer USB ports, and a wide variety of devices is now available using that means of entry to the computer. And many older modern and some senior-citizen machines can be upgraded to offer USB if they don't already provide that facility.

Ch 4

TABLE 4-1: PCI and AGP Bus Specifications				
Bus Design	Bus Speed (MHz)	Bus Width (bits)	Data Movements per Clock Cycle	Maximum Transfer Rate (MBps)
PC/XT	4.77	8	$1/2$	2.39
ISA (8 bit)*	6, 8, 8.33	8	$1/2$	4.17
ISA (16 bit)	8.33	16	$1/2$	8.33
EISA	8.33	32	1	33
MCA-16	5	16	1	10
MCA-32	5	32	1	20
VESA VL	33	32	1	133
PCI	33 MHz	32	1	133 MBps
PCI	66 MHz	32	1	266 MBps
PCI	33 MHz	64	1	266 MBps
PCI	66 MHz	64	1	533 MBps
AGP	66 MHz	32	1	266 MBps
AGP 2X	66 MHz	32	2	533 MBps
AGP 4X	66 MHz	32	4	1066 MBps
AGP 8X	66 MHz	32	8	2133 MBps

The ISA bus, which grew out of the original PC bus, was initially introduced with a 6 MHz bus speed and later improved to 8 MHz. At the time of the introduction of the 16-bit AT bus, the clock speed was set at 8.33 MHz.

TABLE 4-2: PCI and PCI Express Bus Specifications

Bus Design	Maximum Transfer Rate
PCI	133 MBps
AGP 8X	2133 MBps
PCI Express x1	250 MBps
PCI Express x2	500 MBps
PCI Express x4	1000 MBps
PCI Express x16	4000 MBps
PCI Express x32	8000 MBps

Ch
4

The PCI bus: The dethroned champion

The *Peripheral Component Interconnect (PCI)* bus represented a major improvement in performance when it was introduced about 1994. The vast majority of modern machines produced between then and 2006 were based around this bus to link adapters that add function to the system, including video cards, network interfaces, sound cards, and other devices. The PCI bus was also used as the gateway or enabler of another group of subsidiary buses, such as AGP and SCSI.

The original PCI bus was a 32-bit path that operates at 33 MHz. Workstations, servers, and other advanced machines extended that design to run at 66 MHz, use a 64-bit bus width, or both. PCI 2.2 allowed for 66 MHz-signaling, and PCI 3.0 was the final version of the specification, which brought some enhancements but also removed support for devices that demanded 5 volts of power. The PCI-X standard, not widely used in consumer PCs, doubled the data width to 64 bits and increased the maximum data rate to 133 MHz.

In addition to its speed, PCI has the advantage of being able to operate, more or less, independent of the CPU; devices plugged into the PCI bus can move data and instructions back and forth over the bus while the microprocessor is otherwise engaged.

PCI devices must use a PCI slot, which has a different physical and electrical design from ISA, EISA, and AGP. The slots are white, making them a visual contrast from the black ISA slots.

The 64-bit version of PCI uses an extended connector to handle the additional 32 bits of data. Figure 4-1 shows an example of standard 32-bit PCI slots on a motherboard that also offers ISA connectors.

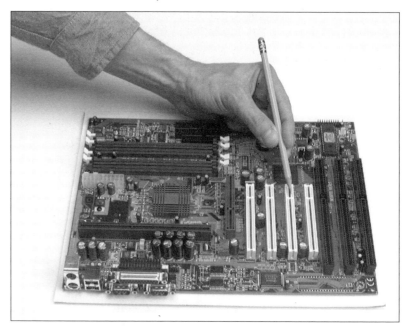

FIGURE 4-1: *On the right side of this crowded ATX motherboard are seven bus slots (four white PCI connectors and three black ISA connectors). Where they come together, there's room for only one adapter, either a PCI or ISA device, but not both.*

The bus, developed by Intel, includes *arbitrated bus mastering* — which is the ability for devices on the bus to operate semi-independent of the microprocessor. PCI also permits *parity checking,* which is the ability to set system configuration without jumpers or switches for all devices in the system, and support for the Plug-and-Play specification that allows the computer to recognize most devices as they are attached to the system.

PCI, in its early versions, was capable of working with no more than three peripheral devices plugged directly into it. Relatively few motherboards were produced using that design. With the introduction of PCI 2.0, the standard took full flight.

For some users, a major advantage of a PCI bus is its ability to share IRQs (interrupt requests), a feature that can make installation of a wide range of adapters much easier to manage. Keep in mind a couple of caveats, however; first, PCI devices can share IRQs with each other, but not with an ISA device that may already be plugged into the system. Second, some PCI devices are better behaved than others, occasionally putting the lie to the shared IRQ theory. My best advice is to conduct a trial-and-error testing process if you choose to share an IRQ among PCI cards. If the system works, be happy; if it grinds to a halt, undo the last IRQ assignment that you made and try something else.

Under current versions of Windows (beginning with the B revision of Windows 95), PCs can use IRQ steering, which gives the operating system the task of dynamically assigning (or steering) IRQs to PCI devices, making use of the Plug-and-Play definitions of newer cards whenever possible.

Typically running at a clock speed of 33 MHz (with some specialized systems at 66, 100, or 133 MHz), the PCI local bus employs a 32-bit data bus that supports multiple peripheral components and add-in cards at a peak bandwidth of 133 MBps (megabytes per second) — a substantial improvement over the 5 MBps peak transfer rate of the standard ISA bus. The actual throughput over a fully loaded, 133 MBps PCI bus is about 90 MBps because of system overhead. This increased bandwidth allows the PCI local bus to provide more than four times the graphics performance of the ISA bus.

Later PCI bus designs include 39 additional signal pins to permit the bus to support 64-bit data transfers. This enhancement increases addressable memory from about 4GB to more than 17GB and improves data transfer speed over the bus. A 64-bit PCI bus ships data among system components 64 bits at a time — not 32 bits — which potentially doubles bus throughput (at least to memory and other devices that can handle 64-bit-wide information). Until implementation of Intel's Itanium 64-bit CPU, Intel CPUs support only 32-bit internal architecture. Other CPU makers, though, have CPUs with internal 64-bit architecture and 64-bit PCI buses.

The PCI local bus, however, offers much more than high bandwidth. It enables peripherals to take full advantage of available processing power without being dependent on processor speed or architecture. It also supports autoconfiguration of Plug-and-Play enabled add-in cards and offers system designers a standardized design path. PCI devices can be either *targets* (devices that accept commands) or *masters* (devices that can perform some processing independent of the CPU and the bus). Finally, PCI provides built-in upgradability to accommodate future technical advances.

The AGP port: Video special

The *AGP (accelerated graphics port)* bus is a high-speed 32-bit bus designed specifically for use with video cards. AGP runs at 66 MHz. The original specification called for one data transfer per clock cycle; subsequent versions transfer two, four, and eight times with each cycle and are referred to as AGP2X, AGP4X, and AGP8X, respectively.

The initial AGP specification and AGP2X provided 3.3 volts to the adapter card; later versions support lower-demand 1.5-volt cards. Later versions of the slot are backward compatible, meaning they will work with cards designed for older AGP specifications, running at the original speed. However, some motherboards may demand particular AGP speeds or may be optimized to an individual specification. Figure 4-2 shows an AGP slot.

FIGURE 4-2: *The AGP slot sits alongside a set of PCI and ISA slots in this Pentium III motherboard.*

High-end graphics workstations may employ an extension to the AGP specification called AGP Pro; this design is intended for cards that have a higher power demand, as much as 110 watts. AGP Pro adds another section of connectors to the front and back end of the slot; adapters designed for the AGP standard need to be carefully positioned in the middle of the overlong AGP Pro slot.

AGP operates independent of the PCI bus, and mostly independent of the microprocessor, thus offloading the heavy demands of a graphics card. As such, a graphics card can have a direct connection to RAM, allowing it to share the large resources there instead of the relatively small allocation of memory on the card; on the other hand, high-performance graphics cards are designed with memory close at hand for maximum speed.

Some of the specifics of the various versions of AGP are shown in Table 4-3.

TABLE 4-3: AGP Standards

Version	Bus Speed (MHz)	Bus Width (bits)	Data Cycles per Clock	Throughput (MBps)
AGP	66	32	1	266
AGP2X	66	32	2	533
AGP4X	66	32	4	1066
AGP8X	66	32	8	2133

Information presented in three dimensions can be particularly memory- and transfer bus-intensive. With today's games, artificial reality, and artificial intelligence applications, 3-D data is becoming more common. Traditionally, the main system CPU has used the computer's bus to move graphical information from your computer's memory to where it belongs on a display adapter. This means that the transfer was limited to a maximum data rate of 66 MHz or less in slower systems. Not only is this bus speed relatively slow by today's computer standards, it's also crowded. Graphical information going to and from your video adapter must share this highway with other data going to and from memory and other peripherals.

AGP technology opens a high-speed pathway between a PC's graphics controller and system memory so that the graphics controller can execute texture maps directly from system memory, rather than caching them in its limited local video memory. It also helps speed the flow of decoded video from the CPU to the graphics controller. AGP is separate from the main PCI bus, so other computer data isn't competing with graphics data for bandwidth. The PCI bus can transfer data at speeds up to 132 MBps. AGP, on the other hand, handles graphical data directly from system memory to the video display adapter at speeds up to 533 MBps (peak; 1 GBps with new support chips) — a significant improvement.

In some systems, AGP exists as integrated circuitry directly on the motherboard rather than as a plug-in card. This form of AGP, introduced with Intel's 810 chipset, has some of the same operating characteristics, although it uses a segment of system RAM for its purposes. The downside is that if you ever choose to upgrade the video circuitry on the board, you have to use a slower PCI card because there is no AGP slot.

The ISA bus: A PC classic

Prior to the arrival of PCI, the predominant design for internal connections to adapters was the *ISA (industry standard architecture)* bus, which was developed from the original PC bus. Its first incarnation used 8-bit computer words moving at a poky 4.77 MHz; it was subsequently improved to 16 bits and 8.33 MHz with the introduction of the PC-AT in 1984. The arrival of the new machine came just as the clone industry exploded, and the bus was widely imitated. Clone makers dubbed the bus the ISA.

ISA slots built on the original PC bus slots, adding a second block of connectors for the additional 8 bits of information.

Modern machines are no longer built around the limited ISA bus. However, the bus is still present in one way or another: either as a "legacy" bus that branches off the PCI bus to allow users to continue using older adapter cards designed for the ISA, or as a hidden bus that communicates with basic components of the PC that have remained essentially unchanged throughout the history of the device, such as the keyboard and mouse.

In Figure 4-3 you can see the larger ISA slots on a mixed PCI/ISA motherboard.

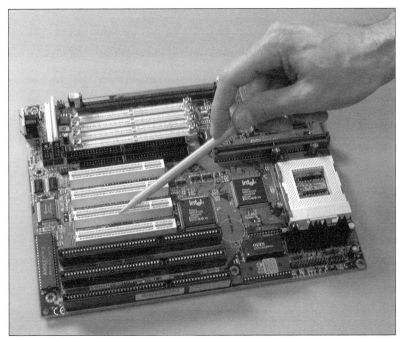

FIGURE 4-3: *The black ISA slots, below the pencil toward the front of the motherboard, are available for compatibility with older adapter cards and adapter cards that don't need the high speed of the white PCI bus slots.*

NOTE

Some manufacturers have begun offering "legacy-free" designs, which is marketing shorthand for PCs that make no attempt to be backward compatible with outdated older technologies. A legacy-free machine may dispense with serial, parallel, and PS/2 ports in favor of advanced USB and FireWire ports. And motherboards may offer only PCI and AGP slots, thus eliminating holdover ISA slots. If you are buying a new machine, a legacy-free design may make sense because modern ports — especially USB — have been linked to nearly every type of peripheral, including keyboards, mice, monitors, printers, and scanners. And nearly every type of adapter card is now available in a PCI version.

PC cards

The Personal Computer Memory Card International Association standard defines a removable credit-card-size device that can be used in a wide range of portable computers and desktops. When it was introduced, users were forced to memorize its tongue-twisting acronym of a name: PCMCIA. Luckily, more sensible heads prevailed and the working title for cards that use the PCMCIA standard was dubbed *PC Card* in 1995.

The PC Card bus branches off a PCI bus. Plug-in cards can be used for memory, tiny hard drives, modems, network adapters, sound cards, SCSI adapters, 1394 FireWire I/O cards, and more. Future versions of PC Card specifications may permit video adapter and even processor upgrades. Some of the details of PC Cards are shown in Table 4-4.

TABLE 4-4: PC Card Standards

Bus	Bus Speed (MHz)	Bus Width (bits)	Data Cycles per Clock	Throughput (MBps)
PC Card	10	16	1	20
CardBus	33	32	1	133

PC Cards are not in common use on desktop PCs, but are ubiquitous on laptops where they are used for modems, network interfaces, and storage. On laptops, PC Cards face challenges from the burgeoning USB interface.

The original PC Card standard was limited by its 16-bit data interface standard. A newer standard, called *CardBus*, supports 32-bit interfaces and the ability to take advantage of internal bus speeds that can be four to six times faster than 16-bit PC Cards. In 2001, the association adopted the CardBay standard, which allows the same connector to bring USB 2.0 functionality to the PC Card format.

CardBus slots can accept 16-bit PC Card devices, but only 32-bit cards can take advantage of the wider format and faster data transfer supported by CardBus. In addition, CardBus devices operate at 3.3 volts (the PC Card uses 5 volts), which can result in lower power consumption and reduced heat.

Both PC Card and CardBus devices use a 68-pin interface that connects the card to the motherboard or to the system's expansion

Ch 4

bus. However, a special tab on CardBus devices prevents you from plugging a CardBus card into a 16-bit PC Card interface.

PC Card slots are available in four types, measured by the thickness of the card they accept. The same standard for slot size is supported by the CardBus, as well. (Be sure to check the capability of your PC Card reader before making a purchase. A properly designed Type III socket will work with Types I and II, as well; a Type II socket also should accept Type I cards.)

- **Type I.** A 3.3 mm-thick slot, commonly used for RAM, flash memory, electronically erasable programmable read-only memory, and other such devices. Type I slots are most often used in personal digital assistants and handheld devices.
- **Type II.** A 5 mm-thick slot, fully I/O capable, used for memory enhancements or for I/O devices, such as modems and network connections.
- **Type III.** A 10.5 mm-thick slot, designed primarily for removable hard drive devices.
- **Type IV.** Now available from some manufacturers, Type IV slots can run two PC Card peripherals simultaneously and can be Plug-and-Play certified.

One of the advanced features of a PC Card and CardBus interface is *hot swap*. In theory, hot swap enables you to insert and remove cards while PC power is on without losing data or damaging the card or system. Not all applications or versions of operating systems, though, can recognize when you have inserted or removed cards, so save your data before trying this feature for the first time.

If you need to read a PC Card directly in a desktop, a number of adapters is available. Perhaps the easiest is a USB to PC Card reader; you'll also find devices that link a parallel port to a PC Card reader. If you can find one in the back shelves of a computer store or deep in the database of an online sellers, a more permanent solution involves installation of a PC Card reader that attaches to the internal bus of your system.

Memory bus

The microprocessor communicates with RAM using the memory bus. In modern machines, this bus branches off the north bridge or memory controller hub. The speed of the bus is related to the design of the chipset and the type of memory in use.

When memory runs at the same speed as the processor bus (as is the case with many modern machines), there is no need for cache memory on the motherboard, which allows the CPU manufacturer to move L2 cache onto the processor cartridge (in the case of Pentium II and early Pentium III CPUs) or onto the processor die itself.

Table 4-5 shows some of the important specifications of commonly used memory designs.

TABLE 4-5: Memory Bus Designs

Memory Design	Bus Speed (MHz)	Bus Width (bits)	Data Cycles per Clock	Throughput (MBps)
FPM DRAM	22	64	1	177
EDO DRAM	33	64	1	266
PC66 SDRAM	66	64	1	533
PC100 SDRAM	100	64	1	800
PC133 SDRAM	133	64	1	1066
PC600 RDRAM	300	16	2	1200
PC700 RDRAM	350	16	2	1400
PC800 RDRAM	400	16	2	1600
PC800 RDRAM Dual Channel	400	32	2	3200
PC1600 DDR SDRAM	100	64	2	1600
PC2100 DDR SDRAM	133	64	2	2133

CROSS-REFERENCE

For more details on RAM, see Chapter 8.

I/O subsystems: Serial, parallel, USB, FireWire, eSATA, and USB

Thousands of valuable devices exist on the side streets off the computer's superhighway: the I/O subsystems used by modems, printers, scanners, and external storage units. Table 4-6 includes some of the specifications for these subsystems. Additionally, I discuss the most commonly used subsystems elsewhere in this book, as follows:

- **Serial.** Chapter 15
- **Parallel.** Chapter 17
- **USB.** Chapter 15
- **FireWire.** Chapter 15
- **eSATA.** Chapter 15
- **SCSI.** Chapter 10

TABLE 4-6: I/O Subsystems

I/O Subsystem	Bus Speed (MHz)	Bus Width (bits)	Data Cycles per Clock	Throughput (MBps)
RS-232 Serial	0.1152	1	1/10	0.01152
IEEE-1284 Parallel	8.33	8	1/6	1.38
IEEE-1284 EPP/ECP Parallel	8.33	8	1/3	2.77
USB 1.1	12	1	1	1.5
USB 2.0	480	1	1	60
IEEE-1394 FireWire	100, 200, 400, 800, 1600	1	1	12.4, 25, 50, 100, 200
SCSI	5	8	1	5
SCSI Wide	5	16	1	10
SCSI Fast	10	8	1	10
SCSI Fast/Wide	10	16	1	20
SCSI Ultra	20	8	1	20
SCSI Ultra/Wide	20	16	1	40
SCSI Ultra 2	40	8	1	40
SCSI Ultra 2/Wide	40	16	1	80
SCSI Ultra 3 (SCSI Ultra 160)	40	16	2	160
SCSI Ultra 4 (SCSI Ultra 320)	80	16	2	320

IRQs: Irksome Essentials

The various pieces of hardware attached to a CPU through a system bus need the attention of the microprocessor to perform services or to supervise the movement of information from place to place. Luckily, not all of the devices need the CPU's attention all of the time. Even if they did, the computer would not be able to deal with more than one thing at a time.

Some devices, such as keyboards, are in heavy use, while other pieces of hardware, such as sound cards or floppy disk drives, may be operated only for a few seconds at a time over the course of a day's work. The computer solution is *interrupts*, which do exactly what their name suggests: They are electronic flag-wavers that grab the CPU's attention when necessary.

Interrupts are signals that run along the wires of the bus. They are carried out in the order of their importance to the system, determined by a pecking order set by interrupt numbers. In computer terminology, these are called IRQs (*interrupt requests*).

All of this information is very important to users of older machines, including dinosaurs and senior citizens; it is mostly of academic interest to owners of modern machines because of the development of Plug-and-Play hardware and accompanying extensions that are part of current versions of the Windows operating system. The hardware and Windows are generally able to rearrange IRQs and DMAs (about which you learn more in a moment) to accommodate most adapter combinations.

Today it is extremely rare for a user to have to manually set IRQs; if you must, you can go to the Control Panel, choose the Hardware tab, and then select the Properties panel. Consult the manufacturer of any adapter card for assistance if Windows reports a conflict in resources that it cannot fix on its own.

The original PCs had a single Intel 8259A PIC (programmable interrupt controller) that was capable of arbitrating among eight requests for attention. The requests were numbered IRQ 0 through 7. The essential system timer was assigned IRQ 0 with the highest priority, and the keyboard used IRQ 1.

As PCs became more capable and complex, it became obvious that additional interrupts were needed to service new devices, including network adapters, sound cards, and more. The PC-AT and all modern machines, therefore, have a second interrupt controller with eight more lines, numbered IRQ 8 through 15. To maintain compatibility

Ch 4

with older hardware and operating systems, the eight new interrupts are cascaded to the first controller over the IRQ 2 line. This results in a total of 15 IRQs, rather than 16.

Because the eight additional IRQs enter into the system between IRQ 1 and 3, interrupts 8 through 15 have a higher priority than IRQs 3 through 7. On a modern machine, the system claims permanent ownership of IRQs 0, 1, 8, and 13. The remaining 11 are open to assignment.

It is important to understand that, on a standard PC, no two devices can simultaneously use the same IRQ without causing serious problems, including a system lockup. In theory, two devices can have the same assignment if they are never used together; this is a dangerous practice, though.

PCI, MCA, and EISA systems are capable of allowing multiple hardware devices to share a single IRQ. On a PCI bus, this sharing is achieved through IRQ or interrupt steering. Multiple devices can be assigned the same IRQ, but an interim process decides which of these devices gets to use the interrupt at any given time.

Most devices come preset to use a particular IRQ; their instruction manuals should inform you which other interrupts they can be set to and how to make the reassignment. Older devices use connector blocks or DIP switches to change interrupts; on some modern devices, you can change their settings with a software command.

In theory, IRQ 7 is assigned to the first parallel port (LPT 1), and IRQ 5 to the second possible parallel port (LPT 2). But for most users and in most situations, the parallel port does not use any interrupts. Therefore, it is common for other devices to lay claim to these two interrupts.

Table 4-7 contains some typical assignments for IRQs on a modern machine.

TABLE 4-7: Typical IRQ Availability on a Modern Machine

Interrupt	Function	Physical Type
IRQ0	System timer	Motherboard
IRQ1	Keyboard controller	Motherboard
IRQ2	Cascade from second 8259A PIC (Programmable Interrupt Controller)	Motherboard
IRQ3	Serial ports 2 and 4 (COM2 or COM4)	8/16-bit slot or motherboard resource
IRQ4	Serial ports 1 and 3 (COM1 and COM3)	8/16-bit slot or motherboard resource
IRQ5	Sound card or LPT2 (LPT2 is parallel port 2)	8/16-bit slot
IRQ6	Floppy disk controller	8/16-bit slot or motherboard resource
IRQ7	Parallel port LPT1	8/16-bit slot or motherboard resource
IRQ8	CMOS setup memory and real-time clock	Motherboard
IRQ9	Available as IRQ9 or redirected to IRQ2; often used for network interface or MPEG video	8/16-bit slot or motherboard resource
IRQ10	Available for use; typically used for USB	16-bit slot or motherboard resource
IRQ11	Available for use	16-bit slot or motherboard resource
IRQ12	Available for use; often used for mouse port	16-bit slot or motherboard resource
IRQ13	Math coprocessor	Motherboard resource
IRQ14	Hard disk controller	16-bit slot or motherboard resource Used for primary IDE controller
IRQ15	Disk controller; used for secondary IDE controller	16-bit slot or motherboard resource

For the record, Table 4-8 contains the typical assignments for IRQs on a dinosaur.

TABLE 4-8: Typical IRQ Assignments on a Dinosaur PC-XT Machine

Interrupt	Function	Physical Type
IRQ0	System timer	Motherboard resource
IRQ1	Keyboard controller	Motherboard resource
IRQ2	Available for use	8-bit slot
IRQ3	Serial ports COM2/COM4	8-bit slot
IRQ4	Serial ports COM1/COM3	8-bit slot
IRQ5	Hard disk controller	8-bit slot
IRQ6	Floppy disk controller	8-bit slot
IRQ7	Parallel port LPT1	8-bit slot

Two devices are not supposed to share the same IRQ; however, in modern machines, this is possible. You will find, however, that although your computer and operating system may support shared IRQs, individual hardware products may not. Read your documentation carefully or call the product vendor to determine whether this sharing is possible. If you try to expand a modern machine with multimedia capabilities, you'll quickly discover that you can soon end up with only a few options to avoid conflicts.

First of all, realize that some IRQs are permanently assigned; the interrupts for system timer, keyboard, COM ports, and disk controllers are immutable.

Modern machines with current BIOS, in concert with modern operating systems beginning with Windows 95B (OSR 2) with Plug-and-Play facilities, can use a facility called *interrupt steering*, also known as *IRQ steering*. Under this scheme, Windows takes over from the BIOS the task of assigning IRQs, seeking to avoid conflicts. And, depending on the nature of the devices, the operating system will allow two or more to share a single interrupt.

If you have any ISA slots and devices, though, these pieces of hardware must be manually assigned to a non-shareable interrupt among the original eight IRQs of the dinosaur PC.

NOTE

Under Windows 95B, Windows 98, and later versions of the Windows operating system including Windows XP and Vista, interrupt steering can be turned on or off from the Device Manager. Double-click the System Devices branch, and double-click PCI Bus. Choose the IRQ Steering tab to enable or disable the feature. In most instances, you'll want to keep the facility enabled; this is a feature ordinarily related to the facilities of the BIOS.

After the fact, you can use a diagnostic program to check IRQ settings, although the reports are not 100 percent accurate because not all devices may be active when you run the test.

One way to track the assignment of IRQs in your system is to consult the Device Manager that is part of the Systems tab of Control Panel in Windows. Under the View menu, check to see the display of Resources by Connection and examine the Interrupts report. Another path to a similar report is through use of the System Information report; to reach it, click Start ⇨ All Programs ⇨ Accessories/System Tools/System Information. View the hardware report and select IRQs. An example of this report is shown in Figure 4-4.

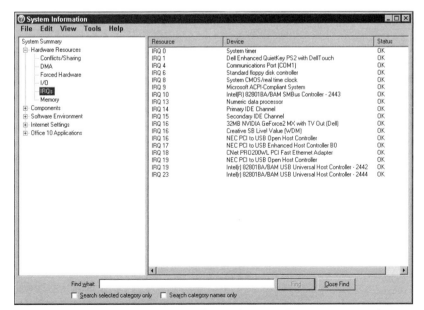

FIGURE 4-4: *The IRQ assignments of a modern machine, as seen in the System Information screen of Windows.*

CROSS-REFERENCE

Appendix D on the CD lists IRQ assignments. Chapter 3 discusses a BIOS that allows users to reclaim IRQs.

DMA: Mind Transfers Made Easy

The other half of the communication process for many hardware devices, including some disk controllers, sound cards, and other I/O cards, is *direct memory access (DMA)*. DMA is a facility that allows transfer of data directly, without intervention by the microprocessor. This allows for greater speed in data transfer and avoids bogging down the CPU in unnecessary tasks.

The dinosaur PC had a single Intel 8237A, four-channel DMA controller capable of 8-bit data transfers. DMA line 0 was reserved by the system for dynamic RAM refresh, DMA 2 was assigned to floppy disk transfers, and DMA 3 was to be used for hard disk transfers.

With the arrival of the PC-AT and other modern machines capable of 16-bit operations, a second DMA controller was added. The output of the first controller is routed to the first input of the second chip.

Therefore, a modern machine has seven DMA lines, numbered 0 through 3 and 5 through 7. The lower lines still are used only for transfers between 8-bit devices and 8- or 16-bit memory; DMA lines 5 through 7 are available for full 16-bit transfers in either direction.

Because of the improved speed of CPUs beginning with the 80286, DMA is no longer needed for RAM refresh operations, and DMA 0 is therefore available for reassignment on modern machines. Similarly, DMA 3 is not used for hard disk transfers on 16-bit machines.

Depending on the type of adapter, some DMA channels can be shared. For example, a network adapter and an I/O device can coexist although the I/O unit wouldn't be available when the network was in use.

Table 4-9 contains some typical assignments for DMA channels on a modern system.

TABLE 4-9: Typical DMA Channel Assignments

DMA Channel	Assignment
0	(16-bit slot) Available.
1	(8/16-bit slot) Available. Typically used by sound card; also used for SCSI host adapter, network interface.
2	(8/16-bit slot or motherboard resource). Floppy controller; also used for tape drive.
3	(8/16-bit slot or motherboard resource) Available. Typically used for LPT1, SCSI host adapter, network interface.
4	Cascade to DMA channels 0–3.
5	(16-bit slot) Available.
6	(16-bit slot) Available.
7	(16-bit slot) Available.

CROSS-REFERENCE

Appendix D on the CD deals with DMA in more detail.

SUMMARY

The first four chapters of this book have explored the basic foundations of the computer. With that initial exploration complete, I move on to discuss the hardware of the PC in the next chapter.

Notes

Chapter 5

Tools Needed:

Basic Projects:

- Phillips or flat-blade screwdriver
- Antistatic strip, wrist strap, or grounding pad

Advanced Projects:

- Tweezers
- Nut drivers
- Needle-nose pliers
- Chip insertion and extraction tools

Bonus Chapter 5:

- A Tale of Five Motherboards
- Dinosaur Time: Clock Card
- Matching Cables and Connectors

Basic Hardware Skills

At this point in the book, you're approaching the moment when you'll lay hands on a computer to take it apart. Before you do, though, let's take an advanced course in anatomy. Let's explore the basic components of the computer in more detail, including the case, the motherboard, cooling fans, expansion cards, memory, and the power supply.

Tools of the Trade

Before you do any repair work on your PC — in fact, before you even think about opening up the innards of your computer — start by assembling the appropriate computer toolkit. I'm not talking about hundreds of dollars here: Most of the tools are part of the basic set you may already have around the house or office; a few special-purpose items may set you back less than $25 from a computer dealer, mail-order house, or well-equipped hardware store.

As you learn in Chapter 6, the most modern of machines on the market today allow most upgrades or repairs to be accomplished without the need of any tools. If you're lucky enough to have a machine like the one I deconstruct in that chapter, you'll be able to open the case and install RAM, adapter cards, and cables with just your fingers. Even some hard drives or CD or DVD drives can just slip into place within plastic or metal latches and bays; a few projects will require the use of a small X-shaped Phillips-head screwdriver and a small flat-head screwdriver.

If you're working on a modern machine that has not quite reached this level of tool-free simplicity, your kit should include a set of Phillips-head screwdrivers (small, medium, and large sized) and an antistatic mat or strap. A Phillips-head screwdriver is properly shaped for the X-shaped slot on the top of screws used to close many cases and to hold internal parts and adapter cards in place. (Most screws used on modern computers also have a hexagonal head; if the Phillips slot becomes stripped — perhaps because of the use of the wrong-sized screwdriver — it can usually be removed with the aid of a nut driver of the proper size.

On any machine — tool-free or older models — you still need to have a way to ground yourself or the machine before you touch the electrically sensitive chips under the covers of the PC. The official way to do this is with an *antistatic grounding strap*, which attaches to your wrist or ankle and connects to an electrical ground. You can purchase a grounding strap for less than $10 from a computer store. Another useful and even less expensive device is a static touchpad (see Figure 5-1) or touch strip that you can anchor on the desktop and connect to a ground.

You can also make your own antistatic device. Run a length of solid copper hookup wire (actually, almost any electrical wire will do) from the center screw of a grounded electrical outlet plate — be careful not to insert the wire into the slots of the outlet itself — and tape the other end to your desktop. Touch the bare end of the wire to discharge any static in your body before touching any electronic parts. In any case, it is also useful to check all the outlets in your office or home to ensure that they are properly grounded. Simple plug-in ground fault detectors are available at Radio Shack or other suppliers for as little as $10. They indicate open grounds, open neutral, hot/ground reverse, hot/neutral reverse, and check the integrity of a ground fault circuit interrupter if present. If they indicate a problem, contact a professional electrician to correct your wiring. (Improper grounds or other wiring problems could lead to a power failure or fire.)

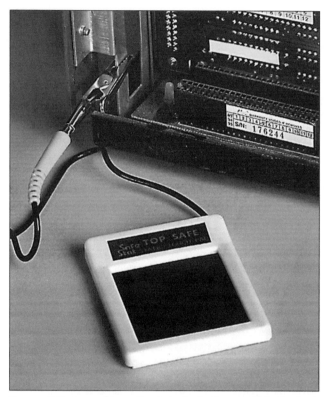

FIGURE 5-1: *A good practice is to install an antistatic device, such as this touchpad, on your desktop. You can also purchase a keyboard mat or touch strip. Get in the habit of grounding yourself before you touch any part of your computer.*

For more advanced work, your computer toolkit should include a set of good quality needle-nose pliers of various sizes, a small-blade straight-edge screwdriver, a collection of nut drivers, one or more tweezers, and a set of chip insertion and extraction tools.

If you are working on some very old equipment, or specialized devices, you may need a set of Torx drivers, which work with special screws that were used by some manufacturers that hoped you wouldn't try to open their magic boxes by yourself. Torx screws, thankfully, have all but disappeared from consumer-grade equipment.

In my office, I also have an IC (integrated circuit) inserter and extractor and several handy parts holders. I'm especially fond of a little spring-loaded tweezers that I can attach to a screw and guide deep into the innards of a computer to mate with its intended hole.

To clean the connectors of adapter cards, keep a small bottle of rubbing alcohol and a set of good-quality cotton swabs. Some people clean connectors with a fresh pencil eraser, although I fear the possibility that this method can result in the accidental discharge of bits of rubber into the slots, which can cause problems with electrical contact.

A low-tech nicety is a small, compartmentalized plastic or wooden box, such as a sewing kit. Mark the compartments with letters or numbers, and keep a notepad and pen in the box. As you remove screws and parts, put them into individual sections and note where they go. Use stickers or labels with corresponding numbers or letters on the computer components.

Want to go even lower-tech? Use an egg carton; it comes all set up with 12 small compartments and you can write notes directly on the cardboard or foam as you store screws and parts.

Advanced Tools

A useful tool for advanced troubleshooters is a simple multimeter that can check DC and AC voltage and DC current; older designs use a meter with a needle, while more modern (and sturdier) devices have digital readouts. Use the meter to check the voltage coming out of a wall socket, proper output from a power supply, and voltage levels on connectors. Some devices also enable you to check the continuity of cables, which can tell you if a wire is broken or shorted. Simple meters sell for as little as $15 to $20 at places like Radio Shack; more sophisticated digital devices rise to about $100. Be sure to study and understand the instruction manual before you use a multimeter.

If you must use a meter on a system that is receiving power, you will need to exercise extreme caution. Be very careful not to short across connectors or traces on the motherboard. You should also take care not scratch the surface of the motherboard, which can result in a break in one of the tiny "traces" that serve as wiring between components. And guard against the possibility of any pieces of conductive metal falling into the inside of the machine; paperclips, screws, and snippets of wire can short out the system.

You can also purchase more sophisticated testers for serial and network cables. An RS232 breakout box for use with older machines still dependent on outmoded serial cables and connectors includes a set of jumper wires to reconfigure cables, DIP switches to cross over connections, and LEDs to monitor signals on a live cable, and sells for about $30. A similar breakout box is available for the eight lines of an RJ45 connector used in Ethernet cable.

A multipurpose cable tester, which sells for about $125, has connectors and circuitry to test a range of wiring devices, including serial, parallel, network, USB, and FireWire cables.

It probably does not make sense to buy a cable tester unless you plan to make a career out of repairing computers; it would be cheaper to have a supply of replacement cables of various types and sizes and use them to test questionable devices and replace them when needed. (This is one very good reason to establish a collection of computer parts that are left over from projects or scavenged from retired systems.)

If you are going to make your own cables, you should invest in a fine-point soldering iron, a set of wire strippers, some needle-nose pliers, and cable crimpers. You also need raw cable and a set of connectors for the cables you want to make. All are available from the same sources already mentioned. Having stated that, I haven't built a cable from scratch in years. Cables are more standardized than they used to be, and most cables are available at reasonable prices from mail-order houses or computer retailers.

CROSS-REFERENCE

Appendix F on the CD presents an encyclopedia of cables and connectors for the PC.

Testing the System Unit Case and Cover

In general, if the case looks all right, it works all right. Not always, though: It is possible for the case itself to cause system troubles.

A poorly designed case with misshapen pieces of metal in the wrong places can cause intermittent electrical shorts. I have come across cases where the bottom (or the side on a tower unit) sat perilously close to soldered component leads on the underside of the motherboard. Sometimes the motherboard actually touched the case. If such a motherboard boots at all, sooner or later the vibration of the disk drives and fans will bring the electrically active motherboard in contact with the metal case. At best, this will cause intermittent shorts or hang-ups. At worst, something may fry.

In another instance, the high-tech and expensive case on a modern machine included a row of small copper fingers that were part of the protection against RF (radio frequency) leakage. Unfortunately, a few of the fingers broke loose in the process of removing and reinstalling the cover, with the result that a few of these pieces of metal were rattling around on the motherboard, just waiting to short out the machine. If your case uses this design, proceed with caution.

The most modern of PC cases now make use of a number of conveniences that allow easier access, surer RF protection, and other niceties. I'm fond of designs where the PC opens up like a clamshell without the need to touch a screwdriver. Some designs for cases (including the ultra-modern one profiled in Chapter 6) use retaining arms or latches to hold adapters as well as blank metal covers for unused adapter slots; take care to make sure they are properly installed at top and bottom to avoid problems with electrical contact on working cards or ventilation air or RF leaks caused by gaps at unused slots.

RF radiation usually does not present any problems for the user, although it may interfere with other electronic devices in your home or office. You can usually detect RF leakage by bringing a television set or FM radio near the PC. If you see a pattern that changes as the PC performs various assignments, or if the reception on the FM radio is affected by a whine or pulsing beat that changes as the PC responds to keyboard commands, you have an RF radiation problem.

Should you fix it? RF radiation is in most cases just an annoyance. In the most severe instances, though — when it interferes with television reception in the home, changes the channel on the office stereo system, or opens and closes your neighbor's garage door — you're going to want to seal up all the openings in the PC case properly. (Be sure not to block air intakes and vents, of course.) Figure 5-2 shows a properly shielded new computer case awaiting installation of internal parts.

FIGURE 5-2: *An untouched older modern mid-tower case. Note the RF shielding that occupies the future homes of hard, floppy, and CD-ROM drives. The metal plates can be removed, and plastic faceplates are supplied to finish off the appearance of the front. In Chapter 6 you can learn about a current modern machine that requires a bare minimum of tools and extra parts.*

The Mother of All Boards

The motherboard holds together all of the essential internal parts of the computer and provides connections to external devices and the power supply. (Some manufacturers and technical types refer to the motherboard as the system board or the mainboard.)

In a desktop machine, the motherboard lies beneath the add-in cards and internal peripherals of the PC. In most systems, several add-in cards stand upright in slots on the motherboard.

Tower systems place the motherboard on its end along one side of the box with add-in cards mounted horizontally. The beauty of a tower is that it can be placed on the floor without requiring real estate on your desk; combined with a thin LCD monitor, you'll regain all sort of space . . . for piles of paper.

An older type of design, used in some low-profile desktop machines, allows placement of adapter cards in a horizontal position. This type of system uses a riser card that stands up in a slot on the motherboard like a Christmas tree, with slots branching off one or both sides for add-ins. The riser card makes for a compact box but a sometimes difficult repair and upgrade assignment.

It's worth your time to examine the design of a PC case to determine how difficult it will be to install peripherals and to access the motherboard itself for the memory and CPU sockets or slots. Figure 5-3 shows an example of a case that requires some additional disassembly before you can work on it.

FIGURE 5-3: *On older cases, you may find it necessary to remove drive cages to make it easier to remove or install a motherboard. Within some compact cases, you may also have to remove the power supply that overhangs the motherboard.*

The components of the motherboard

All PC motherboards include the following in one form or another:

- **CPU (central processing unit, or microprocessor).** This is the brains of the outfit.
- **System ROM BIOS (Read-Only Memory Basic Input/Output System).** The set of instructions that tells the CPU how to control the simplest, basic functions of the hardware.
- **Chipset.** A group of circuits on the motherboard that allow the CPU to control the hardware; CPUs and chipsets must be properly matched and fully supported by the other components of the motherboard.

- **RAM (random access memory).** The active thinking space for the computer. Modern machines have slots that accept memory modules, usually called DIMMs. A small number of older modern machines used a similar design called RIMMs. Older modern machines and some senior citizens may require lower-capacity SIMMs. And dinosaurs may have sockets on the motherboard to accept individual memory chips, or require use of plug-in adapter cards populated with individual chips.
- **Expansion bus.** The interconnecting superhighway that enables you to add devices to the system. Modern machines generally use a 32-bit PCI bus; while the newest of the modern machines have shifted to the faster, more flexible PCI Express which acts like a bus although it has a different structure. With each transition of bus designs, motherboards offered combinations including PCI Express and PCI, and PCI with a few holdover 16-bit ISA bus slots for use with "legacy" devices. The final generation of PCI bus motherboards generally added an AGP (Accelerated Graphics Port) slot that was a separate bus used to connect a special video card directly to the memory bus. PCI Express has removed the need for the AGP system.

NOTE

The newer PCI Express bus uses some of the same concepts as the older PCI bus, but has some key differences including the fact that it transmits data as serial packets rather than in parallel words. And adapters designed for PCI slots cannot physically fit into or use the electrical pathways of PCI Express. In this book, to help avoid confusion, we refer to the two standards by their full acronyms: PCI and PCI Express. When we discuss particular PCI Express slots, our style identifies them by the number of data lanes they offer, as in PCI Express x16.

- **IRQ (interrupt request) lines.** A set of electrical lines used by the hardware in the bus to seek the attention of the CPU.
- **DMA (direct memory access) channels.** A set of channels that can transfer information between devices without the help of the CPU.
- **Input ports.** Connections between the motherboard and input devices, such as a keyboard, a mouse, a scanner, a camera, and other devices. On dinosaurs through older modern machines, these included serial, parallel, and PS/2 ports; most current

modern machines have begun to shed these outmoded, inflexible, and slow ports in favor of multipurpose USB ports and, to a lesser extent, FireWire ports.

- **Output ports.** Connections between the motherboard and output devices, such as a printer, an external storage device such as a hard drive, a modem, and other devices. As with input devices, most current machines have adopted the USB port as the principal means of output to most devices.
- **Network adapter.** A network interface card, or equivalent circuitry built into the motherboard, permits a PC to communicate at high speed over a network or to connect to an individual or shared broadband modem for Internet use.
- **Display adapter.** Circuitry that converts computer information into letters or pictures presented on a monitor. The display adapter can be on an expansion card that plugs into the bus or be part of the motherboard itself.
- **Connection to storage devices.** On the newest of modern machines, Serial ATA (SATA) controllers connect individual hard drives to a controller on the motherboard; several IDE (also known as Parallel ATA) connectors are also offered for use with other internal devices such as CD or DVD readers or writers. On modern machines of an older vintage, the motherboard generally offered a pair of IDE controllers — each capable of working with two devices — for attachment to hard drives and CD or DVD devices. Some machines, especially those devoted to specialized graphics processing or used as servers, offered a faster and more capacious SCSI controller. There was also a separate controller devoted to the needs of one or two floppy disk drives; many current modern machines have dispensed with the use of floppy drives. On older machines, and some modern machines with special needs, the storage controller was resident on an adapter that plugged into the expansion bus instead of existing as a chipset on the motherboard.
- **Setup system.** A means to customize the way the PC operates through switches, jumpers, or software settings held in battery-backed memory.
- **Clock.** The heartbeat of the system, the clock chip or clock crystal sets the pulse with which information moves along the bus.
- **Real-time clock/CMOS battery.** The calendar for the system, keeping track of the date and time as well as system

configuration settings used by the PC at bootup. The small rechargeable or lithium battery keeps the information unaltered even with the power off.

Dinosaur PCs may have the following:

- **A VESA local (VL) bus.** An extension to the memory bus used primarily for graphics adapters that could run faster than adapters in the expansion bus.
- **A math coprocessor.** Or an empty socket for such a chip that, when asked, performs complex math faster than the CPU, freeing the CPU to go on to other chores.
- **OverDrive socket.** On some senior citizens and early modern machines, a means of upgrading the CPU with later models.

CPU

The CPU, also referred to as the microprocessor, is the engine of the computer, the place where data is actually processed. I explore the lineage of CPU chips in Chapter 2; a review appears here in Tables 5-1, 5-2, and 5-3.

TABLE 5-1: Modern Machine CPUs

CPU Chip	Commonly Used with Systems of This Type
Intel Core 2 Duo, Intel Quad Core	PCI Express in combination with PCI slots Future machines will likely offer only PCI Express
Intel Pentium D	PCI Express in combination with PCI, or PCI with AGP
Intel Celeron D	PCI Express in combination with PCI, PCI with AGP, or PCI
Intel Pentium 4	ISA/PCI combination with AGP, PCI with AGP, or PCI Express with PCI
AMD Athlon 64	PCI Express combination with PCI, PCI with AGP
AMD Sempron/Duron	PCI with AGP
AMD Athlon XP	PCI with AGP
AMD Athlon	ISA/PCI combination with AGP, and PCI with AGP

TABLE 5-2: Senior-Citizen CPUs

CPU Chip	Commonly Used with Systems of This Type
Intel Pentium III	ISA, PCI, ISA/PCI combination with AGP, and PCI with AGP
Intel Pentium III Xeon	ISA/PCI combination with AGP
Intel Celeron	ISA, PCI with AGP, ISA/PCI combination with AGP
Intel Pentium II	ISA, PCI, ISA/PCI combination, and PCI with AGP
Intel Pentium II Xeon	ISA, PCI, ISA/PCI combination, and PCI with AGP
AMD K6/2, AMD K6/3	ISA/PCI combination with AGP
Intel Pentium with MMX	ISA, PCI, ISA/PCI combination
Intel Pentium Pro	ISA, PCI, ISA/PCI combination
Intel Pentium	ISA, EISA, VL, PCI
Cyrix 6x86, AMD K5	ISA, PCI
Intel 486DX	ISA, EISA, PS/2, VL, PCI
Cyrix 486SLC	ISA, VL, PCICyrix 486DLC, AMD Am486DX4-100
Intel 486DX2, Intel 486DX4	ISA, VL, PCI

TABLE 5-3: Dinosaur CPUs

CPU Chip	Used with Systems of This Type
Intel 486SX	ISA, EISA, PS/2, VL, PCI
Intel 386SL, IBM 386SLC	Portables using proprietary buses
Intel 386, 386SX	ISA machines, EISA, PS/2s
Intel 286	PC-AT bus
NEC V20, NEC V30	PC bus
Intel 8086	PC bus
Intel 8088	PC bus

Throughout the history of the PC, the CPU has almost always been located in a socket on the motherboard or on a carrier that plugged into a special slot on the board. A few senior-citizen designs moved the microprocessor to a system board card that attached to a backplane bus; this short-lived design was intended to enable easy upgrades of the processor. And a tiny fraction of dinosaurs had the CPU soldered into place as part of the motherboard itself; this design was not widely adopted for a good reason: It limited PC makers as well as users when it came to replacement or upgrade of the processor.

With the arrival of the Intel 386, motherboards accepted CPUs mounted in zero insertion force (ZIF) sockets or additional OverDrive sockets intended for use with upgrade chips.

With the introduction of the Pentium II, Pentium II Xeon, and Pentium III, the processors were housed inside a sealed rectangular single edge contact cartridge (SECC) containing the CPU, secondary cache, and support chips; the cartridge plugged into a slot connector (see Figures 5-4 and 5-5). Intel Celerons, some late-model Pentium IIIs, and the Pentium 4 returned to surface-mount sockets on the motherboard, in two versions: a 423-pin OLGA (Organic Land Grid Array) PGA (Pin Grid Array) package and a 478-pin micro flip-chip PGA package.

Today's most modern processors, including the Intel Core 2 Duo and Intel Core M, were initially introduced in forms that plug into a surface-mounted receptacle called Socket M (or in technical documents as FCPGA6); this mates with 478 pins on the processor. In mid-2007, Intel is expected to introduce new processor designs intended for use with a slightly modified receptacle, expected to be called Socket P.

CROSS-REFERENCE

In Chapter 6, in Figure 6-7, you can see a photo of an Intel Core 2 Duo processor under its massive fan and wind tunnel.

Most modern machines based on Intel chips including Pentium 4, Pentium D, or Celeron D generally use an LGA775 socket to hold the processor flat on the motherboard; the Land Grid Array socket has 775 connectors.

Modern CPUs are usually covered with a heat sink and then topped by a fan that is held within a cover that serves as a wind tunnel to convey the heat generated by the processor directly to a vent in the case.

Ch 5

Motherboards built to use current AMD processors generally use a Socket AM2 for Athlon 64, Sempron, the dual-core Athlon 64 X2, and the Athlon 64 FX. The 940-pin AM2 replaced the similar but incompatible Socket 940 which was employed for Opterons and first-generation Athlon 64 FX processors. The 939-pin Socket-939 was used for certain models of Athlon 64, Athlon 64 FX, Athlon 64 X2, and early Opteron and Sempron models. And finally there is the 754-pin Socket 754 which was used for older Athlon 64 and Sempron chips.

The Socket 754 replaced AMD's Socket A (also known as Socket 462), which was widely used for AMD's first, highly successful, direct competitors to Intel's Pentium 4 series. The 453-pin Socket A was used for AMD Athlon, Athlon XP, and slower Duron and Sempron CPUs. And the earliest of Athlons used Slot A, which stood the processor on its side; Slot A was mechanically the same as Intel's Slot 1 (SC242) but electrically incompatible. Dinosaur-era AMD K6 processors plugged into a horizontal Socket 7 on the motherboard.

FIGURE 5-5: *A Pentium II module includes locking clips on each end; it inserts into Slot 1 like an add-in card. Some senior-citizen machines based on Pentium III and AMD modules used a similar cartridge.*

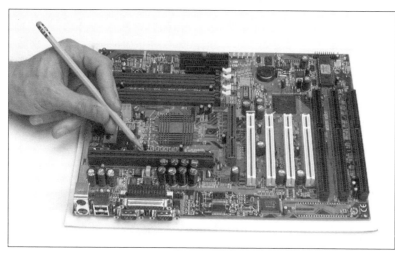

FIGURE 5-4: *A vertical Slot 1 to hold a Pentium II on an ATX motherboard. A supporting frame to hold a heat sink and fan attaches to pins that rise from the board.*

Chipsets

The CPU is supported by a group of special integrated circuits on the motherboard called a chipset. These chips (most manufactured by Intel; other makers include AMD and VIA) interface among the CPU, BIOS, and buses.

In most cases, the motherboard is optimized for a particular chipset, and the support chips are likely to be soldered into place and not changeable.

The state-of-the-art in chipsets for standard Intel-based systems in 2006 was the Intel 975 Express Chipset and its close cousin the Intel 965 Express. These chipsets offer advanced features for modern processors including the Intel Core 2 Duo and Intel Quad Core as well

Pentium 4 HyperThreading processors and Pentium 4 Extreme Edition and Pentium D processors. The chipsets are capable of working with a motherboard that supported as much as 8GB of Dual-Channel DD2 memory, Serial ATA and Parallel ATA storage devices, a system bus of 800 to 1066 MHz, and the PCI Express peripheral bus.

CROSS-REFERENCE

For more details on motherboard chipsets, see Chapter 2.

ROM BIOS

The ROM (read-only memory) BIOS (basic input/output system) provides the most basic level of hardware control while the computer is running. As I have already discussed, computers in the PC family are equipped with a read-only memory, basic input/output system, (ROM BIOS) chip. The BIOS chip contains the nitty-gritty directions your computer needs to connect to a floppy drive, video card, or another device.

On a modern machine, the system's CMOS setup screen and memory are associated with the ROM BIOS.

When your computer is first powered up, it gives itself a quick diagnostic exam; it's called a power-on self-test (POST) and then it executes a set of basic instructions to start, or boot, the motherboard and CPU.

Your computer needs to know what pieces of hardware are installed in it. Modern systems are able to reach out along all of the tendrils of the various buses, disk drive interfaces, and even through external ports to USB, FireWire, and certain other devices to find out every piece of hardware that is installed within or attached to the system; the BIOS then compares what it finds to the list of device drivers and other elements of the operating systems. The concept of "Plug and Play" has been extended to allow the system to reach out to the Internet to find device drivers and updates when necessary.

In certain situations you will have to manually instruct the system about some devices by using a setup or configuration program or by making selections on the CMOS setup screen.

Dinosaurs may need to be instructed about the specifications for every last piece of equipment, from keyboard, floppy disks, and hard drives to video cards, parallel ports, and serial ports. On an XT and some early AT machines, you have to set switches or notify the system in one or another mechanical way including placement of jumpers across pins to enable circuits, setting of tiny dip switches, or using special cables that identify devices by their use of certain pins or wires in the cable.

In the day of the dinosaur, BIOS chips were rarely replaced except if they had failed. Then came a period when computer users were regularly offered upgrades to the BIOS chips, which required that they be pried out of their sockets and replaced.

Today, BIOS chips rarely need to be replaced but they can easily be upgraded in place. Flash BIOS chips can accept a new set of instructions loaded into their memory from a disk or over the Internet; these BIOS chips retain the new instructions when power is turned off.

CROSS-REFERENCE

I explore BIOS replacement and other BIOS issues in detail in Chapter 3.

The ROM BIOS in the original IBM PC computer was a true dinosaur. IBM didn't bother to include directions to enable it to work with a hard disk, because nobody thought users would ever want or could ever afford hard disks. In fact, the original IBM PC came with a cassette port so that users could save data on an ordinary audio cassette recorder, a painfully slow process. If anyone ever actually made regular use of that port, that fact has been lost in the mists of history; however, to maintain compatibility, support for the cassette port continued to be part of the ROM BIOS for many years to follow.

IBM XTs and their clones were a bit smarter. These computers were instructed to search for additional ROMs located on cards plugged into the bus — for example, ROMs on a hard disk controller card or on a video card.

The BIOS chips in ATs and AT clones were even smarter. They knew about hard disks and actually had directions built in for the most popular hard disks then available. The AT computers (ISAs) kept the search-for-other-ROMs feature, too.

EISA computers were smarter yet. They included the full instructions of ISA computers and added to them accommodations for special EISA adapter cards, which transfer data at extraordinarily high speeds. But you, the installer, must tell the EISA computer which EISA cards are installed.

Ch 5

MCA computers, like EISA computers, demand that you run a Micro Channel setup program from the reference disk shipped with your computer whenever you install a new card.

Beginning with the arrival of PCI bus, users were able to access setup screens that are part of their ROM BIOS code. Today's most modern machines include detailed displays that allow configuration of a wide range of hardware components. To save system resources and a bit of power, many of the most modern machines come with unused SATA connectors and other features turned off; they need to be switched on from the setup screen.

Random access memory

Random access memory (RAM), also called system memory, provides a temporary storage area for the operating system, programs, and data.

Nearly all of today's modern machines work with high-speed, high-density memory mounted on modules that plug into special slots on the motherboard. The most common design is a DIMM (Dual In-Line Memory Module). Today's fastest memory for consumer-grade machines are DDR SDRAM (Double Data Rate Synchronous Dynamic Random Access Memory) modules, almost exclusively offered as part of a particular design of DIMM that assures a match between the electrical needs of the memory and the system.

For several years beginning about 2001, some modern machines used a similar but incompatible technology called a RIMM (Rambus In-line Memory Module) for high-speed Rambus memory. Rambus memory is not used in the most modern of machines.

Older senior-citizen machines used lower-capacity SIMMs (Single In-Line Memory Modules). And if you reach way back into the day of the dinosaur you'll find individual memory chips mounted on expansion cards or installed one-by-one directly onto the motherboard.

But back to the future: according to Microsoft, the absolute minimum memory requirement for a modern machine running Windows XP is 64MB of RAM; 128MB is recommended. But I wouldn't attempt to conduct meaningful work on a Windows XP system without at least 256MB of RAM and would prefer at least twice that amount. Earlier versions of Windows could work with smaller amounts of memory, although they would benefit from at least 64MB.

And the Windows Vista operating system starts at a much higher entry point. According to Microsoft, the minimum amount of system memory for Vista is 512MB. I always am leery of setting up a machine based around "minimums" and thus I recommend at least 1GB of RAM for the new O/S and suggest you consider doubling again to 2GB.

The IBM PC, the original dinosaur of dinosaurs, came equipped with as little as 16K or 64K of memory, installed in individual memory chips on the motherboard. Later improvements allowed these first machines to work with as much as 640K of memory — considered a massive amount, and priced as such when it was first offered — but you will still not be able to run Microsoft Windows or any modern software. It is not economically feasible to upgrade such an outdated system; it's cheaper to buy a new motherboard capable of accepting high-capacity memory chips or even better, a new system with modern supporting peripherals.

That original PC limit of 640K of system memory went on to become the basic building block for every subsequent operating system. Over the years various schemes for expanded or extended memory have permitted machines to work with memory that lies above that base or system memory. Such memory is essential for use with Windows and many DOS multimedia programs.

On all machines, the first 64K of memory is filled with housekeeping information (data the computer needs to operate itself). Consider the example of the interrupt vector table, an element of the operating system that tells the microprocessor what to do if a particular piece of hardware requires its attention. The table must be correct and in the proper place for the computer to do any work. (Because of this, most memory-test diagnostic programs can't read from or write to the first 64K of memory without crashing the computer.)

 CROSS-REFERENCE

I discuss memory in more detail in Chapter 8.

Direct memory access

Direct memory access (DMA) channels enable direct information transfer from peripherals to system memory without the involvement of the microprocessor; this change speeds up the transfer and removes some of the workload from the CPU.

Some dinosaur clones did without DMA, but virtually every member of the PC family has used them for modern machines. Older machines required users to become directly involved in assigning specific DMA channels to devices, but modern Plug-and-Play motherboards have mostly automated the process.

DMA is routinely used for most of the peripherals of the PC, with the exception of floppy disk drives; some backup programs, though, are capable of rerouting floppy disk transfer to the DMA channels to pick up speed in making massive archival backups.

On modern machines, DMA is part of the integrated motherboard chipset; on older machines DMA was managed by discrete chips soldered into place on the motherboard, making it nearly impossible to replace them if they fail. Such failures, though, are relatively rare in modern machines. If the DMA chips or the integrated chipset fail, you are probably due for a motherboard replacement.

Bus

The bus is a main information path inside the computer. On older machines, it connects the microprocessor, memory, ROM, and all expansion cards. On more modern machines, it is an interconnection between the microprocessor and a number of special-purpose high-speed buses that bring together all the pieces of the machine. PC buses have gone through an ever-improving progression from 8-bit PC to 16-bit AT to ISA, EISA, MCA, VL, PCI, and PCI Express designs. They are all, though, essentially the same: a series of thin wires, called traces, that run from connectors on the motherboard to control chips and the CPU itself. From early designs up to and including the PCI bus, high-performance buses became wider (capable of handling more parallel pathways) and faster. With the advent of the PCI Express, personal computers took a step back from a parallel superhighway in favor of a high-speed dedicated two-lane raceway.

CROSS-REFERENCE

I discuss the design essentials of computer buses in Chapter 4.

On a typical modern machine, you'll find two important buses. The first is the system bus, also known as a local bus; this connects the microprocessor and system memory. For dinosaur ISA and modern PCI designs, the motherboard connects the system bus through a bridge to peripherals; the bridge is managed by the motherboard's chipset. The PCI Express design is able to communicate directly with the processor at one end and peripherals at the other.

The second bus is dedicated to the needs of memory. With the arrival of high-speed CPUs and RAM, designers sought to isolate the path between the processor and memory and then make it more direct. Current machines use a Dual Independent Bus (DIB), which replaces the single system bus with a frontside bus and a backside bus. The frontside bus connects the system memory to the processor, under the management of the memory controller, and other subsidiary buses to the CPU and system memory. The backside bus serves one purpose: to provide a direct, fast channel between the CPU and Level 2 cache.

Bus connectors for expansion cards

Modern machines are based around motherboards that use the flexible PCI bus; some boards include a few older and slower ISA sockets to work with "legacy" adapters.

Modern buses

The PCI Express design is poised to take over the internal pathways of most modern machines. At the physical level, PCI Express acts similarly to the serial communication used for the Internet or a direct machine-to-machine Ethernet. The various slots on the motherboard connect to a hub on the motherboard which consolidates, divides, or redirects data as needed.

The first wave of motherboards offering PCI Express used a version capable of transferring data as fast as 250MBps on each of 16 bi-directional lanes, for a total potential transfer rate of 4GBps. Actually, in certain applications, devices in a PCI Express can choose to use both wires in each lane to send or receive data in one direction, which can double the transfer rate. This is the underlying specification for a PCI Express 16x slot; plans already call for a 32x slot with even larger and faster designs on the drawing boards.

For the computer manufacturer, one of the advantages of the switchover to PCI Express is that on the logical level, adapters use the same design as PCI, meaning that drivers and software do not need to be rewritten. Hardware makers can easily convert proven PCI adapter designs to work in a PCI Express slot by changing the physical layer — the connector pins and electrical coding and decoding components.

The PCI (peripheral component interconnect) bus was originally implemented as a 32-bit parallel bus running at clock speeds of 33 or

66 MHz; modern machines can work with PCI devices at a system bus speed of 100 or 133 MHz. Among its many advanced features is *bus mastering*, which allows certain PCI devices to take control of the bus and operate independently of the CPU.

Standard 32-bit cards have 120 active connections, with 4 additional pin locations used for "keying" the card into proper position, giving a total of 124 pin locations.

A 64-bit version of the PCI bus is used in high-end servers and workstations; the second 32 bits of information are transported across an extension to the standard card and to the bus on the motherboard— the extension adds another 60 pins for a total of 184.

As each generation of bus has taken primacy in the PC, there has been a period of time during which motherboard manufacturers offered backward compatibility with older designs so that users (and manufacturers) could continue to use devices of the previous generation. For example, as this edition goes to press most modern motherboards are based around the PCI Express design but also offer several PCI slots to permit use with "legacy" devices.

Similarly, when PCI first arrived, most motherboards also offered several ISA slots to permit use of devices designed for that specification. A smaller number of older machines combined PCI alongside an EISA or VL bus.

Dinosaur buses

The ISA (industry standard architecture) bus was developed for the PC-AT computer and its clones. The 16-bit bus, with two connector sockets for each expansion card, uses a 62-pin socket that is mechanically identical to the sockets of the original IBM PC and XT, which was an 8-bit design. This allows most older 8-bit cards to work in a 286, 386, 486, or Pentium ISA bus computer. More importantly for modern computer users, most cards that work with an ISA bus can work in a combination motherboard that shares the faster PCI bus.

The original PC and PC/XT machines used the PC bus, an 8-bit bus with a single 62-pin connector for each expansion card.

EISA motherboards use a versatile bus connector socket that can accept ordinary 8-bit cards, ordinary 16-bit ISA-style cards, or EISA cards.

MCA buses include 16-bit and 32-bit socket designs. Cards for 16-bit devices have 58 fingers, with signals available on each side of the card for a total of 116 connections. Cards for 32-bit devices have 93 fingers, again with connections on both sides of the card for a total of 186 wires. MCA cards generate less electrical interference than other adapters, which enhances system reliability and the integrity of data.

VL, or VESA local, bus systems are extensions to an ISA or EISA motherboard that connect directly to the CPU. Some early designs for local buses used proprietary cards and connectors, but standardization was eventually achieved. VL motherboards place an MCA connector in line with a standard ISA connector; VL cards include pins that plug into both.

WARNING

Avoid touching the gold-plated connectors at the bottom of expansion cards. First of all, you could end up sending a surge of static electricity through the delicate electronic components. And the oil on your hands could speed the corrosion process on the contacts of the card and the connectors. Handle the card by its nonconductive sides or by the bracket.

System setup: Plug-and-Play, DIP switches, and jumpers

From the early days of personal computing up to the era of the modern machines, users had to instruct the system about the various installed parts. As machines have progressed, though, the process of doing so has become simpler; put another way, the machines have become smarter.

Modern machine configuration

Nearly all current machines use a setup or configuration program to write system hardware information to a special block of memory— typically CMOS (Complementary Metal-Oxide-Semiconductor) design— that requires only a tiny amount of power from a small internal battery to hold information. The next generation of modern machines may use a form of non-volatile flash memory that can hold onto information indefinitely and requires power only when it is being read or written to.

The system uses the configuration memory to record the amount of system memory, the type of drives installed (including floppy and hard disk drives, and CD or DVD drives), the video adapter type, and the type and usage of special-purpose I/O ports including internal and external SATA, USB, and older data interchange ports such as IDE/ATA (now renamed as Parallel ATA). CMOS also keeps track of the date and time. CMOS memory chips hold onto their information with the assistance of a small, rechargeable or long-lived lithium battery so that configuration information is not lost while the machine is turned off.

Plug-and-Play

Current versions of Microsoft Windows exchange information with the chipsets of modern motherboards in a process called Plug-and-Play to perform an inventory of all installed and active devices, checking them against a list of device drivers and other extensions to the operating system. Plug-and-Play had a tentative introduction in Windows 95, with more functionality added in Windows 98 and 98SE, and full implementation in Windows 2000, Windows NT, Windows XP, and Windows Vista.

In theory, anytime you attach a compatible device into the system bus, the USB, a bi-directional parallel port, a serial port, or just about any I/O port, the operating system will recognize the piece of hardware and work with you to install proper drivers and make system settings. Similarly, the operating system is able to detect the removal of a card or device that had previously been recognized.

Plug-and-Play is not infallible; you'll need to pay attention to the settings of your system anytime you make a change or run into a problem.

NOTE

Sometimes the cure to a misbehaving (or unrecognized) device is to go to the Device Manager and remove the hardware from the list of hardware in the machine and then reboot the machine to allow Plug-and-Play to discover its presence and install the proper driver. Windows will seek to find device drivers in its own library on your hard disk, check the Microsoft web site over the Internet if your machine is configured for Web access, or ask you to insert a CD or other media that contains the software the operating system requires.

CROSS-REFERENCE

You can find more details about Plug-and-Play later in this chapter and, from another angle, in Chapter 23 when I discuss using Windows for troubleshooting.

Dinosaur DIPs and jumpers

PC, PC/XT, AT, and some later machines used tiny controls called DIP switches or jumper pins to tell the ROM BIOS what hardware was installed on the machine. Technicians or users set the switches or moved tiny plastic-cased jumpers that contained a piece of wire to close the circuit between two open pins; in either method, the result was read by the machine as an indication of details such as the amount of memory, the type of floppy or hard drives installed, the type of video adapter in place, and the presence or absence of a numeric coprocessor.

You'll still find jumpers used on some modern disk drives as a way to identify the device as a master or slave on a PATA cable, and on a handful of older-design adapter cards as a means to turn on or off certain functions. (For example, some outdated sound cards require users to remove a jumper from a set of pins to turn off the onboard audio amplifier if the card is going to be used with external amplified speakers.)

Be sure to consult the instruction manual or support technicians before removing jumpers or setting switches on a motherboard, and make notes on any steps you take so that they can be undone if the system fails to function properly after changes have been made.

NOTE

If you are confronted with hardware that uses jumpers, be sure to hold on to them in case they need to be reinstalled later. One way to keep track of them is to tape any jumpers removed from a device to a safe spot on the interior of the case; be sure to secure them safely so that they do not fall into the electrical connectors or moving parts of the machine.

Clock crystal

The computer's CPU beats to an internal clock that is based on a crystal oscillator that vibrates at a known frequency when electricity is applied. With each beat of the clock, the CPU moves a block of information through its set of microscopic switches. The tempo of the internal clock is measured in MHz or GHz; a megahertz represents one million cycles per second and a gigahertz one billion cycles per second. A 2.6-GHz processor, then, uses an internal tempo of 2.6 billion cycles per second.

The original IBM PC had a clock crystal that beat at a somnolent 4.77 MHz, just under five million beats per second. As I'm writing this book, the fastest CPUs sold to consumers have gone past 3 GHz (three billion beats per second) and Intel, AMD, and other makers are still pushing the speed limit. In recent years, though, chipmakers have changed their technical and marketing strategies to measure speed on the basis of actual performance rather than raw technical specifications.

In general, though, faster is better, although high speed also brings heat buildup and increased RF radiation. As I've already discussed, for these reasons a properly designed case and ventilation system are essential; do not modify a PC case or block its air holes.

Crystal oscillators (also called clock crystals) are usually permanently attached to the motherboard. Some early dinosaurs had crystals in sockets, and some early upgrade kits gave a CPU a quick boost by offering a faster, replacement crystal. On the most modern of machines, the crystal is a component of the chipset. A can-shaped modern crystal oscillator, and its associated clock chip, can be seen in Figure 5-6.

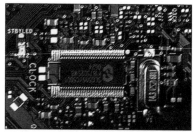

FIGURE 5-6: *A closeup of two critical components of a modern motherboard: at left is the system clock and at right the can-shaped crystal oscillator that sets the beat for the movement of data.*

On modern machines, the crystal is more flexible. It beats at a high speed that is adjusted by instructing the microprocessor to change its "clock multiplier." This adjustment can be made from the setup or configuration screen of most current devices. Some hobbyists make unsanctioned adjustments to the clock multiplier to try to wring every possible bit of performance out of the processor; such *overclocking* is sometimes successful but sometimes can also lead to overheating and damage to the processor or system components. The purpose of this book is to fix your own PC, not cause problems, and for that reason we do not recommend overclocking.

Crystal oscillators on modern machines rarely fail. If you do have a problem with the clock, the motherboard will likely have to be replaced or professionally repaired.

How the computer keeps time

Modern machines also have as many as three interrelated timekeeping clocks:

- The real-time clock, located on the motherboard and powered by the same battery that maintains the memory of the CMOS setup, is continually updated whether the system is turned on and receiving AC power or turned off.
- The CMOS clock is a logical clock stored in the BIOS chip on the system board; when the system is turned off, the CMOS records the most recent date and time but that information is not updated while the machine is turned off.
- The operating system maintains a logical clock that exists in system memory while the computer is operating; the information is not maintained when power is off.

When the computer boots up, the CMOS clock obtains the latest time and date from the real-time clock. After Windows loads, it reads the current time from the CMOS clock and starts its own operating system clock.

Now here's a tricky situation: The operating system clock runs independently of the CMOS. If your system is loaded down with some very computation-intensive tasks, it is possible for the operating system clock to slip a few tenths of a second or more behind the CMOS clock. In some very unusual situations, this can result in some odd system messages or information in saved files.

The operating system clock and the real-time clock automatically reconcile with each other when the machine is shut down or restarted. Current versions of Windows include a function that instructs the computer to synchronize its operating system clock with a national standard clock maintained by government agencies; this feature requires an Internet connection. You can make settings by going to the Control Panel and then choosing Date and Time and the Internet Time tab.

Changing the backup battery

Most modern machines use a long-life 3-volt button battery (model CR2032) to provide a trickle of power to a small block of memory that holds computer configuration information and to power an internal clock and calendar. The lithium battery should last several years before it needs to be replaced; if you purchase a used machine or a new machine that may have sat on a shelf for a lengthy period of time be aware that the clock has literally been running since the battery was first installed.

There are two tipoffs to a dying battery. The most common indicator: the computer fails to keep accurate time while it is turned off, or displays a completely incorrect time and date at bootup. Another signal is odd behavior of the machine that can be traced to incorrect or incomplete settings in the System Setup.

On the modern machine we're examining in this book, the backup battery is located near the memory slots and the heat sink that covers the chipset; you can see it in Figure 5-7. When you buy a replacement battery, be sure to check its expiration date. Look for a new battery, in a sealed package, with a printed promise by the manufacturer of at least several years of shelf life.

Before you replace the battery, open the System Setup program and write down all of the settings in a notebook; in fact, I'd recommend you do this every few months so that you have a record in case of an unexpected failure of the battery or the rare situation where a power surge or a computer virus may scramble the settings.

Once the new battery is in place, enter System Setup and restore settings to those you have recorded in your notebook.

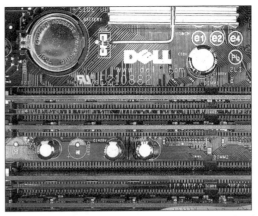

FIGURE 5-7: *The button battery on the motherboard of a modern machine. In this motherboard, there is a notation just above the battery that the + side is supposed to face up. Be sure to check the instruction manual for the details of your particular system.*

NOTE

Replacing a battery is simple, but there are some dangers to the system if the job is not done properly. Be sure to take extra care to discharge any static electricity in your body before you touch the motherboard and the battery. And assure that the battery is properly installed, matching the + mark on the battery to the + mark on the motherboard or the clip that holds it in place (depending on the design of your system). An improperly installed battery can generate damaging heat or even explode. Finally, if you must use a screwdriver or any other tool to pry the battery out of its socket be careful not to touch the system board with the object; doing so could scratch the motherboard and break delicate circuit traces on the system board.

Integrated I/O, display, and audio adapter circuitry on the motherboard

The original concept for a computer motherboard was basically to provide an engine and a set of connections to essential components.

The first IBM PC and most dinosaurs offered the microprocessor, a block of memory, and some very simple basic I/O features. Everything else was added in the form of an adapter card: serial and parallel ports, a video display adapter, a joystick or mouse port, and other devices. So, too, hard and floppy drive controllers began life as separate adapter cards that plugged into the bus.

Over the years, though, many of these functions have become part of the motherboards themselves; in technical terms they have been "integrated" with the processor in the form of the chipset and auxiliary circuits. One advantage of integrating many functions on the motherboard is the capability of the manufacturer to fine-tune and test all the components together and guarantee the complete product — no more worries about subtle incompatibilities between your floppy drive controller and your motherboard.

Integration can also reduce the overall price of a system because chips are much less expensive to manufacture than adapter cards; prices also continue to drop as manufacturers make more and more of a particular design of integrated circuit. Further, the chips generally demand less power than adapters and manufacturers can reduce the number of available slots within the case.

Today, a typical modern machine includes the following components integrated onto the motherboard:

- SATA or PATA connectors and control circuits for data interchange with hard disk drives and CD or DVD drives
- A full set of USB ports that can be used to connect an almost limitless number of external devices that support that specification
- Ethernet circuitry to allow connection of the machine to a local area network or to a broadband modem that serves as the gateway to the Internet

Older modern machines (and some current machines that seek to bridge the widening gap between technological generations) may also include:

- An interface for a floppy disk drive
- Serial, parallel, and PS/2 mouse and keyboard ports to support older devices not compatible with the USB standard

And as price competition has intensified in recent years, PC manufacturers have looked for ways to reduce the bottom line — at least the price that they advertise as the entry level for their machines.

Today, many motherboards for systems ranging from the simplest home computer to advanced office devices offer some of these features on the motherboard:

- Basic to advanced sound facilities
- Basic to advanced video adapter functions, often using a design in which the chips on the motherboard "share" some of system memory as needed to draw graphics, and
- Basic WiFi or Bluetooth wireless communication technology

For many users, the integrated features are more than sufficient for their needs. This is especially true for users looking for basic office tasks including word processing and spreadsheets and for e-mail and Internet access. The video and sound quality is more than adequate.

 NOTE

If you're going to use an integrated video adapter that shares system memory, you can gain an easy and relatively inexpensive boost in performance by adding RAM to your system. Most integrated video chipsets will take as much as 128 to 256MB of available RAM to construct images; I would recommend adding at least that much RAM to your system to prevent the video adapter from being a drag on overall system speed.

But if you're going to be performing digital editing of photographs, drawings, or sound files or playing the most demanding of PC games on your own machine or over the Internet, you'll probably find that integrated features are not powerful enough for your purposes. As an example, on the very modern Dell Dimension 9200 profiled in Chapter 6, the onboard Sigma Tel audio chipset on the motherboard is purposely crippled by Dell to provide only basic functions: you can play streaming audio from the Internet but cannot capture it to an editor, for example. Dell does this so that it can charge extra for an upgraded sound card, not because the integrated chipset is unable to provide the function.

A possible disadvantage to an integrated subsystem is that a problem with an integrated component cannot be economically repaired or replaced except by installing a new motherboard. The solution: work around a failed part or an outmoded part by installing a replacement in the system bus.

The good news is that it is very easy to disable onboard video or audio facilities and install an advanced adapter in one of the PC's bus slots or as an external device attached to a high-speed USB port. On modern machines this is usually done by changing a selection in the Setup or Configuration screen. On older machines you may have to remove a jumper or change a switch setting to physically disable onboard audio or video.

Similarly, it is possible to upgrade an older machine to add USB 2.0 ports (on a system without USB ports, or on one of the relatively small number of systems that shipped with hardware supporting the slower initial standard USB 1.0 or 1.1), or add a faster hard disk controller (upgrading from ATA/33 or ATA/66 to a faster PATA, or adding a new SATA subsystem to use with the latest hard drives).

Just about the only thing you cannot upgrade on a modern machine is the bus itself. If the motherboard came with a set of PCI slots, you cannot adapt it to add PCI Express slots. But wait, let me amend that slightly: adding a USB adapter to a PCI slot extends or expands on a machine's capabilities markedly. It is one of the most effective ways to transform the capabilities of an older modern machine.

An older AT form factor motherboard with onboard I/O is shown in Figure 5-8. On this design, a cable runs from the I/O header on the motherboard to a bracket that mounts in an available slot at the rear of the system.

On ATX motherboards, the serial and parallel ports (as well as USB) are attached directly to the board and line up with openings in the rear of the case. This saves real estate at the slots, reduces the chance for cables to come loose, and adds to the useful standardization of motherboards and PC cases.

And as we'll explore in Chapter 6, the most modern of machines, based around a BTX motherboard, simplify computers in two ways: by integrating many functions onto the motherboard and by dispensing with the need for serial, parallel, PS/2, and certain other forms of specialized I/O subsystems in favor of the high-speed, extremely flexible USB and SATA ports in internal and external versions.

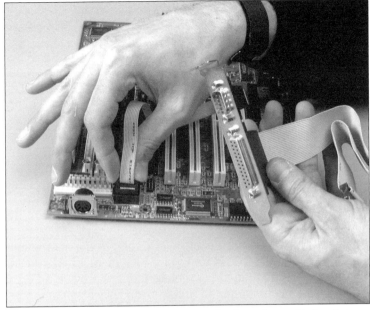

FIGURE 5-8: *On this AT form factor motherboard, a cable leads to a bracket with ports that poke through the rear panel of the case with serial and parallel connectors.*

How the Motherboard Works

The mother of all boards in your PC is the home of the CPU and its supporting chips, including the ROM BIOS. As I've already discussed, system memory may lie on the motherboard or on an add-in card in dinosaur machines or on plug-in SIMM or DIMM modules that are inserted into slots on senior citizen and modern machines. Other elements that may be integrated onto the motherboard include serial and parallel ports, USB circuitry, the video adapter, and floppy and hard drive adapters of various specifications ranging from PATA (ATA/IDE) to current SATA designs. The motherboard is also connected to a power supply that provides low-voltage DC power and a fan that helps keep the closed box cool.

Ch
5

To understand how the motherboard components interact, consider what happens when you turn on the power. What follows is a generic description of a modern machine coming to life.

The computer's first steps are hard-wired into the circuitry. When you flick on the power switch, the power supply takes a few fractions of a second to step down and transform the voltage and to spin its fan; when it is ready, it sends a power-good signal to the clock reset chip on the motherboard. The clock reset chip in turn sends a reset message to the microprocessor. The CPU resets and initializes itself with its ordinary startup instructions; the early steps include the running of a self-test.

The final, hard-wired step as the computer comes to life is an instruction to look in a specific, very high address for further instructions. There, the microprocessor finds a pointer that sends it to the place in memory where the ROM BIOS is located.

At this point, the computer marches according to the instructions programmed into the ROM. It is important to remember that ROMs can be changed; you can upgrade or replace them to provide different instructions to the microcomputer. Today's modern machines often include BIOS chips that bear the name of the seller of the PC (Dell, Gateway, Hewlett Packard, and other major names) but are often re-labeled and customized versions of code developed and maintained by makers that today include American Megatrends, Phoenix (which purchased competitor Award in 1998), and a number of Asian sources including Abit, Acer, Asus, and Micro-Star.

The various BIOS chips all use some form of power-on self-test (POST), but the details may vary from machine to machine. The error messages or informational messages displayed onscreen may differ slightly too. And, many manufacturers take advantage of the customization features of the BIOS I just mentioned to display their own information during the POST process, so instead of the system information I describe next, you may see the name of the manufacturer, a company logo, or other information. You usually can disable this promotional display by making changes to the BIOS settings similar to the way you change hardware device boot order. I cover more BIOS information in Chapter 3.

The POST usually begins by writing the BIOS name, date, and copyright information on the screen; then it checks the keyboard (on many systems, you can see the Caps Lock and Num Lock lights flash on and off). The test usually extends to the controller chip inside the keyboard itself.

From the very dawn of the PC, users have faced this vexing conundrum: how can you diagnose a problem with a component of the machine if the motherboard will not boot up or if the video adapter is unable to display error messages or codes on the screen of a monitor. The initial solution, dating back to the very first IBM PC, was to have the POST use a tiny speaker within the case to send out a Morse Code-like set of beeps to report on its progress or to sound the alarm: various machines used various combinations of long and short beeps during bootup to inform the user of success or failure. Today's most modern machines have eliminated the noisy beeps in favor of a set of colored, numbered, or lettered LED lamps on the front or back of the machine; these serve the same purpose and can provide a great deal of information about problems the computer encounters in the moments before it is able to load and display the operating system. Consult the instruction manual for your PC to learn the specifics of your device.

Once past the basic tests of the POST, on modern machines the utility consults the information found in the Setup or Configuration memory and then interrogates all devices plugged into internal bus slots, memory slots, and internal and external connectors including SATA or PATA drive subsystems, internal and external USB ports, pointing devices, keyboards, and monitors. In general, a device has to be turned on or receiving power from the computer itself to be queried by the system. The system is looking to confirm that all devices are functioning properly; at this point, though, it is not checking the hardware against the set of device drivers that stand between them and the Windows operating system.

On a dinosaur machine, the computer reads the settings of DIP switches or the activation of circuits by jumpers across pins on the motherboard or on devices themselves. Most older machines also have a limited version of a Setup or Configuration utility where you can identify to the machine the presence of a particular type of hard drive or make the basic settings for a video card. On EISA and MCA machines, the BIOS may be able to interrogate devices plugged into the bus to determine their capabilities.

On many a ROM BIOS, the next step is to conduct an inventory and test of system memory; you may see a countdown onscreen as it checks the RAM chips.

The POST also checks many of the other parts of the system, including the CPU itself, the DMA chips, and other critical elements of the system.

The POST checks the floppy drives (the floppy drive light flashes, and the drive spins as it's doing this). If a printer is attached to the parallel port and turned on at bootup, the POST initializes the printer, clearing its memory and preparing it to accept output.

When the POST is done, the ROM BIOS checks for BIOS extensions—those extra ROMs installed on a hard disk controller or on a video card—and follows the initialization instructions in each of these ROM extensions in turn.

The next step is to begin the process of loading the operating system. Here it follows the instructions in the Setup or Configuration memory and looks for the boot tracks on a particular set of devices. On older machines the PC would first check the floppy disk drive, then the hard drive. On more modern machines, the default first step is the hard disk, and from there it can go on to look for the operating system on a disc mounted in a CD or DVD drive, or look on an attached network for a bootable version of the operating system.

As part of your configuration of a new machine, and as part of a regular review of the settings for your machine, you should check the boot sequence settings to make sure they match your needs and wants.

NOTE

It is generally a bad idea to have your computer look for the presence of a bootable disk in the floppy disk drive—if your machine has one, that is. First of all, it is almost impossible to squeeze a modern operating system onto a floppy disk drive. And secondly, this used to be one of the most common sources of virus infection for computers. A virus is certainly small enough to fit on a floppy, and some malicious authors used this loophole as a way to get their nasty efforts onto machines otherwise protected. If your PC has a floppy disk drive, I'd advise you to change the boot sequence to keep that device out of the list of devices checked by the machine at bootup.

And now, finally, the system is ready to load the operating system. In days of old, PCs would look for DOS (the Disk Operating System). Today, current versions of Windows embed their own operating system, although deep down inside there are some of the elements of the very first DOS or code that emulates it.

When the selected drive spins to life, the drive heads look to the boot sector to load operating system files. These files bring the components of the PC to life one-by-one. Modern versions of Windows compare the list of devices found to be physically attached to the system to the list of device driver software it finds on the hard disk drive; these device drivers give pieces of hardware their particular personality while allowing Windows to concentrate on basic functions. Similarly, DLL (Dynamic Link Library) components stand between the operating system and particular pieces of software you have installed in your machine and communicate in both directions.

Motherboard form factors

Though literally hundreds of different motherboards are on the market from dozens of manufacturers large and small, it is by no means a world of anarchy.

Here's why: It all has to do with the modular nature of modern machines. It's a mix-and-match world where a computer maker—Dell, Gateway, Hewlett-Packard, or you—can assemble a machine from off-the-shelf parts. But everything has to work together.

First of all, every motherboard has to be compatible with a particular set of BIOS chips, memory, and the CPU. Second, the connectors on the bus have to be standardized so that they will work properly with any adapter card meant to be plugged into the bus. Next, the motherboard has to match up with the power supply connectors and voltage.

And finally, the motherboard has to be mechanically standardized so that adapter sockets on the board line up with openings on computer cases and so that serial, parallel, USB, and other ports can be accessed from outside the case. And the motherboard has to line up with attachment points in the case. Boards generally use non-conducting standoffs from the metal case, as shown in Figure 5-9.

Think of the automobile industry: General Motors or Ford can come up with a very fancy car with all sorts of special features and spectacular design, but it still must work with the gasoline sold at every service station. Your neighborhood mechanic has to be able to change the oil with the tools in his kit. The wheels have to work with tires available at Goodyear as well as Sears. And the vehicle must fit on Interstate 95 as well as in your garage. Get the idea?

Table 5-4 lists the most commonly used form factors for modern machines. Table 5-5 describes older form factors used in senior citizens and dinosaurs.

TABLE 5-4: Modern Machine Form Factors

Form Factor	Maximum Width	Maximum Depth
BTX	12.8 inches	10.5 inches
MicroBTX	10.4 inches	10.5 inches
ATX	12 inches	9.6 inches
FlexATX	9 inches	7.5 inches
MicroATX	9.6 inches	9.6 inches
Mini ATX	11.2 inches	8.2 inches

TABLE 5-5: Senior-Citizen and Dinosaur Form Factors

Form Factor	Maximum Width	Maximum Depth
NLX	8 to 9 inches	10 to 11 inches
WTX	14 inches	16.75 inches
LPX	9 inches	11 to 13 inches
Mini LPX	8 to 9 inches	10 to 11 inches
Baby AT	8.5 inches	10 to 13 inches
AT	12 inches	11 to 13 inches
PC	8.5 inches	13 inches

The computer industry's solution is something the engineers call motherboard form factors. Over the past decade, most PCs used one or another version of the ATX (Advanced Technology Extended) motherboard standard; beginning in 2005 and accelerating in 2006, many makers switched over to a newer specification, the BTX (Balanced Technology Extended). It is too early to tell if BTX will become dominant or whether a new specification or an adaptation of previous ones will be most commonly used in coming years. Here are the most common in use for modern machines:

FIGURE 5-9: *Motherboard designers have to find a way to support the electrically conductive circuitry without allowing it to touch the metal case. One typical solution is to use insulating plastic standoffs installed from the underside to support the board. Other designs use metal posts and screws that attach to specially isolated attachment points on the board. A replacement motherboard should come with an appropriate set of new standoffs; for unusual cases you can order specialized supports from computer supply houses.*

- **BTX.** Intel was the prime moving force behind the development and standardization of a new motherboard specification; it did so primarily in self-defense because its newer microprocessors were generating so much heat that they were capable of overloading the cooling system of older board and case designs. The primary purpose of BTX was to reorganize the placement of components and to remove impediments so that air could be drawn through the case and out a vent more efficiently. You can see an example of a BTX motherboard in Figure 5-10, and more details in

Chapter 6 where I take apart a modern machine based on that design. As with ATX, there are also specifications for slightly smaller versions (microBTX, nanoBTX, and picoBTX) for use in special-purpose embedded computers or ultra-slim models.

■ **ATX.** The ATX motherboard implemented a major reorganization of the I/O slots at the back of the system, paving the way for a multitude of external enhancement devices, beginning with those that attached to the serial and parallel ports and then, in later versions, ATX was easily adapted to provide USB ports. Figure 5-11 shows an example.

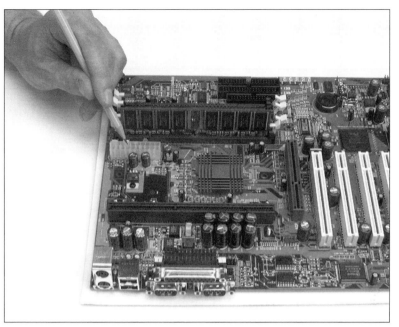

FIGURE 5-11: *On this ATX motherboard, the main power connection sits between the Pentium II module's Slot 1 and the memory DIMM slots.*

Among the features of the ATX is a stacked I/O connector panel that typically includes serial, parallel, keyboard, mouse, and USB connectors; all of these ports are attached directly to the motherboard, eliminating cables and extra hardware. The CPU was moved to a central location to enable the upright Pentium II or Pentium III to install in its own slot without interfering with adapter cards and promoting a better flow of cooling air over increasingly hotter processors. The I/O layout on an ATX board is shown in Figure 5-12.

■ **MicroATX.** A reduced-size version of the ATX specification, permitting smaller desktop and tower systems and less-expensive motherboards.

FIGURE 5-10: *The main feature of a BTX motherboard is the clear pathway between the intake air vent at the front and the outflow vent at the rear. In between is the microprocessor beneath a fan cowling. Other sources of heat, including the chipset (beneath its own aluminum cooling fins), and the video adapter card, are also placed for maximum cooling.*

FIGURE 5-12: *This close-up of the back of a Micro-Star MS-6111 motherboard shows the I/O connectors. The bank of I/O connectors on this ATX motherboard neatly brings together, from left to right, mouse and keyboard connectors, a pair of stacked USB ports, two DB-9 serial ports, and above them a DB-25 enhanced parallel port.*

- **FlexATX.** Developed by Intel as an extension to the microATX specification, FlexATX motherboards are intended as the basis for small closed-box PCs. Among the first uses: the Barbie PC and the Hot Wheels PC.

  Some closed-box designs rely on external expansion and feature no PCI slots, instead relying on USB ports at the front and back panels for simple plug-and-play expandability. Some FlexATX desktop boards have eliminated legacy connectors including PS/2, and MIDI/game, serial, and parallel ports. While most form factors have sought downsizing, the needs for an expanded case and motherboard for use with high-end workstations and servers has brought about the development of the WTX design.

- **WTX.** Its design includes provision for redundant power supplies, extra cooling, and space for a multitude of drives and other internal devices. The interior of the case is designed with

thermal zones to manage the buildup of heat. The motherboard can use a Flex Slot I/O card to move external connections to customized configurations and locations.

Before the arrival of the micro and flex version of the ATX, manufacturers also produced systems based on a pair of low-profile or slimline designs. Some of the early desktop versions of machines based on the LPX were called pizza boxes because of their shape.

- **NLX.** A more recent version of the slimline or low-profile design, this design shrank the size of the motherboard at the same time as it added more space for connectors at the rear of the chassis and allowed for the placement of connectors at the front through the use of a riser card. The internal connector for the riser card was given greater functionality, including electric connections for the PCI bus, ISA bus, power, floppy, serial bus, and other I/O signals.

- **LPX.** Introduced for use in low-profile cases, the LPX is now relatively rare because of limitations in expandability. Expansion cards plug sideways into a single bus riser card that plugs into a single slot on the motherboard. The LPX added standard locations for serial, parallel, video, mouse, and keyboard connectors; the serial ports used smaller DB9 connectors, and the mouse and keyboard used mini-DIN PS/2 connectors.

Through the first half of the history of the PC, nearly all machines used an AT motherboard, which was the successor to the original IBM PC design.

- **AT.** The full-size AT motherboard was introduced with IBM's PC-AT machine and was the largest motherboard offered for PCs. Serial and parallel ports and connectors for video output and the keyboard were generally located on adapter cards that plugged into the bus. An AT motherboard fits only into AT desktop or AT tower cases. Figure 5-13 shows a basic AT motherboard.

- **Baby AT.** Widely used for senior citizens and modern machines, the baby AT keyboard port — usually a large 5-pin DIN connector — was part of the motherboard and matched up with an opening in the case. This board fits in AT and baby AT desktop and tower units.

FIGURE 5-13: *Bare Micro-Star Pentium AT motherboard.*

Testing the motherboard

Very few motherboard components are individually serviceable. Here's a list of some of the pieces and the opportunities (or impediments) to repair:

CPU

Most modern machines have their CPU in a flat socket on the surface of the motherboard. Some older modern machines had a large slot that held a CPU cartridge upright like an adapter card.

Most dinosaur CPU chips are installed in sockets and you can remove them for replacement or upgrade, although some machines, including a family of relatively inexpensive 386SX machines produced in the early 1990s, had the CPU soldered into place.

The CPU itself is usually a pretty stable element of the system; if it survives the initial few hours of use it is likely to last many years. On the other hand, if the system sustains physical damage from an electrical surge or shock, water damage, or severe overheating it often does not make sense to replace just the microprocessor; if the system is still under warranty the most likely repair would be installation of a

new motherboard with CPU in place. If the system is out of warranty, chances are the cost of a new (and usually more advanced) system will be comparable or less than the expense of replacing the motherboard and CPU.

Control chipset

On most motherboards, the clock generator and timer chips, the crystal oscillator (clock crystal), onboard clock chip, CMOS memory, the bus controller, the DMA controller, and all the chip sockets are soldered into place. It's not reasonable to consider replacing them.

Some hobbyists and technically advanced users with specific needs (and a high tolerance for risk) experiment with changing the clock speed settings for a microprocessor (called overclocking) to attempt to wring out higher performance. Doing so brings some risk of overheating or errors. On dinosaur machines, the crystal oscillator was in a socket or stood on a pair of spindly wire legs on the motherboard and some early experimenters upgraded them as faster hardware was available.

Memory

Memory chips of modern machines are held on SIMMs, SIPPs, or DIMMS, and other designs of carriers that plug into sockets; the entire module can be easily changed, but individual chips can't be replaced. RAM chips on dinosaurs can be replaced if they are not soldered into place.

ROM BIOS

On dinosaurs and senior citizens, BIOS chips are usually held in sockets and can be replaced if they fail or for upgrading. On modern machines, BIOS chips may be in a socket or soldered into place. Most hold instructions in flash memory that can be changed in place by reading in new code from a floppy disk or other source.

CMOS battery

The clock/CMOS battery is a simple slip-out/slip-in replacement on most motherboards, but some poorly designed dinosaurs had the battery soldered into place. Today nearly every modern machine has switched over to an easily replaceable button battery like the one used in wristwatches. You may also find a rechargeable battery that is topped off every time the machine is turned on. A third variant, used in some older modern machines, combined a rechargeable battery with a clock module; this was a good idea but one that presented problems if the battery did not last as long as the system around it.

One indicator of a serious problem with a motherboard is the appearance on screen of an NMI (nonmaskable interrupt) error. If an NMI appears once in a blue moon, this might be a situation where a particular unusual combination of hardware, software, and operating system instructions exposes an error that can be ignored. But if an NMI pops up regularly, crashing the system or bringing down an essential piece of software, this is often the signal that something has gone seriously wrong with your PC's motherboard.

An interrupt is a signal from a particular device that it wants the attention of the microprocessor. A nonmaskable interrupt is one that the hardware is not permitted to mask, or ignore, while processing another task. When an NMI occurs, the NMI error message goes up on the screen, and everything is deadlocked until you address the NMI error—no matter what else is going on. If you're lucky, a recurring NMI may be indicating a memory parity error, which would require only the replacement of a memory module.

Removing a motherboard

As I've said, the motherboard itself is a maze of printed circuits, none of which is readily repairable. That's the bad news; the good news is that replacement motherboards—almost certainly even more advanced than the original—sell for about $80 to $200.

To get to the motherboard, start by turning off the computer and unplugging it from the wall. Unplug all external cables from connectors on the rear of the case. Remove the system cover and be sure to ground yourself before reaching into the case. If you've got a digital camera, bring it out and take a series of photos of the system as you find it. Take an overview picture and as many close-ups of connectors and connections as appropriate. In addition, I suggest that you keep a notebook close at hand and make a sketch of the innards of the case to help you put things back where they were. Use sticky-tab papers to mark pieces or make notes on masking tape to identify the parts. Be especially careful to note the polarity of cables, that is, which connector pin is assigned to pin 1 of the connector. Some motherboard connectors include slots or tabs to prevent incorrect connection; others, however, can be inserted either way.

 NOTE

When I'm performing exploratory surgery on a motherboard, I use a felt-tipped marker to place a mark on the cable and another on the motherboard or connector before disconnecting the cable. When it comes time to hook everything back up, simply line up the two marks and you have restored proper polarity.

Assign numbers to any cables you remove and place matching numbers on their connectors. Put screws into envelopes or containers marked with a description of their purpose. Trust me on this one: A few minutes spent organizing the parts you take out can save hours when it comes to putting them all back together again.

In most systems you have to remove add-in cards and some or all of the hard drives, floppy drives, CD-ROM drives, and other internal devices.

On tower cases and some desktops, you may need to unbolt one or more drive cages that hold add-in drives; many of these cages overhang parts of the motherboard. In cramped designs, such as the low-profile cases, you may even have to remove the power supply that sometimes hangs over the motherboard or be very careful when slipping the motherboard out from underneath.

After everything is out of the way, unplug the power supply's electrical cable or cables from the motherboard.

A step-by-step example

Here's a step-by-step walk-through of a typical project; your case may be slightly different:

1. Turn off the power and unplug the PC from the wall. Remove the cover: the most modern of machines now offer cases that permit removal of the cover with the lifting of a latch; another modern design allows the case to open like a clamshell with the push of a release button. The majority of older modern machines and nearly all senior citizens and dinosaurs secure the cover in place with screws; some designs allow the removal of a side panel for direct access to the innards, while the original design for PC cases had screws at the back or sides of the case holding a U-shaped cover that slides over the frame that holds the motherboard and adapters.

(If you do have to remove screws that hold the cover in place, be sure to store them in a safe place. Some suggestions: tape them to the case panel with masking tape, or place them in a labeled egg carton.)

2. Ground yourself. Touch a grounding strip or the center screw of an electrical outlet plate to release static electricity in your body. Even better, wear a properly grounded antistatic wrist strap.

3. Remove adapter cards, marking any cables or wires you must disconnect in the process.

4. Attach labels to all wires connected to pins on the motherboard. All motherboards receive electrical current from the power supply at one or more locations. You'll also find cables that run from disk drive adapters and internal USB and SATA ports. On senior citizen and dinosaur motherboards you'll likely find wires that run to indicator lights on the front panel and internal speakers; on more modern machines these components are usually integrated onto the motherboard itself and match up with openings on the case.

5. Remove the power supply if necessary. A desktop computer case is pretty crowded. It may be necessary — or you may find it easier — to remove the power supply screws and slide the power supply out of the case so you have some working room.

6. Remove mounting screws and lift the motherboard out.

- **Modern machines:** Many modern motherboards are mounted with as few as one or as many as half a dozen small screws, with the motherboard reinforced and electrically insulated at the screw holes. At other places, especially beneath the bus slots, are plastic standoff supports that pop through the board and slip into slots on the case beneath. Look for an insulating washer under the screw heads. Remove the screws, and then slide the motherboard half an inch sideways, moving it away from the power supply. It might make sense to remove the power supply and possibly the drive cage in a smaller case to make room to remove the board. Lift it up and wiggle it out of the chassis. Sometimes it's easier to squeeze the tops of the standoffs and lift the motherboard out. Save the washers and standoffs to mount the new motherboard. You can also purchase new hardware from computer supply houses.

- **Dinosaurs:** Most PC/XT motherboards have nine standoffs (little metal or plastic legs) that attach the board to the bottom of the case. Look for screws on the bottom of the computer that correspond to the nine screws or nuts on the top of the motherboard. You can remove either the top nuts or the bottom screws. Other XT clones use two screws and a handful of insulated plastic pegs. After you remove the nuts or screws, lift the motherboard out of the chassis. Some older systems have paper or plastic insulating washers on the top and bottom of the motherboard at each of the nine standoffs and/or screws. You may need to reuse these insulating washers, the standoffs, and the screws to mount a new motherboard.

Installing a new motherboard

In theory, installing a new motherboard is simply the reverse process of removing the old one. On a current modern machine that adheres to industry-standard form factors, a BTX or ATX motherboard should line up perfectly with the attachment points, electrical connections, and other features of the original board; your chances of success will be near 100 percent if you are replacing a board with an identical model and a bit less if you are upgrading or changing from one manufacturer to another.

On older modern machines and most senior citizens and dinosaurs, anything other than a model-for-model swap opens the possibility of physical mismatches in mounting or wiring. Be sure to study the board you are replacing and be prepared for some creative solutions: some of the systems I have built or rebuilt have required use of shims or other hardware fixes, cable extensions, and the occasional judicious use of one of the most important tools of our time: duct tape. I have never seen a replacement job on an older machine go perfectly smoothly, but I have also never failed to complete the job sooner or later. This is an indoor job, no heavy lifting.

Make sure the motherboard you purchase comes with a detailed and understandable manual; you'll need instructions about electrical connectors, jumpers, DIP switches, and settings. I would turn down a hot new board at a great price but a sketchy instruction manual in favor of a capable motherboard with a good manual and even better, support from the technical desk of the seller.

Ch
5

In some cases, you can read the instruction manual and technical documents for a motherboard before you make a purchase by consulting the web site for the manufacturer.

1. **Prepare the case and motherboard.** Gently place the new motherboard into the case so that external connectors are lined up exactly with the openings at the back of the case; on the most modern of machines, this mostly means the set of USB ports and perhaps the outputs of integrated video and audio if they are part of the motherboard. On older motherboards, you'll need to align ports including keyboard, mouse, parallel, serial, and sometimes other I/O options. Lift up the motherboard slightly to determine where you must install plastic or other nonconducting standoffs so that the new motherboard is secure and can't touch the metal case at any point. The more standoffs you install, the more stable the motherboard will be.

   Most cases have slotted grooves that accept the underside of the standoffs and lock them into place. In some places, you may have standoffs that merely sit atop the bare metal bottom of the case. Don't pass up a chance to add support to the motherboard anywhere you can.

   Find the location on the chassis itself of the one or two brass hexagonal studs that actually hold the motherboard in place. You may have to reposition this metal connector to match a different hole location on the new motherboard.

2. **Set switches or jumpers.** You may need to change the default settings of switches or jumpers on the motherboard to indicate the type or speed of the CPU; on modern motherboards all — or nearly all — adjustments can be made from the Setup screen. Consult the instruction manual.

3. **Install the motherboard.** Once you have determined the proper location for all the standoffs, you can lay the motherboard in the case by sliding the nonconducting standoffs into the grooves of the case. Be careful not to warp the motherboard as you slide it into place; bending the motherboard can short it out or break its electrical traces.

   In most designs, you'll attach the board with one or more screws into a brass stud, using a nonconductive paper or plastic washer between the screw and the motherboard.

4. **Connect electrical cables to the motherboard.** Locate the two white rectangular power leads with 20-pin plugs that come from your power supply. Newer ATX motherboards also require a second connection for a 4-pin set of wires delivering an additional source of 12 volts necessary for some CPUs. Newer BTX motherboards require use of a different, 24-pin plug; be sure to match the proper power supply to the motherboard. It is possible to use an adapter cable to convert an ATX power supply to work with a BTX motherboard or the other way around; more important is the question of whether the power supply you purchase will fit in the space allowed for it within the case and not interfere with components on the motherboard. Stop, look, and think: A mistake here could fry your motherboard. The good news is that it is pretty difficult to make a mistake with electrical connectors. They are keyed so that they should only fit in the proper direction, and they are color coded for position.

   On ATX motherboards, the two connectors line up alongside each other with black wires adjacent to each other. On most cables, the color order goes like this: orange, red, yellow, blue, black, black, black, black, white, red, red, and red. On most motherboards, these leads plug into a connector near the keyboard port at the back end of the board.

   Next, connect the power indicator, turbo, reset, and hard drive light connectors to pins on the motherboard indicated in the manual that accompanies it. The pins are usually marked with numbers or labels printed directly on the motherboard. Pay special attention to the polarity of the plugs you install; the instruction manual usually indicates the color of wire for each pin or whether a particular pin is + or – voltage. In general, power supply wires are as follows: Red or yellow are positive, blue or white are negative, and black is ground.

5. **Install the CPU and RAM.** If the microprocessor and memory are not already on the motherboard, you need to install them now. If I have room to work inside the case, I prefer to perform this step at this stage of the installation; if your case is very crowded, you might want to put the CPU and memory in place before installing the motherboard. Either way, take care not to damage the somewhat delicate pins on the CPU and be sure to take appropriate antistatic precautions.

Read the instruction manual for your motherboard carefully to determine memory options; some boards require banks to be filled in matched pairs, while others may not work with certain types of memory such as EDO. If you want to reuse memory SIMMs from the original motherboard, be sure they are appropriate for the new board.

CROSS-REFERENCE

I discuss ways to adapt certain older-style memory carriers to some new boards in Chapter 8.

Most high-speed CPUs, beginning with late-model 486s and continuing through the Pentium, Celeron, and Athlon families, include a CPU fan to help remove the heat produced by the microprocessor. In our state-of-the-art demonstration system in Chapter 6, the CPU sits within a wind tunnel-like enclosure that is cooled by a large fan mounted on the rear panel of the case. In either case, make sure you connect the fan to the power supply at this stage.

6. **Install add-in cards.** Reinstall expansion cards into appropriate slots on the motherboard. If you are upgrading to a motherboard with a different slot design, make sure your old cards fit into the new board. Each successive generation of bus design is not compatible with previous ones: PCI Express cards will not fit into or work with PCI bus slots, for example. So, too, PCI cards will not work with older ISA slots.

And there are also some other wrinkles: some full-size dinosaur-era PC cards are too large to fit in the 8/16-bit ISA slots on an AT motherboard. Some cards are wider than others, and you need to give some thought to which cards can safely sit next to each other. Cards that include a daughter card, for example, are considerably thicker than cards without this extra circuitry. A disk controller card may not be all that thick itself, but it requires that one or more ribbon cables connect to it. If you place two wide cards or two cards with side-mounting cables side by side it may be difficult to get everything to fit. Just look at the cards that need to reside next to each other and separate the ones that need more than normal space.

And just to make things interesting, most ISA 16-bit cards have their components on the opposite side of those on PCI cards. The place where ISA and PCI come together on the motherboard can be a very crowded neighborhood.

7. **Reinstall drive cages if you have removed them.** Reattach power connections to hard drives and floppy drives if you disconnected them.

8. **Attach data cables.** If your system's hard drive, floppy drive, and CD-ROM drive connect to an EIDE port on the motherboard, you need to attach those cables so that they can communicate with the bus. If the drives connect to an adapter card instead, you probably didn't remove the cables during the installation of the motherboard.

9. **Double-check everything.** Take a few moments to check the inside of the case once more. Look for any unattached cables. There are likely to be a few extra power leads from the power supply, but indicator lights, speakers, fan power leads, and other such elements of the motherboard should all be attached.

10. **Attach external components.** Plug in the keyboard, mouse, and video display.

11. **Turn on the system.** Plug in the computer and turn it on. If you've done everything correctly, your system will display the new motherboard's CMOS Setup screen where you can inform it about the elements of your computer. Consult the instruction manual for your motherboard to understand the specifics of your ROM BIOS.

12. **Check out the system under power.** Careful readers will notice that I haven't asked you to put the cover on yet. Shine a powerful light on your system and study the innards for a moment. Are all the fans spinning? Do you hear any unusual sounds, such as wires touching fans or components vibrating in place? Do you see curls of smoke? I hope not.

13. **Turn off the machine, remove the power cord, and connect cables to external devices once again.** Assuming that the system is running properly, replace the cover carefully. Although it is fine to run the machine for a short period of time without the cover, you need to replace the cover once it is ready to run to avoid damage from dirt and improper cooling and to avoid radio frequency interference to radios, televisions, and other electronic devices.

What if the new motherboard doesn't run?

Stop, look, and listen: You don't want to see smoke or sparks, and you want to hear a power supply fan and the correct audio tones from the speaker. If anything looks or sounds wrong, turn off the computer.

There's not much else to do except to reverse all the installation steps and check and double-check everything you've done. Here are some common reasons why a new motherboard may not work:

- CPU not oriented properly in socket
- Improper settings on switches or jumpers
- Keyboard and mouse cables reversed
- Memory modules not properly seated in slots
- Power supply not properly connected to the board
- Traces on bottom of motherboard shorting out to case

Of course, it is also possible that you have received a bad motherboard, although dead-on-arrival boards are much less likely in these days of modern devices. Once again, though, this is a time when you will be very thankful to be dealing with a reputable vendor who offers technical assistance and/or replacement if necessary.

Working with Expansion Cards

In this section, you learn how to remove and install an expansion card.

CROSS-REFERENCE

I discuss how to remove the system cover in Chapter 1; review that section if you need to.

WARNING

Be sure to turn off the power and remove the power cord before going under the cover. And I recommend using a grounding strap or grounding pad.

Removing an expansion card

An expansion card becomes part of the computer through the bottom connector that plugs into the system-bus expansion slots on the motherboard. The connector picks up electrical power and ties into data communication lines through the slot.

On most systems, the card is held firmly in its slot by a bracket that attaches to the back wall of the system unit chassis with a single screw. In dinosaurs and some modern machines, the other end of the card slips into a plastic groove that holds it in place laterally; high-density integration has enabled modern expansion cards to become smaller and smaller, and today few cards extend all the way across the length or width of a motherboard.

On some modern machines, like the state-of-the-art model I examine in Chapter 6, the entire group of cards is held in place by a single arm that closes over the top of the devices and locks into place.

To remove an expansion card, begin by turning off the machine and disconnecting the power cord. Then remove any external cables connected to the port at the back of the computer.

On an older machine, take out the screw that attaches the card to the system unit chassis and set it aside in a safe place. Some people like to work with magnetized screwdrivers to help hold onto the screw; this is a good idea in theory, so long as you take care not to lay the screwdriver down on a floppy or hard disk drive. The magnetic power of the screwdriver is relatively low, but magnetism is the enemy of data stored on a disk.

Removing these cards doesn't take much force, but watch your fingers — the card bristles with prickly solder blobs and little metal legs. Put your fingers in comfortable places before lifting. It's also helpful to rock the card back and forth slightly from end to end — not side to side — to dislodge it from the slot.

Installing a new card to replace a bad card

Most of the time, the replacement card looks a lot like the card you take out of the system. Unless you are upgrading the machine with an adapter of greater functionality, you replace an 8-bit video card with another 8-bit video card, a 32-bit PCI card with another of the same standard, and so forth. (One modern difference: PCI Express cards come in several variants, depending on the number of serial "lanes" they require for communication. The slots are downwardly compatible: a PCI Express x1 card will fit into and work with an x16 slot, but an x16 card cannot fit into an x1 slot. A similar situation exists with the now-abandoned AGP slot for video cards, which were offered in 1X, 4X, and 8X versions.) Compare the bus connectors on the two cards. If they are the same, just slide the new card into the old card's expansion slot.

Carefully line up the card edge connector with the slot on the motherboard. If the card has external connectors for ports on the back, you may have to angle the card slightly to come under the lip of the PC chassis before you position it above the slots. Also, the bottom of the bracket may need to fit into a slot or past a metal lip that you can't see. Work gently. When the card is properly positioned over the slot, press down firmly, applying even pressure at front and back.

When the card is in place, the screw hole on the card lines up with the screw hole in the back of the chassis — that is the situation whether or not your case requires use of the screw; if you have a modern machine with a latch that clicks into place to hold cards, it is still necessary for the holes to align, even if no screw is installed, so that proper electrical contact is made.. Check the bottom of the card where it goes into the bus connector to make sure the card is fully inserted.

Reinstall the screw if your case requires, or lower the locking bracket. Replace the cover, reattach data and power cords, and test the machine.

Senior-citizen and dinosaur machines

VL and PCI bus designs are generally paired with a separate ISA bus. This enables you to use any ISA cards you want, reserving special high-speed adapters for the VL and PCI slots with their extra connectors.

If you have an ISA 16-bit expansion card, it will fit in either an AT-style ISA computer or an EISA computer.

EISA cards fit only in EISA motherboards, though ordinary 8-bit and 16-bit cards will fit in EISA motherboard connectors.

MCA cards fit in high-end PS/2 computers with the relatively obscure MCA bus. Use only MCA cards in MCA computers; nothing else fits.

If you are installing an 8-bit card with the short, single bus connector, any bus expansion slot in any of the clones will do. These 8-bit cards fit in XT clones, in 286/386/486/Pentium ISA computers, and in EISA computers. Don't worry about long versus short slots; if the board physically fits into the slot, it will work.

NOTE

Some slim-line PC designs call for adapter cards to be installed sideways into a riser card that comes up from the motherboard. The same principles apply to a board inserted into a riser card, except that you will be pushing in toward the center of the riser card instead of down to the motherboard itself. Sometimes it is easier to remove the riser board and install the cards, and then reinstall the riser.

Similarly, PCs using tower cases have the motherboard mounted vertically. With a tower case, it may be easier to turn the PC on its side to remove and install adapter cards.

Plug-and-Play

On some levels, the day when the PC began to move from a technically complex machine that required a high degree of skill and background by those who would repair and upgrade it, to a device closer to an appliance was the arrival of the Plug-and-Play concept in Windows 95 and 98. In theory, Plug-and-Play enables Windows to reach out and interrogate every piece of hardware within and without the system to determine its presence and its need of interrupts, DMA channels, port settings, and other elements of the PC.

Plug-and-Play works through the use of BIOS chips on hardware and a huge list of devices maintained by Windows. In theory, when you turn on your PC, Windows knows everything it needs to know about your system and is able to manage devices so that they do not conflict with each other. With each succeeding version of the operating system, aided and abetted by improvements to system BIOS and the intelligence added to new hardware, it becomes easier and easier to plug in and play a new adapter card to an internal bus, attach an external hard drive or pointing device to a port, or insert a for-the-moment flash memory drive or digital camera or music player into a USB port.

It works like this: the system identifies the presence of hardware that was installed since the last time it was started, or detects the insertion of a device into a hot-swappable port including USB, FireWire, and eSATA. (*Hot-swappable* ports are those that allow you to add or remove a device while the machine is running.)

The operating system will check to see if it already has a driver loaded to work with the new hardware. If it does not find one, it will ask you whether you have already downloaded a copy of the driver from a web site or an installation disk and placed it somewhere on the system. It will also ask if the driver is resident on a CD or DVD (or less commonly now, on a floppy disk) that it can access. The fourth option is to allow the PC to go out onto the Internet to search for the driver in Microsoft's vast library or visit a location you specify that is maintained by the hardware maker. Be sure to consult the instruction manual for new hardware to learn the manufacturer's suggested installation process.

And just for the record, before you permit an Apple fan to rant and rave about the supposed superiority of that system, remember that Apple was able to enforce its will because it was a closed architecture. Manufacturers were forced to comply with Apple's directives, which resulted in higher prices and limits on device availability. The open PC architecture, like most democracies, presented a wild, disorganized, and lively marketplace. It took nearly twenty years before (love them or hate them) Intel and Microsoft and some of their largest customers were able to put into place the various standards that enabled Plug-and-Play.

Modern machines working with current operating systems and hardware are almost certain, sometime between now and forever, to achieve the desired state when all the elements of your PC conform to the Plug-and-Play specification, and all will be well with the world. In the meantime, you can expect to have a mix of Plug-and-Play and old-style devices in your machine and on the market for years to come. Users will still have to configure non-Plug-and-Play devices manually and may even run into some conflicts with automatically set devices.

Each branch of the PC family uses slightly different techniques to tell the computer what parts are installed.

Setup and configuration memory

Nearly every modern machine uses a BIOS that allows the user to make system settings on a configuration screen.

On most machines, the bootup sequence displays a message to remind users how to load the Setup screen. Common choices include the Del key, one of the F (Function) keys, or a key combination such as Ctrl + Esc. If you are unsure of the necessary procedure, consult the instruction manual for your PC.

Most users will only make changes to the basic screen of Setup; be sure to read the instruction manual and consult help screens for assistance. I would suggest you make notes on any changes you make to the Setup so that you can undo them if they cause problems.

You also need to understand the method your particular style of Setup screen uses to record changes you have made. Some require you to press Esc and then a function key; others have a menu option to select to save changes. Be sure you understand the process or your changes may not be recorded.

Dinosaurs based around an ISA bus may use a Setup screen, a setup program run from a special floppy disk, DIP switches on the motherboard, or a combination of one or more of these means.

Early ATs and AT clones used a separate system setup disk. Running the system configuration software program (often called SETUP) lets the user edit the list of drives, memory type, display type, and so on in the CMOS chip. Because the CMOS chip is backed up with batteries, it remembers what hardware is installed in the computer, even when the power is off.

Several problems occurred when putting the setup program on the floppy disk. First of all, the disk could become lost or damaged. Second, the disk was useless if the setting that enabled the computer to recognize the presence of a floppy disk drive was damaged. The next step in the development of PC systems, then, was to put the setup program right into the ROM BIOS.

Before you make any changes to the Setup screen, make a copy of the settings and place it in the instruction manual for your computer. Some setup programs let you print the settings to a file that you can edit within a word processor, or print settings directly to an attached printer. If you can't obtain such an automatic copy, use a pen and piece of paper for the task.

Take care with the entries you make in the setup program; you shouldn't be able to damage your computer with a software setting, but some instructions could make things difficult. Pay special attention to the hard drive setting; enter the wrong hard disk type, and your hard disk and all its data will seem to disappear. It's still there somewhere, so don't panic — you have to correct the setting before the system can find the drive and its contents.

When in doubt, check your computer's instruction manual or call the manufacturer for more details on setup settings.

Power Supplies

The power supply is an electronic device that changes 115 volts of AC (alternating current) from the power line into 3.3, 5, and 12 volts of DC (direct current) for the components of the computer.

You have three important issues to consider when you buy a replacement or upgrade power supply: selecting the proper capacity, getting a good quality unit, and finding the proper shape and size for your case. Make sure to measure your power supply before ordering a replacement.

You can start with two important details: the form factor for the motherboard and an estimate of the minimum and maximum power demands you can expect. Most modern machines are based on either the ATX or the newer BTX form factor; a small portion of current machines is based on motherboard designs that are slightly or significantly different from those standards. An ATX power supply is, by definition, intended to fit within an ATX case and attach to ATX-standard connectors on the motherboard; a BTX power supply is designed for use with BTX boards and cases, but may be able to fit within certain ATX cases and plug into a converter that allows it to plug into an ATX board.

Reduced-size versions of ATX and BTX cases also are available. Dinosaurs used a variety of large power supply designs; the most common dinosaur style is classified as the PC/XT design.

Be sure to investigate carefully any power supply to make sure that it 1) fits in the allotted space and attaches to existing screw holes in the case, 2) has the proper set of power cables that match the needs of the motherboard and devices within the case that receive power directly from the power supply, and 3) provides sufficient power for the needs of the system. The power supply is located inside the computer case and easy enough to find — just look for a big shiny or black box with a fan and a power jack on the back. To remove a power supply, start by unplugging it from the wall and then disconnect each of the power connectors from the supply to the motherboard and internal devices. You might want to label each connector as you remove it to help when you install a new power supply. In most computer designs, the power supply is attached to the case by four screws that come through the rear panel. On some PCs, especially compact desktop units, you may need to remove some adapter cards or device cages to gain access to the power supply.

ATX and BTX supplies are turned on and off by a low-voltage signal from the motherboard that is connected to a button on the case.

Dinosaur PCs used a larger AT power supply which attached to the motherboard with two single-row power connectors. They include a line voltage cable that connects to a heavy-duty, on-off switch on the case or to a switch built into the power supply itself.

Nearly all PCs use off-the-shelf power supplies that can be replaced easily; a handful of models, though, use specially designed supplies that have to be ordered directly from the manufacturer or a parts warehouse.

If you are purchasing a replacement power supply for a high-end machine, make sure it is certified to work with the fastest CPUs that will be installed on the motherboard. The top end of Intel's Pentium 4 series required as much as 225 watts of power; the newer Intel Core 2 Duo processors deliver more processing speed at lower power demands, down around 90 watts. AMD has gone through the same experience, moving toward lower-demand CPUs in its most modern processors.

Following is a description of the most common power supplies in use in modern machines. A small number of PCs uses power supplies of an unusual design or specification; to replace them you will have to contact the PC's manufacturer or search for components from specialty suppliers. The following are the most commonly used power supply designs for modern machines:

- **ATX:** Introduced in 1997. Power is delivered to the motherboard through a single 20-pin connector with a second 4-pin connector specifically for the use of the CPU added in more modern machines. Additional power cables go directly to disk drives, fans, and certain other internal devices; in the most modern of machines, special connectors intended for use with internal SATA devices have been added. Dimensions: $5.9 \times 5.5 \times 3.4$ inches. Power output: $+/- 12v$, $+/- 5v$, $+ 3.3v$.
- **BTX:** Introduced in 2004, arriving in large numbers in 2006. Power is delivered to the motherboard through a single 24-pin connector, and there also is a set of power cables for disk drives, fans, and certain other internal devices. As a newer standard, support for internal SATA devices is common. Most BTX power supplies have the same physical dimensions as ATX devices.

Micro- and mini-versions of ATX and BTX are used in some special-purpose machines. Here are some dinosaur and less commonly used modern designs:

- **SFX:** Introduced in 1999 for some low-profile and all-in-one systems. Power is delivered to the motherboard through a single 20-pin connector. Versions include ones with AC receptacle on the short side (more common) as well as on the long side (used by manufacturers including Hewlett Packard and eMachines for some of their models). Dimensions: 3.9 × 4.9 × 3.0 inches. Power output: +/– 12v, +5v, +3.3v.
- **WTX:** Introduced in 2002 for high-end workstations and servers in tower cases. Power is delivered to a WTX connector on WTX motherboards. Dimensions 6 × 9.2 × 3.4 for single-fan units, and 9 × 9.2 × 3.4 inches for dual-fan units. Power output: +12v, +5v, +3.3v.
- **AT:** Full-size units, used from about 1991 to 1999. Power was delivered to the motherboard with two six-pin connectors. Dimension: 8.35 × 5.9 × 5.9 inches. Power output: +/– 12v, +/– 5v.
- **AT:** Slim-size units, used from about 1994 to 1999. Power was delivered to the motherboard with two 6-pin connectors. Dimensions: 5.9 × 5.5 × 3.4 inches. Power output: +/– 12v, +/– 5v.

How the power supply works (ATX and BTX modern motherboards)

The power supply has a very simple job: to provide clean, smooth power at particular voltages and of sufficient wattage. In the simplest of terms, voltage is the strength of the current and wattage of power delivered. Most physics teachers try to explain this in terms of a pipe carrying water: the voltage would be the rate of flow in the pipe and the current would be the amount of water delivered in a particular period of time. Wattage is the product of voltage and current (12 Volts × 1 Ampere = 12 Watts).

Within modern machines, the demand is for +12 volts DC, –12 volts DC, +5 volts DC, –5 volts DC, and +3.3 volts DC.

It monitors its own power output on startup and sends a power-good signal to the motherboard when the voltages have stabilized at their required levels. The microprocessor resets, and bootup starts when the motherboard receives this signal.

Power supplies are rated by the wattage they support — the higher the wattage, the more peripherals the unit can support. Modern machines typically have a power supply rated at least 200 watts, with 250- and 300- or even 400-watt units increasingly common. Dinosaur PCs had power supplies as small as 65 watts

Most supplies you'll find on the market today use a technology called "switching," which enables the power supply to only draw what is needed. If your PC needs 250 watts, a 400-watt switching power supply will only match the draw. Switching power supplies use electronic circuitry to change voltage from 120 down to 12 or 5 or 3. Older technology used heavy metal transformers to achieve this voltage change, which resulted in heavier and larger power supplies for a given power rating.

WARNING

The electronics inside the power supply are not reparable by amateurs and are usually not worth the expense of a professional repair. A new power supply usually sells for $25 to $50. Do not open the power supply itself.

Modern machines can work with an astonishing variety of devices, and you may find that you have run out of power connectors running off the power supply. Assuming you have enough available power to handle startup power for hard drives and CD or DVD drives, you can use a power cable splitter that connects to a power lead at one end and branches into two available connectors. Within the PC itself, a typical modern CPU demands as little as 50 watts and as much as 225 watts, depending on its speed and design; the newest processors have dropped down a bit to the range of about 90 to 100 watts. A typical high-speed hard drive or CD-ROM uses 20 to 30 watts when it is in full operation, and less when it is powered-on but is not being accessed. Other plug-in devices, such as internal modems and adapters, may ask for 5 to 10 watts apiece. A large bank of RAM may need about that much power as well. A sampling of the power demands of modern common PC components is in Table 5-6.

TABLE 5-6: Power Demands of Modern PC Parts

Component	Wattage	Lines Used
Motherboard (without CPU or RAM)	50 to 100	+3.3V and +5V
CPUs (higher speed generally are higher draw)	10 to 225	+5V or +12V
RAM	15 per GB	+3.3V
Typical PCI or PCI Express adapter card	5 to 25	+5V
High-wattage AGP video card	30 to 50	+3.3V
PCI Express video card	100 to 225	
Ethernet 10/100 NIC card	4	+5V
Floppy drive	5	+5V
CD or DVD drive (higher speeds generally are higher draw)	20 to 30	+5V and +12V
Hard disk drive	15 to 30	+5V and +12V
Case and CPU fans	3 (each)	+12V

Depending on its components, a typical modern machine may draw a total of 90 to 200 watts; high-end machines with fast processors, large blocks of memory, several drives, and other devices may draw as much as 400 watts. The sample machine I write about in Chapter 6, a thoroughly modern PC based around the relatively low-power Intel Core 2 Duo processor, comes equipped with a 375-watt power supply.

To calculate the proper specifications for a power supply, add up the wattage demands of all of the devices in the machine and those you can reasonably expect to add during its life. Then add a cushion of at least 50 percent — some advise as much as 80 to 100 percent — to account for disproportionate demands on the 12-volt output for electrical motors in disk drives, and to allow for varying requirements from devices attached to the USB or FireWire chain on a modern machine. Finally, a power supply generally operates most efficiently and has the longest life when its consistent load amounts to no more than about 70 percent of its capacity.

Check the specifications for any device you have installed in your machine. Most list the number of watts they require. You may see some devices that tell you amperage and voltage requirements instead; to convert to watts, multiply the voltage by the amps.

Your electric company charges on the basis of kilowatt hours, a measurement equal to 1,000 watts over the course of an hour. Rates vary around the country, and bills include a number of components including generation, transmission, distribution, and taxes. To obtain a rough idea of your average cost per kilowatt, divide your total monthly bill by the number of kilowatt hours used that month.

In my office, electricity costs in early 2007 worked out to about 16 cents per kilowatt hour. That means it costs 16 cents to keep ten hundred-watt light bulbs lit for an hour, or about 8 cents to run one of my computers and a monitor for the same period.

That sounds like a great bargain, and it probably is, but the pennies can add up quickly. I figure my main computer draws just under a kilowatt hour each hour it is in use — for the PC, a large monitor, a laser printer, lighting, and necessary musical accompaniment. That's about 16 cents per hour. The machines are on at least ten hours a day, an average of six days a week: that's just under $10 per week, or about $500 per year for electricity. Consider that a high-end new PC sells for about $1,000 and you'll see you are spending a good portion of the cost of a PC for power.

Most modern PCs support Advanced Power Management (APM) or the Advanced Configuration and Power Interface (ACPI). Check the instruction manual for your PC to learn about settings that allow you to manage the power use of your machine.

The biggest possible savings is a setting that powers your monitor down after a reasonable period of inactivity; the monitor can come back to life in a few seconds but in the meantime you can save a few kilowatt hours each week during your coffee breaks, lunch, and meetings.

ATX and BTX power supplies

Standard assignments for the various connectors of an ATX power supply (and the similar BTX supply) are shown in Tables 5-7 through 5-11. Actual wire colors may vary slightly, but the pin assignments are fixed.

The ATX specification added 3.3-volt output to the demands on the power supply. The ATX connection to the motherboard uses a single 20-pin connector plus a 4-pin 12-volt connector for the needs of the CPU. The BTX connection uses a single 24-pin connector. A typical ATX power supply, like the one shown in Figure 5-14, also includes six peripheral power connectors, two floppy drive connectors, one auxiliary power connector, and one 12-volt connector. The

Ch
5

most modern of ATX supplies and most BTX supplies also add several connectors for the use of the downsized power attachment point on an internal SATA drive.

TABLE 5-7: Connector to Motherboard Wire Assignments from ATX and BTX Power Supplies

Pin	Wire Color	Function	Pin	Wire Color	Function
1	Orange	+3.3V DC	11	Orange	+3.3V DC
2	Orange	+3.3V DC	12	Brown	−12V DC
3	Black	Ground	13	Black	Ground
4	Red	+5V DC	14	Green	PS On for remote start
5	Black	Ground	15	Black	Ground
6	Red	+5V DC	16	Black	Ground
7	Black	Ground	17	Black	Ground
8	White	Power Good	18	Blue	−5V DC
9	Purple	+5VSB	19	Red	+5V DC
10	Yellow	+12V DC	20	Red	+5V DC

Note: Connector is MOLEX 39-01-2200 or equivalent.

TABLE 5-8: Peripheral Connectors from ATX or BTX Power Supplies

Pin	Wire Color	Function
1	Yellow	+12V DC
2	Black	Ground
3	Black	Ground
4	Red	+5V DC

Note: Connector is AMP 1-480424-0 or equivalent.

TABLE 5-9: Floppy Drive Connectors from ATX Power Supply

Pin	Wire Color	Function
1	Red	+5V DC
2	Black	Ground
3	Black	Ground
4	Yellow	+12V DC

Note: Connector is AMP 171822-4 or equivalent.

TABLE 5-10: Auxiliary Power Connectors from ATX or BTX Power Supplies

Pin	Wire Color	Function
1	Red	+5V DC
2	Black	Ground
3	Black	Ground
4	Yellow	+12V DC

Note: Connector is MOLEX 90331-0010 or equivalent.

TABLE 5-11: 12V CPU Power Connector from ATX and BTX Power Supplies

ATX Supply (Separate 4-pin connector)

Pin	Wire Color	Function
1	Black	Ground
2	Black	Ground
3	Yellow	+12V DC
4	Yellow	+12V DC

BTX Supply Integrated into 24-pin motherboard connector

Pin	Wire Color	Function
1	Yellow	+12V DC
2	Black	Ground
3	Black	Ground
4	Yellow	+12V DC

FIGURE 5-14: *An ATX form factor power supply.*

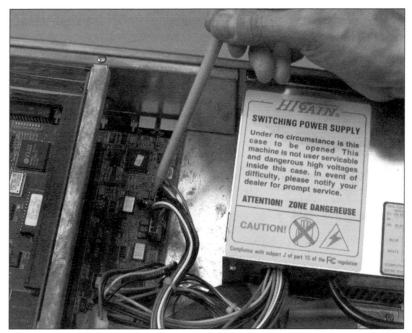

FIGURE 5-15: *On many motherboards, a pair of power supply connectors, marked P8 and P9, provide all the power for the CPU, logic chips, and devices plugged into the bus.*

AT power supplies

PC/XT and AT power supplies have two large six-pin power connectors marked P8 and P9, shown in Figure 5-15, that send voltage to the motherboard. On most such systems, the two connectors attach to a single attachment point, with the black wires on each connector next to each other. There are also five or six smaller connectors that are intended for internal devices such as floppy, hard, and CD-ROM drives. The larger power connectors (see Figures 5-16 and 5-17) generally are used by hard drives and CD-ROMs, and the miniplugs are used by 3.5-inch floppy drives. No matter what the size of the connector, the voltage level and type are the same.

If you find a mismatch between power connector and receptacle, you can purchase converter plugs that change a large connector to a small one, as shown in Figure 5-18.

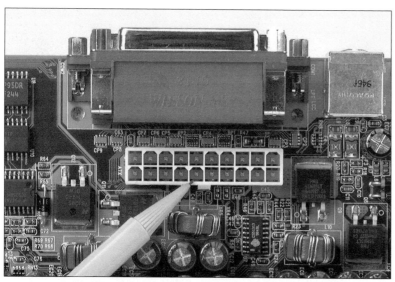

FIGURE 5-16: *On ATX form motherboards, a single ATX Power connector links the board to the power supply.*

FIGURE 5-17: *A four-wire power supply connector has beveled edges that keep it properly oriented. The yellow wire is +12 volts, the two black wires are ground, and the red wire is +5 volts.*

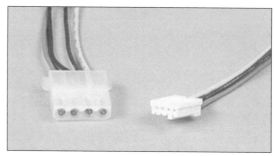

FIGURE 5-18: *Some dinosaurs and other machines may need an adapter to convert a standard power lead to work with a 3.5-inch floppy drive or other modern device that requires the new, miniaturized plug.*

Similarly, you can connect more than one device to a single power cable with the use of a Y-splitter, such as the one shown in Figure 5-19.

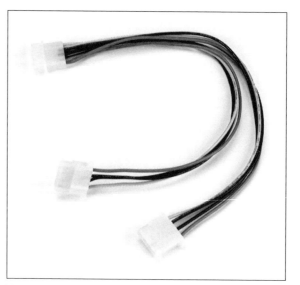

FIGURE 5-19: *A Y-splitter lets you send electricity to two devices using a single lead from the power supply.*

Another power-cable variant splits off a miniconnector to power a small device such as a CPU fan. An example is shown in Figure 5-20.

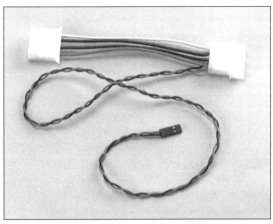

FIGURE 5-20: *This power cable includes a split-off to power a small electrical device such as a fan or power-on indicator light.*

Tables 5-12, 5-13, and 5-14 list the assignments for the wires from a standard AT power supply.

TABLE 5-12: Device Connector Wire Assignments for AT Power Supply

Pin	Wire Color	Function
1	Yellow	+12V DC
2	Black	Ground
3	Black	Ground
4	Red	+5V DC

TABLE 5-13: P8 Connector to Motherboard Wire Assignments for AT Power Supply

Pin	Wire Color	Function
1	Orange or White	Power good signal
2	Red	+5V DC
3	Yellow	+12V DC
4	Blue or Brown	−12V DC
5	Black	Ground
6	Black	Ground

TABLE 5-14: P9 Connector to Motherboard Wire Assignments for AT Power Supply

Pin	Wire Color	Function
1	Black	Ground
2	Black	Ground
3	Blue or White	−5V DC
4	Red	+5V DC
5	Red	+5V DC
6	Red	+5V DC

NOTE

An essential component of any PC system is a high-quality surge protector that stands between the computer and the wall outlet. The surge protector should meet Underwriters Laboratories' UL 1449 standard, with a rated response time of no more than 1 nanosecond. If you use an uninterruptible power supply, that unit should include surge protection as part of its design.

Testing the power supply

Loss of CMOS setup in modern machines is often caused by a bad power supply.

On a typical system, the CMOS chip requires at least 4.5 volts to hold the configuration setup information (date, time, and installed hardware) reliably. It is powered by batteries whenever the computer is turned off. When the 5-volt line climbs above 5 volts, or the power-good line to the motherboard is on, the CMOS battery backup disengages. If a defective power supply sends the power-good signal before the 5-volt line is high enough, the setup information is lost. Be sure to check the batteries first. They tend to wear out after a year of service. If you replace the batteries and run the CMOS setup routine, but the problem still remains, then you probably have a faulty power supply.

Power supplies are not serviceable in the field. Besides, replacements are cheap. If your power supply is not performing correctly, do not attempt to repair it — just throw it away. New power supplies range in price from about $25 to $50. Nearly all power supplies come from obscure Asian manufacturers; I'd pay more attention to the warranty claims of the store or mail-order house than to any brand name for the power supply.

You can easily test the voltages produced by your power supply with a handheld voltmeter. To do this, you must hook the power supply up to 115 volts and to a load of some kind — a disk drive or the motherboard will do. The four-wire connectors are identical, so you can use any one of them to test your power supply while it is hooked into the computer. This is probably the best way to test the power supply because it should perform properly when fully loaded with all add-on boards, drives, and other such devices. You're looking for + 5, −5, + 12, and −12 volts.

 NOTE

If the DC voltages are low, consider the external circumstances before condemning the power supply. It's smart to test the AC line voltage. The minimum acceptable standard is 104 volts AC. If your power is marginal, I recommend you purchase an uninterruptible power supply or a power line conditioner. In fact, an UPS is a smart addition to your computer setup in any case, since it will bridge an unplanned power outage and allow you to shut down your computer in an orderly manner.

Unfortunately, power supplies occasionally fail for only a microsecond, perhaps on bootup or during drive access. In addition, a defective unit may send the power-good signal prematurely, causing the microprocessor to reset while voltages are unstable. Premature reset can cause a problem in almost any part of the computer because random errors may be introduced any place in memory. If you turn the computer power switch off and on again, the same problem may recur, or a different one, or no problem at all, may occur. The ordinary voltmeter does not respond rapidly enough to catch a momentary dip or surge in power. In this case, substitute a known good power supply and retest the machine to confirm the bad power supply diagnosis.

Occasionally, one of the four-wire power connectors fails while the others remain functional. If you suspect a problem with one of the four-wire connectors — because disk drive B: doesn't function at all, for instance — you can try switching the suspect power connector with the known good one from the A: drive. If you establish a four-wire connector as the problem, you can try rewiring a new connector; don't go under the covers of the power supply, though.

Removing and replacing the power supply

Before you remove the power supply, unplug the 110-volt power cord and disconnect the four-wire power supply connectors from disk drives, tape drives, and other devices.

The motherboard receives power from a single long connector or from two multiwire connectors. Examine these connectors closely before removing them and place labels on them to help with reinstallation. They must be reinstalled properly. If you jam the connectors on backward and turn on the computer, you will damage the motherboard.

Typically, you remove four screws that hold the power supply to the back panel of the chassis. With some designs, you need to slide the power supply forward an inch or two to clear the lugs on the bottom of the case and lift it up out of the case.

To install a power supply, perform the steps in reverse order. Make sure you reinstall the power connectors on the motherboard correctly.

Cooling the System

It's a basic law of physics: The faster those electrons zip around within the microprocessor, the more heat they generate. The heat is caused by the friction between the electrical current and the pathways it travels.

The dinosaurs were poky enough so that the little heat they generated could be removed by the flow of air generated by a single fan at the back of the power supply. Air was drawn in through holes at the front of the case and exhausted at the rear.

That solution was good enough for CPUs running from the original 4.77 MHz through the approximate 66 MHz speed of the venerable 486DX2 senior citizen.

But with the arrival of microprocessors faster than 100 MHz, the buildup of heat threatened the life of the microprocessor and other components. There are three solutions to the heat buildup problem:

- Installation of a heat sink atop the CPU. This passive solution uses a vaned metallic device that draws heat up and away from the chip and into the air stream of the system's fan.
- Addition of a powered fan that sits atop the CPU. This fan draws heat away from the chip. In some cases, the fan is combined with a heat sink. Examples of CPU fans are shown in Figures 5-21, 5-22, and 5-23.

■ Increased system cooling. Modern machine cases can include an additional fan at the front of the case as well as a rear-facing fan at the power supply and a chip-top fan.

FIGURE 5-21: *An external fan/heat sink attaches to the outside of the Pentium II/III SECC cartridge. On most motherboards, a supporting bracket is then connected from the cartridge to the motherboard to lock the CPU in place. An electrical connector powers the fan from a header on the motherboard.*

Up through the arrival of systems based on ATX motherboards, most PCs performed their cooling by drawing room air *into* the case at one end and pushing it out another. One large fan was often sufficient to move air through the system. The disadvantage of this design, though, was that dust, smoke, and other particles were drawn into the machine.

The original design for ATX motherboards continued the use of an *inflow* cooling system, but in recent years designers have turned around the fans so that they push air out of vents at the power supply or elsewhere. Faster — and hotter — systems typically include several fans. Modern ATX systems also typically include a cowling with an integrated fan that sits over the top of the CPU.

Your best defense against heat buildup is to select a properly designed case and to follow the chip manufacturer's recommendations on supplementary cooling.

 CROSS-REFERENCE

I discuss the advanced cooling system of a modern BTX motherboard in Chapter 6.

FIGURE 5-22: *This Pentium 133 CPU uses a clip-on cooling fan.*

In one of the machines I built for my office, I added a SIIG DiskFan, shown in Figure 5-24. It installs in a 3.5-inch disk bay and exhausts air from the front midsection of the tower case.

Yet another type of cooling exhausts air through the rear of the computer. An example is SIIG's AirCooler Pro, a dual-exhaust slot fan shown in Figure 5-25. This device attaches to one of the brackets intended to hold an adapter card in the bus; a nonconductive plastic support holds the device in place while an electrical cable connects to the power supply within the case. The two fans on the AirCooler Pro can be extended a few inches into the case and their heads individually directed toward sources of heat; air is exhausted through holes in the bracket at the rear. (Of course, you do need to have an unused Industry Standard Architecture [ISA] or Peripheral Component Interconnect [PCI] slot to hold a fan like this.)

If you're a belt-and-suspenders type, you can add a third level of fan to most cases. Some designs come with brackets and vents on the front of the case enabling installation of a fan to supplement the device on the CPU itself and in the power supply. An example of a case of this design is shown in Figure 5-26.

FIGURE 5-24: *This fan installs in a 3.5-inch disk-drive bay to remove heat buildup from within the case; it receives power from a connector within. The manufacturer recommends installing the fan above the floppy and hard drives to draw off the rising heat from those devices.*

FIGURE 5-23: *On this modern Pentium 4 1.8-GHz system, the CPU and its associated chipset sit beneath a massive heat sink that is in turn covered by a plastic sheath that leads to a fan that exhausts air out of the case.*

If you choose to add another fan to the front of a case, be sure to purchase a quality device that won't add a lot of noise to the system. Any device at the front of the case is usually aimed at the user, and most PCs are already noisy enough. Figure 5-27 shows a lightweight and quiet brushless fan in a plastic housing.

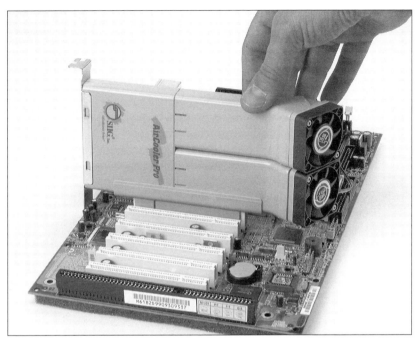

FIGURE 5-25: *The unusual AirCooler Pro's two fans can be aimed at sources of heat within the case; air is exhausted through the rear of the computer. The fan sits atop an ISA or PCI slot. You can also purchase simpler single-fan devices that also attach to slot brackets.*

FIGURE 5-26: *The bare innards of an ATX mid-tower case. The thicket of power cords connects to the motherboard, drives, and other devices that will take up residence within. The capacious case includes bays for four 3.5-inch devices and three 5.25-inch devices. Note the opening for an additional cooling fan at the front of the case.*

Many current motherboards make use of the facilities of the latest Intel chipsets to monitor the condition of the hardware, including a thermistor to check internal temperature of the case and the microprocessor. The system can also control the speed of the chassis fan and other devices to increase cooling when necessary.

For older systems that lack such facilities, you can use separate temperature monitoring devices. One such device is PC Power and Cooling's 110 Alert, an inexpensive piece of equipment that sounds an alarm if the PC's internal temperature rises above 110 degrees Fahrenheit, or alerts you when your CPU fan falters. For information, consult www.pcpowercooling.com.

Ch
5

FIGURE 5-27: *This exhaust fan mounts in available brackets at the front of some PC case designs. It draws power from any power connector.*

Matching Cables and Connectors

I can't begin to tell you how many times I have been faced with a mismatch of cable and connector — the wrong size or shape, an incorrect number of pins, the wrong gender (no offense intended, but a male plug and a male connector won't mate any better than a pair of females).

Before you begin a repair or upgrade project, analyze what you've got at each end: at the connector on the motherboard and at the connector on the device. Here's a step-by-step procedure:

1. Begin by counting the number of pins or holes.
2. Determine the gender you need for both ends of the cable; you need a male plug to mate with a female connector, for example.
3. Study the layout of the pins or holes — 5 over 4 or 34 over 34.
4. Examine the shape of the connector to choose the correct family of hardware from among tiny DIN or RJ plugs, mid-sized DB, and generally larger Centronics designs. (Other families exist.)
5. If you find a mismatch in gender or in size or shape of connector, you have two choices: obtain the proper cable to match your needs, or buy a converter that changes genders or plug design. Check carefully to make sure that any converter or replacement cable meets both the physical (size, shape, and gender) needs of the connection and the electrical requirements (the proper pins have to connect through from one connector to the other.) When in doubt, consult the manufacturer of the device for suggestions on conversion hardware.

CROSS-REFERENCE

Somebody needs to write a book someday . . . an encyclopedia of computer cables and connectors. Until then, Appendix F on the CD is a partial collection selected from the hundreds of pieces of standard and nonstandard hardware out there.

Looking Closely at Modern Motherboards

If you were to browse the virtual shelves of a computer supply store today, you'd find dozens if not hundreds of various modern motherboards for sale; each has a particular technical or price advantage. Do you want a board built for use with an Intel or an AMD processor, for example? (A few years back, the choice of CPU manufacturers was broader, but today these two makers own nearly the entire market for consumer PCs. Even Apple Computer has changed over from its longtime Motorola source to use chips made by Intel; a side benefit of that switchover is easier adoption of Windows as a secondary or even primary operating system on Apple hardware.)

Do you want a state-of-the-art BTX motherboard, or will a modern ATX model suit your needs? What about adoption of SATA controllers for use with hard drives and CD or DVD drives, or will older PATA (ATA/IDE) controllers suffice? Which bus system would you prefer: PCI with an AGP slot for a video card, or the newer PCI Express in combination with a set of PCI slots for legacy devices?

The number of combinations of features is almost without limit. And it is for that reason that you should learn how to read the specifications for the motherboard of a new machine you are purchasing from a manufacturer, understand the makeup of the board in a machine you already own, and be able to appraise the capabilities of a replacement or upgrade board you might buy.

In this section I give an overview of five modern motherboards: one state-of-the-art BTX motherboard (the circuit board used in our sample modern machine in Chapter 6) and four older but still capable motherboards that are used in machines still in active use in offices and homes.

Dell motherboard for Intel Core 2 Duo processors

The state-of-the-art motherboard used for the midrange Dell Dimension 9200 machine profiled in Chapter 6 incorporates dozens of improvements large and small when compared to its cousins of just a few years before. It all begins with the adoption of the BTX form factor which reorganizes electronic parts to improve cooling of high-speed (and heat-generating) components.

To begin with, the BTX design moves the hottest components toward the "front" of the motherboard and directly in the path of a large fan that draws in outside air and moves it through the box to vents at the rear. Dell's design places a large 120mm fan (about 4.7 inches in diameter) fan at the front and a second, smaller fan within a cowling that covers the microprocessor; both are monitored by temperature probes that can instruct the processor to speed up the revolutions when needed or step them down when all is cool.

The motherboard includes three PCI Express slots, in x1, x4, and x16 versions; they vary in capacity by the number of *serial* lanes it has available for communication with the processor. For compatibility with older adapter cards, it also offers a trio of PCI slots. No longer offered is an AGP slot for a video card; graphics card makers are instead offering their fastest devices for use in the PCI Express x16 slot.

FIGURE 5-28: *The Dell Dimension 9200 revealed. The simplified BTX form factor motherboard depends on all-purpose SATA and USB connectors, marking the next generation of systems moving away from parallel data pathways.*

Also part of the migration to ultra-fast serial communication is the adoption of SATA (Serial ATA) pathways for the use of storage devices. The Dell motherboard includes six internal SATA connectors for the use of hard drives, CD or DVD drives, and other devices. SATA replaced the long-used technology of IDE or ATA, now renamed as Parallel ATA or PATA; if you need to maintain compatibility with an older device you can add PATA connectors by making use of one of the PCI slots or you can add a special converter to the connector on the drive that allows it to work with an incoming SATA signal.

Yet another serial pathway is offered with an internal USB connector that Dell intends to be used with "FlexBay" devices installed in bays at the top of the case; typical uses would be for a floppy disk drive or a flash memory media reader for use with digital cameras or digital music players.

Dell also offers a floppy drive connector for use with an old-style drive of that type, and a connector that paired with a cable and bracket to add a PS/2 and serial connector for use with older devices including keyboards, mice, and controllers designed before the advent of the all-purpose USB port.

Finally, there are four memory module connectors that can be filled (in matched pairs) by SDRAM DIMMs.

This motherboard is likely to serve as a bridge between "older" modern technologies and newer ones. Within a few years, we can expect to see the disappearance of superfluous appendages including the floppy drive connector, the PS/2 and serial connector, and eventually the end of the PCI slots in favor of additional PCI Express replacements.

 CROSS-REFERENCE

In Chapter 6, I discuss in more detail some of the specific features of the Intel-made BTX motherboard employed in the test modern machine dissected in this edition of this book.

Intel D850MD motherboard for Pentium 4 with RDRAM memory

Intel's motherboards are, by definition, fully compatible with Intel's microprocessors. The D850MD board was designed as the third element of a matched set, along with the Pentium 4 processor and its supporting Intel 850 chipset.

This board is used by a number of PC manufacturers, including Dell Computer; you can read more about the board in the discussion of the older but still modern Dell Pentium 4 1.8-GHz system we examine in detail in Chapter 6.

The compact board, in the Micro ATX form factor, uses a 478 Pin Grid Array (PGA) socket for Pentium 4 CPUs running at 1.4 GHz and faster. The AGP connector supports the 2X and 4X specifications for high-speed graphics cards. There are just three dedicated PCI connectors, each supporting bus-mastering. And there is one optional Communication and Networking Riser (CNR) connector.

Intel also offers a full-size ATX version of the board, with five PCI slots; in Dell's system, the company attaches a small daughterboard to the end of the mainboard to add two more PCI slots for a total of five.

The basic board, shown in Figure 5-46, is a neatly designed and tightly integrated device.

Intel's 850 chipset mates the Pentium 4's 3.2-gigabytes-per-second bus to 3.2-gigabytes-per-second of memory bandwidth using Dual RDRAM to eliminate memory bottlenecks that would have negatively impacted system efficiency. The two RDRAM channels support up to two RIMMs per channel, four RIMM sockets in total. The system can support memory configurations from a minimum of 128MB to a maximum of 2GB, utilizing 128 Mb or 256 Mb technology and PC600- and PC800-compliant RDRAM RIMMs.

Other features include Intel Rapid BIOS Boot to accelerate the power-on self test (POST), Ultra ATA/100 disk support, support for as many as seven USB ports, AC'97 integrated audio, and an optional Integrated Intel PRO/100 Network Connection. The 4MB flash Intel/AMI BIOS features Plug-and-Play, IDE drive auto-configuration, Advanced Power Management (APM) 1.2, ACPI 1.0, DMI 2.0, and Multilingual support.

The board sends signals to four diagnostic lights on the back of the computer; each light can be yellow, green, or off. The BIOS uses the lights to display ten diagnostic codes that report on the progress of the POST at bootup of the system.

Intel and other makers also produce similar boards based on the Intel 845 chipset, which works with conventional PC133 SDRAM. The 845 chipset, released in mid-2001, was a tacit acknowledgement by Intel that some buyers were resisting upgrading to the Pentium 4 because of its original linkage to RDRAM memory, which is more expensive than SDRAM and was somewhat problematic when it was first released.

FIGURE 5-29: *The Intel D850MD motherboard is a Micro ATX design. To the left of the three white PCI slots is a horizontal connector that can be used to extend to a daughterboard; in the Dimension 8200 computer we examine in Chapter 6, Dell adds two more PCI slots. The four RDRAM memory slots sit below the CPU socket; all four must be populated with RAM or with empty continuity modules.*

FIGURE 5-30: *The Asus motherboard is a compact baby AT, about 9 by 10 inches in size. The zero insertion force Socket 7 includes a thermal sensor below the chip to monitor heat buildup. A flash upgradeable Award BIOS lies to the left of the PCI slots.*

Ch 5

Asus P5S-B Super7 motherboard for Pentium-class processors

The Asus P5S-B, shown in Figures 5-30 through 5-34, is a good candidate to replace an older and less advanced motherboard for Pentium-class CPUs and clones, including Intel Pentium, AMD K5, AMD K6, and IBM/Cyrix 6x86MMX processors. It brings AGP video, ATA/66 IDE connections, and PC100 memory support, all features that were not available when Pentium processors were first introduced.

Ch
5

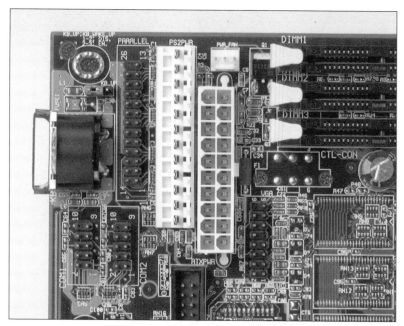

FIGURE 5-31: *The board can be installed in a tiny pizza box system, an AT case, or an ATX case. The AT and ATX cases use different specifications for power supplies and cables. The motherboard includes an old-form AT electrical connector alongside a newer ATX connector.*

FIGURE 5-32: *Beneath the heat sink on this board is an SiS AGPset, a chipset that includes an AGP 2X video adapter; it is set up to use shared system memory. An optional version of the motherboard includes 8MB of SDRAM as local graphics memory, freeing up system resources that would be taken by a shared memory video scheme.*

FIGURE 5-33: *There's a tight fit for cables to attach to the two IDE connectors that sit in the shadow to the right of the last two PCI slots.*

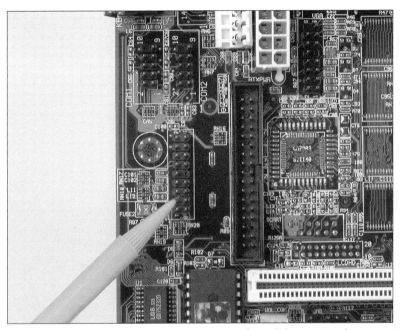

FIGURE 5-34: *To use a PS/2 mouse, USB, or infrared devices on the Asus P5S, you need to purchase and install an optional USB/MIR connector, which attaches to an 18-pin block on the motherboard.*

Ch
5

Micro-Star MS-6182 for Intel Pentium II/III and Celeron processors

A highly evolved model that arrived near the end of the dinosaur era, the Micro-Star MS-6182, shown in Figures 5-35 through 5-40, is an example of a highly integrated motherboard based around Intel's 810 Integrated Graphics chipset, featuring a built-in graphics adapter and a sound chip with multimedia inputs and outputs. For many users, there's not much more to add to this board other than a CPU and memory.

FIGURE 5-36: *The MS-6182 motherboard includes a bank of four LEDs alongside the CPU that report the various startup phases of the motherboard in sequence. Each light can glow red or green, giving a total of 16 possible messages. If the system hangs up, you can examine lights to determine where the motherboard has run into trouble. This is a particularly valuable feature on a motherboard that is so highly integrated. If, for example, the onboard video subsystem fails, you should be able to install a plug-in card in the bus to work around the problem.*

FIGURE 5-35: *The Micro-Star MS-6182 includes most of the elements of a modern machine on the motherboard, including a graphics adapter and audio subsystem. The manager for the system is Intel's 810 chipset, visible in the top center under a large heat sink between Slot 1 for the CPU and the three DIMM slots for memory.*

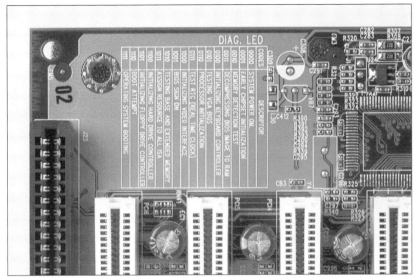

FIGURE 5-37: *Micro-Star lists the meanings of the LED codes right on the motherboard.*

The Intel 810 chipset includes three core components: the graphics and memory controller hub (GMCH), the I/O controller hub (ICHO/ICH), and the firmware hub (FWH).

The GMCH manages the system bus (66 or 100 MHz), a 100 MHz SDRAM controller, and a 2D/3D graphics accelerator.

The ICHO/ICH manages an Ultra ATA/33 and Ultra ATA/66 controller for disk drives, a USB host controller, and the PCI controller.

The FWH implements Intel's 82802 firmware hub for future security and management tasks.

FIGURE 5-38: *The 810 chipset on the MS-6182 supports Intel's definition for an audio/modem riser (AMR), intended to hold advanced audio daughterboards and modems that can link directly to the processor. The integrated Audio Codec '97 will enable developers to use the host processor for basic sound facilities. To the right of the AMR on Micro-Star's motherboard is another slot, the panel link/TV-out Interface designed to work with proprietary multimedia adapters. The Micro-Star motherboard is also available with a Creative Labs sound chip, which offers advanced features including wave-table audio; you can also plug a sound card into one of the PCI slots to expand beyond the basic facilities of the board as delivered.*

Ch
5

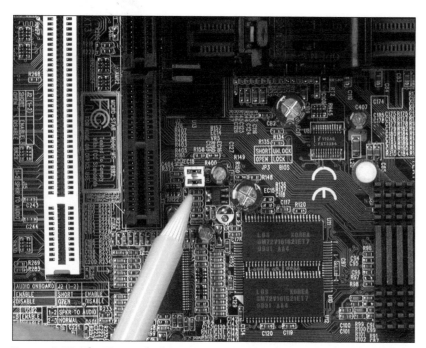

Figure 5-39: *The J2 overclocking jumper on the Micro-Star motherboard is set to detect automatically the proper bus frequency for the CPU. Changing the shorting blocks enables you to force the CPU to operate at 133 MHz, beyond the recommended speed. Many techies happily do so, but Intel and motherboard makers warn that overclocking could result in damage to the CPU and other components.*

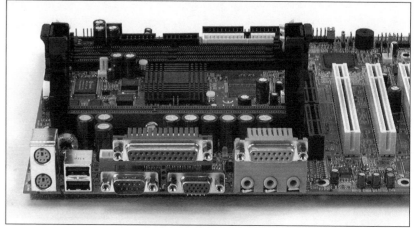

Figure 5-40: *The ATX format motherboard includes a full suite of input and output ports. From the top to bottom, they include a stacked pair with a mouse connector above the keyboard port; two USB ports; a parallel port above a VGA video connector; and a multimedia panel with a midi/game port, line out, line in, and microphone connector. A set of pins on the opposite side of the board can be used to connect a cable that runs to a USB connector on the front of some PC cases.*

Abit BE6-II motherboard for Intel Pentium II, III, and Celeron processors

The Abit BE6-II, shown in Figures 5-41 through 5-46, was near the end of the evolution of motherboards for Pentium II, III, and Celeron CPUs. Built around Intel's 440BX chipset, it offers an AGP video slot, USB ports, five PCI and one ISA slot, and four IDE connectors.

Abit's BIOS includes CPU Soft Menu III, a technology that lets the user configure most of the board's settings from a menu instead of using pin blocks and switches on the motherboard. There are 120 different front-side bus settings for the CPU, for example, from 84 to 200 MHz. You can also ask the BIOS to make its own decisions on the best configuration.

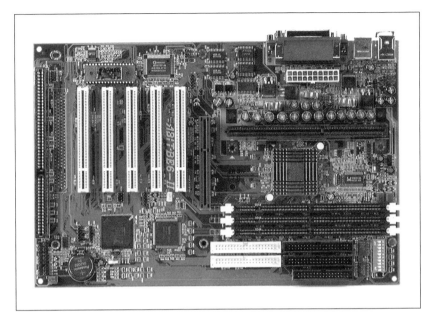

FIGURE 5-41: *The capable Abit BE6-II motherboard is neatly designed, offering more than the usual working space for installing cards and attaching cables. The 440BX chipset lies beneath a heat sink between the memory DIMM slots and Slot 1 for the CPU.*

FIGURE 5-42: *The Ultra ATA/66 chipset on the Abit BE6-II supports as many as eight IDE devices, four at ATA/66's 66.6 megabytes per second (MBps) speed and four at the previous ATA/33 standard. IDE3 and IDE4, the white connectors, use ATA/66; to their right are the black connectors for IDE1 and IDE2, which use the ATA/33 specification. Below IDE1 is the smaller connector for the floppy disk drive. The ATA/66 controller is designed for high-speed mass storage. In general, devices such as CD-ROMs, Zip drives, and Superdrives should use the ATA/33 connectors. You need to add a driver to Windows systems for Ultra ATA/66; the instruction manual gives details on how to update the hard disk driver.*

Ch
5

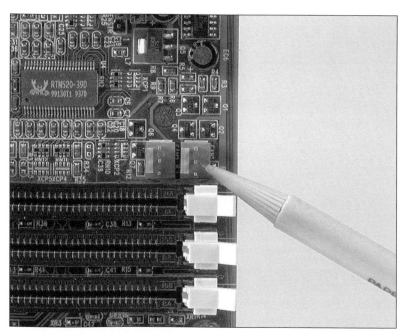

FIGURE 5-43: *Just above the memory DIMM slot on the Abit BE6-II is the header to provide power to the fan on the Pentium II/III or Celeron CPU. Alongside is a second fan header, and there is a third fan header at the front of the motherboard near the CMOS battery. High-speed processors and chipsets can benefit from additional cooling fans attached to components or on the case.*

FIGURE 5-44: *Advanced features on the Abit BE6-II include SB-LINK, Wake on Ring, and Wake on LAN; the headers for each are located, from left to right, below the PCI slots on this motherboard. SB-LINK, when used with a PCI audio adapter that supports this feature, serves as a bridge between the motherboard and the sound card to deliver high-end audio to real-mode DOS games. This solves one of the problems faced by the latest multimedia games that go around Windows to pick up the maximum speed directly from the hardware. If you have an internal modem adapter that supports Wake on Ring, attach a cable to the motherboard to enable the modem to wake up and start the computer when an incoming call arrives. Similarly, if you use a network adapter with a Wake on LAN feature, a cable attachment to the motherboard enables a message sent over the network to wake the computer. You also need a utility program such as Intel LDCM.*

Ch 5

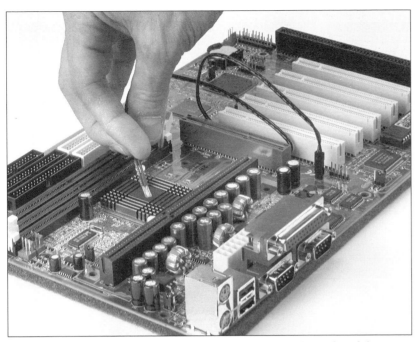

FIGURE 5-45: *The TSYS2 header, above the AGP slot to the right of the PCI slots on the Abit BE6-II, accepts a thermistor sensor cable that can be used to monitor the temperature at a particular location or device within the case.*

FIGURE 5-46: *The main interface between the motherboard and the front panel of the PC's case can be found at PN1 and PN2 at the front of the board, in this picture to the left of the backup battery. Note that the connectors lie at the end of the ISA slot; some older, extra-long ISA cards could make access to the pins difficult. In any case, you want to make attachments to the pins before installing any ISA or PCI cards on the board. PN1 makes connection to the three-wire power LED cable, plus two-wire cables for the keylock (if used on the case), the hard disk drive LED, power-on switch, and hardware-suspend switch. PN2 is the header for the two-wire hardware reset switch, the four-wire internal speaker cable, and a two-wire system suspend LED. Take care to install the cables with the proper orientation. The instruction manual shows + and – orientation for each wire.*

Ch
5

SUMMARY

You've explored the basics of the computer. In the next chapter, I apply a screwdriver to a state-of-the-art PC and reveal its secrets in step-by-step detail.

Notes

Chapter 6

Step-by-Step through a Modern PC

Throughout the history of the PC, the basic components of the machine have remained quite constant.

From the very first IBM PC, the building blocks have included a motherboard and microprocessor, a block of random access memory, a form of non-volatile read/write storage (at first a floppy disk, and now one or more hard disk drives, CD or DVD drives, or flash memory), a video adapter, a power supply, and a case to hold all of the parts.

Today, the most modern machines include the same elements. However, today's engineers have managed to combine two seemingly opposing trends. On the one hand, current motherboards are highly integrated; an advanced board may include disk drive adapters, video adapters, Ethernet circuitry, WiFi capability, audio functions, and a broadening array of high-speed I/O facilities built right in. At the same time, engineers have moved much of the specialized and user-replaceable elements of the machine outside the box, making use of I/O ports including USB, FireWire, and eSATA. The third change is the arrival of the *designer* in the computer world: New machines have a bit of style and the cases are much easier to work within. On many modern machines, you don't even need a screwdriver to remove or install components.

In this chapter, I take apart a state-of-the-art modern machine to identify the parts and show some common repair projects. I also delve into an older but still capable machine for a few essential upgrades.

Touring a Modern Machine

I purchased . . . and proceeded to take apart down to the bare shell . . . a state-of-the-art machine based around Intel's Core 2 Duo processor. I chose Intel's model 6600 CPU, rated at 2.4 GHz with a 4MB cache, and had the machine equipped with 1GB of RAM (two 512MB DIMMs), a 250GB SATA hard drive, and a CD R/W and DVD read-only combo drive.

Although this is not the way I recommend you spend your own money, I bought one of the first machines off the assembly line. (I did this, of course, to get the latest and greatest machine for purposes of the book. If you're looking to save a bit of money or hoping to avoid the almost-inevitable headaches that go with buying the first editions of a new model, I recommend waiting a few months after introduction of a new technology. Let someone else work out the kinks for you. I guess that would be me, in this situation.)

I chose Dell's Dimension 9200 for several reasons: The company is always among the first to market with new technologies and offers a very high degree of customization. They offered to build to order this particular model with any of half a dozen different processors. (I followed my own advice and chose the CPU that was one step down from the top of the line.) I took advantage of a special discount offered by Dell and got the most bang for my bucks with a pair of 512MB DIMMs. I chose to upgrade from the most basic graphics card to a more capable one, but otherwise I ordered a very basic model of a very advanced machine. Figure 6-1 shows this edition's test machine.

NOTE

Just for the record: I'm not endorsing Dell or any other particular PC manufacturer. Prices, engineering, and quality of manufacture and service can change from year to year and month to month in the computer industry. Dell is a good example of a mass-market computer seller; the company offers machines that have the most current hardware and allows a wide degree of customization to online buyers. A savvy consumer shops carefully before committing to a system purchase. In my office, I run a mix of machines from Compaq, Dell, Gateway, Hewlett Packard, Toshiba, and other systems that I have assembled myself using industry-standard parts.

Here's the skinny on the new machine, as delivered and before I upgraded it:

- Intel Core 2 Duo processor 6600, running at 2.4 GHz.
- 1GB of DDR 533-MHz RAM, occupying two of the four available memory slots.
- A highly integrated motherboard based on the BTX design, including six internal SATA ports and three PCI Express connectors (x1,x4, and x16). Since the BTX design and this computer were both offering new technologies for connections, the board offered a few legacy connectors that could be used to support still-capable older devices; these included three PCI connectors, a connector for a PS/2 and serial port for prior-generation keyboards and mice, and a floppy drive connector.
- The motherboard, which was manufactured for Dell and bears that label, uses the Intel 965 chipset and various other Intel components in addition to its processor; in previous years, Dell has used motherboards designed and built by Intel and this well-designed board may be made by that company, or by a maker in close step with Intel's products and design initiatives.
- Built-in support in the hard disk controller for RAID (an acronym for Redundant Array of Independent [or Inexpensive] Disks), which allow users to spread data across multiple disks or make concurrent copies of data on more than one disk; either way, it's a valuable option for people to whom the loss of a file — or an entire hard disk drive — would be an expensive or painful disaster.

- Two internally accessible bays for 3.5-inch hard disk drives, plus two externally accessible bays (FlexBay design that permits insertion and removal of USB devices including floppy disk drives and media card readers from the outside of the case if desired) and two externally accessible 5.25-inch drive bays intended for use with CD or DVD drives.
- Built-in Ethernet circuitry on the motherboard, connected to an external port on the rear of the machine.
- Integrated audio, a Sigma Tel Audio chipset that delivers good performance for external speakers and accepts line in and microphone signals. However, on this model and a number of other systems from Dell, the device driver for the audio chipset has been crippled so sound-editing software cannot capture card output; music comes into the system from the Internet or a CD or DVD in the PC's drive, but it goes only to external headphones or speakers.
- Two front-panel and six back-panel USB 2.0 connectors.
- A 375-watt power supply capable of providing sufficient juice to energy-hungry modern devices including the dual-core processor, a high-speed video processor, a huge block of double data rate RAM, and a base level of power for external devices attached to eSATA, USB, and FireWire connectors.
- A redesigned cooling system (at the heart of the BTX specification) that draws air across the top of the hot microprocessor and through an uninterrupted channel out an exhaust port, dissipating 683 BTU per hour.
- Discretely hidden behind a smoked glass panel on the front of the machine, a set of four tiny numbered lights that give a report on any problems encountered at the machine's startup. The lights are so unobtrusive that it's easy to forget they're there — but if someday your machine stalls before Windows is loaded, you may be quite grateful for the clues they offer to what lies beneath. Once the operating system loads, the computer should run Dell's own diagnostic software, supplied with the machine, as well as other utilities from other makers you may choose to install on the computer.

NOTE

Here are few more technical details about the Dimension 9200, for those readers who have a need to know. The Intel Core 2 Duo processor is regulated by a system clock that beats at a 1066-MHz data rate. The Dell motherboard uses Intel's P965 Express chipset and Intel's 82566DC Gigabit integrated network connection. The board works with 8 DMA channels and 24 Interrupt levels. The BIOS chip holds 4MB of instructions.

The motherboard itself includes a 36-pin PCI Express x1 slot, a 98-pin PCI Express slot that can be used by an x4 or an x8 device, a 164-pin PCI Express x16 slot, as well as three standard 120-pin PCI slots. There are six SATA connectors, a FlexBay Drive USB header for use with optional internally mounted floppy disk drives or other devices, and a pair of connectors that can be used with an appropriate cable and hardware to add a PS/2 and serial port connector to the rear panel of the machine.

The vents at the bottom of the front of the case draw in outside air which is brought across the carefully located sources of heat; air is exhausted through a baffled vent hidden above, shown in Figure 6-2, and through openings at the back and sides of the box.

This machine is also notable for a few things that are not present. First of all, it is the first system covered in this book that does not include a floppy disk drive. That device has been a vestigial organ on many computers for the past few years; modern software is now installed almost exclusively from CD, DVD, or web site download, and the Internet or local area networks make it very easy to send files from place to place within a home or office or around the world. If you've absolutely got to carry around a copy of data (or want a quick and easy way to lock away information) the easy replacements for the floppy disk are a flash memory key (which plugs into a USB port), a recordable CD or DVD, a removable hard disk platter like a Zip or Rev cartridge, or even a small external hard drive (that can be unplugged and moved).

FIGURE 6-1: *Dell combines form and function in its design for the Dimension 9200.*

Ch
6

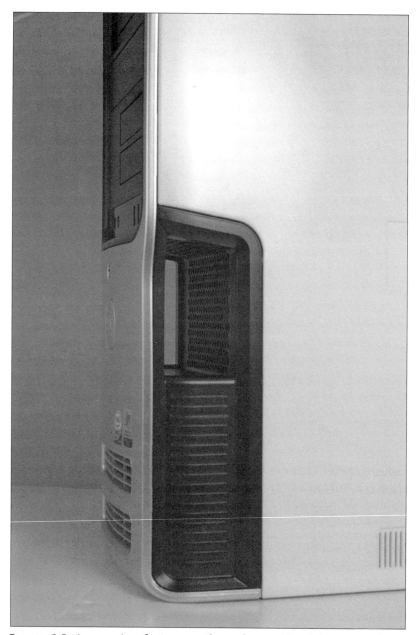

FIGURE 6-2: *An opening that passes through one side of the case to the other baffles the heated air that comes directly off of the Intel Core 2 Duo processor on the motherboard.*

This particular model's motherboard includes a connector for an internal floppy disk drive and pins for attaching a cable to a bracket to hold a pair of PS/2 ports for older-design keyboards and mice; both of those elements will likely be absent from the next generation of motherboards; the USB port can be used for almost any sort of external device.

Missing from the motherboard was support for the hard disk-drive interface that has been standard on PCs for a decade: the ATA (or IDE) standard. Nearly all modern machines are now based around the high-speed serial replacement, SATA. The Dimension 9200's motherboard included six SATA connectors for use with internal CD, DVD, and hard disk drives. If I had needed to add support for an older IDE hard drive, I could have installed a hard drive adapter in one of the PCI slots or used a plug-in adapter that converts an SATA feed to IDE at the hard drive itself. The set of SATA connectors is shown in Figure 6-3.

FIGURE 6-3: *The motherboard includes two groups of SATA connectors, part of the BTX design that is intended to reduce the clutter of wires within the case and help facilitate cooling.*

This new machine fully embraces the PCI Express bus design, with an x16 slot intended as the location for an advanced video graphics adapter and two additional slots (an x4 and an x1) available for future expansion. Missing from the motherboard: an AGP video slot, which held sway as the home of advanced graphics cards in recent years; PCI Express is an improvement over AGP, and the two designs are not physically or electrically interchangeable.

Ch 6

The rear panel shows the powerful simplicity of an advanced machine. As delivered, the USB port is king: Six connectors, shown in Figure 6-4, are for use with keyboards, mice, and external devices; you can attach any of the ports to a hub and split to serve additional devices. (Two more USB ports are on the front, intended for use with temporarily connected devices such as music players and digital cameras.)

Also on the rear panel: an Ethernet port that can be used to connect to a wired or WiFi local area network, or directly to a cable or DSL modem for high-speed Internet access. And on this model, I chose to use the motherboard's built-in audio facilities; the rear panel includes a neatly arranged stack of seven connectors including line-in, line-out, microphone-in, and surround sound ports for rear, center or subwoofer, and side speakers. The connectors can be seen in Figure 6-5. There's also an S/PDIF connector to transmit digital audio to devices capable of working with that sort of signal without going through conversion to analog.

FIGURE 6-4: *The stack of six USB and one Ethernet ports on the rear of the machine are intended for devices that are regularly used, including a keyboard, mouse, and external storage and communication devices. There are also two more USB ports on the front of the machine.*

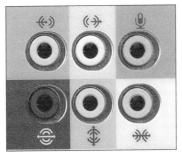

FIGURE 6-5: *The audio connectors for the sound features built into the motherboard on this modern machine.*

The machine, as delivered, included an ATI Radeon X1300 Pro video adapter with 256MB of its own memory, an upgrade from the entry-level adapter. A highly capable card, much improved over adapters available over the course of PC history, it is fully capable of business and Internet applications but stands several notches beneath the specialized (and expensive) cards offered to serious gamers.

Attached to the system through the PCI Express x16 slot, the video card offers two outputs: a VGA connector for a standard monitor, and a DVI for use with an LCD capable of working with a digital signal. The card is capable of driving two monitors at the same time. Depending on settings you make within Windows, the two displays can show the same image (this is called *clone mode*) or you can have a dual display that spreads the Windows screen across both (called *extended desktop mode*).

NOTE

It is possible to convert the output (and physical connector design) of a DVI connector so you can use it with a standard analog monitor. You need to purchase a DVI-to-VGA converter plug or a cable that offers the same connector combination. The standard video card terminates its DVI output with a female connector on the back of the machine and, therefore, the DVI-to-VGA converter has a male DVI plug at one end and a male VGA plug at the other. Check your card design to make sure it follows the regular connector assignment.

Opening the box

The PC is now into its third decade, and designers have finally figured out ways to make PCs about as easy to open and configure as a desk lamp. The Dell Dimension 9200 is the first computer I have worked with — and I have disassembled dozens of them — that required no tools whatsoever to open the box or to add or remove memory, adapter cards, and hard disks. At most, you may need a small Phillips-head screwdriver to lock a drive into a plastic carrier. (Certain designs of CD, DVD, floppy, and media drives require installation of several locking screws.)

There are two reasons why a tool-free case is important. The first is technical and the second is symbolic.

On the technical side, the fact that you can open a machine and install or remove most parts without having to insert a pointed metal object into the case near the delicate and expensive parts is a very good thing. There are three major causes of self-inflicted damage to the internal hardware by computer users: damaging the wires or components with a tool, dropping a tiny screw into a place where it can cause an electrical short, and electrostatic shock. Avoiding tools makes the first two dangers significantly less likely.

As a symbol, the introduction of tool-free cases is a visible affirmation of a claim that has been more honored in the breach than the observance. For years now we have been told that sooner or later, PCs will be as accessible as common appliances. Almost any of us can open a refrigerator and figure out how to move the shelves, adjust the drawers, and even change the light bulb. Back to PCs: That was certainly not the case when users had to remove six or eight screws just

to take off the cover and a few dozen more within the case to remove or install adapter cards and storage devices. (Elsewhere in this book I advise owners of older machines to have a numbered egg carton and a notebook alongside their machine when they open it for internal work. That's still necessary for the vast majority of machines, but not this one . . . and, I hope, not for future machines.)

NOTE

Throughout this book, I advise users to always disconnect the power cord from a computer before opening the case to prevent accidental power shorts and to help guard against tripping over the cord and tumbling the PC to the floor. On the most modern of machines, you have two other reasons to disconnect the power cord: Many new machines (like many television sets) provide power to certain components, such as indicator lights, even when the power is "off." So power flows — and can be shorted out inadvertently — whenever the plug is attached. Another reason to disconnect the power cord on a modern machine is that some network adapters are designed to start the computer automatically when the adapters detect attachment of a network cable that is attached to an active network.

So, here are the steps to remove the cover of this most modern machine:

1. Prepare a clean, solid, and well-lighted work surface.
2. Disconnect the power cable to avoid the chances of electrical shorts or surges, and while you're at it, remove all other cables. On the most modern of machines, once you remove the power cable, press the On button as if you were trying to turn on the machine; this grounds the system by discharging any residual power in capacitors or other electronic devices.
3. Lay the computer on its side with the computer cover facing up. Gently pull back the large, black release catch on the top of the computer. Not quite like a ripcord on a parachute, the catch is attached by an internal cable to a set of locking fingers within the case; when the catch is fully extended, the cover is released and can be pivoted away from the case on a set of three hinge tabs at the bottom of computer.

That's it. No screwdrivers. No egg cartons. No sweat.

The opened case, turned back to an upright position, is shown in Figure 6-6.

FIGURE 6-6: *The Dimension 9200 revealed. At top left are the carriers for the CD/DVD and space for two or three hard drives, a floppy disk drive, a media card reader, and other devices; at upper right is the power supply; at bottom right are the six expansion slots (three PCI and three PCIExpress), and at bottom left are a pair of bays that can hold two more hard drives. In the center of the board, beneath a plastic hulk of a wind tunnel with its own fan, is the Intel Core 2 Duo processor.*

Kicking the tires

Let me quickly assure you: This new machine does not come equipped with whitewalls. As I have noted, the machine's interior represents a major evolutionary advance in the design of the PC, but an owner of a 20-year-old machine will be able to recognize all the basic motherboard elements: the memory modules, the adapter slots, the power supply, the hard drive and other storage devices, and the general purpose of most other connectors and cables within the box.

Nearly all current machines use a power supply that can work with either the 110- or 115-volt standard of the U.S. and Canada (and many other nations) or with the 220- or 230-volt standard that is used in Europe and many other places around the world. Some power supplies are capable of automatically switching between the two ranges of voltage.

The supply on the test bed Dimension 9200 also has a small switch on the back panel that converts the power supply to work with your home's or office's voltage. It has been years since I have seen such a mistake, and most modern machines would likely protect against burnout with a fuse, but nevertheless: The first time you prepare to power up a new machine, or any time any work has taken place near the power supply, check to see that it is switched to the proper setting.

Because the power supply's main task is to *step down* and *rectify* the voltage (reduce voltage to 3.3, 5, or 12 volts of DC power) it is generally very forgiving of a reasonable amount of undervoltage or overvoltage coming out of your wall socket. For example, the supply that is standard with the test machine is capable of working with 90 to 135 volts in a "115-volt" setting, and 180 to 265 volts in a "230-volt" setting. However, that does not mean that I recommend you operate your computer without the additional protection of a surge protector, either as a standalone device or as part of a *UPS (uninterruptible power supply)* battery system that also guards against blackouts. It's an insurance policy I always buy: a $25 surge protector or a $100 UPS to stand as a self-sacrificing sentry against a sudden jolt that could fry a $1,000 PC and the data it holds.

Ch
6

One major area of difference involves the cooling system, something that I discuss in more detail in Chapter 5. A great deal of attention has been paid to dealing with the three largest electronic generators of heat in the box: the microprocessor, the chipset, and the video graphics adapter. In Figure 6-7, you can see the large plastic cowling that covers the processor, and to its right, a finned heat sink that perches atop the chipset. A fan within the cowling directly draws air across the processor and out of the box. A similar heat sink sits atop the processor on the video graphics adapter. Other sources of warming, including the power supply and any internal disk drives, are placed so that the flow of air into and out of the machine draws heat out of the box.

FIGURE 6-7: *The specially designed cooling cowl that sits over the microprocessor is an essential part of the system that prevents a modern machine from overheating.*

Overall, on this particular advanced consumer PC, the cooling system is capable of removing 683 BTU per hour, which is a substantial amount of heat taken out of the box. A *BTU* (the acronym refers to an arcane measure called a British Thermal Unit) is defined as the amount of heat required to raise the temperature of a pound of water by one degree. Going the other direction, in a laboratory setting 143 BTUs are required to melt a pound of ice.

NOTE

Help your computer keep its cool by not compromising the cooling system. Make sure there is at least two inches between the entry and exit vents of the machine and a solid object such as a wall or window or other hardware; this ensures that the full volume of air can get in and out. Every few months — more often if you work in a dusty environment — gently vacuum out the vents. Finally, don't run the machine for extended periods without its cover in place or with any of its internal fans disabled; the cover is part of the overall case design, which is intended to channel air in the most efficient manner.

Adding memory modules

The Dell motherboard includes four connectors to hold memory modules, logically and electrically organized in two banks. Although, in theory, most motherboards for modern machines can operate with any number of the slots filled — one, two, three, or four — most manufacturers recommend that the banks be filled evenly and with matched modules.

Here's what that means:

- A pair of matched memory modules in connectors DIMM1 and DIMM2. (*Matched* means that the two DIMMs have identical specification; in theory you can mix DIMMs from two different manufacturers, although I hesitate to recommend that because there are so many variables amongst the specifications, and in certain rare circumstances this may lead to operating problems.)
- A pair of matched memory modules in connectors DIMM1 and DIMM2, and a second pair of matched modules in connectors DIMM3 and DIMM4.
- Although you can install faster or slower DIMMs in one or the other bank of memory, all the modules operate at the slowest speed installed. For example, if one bank had DDR2 667-MHz (PC2-5300) memory DIMMs and the other DDR 533-MHz (PC2-4200) modules, all the memory will be limited to 533 MHz.
- You should not mix *ECC (error-correcting code)* and non-ECC memory in a system; if the computer boots at all, it is almost certain to crash regularly. Most new machines used in homes, home offices, and small businesses employ the simpler and less-expensive non-ECC design.

There is no requirement that motherboard manufacturers subscribe to a particular layout for the placement of the connectors. On the Dell motherboard I found, after close examination, that the two groups of connectors each included one half of a bank of memory; there were two connectors with white securing clips and two with black securing clips.

Just to make things more complex, DIMM1 was not, as I had first guessed, the connector closest to the top of the motherboard but rather the lowest positioned slot; a careful reading of the instruction manual identifies this slot as the one closest to the microprocessor. There was a 512MB DIMM of memory installed in each of the two white-clipped connectors, for a total of 1GB of RAM.

The particular motherboard in this machine supports a maximum of 4GB of memory (four 1GB modules), which happens also to be the maximum amount of memory that current operating systems, including Windows XP, support. And all operating systems for PCs lock away a part of however much memory is installed in the machine, reserving segments for the use of certain pieces of hardware.

My first upgrade project for this machine involved doubling installed RAM to 2GB, a healthy block of memory appropriate for use with some of the tasks this computer would be assigned, including digital photo editing. I ordered a pair of Crucial Memory DIMMs that matched the ones supplied with the machine; Crucial is the consumer arm of American manufacturer Micron Technology.

DDR2 DIMMs have a locating notch that is slightly off-center; this ensures that the module is installed with the proper side up. The module is shown in Figure 6-8.

After I understood the machine's black-white-black-white (DIMM4-DIMM2-DIMM3-DIMM1) organization for the connectors, the next issue was assuring that the new memory modules were properly aligned; the open locating notch in the module has to line up with a vertical finger in the connector. Once again, I ran into a situation where different manufacturers produced equivalent but not identical hardware.

The two DIMMs Dell supplied were manufactured by Samsung; the eight plastic carriers for the memory itself were installed on the top side of the module, the side facing *away* from the microprocessor. The two upgrade DIMMs from Crucial had their eight plastic memory chips installed on the bottom side of the module, the side facing *toward* the microprocessor.

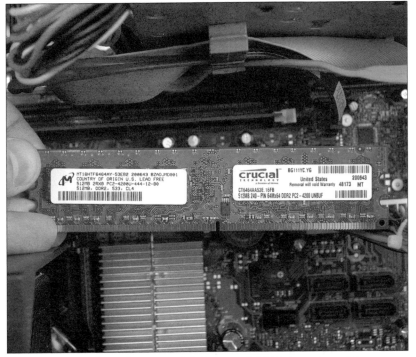

FIGURE 6-8: *The first of two Crucial Memory DIMMs is prepared for insertion into the machine. The locating notch is amongst the connecting fingers at the bottom of the module; it is slightly off center to prevent mis-installation.*

In the overall scheme of things, this is strictly a matter of design. It makes no difference to the computer on which side of the module the memory is soldered, and it makes no difference to you as a buyer. But you have to pay attention: Once you are certain that the modules you have ordered are proper for your machine, regardless of memory module placement, you must take care to align the locating notch properly with the vertical finger in the connector. In Figure 6-9, you can see all four DDR2 RAM modules installed in the Dell machine.

Ch
6

FIGURE 6-9: *The last of four DDR2 modules is installed into place on the motherboard. If you look carefully at the image, you'll see that not all of the securing clips have yet been locked into place.*

I found that inserting the new memory module into DIMM4 (the top connector, with black clips) was difficult; if you look at the photo you'll see that the connector is close to a set of cables at the top of the machine and there is not much room to work. I removed the original memory module, in DIMM2, to open up a bit more space.

Satisfied that all four modules were properly seated, I replaced the cover and started up the computer to test my work. Almost immediately, the diagnostic lights on the front of the machine began to flash a coded message, and the sophisticated self-test for the computer halted the loading of the operating system. Instead, I saw a BIOS Setup screen that warned of a memory mismatch: according to the report, the system had located 1.5GB of memory in three modules rather than the 2.0GB in four modules that I had installed.

I was able to proceed to continue the loading of Windows, and once the operating system was running I was able to run Dell's diagnostic program as well as the exhaustive set of tests that are part of Symantec's Norton SystemWorks. Both found only 1.5G of RAM available to the system.

To shorten the story of a long night, here's the summary of the steps I took to troubleshoot the problem:

- I removed and reinstalled all four modules, checking the seating of the DIMMs and the locking clips. No success.

- I tried swapping the original Samsung modules and the new Crucial Memory modules in the machine. No success.
- I removed the original Samsung modules from the machine and installed only the new Crucial Memory modules in the DIMM1 and DIMM2 slots to determine if the upgrade memory was functioning properly; it was.
- I spent more than an hour on the phone to a Dell support technician (at the scratchy end of a bad phone connection to India). She reviewed all the swaps and reinstalls I had performed, and to my surprise immediately suggested that the brand-new motherboard needed to be replaced. I told her to go ahead and make the arrangements.
- Sometime around midnight, I tried one more reinstall. I took all four modules out of the brand new machine and tilted the case and the motherboard so they were facing down; I took a can of filtered air and held it upright (to prevent inadvertently discharging liquid propellant) and carefully sprayed a few bursts at the connectors. And then I reinstalled all four modules. I replaced the cover, and turned on the machine . . . and watched as the new PC skipped over all warning messages and loaded Windows XP. I checked the Control Panel's System panel and found that my machine was now the proud operator of 2GB of RAM; before collapsing into bed, I assigned a diagnostic program to put the entire machine through an endless loop of tests all through the night just to check if there was some sort of transient error with the board. There were no bad reports the next morning.

So, what happened? There are two likely causes for the problem I experienced:

- It was possible that the previously unused DIMM4 slot was slightly out of alignment, just enough to prevent the new memory module from properly lining up with the electrical fingers the first dozen times I tried. Eventually, my efforts opened up the slot just enough to allow it to accept the new memory.
- There may have been a tiny piece of plastic or dirt that had fallen into the connector, preventing the new memory module (or the original modules, when I tried swapping them) from becoming properly seated. Using gravity and a puff of air may have dislodged it.

Adding expansion cards

This modern machine's tool-free design employs two pieces of hardware that open to reveal available slots, and close to hold installed cards in place. There are no screws required to open the slots for use, and no screws to hold the cards in place. (And, as I have already noted, no chance of dropping a metallic screw into the innards or scratching the delicate motherboard with a screwdriver.)

You can see the two-part retention system for the Dimension 9200 in Figure 6-10.

After you have the machine prepared for modification (clean, well-lit, and stable work surface and all electrical cables removed), place the machine on its side and remove the cover. The ends of the cards that open to external ports on the rear of the PC — also the part of the card that is attached to a metal mounting bracket — is covered by a card retention door. In the Dell design, press the two release tabs on the inside of the door and lift it up and out of the way.

There is a second device, called a *card retention mechanism*, that folds down over the other end of an otherwise barely supported PCI Express x16 card, holding it securely. Release it by pulling in on a latch that attaches to the cooling cowl over the microprocessor.

To add a new device, you merely open both mechanisms to free any existing cards and to reveal the set of metal filler brackets that cover the openings at the rear of the computer. As explored in Chapter 1, these brackets are part of the computer's essential protection against unwanted release of *RF (radio frequency)* interference. Operating a computer without its cover properly installed, or without either an adapter card or a filler bracket in place at the back panel, can result in signal escape; that can cause interference with televisions, FM radios, and other devices; their absence can also disrupt a modern PC's carefully engineered cooling system.

In the tool-less world of this modern machine, the filler brackets sit in place atop a series of small pegs; when the card retention door is lowered over the filler bracket or an installed adapter card, they become locked into place at the back of the computer. It's a simple mechanism, cleverly designed, but you have to make certain that cards or fillers are squarely seated before locking the retention mechanism to avoid misalignment.

FIGURE 6-10: *At right is the card retention door that sits over the adapter card brackets or the filler brackets that cover holes near unused slots. In this picture, only one of the six slots is being used — the PCI Express x16 slot holds a video adapter card. At left is the card retention mechanism that holds the other end of adapter cards in proper alignment.*

 WARNING

Never route a cable over the top of an expansion card, or between the card and the back of the computer. Doing so could prevent the cover from closing properly, resulting in overheating, radio frequency radiation release, or crimping and damaging the cable.

WARNING

When attaching an Ethernet cable to a network card or port, first plug the cable into the network device (hub, router, WiFi gateway, broadband modem, and the like) and then into the computer. This reduces the chance of an electrical surge that could damage the PC. Similarly, take care not to install a telephone cable into an Ethernet port; the phone cord carries a bit of voltage if connected to the phone system, and the two types of plugs — though similar in design and appearance — are not the same size. You could end up damaging the connector or port with a mismatch.

The ATI X1300 Radeon Pro is very capable for graphic functions; it easily powered my two-monitor setup with high-resolution, high-color images and reacted quickly to most drawing tasks. So, too, the built-in sound functions of the Sigma Tel High Definition Audio chipset and associated software drivers offer more-than-acceptable audio features for most users listening to digital music over the Internet or played from CD or DVD sources.

But serious gamers or users with need for especially powerful graphics, audio playback, and editing functions will want to add a faster, more-capable graphics card and a more powerful, flexible sound card. In Chapter 13, I discuss the relatively simple assignment of upgrading the X1300 card to an even-faster card with more memory: the ATI Radeon X1600 Pro with 512MB of memory. Although the X1300 would have been sufficient for use with Windows Vista, I wanted to go one step beyond to configure a machine that stood a chance of remaining current for at least a year after I plugged it into the electrical outlet. I noticed an immediate improvement in the image clarity on both monitors I attached to the video card's output.

The other modification I made was installing a new sound card to expand the capabilities of the audio system and, more importantly, to allow use of advanced digital-editing software; as noted, I found that the integrated sound chipset was not recognized by a number of software applications as the source of streaming audio from the Internet. This is a problem specific to the particular chipset and associated drivers Dell uses for the motherboard; some other computer makers using the same chipset provide drivers that address this issue. (And yes, I tried to install a different computer maker's device driver on the Dell machine; let's just say I was greeted with the sounds of silence.)

In coming years, you can expect to see sound cards developed to plug into a PCI Express slot. (The first round of current modern machines include a x16, x4, and x1 slot.) As this book goes to press, though, internal sound cards are designed to be installed in a PCI slot. The sound card adds a broader range of capabilities, more connection choices for incoming and outgoing audio signals, and a much-improved device driver and audio software control panel.

You can also find a small number of external sound adapters that connect to the PC's USB port. They are very simple to install — literally plug and play — and may not offer significant improvements over a card installed in an internal PCI bus. At least for the moment, the principal advantage of using an external adapter is that installation does not require opening the PC cover.

NOTE

Check with the manufacturer of your computer to see if onboard sound chips need to be disabled through the Setup screen if an upgrade sound adapter is installed. Even if this is not required, you may want to do so anyway to reduce the demand on system resources and to eliminate the possibility that a piece of software will seek to use the original audio chips after you have made them superfluous.

Adding more hard drives

The high degree of integration used on this modern machine's motherboard leaves a tremendous amount of space within its mid-sized case. As delivered, there is only one adapter card — the video adapter — in the six available slots, a single hard disk drive, and a combination CD/DVD drive. There is room for a second CD or DVD drive, and two Flexbay locations that open to the outside for use with a floppy disk drive and a media drive (to work with flash memory devices for cameras and audio players) if you choose.

I ordered the machine with a single 250MB SATA hard drive, the largest C: (root) drive on any of the machines in my office. I prefer to organize my computer with the C: drive as the home of the operating system and applications, and to store data (including text, graphics, and audio) on a separate hard drive.

Ch 6

This, then, was my plan for the new machine:

- The C: drive, as delivered, was to hold the Windows operating system and all applications.
- I would add a second internal hard drive to hold data.
- I would add a third and fourth external hard drive, each connected to one of the machine's USB 2.0 ports, to hold backup copies of all data. Coming out of a business environment, I have for many years employed an old-style backup scheme that leaves little room for disaster: I alternate weekly backups between two different external storage devices. In this way, I always have a set of data that is no more than a week old and I have an earlier version of the backup just in case there is a problem writing or reading the backup file. In addition, I also burn CD or DVD copies of critical data — as often as daily — if I am working on a very important or very valuable project.

The design of the Dimension 9200 encourages placement of one or two internal hard disk drives at the bottom of the case, near the second set of SATA connectors on the motherboard; the intended location of the boot disk is near the top of the machine in a cage that holds the CD/DVD and has space for any devices installed in a Flexbay. Flexbay devices, in Dell's design, are intended to connect to an internal USB port; I could have, through an extended-length SATA cable, put a hard drive there.

To install a drive in the upper disk-drive cage (including a hard disk drive, CD or DVD, a floppy disk drive, or a media reader), designers make it easy to gain access by offering a removable front panel cover. The first step in the process is to open the PC's side cover. Then, the drive panel is unlatched using a push tab. The opened front can be seen in Figure 6-11.

For this project, I chose to add a very fast, very large new SATA drive from Western Digital, the WD Caviar SE16 with a 500GB capacity. This drive, introduced in late 2006, is one of the most advanced consumer disk drives available. The drive includes 16MB of cache with a transfer speed of as much as 300 MBps. You can read more about the drive in Chapter 10.

Of all the gin joints . . . make that of all the disk drives in all the computers I have ever worked on . . . installing the WD Caviar SE16 into the Dimension 9200 PC was the easiest such project I have ever embarked upon, once I got past one little change in my standard procedure.

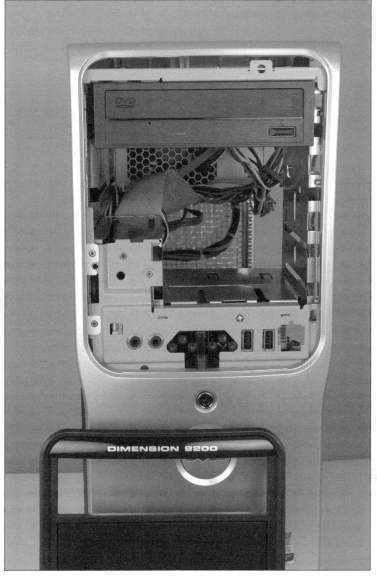

Figure 6-11: *With the drive cover plate removed, you have direct access to the FlexBay compartment. Already installed at top is the CD/DVD drive, and at the bottom a bracket that holds two USB ports, a headphone and microphone connector for the built-in audio, and the diagnostic lights that tell you the condition of the machine at bootup.*

Ch
6

The PC's tool-free case includes a pair of sturdy plastic hard-drive brackets already in place in bays at the bottom. They slide out with the push of a pair of side tabs, and the hard drive slips into the bracket like a foot into a shoe, as seen in Figure 6-12.

The next step is to slide the plastic bracket into the bay and attach the data and power cables for the drive. In Figure 6-13, you can see the new drive already installed at left. I've unlatched and extended the unused extra drive bracket to its right.

FIGURE 6-13: *WD's Caviar SE16 drive, one of the first high-capacity SATA drives, comes with a special cable that adapts it for use with the motherboard's built-in data connector; it also uses one of the Dimension's old-style power connectors instead of the smaller connectors that are part of the BTX form factor. Future drives, as BTX motherboards become more popular, will make full use of the new standard for thin data and power cables.*

FIGURE 6-12: *The advanced Western Digital Caviar drive slides into place in one of the Dimension's drive brackets; the plastic frame locks it firmly without the need for screws or clips.*

Once the hard drive was happily clicked into place and the cables attached (no jumper settings are required on a SATA drive), I replaced the computer cover and powered up the computer, looking forward to a five-minute tripling of the available hard drive space of the machine from 250GB to 750GB. No joy: The computer completely ignored the new drive.

I retraced my steps to recheck the installation of the data cables on the hard drive and at the SATA port on the motherboard, noting which of the six numbered ports I had used. I also checked that the power connector was properly attached at the drive. And before I closed the case, I made sure that both cables were not crimped or pinched by any other components within the case. The computer still declined to acknowledge the new drive.

And then I burrowed deeper into the computer's instruction manual and found a significant difference between the new SATA drive controller and the previous *PATA* (*Parallel ATA* or IDE) design: As delivered, computers using the SATA design are set with unused ports disabled. To use a new drive, I had to enter System Setup at bootup, go to the BIOS Drives section, and change the setting to On for the SATA port used by the device.

NOTE

Just as SATA ports need to be enabled from System Setup to recognize a newly installed drive, you must follow the same procedure for devices installed into an internal FlexBay device, enabling USB for FlexBay.

From that point on, the new WD hard drive performed exactly as I had hoped — faster and larger than any drive in my office. I partitioned it into two logical drives of 250GB each; this offered me two options. First of all, I could have chosen to use one of the logical drives as a RAID drive, automatically creating a duplicate of the data and programs on the C: drive. The second option, which I chose to implement, was to use the first logical partition (D:) as the home of all current application data and the second logical partition (E:) as a deep archive for older files and older versions of current works in progress.

Advanced maintenance on a modern machine

Part and parcel of a tool-less computer case is simple access to other maintenance basics, including replacing the motherboard's backup battery, clearing forgotten passwords, and performing other important, and sometimes essential, tasks. I've already discussed changing the backup battery in Chapter 5.

Clearing forgotten passwords

Hardware-based passwords (which are different from those demanded by software or web sites) are recorded in a small piece of non-volatile memory on the motherboard of many modern computers. If your machine is located in a place where others can use it without your knowledge or approval, it's a good idea to protect the system with a password.

But what happens if you forget the password? Or if the recorded secret code somehow becomes scrambled and no longer responds to your keyboard entry? On most modern machines, you should be able to clear the password memory by removing a jumper or pressing a tiny reset button on the motherboard; consult the instruction manual or manufacturer's online resources for details.

On the Dimension 9200 test machine, a pair of small jumpers is located just above the PCI Express x1 slot, near the back of the board. One is marked CLRPSWD, as in *clear password;* the other is CLRCMOS, and is used to dump any changes you have made to the default settings of the CMOS System Setup.

Once you have properly removed power from the machine and opened the cover, carefully reach into the motherboard and remove the CLRPSWD jumper. I suggest using a piece of plastic tape to attach the jumper to a safe place on the desktop so that you won't lose the tiny piece of plastic.

1. With the jumper open, replace the cover and reconnect power and data cables to the computer and turn on the machine.
2. Allow the PC to progress all the way through loading Windows. (It will skip over any request for passwords.)
3. Once the operating system is running properly, shut down Windows from within the operating system.
4. Turn off the power to the machine.
5. Remove all power and data cables and open up the cover.
6. Replace the jumper between the two pins of the password pins.
7. The next time you turn on the machine's power, you skip past the password section; if you want to add a password, you can do so from the System Setup screen during bootup.
8. Check the instruction manual or online resources for your machine to find its particular method for resetting passwords.

Another solution began in government agencies and large corporations and is now available to consumers. It is the use of biometric readers as a gateway to use of a machine. These pieces of hardware can read a fingerprint or other body components, such as the dimensions of your eye's iris. The hardware may store the information in its own memory or on the hard disk; either way, the PC is instructed not to fully boot until it recognizes that a trusted human being is at the keyboard.

CROSS-REFERENCE

In Chapter 22, I discuss Dell's built-in diagnostic program, which can be invoked before the operating system loads, as well as third-party diagnostic programs that are available to test hardware and software once the system is up and running. These utilities are very useful in finding missing or corrupted elements of software or problems with the Windows System Registry, and will also help you find hardware problems that are caused by software settings.

Understanding Standby, Hibernation, and Power Schemes

Modern machines combine elements of the operating system and coding in the motherboard's chipset to allow users to conserve power and reduce some wear on hardware, which occurs when computers are left unused after a period of time. On most systems, the options are Standby and Hibernate.

In Standby mode, the computer turns off the display and the hard drive after the particular time period you have chosen. When the computer is brought back from this "time-out" condition, it returns to the operating state it was in before Standby.

NOTE

Putting a computer into Standby generally does not protect against losing data or settings if the machine suffers a loss of power; the best defense is to be sure to save all open files before going into a time-out condition. In addition, some peripherals may not support Standby mode, especially (as is the case with the most modern machines) when a card is installed in the PCI Express x16 slot.

If you are running Windows XP or Vista, set the period of time before a machine is ready for Standby by doing the following:

1. Click Start ➪ Control Panel.
2. Choose the Power Options tab.
3. On an AC-powered desktop or tower machine, select a default power scheme from amongst the predefined options, including

   • Home/Office Desk
   • Portable/Laptop

   • Presentation
   • Always On
   • Minimal Power Management

The last three of the options listed here are for when you do not want the machine to quickly or inappropriately shut down. (For example, if you are using your machine to control a PowerPoint or similar presentation, you do not want it to go into a time out because the mouse or keyboard has not been moved in a while.)

Give some thought to the way you use your computer. If you tend to monitor a web site for long periods of time while you work on other projects, you may not want the machine to go into Standby. On the other hand, if you are in the habit of management by walking around, or otherwise tend to step away from your desk for long periods of time, it may make sense to set the machine to choose a time out after 15 or 30 minutes.

To command your machine to quickly go into Standby mode, click Start button ➪ Turn Off Computer ➪ Stand By. To bring a machine back to life from Stand By, press any key on the keyboard or move the mouse.

Hibernate mode is a more complete and safe temporary closing of activity. When a computer is in Hibernate mode, the computer copies system data to a reserved area on the hard drive, and then completely turns off the computer. When you ask the machine to come back to life, the processor instructs the hard disk drive to load the information from storage, restoring it to the state it was in.

To set up a Hibernate mode on a machine running Windows XP or Vista, do the following:

1. Click Start ➪ Control Panel.
2. Choose the Power Options tab.
3. Click the Hibernate tab, and then click Enable Hibernation. The tab tells you the amount of available free space on the primary disk drive, and the amount of space required to store hibernation information.

To exit Hibernate mode, press and release the computer's power button; depending on the complexity of the files you had open and the speed of the hard drive and processor, returning from hibernation may take a few seconds or as much as a minute. (On many machines, a hibernating machine reminds you of its current state by having the power button flash, illuminate in a special color, or both.) You cannot bring a hibernating machine back to life by pressing the keyboard or moving the mouse.

NOTE

In Standby mode, if you set the hard drive to time out before the monitor does, your computer may appear to be locked up. To recover, press any key on the keyboard or click the mouse. To avoid this situation, always set the monitor to time out before the hard drive.

An Older Modern Machine

The previous edition of this book featured a machine that was close to the top of the heap in 2002. That machine, a Dell Dimension 8200 based around a 1.8-GHz Pentium 4 microprocessor, is still a highly capable modern machine five years later (although it lacks the most modern of advances such as SATA and PCI Express slots). As delivered, though, it marked the appearance of USB in PCs, an internal CD-RW, and an AGP4X slot for the video adapter.

That advanced machine, though, did not sustain one significant feature: RDRAM memory. Although that memory design offered some advantages over other RAM designs at the time, a combination of higher cost, technology, and marketing resulted in its short life in consumer machines. RDRAM modules are not physically or electrically compatible with any other memory design, including today's SDRAM. If you bought a machine based on RDRAM, it probably continues to perform well and you can purchase (at a premium) memory to replace or upgrade those modules.

The motherboard used the mini-ATX form factor, which improved organization to the external ports and connectors and accommodated the large cooling tunnel for the hot Pentium 4 processor.

I'm going through the major components of this older modern machine for two reasons: because millions of similar machines are still in use, and because some of its features are at least a generation behind the most modern machine I wrote about earlier in this chapter. The last time around, the modern machine model was a Dell Dimension 8200.

Figure 6-14 shows the machine in its operating glory.

The rear panel of the PC neatly presents a wide range of input and output ports, including serial and parallel ports and PS/2 keyboard and mouse ports, as shown in Figure 6-15. Today's most modern machines rely more on multi-purpose USB ports.

FIGURE 6-14: *The Dell Dimension 8200, an older modern machine, includes a CD-RW and a floppy disk drive on the front panel; there is additional space for a second 5.25-inch drive such as a DVD, and a second 3.5-inch drive such as an Iomega Zip. Behind a lift-up panel at the bottom-front of the system is a pair of USB ports and a headphone jack for multimedia equipment. In this setup, the system is topped by a 40GB external USB drive. Alongside are stereo speakers; a subwoofer speaker sits out of the way, on the floor. The PC, external drive, and monitor are plugged into an uninterruptible power supply that will support the system for enough time to allow an orderly shut down if there is a problem with electricity in the office or home.*

The power supply's cooling fan is located to the right of the electrical connection; below it is the air vent for a second fan that directly cools the Pentium 4 processor on the motherboard within.

Two-thirds of the way down on the right side of the rear panel is a steel hasp that can be used with a small padlock to bolt the case closed.

Ch 6

FIGURE 6-15: *Below the electrical connection are the ports directly attached to the mini-ATX motherboard. From top left, moving clockwise, is a DB-15 serial port, a DB-25 parallel port, a PS/2 mouse connector, two USB ports, and a PS/2 keyboard connector. Some of the most current systems color-code the connectors on cables to make configuration easy.*

FIGURE 6-16: *The panel located to the left of the case-cooling fan holds the small DB-15 serial port, the larger DB-25 parallel port, the keyboard and mouse connectors, and a pair of USB 1.1 ports. Two more USB 1.1 ports are located on the front of the case. By comparison, the more modern machine discussed earlier in this chapter dispenses with the serial, parallel, keyboard, and mouse connectors; they are replaced with eight USB ports.*

The bottom section of the rear panel shows the ports of devices that are plugged into the system bus. The top device is a video card plugged into the system's AGP 4X slot; the video card in the example system includes both a standard analog port for a computer monitor and a circular S-VHS port for use with a television screen.

The next device in the bus, plugged into a PCI slot, is a Creative Labs Sound Blaster Live! Card. In addition to audio input and output connectors, the card includes a larger joystick port.

The third device in the bus is an Ethernet network interface card.

The modern motherboard, which if you read the tiny print on its surface indicates it was manufactured for Dell by Intel, makes use of the PC99 specification color-code connectors. The attached connectors, shown in Figure 6-16, are gathered in a tight cluster in a cutout on the rear panel of the case.

CROSS-REFERENCE

I list the assignments of the PC99 color scheme, and its subsequent updates, in Chapter 1.

The Intel-manufactured motherboard used in the Dell Dimension 8200 includes a set of diagnostic lights on the rear panel, located between the serial and parallel ports and the keyboard and mouse ports. The four lights, labeled A, B, C, and D, can be yellow, green, or off. The codes indicate problems that may occur before the BIOS begins to run, the failure of the BIOS itself, and the most common hardware problems that the BIOS test may uncover, including problems with the memory, the PCI bus, the video controller, and the USB port. (Note that the newer model featured earlier in this chapter has a slightly more capable preboot diagnostic system, and more importantly, the indicator lamps are moved to the front of the machine, where you can see them easily during the startup process.)

This Intel motherboard includes an AGP slot and four PCI slots; the external access to the adapter cards is shown in Figure 6-17. I discuss the computer bus in its various forms in Chapter 4.

The first PCI card in the bus in this system is a Sound Blaster Live! Adapter that includes a MIDI or joystick controller, as well as a full set of ports for incoming line audio from an amplifier or a microphone, in addition to outputs to speakers and amplifiers. Within the case, the card has connectors to an internal CD-ROM for both analog and digital playback.

The third card shown is a network interface card, with an open RJ45 connector. This advanced machine also includes built-in USB ports; as delivered, it offered the capable but relatively slower 1.1 version of the standard; later in this chapter I describe the Plug-and-Play installation of an adapter card in a PCI slot to add four USB 2.0 slots to the back of the machine. Another improvement came with the addition of an ATA/133 adapter that allows use of a Maxtor 160GB internal drive at its full capacity and speed. Two of the USB ports are on the rear panel of the case; a second set, shown in Figure 6-18, is sheltered behind a decorative cover on the front.

CROSS-REFERENCE

You can learn more about USB technology in Chapter 15.

FIGURE 6-17: *The system's ATI video card includes a standard SVGA output to a computer monitor and a small round S-VHS connector that can be used to drive a component television or videotape recorder; an adapter can be purchased to convert S-VHS to standard RCA plug outputs for consumer-grade televisions. The video card uses the AGP4X slot on the motherboard, sitting just above the bank of PCI slots.*

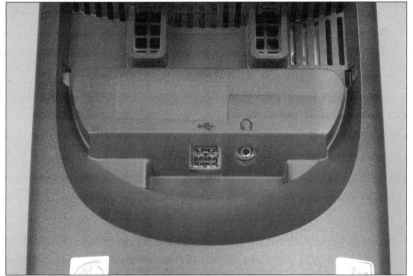

FIGURE 6-18: *Located behind a decorative cover on this modern machine is a second set of USB ports, best used for temporary attachments such as for downloading images from a digital camera, and a headphone connector for system audio; since I upgraded the internal circuitry with a USB 2.0 card, though, I made more use of the new ports on the rear of the machine; to make them easier to reach I attached a powered USB hub.*

The case shell is made of high-grade plastic, lined with metal panels that provide stiffness and shielding against RF leakage. The case opens like a clamshell with the press of a pair of release buttons on the top and bottom, as shown in Figure 6-19. Adapters and drives must still be secured with screws and rails.

CROSS-REFERENCE

I discuss the function of the case in Chapter 5.

When fully opened and flat on the tabletop, as shown in Figure 6-20, the case reveals the motherboard. The exterior plastic shell of the case covers a sturdy steel frame within. Each of the devices installed in a drive cage slides in and out on plastic rails; the case comes with extra rails for future upgrades to the system.

FIGURE 6-20: *Rising at a 90-degree angle are three drive cages. One holds devices that require external access through the case — the CD-R drive and an open slot that could hold a DVD drive, Zip drive, or other device. A second drive cage holds the floppy disk drive. A third drive cage has room for two internal hard drives. Each of the cages comes equipped with plastic rails that attach to drives before installation; this allows drives to slide in and out of the cages easily and permits precise positioning.*

FIGURE 6-19: *To open this model of modern case, remove all external cables and place the unit on its side. Push buttons on the top and bottom release catches that hold the two halves of the case together.*

Turned on its side, as shown in Figure 6-21, other components of the system are visible. The interior is dominated by the metal case for the power supply located at the upper-left; below it is the plastic cowling that sits atop the CPU to create a wind tunnel effect.

CROSS-REFERENCE

You can learn more about the power supply in Chapter 5.

FIGURE 6-21: *The power supply is shown at the upper-left. An extra-long wiring harness provides DC power to the drive cages at right and to the motherboard below. On this modern microATX motherboard, electrical power goes to the board at two locations.*

FIGURE 6-22: *The main power connection to the system on a microATX motherboard, marked as P1.*

Figure 6-22 shows the main wiring harness that supplies the bus, many onboard peripherals, and powered I/O chains, such as FireWire and USB. Figure 6-23 shows the secondary connection from the power supply to the motherboard, supplying the Intel Pentium 4 CPU, RDRAM memory, and associated chips.

Directly below the power supply is a large plastic cowling that sits atop the Pentium 4 CPU on the motherboard; the assembly extends to a fan that mounts at the back of the case, thus creating a wind tunnel to cool the 1.8-GHz microprocessor.

FIGURE 6-23: *The secondary power connection on a microATX motherboard, used by the CPU, and marked as P2.*

The highly integrated Intel motherboard, as shown in Figure 6-24, makes it easy to install new adapters and memory modules. Intel is the single largest manufacturer of motherboards; its boards and CPUs power the machines offered for sale by many brand name resellers.

As Figure 6-25 shows, I've removed the fan cowling. The cowling allows system designers to use a larger fan on the rear panel of the case instead of a smaller unit clipped directly to the CPU. The result is a wind tunnel that isolates a stream of exhaust air from the larger and less-channeled interior of the case.

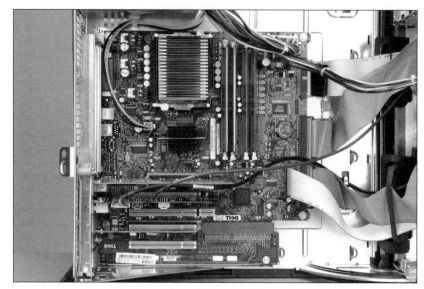

FIGURE 6-25: *Beneath the cooling fan assembly, the Pentium 4 sits beneath a massive heat sink that draws heat away from the microprocessor and into the stream of air moved by the case fan. The heat sink is held in place by clips at top and bottom.*

Peeling away the heat sink, the final layer of protection, the Pentium 4 microprocessor is revealed in Figure 6-26.

CROSS-REFERENCE

I discuss microprocessors in more detail in Chapter 2.

FIGURE 6-24: *Four slots for memory modules sit above the cooling fan assembly for the microprocessor. This motherboard uses RDRAM modules, called RIMMs; in this design, modules must be installed in pairs, and unused slots must be occupied by empty cards that complete the continuity of the circuit. Located to the right of the fan assembly are the five expansion slots. In this mostly tool-free design, the cards are held in place by a plastic lever that locks over the top of the installation brackets.*

FIGURE 6-26: *A small horizontal chip holds the system brain in a zero-insertion force socket; that design, which was a throwback to older microprocessors in PC history, requires addition of a heat sink, cooling fan, and wind tunnel cowling to draw away heat.*

To replace the CPU for repair or upgrade, the guillotine-like latch at the top of the socket is unhooked and lifted to release pressure on the pins of the microprocessor, as shown in Figure 6-27.

FIGURE 6-27: *Its latch open, the Pentium 4 can be removed. Most motherboards can only be upgraded within the same family of chips, although computer equipment manufacturers have proved ingenious over the years in coming up with adapters that permit use of CPUs that were not planned for when a particular motherboard was designed.*

RIMM modules with RDRAM, like the one shown in Figure 6-28, are similar in shape to DIMM modules that hold SDRAM. RIMMs, however, are covered with a heat sink to keep them cool. RIMMs use Rambus memory based on CMOS DRAM that at the time of their introduction provided sustainable system throughput as much as ten times faster than standard SDRAM, although that gap in performance has been eliminated in more modern SDRAM designs.

CROSS-REFERENCE

I discuss memory technology in Chapter 8.

Ch
6

FIGURE 6-28: *Memory modules, like this 128MB RIMM, plug into special sockets on the motherboard. The sockets for RIMMs and DIMMs are "keyed," requiring that modules be installed in the proper orientation; match the gaps or extra fingers on the module with the corresponding position on the socket.*

FIGURE 6-29: *Continuity modules complete the electrical circuit on a system based on RDRAM. Essential to the operation of the system, they hold no memory. On most systems based on RDRAM, the pair of sockets closest to the CPU—usually identified as Bank 0—must be populated first.*

RIMM modules use pipelining technology to send four 16-bit packets at a time to a 64-bit CPU. On a system based on RDRAM, unused memory sockets must be filled with continuity modules, like the one shown in Figure 6-29.

To add a new adapter card or replace an existing one within this advanced case, you open the latch over the brackets, as shown in Figure 6-30. In this system, the only place you'll need to use a screwdriver is to install devices in the drive cages or to remove the power supply.

In this class of machines, a separate AGP (accelerated graphics port) slot was offered for the use of a video adapter. The high-speed 32-bit bus was designed specifically for use with video cards. The original specification called for one data transfer per clock cycle; subsequent versions transfer two, four, and eight times with each cycle and are referred to as AGP2X, AGP4X, and AGP8X. The test machine for this book's seventh edition offered an AGP4X slot; that was quickly supplanted by AGP8X in later models. Today, most modern machines offer PCI Express x16 slots instead of AGP.

FIGURE 6-30: *The retaining latch for adapter cards on this advanced case has been opened, allowing insertion or removal of cards held in place in the expansion slots. On most other systems, the brackets are held in place by screws that connect to the frame of the case. The cables connected to the second adapter card from the top link the sound card to the CD-R drive.*

FIGURE 6-31: *The AGP slot on Dell's Dimension 8200 system includes a plastic locking bracket that hooks into an L-shaped notch on the card to lock it in place and provide stability.*

CROSS-REFERENCE

I explore AGP in detail in Chapter 4.

The AGP 4X slot shown in Figure 6-31 has 172 pins. Some systems include built-in video capabilities on a chipset that is electrically connected to the processor in the same manner as an AGP bus slot would be designed; this provides good speed for the video subsystem but offers limited flexibility when it comes to upgrades or replacement.

The AGP card used in this system, as shown in Figure 6-32, is based on the nVidia GeForce2 chip, a processor that was widely used in a number of older brand-name and generic video cards. It came equipped with 32MB of memory, which is more than adequate for most users but would not permit use of this machine with the full set of Windows Vista features.

A more modern video card with 128MB or 256MB of memory is one worthy upgrade for this machine. A word of warning: The card has to match the machine's AGP4X slot; an AGP8X card would not install in the slot or meet the system's electrical requirements. (By comparison, the original video card on the Dell Dimension 9200 written about earlier in this chapter offered 256MB of memory, and the upgraded replacement I installed doubled that to 512MB.)

CROSS-REFERENCE

You can learn more details about video cards in Chapter 13.

FIGURE 6-32: *This AGP card includes 32MB of memory, soldered in place in four chips above and to the right of the nVidia processor. The card also offers a feature connector, located at the upper-left, for use with other video circuitry, such as a TV tuner or a hardware-based DVD decoder.*

FIGURE 6-33: *The Sound Blaster Live! Card includes 13 connectors for various audio devices. Six are accessible from the outside of the case; the others require internal connections to devices such as a CD or DVD drive or a telephone answering device (sometimes part of the circuitry of a modem card).*

The sound card on this system, as shown in Figure 6-33, is a Sound Blaster Live! from Creative Labs, a capable device for most users; serious audiophiles and professional sound engineers will use cards with an even broader range of MIDI samples and signal processing circuitry.

CROSS-REFERENCE

I discuss sound cards in Chapter 19.

With all of the adapter cards removed, the bus of this modern machine is fully revealed in Figure 6-34. The four white slots are for use with PCI cards (including one with extensions for a 64-bit universal PCI adapter, not commonly used in consumer machines). The black slot at top, with its plastic retaining hook, is for use with AGP video cards.

FIGURE 6-34: *The Intel motherboard used in this advanced system is adaptable for use in compact systems, including just two PCI slots on the main board itself. A small expansion board attaches to a connector shown at the bottom of this picture, adding two more PCI slots.*

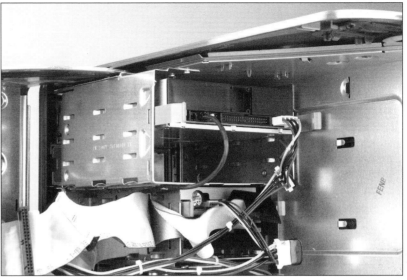

FIGURE 6-35: *CD and DVD drives of all designs include three groups of connectors. On this Matsushita CD-R, located from left to right are two plug-ins for audio output — digital and audio; a set of pins to accept a data cable that communicates with the bus, and a power input block.*

The machine includes a CD-R drive, installed in the upper drive cage, as shown in Figure 6-35. The cage includes space for two 5.25-inch drives; the second space can be used for a DVD or tape drive. With the use of special hardware, you can adapt it to hold a 3.5-inch device, such as a Zip drive or an additional hard drive.

Upgrades for an older modern machine

Our older modern machine started life well equipped for most users: a Pentium 4 processor running at a 1.8-GHz clock speed, 256MB of RDRAM memory, four USB 1.1 ports, a 40GB ATA/100 hard drive, and a CD-R. However, things change.

CPU speeds advance every few months — zooming past 2 GHz and heading toward 4 GHz as this book goes to press. More memory is almost always better than less. Four USB ports is probably more than enough when attached to hubs that allow it to work with dozens of devices; however, nearly all machines sold before early 2002 don't support the 40-times-faster USB 2.0 standard.

Like memory, you can always find a use for more hard disk storage. And faster is always better when it comes to reading and writing huge files to that disk.

In my office, I regularly make use of large digital images (including the photos in this book) and audio files, so my priorities for upgrade are large storage devices — internal and external — and data controllers capable of reading and writing the files as quickly as possible. And so, off go the covers and into the bus and card cages for these projects:

- Installation of a USB 2.0 adapter to support a 40GB external hard drive and future high-speed devices
- Adding a FireWire adapter to allow direct high-speed connection to professional digital camcorders and cameras
- Installation of an ATA/133 hard drive adapter to support the transfer rate and capacity of a 160GB hard drive

 CROSS-REFERENCE

I explore a USB 2.0 adapter in more detail in Chapter 15.

I used a card from Keyspan that offers four external and one internal high-speed USB ports that are capable of transferring data at as much as 480 MBps in combination with USB 2.0 drivers from Microsoft.

For devices to operate at the USB 2.0 speed, all the components in the chain must be compatible with the newer standard. If you use a USB hub to expand the number of ports and provide additional electrical power to the circuit, the hub must include USB 2.0 circuitry to operate at 480 MBps.

Older devices, including hubs, are compatible with USB 2.0 ports and drivers, but they will run at the original USB 1.1 speed of 12 MBps.

After the card and current software drivers were installed, I was able to attach and immediately use a Maxtor 40GB external USB hard drive for backup purposes. Within the box is a 5,400 RPM 3.5-inch IDE drive with a 2MB cache buffer. Unlike many other USB devices, the drive requires its own power supply because of the needs of the drive motor.

The next enhancement to the system was the installation of a Belkin FireWire card that adds three 400 MBps ports for use with digital video devices, scanners, hard drives, and other peripherals. FireWire is an implementation of the IEEE 1394 standard.

The card, shown in Figure 6-36, is a Plug-and-Play device that installs in the PCI bus; I also installed a FireWire hub, as shown in Figure 6-37, to expand the number of available ports and amplify electrical current on the chain.

 CROSS-REFERENCE

I cover FireWire technology in more detail in Chapter 15.

Like USB, FireWire can divide the available bandwidth *isochronously*, dedicating a particular slice of the spectrum to particular devices — useful in such applications as streaming video. FireWire can also operate *asynchronously*, a more flexible means of communication for devices that can accept information broken into packets and able to deal with sometimes-changing conditions along the shared cable as other devices request access to the stream of data.

FIGURE 6-36: *Belkin's FireWire PCI Card allows hot-swapping of devices. Just as with USB, a series of FireWire devices can be daisy-chained to each other. Unlike USB, though, the result is a peer-to-peer network between and among the devices on the node without active control by the PC; devices can even communicate with each other without management by the computer. The design also permits two computers to share a single peripheral.*

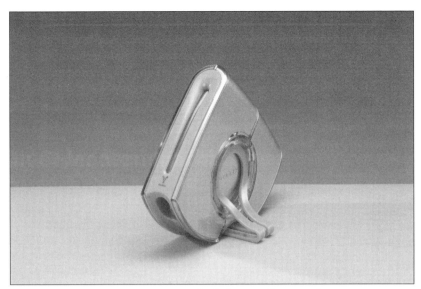

FIGURE 6-37: *This six-port FireWire hub from Belkin can draw its power from the bus or amplify available electrical current for devices through the use of a power block. The rear panel contains five ports; another port is hidden behind a panel on the front. A docking ring on the side mates the hub to additional hubs, routers, and other devices from the same manufacturer.*

The next project was to burst through a pair of barriers on hard drive capacity and speed of transfer.

CROSS-REFERENCE

I discuss hard drives in detail in Chapter 10.

I installed Maxtor's DiamondMax D540X, a 160GB hard drive that also introduced the Ultra ATA/133 standard (developed by Maxtor) that permits data transfer of as much as 133 MBps to and from the interface. The drive, shown in Figure 6-38, slipped into place below the original 40GB hard drive in the system.

The chipset included as part of Ultra ATA/133 breaks through the 137GB barrier for ATA hard drives, allowing a new top end of 100,000 times more data: 48-bit addressing permits a single drive with more than 144 *petabytes* (144 million gigabytes) of storage.

The interface uses the same 80-conductor, 40-pin cable used for ATA/100 and provides backward compatibility with all parallel ATA devices, including Ultra ATA/33, ATA/66 and ATA/100. The interface includes a set of tightly controlled specifications for trace lengths and timing parameters, an essential element of any high-speed parallel interface.

Motherboards are expected to add support to ATA/133 (as well as the developing Serial ATA standard). In the meantime, Maxtor and licensed manufacturers will offer adapter cards, like the one shown in Figure 6-39, to update systems.

FIGURE 6-38: *In our demonstration system, the 160GB hard drive shares a drive cage with a 40GB drive; both devices are attached by cable to a new ATA/133 adapter card, although the smaller drive will be limited to its original 100 MBps transfer rate.*

Ch 6

FIGURE 6-39: *The ATA/133 adapter card included drivers to update Windows 98 and later operating systems to work with the new standard.*

SUMMARY

Now it's time to go shopping! In the next chapter, I look at shopping strategies and sources.

Ch
6

Notes

Chapter 7

Shopping for PC Parts

I've got some good news and some bad news. First the good news: Today's modern machines are, by some measures, more than a thousand times faster than the original dinosaurs of the early 1980s and cost one-third to one-quarter as much. (If only other products followed the same pattern, we'd all be driving $29.95 Porsches and watching 60-inch HDTV plasma screen TVs given away as door prizes with the purchase of a tank full of gasoline.)

In recent years, CPUs have doubled in speed every one to two years. Hard disk drives have increased greatly in size and speed; today, you can purchase a relatively gigantic 100GB hard drive for less than the price of a 1GB drive of just a few years ago. The price of memory has dropped so much that it is no longer much of a significant issue in calculating the cost of repairs and upgrades.

Now the bad news: With prices on almost every part of a modern machine plummeting so fast and so often, it is generally foolish to even bother to repair a major component of a senior citizen or a dinosaur. Only when you come to the world of modern machines is it sometimes worthwhile to perform major surgery.

This reality does not mean that you shouldn't replace or upgrade a hard drive, install a new video adapter with improved features, or add RAM or (if possible) a new CPU to an underpowered older machine. Just pay attention to the bottom line. This chapter helps you to calculate cost-benefit bottom lines for repair jobs and explore bare-bones computer recycling projects.

My Dream System

Every time this book goes through a major revision, I present a state-of-the-art system. And every time, the system is out of date before the ink dries on these pages. That's good news, of course. But just keep in mind that what is fresh and fast today is guaranteed to appear old and slow (and less expensive) in six months' time. There's nothing we can do about it, and we really shouldn't want the process to slow down; we are the beneficiaries of the rapid progress in technology and the constant downward pressure on prices.

If I could design a system, it would include the latest *proven* technology and the best *consumer* hardware on the market. Later and greater toys will always come along, but I'm looking for a rocket I can ride right out of the box. At the same time, though, I'm always looking for the best deal. For that reason, I usually recommend buying a system that is one notch, or one generation, below the latest and greatest. With that in mind, here's the system I would put together today:

- Intel Core 2 Duo Processor E6600 (2.4 GHz, 1066 FSB)
- BTX form factor motherboard
- 512MB ATI Radeon X1600 Pro graphics card
- 20-inch widescreen digital flat-panel LCD display
- 1GB Dual Channel DDR2 SDRAM at 667 MHz
- 250GB Serial ATA 3GBps 7200 RPM hard drive
- 1X, 8X, and 16X PCI Express slots plus three standard PCI slots
- 10/100/1000 Fast Ethernet NIC
- 48X CD-RW Drive
- 16X DVD +/- RW drive with double-layer write capability

- Sound Blaster X-Fi XtremeMusic digital sound card with Dolby Digital 5.1
- Microsoft Windows XP Home or Windows Vista Home Premium

The price, in early 2007, delivered to my door, was less than $1,000. If I wanted to add a 20-inch widescreen digital flat panel LCD display, the whole price for this drag racer of a system would reach about $1,350.

As you already explored, since the birth of the PC, prices have trended downward almost without interruption at the same time as speed and capability have gone up. In the four years since I last calculated the price of a realistic high-end machine, the price of my dream has dropped by about 50 percent at the same time as the processor and motherboard speed has doubled. And for that half-off price, I could buy four times as much RAM, a video adapter that runs about four times faster and comes with four times as much video memory, and a hard drive three times as large.

And the cherry atop the whipped cream: At the time I priced this system, the Intel Core Duo processor had just been introduced to the market; by the time this book is in your hands I am certain that the same system will cost a few hundred dollars less or offer a larger hard drive or more memory or an improved video card for the same price.

In this book's seventh edition, I specified a system like this: a 2.0 GHz Pentium 4 processor, a 64MB 4X AGP graphics card, 256MB of PC800 memory, an 80GB hard drive, a 16X/10X/40X CD-RW drive and a 16X read-only DVD drive, an Ethernet port, and an Iomega Zip internal drive. The machine would have come equipped with Microsoft Windows XP Pro. The retail price for this system (without monitor) in early 2002 was about $1,850. To this I would have added a 19-inch flat-screen Trinitron monitor for a desktop (about $450), or a 21-inch Trinitron monitor for graphics work (about $750). Bottom line: $2,300 for a desktop or $2,600 for a graphics workstation.

Just as an exercise, as I researched this edition, I tried to find a machine close to the model used in the previous edition; the closest I came was a more-capable PC with a 3.0-GHz Pentium 4 and 512MB of RAM (twice the memory), with an included 15-inch analog LCD. The price: $499 delivered, or a 78-percent discount from 2003 prices. That's a pretty potent machine — I was willing to recommend less in 2002 — but today the gap between the bottom of the market and a reasonable high-end PC is a few hundred dollars. Spread that over a PC's typical three-year lifetime, and the cost per day for the very best is very little.

NOTE

And just for the record, in the sixth edition of this book, I specified a dream machine that was the available state-of-the-art in 2000. It included an 800-MHz Pentium III with a front-side bus of 133 MHz, a 27GB hard drive, and a 21-inch monitor. This machine, arguably somewhere between one-third or one-quarter as capable as today's dream machine, would have cost about $3,000 in 2000.

Current Versions of Windows

The vast majority of modern machines use a version of Microsoft Windows as the operating system, the underlying program that bridges the needs of the computer's software and the capabilities of its hardware. Today the latest and possibly the greatest version of Windows is Vista, introduced at the start of 2007.

In a bit of electronic tail-wagging-the-dog, it is the demands of the operating system that defines the hardware on which it runs. Those few machines that use an alternate system, such as Linux, generally require about the same basic minimum configuration as Windows. (There is not a huge incentive to produce less-demanding operating systems when — as we have seen — hardware prices continue to go down as their capabilities go up. For many users, Windows XP (introduced in late 2001) will continue to be the operating system of choice for several years after widespread introduction of Windows Vista. First of all, not all machines will be capable of working with the new OS, and secondly, not all users will want (or need) to upgrade.

And then there are the cautious users who make a practice of never upgrading their operating system until a new version has been out on the market for six months to a year to allow for patches, updates, and service packs to fix what seem to be inevitable problems with new versions. That's not a bad strategy at all: Let someone else be the guinea pig.

Windows Vista

Microsoft plans to issue Windows Vista in a number of versions for business, server, and personal uses. As the market develops, there may be other versions added. Here is the initial lineup, as released in 2007:

Ch 7

- **Windows Vista Business.** Aimed at organizations of all sizes, the business version also will include a new user interface named Windows Aero, which delivers a professional-looking, transparent glass design, with subtle effects such as dynamic reflections and smooth animations, along with Windows Flip and Flip 3D desktop navigation features. Windows Vista Business also includes features that are intended to make it easier to manage and search through huge volumes of business documents. Also offered is Windows Tablet PC technology for handwriting recognition and interaction with a digital pen or fingertip instead of a keyboard.
- **Windows Vista Enterprise.** For large global organizations and operations with highly complex IT infrastructures, Windows Vista Enterprise includes all of the features of Windows Vista Business plus higher levels of data protection using hardware-based encryption technology (called BitLocker), enhanced compatibility with applications developed for earlier versions of Windows (in a feature called Virtual PC Express), and the ability to standardize on a single worldwide deployment image. Microsoft said that Windows Vista Enterprise will be available only to customers who have PCs covered by Microsoft Software Assurance or a Microsoft Enterprise Agreement.
- **Windows Vista Home Basic.** This entry-level version of the operating system is intended for consumers who concentrate on basic computing needs including browsing the Internet, corresponding through e-mail, and performing basic document creation and editing tasks. The operating system includes new tools and technologies such as a new Search Explorer, Sidebar, and Parental Controls.
- **Windows Vista Home Premium.** A more advanced home version, it adds the Windows Aero user interface as well as specialized Windows Media Center facilities, allowing users to record and watch television (including high-definition TV) and provides the software side of a connection to Microsoft's Xbox 360 game system. Also offered is integrated search throughout the operating system, helping users organize and quickly find large collections of documents, pictures, movies, videos, and music. Other features include Windows Tablet PC technology and integrated DVD burning and authoring.
- **Windows Vista Ultimate.** The full bells-and-whistles version brings together all the entertainment features, mobility features, and business-oriented features available in Windows Vista.

All of the new operating system versions are available for either 32-bit or 64-bit systems. If you purchase a boxed version of the operating system from a retail store or web site, the included DVD has all the various versions; you'll be able to unlock and use the appropriate edition based on the license (and serial number) you have purchased. There were no immediate plans to offer the operating system on CD.

In emerging markets Microsoft also will offer Windows Vista Starter, a 32-bit version designed specifically for lower-cost computers. This version is intended to provide an easy-to-use and more affordable entry point to the Windows Vista family of products.

Windows Vista minimum configuration

New, improved, and more demanding than ever: Windows Vista has a set of minimum requirements that a few years ago would have sounded like the computer equivalent of a race car but today represent a merely ordinary modern machine. Windows Vista is Microsoft's first operating system that is designed to adapt its onscreen bells and whistles to take advantage of the hardware on the machine on which it is installed. Any machine declared by its manufacturer (or determined by the user) to be Windows Vista Capable will be able to run the operating system's core elements; a machine that is Windows Vista Premium Ready can deliver advanced features including the Windows Aero user experience.

Microsoft offers a piece of downloadable software that will examine your existing machine and report on whether it is worthy of an upgrade to Vista. The Windows Vista Upgrade Advisor was offered at www.microsoft.com/windowsvista/getready/upgradeadvisor.

Here are Microsoft's absolute minimums for a **Windows Vista Capable PC:**

- **CPU:** An 800-MHz or faster 32-bit (x86) or 64-bit (x64) processor.
- **Memory:** 512MB of RAM for basic functions.
- **Storage:** At least 15GB of free space on a drive of at least 20GB in size.
- **Storage:** A CD-ROM or DVD drive. (A DVD drive is required for installation of Vista to an already-configured PC.)
- **Graphics:** Super VGA (800 × 600) or higher resolution video adapter, capable of working with DirectX 9.0 or later.
- **Internet access:** High-speed broadband Internet recommended for updates and patches.

Ch
7

For full functionality, Microsoft set the bar for what it calls a **Windows Vista Premium Ready PC.** Here's the minimum you need to get all of the bells and whistles:

- **CPU:** A 1-GHz or faster 32-bit (x86) or 64-bit (x64) processor.
- **Memory:** 1GB of RAM for basic functions.
- **Storage:** At least 15GB of free space on a drive of at least 40GB.
- **Storage:** A DVD drive.
- **Graphics:** Super VGA (800 × 600) or higher resolution video adapter with at least 128MB of graphics memory, capable of working with DirectX 9.0 or later.
- **Audio:** A current sound card or adapter.
- **Internet access:** High-speed broadband Internet recommended for updates and patches.

Features available in specific premium editions of Windows Vista, such as the ability to watch and record live TV, may require additional hardware.

And for the record, Microsoft's "footnotes" for its definition of Windows Vista machines include this: Audio Processor speed is specified as the nominal operational processor frequency for the device. Some processors have power management that allows the processor to run at lower rate to save power.

Windows Aero requirements:

- DirectX 9 class graphics processor that supports a WDDM driver, supports Pixel Shader 2.0 in hardware, and supports 32 bits per pixel.
- Adequate graphics memory is defined as 64MB of graphics memory to support a single monitor less than 1,310,720 pixels, 128MB of graphics memory to support a single monitor at resolutions from 1,310,720 to 2,304,000 pixels, and 256MB of graphics memory to support a single monitor at resolutions higher than 2,304,000 pixels The graphics memory also must meet minimum bandwidth requirements, as assessed by Windows Vista Upgrade Advisor.
- A DVD-ROM may be external or internal to the system. It is also worth noting that the operating system's initial release will be distributed on a DVD, not a CD. If you are upgrading a machine that has just a CD, you may need to upgrade to an internal or external DVD drive to install Windows Vista.

Upgrading to Windows Vista editions

If your machine meets the minimum requirements for Windows Vista, you can take one of two paths to upgrade from a previous current version (Windows XP or Windows 2000): an in-place upgrade or a clean install.

An *in-place upgrade* means that you can install Windows Vista as a replacement for the previous operating system, retaining your existing applications, settings, and files. A *clean install* requires you to back up all of your files and settings to another device (most commonly, to a secondary hard drive or a set of DVD discs) before installing the operating system; once it is in place, you need to reinstall all of your software applications and then load backed-up files and settings.

Before you attempt an upgrade, check the web sites and help desks for all of your major software applications to make certain your most important software and utilities will function with Windows Vista; in some instances you may need to upgrade applications along with the operating system.

Here is Microsoft's description of upgrade procedures for Windows Vista:

	Vista Home Basic	Vista Home Premium	Vista Business	Vista Ultimate
Windows XP Professional	Clean	Clean	In-place	In-place
Windows XP Home	In-place	In-place	In-place	In-place
Windows XP Media Center	Clean	In-place	Clean	In-place
Windows XP Professional x64	Clean	Clean	Clean	Clean
Windows 2000	Clean	Clean	Clean	Clean

In general, however, I recommend a clean installation on all platforms. With Windows it is good practice to refresh your installation periodically (every year or so, depending on usage, new applications installed, and so on). Why not just start Vista clean?

Ch 7

WARNING

In some cases an in-place installation can cause problems with legacy files, resulting in application problems or system slow down.

Windows XP minimum configuration

Windows XP was notably more stable than earlier operating systems and if your PC had the horsepower to let it run at full throttle, it is a bit faster than Windows 98SE. You'll experience far fewer system crashes, and although the occasional application — including some from Microsoft — will crash, Windows XP offers some tools that allow you to save files in progress and even keep the rest of the operating system running if a program dies.

Microsoft has continued support for older operating systems for at least two years after introducing a new OS; under that calendar, you can reasonably expect Windows XP support until at least early 2009.

Three versions of Windows XP were available. The original releases were XP Home and XP Professional. There is also an adaptation of the Home version called Windows XP Media Center Edition that includes some specialized features for use with advanced audio and video hardware including TV tuners, Internet radio and music sources, and home entertainment centers.

The Professional edition adds support for machines with multiple processors and adds a suite of management tools and the ability to access your desktop remotely. Among the added tools are IntelliMirror, a desktop settings and software administration package for corporate networks, and security features, including file-level access control and file encryption.

Although the Home edition works with no more than five computers in a peer-to-peer network, Windows XP Professional expands its reach to ten machines. Larger networks should work with server software.

Most benchmarks showed that Windows XP is noticeably faster than Windows 95/98, but just a bit speedier than Windows 2000 Professional. For many users, the biggest improvement came in a different area — reliability. Windows XP is much more stable than Windows 95 or 98; when applications do crash, they are not likely to halt the operating system. Windows XP and Office XP also work together to save data automatically in the event of a problem.

On the hardware side, Microsoft says Windows XP supported some 12,000 devices in its original release, including drivers for the top 1,000 best-selling devices. If you have any doubt about other products, consult their manufacturers before upgrading to Windows XP.

Here are the minimum requirements for installing XP:

- **CPU:** PC with 300 MHz or higher processor clock speed recommended; 233 MHz minimum required. Intel Pentium/Celeron family, AMD K6/Athlon/Duron family, or compatible processor recommended.
- **Memory:** 128MB of RAM or higher recommended. The operating system should work with as little as 64MB, but performance will be limited and some features may not work. For the best performance, a minimum of 256MB is suggested.
- **Storage:** 1.5GB of available hard disk space. CD-ROM or DVD drive.
- **Graphics:** Super VGA (800 × 600) or higher resolution video adapter and monitor.
- **I/O:** Keyboard and Microsoft mouse or compatible pointing device.

My personal recommendation: Stock your Windows XP machine with at least 256MB of RAM and go to 512MB or 1GB if you can.

One significant change introduced by Microsoft with Windows XP is an "activation" process for the operating system. When installed, you must turn on each copy of Windows XP by registering it with Microsoft by Internet or over the telephone. An Internet connection, especially a high-speed broadband link, is very useful in keeping your operating system up to date with security fixes and new features.

Your copy of Windows XP is then uniquely associated with a particular computer, making it officially impossible to use the same disk to upgrade more than one machine. (It has always been against the license agreement to install and use one copy of the operating system on more than one machine, although the prohibition has been widely ignored.)

If you purchase a new machine with the operating system installed, it should come with the new version of Windows linked to the machine's BIOS, which should avoid the need for reactivation unless Windows XP needs to be installed on a new hard drive.

On older PCs upgraded to Windows XP, the operating system will be linked to a set of specific pieces of hardware, including a network adapter (if installed).

Ch
7

Under Microsoft's scheme, certain significant changes in hardware would result in the operating system requiring you to reactivate the installation by telephone or over the Internet.

The Obsolescence Factor

The hard fact of computer life is this: Between the time you select a PC part at the back of the store and to the time you carry it to the checkout counter, it is already outdated and devalued. New products are constantly spilling out of the laboratories and factories and the very last place they appear is on the shelves or in the mail-order catalogs.

However, it is also true that if you keep waiting for the latest and greatest, you will always be waiting. Sooner or later you've got to jump in and make a purchase.

The way I see it, in most cases, you face three options when it comes to buying a new machine:

- **Money is no object:** Buy the hottest new technology as soon as it is offered to the public. You'll pay top dollar and likely have to put up with some troublesome bugs and incompatibilities until software catches up with hardware, but for a period of time — perhaps a month or two — you'll be as current as the magazine covers.
- **The savvy consumer:** Buy one step behind the state-of-the-art. You may end up with a slightly slower or smaller device, but you'll benefit from the inevitable price reduction when an item moves just a bit out of the spotlight. For example, as this book goes to press, the hottest new things are the Intel Core 2 Duo and the Intel Quad Core and machines based on chips in those series command the highest prices; the best price/performance ratios, though, are for systems based one or two notches behind. The two options: Buy one of the slightly slower versions of the Core 2 Duo or Quad Core rather than the top of the line, or buy a system built around a Pentium D or Pentium 4 chip. The lesser or older chips are potentially about 20 to 40 percent slower for a small number of particular types of operations, but are priced several hundred dollars below the top of the line.
- **Money is the name of the game:** Buy the cheapest closeout products. You can find some incredible savings if you're willing to help a retailer or mail-order operator clear out back inventory. However, the truth is that saving money like this can become more expensive — in time and money — down the road. Settling

for an Intel Celeron in the age of the Intel Core Duo can mean that the latest and greatest operating systems or software will run noticeably slower than they would on a state-of-the-art machine. Buying an inexpensive smaller hard drive can be penny-wise and pound-foolish if you end up having to pull it out in six months because it is much too small for your applications. Also, you may end up with hardware that is no longer backed up with technical support by manufacturers.

The Rules of the Computer Shopping Game

You can pay $3,000 for a poorly designed, ill-configured, and otherwise inappropriate machine, or you can pay half that price — or less — for the perfect speedster. It's all related to your skills as a shopper.

Here are Sandler's Basic Rules for Computer Shopping:

1. Do your own research in this book, in computer magazines, and online before making a buying decision.
2. Ask lots of questions before you place your order.
3. Make the rapid pace of improvement work to your advantage: Buy the latest and greatest for the longest active life or buy one step behind the curve for the best price-performance.
4. Always pay with a credit card.

I explain the reasons behind the rules in the following sections.

A Bang-for-the-Buck Price Matrix

Is a machine that runs 10 percent faster on your desktop worth 50 percent more at the checkout counter? Is twice the storage space worth three times the price? Maybe yes — if you're running a very complex, mission-critical piece of software for your business. Maybe yes — if you're a maniacal game player and have money to burn. For the rest of us, sometimes it pays to search for the sweet spot — the combination of hardware that gives you the most bang for your bucks.

It is the very nature of technology's progress that yesterday's top of the line is today's most bang for the buck. As I noted earlier, as this book goes to press, the top of the line in consumer-level PCs are the Intel Core 2 Duo and the Intel Quad Core just behind it in the pipeline; the sweet spot, a savings of a few hundred dollars, is a still super-speedy late-model Pentium 4 or a Pentium D Duo-Core chip. By the end of 2007, the Pentium 4 may be out of the mix and the sweet spot may be the "old" Core 2 Duo.

In previous editions of this book, I discussed how it was theoretically possible to save a small amount of money by building your own PC by assembling parts purchased at retail. With this edition, though, it is time to acknowledge the reality: PCs have become commodities. It is now almost always less expensive to buy a pre-assembled machine than to buy it piece-by-piece; put another way, the sum of the parts is greater than the whole. The reason, of course, is that PC companies (it's not really accurate to call them manufacturers) buy components at wholesale prices. And like it or not, they are able to scour the world in search of the least expensive power supply, motherboard, memory, hard disk drive, and other components.

The good news is that low prices do not necessarily mean poor quality. A good PC company does not want to sell machines that break down while they are still under warranty or even a few years after that date; they want to make a profit — even just a small one — on every machine they sell, and they want to hold on to satisfied customers over the years.

At the same time, the major suppliers of parts have found ways to stay in the game while cutting costs. For example, Intel supplies many of the motherboards used by major computer companies, including Dell; the boards may have been designed and built almost anywhere in the world. Similarly, the major hard disk drive makers have factories in what may sound like unusual locations like Thailand.

Where to put your money down

Should you buy a new computer from a web site or should you lay hands on a working unit at a retail store? What about purchasing major upgrade or repair components?

Every PC owner has his or her own comfort level. Speaking for myself, I am perfectly comfortable with ordering items over the telephone — from a set of screwdrivers to a complete PC system costing several thousand dollars. Even better is ordering over the Internet, which allows me to research products and easily compare one web site's offerings and prices with another's.

For computer configurations, the Web is a fast and easy way to build a custom system, check the price and specs, add and remove components, and keep at it until you have just the system you want. Most computer manufacturers and parts supply houses have online configuration programs that allow you to mix and match parts and compare bottom lines.

Other folks, though, like to touch the hardware and squeeze the cellophane, preferring to make their purchases at a retail store.

Which is best for you? Table 7-1 presents the pluses and minuses of shopping in person or by phone or keyboard.

What about mail-order fraud? First of all, most mail-order operations are honest, and you can count on them to deliver. However, you can do one very important thing to increase your leverage: Always pay with a credit card and always carefully monitor your credit card statements. The bank that issues your credit card is required by law — and bound by good customer-service practices — to help you receive goods for payment. If you order a product and it does not arrive but a charge is posted to your account, contact the issuer of your credit card immediately and follow its procedures to protest the charge.

What about support? It has been my experience that you can obtain excellent — or lousy — technical support from any source, whether an Internet outfit or a local retail store. Besides, most electronic equipment is extremely reliable. If it passes the infant-mortality stage of, say, the first six to eight weeks, it should last years. Almost all systems and components carry at least a 90-day warranty; many have one- and two-year buyer protection warranties. If a system or component fails during the warranty, the seller usually will simply replace it, so the issue of repair isn't all that serious. After the warranty period, you're on your own anyway, and that's why you're reading this book.

In addition, consider the packaged in-home or in-office repair service included with many systems from companies such as Dell and Gateway. If you buy a machine with this kind of warranty, a phone call usually brings a service person to your doorstep within 24 hours. If you bought from a local retail store, you will likely have to disconnect the machine and carry it into the store for service. What you decide to do depends on your personal level of comfort with doing some of your own work, or how well you know the company or person selling you the machine.

Most major computer companies now offer different tiers of support. For example, you may be offered a basic warranty of just 90 days on a company's least-expensive model, with higher-priced models coming with a year's warranty and phone support. And then you may be offered the chance to purchase an extended warranty and multi-year service contract. And some companies have separated the warranty from phone support; you may be offered the right to call a technician to seek assistance in troubleshooting hardware and even software . . . for a price. Be sure that you understand the terms of any warranty or support policy. On-site service may not extend to all parts of the machine or to all locations. You may be asked to ship products to a depot for service, which may cause a disruption in your office or home use.

I always ask lots of questions before I make a purchase. If I'm not satisfied with the answers, I take my business elsewhere. In other words, if company representatives are not very helpful before you make a purchase, what makes you think they'll be of assistance after they have your money?

TABLE 7-1: Internet, Telephone, and Mail Order versus Retail Stores	
Internet, Telephone, Mail Order	**Retail Store**
+ Generally lower prices	– May be more expensive, although computer superstores approach mail-order prices
+ May have larger selection	– Sometimes more limited in selection
+ May offer the latest technologies, updated almost daily	– Models on sale may be several months or more behind the latest technology
+ The buyer should be able to order a customized machine	– Most retailers offer a limited selection of models and variations and are not set up to allow internal component customization
+/– The best mail-order houses have first-rate free technical support; some, though, are only order-takers	+/– The best retailers offer onsite technical experts or toll-free help
+/– The best outfits have liberal return and replacement policies	+/– The best outfits have liberal return and replacement policies
+ May not charge sales tax in some states	– Will charge sales tax if one is in effect in the state where the store is located
– Adds shipping charges	+ Take home your package immediately, and without a shipping charge
+/– Convenience factor: Overnight courier delivery to your home or office for extra charge	+/– Convenience factor: Immediate pickup if you drive to the store

The upgrade upset

A more logical task than building your own system is replacing the parts of a machine that have failed or become hopelessly outdated. A careful shopper can save hundreds or even thousands of dollars by reusing pieces of an older computer that are still working, substituting only what needs to be replaced.

A careful shopper can also replace a bad motherboard for a few hundred dollars and reinstall memory, hard drives, and adapter cards from the previous system. And while you're at it, you can often upgrade the microprocessor to near state of the art for just a few dollars more. But sometimes the cost of an upgrade or a repair amounts to a substantial proportion of the cost of a new machine . . . or even surpasses the price tag for a replacement. When does an upgrade make sense? The bottom line is different for every user and every user's pocketbook, but in general, it is worth upgrading a PC when several major components are worth recycling. For example, if you have a current motherboard with a PCI bus, an AGP graphics slot, and a capable BIOS, it might make sense to consider adding memory and fixing a failed power supply. Figure out the replacement cost for the components of your machine and subtract them from the price of a new system.

For most modern machines, the most bang for your buck is to install additional RAM and possibly a new hard drive as a replacement or second storage device. If you already have a modern CPU (a Pentium 4, for example), it probably does not make economic sense to purchase a faster microprocessor (and its cooling system). A better use of your money is to purchase additional RAM. More memory allows the microprocessor more working space, especially if you are calling upon the CPU to manage more than one software application at a time.

The motherboard trap

If you've read this far in this book, you are a good candidate for the most major of repair and upgrade tasks: changing the motherboard. The job is not all that difficult, but it does require a great deal of attention to detail. If you're the sort of person who can read a roadmap in a strange place, keep track of half a dozen different sets of screws, clips, and wires, and don't mind blazing a sometimes uncharted path from time to time, replacing the motherboard can be an entertaining electronic puzzle.

Before you buy and install a new motherboard, though, consider the hidden costs of the change. A new board may use a different bus — PCI instead of the ISA slots on an older machine, or PCI Express instead of AGP and PCI on a more recent model, for example — which may limit your ability to reuse older components. Also, the type of memory configuration that your old motherboard uses may be different from the type that the new motherboard needs. Also, its CPU socket or slot may not work with a previous microprocessor.

A replacement board that uses the ATX or the newer BTX form factor design that includes I/O ports directly mounted on the motherboard, may require a new case as well.

And then you must consider the other costs of an upgrade: Even if the bus doesn't change, will you want to upgrade to a better graphics card, a larger hard drive, or a faster CD-ROM?

If you're buying a new motherboard that uses a different form factor than the one you are replacing, I suggest buying your motherboard and case from the same supplier; this way, you have a reasonable expectation that the motherboard will actually fit and mount in the case, and you can have some hope that the seller's technical staff can assist you.

You can tell from this discussion that the overall cost of upgrading the motherboard may, in some cases, be higher than simply purchasing a packaged system complete with warranty and state-of-the-art everything. Again, do some online comparisons from packaged system houses and from the component shops before you decide on the next step toward upgrading. Although I am very comfortable upgrading machines from the motherboard up, I frequently decide to leave well enough alone and buy a new machine as my upgrade. All my computers are networked, so I usually leave the old machine on the network as a backup disk server or printer server, or use it to conduct other tasks that it can do very well in the background, even though it is slower and older than I personally want to use for my day-to-day work.

The bare-bones kit solution

One route to upgrading your system is to buy a bare-bones kit that includes a motherboard and CPU preinstalled in a case with power supply.

If you buy from a reliable source, you are relying on the expertise of the seller in matching the right CPU to the motherboard, the proper motherboard to the case, and mating the board to the half dozen power leads and connectors of the power supply and case. Figures 7-1 through 7-3 show good examples of basic bare-bones systems.

It's up to you to install a floppy drive, hard drive, RAM, and video card. The drives and video cards should easily transfer from one modern machine to another. Memory may or may not be easy to move; new motherboards may use DIMMs instead of SIMMs or may demand faster chips than you have on your older machine.

Once again, it's time to sit down and add up the costs of new equipment and compare them with the price of a new system.

One of the better suppliers of bare-bones systems is TigerDirect (www.tigerdirect.com). Their prices are competitive with other suppliers — although you may still end up paying a bit more than if you purchased a preassembled machine from a major PC company. The advantage of a bare-bones system like those sold by Tiger is that you have a very wide range of options when it comes to selecting components; you aren't limited to choosing from just those offered by Dell, Gateway, HP, Compaq, or other system sellers. The disadvantage is that individual components are sold at retail prices. Keep a close eye on the bottom line, and look for special sales.

Don't overlook the fact that you also have to install an operating system and applications on the computer. You can transfer some from your old machine — most software licenses permit you to move the program from one system to another, as long as it does not end up running on both. If you have to pay for a new version of Windows and a suite of applications, be sure to figure in that cost and compare it to the software and operating system package that is often included with new computers.

Ch
7

FIGURE 7-1: *This Tiger bare-bones case includes convenient side-panel access to the motherboard. The panel removes with just two screws.*

FIGURE 7-2: *A senior-citizen bare-bones system, delivered with the motherboard and Pentium II processor in place. It's up to you to add memory, drives, and other internal peripherals and then bring it all to life with an operating system and application software.*

One of the systems I put together a few years ago was based around an AMD-K6 MMX processor running at 200 MHz — a clone of the Pentium MMX processor. The bare-bones package included an AT PCI motherboard with the AMD processor already installed in a Socket 7 carrier. The board included support for four 72-pin SIMMs or two 168-pin DIMMs, 512K of L2 cache, a dual-channel EIDE controller, two high-speed serial ports, and an ECP/EPP parallel port.

I added a floppy drive for installation of software and device drivers, a 6GB IDE hard drive, an SVGA video card, 32MB of RAM, a 24X CD-ROM, a basic sound card, a mouse, and a keyboard. The cost of the system and parts would have been about $800 for all-new equipment, but I saved about half of that cost by recycling bits and pieces from other machines around the office.

FIGURE 7-3: *Under the side panel of a Tiger K6 bare-bones case.*

But from the standpoint of a recycling project, such a project is a quick and easy way to upgrade a senior citizen or older modern machine — or at least some of its parts — to a zippy middle-of-the-road desktop.

SUMMARY

You've looked at the basics of upgrading systems in this chapter. The next chapter examines the essential area of computer memory: your PC's thinking room.

Chapter 8

Tools Needed:

- Phillips or flat-blade screwdriver
- Antistatic strip, wrist strap, or grounding pad

Memory

Memory is your computer's workspace. To a great extent, the effectiveness of your computer is related to the amount of random access memory it has. Given a choice between an adequate CPU with lots of RAM (random access memory), and a speedster CPU with insufficient RAM, I say, "Thanks for the memory."

System memory has been something of critical importance throughout the history of computers. More so than ever, today's high-speed, multitasking, graphics-rich machines demand huge amounts of memory. The first IBM PC, the dinosaur of dinosaurs, shipped with as little as 16KB of RAM. With the arrival of Windows Vista in 2007, current machines should have a minimum of 1GB of RAM to take advantage of all of the features of the operating system, an increase of about 60,000-fold. If you're working with a still-capable older modern machine and running Windows XP, a realistic minimum is 512MB, although you can still work with 256MB. Older operating systems like Windows 98SE could get by with as little as 64MB, at the price of rather sluggish response.

Let me stop for a moment to explain a critical distinction: Data or instructions stored in chips are said to be stored in *random access memory (RAM)*. *Random access* means that the processor can jump directly to a particular bit of data. Think of RAM as the computer's desktop, where it temporarily gathers and works on the work of the moment. If the computer needs the date and amount of a check you wrote six years ago, it can reach across the equivalent of a huge compartmentalized flat table to grab the information it needs.

Data or instructions located on a disk drive are said to be located in *storage*. Think of storage as the file cabinet crammed with all of your work transactions, as well as the instruction manuals for all the devices in your home or office. Sometimes you pull pieces out of the cabinet to work on them at your desk, but they always retain a relationship to their place in the file.

Storage is not quite as quickly accessible because a disk drive's read/write head must wait for the sector on the spinning disk to move into position.

CROSS-REFERENCE

I explore various forms of storage—from floppy disks to hard disks to removable disks to CD-ROMs and DVDs—in Chapters 9 through 12.

I need to add one more point to complete this analogy: At the end of the day, your computer desktop is swept clear and dumped into the trash, while the file cabinets are closed and locked away until they are needed next. In our computer analogy, RAM is a *volatile* temporary workspace that goes away when power is turned off, while the disk drives are more or less permanent storage. (Later in this chapter I give some details of two forms of RAM—not yet used as system memory—that are *non-volatile,* meaning they do not disappear when the power is turned off.)

When I first began writing about personal computers in 1982, a 16K block of memory sold for about $100. A bit later, an add-in card with 256K of memory had dropped in price to $995, the equivalent of about $4,000 per megabyte.

At the time of this writing, you can purchase a 256MB SDRAM module for as little as $30, about 12 cents per megabyte or about two-tenths of a cent for 16KB. Or at today's prices, the memory on that early $995 quarter-of-a-megabyte expansion card would sell at retail for about 3 cents. Aggressive retailers in early 2007 were selling 1GB DDR2 modules—the state-of-the-art in consumer memory—for as little as $80, the equivalent of about 8 cents per megabyte.

Although supply and demand and new technologies bring occasional upticks in price, over time the trend in cost of RAM has been consistently downward. In fact, if you were to look at prices on a graph, memory costs would look like the downside of a ski jump. Memory has become a relatively inexpensive commodity for PCs. The bottom line: You have no reason to skimp on memory for a modern machine. In this chapter, I introduce you to the various types of memory—an area of continuing improvements in size, speed, and cost—and give you a few hints for dealing with common memory problems.

A History of Memory

By one way of thinking, the first computer was the ancient abacus, which used beads on strings to represent its memory for stored numbers; the human brain managed the manipulation of this stored information.

The Aztecs used an abacus-like device, called the nepohualtzitzin, a millennia ago, about 900-1000 A.D. Counters were made from kernels of maize threaded through strings on a wooden frame. A Chinese device called suan-pan appeared about 1200. It later spread throughout Korea and Japan.

In England in the eighteenth century, Charles Babbage worked on his "difference engine"—a device that looked like a cross between a grasshopper and a knitting loom with cogs and wheels. Not coincidentally, about the same time, Joseph Marie Jacquard developed a programmable knitting loom in France. The positions of those cogs and wheels, and the pins and stops of the loom, served as the programmable settings for the mechanical engines.

The first modern computers were still heavily mechanical, using similar wheels, cogs, and strange assemblages of magnets on wire that would flip one way or another to indicate a bit of information.

Today's computers are almost entirely electronic (with the exception of spinning disk drives and fans), but the memory that they use is essentially an analog of those knitting looms or magnetic cores: RAM consists of electronic circuits that can electrically flip one way or another to indicate 0s or 1s used by the computer to store information.

Within today's modern machine, nearly all current motherboards use *dual in-line memory modules (DIMMs)* that hold massive amounts of memory—as much as 2GB at the time of this writing—on a single circuit board that plugs into an ever-faster direct connection to the CPU. These DIMMs can hold various types of memory, including DRAM, EDO, SDRAM, DDR, and DDR2. An example of a modern DDR2 DIMM, holding 512MB, is shown in Figure 8-1.

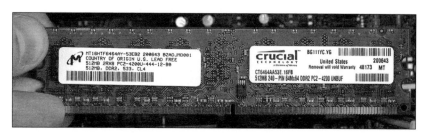

FIGURE 8-1: *A modern DDR2 memory module on a 240-pin DIMM from Crucial Technology; the memory chips themselves are on the opposite side of this device. The company does an excellent job of labeling the type of DIMM and memory, making it easy to identify the device. You can also enter the part number, on this module located directly below the Crucial logo, into a database on the company's web site (*www.crucial.com*) to learn more about the memory.*

The first dinosaur PCs—introduced in the 1980s—had rows of individual memory chips on their motherboards. They were small (each chip was 1K, and nine chips comprised a computer word plus an error-checking parity bit) and they were expensive.

Soon after the dawn of the dinosaur, designers began to run out of space on the motherboard for rows of chips. The next step in the evolutionary process was to move memory to expansion cards that plugged into the system's bus; the upright cards held rows of chips mounted in sockets.

As designers began to pack more and more memory into a single chip, a new carrier was devised—the single in-line memory module (SIMM)—which was a miniature circuit board that could hold thousands, and later millions, of bytes of memory. At that time, memory moved back to the motherboard, with the addition of SIMM sockets that had a direct connection to the CPU. Figure 8-2 pictures an older, small SIMM.

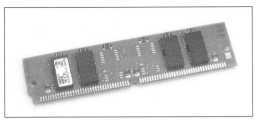

FIGURE 8-2: *An older 4MB SIMM.*

Later improvements to motherboard design allowed larger SIMMs with higher memory capacity. An example of a pair of 72-pin SIMMs is shown in Figure 8-3.

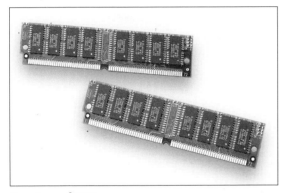

Courtesy of PNY

FIGURE 8-3: *A pair of 128MB 72-pin SIMMs, used in dinosaurs and some senior citizens. Note the positioning notch at the lower-left end of each SIMM, which corresponds to the number 1 pin.*

The next step in the evolution of memory modules was the introduction of 168-pin DIMMs, which allowed the system to read from both sides of the connector, effectively doubling the capacity of memory that could be mounted. Figure 8-4 shows a 168-pin DIMM. As I note earlier in this chapter, today's most common DIMM configurations uses 240 pins and can hold much greater amounts of RAM.

Courtesy of PNY

FIGURE 8-4: *A 168-pin EDO DIMM. The module has an extra notch among the pins near the number 1 position. The notch is moved slightly on an SDRAM module to identify that type of memory.*

Another memory technology, RDRAM (Rambus memory), had a brief moment at the top of the technology heap in 2001 and 2002, and even into 2003 some servers were shipping with RDRAM memory. In the first quarter of 2005 the Rambus company announced that, industrywide, some 500 million RDRAM devices had been shipped, and even in 2006 there was some call for the technology, but RDRAM was surpassed in technology and price by advances in DDR and DDR2 SDRAM and is little used in PCs today. RDRAM is installed on a RIMM module, mechanically similar to a DIMM but with differing electrical properties.

A Short Course in Memory Logic

If computers are so smart, how come they only understand two things: 0 and 1? The answer is that machines are not at all smart, but they are fast. Computers do their work using an alphabet made up of just those two symbols. And even the meaning of these symbols is different for the machine: 0 means there is no value assigned, and 1 means there is a value assigned. You can also think of 0 as *no* or *off,* and 1 as *yes* or *on.* (This explains, by the way, the cryptic marking on some computer power and setup switches: 0 means off and 1 means on.)

The machine uses the 0s and 1s to construct numbers using the binary mathematical system. It's not anywhere as complex as it seems. Each place in a binary number is a power of 2 (1, 2, 4, 8, 16, and so on). Each position is either on or off. Here's a quick and painless lesson.

In binary notation, the number 154 is represented as follows:

```
1 0 0 1 1 0 1 0
```

The way to translate that number in decimal terms is to read it from *right to left* this way:

```
No 1s, one 2, no 4s, one 8, one 16, no 32s, no 64s, and one 128
```

or

```
0x1 + 1x2 + 0x4 + 1x8 + 1x16 + 0x32 + 0x64 + 1x128
```

As you can see, deciphering this value as 154 is a lot more work in binary math, but it is a lot simpler for the machine to manipulate values when they can only be on or off. A computer makes up for the relative awkwardness of its counting method with its blazing speed.

In a computer's binary system, numbers are divided into groups of eight binary digits called a *byte.* Each of the positions in the byte is called a *bit,* a term derived from the term *binary digit.*

As microcomputers have advanced from dinosaur to modern machine, the size of the collection of data bits that is processed as a unit (the CPU's *register size*) has increased. The original microcomputer CPUs only had the horsepower and bandwidth to deal with 8-bit data. Subsequent improvements have pushed register sizes to 16 bits (80286 CPUs), 32 bits (386, 486, and Pentium CPUs), and 64 bits for most current CPUs in consumer machines.

The bigger the register size, the bigger the chunk of information processed by the CPU. At the same time, the memory in your PC must be fast enough to keep up with the demands of the CPU. So, along with the increase in register size, the size of the memory bus, which transfers data between the CPU registers (or in modern CPUs, the primary, or internal, cache) and memory, has also grown. (In modern CPUs the memory bus transfers data between the primary, or internal, cache and memory.)

A 30-pin SIMM can move 8 bits at a time with each transaction between the CPU and its memory (each transaction is called a *bus cycle*). This rate was just fine for a dinosaur. The next step up was a 32-bit CPU such as a 486 processor. The earliest devices in this class

of senior citizens used four 30-pin SIMMs per bank to deliver 32 data bits at a time to the processor. Later motherboards moved to 72-pin SIMMs, permitting the 486 processor to simultaneously draw all 32 bits from a single SIMM bank.

With the arrival of the 64-bit Pentium, early motherboards continued with 32-bit SIMMs; they had to be installed in pairs, comprising a *memory bank.* The CPU communicated with a bank of memory as if it were a single logical unit.

Most current motherboard designs use 240-pin DIMMs that are 64 bits wide; older modern machines used 168-pin DIMMs. Either way, a single module delivers a full 64 bits to the memory bus. (The arcane RDRAM system used RIMMs with narrower 16-bit data paths that can transmit data very quickly using *pipelining technology* to send four packets at a time, thus allowing a 64-bit CPU to process the data as if a single 64-bit chunk had arrived.)

 NOTE

You need to buy memory upgrades in the correct configuration. The manual that came with your computer should be quite clear about what you need, but you may also need to contact the manufacturer. Or, consult with a memory reseller; most maintain databases of motherboards that can identify your machine's specific needs.

Computer users live in a sort of netherworld beneath the decimal-based world of humans, where numbers are expressed in powers of 10, not coincidentally the number of fingers on two hands. You know that 1,000 is 10 times 10 times 10. And you also recognize that the Greek word *kilo,* abbreviated as K, stands for 1,000 when you refer to decimal numbers, and similarly that *mega* stands for 1 million and *giga* for 1 billion.

But as I have just explained, computers calculate based on the powers of 2, as in 0 or 1. So while it makes sense to denominate the money in your wallet in numbers that are divisible by or multiples of 10, as in $1, $5, $10, $50, and $100 bills, when it comes to computer memory the engineers think in terms of computer bytes of 256. When I first began writing about computers, memory was sold in pieces as small as 4 or 8 *kilobytes;* today the more common numbers are 128, 256, and 1,024 *megabytes.*

K, M, and G are used somewhat confusingly as adjectives in front of both decimal and binary numbers. When used to describe capacity for memory storage, K stands for 1,024. Table 8-1 is a cheat sheet to help you think of binary terms in decimal equivalents from kilobits through yottabytes; somewhere out there, someone is already thinking about numbering schemes that go beyond the yotta, which for the record is 2 to the 80th power or a million trillion megabytes.

TABLE 8-1: Decimal Values of Binary Abbreviations

Abbreviation	Meaning	Value in a Binary Number
Kb	Kilobit	1,024 bits
KB	Kilobyte	1,024 bytes
Mb	Megabit	1,048,576 bits
MB	Megabyte	1,048,576 bytes
Gb	Gigabit	1,073,741,824 bits
GB	Gigabyte	1,073,741,824 bytes
Tb	Terabit	1,099,511,627,776 bits
TB	Terabyte	1,099,511,627,776 bytes
Pb	Petabit	1,125,899,906,842,624 bits
PB	Petabyte	1,125,899,906,842,624 bytes
Eb	Exabit	1,152,921,504,606,846,976 bits
EB	Exabyte	1,152,921,504,606,846,976 bytes
Zb	Zettabit	1,180,591,620,717,411,303,424 bits
ZB	Zettabyte	1,180,591,620,717,411,303,424 bytes
Yb	Yottabit	1,208,925,819,614,629,174,706,176 bits
YB	Yottabyte	1,208,925,819,614,629,174,706,176 bytes

Determining How Much Memory You Need

Hmmm . . . how much money do you need? Most of us would answer that we'd like a whole bunch of money, but we recognize that eventually we'd probably reach the point where we have enough to do everything that we need to do, in style.

The same holds true with memory. Here are some truths :

- More memory is better than less memory. In general, an increase in memory speeds up your machine and the applications running on it.
- What seemed to be way too much memory a year or two ago seems like way too little today.

- Eventually, you'll reach a point where you have enough and could even slow down the machine slightly, because of the sheer number of places the processor must examine to find data or, if you go beyond the ability of the motherboard's cache memory, to manage the data.
- If you're working with a current motherboard that uses DDR2 memory (and certain late-model DDR designs), the system includes a feature called *dual channel* that permits the system to interleave the bandwidth of two modules at the same time. To take advantage of this, you need to install modules in pairs; if you're adding 1GB of RAM, you need two 512MB modules rather than a single 1GB unit.
- You can end up slowing down your machine, cause it to crash while running, or even causing it to refuse to boot by not paying close attention to the chipset and motherboard's requirements for pairing and matching. You may find that your modern motherboard can work with just a single DIMM in one of its (usually) four slots, but as I've noted, most modern motherboards require or recommend that memory be installed in matched pairs.
- Although slightly different speed modules may be mixed in among the two or four DIMMs, in most cases all of the memory operates no faster than the slowest module. And memory that is faster than the motherboard's capabilities operates at the chipset's speed limit.
- If you install more memory than your system will ever use, you're wasting money and system resources and generating excess heat.

The first IBM PC shipped with as little as 16K of RAM. A motherboard fully populated with individual memory chips totaling 64K was considered a high-end rocket. (Remember that 64K is 64 thousand bytes of RAM, not 64 million bytes; today, even 64MB is much memory to expect decent performance from current versions of Windows.) The principal reason that today's machines require so much more memory is that we have moved from a text- and command-driven DOS interface to a Windows graphical user interface. The price of user-friendly interfaces, graphics, sound, and even motion video and animation in standard office applications and games requires PCs with more memory. Current operating systems require a huge amount of working space for their own operations and additional memory to permit multiple applications to run. With today's low prices, it doesn't make sense to save a few dollars and sacrifice speed and functionality as long as you keep in mind the previously listed truths.

Ch 8

Windows XP officially requires a minimum of 64MB, but you should consider at least 256MB to be able to run multiple applications simultaneously and, in my opinion, consider a more realistic minimum of 512MB to 1GB. The Windows Vista operating system raises the bar again, with its basic edition requiring 512MB and its premium version starting at 1GB; I have outfitted my newest machine with 2GB of RAM to work with Vista.

And for the record, if you're working with the outdated Windows 95/98 operating system, the entry level is 32MB of RAM, with 64MB a more reasonable starting point. If you run graphics software or habitually keep multiple applications open simultaneously, step up to at least 128 MB or 256MB.

It is important to note that motherboards and associated CPU chipsets have a limit on how much memory they can manage electronically, and there is also a physical constraint on the number of slots available to hold memory modules. Start by consulting your system's technical specifications to determine the physical limit. As this book goes to press, the newest of modern machines, based on Intel's 965 chipset, generally support a maximum of 4GB; this can be accomplished with four 1GB DIMMs or two 2GB modules. These systems also have a *minimum* memory requirement of 512MB. Because there are limited memory slots on the motherboard (usually four), if you're upgrading an existing machine you may find yourself in the unpleasant situation of having to remove low-capacity memory modules and replacing them with larger-capacity blocks of memory. As an example, if you have a machine that has four 32MB modules in place, it probably makes the most economic sense to remove at least two if not four and replace them with matched pairs of larger capacity memory sticks.

If you have a lot of old memory, don't throw it away; consult the back pages of computer magazines to find brokers who purchase used memory to recycle to less-demanding users. Or you may be able to donate the memory to community organizations that may have a need for older technology.

Buying Memory

Modern operating systems, applications, and CPUs demand much more available memory. As I've noted, although prices can fluctuate wildly because of international events and economic conditions, overall, the price of RAM has dropped precipitously in recent years.

You'll usually find the best prices on memory at places that treat it as a commodity: online stores, catalog marketers, and computer superstores.

Sometimes the pricing of modules doesn't seem to follow logic; for example, you may see situations where a 256MB DIMM is more expensive than a 512MB module. The reason is simple supply and demand. As prices of memory drop, lower-capacity modules are less in demand than higher-capacity ones. All modules, though, have some fixed costs: the printed circuit board, its connectors, packaging, shipping, and marketing.

Going the other direction, the largest capacity memory modules usually represent the latest technologies and are usually priced at a premium. As this book goes to press, a single 2GB module is priced considerably higher than two 1GB modules.

As with hard drives, at any particular moment there is usually a "sweet spot" in the price curve. Compare available modules and look for the point at which the cost per megabyte goes up instead of down.

Today's memory modules, purchased from a trusted source, are fully tested and considerably more reliable than previous hardware. The chips themselves are less likely to fail than the module that holds them, the socket on the motherboard, or the wiring to that socket. Therefore, one large module is generally more reliable than two or four smaller modules whose combined memory equals the memory of the large module.

One caveat, though: Most modern machines require installation of memory in matched pairs. So, go large and go identical.

Memory makers speak of infant-mortality failure modes for chips; this unpleasant term means that, like most other electronic elements of your system, memory that survives its first few weeks in your system is likely to last a long time. According to PNY Technologies (www.pny.com), one of the leading memory resellers, the failure rate of memory once it has left the factory is less than 20 pieces per million; the risk lies in solder points, contacts, wiring, and sockets. The fewer of these involved, the better for the user.

And then there's a bonus in cost: As long as you are shopping in the middle of the market, among the sizes and types in the largest supply and ordinary demand—a larger module generally costs less per megabyte than a group of smaller ones because less hardware is involved.

An insider's view of memory

The good news is that memory is more or less Plug-and-Play; the bad news is that you have dozens of different types, sizes, and speeds of memory to choose from. And just to make the situation more complicated, some machines happily allow you to mix and match similar types, while other PCs choke and die if you give them anything but one specific type of memory.

Your best defense is to carefully read the instruction manual that comes with your computer or motherboard; call the PC manufacturer's support desk if they still offer one or consult the company's web site for advice and assistance as well. It may be valuable to take off the covers of your PC and examine the layout of the motherboard. You need to know what types of memory are installed and whether there are any open chip sockets (dinosaurs), SIMM sockets (senior citizens and older modern machines), or DIMM (or RIMM) sockets in current modern machines.

Motherboards typically have four memory sockets, or slots. Some may have only two, while some older modern machines and senior citizens bridged the gaps between what were at one time old and new technologies by offering several DIMM and several SIMM slots. Sooner or later, though, you'll reach the limits of the board.

As much as it may pain you to do so, it may make sense to replace older, slower, and smaller memory modules with newer, faster, larger, and less-expensive replacements.

Several memory resellers have tips and technical information about memory on their web sites. Here were some of the offerings in early 2007:

- Corsair Memory: www.corsairmemory.com
- Crucial Technologies: www.crucial.com
- Kingston Technology: www.kingston.com
- PNY Technologies: www.pny.com

PNY also offers a database of specifications for many PCs, requiring you to determine for yourself what is already in place. Crucial offers a very capable system scan utility on its web site that can look into your machine and report on the type and number of memory modules installed, tell you if there are open slots, and suggest available upgrades that the company guarantees to work with your motherboard. As this book went to press, the other manufacturers offered memory configuration databases that allow you to look up the specifications for your machine, but this can present some problems. For example, this process will not tell you if your machine was properly configured at the time you bought it or if any subsequent replacements or upgrades met the proper specifications.

You should also check the web site for your PC manufacturer; it may offer a tool that inspects your machine and reports on what is installed within.

Counting the chips

For many users, the mathematics of memory is a black art best not examined too closely. Most of us in the industry can't disagree: this is an example of a situation where the technical types have taken over the design and the nomenclature for a product. In this section, I try to clear up the muddle.

A *memory module* — a SIMM, DIMM, RIMM, or other such design — is a carrier for a group of chips. The size of the module is expressed as the sum of the capacities of all of the chips it holds. However, any memory that is used for other functions, such as error checking — including parity schemes — is subtracted from that sum.

The *capacity* of a modern memory module is expressed in megabytes, meaning millions of 8-bit bytes; today's largest consumer-grade modules have moved into gigabyte (billions of bytes) range, with 1GB and 2GB modules available. The first 4GB SDRAM modules were on the market in late 2006, but the price reflected the small demand: about $1,600 per unit, or three times as much as a still-pricey 2GB module.

Regarding the memory chips that make up the module: the *chip density* is measured in megabits, or millions of bits. Each memory chip is made up of hundreds of thousands or millions of cells that hold one bit of information. A 64-megabit chip has 64 million cells.

In some memory chip designs, the chip density is expressed as a description of the organization of the cells in width and depth; for example, this same 64-megabit chip may be called an 8M-by-8, or a 16M-by-4 device. A chip of larger capacity may be expressed as 16M-by-64 for 1,024 megabits.

To calculate the size of a module, determine the chip density in megabits and then multiply that result by the number of chips on the module. Then divide the total number of megabits by 8 to yield the module capacity in megabytes. Or look at the label and hope that the manufacturer has done the math for you and laid it out in a form you can understand.

Speed, parity, and other features

There is a dizzying variety of memory types, speeds, and special features. The bad news is that most variations are incompatible with each other; as we've discussed, the good news is that some memory manufacturers and resellers are offering some valuable tools to help you buy the proper replacement or upgrade modules.

Memory modules are marked with their speed and capacity, although the format for doing so has changed with each new technology, and also can vary from manufacturer to manufacturer.

In general, current DDR and DDR2 speeds (as well as older SDRAM) are marked with a MHz (megahertz) speed or with a PC rating such as PC133. The higher the speed rating, the faster the chip or module can operate.

Another element of the specifications for a memory module is whether it has some form of error-checking or error-correcting capability. Basic memory does not offer this facility, trading off the very rare occurrence of an error in favor of greater speed and lower price; this sort of memory is usually called *non-parity.*

If your motherboard demands the use of *parity* or *ECC (error-correcting code),* you have to use that memory design.

If the label does not indicate if memory is parity or non-parity, you should be able to determine the module's design by counting the large RAM chips on each stick. If the number of chips can be evenly divided by three or five, the module uses ECC or parity. (If the module has four or eight RAM chips, it is non-parity.)

One other significant specification is CL or CAS, which stands for Column Address Strobe Latency, which is the number of clock cycles that pass after a command is received before data begins to flow. Lower latency is faster than higher latency; CAS2 is faster than CAS3. However, as with memory transfer speed, a memory module cannot operate faster than the capabilities of the machine. If a motherboard is designed for CAS3 modules, it will not benefit from CAS2 memory and may even run into problems because of a mismatch.

Checking memory from within Windows

You can watch the digit counter fly as your machine boots up, but detailed information about how much memory is present in your system and how it is allocated can be determined once the machine has booted Windows.

If you are running a current version of Windows (anything from Windows 95/98 and later, including XP and Vista), there are three easy ways to take a reading of your system's memory capacity.

One way is to click Start ⇨ Settings ⇨ Control Panel and then to double-click the System icon. On the General tab you will see the basic information about your machine: the version of Windows (including any Service Packs that represent major updates); the name

of the person or company registered with Microsoft as owner of the operating system; the serial number for the operating system, and finally a basic report on the type and speed of the processor and the amount of RAM recognized by the system. An example of a Windows XP report on the test machine for this book is shown in Figure 8-5.

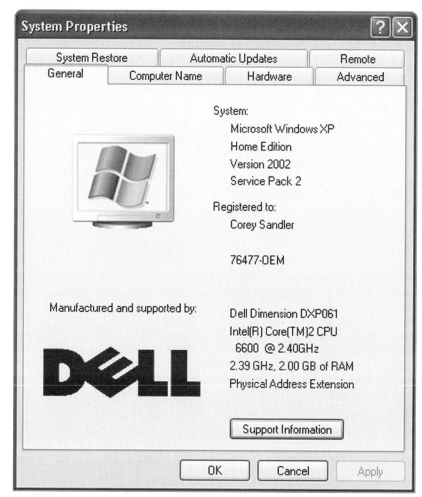

FIGURE 8-5: *The System Properties report for a modern machine with an Intel Core 2 Duo, model number 6600 running at 2.40 GHz, with 2GB of installed RAM, as displayed by Windows XP.*

For more detailed information, request a report on system information. Under current versions of Windows, you can find the System Information utility under Accessories/System Tools. You can also get to a nearly identical report from within most Microsoft brand applications such as Word; click on the Help pulldown menu, then choose About Microsoft Word (or whichever application is in use), and then select System Information. There are also utilities from third party software makers that probe the internals of your machine.

The Windows System Information utility generates a report like the one shown in Figure 8-6 that tells you the Total Physical Memory of your system, as well as the Available Physical Memory that is free for use. If the percentage is low — below 25 per cent — you're likely to run into performance problems as the system is forced to use the slower swap file on disk to store parts of its processes.

If you are having memory problems, check the settings for Virtual Memory in the system; this technology extends the working room for your computer from its system RAM onto a dedicated portion of one of your hard disk drives. The computer uses the hard drive as a scratch pad when it needs more room than it has available in RAM.

To examine the Virtual Memory settings under Windows XP (other current operating systems are similar in their pathways), follow these steps:

1. Go to the Control Panel and click the Systems icon to display the Systems Properties screen.
2. Choose the Advanced tab.
3. In the Performance section, click the Settings radio button. Here you see the Performance Options page.
4. Click the Advanced tab there to display the options shown in Figure 8-7.

To alter the preassigned size of the paging file, click the Change button on the Performance Options screen's Advanced tab. You next see the Virtual Memory report, as shown in Figure 8-8.

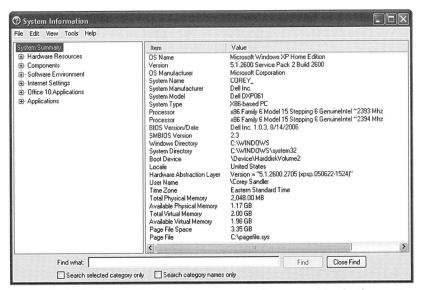

FIGURE 8-6: *The System Information screen offers a wealth of information about the hardware, software, and operating system of your machine. The top-level view includes details of the version of Windows, the identification of the manufacturer and model number of your machine, the microprocessor, and memory.*

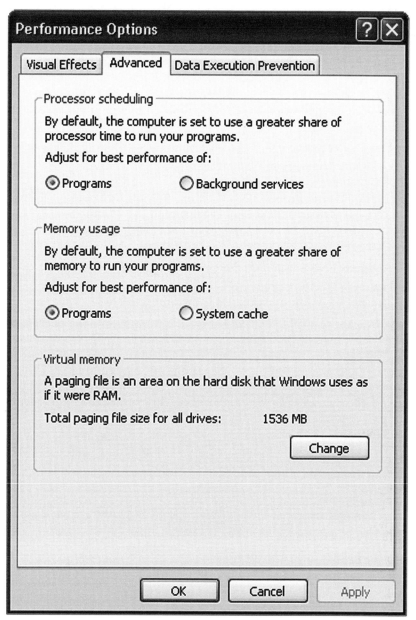

FIGURE 8-7: *On the Performance Options screen within Windows XP, look at the Virtual Memory section to see the total paging size for all drives.*

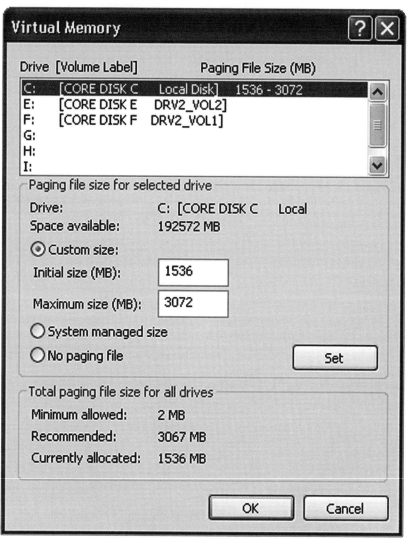

FIGURE 8-8: *On the Virtual Memory report (this is the Windows XP version) you can set a custom initial and maximum size or you can allow Windows to make its own decisions by selecting a system managed size. In general, the maximum custom size should not be smaller than the system's recommendation.*

To see an expanded memory report, including a nifty set of moving graphs and bar charts, go to the Windows Task Manager available under Windows XP; a similar facility is offered in Windows Vista. To display the screen, do the following:

1. Save any open documents to disk. (You do not need to close their associated programs; in fact, if you want to understand how much of a load you machine is juggling, keep all of your regular programs running, including your Internet browser, antivirus utility, and a word processor or other productivity application.)

2. Press the Ctrl-Alt-Del key combination. Windows temporarily suspends operations and displays a black screen with a choice of utilities, including Task Manager (used to see which programs and utilities are running, and allowing a selective shut down of applications).

3. Choose Task Manager and then click the Performance tab. For your purposes here, you're interested in the Physical Memory report, which shows the total amount of memory in the machine, the available memory after applications and the operating system have latched onto chunks, and the machine-managed system cache. An example of the Performance report from Windows XP Pro is shown in Figure 8-9.

About half of the total memory of 2,095,076 bytes (about 2GB) is available on this modern machine, which is running Microsoft Word, Internet Explorer 7.0, and the MailWasher Pro mail manager. And because the state-of-the-art machine that is the test bed for this book employs the Intel Core 2 Duo processor, the operating system reports on the activity level of each of the two virtual CPUs in that chip.

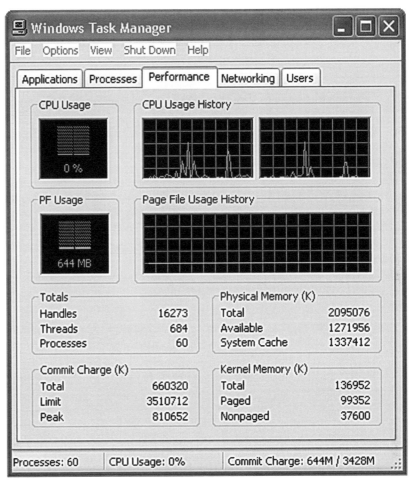

FIGURE 8-9: *The Windows XP Performance report from the Task Manager.*

Where do you put your memory?

As previously noted, way back in the days of the dinosaurs, memory chips were mounted directly on the motherboard. Some very early designs had them soldered into place, a bad decision which made it very difficult to replace them if they failed. These were quickly supplanted by rows of small sockets to hold the memory.

Ch 8

Check the instruction manual for your motherboard to learn about specific needs for memory upgrades. In Table 8-2, you can learn the details of the most commonly used memory modules over the more recent history of the PC.

Module Type	Number of Pins	Type of Memory Supported
SIMM	30	FPM, EDO
SIMM	72	FPM, EDO
DIMM	72	SO-DIMM
DIMM	144	SO-DIMM
DIMM	168	FPM, EDO, SDRAM
DIMM	184	DDR SDRAM
RIMM	184	RDRAM
DIMM	200	SO-DIMM
DIMM	240	DDR2 SDRAM

TABLE 8-2: Memory Module Sizes

The capacities of the early memory chips were small, and they were expensive. And remember that the motherboard of the original PC was only designed to hold 64K of RAM, which was considered more than any user would ever reasonably need.

As operating systems and applications became more demanding and the hardware more accommodating, memory expansions began to move to add-in cards that plugged into the PC's expansion bus.

When machines became faster and faster, memory moved back to the motherboard, which enabled a speedier direct connection to the CPU. Memory in high-capacity modules was plugged into sockets on the motherboard. The first industry-standard carrier for a block of memory was a SIMM (Single In-Line Memory Module). This small printed circuit board was originally available with 30 electrical contacts and fit in a 30-pin connector, or slot. The next step was the arrival of larger and faster 72-pin SIMM modules for 72-pin sockets.

The next progression in DIMM design brought forth motherboards with sockets intended for use with 168-pin DIMMs or 184-pin RIMMs or DDR modules, which put more memory in a smaller amount of real estate. They also provided better performance in high speed, wide-word machines because more information can be transferred in parallel from a single module.

In Chapter 6, I show the very similar installation process for a current modern machine using 240-pin modules holding DDR2 memory.

A NOTE ABOUT METALS

Some PC users search for gold on the contacts of memory modules. Most SIMMs have tin leads, while DIMMs and RIMMs usually have gold leads. (Here I'm talking about leads as the connecting pins on the module; the word is pronounced as if it were spelled *leed*.

If you plug a tin-plated module into a socket with gold contacts, or the other way around, you face a slight risk that oxidation may occur between the two metals and this could damage the socket or the module resulting in memory failures. It is possible for oxidation to cause problems in a period as short as a year, or it could take more years than your PC's useful life.

Don't ask for trouble here. Match the metal on the contacts to the metal in the socket: tin with tin, or gold with gold.

If you do end up with a mix, you may want to schedule semi-annual cleaning sessions with an electrical contact cleaning solution; never polish the contacts dry because this can generate damaging static electricity. Keep in mind that the memory modules themselves are designed for only a finite number of insertions and removals before the plating may be damaged — most modules can withstand just a few dozen ins and outs. It's a better bet to avoid the problem in the first place.

And while I'm on the subject, you may also see reference to certain electronic devices being "lead free." In this usage, the word is pronounced as if it were spelled *led*, and refers to the metallic element. Modern environmentalists are seeking to remove the dangerous heavy metal from as many sectors of our society as possible; the goal is to reduce or eliminate the danger to health from production of devices with lead and the disposal of lead when they reach the end of use. Manufacturers are encouraged (or required by law in some situations) to use lead-free solder and components in putting together electronic parts.

Current Memory Technologies

The race to come up with the fastest, largest, and (usually) least expensive memory technology continues. This race is all to the benefit of the user, but the result is a sometimes bewildering array of memory types.

The latest great new thing is DDR2, which is the second generation of Double Data Rate memory. As this edition goes to press, DDR2 is used in almost all new systems and is poised to expand into greater bandwidth with the fastest memory buses yet seen in consumer-level PCs.

The previous champion had been DDR, which you may see in some descriptions as DDR1. DDR when first introduced was comparable in bandwidth to dual-channel RDRAM despite apparent differences in bandwidth. RDRAM memory has a slightly greater latency than DDR or standard SDRAM; latency is the amount of time a system has to wait after a request for transfer of data from a new page of memory.

In any case, a doubling of memory bandwidth does not usually result in anything near a doubling of system performance in the best cases because a well-designed modern system is drawing a high percentage of its data from L1 and L2 caches once an application is up and running.

The ultimate measure of the utility of a memory design is its bandwidth—the total capacity of the channel, determined by multiplying the speed of the memory bus by the number of data cycles per clock cycle and the width of the memory bus. You'll find a comparison for modern memory designs in Table 8-3.

And the true bottom line is this: Modern memory technologies are not interchangeable with each other. If your motherboard is designed for DDR2, as most new ones are, that's the only type of memory you can use. The same goes for DDR or RDRAM.

Table 8-3: Bandwidth for Modern Memory Technologies

	Memory Bus Speed	Data Cycles per Clock Cycle	Effective Data Rate (Bus Times per Cycle)	Memory Bus Width	Bandwidth
PC66 SDRAM	66 MHz	1	66	8 bytes	533 MBps
PC100 SDRAM	100 MHz	1	100	8 bytes	800 MBps
PC133 SDRAM	133 MHz	1	133	8 bytes	1.1 GBps
PC600 RDRAM	300 MHz	2	600	2 bytes	1.2 GBps
PC700 RDRAM	350 MHz	2	700	2 bytes	1.4 GBps
PC1600 DDR	100 MHz	2	200	8 bytes	1.6 GBps
PC800 RDRAM	400 MHz	2	800	2 bytes	1.6 GBps
PC2100 DDR	133 MHz	2	266	8 bytes	2.1 GBps
PC2700 DDR	166 MHz	2	333	8 bytes	2.7 GBps
PC800 Dual Channel RDRAM	400 MHz	2	800	4 bytes	3.2 GBps
PC3200 DDR	200 MHz	2	400	8 bytes	3.2 GBps
PC4000 DDR	250 MHz	2	500	8 bytes	4.0 GBps
PC2-3200 DDR2	200 MHz	2	400	8 bytes	3.2 GBps
PC2-4200 DDR2	266 MHz	2	533	8 bytes	4.2 GBps
PC2-5300 DDR2	333 MHz	2	667	8 bytes	5.3 GBps
PC2-6400 DDR2	400 MHz	2	800	8 bytes	6.4 GBps

Double data rate 2 (DDR2) SDRAM

DDR2 offers improvement over DDR resulting in much higher bandwidth. Like DDR, it can transfer data on both the rising and falling edges of a clock signal, delivering double the amount of data transfer for the same data rate. In addition, DDR2 picks up more efficiency through improvements to the electrical interface itself, as well as advanced chip and driver designs.

When introduced, DDR2 was capable of working with bus frequencies of 200, 266, 333, and 400 MHz; DDR had topped out at 200 MHz. The effective data rate for DDR2 began at 400 Mbps — the top end of DDR — and as this book goes to press has been extended to 533, 667, and 800 Mbps.

One way this form of memory gains clock speed is through lower operating voltage (1.8 volts for DDR2 versus 3.5 volts for DDR); it requires less time to generate a wave of lower voltage than higher voltage. This is also why CPU voltages have recently been reduced. And a benefit of low voltage is that it helps the overall effort to reduce the generation and buildup of heat on the motherboard and within the PC case.

As electronic parts become faster, the laws of physics become more important; the shorter an electrical path, the less chance of delay or errors caused by resistance or imperfections. DDR2 packaging shrinks wires and connectors another notch by using a technology called *Fine Ball Grid Array (FBGA)*, a small but important improvement over DDR's *Thin Small Outline Package (TSOP)*.

The dimensions of both DDR and DDR2 modules are almost identical; each is 5.25 inches long. DDR typically stands about 1.25 inches tall, while DDR2 is 1.18 inches tall. DDR2 modules are packaged on a 240-pin DIMM, and require a corresponding socket on the motherboard. They are not physically or electronically compatible or interchangeable with DDR modules, which are packaged on a 184-pin DIMM. Each module has a single positioning notch on the bottom; the DDR2's notch is close to the center, while DDR memory sticks have a gap that is noticeably off-center.

As this book goes to press, there are four common designs for DDR2 chips:

- DDR2-400. The chips run with a front-side bus of 100 MHz and an I/O clock of 200 MHz.
- DDR2-533. The chips run with a front-side bus of 133 MHz and an I/O clock of 266 MHz.
- DDR2-667. The chips run with a front-side bus of 166 MHz and an I/O clock of 333 MHz.
- DDR2-800. The chips run with a front-side bus of 200 MHz and an I/O clock of 400 MHz.

When the chips are brought together to form a memory module that moves eight bits (one byte) at a time, the nomenclature becomes:

- PC2-3200. DDR2-400 chips with a bandwidth of 3,200 MB/s.
- PC2-4200. DDR2-533 chips with a bandwidth of 4,267 MB/s.
- PC2-5300: DDR2-667 chips with a bandwidth of 5,333 MB/s.
- PC2-6400: DDR2-800 chips with a bandwidth of 6,400 MB/s.
- PC2-7200: DDR2-900 Chips with a bandwidth of 7,200 MB/s
- PC2-8000: DDR2-1000 Chips with a bandwidth of 8,000 MB/s

The downside of DDR2 is that it has a latency of nearly twice that of DDR; *latency* is the amount of time the computer must wait before the memory controller obtains a specific bit or byte of information from RAM. For this reason, a DDR2 and a DDR of identical bandwidth (the two standards meet at PC2-3200 and PC-3200) may show little difference in throughput or even a slight advantage to the older technology. However, once DDR2 moves into faster bus speeds — beyond those offered by DDR — it can push more data with sheer brute force. And DDR2 will pick up even more speed when it can use the advanced dual channel feature of the most modern of motherboards and chipsets; this technology allows the system to read from a pair of modules at the same time. To be accurate about it, the two channels of memory are *interleaved* with each other, which helps reduce the effects of DDR2's slower latency.

To benefit from this feature, both modules in a bank of memory must be identical in size and speed. For this reason, if you want to add 1GB of memory to your DDR2-based system you are better off buying a pair of 512MB modules instead of a single 1GB stick.

And on the distant horizon as a possible next step is *QDR (Quad Data Rate SDRAM)*, which doubles the data rate again; however, engineers have run into significant problems in producing the chips. No consumer products use this form of memory as this book goes to press. However, late in the third quarter of 2006 one vendor (known for pushing the speed envelope), OCZ Technology, announced DDR-2 memory running at 1100 MHz. Dubbed the PC2-8800, these modules operate at higher voltage than other DDR-2 modules. As initially announced, they will be available in 2GB (2 × 1,024) memory kits or single 1GB modules.

BUFFERED OR REGISTERED MEMORY

Modern memory is very fast and highly reliable; for that reason, PC designers generally use a form of memory that is not quite as stable as it could possibly be. The tradeoff: lower cost and higher speed.

On the other hand, if a modern machine is intended for use in a situation where the highest priorities are data security and crash prevention, other technologies are available. What kind of situation? Machines used in stock market and other high-finance operations, PCs that control medical equipment, servers in large office settings, and computers that manage expensive factory or laboratory processes.

The solution usually involves *registered* memory, sometimes called *buffered* memory. These chips include registers, or buffers, that hold retrieved data for one clock cycle before it is moved over the bus to the CPU. The fact that data is allowed to settle in a register, even for just a tiny fraction of a second, improves its stability.

Another technology, often combined with buffering, is *ECC (error-correcting code)* memory, which has additional circuitry that examines data received by and sent from the module to attempt to detect errors and make corrections. ECC uses algorithms that can alert the system when a memory block has been corrupted. If the information can be repaired, the system will do so; otherwise it requests a re-send.

Double data rate (DDR) SDRAM

The previous generation of SDRAM was DDR (double data rate) memory. Like the original form of SDRAM, the operation of DDR is synchronous with the system clock. However, DDR reads data on both the rising and falling edges of the clock signal while SDRAM only carries information on the rising edge of a signal. This permits a DDR module to transfer data about twice as fast as SDRAM; on a PC133 bus, this permits an effective rate of 266 MHz. This doesn't mean your

system will run twice as fast, but your memory will, and that is bound to improve the overall performance of your PC.

DDR DIMMs are not compatible with systems designed for SDRAM or RDRAM; the modules have different electrical layouts and different key notches so that they won't fit into the wrong socket. The modules have 184 pins, compared to 168 pins on an SDRAM DIMM. Less commonly used DDR SO-DIMMs have 200 pins, compared to 144 on an SDRAM SO-DIMM.

As a derivative of SDRAM, the DDR memory bus runs at standard rates of 100 MHz for PC1600, 133 MHz for PC2100, and 166 MHz for PC2700. But because the modules run at a double data rate, the industry convention is to refer to the effective data rates of 200, 266, and 333 MHz. Multiplying the data rate times the memory bus width of 8 bytes yields the naming conventions for DDR modules. For example, PC1600 operates a double data rate on a 100-MHz bus with 8 bytes: $100 \times 2 \times 8 = 1,600$.

Synchronous DRAM

The first round of modern machines were based on what was an advanced technology at the time, SDRAM (synchronous dynamic random access memory), a scheme that uses a clock coordinated with the CPU so that memory cycles are synchronized. The result is improved efficiency. The synchronous clock enables SDRAM to read and to write information with no wait states: one clock cycle per access up to 100 MHz.

As with DDR and DDR2 versions of SDRAM, it is important to purchase memory fast enough for your CPU and system bus. On older modern machines, SDRAM DIMMs meant for 66-MHz operation were usually rated at 10ns, DIMMs for a 100-MHz bus at 8ns, and for a 133-MHz bus at 7.5ns. Memory manufacturers labeled SDRAM with an indicator of their match to the front-side bus: PC66, PC100, and PC133.

SDRAM does not need to be installed in pairs. You can add any size of memory module, as long as you do not exceed the system specifications.

In most cases, you will get the best performance from your PC if you put the largest module (in megabytes) in the lowest-numbered slot on the motherboard — usually, but not always, the slot nearest the CPU socket. For example, if your computer has a 32MB module in place and you want to add 128MB, you should move the smaller module to slot 1 and place the 128MB module in slot 0.

Generally you can mix PC66, PC100, and PC133 memory in the same system. However, all of the memory in the PC will run at the slowest memory module's speed. Note, too, that some systems won't run properly with a mix of memory speeds; consult your instruction manual or system manufacturer for details.

You may come across "registered" SDRAM. This specialized type of memory process signals slightly differently from standard SDRAM; it contains a register that delays all information transferred to the module by one clock cycle. Registered SDRAM is intended primarily for use in servers that have huge banks of memory.

Most PCs will only accept unbuffered SDRAM. If your motherboard does support registered SDRAM and you choose to use that type, all of the modules in the PC must be registered; unbuffered and registered modules are not interchangeable.

Coming attraction: Magnetic RAM

On the horizon as a possible replacement for DRAM in computers: magnetic RAM. One such technology is Magnetoresistive *Random Access Memory (MRAM)*. This non-volatile memory does not require near-continuous electrical refreshing.

As you have seen, DRAM uses tiny capacitors to hold a charge to indicate a value of 0 or 1; if the capacitors are not refreshed a few hundred million times per second or so, they lose their charge. And when the power to the machine is shut off, the contents of DRAM are completely lost. As the capacity of dynamic memory chips becomes larger, the cells become smaller, refresh intervals become shorter, and power demands and heat production increase.

MRAM is constructed with two ferromagnetic plates separated by a thin insulator; one plate is permanently magnetized to positive or negative, while the other plate can be changed by a brief burst of electrical power. Within the chip, millions of cells are laid out in a grid and are addressed by their coordinates.

Magnetic memory requires application of power only when a particular cell is written to or read. In current designs, the writing process requires a burst of a bit more power than is required for DRAM, but once the information is in place it sits there unchanged; the same happens when a cell is written, with a one-time query to a particular location to determine whether it holds a 0 or 1.

By one estimate, MRAM's power consumption may turn out to be as little as 1 percent that of DRAM. This is good news for users of PCs, and especially those with for battery-powered laptops. And in the laboratory, scientists have produced MRAM with access times as low as about 2 nanoseconds, a little faster than standard DRAM. Early in third quarter 2006 one memory producer, Freescale Semiconductor, Inc., announced it had started volume production of 4-Mb MRAM memory. These chips are much slower than DDR2 memory and don't store enough data to replace current PC memory, but volume production of these chips validates the technology. These low-capacity chips likely will appear first in automotive and other embedded applications, but they could pave the way for interesting PC technology over the next few years.

Many PC users are already working with another form of non-volatile memory, Flash RAM. These small blocks of memory, often packaged as USB "keys," use voltage pulses that make a physical change to a memory location to indicate a 0 or 1; flash memory is slower than DRAM or MRAM because the device must build up a charge in a capacitor-like charge pump for each use. And, in theory, flash memory devices have a finite life; after a certain number of write cycles they lose the ability to change from one state to another.

For that reason, MRAM may first appear as a replacement for flash memory, but some engineers expect it to arrive as system memory within computers in coming years.

Rambus (RDRAM) memory

RDRAM, a proprietary memory technology developed by Rambus, Inc., burst on the scene in 1999 and for a few years was the fastest RAM in consumer machines. Today, though, it has been surpassed in speed and bettered in price, lower power demands, and heat production by DDR and DDR2.

Rambus is a CMOS DRAM that can provide sustainable system throughput three to four times faster than standard SDRAM, up to 3.2 GBps using dual Rambus channels.

Rambus memory sends less information on the data bus (only 16 bits wide, as opposed to the 32 or 64 bits bus of a modern motherboard) but it sends data more frequently. Like DDR, Rambus memory also reads data on both the rising and falling edges of the clock signal, permitting transfer speeds of 800 MHz and higher.

Rambus carriers are known as RIMMs (Rambus inline memory modules), which are mechanically similar to DIMMs, but they don't use the same electrical connections.

Memory modules must be installed in pairs of matched memory size. On an RDRAM motherboard, all of the memory slots are wired in series, meaning that each memory slot must be populated with a RIMM, or with a special continuity module that completes the circuit. Memory modules have a metal cover on one side to serve as a heat sink; continuity modules are bare circuit boards.

In theory, an 800-MHz data flow should be more than twice as fast as that of a DDR operating at 266 MHz. However, Rambus modules take longer to start moving the first block of data than a DDR system; technically, Rambus memory has a higher latency. The reason for this is the serial wiring that connects the memory slots. The first bit of data must pass through each RIMM module before it reaches the bus.

The best use of the speed of a Rambus system is to transport lengthy streams of data — in a game or streaming video application, for example.

When Rambus was introduced, motherboards with more than two RIMM modules ran into technical problems with Intel's original chipsets. Thousands of motherboards were built with three sockets and were ready to be shipped before Intel notified manufacturers of a two-RIMM limit. Some manufacturers scrapped the boards they had built and reissued new, two-RIMM boards. Others reworked the third RIMM socket to disable it.

Later, motherboards intended for use with Rambus modules were based around the Intel 850 chipset and typically included four sockets for memory.

Manufacturers must pay a royalty to Rambus to produce RIMMS; that's one reason RIMMs are more expensive than SDRAM or DDR memory; another reason is that Rambus chips themselves are a bit more costly to make. In the end, it was this economic disadvantage that stalled acceptance of Rambus and allowed DDR and DDR2 SDRAM to take over the market. Today no new consumer machines are based on RDRAM, but the design is employed in some video-game machines and special-purpose computers.

EDO and burst-EDO RAM

Extended-data-out memory (EDO RAM) and burst-EDO memory were updates to the previous speed champion, fast page-mode (FPM) memory. FPM memory was more than adequate for 486 processors, but not quite up to the demands of the faster memory bus speeds of Pentium-based systems.

The difference comes down to a matter of persistence of memory: FPM loses data after it has been read, while EDO holds the last data request in a buffer while reading the next request. EDO's extended memory enables the bus speed to match the Pentium, which runs at 60 MHz or, more commonly, at 66 MHz, twice the realistic speed limit for FPM and 486-based systems. Newer 100-MHz bus systems with synchronous memory designs require even more performance out of their memory chips.

You need a motherboard and controller chipset that recognizes EDO memory; Intel introduced such facilities with its Triton chipset. In a real-world environment, EDO should offer a 10 to 15 percent speed advantage over comparable FPM chips.

EDO memory works with most current PC controllers, and you can mix it with FPM memory as long as the two types of memory reside in different banks. In my office, I upgraded an older machine by adding 8MB of new EDO RAM to 8MB of older FPM memory. Putting the EDO RAM in the first bank speeds loading of Windows 95 a tiny bit.

Another form of memory is burst extended-data-out (BEDO) DRAM, a form of EDO that uses pipelining to achieve better throughput performance. The throughput of BEDO and SDRAM is about the same, they just use different technologies to achieve the improvements. However, Intel chipsets don't support BEDO DRAM, so SDRAM has won out over BEDO DRAM with most system manufacturers.

Memory Modules

As previously explored, machines dating from the late dinosaur era through modern times aggregate their memory on modules that plug into special sockets on the motherboard. The oldest of the dinosaurs accepted individual memory chips on the motherboard or on an adapter card that plugged into the bus.

If you are seeking to keep alive one of these ancient dinosaurs, you'll have to search the bins of used computer stores or the back bins of supply outlets.

The first widely-used memory module was a 30-pin SIMM, followed by more capacious and speedier 72-pin SIMMs. You should be able to find some types and sizes of this type of module from major memory suppliers such as Crucial, Kingston, or PNY.

240-pin DDR2 DIMMs

DDR2 modules have 120 pins on each side of a module that is nearly identical in size and design to DDR sticks. The exception: DDR2 have a positioning notch that is very close to the center of the module, while DDR have a gap that is off-center. The DDR2 modules are also electrically incompatible with DDRs, operating at a lower voltage. DDR2 modules can usually be installed one module at a time, although most manufacturers recommend upgrades with identical pairs.

184-pin DDR DIMMs and RDRAM RIMMs

DDR SDRAM and Rambus RDRAM uses a memory module with 184 pins.

DDR DIMMs and RDRAM RIMMs are similar in mechanical construction but incompatible in electrical design and can't be interchanged, nor used in older machines designed for other memory technologies. DDR can usually be installed one module at a time. RDRAM, though, must be installed in equal-size pairs and unused sockets must have a continuity module in place to complete the serial circuit required by the RDRAM specification.

168-pin DIMMs

A class of older modern machines and many senior citizens used 168-pin DIMMs, high-capacity modules that are 64-bits wide. Because the memory matches the needs of the memory bus, you can install DIMMs one at a time in a Pentium-class machine.

NOTE

Some senior-citizen motherboards bridged a technology gap by accepting both DIMMs and SIMMs. Some required you to use one or the other type. If the motherboard permitted you to mix memory types, you may need to set a jumper on the motherboard to indicate which socket to use as base memory.

Prior to the arrival of DIMMs, memory chips had almost always required 5 volts of power. Some early modern-machine motherboard designs continued with 5-volt modules, but most current motherboards are less demanding, requiring 3.3 volts. The position of a notch on the DIMM indicates the voltage demands of the module and should prevent users from using the wrong type of DIMM module.

It is possible to force a DIMM into place, probably ruining the motherboard in the process. Take care to buy the proper voltage DIMM (you have to go out of your way to find the relatively rare 5-volt modules).

When 168-pin DIMMs first arrived, they were populated with DRAM. Today, nearly all use high-speed SDRAM. You will also find EDO and DDR memory; most motherboards do not permit a mix of memory types; be sure to consult the instruction manual to learn if there are any allowable combinations of SDRAM, EDO, or DDR.

Most motherboard designs of this era performed buffering themselves. If your 168-pin DIMM contains buffered memory, the module is differentiated with another notch amongst the pins, and again, you should take care not to force a module into the wrong type of socket.

NOTE

I give the details of older technology SIMMs in Bonus Chapter 8 on the CD.

About Memory Speed

Measuring the true speed of memory is a bit like nailing Jell-O to the wall; first, you must understand that RAM is very fast at what it does. In a modern machine, the most significant difference between one type of memory technology or another is the speed of the memory controller (part of the chipset) and the bus used to move data from one place to another.

Here's a brief review of a few of the basic building blocks of the PC. The CPU or microprocessor is the brains of the operation, where computing takes place. The CPU is supported by the chipset; among its functions is the memory controller, responsible for overseeing the flow of data between the memory and the CPU and back again.

The data highway on the motherboard is the bus, a set of parallel wires connecting the CPU, memory, and other devices, including those responsible for input and output. The motherboard also is home to the memory bus from the memory controller to the memory. The design for the memory bus on current modern machines includes a frontside bus (FSB) from the CPU to main memory and a backside bus (BSB) from the memory controller to L2 cache.

When the microprocessor requires data from memory, it issues a command to the memory controller, which fetches the information from memory and at the same time sends a message to the CPU to report when the data will be available.

The issuance of the command, its management by the controller, the report back to the CPU, and the actual movement of the data are all part of the memory system's overhead; the time for the retrieval of the data from memory is related to the speed of the processor, the chipset, and the memory bus that interconnects them all.

Older memory chips and modules were rated with access times ranging from 100ns to 50ns; the lower the rating, the faster the memory chips were in response to commands.

With the arrival of *Synchronous DRAM (SDRAM)* technology memory chips were fast enough to synchronize their cycles to the computer's system clock, the drumbeat that allows all of the disparate parts of the PC to work together. Each rise and fall of the clock signal is considered one clock cycle; a 133-MHz clock generates 133 million clock cycles per second.

Some components of the computer are fast enough to perform their work on a single clock cycle, while others require multiple cycles. And modern CPUs typically run much faster than the bus, at what is called a clock multiplier.

The physical location of main memory also helps determine the speed of memory in a system. The faster the clock speed of the microprocessor and the memory bus it employs, the greater the effect on even tiny differences in distance.

Among the techniques used by engineers to speed the reaction of memory are *interleaving, pipelining,* and *bursting.*

When memory is *interleaved,* the processor alternates its attention between two or more memory banks or cell banks within a memory chip. Each time a block of memory is addressed by the CPU, it requires about one clock cycle to reset itself; by moving on to a different bank the CPU can work with that memory without pausing for the clock cycle.

SDRAM and some other memory chip designs include two independent cell banks that allow the same sort of process, permitting a continuous flow of data without pauses for resetting.

In a *pipelined* system, a task is divided into small overlapping tasks with pieces of the work completed at different stages.

Bursting is a technology in which the CPU makes an educated guess on what data or instructions it expects to need next; it grabs not only the block of information it needs but also other addresses that are contiguous to it because of the likelihood that additional data is located nearby.

Cache memory

In this section, I examine a most productive way in which a modern computer "cheats" to pick up speed. Cache memory is a small block of very fast memory that is physically located very close to the CPU. All modern CPUs include a small amount of cache built right into the processor die or the cartridge that holds the processor; this is called primary or Level 1 (L1) cache. Secondary cache, also called Level 2 or L2 cache, is another level of cache memory available to the CPU.

In some systems without an L1 cache, the L2 cache functions as primary cache. L2 cache can be an integral part of the CPU or can reside on separate chips positioned close to the CPU. The fastest L2 cache is part of the CPU package because data transfer distance is reduced.

The Intel Core 2 Duo model 6600 processor used in this book's example machine offers a comparatively gigantic 4M L2 cache that can be shared by the two cores or allocated unevenly as needed. (By comparison, Pentium 4 processors had between 256K and 1MB of L2 cache; the first of Intel's Quad Core CPUs offered 8M of L2 cache for its four cores.)

Because it is so close, and because the CPU does not have to go through the memory controller to get to it, the contents of cache memory are more quickly available. I'm talking about nanoseconds here (billionths of a second), but a few billionths here and a few billionths there quickly add up to some real time on a high-speed system.

Memory designers base their designs on what they call the "80/20" rule, which calculates that about 20 percent of the instructions, applications, and data on a typical computer is in use about 80 percent of the time. Among the most often-used bits of code: low-level instructions on saving or retrieving files, recognizing input from the keyboard, and, increasingly, Internet-related commands.

When the CPU makes an instruction, the memory controller saves a copy to cache; the most recently used bit of data is assigned the highest priority. When the cache is full, the oldest bit of data is overwritten.

Within older machines, cache memory was offered as a part of the motherboard, mounted in a socket near the CPU. Some current modern motherboards include a design that adds another level of cache, referred to as *L3.*

Cache memory is managed by a cache memory controller. When this specialized chip retrieves an instruction from main memory, it also grabs hold of the next few instructions and places them in memory, working under the logical assumption that adjacent instructions will also be called upon. The better the algorithm used to manage the cache controller, the more efficient the use of the cache and the better the speed for the CPU.

In my previous discussion of memory, I described RAM as the computer's desktop. Think of cache as a notepad for jotting reminders. If you keep your notepad right in front of you, when the phone rings, you can pick up previous topics and ask the caller the right questions without wasting time looking for a file. Likewise, when the CPU needs something and finds it in the cache, processing speeds can improve by at least 10 to 20 percent over the same machine without cache.

Cache memory also is a little different from conventional system memory. Whereas most system memory is dynamic (DRAM), meaning that the information it stores must be updated continuously, cache memory is usually static memory (SRAM), meaning that once the data is written into memory, it stays there until it is replaced or the system is powered down. This provides for fast performance and low overhead because neither the CPU nor the memory subsystem has to spend cycles keeping the memory refreshed. SRAM is more expensive than DRAM, and its benefit is only seen in relatively small amounts of memory, which explains why the entire system's memory is not constructed from static RAM.

Unlike the system memory, PC cache can't be easily upgraded. If the cache is part of the CPU, the only way to add more L1 or L2 cache is to replace the CPU with a compatible more-capable processor. If a separate cache module is installed on the motherboard, consult your motherboard manual or machine maker to determine if your system is one of a relatively small number of boards that can work with more than one specification for cache.

ReadyBoost Memory in Windows Vista

One of the new wrinkles in Microsoft's Windows Vista operating system is the ability to quickly add a block of memory to your system by plugging in an external flash memory device, such as a USB key or memory card or stick like those used in digital cameras and audio players.

Windows ReadyBoost technology uses flash memory as a temporary storage cache for disk reads, placing that information in a form that is quicker to access than if it were kept on a hard disk. Actually, the operating system offers a bit of redundant protection: A copy of disk reads is placed within attached flash memory at the same time as it is written to a reserved segment of your hard disk drive; in technical terms this is known as a *write-through cache.* This protects against data loss if the flash memory key is removed from the system.

Another level of protection is the automatic application of encryption to the data stored on the flash memory. Because of this, it would be very difficult, if not impossible, for someone to read the contents to learn the activities that have taken place on your machine.

Flash memory is slower to respond than system RAM, and also theoretically slower than reading from a modern hard disk drive. However, Microsoft points out that this is more a factor in reading large, sequential files such as music or streaming video. To deal with this, the ReadyBoost technology automatically diverts Vista's attention from the flash memory to the hard drive when it is called upon to read such oversized files.

When it comes to small blocks of information, the situation is often the reverse. Because a hard disk drive's read/write heads have to be moved to a particular location and then wait for the spinning platter to bring the needed data into view, drives lose their performance edge here. The system can find small files quickly on flash memory devices and make up the difference in read/write speed.

Not every flash memory device, though, will be fast enough for use with Windows Vista in this way. According to Microsoft, the entire block of memory must be capable of random access reads at least as fast as 2.5 MBps for 4K blocks of data and 1.5 MBps for 512K random writes. When you attach a flash memory device into a system running Vista, the operating system executes a quick performance test; if the memory is too slow, a message informs you that it can only be used for storage of data and not as a ReadyBoost extension of system memory.

Early models of flash memory devices are not likely to work with ReadyBoost; some units were sold with a mix of fast and slow memory for different purposes, and these are probably incompatible with the new technology. You can expect that memory manufacturers will begin to label their products as "Vista Ready" or "ReadyBoost Ready."

Finally, there is the question of how much memory you can add to your machine. The minimum amount of flash memory for ReadyBoost purposes is 256MB, and any amount beyond that offers performance improvements. The maximum is 4GB.

With the initial release of Windows Vista, Microsoft recommended that the way to get the most benefit from ReadyBoost is to match the capacity of the flash memory device to the amount of installed system memory. Thus, if you have 2GB of RAM in the machine, you get the best performance by installing 2GB of ReadyBoost-compatible flash memory. The flash memory has to be all in one device; if you install two 1GB USB memory keys, for example, Vista only recognizes one of them (the device with the earlier alphabetic drive identification) as available for ReadyBoost.

As soon as a device is plugged into a machine running Vista, the operating system asks if you want to speed up your system using the memory or use the memory as a place to hold files; if you click OK the device is tested. You are then taken to a Properties screen for the memory and a new tab that supports ReadyBoost. Here you can adjust the amount of space you want to allow the system to use for cache; you can devote all the memory to that purpose or divide the memory between cache and file storage.

Memory Problems

Your best defense against memory problems is to purchase quality modules, test them after installation using a capable diagnostic program, and test them again with the diagnostics from time to time.

The second line of defense: Make certain your system is properly cooled. All case fans should be operational; nothing should be installed within the box that interferes with the flow of air over memory modules; the exhaust vents should be vacuumed every few months; and furniture, walls, or other equipment should be away from the vents.

The third line of defense: Make sure your machine is safeguarded against power surges with a capable surge protector or a *UPS (uninterruptible power supply)*. And any time you work within the case, make sure you have discharged any static electricity in your body by grounding yourself or by wearing an antistatic strap, or both.

When you think about it, there are two times when memory can cause you a problem. The computer may be unable to find usable memory when it is first started, or memory may fail after the machine is up and running.

Nearly every PC from the birth of the species has included a memory check as part of the POST (power-on self-test) that occurs when a machine first boots up. Under the control of the BIOS, the system quickly counts all the memory it can find in the system. This process is not the same as a full test of the capabilities and accuracy of each chip that occurs when you run a diagnostic program. If your machine won't start, you'll have to find a way to troubleshoot the memory or the motherboard.

The other type of memory error can be much more annoying — a fatal crash of your system in the middle of your work. (You do have your word processor set up to make backups every five minutes, right? And you do have backups of your data on an external disk drive or a DVD that could easily be brought over to a new machine on a temporary or permanent basis, correct?)

Errors at startup

If your computer fails to allow you to get past the POST, reboot immediately and see if the problem happens again.

If you are able to get past the POST, proceed to your operating system and run a full diagnostics check of the memory. If the diagnostic program reports no problem, you may have an intermittent problem with memory. As long as the problem occurs rarely and does not interfere with your work, you can continue to use the machine.

If the POST again reports a problem and refuses to let you continue into bootup, shut off the machine, let it cool off for about 15 minutes, and then try again. If the system performs without problem when it is cool, you may have a failing memory chip or a module that is not making good contact with its connectors. Heat causes parts of the system to expand, which can cause loss of connection. You might also have a problem with the cooling system, including failed fans or blocked vents.

If you suspect a mechanical problem with the system, turn off the machine and unplug the power cord. Remove the cover. Ground yourself before reaching into the system and then gently push down on memory chips or modules in the PC. Look for memory that may have worked its way out of the socket.

If you have more than one block of memory, try swapping the low-end and high-end memory modules. If the machine now boots, you have a problem with the block of memory you moved.

If your diagnostic program reports a failure of a block of memory, it's time to replace the RAM. There is no way to repair memory, and memory modules for current machines are very inexpensive.

Errors after bootup

You're typing along in your word processor and all of a sudden everything freezes. Or the screen suddenly clears and is replaced with the ominous Blue Screen of Death with a cryptic error message.

I won't burden you with unnecessary explanations about how operating systems handle memory or other memory matters that concern programmers; numerous books cover the technical side of memory. Instead, I focus only on fixing the suddenly forgetful machine.

First of all, if the problem occurs just once, or rarely, chalk it up to some unusual combination of software settings and memory usage, and proceed merrily on your way. (You should, though, make certain that you have instructed your word processor and other applications to save your work automatically on a regular basis — my very reliable machines are nevertheless set to save versions of work in progress every three minutes, meaning that the most I could lose is whatever I have accomplished in the last 179 seconds or so.)

If the problem recurs, try to identify a pattern: Does the system always freeze when you load a particular program or perform a particularly complex task? It may be that you are pushing your system to use more memory than it usually asks for, and there may be problems with that block that are not often exposed. A thorough test with a diagnostic program should help. There may be a conflict with other programs that reside in a particular block of memory not ordinarily used by your application.

If you can cause the problem to reoccur on command from within a particular piece of software, contact the technical support department for the application for advice on possible software memory settings that may cure the problem.

If the error seems related to Windows settings, you can reinstall the operating system to see if this will cure the problem. Windows 95 and Windows 98 will reinstall over a previous copy; consult the instruction manual or call technical support for assistance.

SUMMARY

You've completed a tour of RAM, the temporary working space of the computer. From here, you move on to storage memory, including floppy and hard drives, removable media drives, and CD-ROMs.

Notes

Chapter 9

Tools Needed:

- Phillips or flat-blade screwdriver

Floppy Drives

The floppy disk drive was once a technological marvel that was an essential part of the first personal computers. The disk — which was "floppy" in that it lived within a precariously bendable holder — was the primary way for early users to load programs into a PC and to store data created by the computer. Although refrigerator-sized, hugely expensive hard disk drives were in use at commercial sites, the first PCs — the Apple II, the Tandy TRS-80, and the IBM PC among them — avoided the expense and complexity of these devices.

The original IBM PC was shipped with one large, 3-inch-tall, single-sided, standard-density floppy disk drive, capable of holding a grand total of 160K of information on a fragile 5.25-inch floppy disk. The drives were quite slow at transferring data and — just to make things interesting — were prone to mechanical failure. By the time floppy disks reached commercial maturity a decade later, drives stood less than an inch tall, could hold nearly ten times more data on a 3.5-inch disk, and were encased in a hard plastic protector.

Floppy disks, once they reached the point where they could hold 1.44MB of data, became the medium of choice for the first informal networking of data between machines: the "sneaker net." A user could copy a file onto a floppy disk and carry it across the room (or mail it) to another user or another machine.

The important distinction here is the difference between a removable media and a fixed disk drive. Removable storage devices began with cassette tapes and floppy disk drives and have since moved on to supersized versions; fixed drives are primarily hard disk drives.

Today, floppy disk drives are a vestige of the past; current modern machines no longer come equipped with one. Here's why:

- Nearly every modern machine now comes equipped with a CD drive that can read and write as much as 650MB to 800MB of data, and this device has become the preferred method of loading most new programs and storing huge graphics and other files.
- Modern machines (and current Windows operating systems) easily connect to an Ethernet that allow computers to exchange files, share programs, and divide access to devices including high-speed modems, WiFi routers and gateways, and printers.
- The combination of the commercial arrival of two advanced technologies — the fast and flexible USB port and inexpensive, non-volatile flash memory — gave rise to the flash memory drive. For less than $30 (at 2007 prices) you can buy a flash drive (also called a *memory key*) with 1 or 2GB of storage. Plug the key into a USB slot and treat it as if it were floppy disk drive; when you're through you can pull the key out of its USB slot and bring it to another machine for uploading or put it in your pocket and hit the road. (Some companies have begun using encrypted data on flash memory keys as a means of storing critical information; the keys can be removed from desktops and laptops and locked away in a safe.)

Some older modern machines used replacement technologies that sought to improve on the floppy disk while maintaining some level of compatibility. In Chapter 11, I explore the capable SuperDisk technology that captured a small slice of the storage market from about 1997 until 2000 when it, too, faded away. Other would-be replacements included Iomega's Zip Drive. This chapter, then, is aimed at owners of senior-citizen machines and the small handful of modern machines where a floppy disk drive is still relevant. If you don't have a floppy disk drive in your PC and don't need one, you are excused from Chapter 9 and can move on to Chapter 10.

The Ghost of a Once-Marvelous Technology

On some of the most primitive of the dinosaurs, a single 5.25-inch floppy disk drive was intended to hold the operating system, a simple application, such as a word processor or spreadsheet, and a small amount of data files. Soon, PC users moved on to a basic setup that consisted of a pair of double-density drives — one for the operating system and the application program, and a second for data storage.

With the arrival of the PC-XT came the first widespread use of hard disk drives for PCs. At that point, most of the previous assignments for the floppy disk drive were taken over by the hard drive, which stored the operating system, applications, and data. The floppy disk drive — by this time expanded in capacity but reduced in size — was relegated to a means to load new information and applications onto the hard drive and to easily transfer data from one machine to another, and as an emergency boot device in case the hard drive failed or its contents were damaged.

In the early days of PCs, a handful of applications attempted to prevent unauthorized copying by requiring that the floppy disk drive hold an official copy of the program, even if you were operating from the hard drive. That annoying feature is all but gone from modern machines, although you may still see some hardware-based security measures, such as software that will run only if you plug a cable or connector with security firmware into the serial or parallel port.

By the time that modern machines gained full acceptance, floppy disk drives were still the source of new programs and data. High-density designs took on a new role — that of a low-cost backup. Today, CD-ROMs and Internet downloads have taken over the role of loading huge programs and operating systems.

Today, the floppy disk's principal role is to serve as an emergency boot drive when the hard drive is in trouble; even that task, though, has been taken over by other devices, including bootable CD or DVD drives and systems that can seek out boot tracks over a network.

You can easily operate a PC without a floppy disk drive; if you absolutely need one to make use of old files, you may be able to install an internal floppy disk drive in some older modern machines that have a *floppy disk drive (FDD)* controller on the motherboard. That circuitry is gone on the most modern of machines, but you can purchase an external floppy disk drive that attaches to the computer through the USB port.

Understanding Storage Technologies

Before exploring floppy disk drives, I want to take a moment to distinguish the various disk storage technologies available for use on PCs:

- Removable and fixed media
- Magnetic and optical storage
- Random access and sequential storage

Removable versus fixed media

The distinction between fixed and removable media still makes sense from a troubleshooting perspective. Fixed media are sealed. If anything goes wrong with either the media or the media-access machinery, you have to replace the entire hard disk. If something is wrong with a floppy disk but the drive itself is okay, simply throw away the bad disk. Or, if the drive fails, throw away the mechanism and use the disk in a new drive.

The original IBM PC was capable of controlling one or two single-sided disk drives and a cassette tape drive. Both disk drives and the cassette drive used removable media — you could replace the disk in your disk drive with another or insert a different cassette in the tape recorder.

The cassette drive option was a joke from the moment of its release — it was painfully slow, of questionable reliability, and rarely used. IBM included the cassette drive interface because the first personal computers for hobbyists, including devices from Commodore and Radio Shack, used this means of loading and storing the simple BASIC language programs that users wrote for themselves. Soon after the cassette drive's release, though, IBM began to think beyond the hobbyist to the business user and the cassette port disappeared. Floppy disks became the basic vehicle for distributing PC software and were the first reliable means of data storage.

The first of the dinosaurs used a floppy disk capable of storing 160K of information under DOS 1.0. That was quickly upgraded to 180K with a revision of the operating system. The floppy disks themselves — 5.25-inch-square, thin, black plastic envelopes over a fragile circle of plastic coated with metallic particles — were easily damaged and held too little data to satisfy either programmers or users.

About a year into the life of the PC came the first double-sided floppy disk drives with read/write heads that were capable of looking at both sides of the spinning disk. These drives doubled capacity to 360K, which seemed capacious at the time but is woefully inadequate in modern times.

In 1983, IBM introduced the XT, the first member of the PC family with a hard disk (or *fixed disk*, as IBM preferred to call it), which distinguished the new sealed medium from the removable floppy drive diskettes.

A few years later came the first 3.5-inch floppy disk drives, an improvement that had its genesis in the Apple Macintosh. Though they are called floppy disks, the circle of thin magnetized plastic is encased within a hard plastic shell, nicely protected by a sliding cover. The initial 3.5-inch disks doubled the capacity of removable floppies to 720K. In ensuing years, both 5.25-inch and 3.5-inch disks doubled again in capacity through the use of high-density magnetic material and new electronics.

Table 9-1 provides a history of the floppy standard.

TABLE 9-1: A PC Floppy Disk Chronology

Floppy Drive Type	Capacity	PC Usage
Single-sided 5.25 inch	160K	Original IBM PC
Single-sided 5.25-inch	180K	Original IBM PC, upgraded DOS
Double-sided 5.25-inch	360K	PC, PC-XT Standard density
3.5-inch	720K	PC-AT
High-density 5.25-inch	1.2MB	PC-AT, modern machines
High-density 3.5-inch	1.44MB	Older modern machines
Quad-density 3.5-inch	2.88MB	A relatively rare standard used in a small number of older modern machines

Short-lived alternates to the floppy disk drive

In the early 1990s, IBM introduced super-high-capacity floppies capable of storage of 2.88MB; they were offered in IBM's own PS/2 series of machines and a handful of competitive machines, but the market did not embrace them. Owners of machines with these high-capacity floppy drives may have to deal with IBM or search the backrooms of computer dealers to replace the devices and fresh media.

A standard that was more widely embraced — and still supported — is the high-capacity Zip drive, developed by Iomega. Zip disks, slightly larger than a 3.5-inch floppy, can store 100MB, 250MB, or 750MB of data, depending on the model you choose. The original devices from Iomega attached to internal controllers on the motherboard; current models are external and attach to a USB port. In 2006, the external drives sold for less than $100.

On senior citizens and some older modern machines, systems were unable to use Zip drives as a boot device; that shortcoming has been fixed in current BIOS systems.

The current state-of-the-art in removable disk drives is Iomega's Rev systems, which can hold as much as 70GB of data on a durable, removable disk. The drive is offered with software that can automate backup tasks to protect essential data. In 2006, the drive sold for about $500 and individual disks cost about $60.

An older technology was Imation's LS-120 SuperDisk, which could hold as much as 120MB of data, and a less-often-seen variant called the LS-240 with double the capacity. One advantage of this system was that SuperDisk drives could also read and write to standard 3.5-inch floppy drives of 1.44MB capacity. A number of computer makers offered SuperDisk drives in PCs in the late 1990s, but the standard did not garner wide acceptance. New production of drives and disks has been ended, but you may find equipment in closeout or used equipment markets.

 CROSS-REFERENCE

I discuss Rev, Zip and SuperDisk drives in more detail in Chapter 11.

Magnetic versus optical media

As PCs have evolved, the original method for data storage used technologies based on magnetism. An electronically controlled read/write head is instructed to record an indication of 1 or 0 across the length of a floppy or hard disk track, down the length of a tape, or on a removable platter of a hard drive cartridge.

Here's how magnetic recording works:

1. An intelligent controller instructs the storage device to vary an electrical current that is fed into an electromagnetic recording device.
2. The head produces a stream of positive or negative electrical signals that represent the 1s or 0s of digital information.
3. The information is written onto a medium that is coated with metallic particles that are able to hold onto a magnetic setting.
4. The medium moves under the head, either spinning (disks) or streaming past on rollers (tapes).
5. The controller reserves a special portion of the disk for itself for writing a special record to keep track of which files were recorded in particular places.

Later, the user can ask the drive to run the same section of the disk or tape under the head. As the changing magnetic field passes beneath the head, it induces a variable current flow, re-creating the original current flow used to write the data to the disk or tape.

Magnetic recording technology predates the dawn of the PC by many years. Audio tape recorders read and write the same way, and the ubiquitous VCR machines of our time use the same concept, differing principally in the pattern that the recording heads use to store information.

Although magnetic recording remains the principal means of storage for PCs, a large number of users make increasing use of optical media to write and read data: CD and DVD devices in various read-only, read-and-write, and read-and-rewrite versions. Today, most new software is delivered on CDs or DVDs for uploading to systems; that's a good thing since many applications are now hundreds of megabytes, making the old-fashioned floppy disk woefully inadequate for the task.

CROSS-REFERENCE

See Chapter 12 for more details about CD and DVD technology.

Random access versus sequential media

There is an important distinction between random-access and sequential media. Before I talk about computer technologies, think in terms of devices within your home. The cutlery divider in your kitchen is a random-access device; I'm going to assume you're a reasonably neat person and have placed the knives in the knife compartment and the spoons in the space designed for them, so you can reach right in and grab a fork or a knife without problem. If you're old enough to have ever played a record on a turntable, that is also a random-access device: You could pick up the arm and the needle and move it directly to a track to play a particular tune.

Now consider sequential media. At home, the one that you are most familiar with is a VCR tape. If you record three episodes of "Who Wants to Repair a Millionaire's PC" on one tape, you have to fast forward through the first two hours to get to the third show; if you want to go back and watch again the scene where the automated champagne cooler is connected to the USB port in the opening scene, you have to rewind and wait for that particular piece of tape to be under the machine's read head. In the computer world, floppy diskettes, hard drives, removable disk cartridges, CDs, and DVDS are all random access media. Data is easy to find. It's easy to write new data to an empty portion of the disk. And the drive read/write mechanism can quickly, directly move from one location on the disk to another. It's not quite instantaneous, though; all storage devices are measured in terms of their average seek and access speeds. The *seek speed* is the average amount of time, in milliseconds, it takes the read head to move to the location of the data. The *access time* includes the time it takes on average to transfer the located data.

On the other hand, computer data tapes used for backing up systems are sequential, similar to audio and videotapes. Most tapes use a storage design referred to as *serpentine*. They record several tracks on the tape, moving from one end to the other and then making a U-turn and continuing on the next track in the opposite direction. They are relatively inexpensive and capable of storing huge amounts of data — as much as 19TB (19 Terabytes is equal to about 19,000 Gigabytes) of information in some forms — but they are slow and difficult to use if you need to retrieve a particular piece of information.

Floppy Disks

Floppy disks — the material within the outside protective casing — are made of plastic (usually Mylar) coated with a ferric oxide capable of holding a magnetic charge. The plastic is flexible — hence the name floppy. Because of this, the plastic and coating are easily damaged. Although it is enclosed in a square protective jacket, the disk can still be damaged.

Ways you don't want to abuse your floppy disk

Here are some things you *don't* want to do with a floppy disk:

- Roll over it with your chair
- Use it as a coaster for a cup of coffee
- Spill a Coke over a stack of disks
- Bend a floppy in half to fit it in an envelope
- Staple a 5.25-inch floppy disk to a file folder

Trust me, users have performed every one of those acts — and many more even stranger. The most infamous of all disk-destroying acts is attaching a floppy disk to the side of a file cabinet with a magnet; you probably won't lose the disk, but you'll almost certainly lose some of its contents. Also, be aware of less-than-obvious sources of magnetism, including some scissors, screwdrivers, and electric motors, such as those powering pencil sharpeners. Speaker systems and monitors also give off some magnetic radiation, although modern models have shields to reduce the chances of damage; still, it is not a good idea to place a floppy disk on a monitor or speaker.

Because they're enclosed in a stiff cover that prevents casual contamination, 3.5-inch floppy disks are sturdier and less sensitive to extraneous magnetic fields. Under their high-tech cover, standard 3.5-inch disks use the same read/write technology as 5.25-inch floppies.

The relatively rare, extra-high-density (2.88MB size) 3.5-inch floppy disks use a different coating — barium ferrite — plus a special perpendicular recording technology and twice as many sectors per track as high-density (1.44MB) floppy disks. The 2.88MB drive can read 1.44MB and 720K floppies as well because it has a separate recording head to maintain compatibility with the older 3.5-inch disk. Because this is a non-standard piece of hardware, the manufacturer has to supply a device driver to use the 2.88MB drives with older ROM BIOS chips and operating systems that have never imagined such a technology.

Figure 9-1 shows a floppy disk drive with standard connection to an internal controller. If a modern machine does not include a floppy disk drive, the easiest way to add one is to attach an external drive to a USB port or hub.

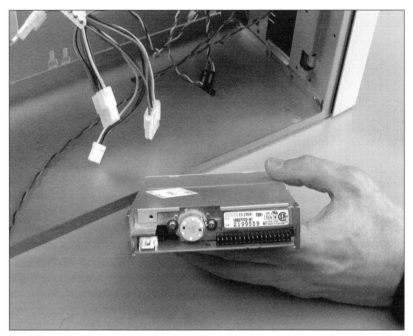

FIGURE 9-1: *A standard internal replacement floppy drive, showing connectors.*

How floppy disks work: Welcome to the Super Bowl

Imagine a circular stadium, with 40 or 80 concentric rows of seats; these are the tracks of a floppy disk. The stadium has 9, 12, or 18 aisles radiating out from the center, which split the stadium seats into sections (the disk's sectors). The stadium owner sells tickets only to groups, and only in multiple-sector, single-row blocks (clusters). If the group doesn't have enough spectators (bytes of data) to fill a complete block, that's tough; the rest of the seats in the cluster just have to go to waste and stay empty.

To help visitors or late arrivals find their group, the stadium owner keeps a master chart at the ticket office showing where each group has been seated. This chart also tells the stadium owner which clusters are still available and which clusters are unusable because some seats in the cluster are broken.

Here's the technical description:

When you insert a 3.5-inch floppy disk into the drive and close the door, the drive mechanism engages with a small slot on the bottom of the disk so that it will spin true. The process of inserting the disk pushes back a sliding cover over the media within the plastic case. At the same time, two read/write heads — one for the top surface of the floppy (side 0) and one for the bottom surface (side 1) — move into position, pressing lightly on the disk. The heads are now prepared to read the magnetic marks on the disk or to write new ones.

NOTE

The read/write heads touch the disk media—this is very different from the design used by hard drives and most removable media storage devices, which float the heads above the surface. Floppy drives spin at only 300 RPM (for 3.5-inch disks) or 360 RPM (for 5.25-inch drives), and the media surface is coated with Teflon or similar compounds to reduce friction. However, over time, the surface of the disk does become degraded. No hard-and-fast rule exists for the expected lifetime of a floppy except this: They don't last forever.

The drive moves these read/write heads according to commands from the controller card. In turn, floppy disk drive controllers get their read or write instructions from DOS or the operating system. These instructions are quite explicit. For example, DOS may tell the floppy disk drive controller to instruct the floppy drive to move the read/write head to track 15, sector 5, and read the contents of that sector.

The floppy disk drive controller is not a particularly sophisticated device. It doesn't have to keep track of the contents of a disk; DOS does that. It doesn't have to know what parts of the disk are empty and available to store new data; DOS does that, too. Nor does it have to decide which read/write head on the drive it is going to activate. The floppy disk drive controller does, however, have to change the DOS-instruction move to track 15 into on/off signals that control the stepper motor that moves the heads from track to track. It also has to know what sector of the floppy disk is under the read/write head at any moment.

For 5.25-inch drives, the floppy disk drive controller locates sectors with the aid of an index hole punched in the floppy disk jacket and in the disk within. When the floppy disk spins, the two index holes line up once every revolution and an electric eye in the disk drive sends a signal to the floppy disk drive controller each time they line up. Knowing where the index mark is, the controller then counts the sector markers until the desired sector is under the read/write head. The controller reads the data in the sector, separating housekeeping bits from the actual data, and returns a clean stream of data to the microprocessor across the bus.

A 3.5-inch drive works in a similar fashion, except that the mechanism knows where it is on the spinning track because of a notch in the center metal spindle of the inner plastic disk. The rotor on the drive motor engages directly into the notch.

R.I.P. 5.25-inch drives

In this section, I make mention of both 5.25-inch and 3.5-inch floppy disk drives. However, the 5.25-inch disk format is all but dead — all new machines have abandoned that older form, and very few modern machines even offer the 3.5-inch drive except as an add-on peripheral.

The only reason to install a new 5.25-inch drive or replace an older one is if you have a large stack of 5.25-inch disks with important information recorded on them. If you have only a few such disks, perhaps you can find a friend or coworker who has a machine with both 5.25-inch and 3.5-inch drives installed and transfer the information to the smaller disks.

At one point in the evolution of the PC, some makers sold combo drives that included both 5.25-inch and 3.5-inch drives in a single slim body that occupy just a single bay in your PC. In any case, you'll find it very difficult to find replacement 5.25-inch drives now; your best bet is to search the bins of the used computer stores, online hobbyist sites, and the back closets of your office.

Tracks and sectors

The surface of the floppy is divided into circular tracks and then into sectors so that data can be stored in a particular location and easily found again. Imagine the floppy rotating in the floppy drive, like a record on a turntable. Hold an imaginary felt-tip marker half an inch from the outer edge of the record and gently lower it onto the surface. The circle drawn on the surface of the record is track 0. If you could accurately move the marker just 1/50 inch toward the center of the record, that new circle would be track 1, as shown in Figure 9-2.

Constant Angular Velocity

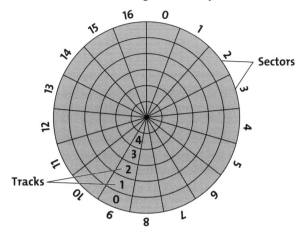

Constant Linear Velocity

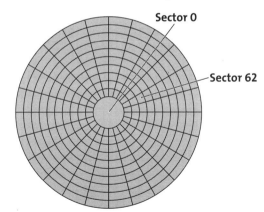

FIGURE 9-2: *Bottom: The spiraling constant linear velocity (CLV) method used by CD-ROM drives. Top: A standard hard or floppy disk with sectors and tracks records data by using the constant angular velocity (CAV) method.*

You might imagine that information is written uniformly across the entire surface of a floppy disk, but that is not the case. A dinosaur 5.25-inch 360K floppy disk, for example, has all 40 tracks packed tightly together in a band less than an inch wide near the outer edge of the disk. This makes sense because the longest (most spacious) tracks are near the outer edge of the disk. At 48 tracks per inch (TPI), these 360K disks are called *double-density*. By comparison, 1.2MB floppy disks jam 80 tracks in the same band less than an inch wide. These high-density 1.2MB floppies have 96 TPI. Both the 720K and the 1.44MB versions of 3.5-inch disks have 80 tracks and are 96 TPI.

A track is a very large space. On a 360K floppy, for example, a single track holds more than 4,600 bytes of data. The track is divided into nine sectors. Each sector on a 360K disk holds 512 bytes of data—a more manageable size for the computer to deal with. A 1.2MB disk has 15 sectors, each with 512K of data. A 720K disk has nine sectors, each with 512 bytes of data per sector. A 1.44MB floppy records twice as much data per track, cramming 18 sectors onto each track.

Here's the calculation for the total amount of data storage available on a disk:

Tracks × Sectors × Bytes per sector × Number of sides = MB data

For example, for a 1.2MB floppy, 80 tracks × 15 sectors × 512 bytes per sector × two sides of the floppy = 1.2MB of data.

Table 9-2 compares the TPI and sectors per track in double-density versus high-density disks for both 5.25-inch and 3.5-inch disks.

Directory and FAT

When you format a disk, DOS creates a file allocation table (FAT) and a directory on track 0 so that stored data can be located on the disk. The directory contains the filename, size, date, time of last modification, file attributes, and physical location of the first part of the file. The FAT contains information about each cluster.

TABLE 9-2: Physical Disk Configuration for Standard Floppy Disk Types

Type	Size	Capacity	Tracks per Side	Sectors per Track	Bytes per Sector	Compatible OS
Double density	5.25-inch	360K	40	9	512	DOS 2.0 or later, all Windows
High density	5.25-inch	1.2MB	80	15	512	DOS 3.0 or later, all Windows
Double density	3.5-inch	720K	80	9	512	DOS 3.2 or later, all Windows
High density	3.5-inch	1.44MB	80	18	512	DOS 3.3 or later, all Windows
Extra high density	3.5-inch	2.88MB	80	36	512	DOS 5.0 or later, all Windows

A *cluster* is a conveniently sized group of sectors used to store information. There are typically one or two sectors per cluster for a floppy drive (one sector for 1.2 and 1.44MB disks, and two sectors for older 360 and 720K and the relatively rare 2.88MB disk) and four sectors per cluster for a hard drive. All reading and writing on disks is done in whole-cluster increments. If only half a cluster is filled with data from File A, the rest of the cluster is left blank.

As noted, the FAT stores information about the contents of each cluster. The FAT is a numeric list of all the clusters, with space for a coded entry for each cluster. A zero in an empty cluster's FAT indicates that the cluster is available for use. Physically defective areas on the disk are marked bad by locking out the appropriate clusters in the FAT. Clusters with a nonzero FAT entry contain data.

A file appears to DOS as a chain of clusters. The first cluster is entered in the directory, along with the filename and other directory information. The FAT entry for that first cluster shows the number of the next cluster in the chain. The last cluster containing data for File A is marked as the end.

The brains of the disk reading-and-writing process are in the floppy drive controller, which is an interface between the computer bus and the floppy disk drives. The controller gets read/write instructions from the microprocessor and data from the bus and then sends both down a ribbon cable to the drives. Working the other way, the controller instructs the floppy drive to locate a particular block of data and then picks it up and sends it across the PC's bus.

Dinosaur PCs used separate floppy and hard drive controllers. Senior citizens offered combination cards that featured both floppy and hard drive controllers. And nearly all older modern machines included an FDD controller on the motherboard, along with a pair of independent *hard disk drive (HDD)* connectors on the motherboard. Because the electronics for each subsystem are independent, one system may fail while the other continues to work properly.

If your modern machine lacks an FDD controller and you want to continue to use floppy disks, attach an external disk drive that uses the flexible USB port; no special controller is needed within the computer in this type of setup.

Figure 9-3 shows the connectors on an older modern machine's motherboard.

The Brains of the Outfit: The Floppy Disk Controller

The floppy drive contains the motor and mechanism necessary to spin the disk and move the head to any desired track on the disk. It also has drive-door-closed (for 5.25-inch drives) or disk-present (for 3.5-inch drives) sensors, and write-protect sensors.

FIGURE 9-3: *A floppy disk connector is near the memory slots on this older modern machine's ATX format motherboard. The port can drive two floppy drives on a single cable with a pair of connectors.*

Testing floppy drive components

A floppy drive subsystem has four basic components:

- Disk drive controller
- Disk drive
- Cable
- Disk

If you're having a problem with a floppy disk drive, you need to test each component in turn to determine whether it is causing the problem. I'm going to turn the order of the preceding list on its head to make the troubleshooting process a bit easier.

The best way to test various pieces of equipment is with a combination of a capable diagnostic program and some old-fashioned logic.

CROSS-REFERENCE

I discuss diagnostic and troubleshooting programs in detail in Chapter 22.

Testing the disk

As with any other mechanical element of your computer, it is only a matter of time before a floppy disk or a floppy disk drive fails. It's not a case of if, but when. Obviously, you should never keep only a single copy of any critical data in one place. Back up any data held on a floppy disk to another floppy disk, to a hard drive, or to any other backup medium.

Here's how to conduct a simple test of a floppy disk: Format it and then copy a file to it. If you get an error message — General failure reading, Data error, or Track 0 failure — try another disk, preferably a new one. Disks die over time; if two or more disks don't work, then the problem almost certainly lies elsewhere.

Make sure that you're using the proper type of disk. If you try formatting a high-density disk in a dinosaur low-density drive, you might get a Track 0 bad message, even though the disk is okay. It's just the wrong type of disk for the drive heads.

Many system diagnostic programs include a test of the floppy disk drive controller and the drive itself. Functions include examining a floppy disk sector by sector, persistently reading and rereading the sector. They check the *cyclic redundancy code (CRC),* a mathematical algorithm that should show any data corruption in the sector. A CRC number can be calculated from the data read and then compared with the CRC recorded in the sector for when the data was originally written to disk. If the CRCs don't match, the data recovery program looks at the error correction code (ECC). The ECC algorithm points to the specific bad bit or bits in a corrupted sector. Norton Utilities and PC Tools also contain data recovery utilities to help the frustrated user recover accidentally deleted files or whole directories.

CROSS-REFERENCE

Chapter 21 covers floppy disk and hard disk data recovery options, particularly the many diagnostic programs that recover data from suspect floppies.

If you're not sure whether you have a damaged floppy, continue reading.

Check the suspect disk in a second floppy drive. Find a disk drive known to be good of the same type as the suspect drive. If you're having problems reading the disk in a 1.2MB drive, for example, try another 1.2MB drive. If the disk works fine in one drive but acts poorly in another, then the problems are probably caused by malfunctions in the system unit hardware — the floppy drive or the disk controller, for example — rather than by a bad disk.

CROSS-REFERENCE

See the troubleshooting charts in Appendix A on the CD for diagnostic assistance.

WARNING

On a dinosaur system, be careful not to mix versions of DOS on the same computer. For example, FORMAT.COM from DOS 5 does not work with DOS 6.2, and raveling such a combination can be a complex mess.

Testing the cables

If the machine has recently been worked on, check to make sure that the floppy drive cable is properly installed. If it is correctly in place, check to make sure that the A: drive, and only the A: drive, has a terminator. If both the cable and the terminator are okay, then break out your diagnostic disk and see whether the drive works.

If the diagnostic disk program says that the drive is bad, replace the cable before junking the drive. Run the floppy drive test again. If it still says the drive is bad, replace the drive.

Testing the floppy drive

The proof of a floppy drive is in the reading. Start by placing a known good disk of the proper disk size and density in the suspect drive and see whether you can read a directory of the disk.

If the drive can't read a floppy that you know is good, go to the troubleshooting charts in Appendix G of this book. Begin at the START chart and work your way through until you locate the problem.

If your dinosaur machine has two drives — a 3.5- and a 5.25-inch drive, for example — and one of the two drives is working, the problem almost certainly does not lie in the disk controller but is instead due either to a cabling problem or to a dead drive.

If your older system has two floppy disk drives — regardless of whether they are both 5.25-inch drives, both 3.5-inch drives, or one of each — one important test is to swap their data cabling. Start by turning off the power and removing the plug, and then take off the cover of the PC. Locate the floppy drives, their associated floppy disk controller, and the cables that interconnect them. Remove the data cable to Drive A: and mark it with a piece of tape or a soft marking pen; do the same with the data cable for Drive B:. Now reverse the assignments of the two drives, making the former Drive B: your first drive.

Power up the system and see if either of the floppy drives now works. If the formerly inoperative drive is still unresponsive and the other drive continues to work properly, you have a dead drive that must be replaced. If both drives now work, the problem may have been caused by improperly seated cables. Or, if you had just installed new drives before the failure, the problem may have been caused by improper termination settings on the drives. If the drive that worked before now does not work, you have a bad cable. Replace it.

Another potential source of the problem is an intentional or unintentional change made to the CMOS settings of your computer. Consult the instruction manual for your PC to learn how to get to the screen and check that the configuration screen properly indicates the type or capacity of floppy drive installed. CMOS settings can be damaged by static electricity, by failing batteries, and occasionally by ill-behaved software.

If the drive still reads and writes unreliably, the problem may be caused by a loose connection on cables or an intermittent failure of the drive electronics. Test utility programs read and write to a disk, repeatedly checking data accuracy at every point on the data storage surface.

Determining if a drive is out of alignment

If you are experiencing more and more data errors with a drive — especially with disks written on another machine or with older files that you recorded some time before — your floppy drive may be going out of alignment.

Alignment means that the heads of the drive are physically aligned with the tracks on the floppy disk, and the heads write information at the proper *level* (an electronics term roughly equivalent to volume on your stereo).

WARNING

It is possible to have a brand-new disk drive that is out of alignment when you first start using it. You may not realize the problem until you swap disks with someone else or run a diagnostic program.

One way to test the alignment of your drive heads is to purchase a diagnostic program that comes with a preformatted test disk that is used as a reference point for tests. But before you do so, consider that realigning a floppy disk drive is not a job that you can do without some expensive tools and testing devices. And the cost of replacing an old floppy disk drive — less than $20 — is sure to be lower than the charge made by a PC repair shop to perform a realignment.

Testing the disk drive controller and power supply

If a new drive flunks tests and you have checked the cables, you may have a failed controller. The next step down the chain calls for replacement of the controller and retesting. If the drive is still bad, you should try installing a power supply that you know to be good. If the controller and drive are good, you have no choice but to replace the motherboard.

On nearly all older modern machines, the controller for the floppy disk drive is a component of the motherboard; if you are running Windows, the first place to check is the System report of the Control Panel. Make certain that the controller is recognized by the system, and that Windows does not report any conflicts for the necessary system resources it requires.

You should also make sure that your BIOS is set up properly to recognize a floppy disk drive controller. Occasionally a power surge or a misbehaving piece of software can corrupt the settings in the CMOS memory for the BIOS.

In rare circumstances, a problem with the system's power supply can cause problems with floppy disk drives; this was more of an issue with dinosaur systems with small power supplies and inefficient motors on the drives. If your power supply is failing, you're likely to experience numerous concurrent problems, including errors on hard drives, memory errors, and system shutdowns. You can test the output of a power supply, or replace it with a unit known to be good to see if this is the cause of the problem.

NOTE

If you are trying to replace a dinosaur full-size drive, you may be out of luck in searching for a direct replacement. You can, though, find adapter hardware that enables you to install a tiny drive in a large space.

Testing the disk controller

Test the floppy disk drive controller the same way you test a floppy drive. First, make sure that the drive formats disks properly, and then use a diagnostic program to see whether the drive reads and writes properly for hours at a time. If the drive functions properly, then the drive controller must be working okay.

In a two-floppy-drive older machine, if one floppy drive works and the second one doesn't work the controller is not likely to be at fault. Conversely, if both drives are bad, it usually means a bad controller, not simultaneous drive failure. The same circuits are used to control both floppy drives, but the hard disk controller has separate circuitry. Therefore, a working hard disk tells you nothing about the state of the controller card, even if the same card controls both floppy and hard drives.

If the floppy disk controller is built into the motherboard of an older modern machine or a senior citizen, you should be able to disable the onboard electronics and install a new controller into a bus slot. When I say "new," I actually mean a "replacement" controller card that you'll likely have to find on the used market or from a surplus equipment reseller; they are simply no longer being manufactured. When these plug-in controllers were on the market, they sold for as little as $15, and replacement internal floppy disk drives for as little as $20.

Check the system BIOS to find a setting to turn off the built-in floppy disk controller. Some senior citizens and dinosaurs may require you to change a jumper or throw a switch on the motherboard to disable the built-in controller.

If your machine has a USB port, a simpler solution is to install an external floppy disk drive that attaches in that way; you don't even have to disable the built-in FDD controller, although you probably should do so to free up system resources devoted to it. Most modern machines can be upgraded with a USB adapter; you'll also need to run a version of Windows that is at least as current as Windows 98SE.

If you have a dinosaur machine, you may not be able to use high-density floppy disk drives. Check with the manufacturer of your machine to see if the machine will accommodate more modern drives. You may need to update the ROM BIOS.

If you are looking for a replacement for a failed 5.25-inch drive for a dinosaur or senior citizen, you are not going to find them easily. Some specialty computer repair outlets may have some in stock, but your best bet may be to search for used parts.

Installing an Internal Floppy Disk Drive

The first step is to remove the old drive. It is often easier to remove the cables (a ribbon cable and a four-wire power cable) after the drive is loose. Examine the cables carefully before you disconnect them so that you will be able to reinstall them properly. Mark them with a piece of tape or a soft marker to help identify them for reinstallation later.

You also have to remove the four-wire power connector that comes from the power supply. Hold the connector (not the wires) and firmly pull it out of its attachment point on the drive.

On most dinosaurs, the floppy drives are mounted directly to the chassis. To remove the drive, you must remove the machine screws on the sides of the drive. Occasionally, the screws are installed from below. If that is the case, turn the computer on its side and look for holes in the bottom of the chassis to access these screws.

On most older modern machines, floppy drives are installed with rails that slide into slots in the drive bays; however, designs vary. Some use a small metal clip that is screwed onto the front surface of the chassis next to the drive. Remove this clip to slide the drive out of the chassis — like a drawer sliding out of a cabinet. On other systems, the drives are held in place with screws on the side or bottom. After you remove these screws, the drive slides out on rails.

Within some PCs, especially those with slim-line or other low-profile designs, you may need to remove other parts of the system — the power supply, adapter cards, riser cards — to gain access to the cage holding the floppy disk drives.

Another issue, which is easily solved, involves installing a 3.5-inch floppy drive in a wider 5.25-inch drive bay. See Figure 9-4 for details.

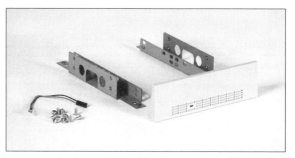

FIGURE 9-4: *To mount a 3.5-inch hard or floppy disk drive into a 5.25-inch drive bay, you need to install mounting rails. Some drive makers include them in installation kits. You can also purchase standard and specialized rails from computer supply companies, such as Dalco Electronics.*

Setting switches/jumpers on the new drive

Most floppy drives have jumpers or DIP switches to set the floppy's drive selector and terminating resistor options, as shown in Figure 9-5.

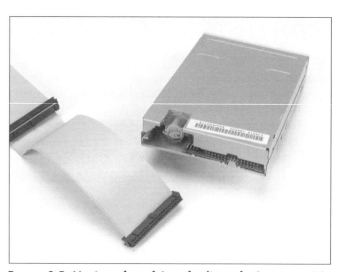

FIGURE 9-5: *Most modern drives don't need a jumper setting.*

However, on senior citizens through modern machines, you should not have to make any change to the floppy disk drive as delivered — the jumper block comes preset for use in PCs. In fact, to make things simple, the standard setup for the final evolution of floppy drives was to leave the jumper block without any jumpers in place.

If you have two floppy drives connected to the controller in your system, the drive selector (DS) on both Drive A: (the first drive recognized by the system) and Drive B: (the second drive in the system) must be set to the second drive option. This may not seem to make sense, but the machine won't confuse the two drives when they're set to the same DS; the twist in the ribbon cable straightens everything out.

As I've previously noted, the floppy controller cable takes care of identifying each of the drives properly. The A: connector is at the end of the cable, nearest to the twist in the wires; the B: connector is in the middle of the cable.

NOTE

Consult the instruction manual that comes with your new floppy drive for the particular settings for that drive and for the location of the jumpers or switches.

The floppy drive data cable has three connectors: one for Drive B: (which is straight-through), one for Drive A: (which has part of the ribbon cable twisted at the end), and one for the floppy-drive controller. The cable, not the DS jumper, determines which drive the machine sees as Drive A: and which as Drive B:.

Checking terminating resistors

Older PCs and floppy drives — especially 5.25-inch drives — require a terminating resistor on the drive attached to the end of the data cable. The resistor helps set the proper electrical levels for the signal. Most (but not all) 5.25-inch drives come with the resistor in place; if you are installing a floppy drive as the first drive on the cable, you may need to remove the resistor.

NOTE

Consult the instruction manual that comes with your floppy drive or call the manufacturer to determine whether your drive has the resistor in place and whether it is necessary to remove it.

Nearly all 3.5-inch internal drives have a built-in termination that does not have to be set by the user. Again, check the manual.

Sliding in the drive and connecting cables

After you configure the drive, you can install it. You should be able to reuse the rails and machine screws from the drive you are replacing, but not all floppy drives have the same physical dimensions or screw hole locations.

Screw the replacement drive down firmly but not too tightly, or you may strip the threads. After you secure the drive in the chassis, connect the ribbon cable. Most 5.25-inch drives use flat edge connectors to mate with a data cable; most 3.5-inch drives use pin connectors. Reconnect the four-wire power connector.

Most current 3.5-inch drives use small, half-inch connectors that click in place, held by a plastic clip. If you have an old-style floppy drive to mate to a modern power supply or the other way around, adapter cables are available to convert the older, large connectors.

Floppy disk drives require a data cable and juice from the power supply. The device that is intended as Drive A: takes the connector at the end of the data cable; if you have a Drive B:, it attaches to the connector in the middle of the cable. Modern disk drives generally use a 34-pin male connector that mates to a 34-pin female plug on the cable; older drives used a 34-pin edge connector. To deal with this occasional incompatibility, floppy disk drive cables are available with redundant female and edge connectors. Note that these connectors are not rectangular — two corners are cut off on a diagonal. Examine the socket on the floppy drive before installing the connector. It is difficult, but not impossible, to force the connector in improperly; the result will most likely be a destroyed disk drive and possibly a damaged power supply.

After you install the replacement drive, turn on the machine and test the drive rigorously. If it passes all the tests, you're finished. If it doesn't pass all the tests, recheck everything carefully, looking especially for incorrect switch settings and incorrect or loose cables.

Figure 9-6 shows a vertical case in which the 3.5-inch floppy slides into place in a snug lower-drive cage. On some machines, you may need to install mounting rails to convert a space intended for a 5.25-inch drive and a faceplate to fill the space around the front bezel of the case.

FIGURE 9-6: *The 3.5-inch floppy fits in the lower drive cage of this vertical case.*

Installing a Floppy Drive Controller

For dinosaurs and senior citizens, the first step in installing a replacement floppy drive controller is to remove the old controller card.

Fixing a problem with a controller on the motherboard

If you suspect a problem with the onboard floppy disk drive controller, you should begin by checking the BIOS Setup screen for your system. Many modern machines use advanced BIOS code that lets you turn the FDD controller on or off from the keyboard. In some instances, power supply or battery backup problems can introduce errors to the CMOS memory of the machine.

Consult the motherboard instruction manual to determine whether you need to move a jumper, set a switch, or make a change to the configuration Setup screen for the BIOS. A small number of older modern machines automatically disabled an onboard FDD controller if they detected the presence of a new controller installed in the bus.

If the FDD has been turned off, reset the option in the CMOS and reboot the system to see if this fixes the problem. Try a floppy disk drive known to be good with the controller, or move your floppy disk drive to a machine with a controller that's known to be good to isolate the problem.

If you decide that the FDD controller on the motherboard is bad, disable it from the BIOS Setup screen. On some systems, you may have to disable it by moving a jumper on a switch block on the motherboard. On a few other systems, plugging a replacement FDD controller into one of the slots on the bus automatically disables the onboard controller.

Replacement disk controllers, usually combined with IDE hard drive circuitry (that you can disable to avoid conflicts if necessary) are available from parts suppliers. Simple add-in cards for IDE sell for about $20 from electronics suppliers; you'll also find controller cards that add multiple I/O functions including high-speed serial ports, SCSI ports, and game ports.

Replacing the controller card

Press the card down into the motherboard bus connector. Some controller cards are extra long and only fit in a particular slot on your machine; other than such physical considerations, a disk controller card works in any ISA slot. There were relatively few controller cards manufactured to install into PCI slots; by the time that advanced bus had arrived, the FDD had moved to a spot on the motherboard itself; that's the reason you may have to scour the bins of used computer equipment stores or search the Internet to find an ISA adapter card.

After you install the card, connect the ribbon cable and reattach the screw that holds the card to the system unit chassis. In some installations, it may be easier to attach the ribbon cable before you place the controller in the slot. Figure 9-7 shows the proper way to attach a floppy disk cable to the motherboard. Test the machine. If it works, replace the cover and you're finished. If not, recheck the cable; the next chapter tells you how.

SUMMARY

In this chapter, I covered floppy drives, a technology that has all but disappeared from current modern machines. If you've got an older modern machine, or need to maintain compatibility with other old machines or old files still stored on floppy disk drives, this equipment is still relevant. In the next chapter, I explore the huge capacity and high speed of hard disk drives.

Ch 9

FIGURE 9-7: *An FDD connector and one of two HDD (EIDE circuitry for hard drives or CD-ROM drives) on an integrated motherboard. If you hold the drive-connector end of the floppy disk drive cable in one hand (note twisted section of cable between the fingers of the left hand), you'll be sure to plug the proper end of the cable to the FDD connector.*

Chapter 10

Tools Needed:

- Phillips or flat-blade screwdriver
- Antistatic strip, wrist strap, or grounding pad

Media Hard Drives

Hard disks were once a very expensive, very fragile luxury. When the first mainframe computers — the size of a tractor trailer — were installed at universities, government agencies, and major businesses, they used various sorts of physical storage: paper tape, punch cards, and huge rolls of magnetic tape.

The first hard drives were refrigerator-size tubs that were babied in air-conditioned glass houses; each one of the whirring drives might hold a few hundred thousand bytes or perhaps a megabyte. I used to spend some time in one such data center at a newspaper where I worked; it looked and felt like the interior of a power dam. For the record, IBM shipped the first hard disk drive in 1956; the RAMAC 305 was capable holding a whopping 5MB of data and sold for about $50,000. There were fifty 24-inch-diameter platters in the big box.

The next significant step in the evolution of hard disk storage came in 1973 with the introduction of IBM's model 3340, which was given the nickname of a "Winchester" driver because at one time during its development, it was expected to include a pair of 30MB drives; someone saw a link to the famed Winchester 30-30 rifle of the 19th century. (Some of us old-timers in the computer industry referred to all hard disk drives as Winchesters for at least the first decade of the PC's history.)

When the first PCs were introduced in the late 1970s and early 1980s they did without hard drives. My first IBM PC came equipped with a pair of 160K floppy drives. One floppy held the operating system and a small word-processing program, and the other held the data files.

If you really wanted to buy a hard drive for your PC, some makers began to shrink drives from refrigerator-sized to television-sized and finally to about the size of a small suitcase. These early hard drives delivered what was considered a huge amount of storage at an acceptable price: A typical early hard drive offered 10MB of storage and only cost a few thousand dollars!

In 1980, IBM again broke new ground with the introduction of the first gigabyte hard drive. Intended for use with mainframe and minicomputers, the refrigerator-sized box weighed about 550 pounds; the list price was about $40,000. Today, hard drives are by comparison almost free. As this book goes to press, the best bang for the buck is a huge 500GB hard drive, selling for about $150. (To save you the math, that's about $3 per gigabyte or three cents for 10MB.) They're also a generally very sturdy and long-lived necessity. Hardly any of the things we take for granted today are possible without gigabytes of storage on a tiny hard disk drive.

Over the life of the PC, hard drives have become larger in capacity, smaller in size, faster in speed, and lower in price. Today, I consider the entry-level size for a hard drive to be 80GB, but I recommend spending a small amount more for a drive of at least twice that size. In this chapter, I explore hard drive technology and organization. Then I tell you what you need to know about today's most common hard drive interfaces: Serial ATA (SATA) and Parallel ATA (PATA, or as it was previously known, IDE).

In the appendix to this chapter, I cast a backward glance at dinosaur-era standards, ST506 MFM and RLL drives and controller cards, as well as ESDI drives and controller cards. You'll also find information on SCSI drives in the appendices.

And I also discuss the unpleasant facts of hard disk mortality. Here's a preview: If you're lucky, your hard drive will have a full, healthy, and productive life. And then it will die. Be prepared.

How a Hard Disk Works

All hard disks share the same basic construction. A small motor spins finely machined disks (usually made of aluminum or a high-tech glass and ceramic mix) at a precise speed. The disks — called *platters* — are coated with an oxide of magnesium, chromium, iron, or other metal particles capable of holding a magnetic charge. Because you can't remove the disks or bend them like the insubstantial media in a floppy disk, these devices are called *hard disk drives* or *fixed disks*.

Above and below each platter, a read/write head glides on a cushion of air very close to the surface of the platter. To write data, the heads magnetize tiny points on the tracks of the platter, using changes in polarity to encode data. To read data, the heads detect the changes in polarity on the disk as the 0s and 1s of binary information. In consumer hard drives, all the heads of the drive are mounted on the same assembly, and they move in and out — from the 0 or outer track to the inner track — on the same actuator mechanism.

If a modern drive has two platters, it usually has four read/write heads and four data surfaces; a three-platter drive would have six of each, and so on. Along with the data, an index to where data is stored is recorded on the disk. In technical terms, this is called an *embedded servo*, as shown in Figure 10-1.

One design for high-performance and high-capacity drives had several heads on a head assembly, with each head covering a smaller zone on the disk. The specs for this sort of drive might indicate something like 4 platters, 8 data surfaces, and 16 or more heads.

Under the covers of a disk drive

Modern hard disk drives usually have more than one platter, stacked one above another like dishes in the cupboard. There's just enough room between the platters for a read/write head to float above (or below) the disks, kept aloft by a cushion of air generated by the spinning disk.

I've opened up the covers of a hard drive in Figure 10-2. (Remember what I said about the mortality of hard drives? This model gave up the magnetic ghost after three years of hard use.) Hard drives are shipped to consumers with sealed covers and high-tech air filters to exhaust heat; this is done to avoid tiny specks of dust that can sit like boulders on the platter as it spins just beneath the read/write head.

FIGURE 10-2: *The innards of this hard drive include three platters. Six read/write heads reside on the head assembly that moves in and out on a cushion of air above the platters.*

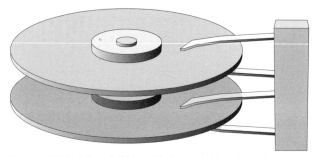

FIGURE 10-1: *A hard disk with two platters has four recording surfaces, so the hard disk needs four read/write heads. The heads move together, in and out across the platter surface.*

The main element of a standard read/write head is a tiny magnet. One common design is made of turns of copper wire on a ring of ferrite; there is a hairline gap on the side of the ferrite core facing the disk. When current is passed through the coil, the disk surface under the gap is magnetized.

To read information from the disk, the device's electronics sense the current caused by the passage of the magnetized sections of the disk as it spins beneath the gap. The electronics sense the transition from one polarity to another.

The signal pulses are amplified and converted from the analog waves detected by the read/write head, and then converted to precise digital pulses of 0 or 1. This is a potential point of failure on a disk drive: If the platter is unable to hold a strong, identifiable marking or if the write head is unable to put one in place, the decoding circuits may mistakenly identify a 0 as a 1.

The next step is to separate the data pulses from the clock pulses. A clock signal is a string of precisely spaced pulses that serve as timing references for other signals, including drive control and positioning.

The disk controller examines the sector address, and if it matches the address the computer is looking for, the processing continues. If not, the data is ignored.

If the sector is correct, most interfaces then perform some level of error detection. (Modern devices employ a scheme called *cyclic redundancy checking*.) The system computes an error-checking value that it compares to the value that was recorded along with the original value. If it finds an error, the controller tries again.

At this point, on a Serial ATA drive the stream of data moves directly to the controller on the motherboard as a serial stream of bits — one bit behind the other. On an older Parallel ATA (IDE) drive, or even more outdated EIDE and SCSI designs, the stream of data bits must be converted from serial form to a parallel form, with individual bits assigned to discrete wires in a cable; the conversion is performed by the drive's integrated electronics (the origin of the IDE acronym) in a circuit called a *data separator*.

Hundreds of hard disk and controller models are available, each with various idiosyncrasies and (on older models) different switch settings and jumpers. Although modern drives are much simpler to configure — especially SATA drives that connect directly to a SATA port on the motherboard without the need for further identification — it is still absolutely essential that you consult an instruction manual from your disk drive manufacturer.

If you are transferring a known-good disk drive from one machine to another and are missing the documentation, you should be able to obtain information from the manufacturer's web site. Many of manufacturers' Web pages also include downloadable device drivers and other software.

The BIOS included in most modern machines generally supports an auto-detect mode that will help you set up a new drive easily, and that is generally the best way to proceed with the installation of a new or replacement drive. Certain combinations of BIOS and drive require you to enter settings manually; the drive maker should be able to assist.

NOTE

If you're moving a hard disk drive from one machine to another, check to see how the old machine's BIOS identified the drive before you remove it. If it was able auto-detect the settings, there's nothing to learn. But if the previous installation included specific settings for capacity, number of platters, heads, and other data, make note of them; you may need to enter these in the new machine's BIOS if that device also cannot auto-detect the specifications of the drive.

The true capacity of a hard drive

A hard drive advertised as a 1GB device (a very small drive by today's standards, but it serves this example well) may actually be a 1.1GB drive, or it may be capable of holding a mere 900MB of data. No hard-and-fast rule exists for stating data capacity, and in any case, the raw capacity of any drive is reduced by the formatting structure applied by the operating system.

All hard drives must be formatted to be used in a computer — the act of formatting adds control information and magnetic markings for the data structure. Also, in the process of formatting, the drive electronics may find that some sectors of the drive are unable to store data reliably and will list them in a table that the disk drive controller consults. Figure on an overhead of about 10 percent from the raw capacity of a drive. In other words, you can expect to be able to use only about 90 percent of the drive's stated capacity.

Ch
10

Some drive manufacturers list formatted capacity in their specifications, and this figure should provide a reasonably accurate means of comparing one drive to another.

If you want to do it yourself, here's the proper mathematical formula:

number of cylinders × number of heads × number of sectors × number of bytes/sector = hard disk capacity

The number of bytes per sector is most commonly 512.

The second problem involves the sometimes-loose way in which computer people use the kilo, mega, and giga prefixes; those terms are commonly used for 1 thousand, 1 million, and 1 billion, respectively, but the math is incorrect if you use them for memory. And because the data in memory is what the computer writes to the hard disk, you'd think hard disk size would be measured the same way. But because computers use binary math, based on powers of 2, memory chips are made in quantities that are powers of 2. And the tenth power is 1,024, close enough to 1,000 for computer users to use the term kilo when referring to memory, as in 1 kilobyte. Thus, a megabyte is 2 to the 20th power, or 1,024 × 1,024 or 1,048,576 bytes; and a gigabyte is 2 to the 30th power, or 1,024 × 1,024 × 1,024 or 1,073,741,824 bytes — at least, for memory.

But for hard disks, whose sizes have grown astronomically and are not constrained by the powers of two, marketing has prevailed over the meaning of megabyte and gigabyte. Hard disk sizes are almost always advertised with those terms meaning 1 million and 1 billion bytes. (After all, in all other cases except computer memory,

the old Greek meanings prevail; kilo means one thousand, as in a 75K salary; mega means a million — an 800-MHz CPU for example; and giga means a billion.) And if you're a manufacturer with a drive that holds 1,073,741,824 bytes, would you advertise it as a 1GB drive or a 1.07GB drive?

Today most drive manufacturers advertise capacity in digital terms — meaning a 40GB hard drive contains 40 billion bytes, which converted to binary accounting would equal about 37.25GB. Either way, it's a lot of space, but the only way to know whether a particular disk-drive manufacturer uses true binary accounting for determining the size of its drive is to study the drive's specs carefully.

And, ever mindful of the quest for the never-arriving horizon, technicians have already come up with labels for collections of huge amounts of data beyond mere gigabytes. A list of numbering terms is in Table 10-1.

And you should be aware of a third wrinkle: Many hard disk drive makers now include diagnostic utilities and sometimes trial versions of applications that you can work with for a particular period of time or a specified number of uses. Unless you remove the software from the drive by reformatting it or using a Windows-based uninstall utility, the drive's usable capacity will be less than you thought. (The same applies to hard drives that are delivered with new computers; the PC maker may tell you the machine comes with a 250GB hard drive, but that does not include perhaps 10GB of space already taken over by the operating system, utilities, and any software — licensed or trial versions — provided with the hardware.)

TABLE 10-1: Data Numbering Scheme

Name	Number of Bytes	Powers of 2	If We Spoke Plain English
1 kilobyte	1,000 bytes	2^{10}	1 thousand bytes
1 megabyte	1,000,000 bytes	2^{20}	1 million bytes
1 gigabyte	1,000,000,000 bytes	2^{30}	1 billion bytes
1 terabyte	1,000,000,000,000 bytes	2^{40}	1 trillion bytes
1 petabyte	1,000,000,000,000,000 bytes	2^{50}	1 quadrillion bytes
1 exabyte	1,000,000,000,000,000,000 bytes	2^{60}	1 quintillion bytes
1 zettabyte	1,000,000,000,000,000,000,000 bytes	2^{70}	1 sextillion bytes
1 yottabyte	1,000,000,000,000,000,000,000,000 bytes	2^{80}	1 septillion bytes

Hard Drives: Bigger . . .

The PC-XT was IBM's first PC with a hard drive. Introduced in 1982, it came equipped with a 10MB hard drive with an access time of 80 milliseconds (ms); the drive was considered huge and fast. Two years later, the capacity of the new PC-AT was doubled, and the access time cut in half.

In early 1996, a basic hard drive size for a Pentium machine was 540MB with a 13 ms access speed. A year later, when the fourth edition of this book was published, a serious Pentium user would expect a hard drive three to five times larger, nearly half again as fast, and half the price.

By the fall of 1998, the jump in available capacity — and in consumer expectations — had accelerated even as prices continued to drop. Then, few modern machines were sold with less than 4GB of storage, and it was easy and relatively inexpensive to add drives of 6, 9, or even 11GB to a computer. In 2000, as I prepared the sixth edition of this book, the basic hard drive for an upper-end machine was in the 10 to 12GB range, and the price for a 20GB drive was about $170, and 27GB drives cost a mere $250 or so.

In 2002, the cost of a 40GB drive had dropped below $100, and a state-of-the-art 160GB drive sold for about $320.

And by late 2006, hard drives had dropped to levels almost unimaginable at the dawn of the PC era. The entry level for most modern machines had reached 80GB and you could purchase a fast and reliable model of that size for about $50; at the top end of consumer market, disk-drive manufacturers were offering drives of 500GB and even 750GB. In four years, prices had dropped as much as 80 percent.

As with almost all electronic devices, the sweet spot — the best bang for the buck — existed one or two steps down from the newest, fastest, and (in the case of hard drives) largest products: 320GB or 500GB hard drives were the best deals.

Let's look first at the march of disk drive capacity and speed over the years. Table 10-2, based on typical systems, includes ratios to compare capacity and access. The capacity ratio column shows that a 160GB hard drive, becoming common on midrange machines as this edition goes to press, is something on the order of 16,000 times larger than the clunky device in the dinosaur PC-XT. The access speed for today's much larger drive is about nine times faster.

TABLE 10-2: A History of Typical PC Disk Drive Capacity and Speed

Model	Typical Capacity	Access Speed (Lower Is Better)	Capacity Ratio (Higher Is Better)	Access Speed Ratio
IBM PC-XT (1982)	10MB	80 ms	1	100 percent
IBM PC-AT (1984)	20MB	40 ms	2	50 percent
IBM PS/2 (1987)	115MB	28 ms	11.5	35 percent
486 Clone (1990)	320MB	15 ms	32	19 percent
Pentium (1995)	540MB	13 ms	54	16 percent
Pentium (1997)	2.5GB	12 ms	250	15 percent
Pentium II (1998)	4GB	12 ms	400	15 percent
Pentium II (1998)	6.5GB	8 ms	650	10 percent
Pentium III (2000)	10GB	7.6 ms	1,000	9.5 percent
Pentium III (2000)	17GB	8 ms	1,700	10 percent
Pentium III (2000)	20GB	7.6 ms	2,000	9.5 percent
Pentium III (2000)	28GB	8 ms	2,800	10 percent
Pentium 4 (2002)	40GB	8.7 ms	4,000	11 percent
Pentium 4/Pentium D (2006)	160GB	8.9 ms	16,000	11 percent
Pentium Core Duo (2006)	320GB	8.9ms	32,000	11 percent
Pentium Core 2 Duo (2006)	500GB	8.9ms	50,000	11 percent

Notice what has happened to capacity and access times. Capacities for typical consumer hard drives have grown as much as 32,000-fold (or more, with the latest drives that are as much as 750GB in size) compared to the PC-XT days of 1982, while access times are only about nine times better. That seems incongruous until you look at both figures together. Consider that the drive mechanics are sorting through at least 32,000 times more data.

It is also worth noting that since 1998, access times haven't improved appreciably. The industry has reached a mechanical plateau, of sorts, in how fast a mechanical device can move over a disk surface that is packed as densely as these drives are packed. Some of the new technologies that I talk about later in this chapter could get over that plateau within a few years.

. . . Faster . . .

Just what is hard drive speed? It all comes down to this: When you enter a command from the keyboard or when a program issues an instruction, how long does it take for the disk drive subsystem to deliver the information to the microprocessor or the video adapter?

One of the components of speed is the rotational speed of the drive. Older hard disks typically spin about ten times faster than a floppy disk drive, usually in the range from 2,400 to 3,600 rpm. Most mid-range, newer drives spin at about 5,400 rpm, although 7,200 rpm devices are now the standard for consumer machines. And special-purpose graphics and advanced business machines may use 10,000 rpm hard drives, which are generally more expensive and have not yet reached the same large capacities of slower drives.

All things being equal, 7,200 rpm drives increase overall system performance by about 5 to 34 percent over 5,400 rpm drives. If your machine is used to stream video or in graphics-intensive applications, you can expect even more benefit from a faster drive. Why doesn't system performance automatically improve by 33 percent, since the drive spins that much faster? The answer lies in the fact that drives are still constrained by the capacity of the bus to carry information and can also be slowed down by other processes that demand the CPU's attention. And the software you use also makes a difference; the more sustained the data transfer, the more the machine benefits from a faster drive. If you're just using the computer to load a word-processing document that stays in RAM for a few minutes (or a few hours) before it is returned to hard disk storage, the impact of drive speed is very minimal on your overall productivity.

One other factor: Faster drives generally consume more power, generate more heat, and are louder than slower drives. Hard drive manufacturers have devoted a great deal of resources to dealing with each of these problems, but buyers need to be aware that performance comes at a price.

This edition ends coverage of new SCSI or Fibre Channel interface hard drives. In the early 1990s, SCSI represented a legitimate competitor to the ATA hard drive interface for advanced users; today, though, a combination of technology and pricing improvements have made Serial ATA the drive of choice for modern machines. Older modern machines can benefit from advances on Parallel ATA drives (formerly called IDE drives.) You'll find information on SCSI, along with dinosaur interfaces, in this book's CD.

Four physical factors have the largest impact on the usable speed of a hard drive: physical seek time, latency, data buffer size, and transfer rate.

- **Seek time.** The average time required to position the read/write head of a drive over a specified track on the drive. The time varies based on the location of the track and the position of the head before it begins to move. In other words, moving from one track to the adjacent track is quicker than moving from the innermost track to the outside track.
- **Latency.** The average time it takes for the rotating drive to bring the data under the read/write head. Latency is related to the speed of the drive.
- **Data buffer size.** A data buffer is a specialized block of memory used to hold data being transferred from one device to another to help compensate for differences in transfer rates between devices.
- **Transfer rate.** The speed at which the collected information is pumped out of the drive to the computer bus or accepted from the bus.

A measure of the first two factors is *average access time*. The word average is an important component of that specification. Access time is supposed to mean the amount of time required for the read/write head mechanism to find the track or cylinder that holds the desired data (this is called *average seek time*), plus the time required for the head mechanism to become stable over the location of the data (called *settling time*), plus the average time required for the proper data to spin under the read/write head (called *rotational latency*). Latency is directly related to the disk drive's speed of rotation.

Expressed as a formula, access time would be: *average access = average seek + settling time + latency*. Some manufacturers have dropped latency from their access time claims, and some ignore settling time. Be sure you are comparing fast apples to fast apples when you look at drive speed.

A drive manufacturer can fudge the numbers by calculating how fast the drive can get to a bit of information that is already directly under the read/write head. Such a number is all but useless as an indicator of true access time.

The final — and important — component of drive speed is data transfer. Data transfer is the rate at which a drive or controller dumps the information it has retrieved to the computer bus. This is an area that often has great mismatches — a slow data transfer system can cause quickly accessed data to back up on the hard drive side of the controller; a fast data transfer system can stand idle most of the time, waiting for a slow disk drive to find and pick up the requested data.

In general, data transfer speed depends on the rotational speed of the drive and the type of interface used to transfer the data.

Today, the most common interface in new machines is Serial ATA, which offers transfer speeds of 150MBps in its initial release, with specifications drawn for a 300MBps version. SATA was adapted from the parallel circuitry Ultra ATA/133 standard, which reached a top transfer speed of 133MBps. With the arrival of SATA, marketers renamed Ultra ATA/133 as Parallel ATA, or PATA.

Now that I've (sort of) cleared up the issue of speed on a drive, you should bear in mind one more issue: The stream of data that comes off a hard drive includes more than just the information you are looking for. The data includes formatting data and, on some drives, padding bits that mean nothing but are used to deal with speed variations at the narrow or wide parts of the disk. On most modern drives, integrated electronics take this information out of the data stream; on older designs, the drive controller card removes extra information. Either way, a full ten-gallon bucket of data may contain only eight gallons or less of usable information.

. . . and Cheaper

Almost as amazing as has been the upward march of technological advances has been the downward plunge of hard disk drive prices.

I first began writing about IBM PCs and early clones in 1982, soon after the birth of the PC, when I was the first executive editor of *PC Magazine*. Here's a random selection of prices for hard drives from the October 1982 issue of *PC Magazine:* A 5MB (megabyte, not gigabyte!) Winchester in a box about the size of the PC it sat alongside, $1,899. A 19.2MB Winchester (actually a pair of 9.6MB drives) in a huge metal box, $2,799.

In 1996, a 1GB IDE hard drive seemed like a fantastic bargain at about $375. A year later, newer and improved versions of the same capacity drive were priced at about $170.

In early 2002, the best deal on hard drives was for devices 40 times larger and about half again as expensive: a 40GB drive for less than $100. In 2006 a drive of that same capacity sold for about $40; for just over $100 you could purchase a 320GB whopper or continue up the scale to 500GB for about $150.

Here's one last exercise: I omit access speeds because it's simply too difficult to compare early PC buses, controller cards, and processors to modern-day systems. I can, though, compare the approximate cost per unformatted megabyte, as shown in Table 10-3 for IDE drives. Taking the most extreme example, the cost of hard disk storage has declined from about $380 per megabyte in 1982 to two cents in 1998, to a sweet spot of about three-hundredths of a penny in 2006. I've also calculated the approximate cost per gigabyte, which shows the astounding equivalent prices for the first drives offered to PC users.

The price per MB or GB shows an inexorable downward march, and there is no reason to believe this will stop. However, it is not always the case that the most bang-for-the-buck (the sweet spot) comes with the absolutely largest disk drive on the market. Instead, look one or two notches down from the largest or fastest drive to get the best deal . . . and keep in mind that newer, larger drives are always on the horizon.

Back in the early days of the PC, it hardly seemed necessary to have a hard disk. After all, word processors fit on a single floppy disk, and Pac-Man was considered the state of the art in multimedia.

If you install Windows Vista Premium with all of its bells, whistles, and see-through graphics, you need at least 15GB of space just for the operating system. In theory, Windows XP Home Edition asked for a mere 1.5GB, although various add-ons and service packs doubled that demand. And for the record, Windows 98 required somewhere in the range of 300MB, about five times as much as Windows 95 before it.

Today, it is not uncommon for a suite of programs such as Microsoft Office XP to occupy from 210 to 245MB of disk space. Microsoft Windows 95 demanded as much as 65MB for a full installation. Upgrading to Windows 98 could take up to 300MB. And Windows XP demands as much as 1.5GB of space all by itself.

TABLE 10-3: A History of ATA (IDE) Hard Disk Prices

Year	Capacity	Price	Cost per MB	Cost per GB
1982				
	5MB	$1,899	$379.80	$379,800.00
	19.2MB	$2,799	$145.78	$145,781.30
1995				
	428MB	$183	$0.43	$427.57
	722MB	$253	$0.35	$350.42
	1GB	$375	$0.37	$375.00
1997				
	540MB	$139	$0.26	$257.41
	1GB	$170	$0.17	$170.00
	2.7GB	$300	$0.11	$111.11
1998				
	2.1GB	$129	$0.06	$61.43
	6.4GB	$219	$0.03	$32.81
	12GB	$280	$0.02	$23.33
2000				
	6.4GB	$120	$0.02	$18.75
	17GB	$170	$0.01	$10.00
	20GB	$212	$0.01	$10.60
	28GB	$270	$0.01	$9.64
2002				
	10GB	$70	$0.007	$7.00
	20GB	$80	$0.004	$4.00
	40GB	$100	$0.003	$2.50
	80GB	$175	$0.0025	$2.19
	160GB	$320	$0.002	$2.00
2006				
	40GB	$40	$0.001	$1.00
	80GB	$50	$0.00062	$0.62
	160GB	$70	$0.00044	$0.44
	250GB	$85	$0.00034	$0.34
	320GB	$110	$0.00034	$0.34
	500GB	$150	$0.00030	$0.30
	750GB	$340	$0.00045	$0.45

Ch 10

And all of this is before you put any data files on your disk; on my system, I commonly use Adobe Photoshop CS2 to work with photo files as large as 36MB each.

In 2006, the best storage price-performance value seems to be Serial ATA hard drives of about 250 to 500 GB. Smaller drives are available, but their cost per GB is higher. Going the other direction, massive hard drives are much less expensive than they were in earlier times, but because of their special media or electronics, they have a higher cost per gigabyte. In Figure 10-3 is an example of a 20GB Parallel ATA drive. Today's high-speed Serial ATA drives are similar within the case, but use the much simpler cabling scheme of SATA; an example of a SATA drive is shown in Figure 10-4.

FIGURE 10-3: *A 20GB Parallel ATA drive, which sold in 2000 for about $212 and in 2002 for about $80, was at the bottom of the available range of drives in 2006, selling for less than $40 if you could find a dealer who bothered to stock drives with capacities that small.*

FIGURE 10-4: *A new 500GB Western Digital SATA hard drive slides into a waiting bay on the front of a modern machine. The 7,200-RPM drive includes a 16MB cache and is capable of transferring data at transfer speeds of as much as 300MBps.*

Although it may seem risky to put so many eggs in one basket an entire business, your entire lifetime collection of photos or financial documents, or your great American novel on one hard drive — the fact is that modern drives are many times faster and much more reliable than the old behemoths. My preference is to use large, fast drives and to be absolutely religious about maintaining multiple backups on other disk drives or on removable storage media, such as DVDs, CDs, or other forms of external storage.

Form Factor: What Fits Where?

Most modern hard disk drives for desktop computers are designed to install into a 3.5-inch bay within the computer; because hard disk drives do not require access from the outside, they can be installed just about anywhere within the case. (By contrast, CD or DVD drives require a 5.25-inch bay with an opening to the outside of the case for the insertion of discs; a floppy disk drive, if you have one in your machine, needs a 3.5-inch bay with an outside access slot.)

That said, it is easy to adapt a 5.25-inch bay to hold a 3.5-inch device; going the other direction, though, defies the laws of physics. If you need to use a 5.25-inch bay for a smaller device, the bay can easily be adapted with rails and carriers. Some drives include the extra hardware, while in other cases, you have to pay a few dollars extra for a metal or plastic carrier; in Figure 10-5 you can see a new drive installed in a carrier.

An old-style PC case with a metal drive cage accessible only from the interior is shown in Figure 10-6.

Notebook computers usually use tiny 2.5-inch hard drives with increasing capacities and low power requirements. They are priced at a premium over full-size drives. There is no reason to install one of these drives in a typical desktop system, unless you happen to have an extra drive lying around on a shelf. Today's modern machines typically have two externally accessible 5.25-inch bays and from two to four (and occasionally more) internal 3.5-inch bays for hard drives.

FIGURE 10-5: *The tool-free Dimension 9200 case that is our example machine provides click-on plastic carriers for slide-in installation.*

The good news is that as hard disk drives have become smaller, faster, more capacious, and considerably less expensive, they have also become more and more reliable. Some users make the mistake of looking at the older drives with their large cases and heavy motors and assume that bigger means sturdier; actually, the miniaturization of drives has brought simpler, less power-hungry circuitry and motors. One of the benefits of a lower power draw is less generation of heat, which is a danger to all things electronic and mechanical; at the same time, computer manufacturers have greatly improved the cooling systems within the case. And the vast improvement in data density has been accompanied by improved platter surfaces and tiny, lightweight read/write assemblies that are much less likely to suffer a catastrophic crash.

A typical user who takes proper care of the system and provides the hard disk drive with a reliable source of electricity can expect a life of five to ten years or more from a hard disk. But that's not to say that you also might not suffer a catastrophic failure after a few weeks.

Therefore, my cautious recommendation is to always act as if your hard disk drive will fail at any moment, taking with it all of your work.

Hard disks are sealed boxes with high-tech filters designed to prevent particles of dust from clogging the heads or damaging the disks. They are not intended to be opened for service outside of a clean room, and it is not realistic to consider repairing a failed hard disk drive. (The only exception: If you end up in the unfortunate situation of having $10,000 worth of otherwise irretrievable data on a $90 drive, it may be possible to find a professional data recovery service that can make temporary workarounds to get the data off the failed disk and onto a new, working model. It's an expensive solution, and one that could and *should* be avoided by careful attention to backups of your data.)

The value of your data is almost always much greater than the value of your hard disk drive and even your computer itself. For example, this manuscript represents months of work, and you can bet that multiple copies of the files are stored away from the computer on which I'm writing it. My office procedure is to make backups of live files on the hard drive on an external hard drive during the course of a day and then to burn a CD or DVD with the complete set of current files every other day.

In other words, I do whatever I can to avoid the possibility of having to pay for a disaster recovery service. (More about this later.)

FIGURE 10-6: *The Parallel ATA 3.5-inch hard drive in the middle of this photo is installed in a drive cage of the same width; some systems may require the use of mounting rails to adapt the smaller device to a wider bay. Some technicians test the drive before screwing it into place in the drive cage. At the bottom of the photo is a floppy disk drive that will be installed in the same cage.*

The Hard Life of a Hard Disk

I want to start with a harsh fact of life: Hard disks do not last forever. They are electromechanical devices with a motor that spins a disk, an actuator that moves the read/write head to various positions on the disk, bearings that support the spinning platter, and electronics to control the drive and communicate with the rest of the computer.

What could possibly go wrong?

Hard disks are similar to floppy disks, but the technology is more advanced in every way. Hard disks spin faster, pack in more data per inch, move from track to track more quickly, and accommodate multiple platters in each drive unit.

As with other electronic items, from calculators to digital watches, each generation of hard disks is smaller, faster, and more powerful. Half-height models, which replaced the 3-inch-high hard disks of the 1980s, have now given way to mini-monsters less than an inch high. And laptop computers are being delivered with half-inch-tall hard drives with capacities of tens of gigabytes; a properly designed laptop computer uses specially cushioned drives that protect from the unusual insults a portable PC may have to endure. There are also tiny Microdrives, developed by IBM and now manufactured by Hitachi, Sony, and other makers, that pack as much as 12GB in a 1-inch square that can be used in a CompactFlash slot or a PC Card Type II device.

The internal mechanical elements of the drives — always the Achilles heels of data storage devices — are improving.

More precise and reliable voice coil servo mechanisms have generally replaced cheap stepper motors in high-density, high-capacity hard drives. A voice coil mechanism uses servo track information to determine where to move the head in precise increments without the use of preset steps. A servo track is a marking on the drive platter itself; the voice coil moves relative distances from that servo track to find information.

Older drives used a stepper mechanism to move the read/write head in fixed increments, or steps, across the disk surface. The mechanical nature of a drive based on a stepper mechanism delivers precise positioning when the drive is new, but wear and tear can end up throwing the drives out of alignment.

Treat your hard disk gently. It is a delicate, precision-tooled mechanical device and is easily damaged. Dropping a hard disk might crash a read/write head into a platter. Even if the head is not damaged, the portion of the disk that made contact with the head could be injured and made unreadable.

WARNING

One of the biggest threats to laptop computers is the airline security line. At most airports around the world you are required to take the machine out of its protective carrying case and place it in a plastic tub that passes through an X-ray machine. Risk 1: It gets dropped when you remove it from the case. Risk 2: It gets damaged by a malfunctioning metal detector. Risk 3: It gets dropped when it is on the other side of the scanner. Risk 4: Someone steals it while you're lacing your shoes. There's not a lot you can do about any of these risks other than to be very vigilant . . . and to make sure you have backups of essential data stored somewhere other than in your computer case. If I'm going off on a long trip, I make copies of my data files on a CD, DVD, or a flash memory key before I travel.

Preparing for disaster

I recommend that you read this chapter before you need to be rescued. And then, when death is in the house, reread this chapter with the security of knowing you have put away safe backups of everything you should save.

Permit me to begin with a sermon. Call it "Sandler's Top Three Tips for Safe Computing:"

1. Back up your data regularly.
2. Perform Step 1 at least once a week, more often when you are in the middle of a critical assignment.
3. See Steps 1 and 2.

In addition to making backup copies of your data, I also recommend that you regularly run disk drive diagnostic and repair utilities. These programs analyze your drive, ensure that the surface is reliable, and lock out any questionable areas.

CROSS-REFERENCE

After you have read this chapter, read Chapter 21 to learn how to salvage useful data stored on an ailing hard disk.

Automatic disk monitoring

If your computer is so smart, why doesn't it keep an eye on the health of its hard drives while they are running? That's a fine idea, and one that is embraced by a number of software utility makers, including Symantec with its Norton SystemWorks utilities.

There is also a hardware/software system developed by IBM in 1992 called Self-Monitoring, Analysis, and Reporting Technology (SMART). Hard drives using this design — which has been adopted by many hard drive manufacturers and supported by Microsoft in current versions of Windows — includes technology that allows machines to give themselves regular checkups throughout their lives, communicating any actual or impending problems to the user.

SMART software resides in the controller on the disk drive and on the host computer. Software on the drive monitors the internal performance of the motors, media, heads, and electronics of the drive; programming on the computer monitors the overall reliability status of the drive.

Manufacturers adjust the parameters of the software to reflect the projected life and performance of a particular drive. If the SMART system predicts the imminent failure of the drive, it issues a warning and offers advice on protecting existing data. Some advanced systems are able to notify network administrators of potential problems and even to automatically initiate relocation of critical files and backup of data to other storage devices.

Your machine's BIOS must support SMART diagnostics, or you must run application software that can interrogate the system. Appropriate software includes Norton Disk Doctor.

Another version of this sort of protection is the Data Lifeguard features offered by Western Digital on many of its modern drives. Included are shock and environmental protection, real-time embedded error detection and repair, and Data Lifeguard Tools that coordinate with the hardware to check the performance of the drive and make many repairs. The home screen for the utility is shown in Figure 10-7.

And if you're willing, try to wrap your brain around some of the real complexities of a hard drive with a very technical, powerful tool like SpinRite, offered by Gibson Research Corporation. This product provides early warning of impending disaster and, in certain circumstances, can allow you to prevent a failure or recover from one. You can learn about SpinRite at www.grc.com.

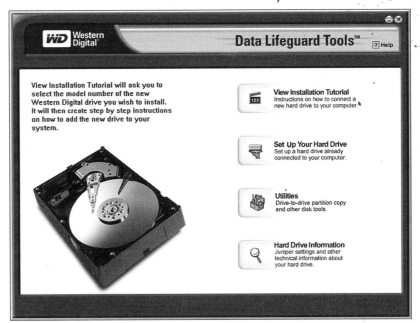

FIGURE 10-7: *The Data Lifeguard Tools include installation assistance as well as detailed information about all installed drives and the ability to repartition an active drive without losing data already in place.*

RAID Systems

For the ultimate in automated belt-and-suspenders data protection, consider conducting a RAID on your system. RAID is an acronym for Redundant Array of Independent (or Inexpensive) Disks. The idea is this: Doubling up the hard disk drives in your system and, in the most common implementation making simultaneous copies of data on separate drives (called mirroring), or spreading data across two drives (called striping). The work is done by a special version of disk controller.

As far as I am concerned, the most valuable type of RAID system for consumers is mirroring system (RAID 1), which gives you two identical hard drives at all times; if one gives up the ghost because of mechanical failure, the other will be available and can be copied onto a replacement drive. Note that I have qualified the type of failure: A mechanical problem include unhappy happenings with the drive motor, the read/write arm actuator, or the bearings. Not included in this list are problems caused by an electrical spike that makes its ways past the power supply, across the motherboard, and into the electronics of the drive; your essential protection against this sort of failure is the purchase and use of a good-quality surge protector or UPS.

Here are the two most common implementations of RAID technology:

- **RAID 0. Striped Disk Array.** Data striping spreads out the blocks of each file across multiple disk drives but does not create duplicate or redundant files. This is a system that is aimed mostly at boosting speed; if one drive fails you will lose the data on that drive and may even have trouble recovering data from the surviving disk.
- **RAID 1. Mirroring and Duplexing.** This design creates duplicate data blocks on each of two separate and independent disk drives. The system offers improved read speed and a write speed equal to that of a single disk. To you, the second drive is invisible, just chugging away in the background providing the security of automated backups.

Many modern machines now come equipped with an integrated RAID controller as part of the motherboard; that was what I found with the Dell Dimension 9200 that is our example machine in this book. Users can choose to enable the RAID functions or ignore their presence. If your machine was not originally equipped with a RAID subsystem you can easily add one with an adapter card that takes over the functions of the disk drive controller. System recovery software eats up about 10 to 12GB of space on each machine.

The plummeting price of hard disk drives makes this sort of redundant protection very inexpensive; in 2006, computer makers offered multi-disk RAID 1 systems for as little as $100 more than the cost of a one-drive system. As a user, your only concern should be that the system has sufficient electrical power for the second drive and has a proper cooling system to exhaust the heat produced by the additional drive.

Windows ReadyDrive

One of the new features that is part of Windows Vista is a technology called ReadyDrive that works with special hybrid hard disk drives that include a block of non-volatile flash memory that can be used to hold information that allows a computer to shut down the motor that spins a hard drive and read and write to a block of flash memory built into the drive. Other benefits of ReadyDrive include using the same flash memory to resume faster from hibernation or sleep mode, or to boost system startup.

Vista manages the contents of the non-volatile memory, optimizing the speed of the system and reducing use of power; this last feature is expected to make *H-HDDs (hybrid hard disk drives)* especially popular on laptop machines. Once you open a file, Windows Vista can direct that a copy be placed in the flash memory cache, allowing the hard drive to stop the spin of its platters between saves. Standard settings in Vista also instruct the system to save data required early in the bootup process to the flash memory cache on an H-HDD.

Although the new technology may reduce some wear and tear on the hard drives and draw less power overall, some experts are concerned that flash memory is somewhat prone to failure over time. The cells of flash memory are generally expected to lose their ability to record information after being used between several thousand times and several tens of thousands of time; this raises the possibility that the non-volatile RAM on an H-HDD may fail well before the hard disk drive to which it is attached is ready for retirement.

One of the first companies to announce plans to support the new technology was Samsung; other makers will likely follow and may come up with ways to deal with concern about the life span of the flash memory. One possible solution: install the flash memory in a user-replaceable module. And engineers are expected to allow the user to disable the flash memory to revert the hard disk drive to normal operation.

Buying a Hard Drive

Today's leading hard drive manufacturers include Fujitsu, Hitachi, Maxtor, Samsung, Seagate, and Western Digital. In recent years IBM sold its hard drive manufacturing facilities to Hitachi, and Toshiba has chosen to concentrate on tiny, low-power drives for use in laptops and even-smaller electronic devices. Products from any one of these companies are all comparable, and because hard drives have been changing so much, it's hard to recommend a specific brand. I list the web sites for major hard drive manufacturers in Table 10-4.

You can take steps, though, to try to ensure that you buy the most reliable and current technologies:

- Read the most recent reliability surveys and reviews in computer magazines.
- Include the support policy and the warranty period and terms in your buying decision. In general, a device with a generous technical support policy and warranty is of better quality; companies offer better after-the-sale support and warranties if they don't expect many of their customers to have to use them.
- Look at the specifications for machines offered for sale by major computer manufacturers, including Gateway, Dell, Hewlett-Packard, and Compaq, to see what brand of hard drives they are currently shipping with their systems. It is not in the interests of mass-market sellers to ship hard drives that have a high failure rate.
- Buy the hard disk drive that is one step down from the latest hot model. This strategy almost always saves you some money and keeps you away from any unproven technology. (This advice applies to any computer purchase.)
- Consider the price-performance ratio of whatever you buy. The easiest way to compute this for a hard drive is to calculate the cost per megabyte or gigabyte. As we've already explored, if you look at a range of hard drive sizes, you'll usually see a sweet spot a few notches down from the largest or fastest device. For the same reason, it does not make economic sense to buy the smallest available drive; there is a basic cost for the drive case, electronics, packaging and marketing, and you might as well apply that to more storage room rather than less.
- Buy from a reputable dealer who stands behind the sale. I never buy closeout or final-sale products unless I am absolutely certain of their quality. I'd rather spend a few dollars more and buy from a dealer or Internet company that promises to buy back a faulty product or exchange it for a good one. The best retailers make an unconditional guarantee: If you're not happy with a product, they take it back. No ifs, ands, buts, or time limits (within reason).

TABLE 10-4: Support and Information Web Sites of Major Hard Drive Makers

Vendor	Contact Information	Mergers and Acquisitions
Fujitsui	www.fujitsu.com/us/services/computing/storage/hdd	—
Hitachi	www.hitachigst.com/portal/site/en	—
IBM hard drive division	www.storage.ibm.com/hdd	—
Maxtor	www.maxtor.com	Quantum; In mid-2006, Seagate acquired Maxtor with plans to continue the Maxtor brand
Samsung	www.samsung.com	—
Seagate	www.seagate.com	Conner, Maxtor
Toshiba	www.sdd.toshiba.com	—
Western Digital	www.wdc.com	—

Mean time between headaches

There are several supposed quantifications of the expected life span of a hard disk, although I don't recommend setting your watch by any of them. Instead, use them as a way to compare the relative sturdiness of various devices.

MTBF stands for *mean time between failures*; a similar measure is MTTF, which stands for *mean time to failure*. Both statistics are presented in terms of hours. In the 1990s, a typical disk drive might have a listing of 40,000 to 100,000 hours; as this book goes to press, many drives are accompanied by claims of an MTTF of 300,000 hours.

Think about what those numbers are supposed to specify: a mean (average) time to failure of about 30 years of continuous use.

Another measure is Start/stop, which estimates the expected lifetime of the drive in terms of the number of times it is turned on and off; engineers refer to this as "loading" and "unloading" the springs that position the read/write head. A high-end modern drive may promise a Start/stop life of 50,000 or more cycles.

Yet another measure of the quality of a disk drive is its reported Error Rate, an estimate of how often the drive will pass through a non-recoverable misread of stored data. A modern drive's specifications might claim an error rate of 1 in 10E13, which means once in every 100 trillion bits. If you were to read the entire contents of a full drive one thousand times, you could expect an error in a single bit—and further expect that your disk controller or one of your applications will catch the error and ask for a resend of the data, fix it, or alert you to the problem.

So, how in the world can a manufacturer rush to market with a hot new disk drive—at most a one- or two-year research and development project—and claim that a device should last 30 years? There is obviously no way for manufacturers to put a drive in a closet and run it for that long to see when or if it fails. Instead, drive manufacturers follow two testing tracks. One is to put drives through an intense simulation of heavy use that exercises all of their parts over a few weeks or months. The second testing regime uses a computer model that looks at every nut, bolt, chip, and platter and calculates expected lifetime based on supposedly known reliability of the parts.

You can consult the specifications for any current and most older hard drives on the web sites of the major manufacturers. An example of the specifications for a modern drive, a 500GB WD Caviar SE16 from Western Digital, is listed in Table 10-5 and shown in Figure 10-8.

If you are purchasing a new hard disk controller to go along with the drive, consult dealers, as well as the drive manufacturer, for their recommendations. This is less of an issue if you are attaching the drive to the built-in Serial ATA or Parallel ATA (IDE) controller that is part of the motherboard on many modern machines. You need a new controller only if the built-in controller has failed or if you want to step up to a higher-performance design. For example, you might choose to install a SATA controller in an older modern machine to gain the speed and convenience of a serial connection.

Figure 10-8: *A modern Western Digital SATA drive ready for installation.*

NOTE

As far as I'm concerned, the MTBF ratings are interesting if true, but much more important is how well the hard drive manufacturer stands behind the product. If a drive has a supposed MTBF of 100,000 hours but is under warranty for only 90 days (2,160 hours at most), I don't have reason to believe that the manufacturer has much faith in its own product. Look for drives with two- or three-year warranties, which are reasonable periods of use for a hard drive.

And when you receive your new drive, I recommend that you examine it carefully. Look at the date of manufacture, which is usually listed on a sticker on the drive; if it's more than a year old, you should be suspicious about the quality of the drive. The drive may be a white elephant that has been sitting on the shelf for an unusually long period of time. And, in some rare cases, disreputable repair shops or dealers have been known to try to pass off a remanufactured or returned drive as new.

TABLE 10-5: A Modern Hard Drive Specification Sheet

Configuration

Interface	Serial ATA
Capacity	500GB
Buffer size	16MB
User sectors per drive	234,441,648

Performance

Rotational speed	7,200 RPM (nominal)
Average latency	4.2 average ms

Seek Times

Average read seek	<8.9 ms
Average write seek	10.9 ms
Average track-to-track seek	2.0 ms
Average full-stroke seek	21.0 ms

Transfer Rates

Buffer to host (Serial ATA)	300 MBps maximum
Buffer to disk	740 MBps maximum

Reliability

Error rate (nonrecoverable)	1 in 10 trillion
Start/stop cycles (load/unload at 40° C)	50,000 minimum

Power

Requirement	+5 VDC (+/−5%), +12 VDC
Read/write 12 VDC	450 mA
Idle 12 VDC	430 mA
Read/write 5 VDC	800 mA
Idle 5 VDC	730 mA
Power dissipation read/write	9.5 watts
Power dissipation idle	8.75 watts

Physical Size

Height	1.028 inches
Width	4 inches
Length	5.787 inches
Weight	1.32 pounds

Environmental Characteristics

Operating

Ambient temperature (operating)	41 to 131° F
Ambient temperature (non-operating)	−41 to 149° F
Relative humidity (noncondensing)	5% to 95%
Operating shock (read)	65G, 2ms
Non-operating shock	250G, 2ms

Some older drives were accompanied by a bad track table generated at the factory; more modern drives do the same but keep the information hidden. No drive is perfect, but low-level formatting locks out the bad tracks. The percentage of bad tracks should not exceed a few percent of the total capacity of the drive.

CROSS-REFERENCE

See Chapter 21 for more information on safeguarding hard disk data.

Hard Disk Data Structure

An operating system divides a hard disk into two sections: the system area and the data area.

The system area carries essential programs and directories that help the computer operate and keeps records of how information is stored on the disk.

The system area also includes a *boot sector* that holds a short program that gives the computer the basic instructions it needs to bring itself to life (the term boot comes from the phrase, "lifting yourself up by your own bootstraps," which is a colorful way to look at what the disk operating system is performing when it first starts).

The original operating system for PCs was called DOS (pronounced *DAH-SS*) and was the foundation of the immense Microsoft fortune. DOS went through a number of iterations as a command-driven operating system (users told the machine what to do by typing instructions at a "system prompt." It was then superseded by the first versions of Windows (also from Microsoft) which is classified as a graphical user interface. Current versions of Windows have their own rewritten basic operating system, but in action, that operating system mimics the functions of DOS.

Information in the boot sector includes how much, if any, of the disk belongs to the operating system and where the system boot files are located. The boot sector may contain a *Master Boot Record (MBR)* and a *Volume Boot Record (VBR)*, or a Volume Boot Record alone. A VBR is the first sector of an *unpartitioned* data storage device (usually a floppy disk drive, a USB memory key, or a small hard drive), or the first sector of a particular partition on a data storage device that has been partitioned. Either way, the VBR contains code to load and invoke the operating system that is present on that device or within that partition.

An MBR is the first sector of a *partitioned* data storage device, containing the code that identifies the location of the active partition and instructions on how to invoke its Volume Boot Record.

As far as the computer is concerned, the BIOS does not distinguish between an MBR or a VBR when it boots up; all it does is locate and run the first sector of the storage device. On the positive side, on dinosaur computers this allowed the floppy disk to be used as a boot device and on modern machines it permits booting (in some BIOS designs) from a USB memory key or the running of simple utilities from a floppy disk drive. On the downside, the dumb reliance of the machine on loading and running whatever it finds in the first sector of whatever storage device it looks at first is one of the more dangerous vulnerabilities of PCs; if a virus can take up residence in the boot sector it will be loaded and executed before Windows or antivirus software can detect its presence.

For that reason, you should go to the BIOS Setup screen and disable the system from booting from any device other than the hard disk drive; you can make alterations to the boot device order as needed if you want to start the machine from a floppy disk, CD or DVD disc, or other device. And, of course, you should also install a capable antivirus program and keep it current; though it may not be able to detect the initial loading of a virus from the boot sector, it should be able to freeze the system and warn you if it detects the presence of a virus once the system is running.

The boot sector is recorded on track 0, a fixed location on the disk. If that sector is in some way damaged or the files corrupted, you will have to find some other way to boot the system.

The next section of the disk holds the file attribute tables (FATs), the critical description of the organization of the disk. The tables are basically arrays of numbers that indicate, for example, that cluster X is linked to cluster Y, cluster Z is unusable, and cluster W is free. The system offers some measure of protection by maintaining a pair of identical FATs.

If the boot cluster is damaged, the operating system will not be able to recognize the disk and will display a message such as Non-System Disk, if it can give any message at all. Usually the machine just locks up. If the FAT is slightly damaged, the means to resolving the problem depends on the operating system version that you are using.

Under dinosaur versions of Windows, you can use the limited facilities of the DOS command CHKDSK or the improved DOS program SCANDISK to attempt repairs. CHKDSK, which dates back to the very early versions of DOS, has been in place in the underlying system for Windows from the very start. Under Windows 95/98, Microsoft recommended the use of the enhanced SCANDISK program. With the arrival of Windows XP, Microsoft updated CHKDSK, including facilities that make repairs and display information about partitions that use the NTFS system. For more information on using CHKDSK, see Chapter 22.

There are also a number of third-party data-recovery programs that may be able to reconstruct the pointers (the directions to the next cluster in the chain). If the FAT is completely unreadable, the pointer information and whatever is on the disk may be lost or may be very difficult to retrieve. Even though the information is actually still on the disk, this system has lost its index to what is where.

Some advanced disk repair tools begin by creating backup copies of the FAT which can be stored at a different location on the hard drive, or even on a different disk including an emergency recovery disk. In case of loss of the original file attribute table, the backup copy may be reinstalled. Another possible means of getting information off the disk involves brute force: a search for the scattered fragments of a file spread across a disk. The larger the file and the larger the disk, the more difficult the task of putting a document back together again.

The last part of the system area is the root directory, which begins at cluster 2. It contains the names of the root directory's files and sub-directories and indicates the pointer in the FAT that is the marker for the first cluster of each file. If the root directory is badly damaged, data on the disk cannot be retrieved.

Subdirectories are just lists of filenames, file sizes, file creation dates, file attributes, and first cluster numbers. In other words, a subdirectory is structured just like the root directory but is itself a file.

And here's a secret of most current operating systems: When you delete a file you're not actually erasing it from the disk. Instead, the operating system merely removes the file name from the table of files it maintains as an index. Under DOS and Windows versions up through and including Windows 98, the first letter of the filename was merely changed from its original character to the hexadecimal value E5 (E5H in computerspeak), and the FAT pointer is zeroed out. Later versions of Windows have slightly changed the process, but the concept remains the same.

That is how undelete programs like the Windows Recycle Bin perform their magic: So long as no new file has written over the same space, the program can change E5 or whatever other renaming has been done back to an alphabetic character that is recognized by the software that manages the FAT. The next step is to figure out what the first cluster number should be, and the file will once again appear in the disk directory and be available.

There are two things to learn from this magic trick: A "deleted" file is still available for undeletion (for a while) and can be recovered if not already overwritten, and if you want to make certain that some highly sensitive information (such as passwords, banking information, and the like) is truly unreadable, consider purchasing a secure deletion program that physically overwrites a file with garbage characters.

What goes where: The logical structure

When you think about a hard disk drive, it is also very important to understand its logical structure: what goes where.

Hard disk drive platters are logically divided into cylinders and sectors. Data on a hard disk is stored in concentric circles, called *tracks*. Across each track, the data is subdivided into small units of storage called *sectors;* the standard PC format packs 512 bytes per sector.

A *cylinder* is defined as the same track on each platter. (If you were to cut the hard disk along the thin edge of all platters with a circular cookie cutter, you would end up with a set of cylinders spread across more than one platter.) Each bit of data is located in a particular sector (pie slice), on a particular track (concentric data storage ring), on the top or bottom of a particular platter. The outermost track

on every platter is cylinder 0. The next track is cylinder 1, and so on; see Figure 10-9.

Over the history of the PC, there have been a number of technologies employed to package information but one dominated the early years and another has taken over for the past decade. The older and less efficient methodology was modified frequency modulation (MFM), which is still used in floppy disk drives. Almost all current hard disk drives, CD, DVD, and many other types of modern storage employ run length limited (RLL) encoding.

Before the arrival of the first PCs, one of the first schemes for computer storage was FM (frequency modulation). Engineers developed a modified frequency modulation system that could store twice as much information in the same space, and MFM was introduced as the design behind floppy disks and some of the very first hard disk drives for personal computers. On a PC floppy disk, where it was referred to as double density, MFM encoding stores 17 sectors per track.

When first introduced, RLL encoding nearly doubled the density to 26 sectors per track packing as much as twice the amount of data into the same area. RLL records groups of data as a block.

When it was first introduced, RLL required a higher quality surface, now adopted for all drives and encoding techniques. Either way, the data-coding scheme is built into the controller hardware, not the hard disk.

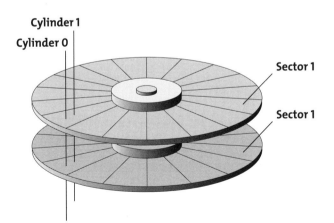

FIGURE 10-9: *Large files are recorded across cylinders instead of across tracks to minimize the amount of movement the read/write heads have to make to retrieve data.*

We do not need to delve any deeper into the highly technical differences between the two means of recording. It's more important to know the capacity of the drive and the type of interface — SATA, PATA (IDE), EIDE, SCSI, and so on — that it requires.

To the operating system, the data recorded across sectors, platters, and cylinders appears as a continuous stream of information. In other words, what you see as two platters with four sides, the operating system sees as one long length of tape.

The operating system sees the data as a continuous stream, like the music on a cassette tape. Tracks 0 and 1 are the outermost tracks on a platter: Track 0 is on the top surface, and track 1 is on the bottom surface. Tracks 2 and 3 are also the outermost tracks but lie on the second platter of this hard drive. This makes sense because the read/write heads move together. Moving head 0 into position to read track 0 also moves the other heads into position to read the outermost tracks on the other platters (see Figure 10-10).

To the operating system, the disk is a large string of clusters. Data is read from and written to the disk in sector increments, and the operating system allocates space by the cluster, not by the individual sector.

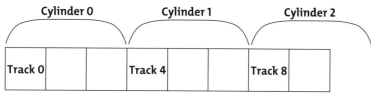

FIGURE 10-10: *A depiction of a typical recording pattern used by a PC.*

This is not a minor matter. The larger the capacity of a physical or logical drive, the larger the cluster size it uses. As an example, on a 1GB drive or logical volume, the cluster would ordinarily be 32K.

That's fine if you are storing files that are 32K, or 64K, or some other exact multiple of the cluster size. But if you store a setting file that is a mere 10 bytes in length, it will nevertheless occupy a 32K cluster with room for 32,768 bytes. Similarly, if a long file spills over its allotted 32K space by just a few characters, it will occupy two clusters, or 64K.

For this reason, it is quite possible to run out of storage space on a 1GB drive with just 700 or 800MB of data, or a 100GB drive could be filled with 70GB of data. Therefore, if your drive is filled with a large number of short files, your usable space is going to be less than the full capacity. One way to reduce the cluster size is to reduce the partition size — in other words, to subdivide the drive into smaller logical drives. You can adjust the partitioning of your hard disk drive at the time the disk is first prepared for use (without any data on the disk). Or you can use one of a number of capable utilities that allow you to repartition a drive already in use without losing data; among products that can do this are Norton Partition Magic from Symantec (www.symantec.com) and Partition Commander from VCom Products (www.v-com.com).

Within Windows XP and Windows Vista, the DISKPART utility is offered from within the Recovery Console for repair of a damaged disk or adding or deleting a partition on a hard disk. Older versions of Windows employed the limited facilities if the FDISK command.

Formatting a Disk

In its raw form, a hard disk platter is merely a disk with a magnetizable coating; think of it as a gigantic blank piece of paper without rules or any other way to organize the information that will be recorded on it and no way to easily retrieve a particular bit of data.

The key to the kingdom here is *formatting* the disk to apply a structure.

A hard drive requires two separate types of formatting; between the two steps, the disk must also be subdivided. In this section, we explore these three steps:

- Low-level formatting
- Partitioning
- High-level formatting

When you first turn on your PC, what you have is an extremely capable group of electronic components without a clue as to what to do.

As a convention that dates back to the birth of the personal computer, though, manufacturers tell the processor to always look to a particular place in memory — the address is FFFF0h — for its basic instructions.

Similarly, every startup hard disk has a consistent place where the processor can consult to find out essential information such as the number and type of partitions, as well as the bootup instructions that begin the process of loading the operating system. This startup location is called the master boot record or the boot sector.

The master boot record is always located at cylinder 0, head 0, and sector 1.

The elements of the master boot record include the master partition table, a tiny table that describes the partitions of the hard disk. There is room for only four physical partitions, also called primary partitions. Any additional partitions on the drive are logical partitions that are managed by the operating system and linked to a primary partition.

The computer looks to one of the primary partitions for bootup information and the operating system code; this is called the active primary partition.

The other critical element of the master boot record is the master boot code, which holds the small initial boot program that is loaded by the BIOS to start the boot process.

Low-level formatting

Low-level formatting applies magnetic signposts to divide the platter's tracks into sectors, setting the spacing between the sectors and tracks and applying codes to indicate the beginning and end of each sector (the sector header and trailer).

Current Serial or Parallel ATA () and SCSI drives can be set up with 17 to 1,000 or more sectors on each track. Dinosaur drives using original ST-506 MFM controllers had 17 sectors per track; as early drives moved on to RLL encoding, they were set up with 25 or 26 sectors per track.

In the original scheme of things, each track on a drive had the same number of sectors. Although this offered the elegance of simplicity, it was also wasteful of valuable real estate. This is because the outer tracks of the hard drive have a lot more space than the inner ones.

Modern drives therefore use *zoned-bit recording*, which varies the number of sectors per track, packing more of them in the outer tracks. The scheme assigns *data zones* of varying size to the drive. The fact that there is more data recorded on the outer tracks while the drive spins the platter at a constant speed means that the data transfer rate is significantly faster when the heads are positioned at the outside edge of the platter. Hard drive specifications usually indicate a maximum and minimum transfer rate for this reason; depending on the speed of rotation, the outer tracks can transfer data nearly twice as fast as inner tracks.

ATA and SCSI drives receive their low-level formatting at the factory, and for the purposes of this book, I'll leave the complexities of that job to the hard drive makers.

Partitioning the disk

The next step in preparing a disk is to assign logical units and file systems. If we were talking about real estate here, we'd be discussing the plot plan that divides up a piece of property into coordinates that can be mapped.

A partition is the basic container for data; each exists in a specified physical location on the drive and functions almost as if it were a single hard drive.

Under current versions of Windows, each hard disk must have at least one partition. A disk can have as many as four primary partitions, or three primary partitions plus one extended partition and multiple logical drives. Each primary partition can use the same or differing file systems. A *primary partition* can be designated as an *extended partition* that can be further subdivided into *logical partitions*.

A PC must include one bootable partition for startup. Under DOS and Windows, only primary partitions are bootable. By default, the boot drive is assigned C: as its drive letter.

CROSS-REFERENCE

See Chapter 22 for third-party partition software programs that go beyond Microsoft's standard specifications and that permit you to perform tasks, such as repartitioning a drive without losing the data in place.

Partitioning lays out a road map of the subdivisions of the disk. Depending on the capacity of the disk and the capability of the BIOS on your motherboard, you can have just a single partition or many. If you create more than one partition on a disk, partitions added after the first one are "logical" volumes, each with its own drive letter and name, even though they exist on a single physical drive.

After a disk has been partitioned, it must be formatted, which applies an index that the hard disk controller will use to store and retrieve information.

Windows 95 and 98 and the MS-DOS operating system that underlies them permit a system to have a total of 24 partitions. All 24 can be on the same drive, or they can be spread across many drives. (Why 24? It's a matter of alphabet logic: Physical and logical drives are identified by letters. A and B are reserved for floppy disk drives, which leaves 24 for hard drives.)

Some third-party partitioning software programs permit the use of more than 24 partitions, and Microsoft may extend the operating system's capabilities in future releases. Only one partition can be active, meaning it is the part of the drive where the operating system will look for the elements it needs to boot the system to life.

Windows Vista, Windows XP, and Windows 2000 assign drive letters differently from the design for Windows 98, Windows Me, and Windows NT 4.0. Basic drives, which are located on physical drives within your local computer, are subject to the same 24-volume limit (plus the A and B floppy drive reservations).

But the latest Windows versions also permit mounted drives, which are volumes attached to an empty folder on an NTFS volume. Mounted drives function like any other volume, but they are identified by a label or name instead of a drive letter. They are not subject to the volume limit, and include other advanced administrative and networking features that are beyond the scope of this book.

Microsoft's utility under DOS and Windows versions through Windows Me is called FDISK, and you find it in the system utilities folder of a Windows installation. You can also obtain a copy from the Microsoft web site; if you have created an emergency boot disk for a Windows system, you will find a copy of the file there.

Under Windows XP, the partitioning utility is called DISKPART; a similar utility is offered by Windows Vista. On an already-partitioned drive, DISKPART is only available when you are using the Recovery Console. You can also access the Computer Management utility from within Windows; from the Control Panel, choose Performance and Maintenance and the Administrative Tools (you must be signed in as the administrator to make changes). Now select the Computer Management shortcut, highlight Storage, and then choose Disk Management. From the screen shown in Figure 10-11, you can choose a drive and, from the Action menu, add or delete a partition.

If you are performing a clean install of Windows XP, the recommended method is to boot the system from Microsoft's distribution disc; to do so, you may have to change the boot sequence setting in the BIOS to go to the CD first. The automated installation process takes you to a Setup screen that leads to a partitioning utility. There you can create or delete partitions, choosing among NFTS, FAT32, and FAT, and assign space to them. After the partition is completed, you're prompted to format the subdivision; you can choose between full (including a scan of the disk for bad sectors) and fast.

FIGURE 10-11: *The Disk Management screen of Windows XP permits adding and deleting partitions on an existing disk.*

If you install Windows on a partition formatted by using the Quick option, you can later check the health of the disk by running the chkdsk /r command. Choose Start ⇨ Run and then type **chkdsk /r**.

Finally, many hard drive manufacturers include a copy of FDISK or DISKPART or their own version of partitioning software as part of their hardware kit.

The software writes a master partition boot sector to cylinder 0, head 0, sector 1. Recorded here are the starting and ending locations of each partition on the drive.

If you choose to have only a single partition on your drive, the utility will create only a primary partition, which will be the active or boot partition of the drive.

If you choose to have multiple partitions on your drive, FDISK or DISKPART will create a primary partition with a single active partition plus an extended partition that is divided into one or more logical volumes.

The minimum size for a partition is 1MB. (Older, small drives of less than that size will have all available space assigned to the primary partition.)

Under Windows 98 and later versions, the maximum size for a partition is as much as 2 terabytes (2,048GB), although hard drive manufacturers often offer workarounds that permit larger partition sizes for users that want a huge amount of real estate under a single drive letter.

Older versions of Windows and DOS will not allow partitions larger than 32MB without special software; again, you may find special versions of FDISK in the hardware kit from drive makers.

If you choose to create a second or further partition, it is called an extended partition, and it uses the space remaining after the primary partition. Extended partitions are labeled with letters from D through Z.

Today nearly every hard drive manufacturer provides a utility that automates the process of partitioning and formatting a new drive installation; one example is the Data Lifeguard Tools that accompanies current Western Digital drives. Some of the utilities work in conjunction with a Windows installation or emergency startup disk that contains the Microsoft programs FDISK and FORMAT, while others use third-party programs that perform the same functions.

Also very useful is a utility to help transfer data from an old disk to the new one. This sort of utility is also available as a standalone product; one example is Copy Commander from VCom, or that company's SystemWorks suite, which includes Copy Commander and other utilities. Whatever method you use — including a manual collection of files — be sure to include all essential data as well as settings, templates, favorites, address books, and e-mail.

Follow the instructions the drive maker provides. If you are installing a secondary drive in a system, most hard drive software requires you to make some changes to the BIOS and possibly the primary drive before the new hardware is put in place.

In Appendix C on the CD, I also discuss PCmover from Laplink (www.laplink.com). This product moves data files as well as many or all programs and settings from an old computer to a new computer using a USB cable or an existing network connection.

After installing the drive, follow the maker's instructions on continuing the process for partitioning and formatting. After you complete that, you can move data from the old drive to the new.

NOTE

Over the years, some computer manufacturers made modifications to the standard BIOS Setup screens to customize them to a particular configuration or product line, simplifying the options on systems marketed to entry-level computer users. In many cases, this causes no problems in ordinary use but may limit upgrading options further down the road. One example I came across was a Compaq computer (now firmly in the senior-citizen class) that was based on an Award BIOS. When I wanted to add a second hard drive to the system, I found the BIOS had no provision for defining a new hard drive. The solution: I opened the case and examined the motherboard to find its model number. I then visited the manufacturer's web site and found an available download of a flash update to the BIOS that added definable hard drives as well as a number of other modern facilities.

Operating system partition limitations

Here is what to expect per OS:

- **DOS 6.22 and earlier.** Versions of DOS that predate the underlying code of Windows 9*x* do not support hard drives larger than 8.4GB.
- **Windows 95 A.** Windows 95 version A (standard version) supports extended interrupt 13, allowing it to work with hard drives larger than 8.4GB up to a maximum of 32GB. However, the FAT16 file system used by the original release of Windows 95 requires that partitions be no larger than 2.048GB in size; therefore a 10GB hard drive must include at least five partitions. Although some third-party utility makers have come up with ways to expand the capability of Windows 95A to larger drives, a better bet is to upgrade to Windows 98 or later. Note that **Windows 95 Upgrade**, sold by Microsoft to migrate drives from Windows 3.1 or MS-DOS is not considered a standard version and does not update the PC's file system; therefore, a Windows 95 Upgrade will not support drives larger than 8.4GB.
- **Windows 95B (OSR2), Windows 95C, and Windows 98.** Windows 95B (OSR2), Windows 95C, and Windows 98 support extended interrupt 13, allowing the use of drives larger than 8.4GB. Windows 95 systems are still officially limited to 32GB,

although third-party utilities can extend their capabilities. These operating systems also support FAT32, which permits the creation of partitions larger than 2.048GB. FAT32 can only be used on hard drives whose capacity exceeds 512MB.

- **Windows 2000.** Windows 2000 supports FAT16, FAT32, and NTFS file systems. Under FAT16, partition sizes are limited in size to 2.048GB. The FAT32 file system supports up to 2TB (terabytes).
- **Windows NT 3.5.** Windows NT 3.5 does not support drives greater than 8.4GB.
- **Windows NT 4.0.** Windows NT 4.0 will support drive capacities greater than 8.4GB if the operating system has been updated to NT 4.0 Service Pack 3 or NT 4.0 Service Pack 4.
- **Windows XP and Windows Vista.** Under NTFS, volumes can be 2TB or larger. Under FAT32, you can format a volume up to 32GB; larger volumes are possible with third-party utilities.

High-level formatting

Logical or high-level formatting applies a file structure that the operating system uses to index the contents of the drive. Over the history of the PC, three common index structures have been used: FAT (in similar FAT12 and FAT16 versions, and the VFAT extension that recognized long filenames), FAT32, and the newest design, NTFS. The history of file systems is shown in Table 10-7.

An important element of the format is the *cluster* size, also called the *allocation unit*. The cluster is the smallest subdivision of the disk, used by the operating system for its index. Larger cluster sizes allow the operating system to work faster, because it has fewer units to keep track of; the bad news is that larger cluster sizes are generally wasteful of space. For example, if the system uses a 32KB cluster, a tiny file of a few hundred bytes would have its own 32KB space; a file of 33KB would demand two clusters, or 64KB of space.

NTFS is the preferred file system for Windows XP and Windows Vista. According to Microsoft, NTFS's advantages include the ability to recover from some disk errors that would prove fatal or at least

problematic for drives using FAT32. NTFS also offers greater support for larger hard disks, and improved security including functions to use permissions and encryption to restrict access to specific files,

If you use FAT32 with Windows Vista you will not be able to create a volume greater than 32GB, and you will not be able to store a file larger than 4GB on a FAT32 volume.

According to Microsoft, the main reason to use FAT32 with Windows Vista or Windows XP is if you have a computer that will sometimes also run Windows 95, Windows 98, or Windows ME. In that situation, you will need to install the earlier operating system on a FAT32 or FAT volume and ensure that the volume is a primary partition (one that can host an operating system). If there are other volumes you will need to access when using an older version of Windows, they must also be formatted with FAT32; the outdated versions of Windows will be able to access NTFS volumes over a network, but not directly on your computer.

Windows 2000 should be able to work with FAT files, while Windows NT 4.0 with Service Pack 4 will have access but with some limitations on features.

TABLE 10-6: File Systems Used by Windows

Operating System	File System
DOS and Windows 3.x	FAT
Windows 95	FAT, VFAT
Windows 95 OSR2, Windows 98, Windows Me	FAT, FAT32
Windows NT v.3 and earlier	FAT, HPFS, NTFS
Windows NT v. 4	FAT, NTFS
Windows 2000, Windows XP	FAT, FAT32, NTFS
Windows Vista	FAT32, NTFS

Each succeeding version of the file system brought new facilities that allow larger partitions, volumes, and filenames. A summary of some of the basics of each file system is shown in Table 10-7.

TABLE 10-7: File System Capabilities

File System	FAT (FAT12, FAT16)	FAT32	NTFS
Operating system compatibility	MS-DOS, all versions of Windows	Windows 95 OSR2. Windows 98, Windows Me, Windows 2000, Windows XP, Windows Vista	Windows Vista, Windows XP, or Windows 2000 can access files on an NTFS partition; a computer running Windows NT 4.0 with Service Pack 4 may be able to access some files
Volume size	Floppy disk size to 4GB	512MB to 2TB	Recommended minimum volume size is 10MB with maximum volumes of 2TB and larger
File size	2GB maximum	4GB maximum	File size limited only by size of volume
Notes	Does not support domains*	Does not support domains*	Cannot be used on floppy disks

In file system terms, a domain is an advanced feature that permits identification of group of computers that are part of a network and share a common directory database. A domain is administered as a unit with common rules and procedures.

FAT16

The file system introduced with DOS 3.1 and maintained through early versions of Windows limits partitions to no larger than 2.048GB in size. Table 10-8 shows the FAT (file allocation table) cluster sizes under FAT16.

TABLE 10-8: FAT16 Cluster Size on Hard Drives

Drive Size (Logical volume)	Cluster Size
0–15MB	4K
16–127MB	2K
128–255MB	4K
256–511MB	8K
512–1,023MB	16K
1,024–2,047MB	32K
2,048–4,095MB	64K
4,096–8,191MB	128K (NT v4.0 only)
8,192–16,384MB	256K (NT v4.0 only)

FAT32

Microsoft's FAT32, used in Windows 98 and Windows Me, and available as an alternative file system in Windows 2000, Windows XP, and Windows Vista is based on a 32-bit file allocation table. FAT32 was introduced a few years into the life of Windows 95, in versions identified as Windows 95B or OEM Service Release 2. Microsoft also posted a partial patch to Windows 95 on its Web page.

Table 10-9 shows the FAT (file allocation table) cluster sizes under FAT32.

This file format can yield several hundred megabytes of additional storage over the conventional, 16-bit FAT because space isn't wasted with fixed large cluster sizes. In addition, you might see improved drive performance, perhaps as much as 50-percent improvement in some situations, according to Microsoft.

To convert a FAT16 file directory to FAT32 in Windows 98, use the built-in utility, Drive Converter: Choose Start ⇨ Programs ⇨ Accessories ⇨ System Tools ⇨ Drive Converter.

This action launches a Windows wizard that steps you through the process. Before proceeding, be sure to click the Details button to read about what FAT32 means to your current configuration.

After you move into the 32-bit file world, you can't go back unless you're willing to reformat and repartition your drives. This, of course, means reinstalling all software — including Windows — and restoring your data files. You also cannot uninstall Windows after converting because earlier versions of Windows won't work with the new file system.

Older utilities — including drive compression, data recovery, and the like — will need to be updated.

Data on removable drives may not be accessible from other machines unless they also use the FAT32 file system.

TABLE 10-9: FAT32 Cluster Size on Hard Drives

Cluster Size	Minimum Partition Size	Maximum Partition Size
512 bytes	0	260MB
4KB	260MB	8GB
8KB	8GB	16GB
16KB	16GB	32GB
32KB	32GB	64GB

NTFS

Windows XP and Windows 2000 allow users to choose from among three file systems: FAT, FAT32, and the advanced (and recommended) NTFS. Windows Vista also recommends use of NTFS, allowing for support of the FAT32 file system if necessary.

NTFS works best with large disks, an improvement over FAT32. Other features are aimed at network administrators, including the ability to use Active Directory for control of distributed computing environment. NFTS also permits access control on files and folders.

Table 10-10 shows cluster sizes under NFTS.

If you're upgrading to Windows XP, that operating system includes utilities that make it easy to convert partitions to NTFS from FAT, FAT32, or the older version of NTFS used in Windows NT. The conversion keeps files intact.

A FAT or FAT32 volume can be converted to NTFS from within Windows XP or Windows Vista. Although the process protects against the possibility of corruption or data loss during the conversion, Microsoft recommends backing up data contained in the volume before converting.

To convert an existing FAT or FAT32 volume to NTFS, do the following:

1. Click Start ⇨ All Programs ⇨ Accessories ⇨ Command Prompt.
2. At the command prompt, insert the drive letter you want to convert in this command: `convert driveletter: /fs:ntfs`. For example, type the following command to convert Drive E from FAT to NTFS: convert e: /fs:ntfs. If the operating system is on the drive that you are converting, you will be prompted to schedule the task when you restart the computer because the conversion cannot be completed while the operating system is running.
3. In response to the message at the command prompt, type in a volume name and press Enter.
4. After you receive a Conversion Complete message, quit the command prompt.

Under Windows XP, if you do not need to maintain files created using an earlier file system, Microsoft recommends that you *format* the partition with NTFS (erasing all data within the partition) rather than *convert* it from the earlier system.

After converting a partition or drive to NTFS, you cannot change it back to FAT or FAT32 without reformatting, which will erase all data. If you have to take this action, be sure to make copies of any files you want to keep.

TABLE 10-10: NTFS Cluster Size on Hard Drives

Cluster Size	Minimum Partition Size	Maximum Partition Size
0.5KB	0	0.5GB
1KB	0.5GB	1GB
2KB	1GB	2GB
4KB	2GB	4GB
8KB	4GB	8GB
16KB	8GB	16GB
32KB	16GB	32GB
64KB	32GB	64GB

The default maximum cluster size under Windows XP is 4KB. It is set for that small size because NTFS file compression cannot be performed on drives with a larger allocation size. You can manually override the default setting by using the /A: option for command-line formatting or by specifying a larger cluster size in the Format dialog box in Disk Management.

Older versions of Windows: Using FDISK

Under Windows 95/98 and Me, to manually partition and format a drive, boot the system from the startup disk. Then type **FDISK** and press Enter.

The first task is to set up a primary DOS partition. Choose Option 1 (Create DOS Partition or Logical DOS Drive). From the succeeding menu, choose Option 1.

You must instruct the system whether to devote the entire C: drive to the primary partition or to subdivide the drive. For simplicity, some users make the entire drive the primary partition; others prefer to organize the drive with C: devoted to the operating system and programs, and subsequent partitions used for storage of various types of files.

If you want to subdivide the drive, specify the amount of drive space you want to partition in either megabytes or a percentage of the entire drive, using a % (percent) sign.

Next, you need to make the primary partition active, holding the bootup files and instructions. From the main FDISK menu, choose Option 2 (Set Active Partition).

To create an extended partition, choose Option 1 again, and then choose Option 2 (Create Extended DOS Partition). Enter a percentage of the drive or the number of megabytes for this partition. Do not attempt to make this partition active; only one can be active.

After you create an extended partition, you can further divide it into logical drives. To do so, select the Create Logical Drives option from the extended partition menu. Follow the on-screen instructions to assign drive letters to your partitions. Bear in mind that if you choose D:, you will end up pushing the designation for any installed CD-ROM drive to higher in the alphabet; this should not cause problems but may result in some confusion when other programs, including installation utilities, assume that the D: designator refers to your CD-ROM.

You can double-check the results of your work by choosing Option 4 (Display Partition Information).

FDISK virus repair

The master boot record is a very attractive target for malicious virus makers; you should guard your machine with antivirus software and take other steps to protect the data recorded there.

Current versions of FDISK include two safety utilities that can help protect against accidental or malicious damage to your partition table.

If the master boot record is damaged, you can instruct FDISK to rewrite it based on the existing partitions on the drive, without damaging them or deleting the data records. To perform this task, boot from the startup disk and go to the A: prompt. Then type **FDISK /MBR** and press Enter.

You can also create a backup copy of the partition table on a floppy disk. From the DOS prompt, type **MIRROR /PARTN**.

The MIRROR utility copies the partition table to a file called `PARTNSAV.FIL`.

To restore this partition information, go to the DOS prompt and type **UNFORMAT /PARTN**.

Repartitioning a hard drive using FDISK

Follow these steps to repartition a hard drive by using FDISK:

1. Boot the computer from your Windows startup disk, a Microsoft boot disk, or other startup disk.
2. Select the option to Start Computer with CD-ROM support.
3. The first step is to clear the Master Boot Record, which holds the partition records. At the A: prompt, type **FDISK/ mbr** and press Enter.
4. Now, you begin the process of removing the existing partitions. At the A: prompt, type **FDISK** and press Enter. On most modern machines, the operating system will ask if you want to use large disk support, which means to adapt the BIOS to work with, well, larger disks. Type **Y** and press Enter.
5. From the menu, select Option 3 (Delete the Partition) and press Enter. From the succeeding menu, select Option 1 (Delete the PRIMARY Partition).
6. Next, you're asked to confirm the partition to remove; type **1** and press Enter, and then enter the Volume Label for the partition to be removed. If it has no name, press Enter to move on.
7. At this point you have removed all partition information on the drive and made any data inaccessible. Now you need to repartition the drive. From the main menu select Option 1 (Create Partition). At the next screen, choose Option 1 (Create the PRIMARY DOS Partition).
8. The utility asks if you want to use the maximum partition space for the Primary Dos Partition. Type **Y** and then press Enter.

9. Your hard drive is now partitioned. Press the Escape key to return to the A: prompt.
10. The final step is to reformat the hard drive. Be sure to add the necessary system tracks. From the A: drive, type **Format C:/s** to do both.

⚡ **WARNING**

Using FDISK on an existing hard drive deletes the records for everything previously stored.

Recovery Console (Windows 2000, Windows XP, and Windows Vista)

FDISK was replaced by the DISKPART utility under Windows XP; a similar utility is offered in Windows Vista. The diskpart command enables users to manage disks, partitions, or volumes.

Advanced users of Windows 2000 and Windows XP can perform surgery on drives — including formatting, writing data or recovery files or drivers to and from a drive, reading the data on an otherwise-inaccessible disk, and other power-tool tasks — by using the Recovery Console. You can also repair a damaged boot sector.

Two powerful uses of the Recovery Console are to repair a system by copying a file from a floppy disk or CD-ROM to the hard drive outside of Windows, and to reconfigure a service that is preventing the computer from starting properly.

You must be an administrator to use the Recovery Console.

If you are unable to start your computer, you can run the Recovery Console from the Windows XP or Windows 2000 Setup CD. Follow the text prompts to the repair or recover option.

Or, you can install the Recovery Console on your computer to make it available anytime Windows is in the process of starting. A Recovery Console option is then added to the list of available operating systems at startup. A similar utility is offered in Windows Vista.

 CROSS-REFERENCE

I discuss the Recovery Console in more detail in Chapter 22.

Alphabet Soup: Hard Drive Interfaces

Up to this point we have concentrated on the construction and organization of a hard disk; although newer drives are faster and much larger than their predecessors there has not been much change in their essential design: one or more spinning platters with a set of one or more read/write heads that put down a magnetic marker or read an existing one. The major area of change in technology has been a steady improvement in the interface between the hard drive and the computer: the faster and more efficient the interface, the greater the throughput of information to or from the disk.

Think of a faster interface as a larger pipe, capable of handling higher pressure. That works when you consider the interface in logical terms; in reality the pipe has actually become much smaller in recent years but also considerably more efficient. The vast majority of modern machines and most senior citizens and dinosaurs used one or another form of parallel communication: the individual bits of a computer word moving across the system bus on individual traces or wires were transported to the hard disk in the same manner before being converted to a serial stream of 0s and 1s for writing data. The system functioned in reverse going from the disk to the system.

Since 2005, most current modern machines have made the change to the smaller but more efficient pipe of a serial connection. Data is converted on the motherboard (or in an adapter card plugged into the bus) from parallel communication to a serial stream. A small and flexible cable with essentially two signal wires — one for each direction — connects to the hard disk.

A hard disk interface is based on an industry standard that describes the adapter card, the cable, the electronics on the hard disk itself, and the electrical signals running between the hard disk and controller. In roughly chronological order, the PC has been host to ST506, ESDI, SCSI, IDE (also known as ATA), the enhanced EIDE standard (Enhanced IDE, also called ATA-2), Ultra ATA (based on Ultra DMA/33), Wide SCSI, and Serial ATA.

As I have noted, with this edition we have removed coverage of SCSI drives which are no longer common on current modern machines; you'll find coverage of SCSI drives (as well as dinosaur ESDI and ST506 devices) in the appendix of the book. At the same time we have added expanded coverage of Serial ATA drives and interfaces which have become the standard on new machines.

Nearly all modern machines use an ATA interface, either in the form of an advanced Serial ATA design or based on the older Parallel

ATA or IDE design. All ATA drives, whether serial or parallel, employ IDE (Integrated Drive Electronics), meaning that the controller is built into the drive rather than on a separate controller card. For our purposes, IDE and ATA are the same thing; the controller uses the ATA specifications and the storage device uses Integrated Drive Electronics (IDE) to manage the flow of data in either direction. Today's principal distinction is between Serial ATA and Parallel ATA.

Older advanced machines and some special-purpose machines (including those employed in graphics and audio processing) may offer a SCSI interface. Another advanced technology is Fibre Channel, employed in disk arrays used in engineering, video editing, graphics, and sound applications.

Each hard drive interface handles the actual data storage in its own way.

ATA drives allow ordinary computer bus signals on the cable running from the adapter card to a compatible hard drive with its own electronic controller (the IDE). A Serial ATA interface connects to a SATA drive using a serial cable with data moving one bit behind the other; a Parallel ATA interface sends eight bits of information across individual wires from the bus to the drive where the data is converted to serial form for recording on the drive.

SCSI uses a separate bus (its own data and control signal path) to carry the data signals and control signals from adapter card, to hard disk, and back again. The SCSI bus is so separate, in fact, that most SCSI installations tell you to set up your computer as if no hard drives were installed. SCSI doesn't want the computer messing around with its bus, its data, or its hard disk.

Prior to the arrival of ATA drives in 1986, most early PCs used a design called ST506/412, which was introduced with the original IBM PC and still used until about 1988, and a specification called ESDI, in use from about 1983 through 1991.

The ST506 specification expected the user to instruct the computer's ROM BIOS how many heads and cylinders are on the hard disk, which read/write head should read what data, and what track on the hard disk this head should read.

These hard drive interfaces all do the same basic job (store and retrieve data, and connect to the computer motherboard) but in such different ways that none of the parts are interchangeable. SCSI drives insist on a SCSI adapter and cable; an older ESDI hard disk controller card won't work with a modern ATA drive. An SATA drive can work with an adapter that stands between it and a Parallel ATA controller, although this adds expense and slows down data transfer a bit. In addition, troubleshooting and installation techniques vary from interface to interface.

Examining Your Hard Drive and Interface

If you don't know what type of hard drive is within the case of your PC, you can consult the Hard Drive section of the Device Manager within Windows where you can learn about the type of drive installed. You can also look at the Drive Controller section; look for a listing for an IDE or SCSI controller and driver. Most capable diagnostic programs will also produce a report that includes details of your storage system.

You can also open your computer to examine the drive, its controller/adapter, and their associated cables. Remove the cover and find the hard drive — a solid, rectangular, metal device that is usually mounted in a bay at the front of the chassis, although some designs suspend it elsewhere inside the case.

On most older modern machines you'll find a four-wire power cable and one or two ribbon cables are attached to the back of the hard disk: these are hallmarks of a Parallel ATA (IDE) drive. IDE ribbon cables have 40 or 80 wires. SCSI ribbon cables have 50 wires. Both of these cables are straight-through in design, with pin 1 at one end equal to pin 1 at the other. (See Figure 10-12.)

Your floppy disk drive or drives also have a four-wire power cable and a ribbon cable, but it is easy to tell floppy disk drives from hard drives: Each floppy drive has a door in front to insert the floppy disks — a hard drive doesn't. A floppy drive cable has a twist with seven wires split off from the rest of the ribbon, flipped over, and clipped into the Drive A: connector. (See Figure 10-13.)

Newer modern machines offering a Serial ATA interface and drive employ thin data cables — one for each drive — and a thin bundle of power cables.

Dinosaur tech: Because ESDI is simply a faster version of the ST506 interface (but incompatible with ST506), ESDI and ST506 drives and cables look the same. ST506 and ESDI interfaces both use two ribbon cables. One is 34 wires wide (the controller cable) and the other is 20 wires wide (the data cable). You can follow the ribbon cables back to the hard disk controller card. If you have two cables and your hard disk is less than 50MB, you probably have an ST506 interface. (The handful of exceptions includes a few small ESDI drives from makers no longer among the major players today: Micropolis, Rodime, and Microscience.) If the hard disk is more than 200MB and has two data cables, it is almost certainly an ESDI drive. Between 50 and 200MB is a gray area, because both ST506 drives (also called MFM and RLL drives) and ESDI drives have been manufactured in this size range. It makes sense to call your computer dealer or the hard drive manufacturer if you have any doubts.

A dizzying alphabet soup of standards and specifications govern the recording and retrieval of data on a hard disk. For your purposes, it doesn't matter whether your drive uses MFM (modified frequency modulation) or RLL (run length limited) schemes for recording, or ST506, ESDI, IDE, EIDE, or SCSI disk controllers: The hard drive platters and heads are the same.

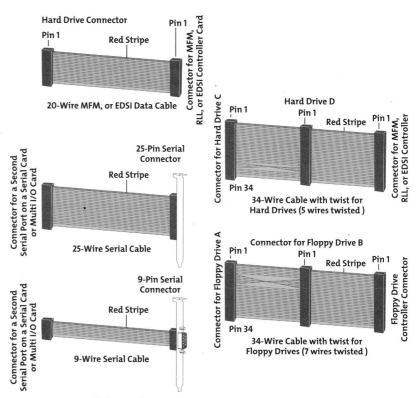

Figure 10-13: *At left are three more straight-through cables. At right are two ribbon cables with a twist to change drive selection on older hard drives and floppy disk drives.*

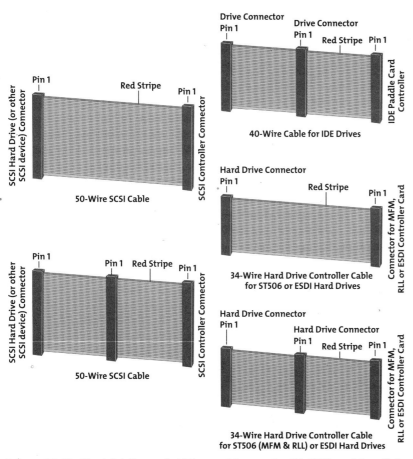

Figure 10-12: *Straight-through ribbon cables used with SCSI and Parallel ATA and older hard drive connectors.*

Modern Machine Hard Disk Drives and Interfaces

The good news is that modern machines can work with just about any drive interface previously used for PCs. The bad news is that you've got a whole bunch of choices and configurations to deal with. Table 10-11 lists the maximum possible transfer rates for modern interfaces.

TABLE 10-11: Transfer Rates for Hard Drive Interfaces

Interface Design	Year Introduced	Maximum Theoretical Transfer Rate
ST506	1980	0.625 MBps
ESDI	Mid-1980s	2.5 MBps
IDE (ATA-1)	Late 1980s	2–3 MBps
SCSI	1986	10 MBps
EIDE (ATA-2, ATA-3)	1995	11.1 or 16.6 MBps
SCSI-2 (Fast SCSI-2)	1989	20 MBps
Ultra SCSI (SCSI-3, (Ultra SCSI Wide)	1992	20 MBps or 40 MBps
Ultra ATA (ATA/33, ATA-4, ATAPI-4)	1998	33.3 MBps
Ultra2 SCSI	1997	80 MBps
Ultra ATA/66 (ATA-5, ATAPI-5)	1999	66 MBps
Fibre Channel	1988	100 MBps
Ultra ATA/100 (ATA-6, Parallel ATA)	2000	100 MBps
Ultra ATA/133 (ATA-7, Parallel ATA)	2001	133 MBps
Ultra3 SCSI (SCSI 160)	1999	160 MBps
Fibre Channel Dual Loop	2000	200 MBps
Ultra320 SCSI	2002	320 MBps
Serial ATA	2003	150 or 300 MBps

Serial ATA: The Beauty of Simplicity

A Serial ATA subsystem (controller, cabling, and drive) is a bit faster and much simpler to implement than Parallel ATA (IDE) or other older designs. In truth, though, it is the simplicity of the cabling that is its biggest appeal. Serial ATA follows the trend away from parallel wiring to improved serial communication.

SATA is available under Windows Vista, XP, or 2000 with a SATA motherboard or with a SATA adapter installed in a bus slot. Earlier versions of Windows, including Windows 98SE and 98, are not compatible with SATA hardware.

Consumer-grade hard disk drives have not delivered marked improvements in transfer speed in recent years; the emphasis has been on producing larger and larger capacities at lower and lower prices and for most users that is a tradeoff worth making. The theoretical maximum speed of current SATA drives and controllers is 3 GBps (actually 2.4 GBps once overhead is subtracted): a speed rarely, if ever, reached by current drives.

For many years, designers have been aware of the limitations of the ATA interface. The principal issue is the inherent difficulty of maintaining proper timing of the individual bits of a computer word or byte traveling alongside each other on parallel wires. ATA (which some designers have redubbed *parallel ATA*) has been inching forward in potential transfer speed, most recently advancing to 133 MBps in Maxtor's ATA/133 hardware.

As you have seen, parallel wiring—which sends each bit in a computer word alongside others, each on a separate wire—started out with a speed advantage. In theory, in parallel communication, all eight bits in a computer word arrive at the same time. By comparison, to send eight bits down the length of a serial cable, the bits had to be stacked up one behind the other and bracketed on each end by a set of markers to differentiate one word from another.

The advantage for parallel communication, though, began to disappear as speeds began to increase exponentially. Minute differences in the quality of the wires in the parallel cable or fluctuations in electrical power can affect the orderly arrival of the bits. If one bit arrives a few milliseconds behind the others it can result in a loss of communication.

The parallel ATA design uses a somewhat unwieldy cable with 40 or 80 wires (ATA/66 and later standards use 80 conductors) and 40 pins in the connector. In many installations, the cable has to be twisted 180 degrees between devices; data transmission can be affected if a crimped cable shorts out some of the wires. At the motherboard end, 26 signal pins go into the interface chip. The ribbon cables are 2 inches wide and can be no more than 18 inches in length.

Disadvantages of parallel ATA include:

- The large and cumbersome 40- or 80-wire cables and 40-pin connectors create clutter within the machine, and the broad ribbon cables can interfere with effective cooling within the case.
- The need for 5-volt electrical signals on 26 wires goes against the trend that seeks lower-voltage integrated circuits on the motherboard.
- The practical length limit of 18 inches in length for parallel ATA cables can complicate internal and external expansion.
- A lack of full data checking is less valuable to the user. The original ATA standard had no data checking at all, and current versions offer only limited data protection with CRC algorithms.

Ultra ATA-100 and the less commonly used ATA-133 standards most likely represent the top end for parallel ATA communication, delivering maximum burst data transfer rate of 100 MBps or 133 MBps respectively.

Serial ATA uses the same protocols as parallel ATA but with different connecting and decoding hardware, including a considerably thinner cable. The data cable also demands less voltage on fewer wires, which allows chipset manufacturers to produce smaller, less expensive devices. The new standard is intended to be 100 percent *software* compatible with earlier systems, requiring no changes to software and operating systems.

The initial release of devices for Serial ATA began at a data transfer rate of 150 MBps and almost immediately doubled to 300 MBps; another doubling, to 600 MBps, is expected by 2007 or 2008. An example of a current SATA drive was shown earlier in this chapter in Figure 10-4.

As this book goes to press, SATA hard drives are widely available and have become the standard design for storage on new modern machines; manufacturers have just begun to introduce CD and DVD drives that can connect to a SATA interface. Because of that lag, we can expect to see motherboards offering a combination of serial and parallel ATA connections for a while until CD and DVD drives are more available.

The beauty of the simple seven-wire cable and connector of a SATA system and the fact that each hard drive has its own cabling make it very simple to configure a system; this replaces the nearly two-inch-wide 80-wire "ribbon" cable for Parallel ATA. The ribbon cable typically was used for two devices (a master and slave) and required an awkward routing from the motherboard to the devices that sometimes required a twist midway. In addition to the awkwardness of the cabling design, the wide ribbons also interfered with cooling the interior of the PC's case.

Finally, the developing External SATA market adds one more convenience: like USB devices, an external drive attached to an E-SATA connection can be *hot swapped* — attached or detached while the system is running.

A SATA subsystem gives each device its own cable and its own dedicated bandwidth (essentially a bus). Although this may seem like a step back from the shared facilities of Parallel ATA (just as serial communication, on the face of it, would seem to be less capable than a parallel interface), the cost of adding individual controllers on the motherboard has dropped to almost inconsequential levels.

The SATA data cable has seven conductors and a thin 8mm connector (about one-third of an inch wide) at each end; cables can be as much as a meter (39 inches) long, which allows them to be nearly snaked around devices and tucked away out of the airstream within the case. By comparison, a Parallel ATA ribbon cable carries 40 or 80 wires and is limited in length to 18 inches. SATA data cables are also keyed so that they can only plug in the proper orientation; Parallel ATA cables were marked with a red stripe on one side but could easily be misinstalled.

The specified power cable for a SATA device has 15 wires and cables in a small and thin connector. The reason for so many wires is that the standard allows for three different voltage levels for various types of devices; the connector carries 3.3 volts, 5 volts, and 12 volts plus ground wires. Within a SATA device two or more of the voltage pins can be combined to provide additional current.

Some older SATA drives also offer a larger 4-pin Molex connector to take electricity from a power supply that was designed to work only with Parallel ATA devices. Another way around that sort of problem is to use a PATA to SATA power connection adapter.

Current SATA drives are identical to Parallel ATA devices when it comes to the drive platters, read/write heads, and motors but use a different electronic design to package the data that goes to or comes from the motherboard. A native SATA drive — most common now — has electronically specifically designed for use with a serial controller; a *bridged* SATA is an adaptation of a Parallel ATA drive with the addition of a bridge chip to convert between parallel and serial.

Although I don't discuss SCSI drives in this edition, for the record, Serial ATA drives can attach to and communicate with *Serial Attached SCSI (SAS)* controllers, using a SAS cable. Going the other direction, though, SAS disks cannot be used with a SATA controller. In Table 10-12 I show some of the specifics for current hard disk drive interfaces.

Serial ATA advantages

The Serial ATA standard uses only four signal pins to carry data in a thin cable similar in appearance to a telephone cable. The smaller cable can be as long as 1 meter (39 inches), allowing for simpler design within the case and improving the system's airflow and cooling. The initial release uses 500 millivolt ($\frac{1}{2}$ volt) signaling, one-tenth the 5-volt demand for each of 26 data wires in a parallel ATA cable.

Designers promise that ultrafine traces (the equivalent of wires) on motherboards that will be available in coming years will allow use of much lower voltage for data transmission, and plans are already in place for Serial ATA connections that will work with signaling voltages of as little as 250 millivolts ($\frac{1}{4}$ volt).

Devices attached to a parallel ATA interface are set up in pairs sharing a common cable in a master-slave relationship; both devices share the available bandwidth, and in some situations, both may be contending for access and data transfer at the same time.

On the other hand, Serial ATA is set up as a point-to-point interface with each device directly connected to the host with its own cable and each is able to use the entire bandwidth. There is no need to worry about master-slave settings or conflicts between devices with differing demands on the interface. The cables are also designed to be impossible to install improperly in the connector.

Finally, Serial ATA can be set up to be hot-pluggable, allowing devices to be attached to or removed from a system while it is running.

We have seen similar moves to high-speed serial communication in USB and FireWire (IEEE 1394) buses now in wide use on PCs for external devices.

Mixing Serial and Parallel ATA

The first Serial ATA hard drives were priced just slightly higher than parallel equivalents; the cost differential has disappeared because of the industry-wide switch to that specification, and in some cases Parallel ATA drives may cost a bit more because they are facing shrinking demand. Future advancements in speed and capacity will likely show up first in serial versions of hard drives and make their way to parallel drives a bit more slowly.

Because of the tens of millions of still-capable machines that use them, it will take a long time before Parallel ATA drives are no longer considered modern equipment. However, few new PC designs are likely to be based around the older standard.

If you want to add a Serial ATA drive to a system that does not directly support that communication standard, you need to install an

TABLE 10-12: Transfer Rates for Current Modern Machine Hard Drive Interfaces				
Interface Design	Potential Maximum Transfer Speed	Typical Net Transfer Speed	Maximum Cable Length	Maximum Devices Per Channel Without Hub
SATA 3.0 Gbps	3.0 Gbps	2.4 Gbps (300 MBps)	18 inches	1
eSATA	3.0 Gbps	2.4 Gbps (300 MBps)	78 inches	1
SATA 1.5 Gbps	1.5 Gbps	1.2 Gbps (150 MBps)	18 inches	1
PATA (Ultra ATA/133)	1.064 Gbp	1.064 Gbps (133 MBps)	18 inches	2
FireWire 800	800 Mbps	768 Mbps	14.5 feet	63
USB 2.0	480 Mbps	375 Mbps	16 feet	127

adapter card. Nearly all current motherboards come with a SATA controller; older modern motherboards can add SATA through use of a plug-in adapter card like the one shown in Figure 10-14. The Addonics card, which plugs into a PCI slot, adds four SATA ports that support first-generation data rates of as much as 1.5Gbps. Built-in intelligence on the board permits the four ports to act independently or as part of a RAID set.

Addonics, shown in Figure 10-15, that has a SATA power and data connector on one side and a choice of two types of USB connectors on the other. One USB connector is a type B plug for use with a standard cable and the other a pin-header for attachment to a compatible header on the motherboard.

FIGURE 10-15: *This tiny adapter from Addonics mounts directly on the back of a SATA drive, allowing connection of a cable to permit you to use the drive with a USB 1.1 or 2.0 controller.*

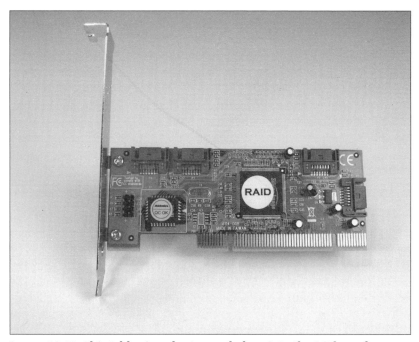

FIGURE 10-14: *This Addonics adapter card plugs into the PCI bus of a modern machine to add four internal SATA ports; in the photo, two ports can be seen at the top near the mounting bracket, and two others are to the right, at the corner above the card's connector. The card can also be configured to function as a RAID controller to create redundant copies of data on multiple disks or to spread data over more than one disk.*

SATA 1.5 Gbps

The original specification for Serial ATA interfaces, also known as SATA/150, runs at 1.5 GHz; because of the need for marker bits in the serial stream of data the potential maximum efficiency is 80 percent, yielding a throughout of about 1.2 Gbps. Relatively few systems were shipped with this first implementation.

SATA 3.0 Gbps

The enhanced SATA specification, which followed quickly on the heels of the original standard and is much more widely used, runs at 3 GHz and yields a maximum potential transfer of 2.4 Gbps.

You can also go the other way if you need to make a SATA hard disk drive or optical drive work as an internal or external USB device. One device to make the changeover is a small circuit board from

In theory, older and newer devices can be interchanged on the same computer: a SATA 1.5 drive will run at that speed if attached to a SATA 3.0 controller, while a SATA 3.0 drive will be forced to transfer data at half-speed if connected to a SATA 1.5 controller.

If you have an older modern machine or an older SATA device, check the documentation to see if (as is occasionally necessary) you must set a jumper on the drive to match the speed of the controller or if the device is smart enough to handle this automatically. All current SATA 3.0 controllers and drives are able to auto-detect.

Future tech: SATA 6.0 Gbps

Plans call for another doubling of SATA speed, perhaps as soon as 2007. SATA 6.0 Gbps would run at 6.0 GHz with a potential throughput of 4.8 Gbps. A faster top end for transfer is always better than a slower one, but experts point out that the limiting factor is the ability of a hard disk drive to pump out or receive data, and currently most drives are capable of only about half that rate.

IDE (Parallel ATA) drives and adapters

The key to understanding IDE controllers lies in the name: The drive electronics are integrated onto the drive itself. IDE connectors are host adapters that serve as ports into and out of the computer bus; the controller exists on the drive. This placement enables customization and upgrades by the drive manufacturer.

IDE controllers generally use one of the ATA standards, the latest of which are Ultra ATA/133, Ultra ATA/100, and Ultra ATA/66.

Older modern PCs with Parallel ATA controllers come with one or two IDE connectors on the motherboard. You can plug as many as two devices into each cable that attaches to the connectors. See Figure 10-16.

Current modern PCs using Serial ATA technology have one controller for each hard drive — as many as four on the motherboard — and a dedicated cable for each device. To work with most CD and DVD drives, the motherboard also has one or more Parallel ATA controller dedicated to those devices; within the next few years SATA versions of CD and DVD drives are expected to become the standard in new machines.

If you don't want to use the motherboard's built-in controller, or to work around a failed controller, the system BIOS configuration/setup program should let you turn off the onboard IDE electronics and

replace it with an adapter card that plugs into a PCS slot. If the hard disk controller is not part of the BIOS, the motherboard should include a jumper block or a switch that disables the controller and recognizes a new controller plugged into the bus.

You might also choose to upgrade an older modern machine with a newer hard disk controller; various manufacturers offer Serial ATA or Parallel ATA controllers that plug into the bus; these replacement cards sell for as little as $20 to $30.

FIGURE 10-16: *IDE connectors on an ATX motherboard with the secondary connector nearest the rear of the board.*

IDE systems put the brains on the hard drive itself. The host adapter merely sends signals from the drive across the bus. On the older Parallel ATA technology the data moves across individual wires to the drive; on a newer SATA controller and drive, the signal is streamed to the drive as a serial signal. The adapter, unlike earlier ST506 or ESDI hard disk controllers, does no data encoding or decoding. The drive's electronics also take responsibility for control signals for the read/write heads on the disk.

At the heart of the definition of IDE is the concept of the independence of the drive from its PC host. IDE drives use special registers for commands from the PC; the drives themselves have address-decoding logic used to match bus signals to the drive. In this way, a PC designer can locate an IDE subsystem at any port address with relative ease.

Because of the rapid increase in the number and types of IDE drives and to maintain compatibility with older drives and ROM BIOS chips, most modern machines do not have a drive type preconfigured in the BIOS that matches the IDE drive. Follow the drive manufacturer's instructions; depending on the system, you'll either set up the device as a user-defined drive type or allow the BIOS to automatically detect the specifications of the drive. If you want to use all the storage space available on your IDE drive, you have to tell the CMOS setup program that the IDE drive is a user-definable drive type.

Engineers introduced a series of improvements to the Parallel ATA or IDE standard over the years; most older modern machines use ATA/100 or ATA/133 specifications; both of those high-speed protocols, as well as the older ATA/66 design, are downwardly compatible with older IDE and ATAPI devices using the ATA/33 protocol.

Ultra ATA, DMA/33, EIDE

The original IDE drive specification suffered from a few handicaps. As designed, IDE circuitry could not work with hard drives larger than 528MB, which seemed huge at the time but is way too tiny to hold even the operating system these days. Another problem was a limit of no more than two devices per IDE connector. Finally, IDE was at first only intended for use with hard drives, meaning it could not work with CD-ROM drives and tape backup devices. An example of an Ultra ATA cable is shown in Figure 10-17.

Western Digital lead the effort to enhance the IDE specification, coming up with an improved variant that was named, logically, enhanced integrated drive electronics, or EIDE. Today EIDE is variously called Fast ATA, Fast IDE, ATA-2, ATA-3, and Ultra ATA. In this book, I have chosen to use the latest name, Ultra ATA.

Ultra ATA became widely available in 1998, offering data transfer rates up to 33 MBps when the proper drive was paired with an Ultra DMA/33 motherboard and controller. Ultra ATA is completely backward compatible with older Fast ATA-2 (EIDE) systems and can be used in legacy systems, albeit at the slower speed.

FIGURE 10-17: *An Ultra ATA cable is an unusual bridge between two specifications. It uses a 40-pin, 80-wire connection; the extra 40 wires serve as ground connections to help the parallel data stay in proper marching order. The blue connector must be plugged into the motherboard; the black end connector is used for the master drive on the cable, and the gray middle connector for a slave drive, if present. In this picture, the high-density Ultra ATA cable sits above its ATA/33 cousin.*

Most controllers can work with as many as four drives, with two on each channel. The drives can be all EIDE, all IDE, or a mix. In some systems, the entire EIDE channel will be limited to the maximum speed of the slowest device attached.

With this version of the specification, IDE included the ATA Packet Interface (ATAPI) specification that extends control to other types of devices. ATAPI drivers are available for CD-ROM drives, tape drives, and removable storage devices such as Iomega Zip drives.

The enhanced IDE standard deals with most of the limitations of IDE. It includes support for the following:

- As many as four devices from one controller, with the addition of a second connector that enables two devices on each of two channels.
- CD-ROMs and nondisk devices, as well as hard disk drives.
- High-capacity disk drives, up to 8.4GB in a single volume on a hard disk.
- High-speed host transfers, beyond that of the ISA bus. This enables a device to take full advantage of a VL or PCI local bus with data throughput of up to 11.1 MBps, which compares favorably with SCSI transfer rates of 10 MBps.

And, more importantly, Ultra ATA retains compatibility with ATA devices.

Ultra ATA/66 and Ultra ATA/100 interfaces

The Ultra ATA/66 or Ultra ATA/100 enhanced IDE interfaces (also known as Ultra DMA/66 or Ultra DMA/100) double and triple the Ultra/33 burst data transfer rate to 66.6 MBps and 100 MBps, respectively.

Both of these interface standards describe how fast information can flow from your hard drive's data buffer (RAM) to your computer system; it is not a measure of how fast the hardware can actually pass data off of the disk to the system. You also need the Intel 820 chipset or a later (higher-numbered) chipset or a competitive equivalent to support the advanced standards; you can also purchase a third-party hard disk controller with its own onboard support for this high-speed IDE mode.

Although an Ultra ATA/66 and Ultra ATA/100 cable look like a conventional 40-conductor IDE interface, they are electrically different. The connectors still hold only 40 pins; there are 40 additional ground lines between each of the standard 40-pin ATA signal lines and ground lines to improve signal integrity by reducing crosstalk across data lines.

The specification calls for the connector at the drive end to be colored bright blue in order to help differentiate this interface from others in your system. You can use the new interface cables with conventional IDE drives, but, of course, you'll only get 33 MBps or less performance.

In order to run data transfer in Ultra ATA/66 or Ultra ATA/100 mode, you need the following:

- A storage device capable of working with the Ultra ATA/66 or Ultra ATA/100 standard
- A system board and BIOS compatible with the advanced standards
- An 80-conductor cable designed for the Ultra ATA/66 or Ultra ATA/100 standard
- An operating system capable of DMA transfers — support began with Windows 95 (OSR2) and continues in Windows 98, Me, 2000, XP, and Vista.

In a capable system, both the motherboard and the hard drive can detect the presence of the required 80-conductor cable.

Ultra ATA/100 increases the data transfer rate and adds some enhancements to error checking. These drives also work with an expanded command set intended to work with future interfaces and enhancements.

All Ultra ATA/100 and Ultra ATA/66 drives are backward compatible with earlier ATA standards. However, some older ATA host controllers and motherboards may not work properly with Ultra ATA drives; the major disk drive manufacturers offer a utility program that sets the most advanced Ultra ATA drives to Ultra ATA/33 or Ultra ATA/66 mode to maintain compatibility. Changing the transfer mode affects only the external maximum (burst) transfer rate of the device; internal performance is not affected by the external transfer mode, so the overall sustained transfer rate is only slightly reduced.

Ultra ATA/133

Maxtor introduced the Ultra ATA/133 interface in 2001, delivering a 33-percent boost to 133 MBps in the top speed for data transfer to and from the interface. The interface uses the same 80-conductor, 40-pin cable used for ATA/100 and provides backward compatibility with all parallel ATA devices, including Ultra ATA/33, ATA/66 and ATA/100. The interface includes a set of tightly controlled specifications for trace lengths and timing parameters, an essential element of any high-speed parallel interface.

In 2007, it seems as if this is as far as Parallel ATA standards are likely to go; Serial ATA has almost completely replaced the older specification in new modern machines. That doesn't mean that some laboratory is not at work on some future technology that might overcome the limitations of parallel communication at high speed and bring it back to the forefront.

The Ultra ATA/133 standard was not as widely used as previous ones because of the patent held by Maxtor; a number of other companies did obtain licensing for Ultra ATA/133 interface technology for systems and chipsets.

Even with faster potential transfer rates, however, the real interface transfer rate is actually as much as one-third slower because of overhead; one estimate is that a 32K block of data has a transfer efficiency of about 62 percent on an ATA/100 interface, meaning an effective transfer rate of 62 MBps, which is a lot closer to the maximum media data transfer rate.

According to hard drive manufacturer Maxtor, hard drive performance has been improving at about 40 percent per year, and the transfer overhead becomes more and more of an issue with larger drives and higher speeds.

Drive designers consider ATA/133 an important accomplishment because it matches the PCI bus data rate of 133 MBps exactly. In theory, even faster data transfer rates are possible, although there are obstacles, including finding a way to deliver backward compatibility to earlier interfaces. Current plans involve new designs for cables and connectors that won't work with the existing ATA interface.

For some users, the most important new element of the ATA/133 specification is breaking through the 137GB barrier for ATA hard drives. Over the history of the personal computer, there have been nearly a dozen barriers that set a maximum size for hard drives, beginning with an original limit of 528MB.

The 137GB barrier was in place because the original ATA interface provided only 28 bits of address for data, which meant that a hard disk could have no more than 268,435,456 sectors of 512 bytes of data.

ATA/133 doesn't just break through the barrier — it smashes it to bits, with a new top end of 100,000 times more data: 48-bit addressing permits a single drive with more than 144 *petabytes* (144 million GB) of storage. (A *petabyte* is 2^{50} bytes [1,125,899,906,842,624], or 1,024 terabytes.)

And the accompanying ATA/ATAPI-6 definition also permits a boost in the maximum amount of data that can be transferred with each command for ATA devices from 256 sectors (about 131KB) to 65,536 sectors (about 33MB). This new capability will be used in multimedia applications including streaming audio and video.

However, the hardware top end of 144 petabytes is not yet matched by current operating systems. Because they are based on 32-bit addressing, Windows 95/98, Me, 2000, and XP cannot work with drives larger than 2.2 terabytes (2,200GB).

To work with the ATA/133 specification, systems need a compatible hard disk controller; Maxtor supplied a plug-in adapter with its early models of 160GB hard drives, ahead of the arrival of adapter cards from other manufacturers. Many BIOS chips also have to be updated in order to work with the advanced standard.

Testing IDE (ATA) Drives and Their Adapter Cards

In general, ATA drives work or they don't. That's especially so for SATA drives, but I start here with Parallel ATA drives, which have a few special wrinkles. There are four likely points of failure:

- The hard drive can fail.
- The hard drive controller can fail, or be disabled by a conflict over system resources.
- The cable between the controller and the drive can become dislodged, crimped to the point of failure, or misinstalled.
- The power supply for the drive can fail.

Parallel ATA

One cause of a failure to communicate for a Parallel ATA drive is if you fail to properly identify each device on the cable as either a primary or secondary (also known as a master or slave) device.

On many Parallel ATA drives, you identify devices by setting a pin block on the rear of the drive. Consult the instructions that come with drives for proper settings.

On other systems, devices receive their primary or secondary identification depending on which of the two connectors on the cable they use; these "cable select" systems use the connector on the end of the cable for the primary device and the connector between the two ends of the cable for the secondary device.

If the drive won't read or write and the installation is new, recheck the drive jumpers and the cables. If the drive doesn't even spin, you may have a bad power connection, or you may have put the ribbon cable on upside down so that the red stripe is away from pin 1.

If the drive does not seem to be spinning (no flashes of the disk activity light if your computer has one, or a silence where there used to be a whine), ensure that the power cable is properly attached to the drive. For a Parallel ATA drive, the power arrives through a one-inch-wide white connector with four heavy wires; it clicks into place on the drive with a positioning slot intended to prevent reversing the wires. The other end of the power cable goes directly to the power supply, a large silver or black box in one of the corners of the case.

Serial ATA

Among the simplicities brought by newer SATA drive is the use of a single controller and a single data cable for each device. There is no need to identify a drive as primary or secondary.

Another improvement involves a key slot that prevents improper installation of the data cable. Unless you really go out of your way to force a cable onto its connector, it is not going to plug in the wrong way. If the drive does not seem to be spinning, ensure that the power cable is properly attached to the drive. For a Serial ATA drive, the power arrives through a thin wafer white connector with 15 thin wires; it clicks into place on the drive with a positioning slot intended to prevent reversing the wires. The other end of the power cable goes directly to the power supply, a large silver or black box in one of the corners of the case.

Installing an ATA adapter card

Current modern machines have two to four Serial ATA ports built into the motherboard; each interface is intended to serve a single device. At this time, CD or DVD drives that can work with a SATA interface are rare, and for that reason as this book goes to press we are in a transitional period; most motherboards also offer one or two Parallel ATA ports that can be used for optical drives (or to support an older PATA hard disk drive.

Older modern machines have two Parallel ATA ports built into the motherboard. All you have to do is connect one or two drives to the IDE connector on the motherboard.

Because the ATA interface (either serial or parallel) is built into the circuitry of the motherboard, if there is a failure of the port you'll have to find a way to work around the old connector. Similarly, if you want to change an older motherboard to add Serial ATA (or to add Parallel ATA to a current motherboard for downward compatibility) you'll need to install an adapter card in an available bus slot. Parallel ATA adapters have been available for many years; add-on Serial ATA adapters are more recent products and require the use of the Windows XP or Windows Vista operating system.

On some systems, you may need to disable the built-in disk controller circuitry on the motherboard by moving a jumper or a switch; on some modern machines you can disable the onboard electronics from the Setup control panel. Some systems automatically disable built-in circuitry if a new adapter is detected in the bus. Consult your PC's instruction manual or the manufacturer for details.

NOTE

On some early modern machines, when you disable an onboard IDE interface, each time you boot Windows you will receive a repetitive and annoying reminder that you have new hardware for which there are no drivers. When you do reboot, just click Cancel when Windows asks if you want to search for the appropriate drivers for this new hardware. If you're lucky, the maker of the system BIOS will offer an update that you can download and install.

Removing an existing ATA connection

If you must remove or work around an existing ATA host controller, take all appropriate steps before touching the interior of the case: unplug the PC and ground yourself.

If you are taking out a bus card, remove the screw holding the card to the rear of the computer chassis and pull the ATA paddle card straight up out of the bus connector. If you are disabling a controller on the motherboard, check with the PC's maker to see if you need to change the position of any jumpers or switches.

Examine the cables attached to the old card or the connector on the motherboard. Mark the cables with a small piece of masking tape or clear tape and identify them by writing on the tape with a soft marker; you should also take notes before you disconnect them so that you will be able to reinstall them properly.

On many machines, a small two-wire cable runs from the controller in the bus or from the motherboard to a hard-drive activity light on the front panel of your computer case. It pulls right off the controller card or the motherboard and slides into place on the equivalent pins on the new card.

Dinosaur note: EIDE adapters sometimes are installed in PCI local bus slots. XT-style 8-bit adapter boards with a ROM on the paddle card go in older machines to drive XT-style IDE drives.

Installing a Parallel ATA cable

Most Parallel ATA cables have three connectors. One attaches to the ATA port on the motherboard or on an adapter card in the bus, and the other two are available for connection to Parallel ATA (IDE) drives.

It is possible to install a Parallel ATA cable incorrectly, if you ignore all of the identifying markers. Don't feel bad if you do, though; most experts, including this author, have reversed a ribbon cable more than once and been confronted with a non-working hard disk drive. In almost all instances, though, the only damage is to the ego; once the cable is properly installed, the drive should be recognized and ready to perform work.

Here are the official markers: The cable ends are color-coded in blue for the motherboard end, black for the master ATA drive, and gray for the slave drive that attaches to the middle connector. In addition, most controllers (and some drives) have the number 1 stenciled next to the Pin-1 end of the cable connector. The cable has a red or blue stripe along one edge. Put this edge toward Pin 1 on the drive and the controller. Finally, the connectors are usually keyed to fit in only one direction; one of the openings on the cable's connector is filled in and should make it difficult to seat the cable improperly if the filled-in hole meets a protruding pin in an upside-down installation.

That is, as I say, the "official" markers on a Parallel ATA cable. However, as I write these words I have on the desktop in front of me a mint-condition ATA cable that uses three identical *white* connectors. It does have a red stripe on the Pin-1 end.

You need to know if your controller employs standard or cable select logic to identify devices. In a standard system, it doesn't matter which data connector you use for each drive; the selection of a master or slave drive is made with jumpers or switches on the drives themselves. In a cable select system, the connector you use (middle or end) determines whether a drive is primary or secondary.

Installing a Parallel ATA drive

Jumpers on a Parallel ATA drive tell the system if the device is one of the following:

- The only drive installed in the computer
- One of two drives installed and assigned as the first drive, or master

- One of two drives installed and assigned as the second drive, or slave
- A drive in a system that uses cable select to identify first or slave drives based on which of the two connectors they use

If you're adding a second drive to your system, do your research on web sites and instruction manuals. You want to end up with compatible drives and be able to boot off the drive of your choice. In some rare instances, some drives may not be able to be slaves to another drive's master, or vice versa.

As you might imagine, if you have two identical drives or two similar drives from the same manufacturer, you stand a better chance of setting jumpers properly. That doesn't mean you can't mix a Seagate with a Western Digital — just take care to read the instruction manuals of both drives.

If you're installing a new drive and controller package, check with both manufacturers to be certain they will work together.

Removing a Parallel ATA drive

Remove the system cover. Study the 40-pin ribbon cable at the back of the hard disk, mark it with tape or a soft marker, and make notes so that you'll be able to reinstall it properly. Pay special attention to the red stripe on the flat cable — this indicates the Pin 1 position on the cable to help orient it correctly in the connector. Disconnect the ribbon cable and the four-wire power cord from the hard disk.

On some space-saving desktop cases, you may need to remove the power supply and/or other components, including other drives, to gain access to the bay; this is especially true with space-saving desktop PC cases.

Some modern machines use metal or plastic rails screwed to the side of the hard disk that make it possible to slide the disk in and out of the chassis like a drawer. Some such installations hold the disk in place with clips on the front of the chassis that hold the hard disk. Remove the screws holding the clips in place or squeeze the spring-loaded clips and then slide the hard disk out.

Other drives are held in place by one or more screws on the sides of the drive. Regardless of which system holds your hard disk in place, save any rails, clips, or screws you remove; you will need them for the new hard disk.

On standard systems, set the jumpers or the switches on the drive to distinguish the first drive (called the master) from the second drive (the slave). Consult your instruction manual or call the manufacturer of the drive for assistance if necessary.

Sliding in the drive and connecting cables

Slide the hard disk into the chassis using either rails attached to the side of the drive, or guides that exist in the drive bay. Some systems click into place, while older machines require the use of one or more screws to secure a drive in the bay. Connect the 40-pin ribbon cable. Be sure to connect pin 1 on the ribbon cable to pin 1 on the hard drive. If you have two ATA hard disks in your system, they will probably share the ribbon cable.

Plug in a four-wire power cable from the power supply. Note that the power supply cable connectors are not rectangular. Look at one carefully; two corners have been cut off on a diagonal. Examine the socket on the hard drive carefully and be sure to install the power connector correctly.

Installing a Serial ATA cable

A slender seven-wire Serial ATA cable has two identical connectors. One attaches to the ATA port on the motherboard or on an adapter card in the bus, and the other connects to a Serial ATA drive. It is very difficult to install a Serial ATA cable incorrectly; the connectors have a protruding bump on one side that is intended to mate with a corresponding slot on the receptacle on the controller or drive. You have to work very hard to force a SATA connector in place incorrectly.

Installing a Serial ATA drive

Because each SATA controller is intended to work with only one drive, there is no need to identify a drive as primary or secondary, master or slave. A new SATA drive should come from the factory already configured; very few unusual configurations require a change to any of the jumpers on a serial drive. Your only assignment is to plug the drive you want identified as the system's first in the lowest-numbered controller on the motherboard (usually identified as 0, but sometimes as 1).

Since Serial ATA is a very modern design, most PCs designed to use them have advanced drive bays with plastic rails or even slide-out drawers. Insert the drive in the bay and click or screw it into place.

The data cable installs in only one orientation; the same goes for the power cable from the motherboard.

Removing a Serial ATA drive

Remove the system cover. Mark the seven-wire SATA cable with a tape label to help you install a replacement properly. Disconnect the data cable and the power cable and set them aside. Remove screws or clips that hold the drive in place and slide it out.

Sliding in the drive and connecting cables

Slide the hard disk into the chassis using either rails attached to the side of the drive, or guides that exist in the drive bay. Some systems click into place, while older machines require the use of one or more screws to secure a drive in the bay. Connect the thin seven-wire data cable; it only fits in one orientation. Plug in the SATA power cable from the power supply. The thin connector is notched so that it installs only in the proper orientation.

Using Setup to tell your computer about the hard disk

Begin your configuration process by seeking information from the instruction manual for your new drive. Nearly all current hard drives come with an automatic installation program on diskette which may take care of all of the details. However, on some modern machines and certain hard drives, even with this program, you may have to make settings in the BIOS. The most common BIOS setting is to instruct the system to auto-detect the drive; the BIOS communicates with the drive to determine the proper settings.

If your BIOS will work with auto-detect, you can skip to the next section of this chapter. Otherwise, read on.

On an older system, you will have to choose settings. Once again, consult the instruction manual for the hard drive for specific details. When you enter your computer's Setup screen, you see a list of supported hard disks, complete with number of cylinders and heads. This list was stored in the ROM BIOS when it was manufactured. You may find that the exact IDE drive configuration that you have will be in this hard disk list, especially if you're dealing with a senior citizen or an older modern machine BIOS manufactured before 1990.

Ch 10

Many IDE drives don't fit into the standard drive list, anyway. They may, for example, break a cardinal rule of BIOS-supported hard disks by putting more sectors on the large outer tracks than on the small-diameter inner tracks. The good news is that the drive you select on the Setup screen doesn't have to match the physical configuration of the IDE drive, just the logical configuration.

Multiply heads by cylinders by sectors per track to determine the number of cylinders on a hard disk (this is the logical size). An 84MB IDE drive with 6 heads, 832 cylinders, and 33 sectors per track would have 164,736 sectors. If you select a hard drive type from the BIOS list that contains the same 164,736 sectors (or fewer), the drive will work. It will work even if the drive you pick has 8 heads and 624 cylinders (a different physical configuration) because the IDE drive electronics translate your computer's instructions to read a particular logical sector (in the drive the computer believes is installed) to the actual head-and-cylinder situation in the IDE drive.

If you must choose among a limited list of drive types, pick one as close as possible to your actual IDE logical size (total number of sectors), but pick one a bit smaller rather than a hair too large. Newer ROMs now support a user-definable drive with user-defined cylinder and head counts. Thus, you can easily match the logical size of your IDE drive to the logical size of your user-defined drive by picking an ordinary number of heads (for example, 8) and an ordinary number of sectors per track (17, 39, and 53 are typical values) and calculating the nonstandard number of cylinders you need to make the total number of sectors on the drive less than or equal to the actual number of sectors on your IDE drive.

If you don't have a reasonable size match to choose from, and you don't have (or can't use) a user-definable drive type, it makes sense to get a newer BIOS rather than wasting a quarter or a third of your IDE drive's capacity by entering too small a drive in your computer's CMOS Setup.

NOTE

In some situations, less-than-current network software may not run properly on user-definable drives. Check with your LAN supplier if you have any questions.

Internal Versus External Hard Disk Drives

The original Winchester hard drives were huge washing machine-sized boxes that sat outside the even larger computers they served. (The name Winchester dates back to IBM's design for a drive subsystem with 30MB of fixed-disk storage and 30MB of removable storage; they were called 30-30s, calling to mind the famous Winchester 30-30 rifle.)

With the advent of the personal computer, nearly all hard disk drives moved inside the PCs they were associated with. That is still the situation with the primary hard disk drive for modern machines, but with the arrival of advanced high-speed I/O systems many users no longer bother opening the case to install a new hard drive and instead add an external drive.

Here's why an external drive may make sense:

- Convenience. Adding an external drive is as simple as plugging in a new mouse or keyboard. You'll need to attach the drive to an I/O port and provide electrical power; your operating system may recognize and immediately work with the drive or you may have to add a device driver provided by the drive maker.
- Expansion beyond internal limits. Some modern machines have room for only one or two hard disk drives in internal bays.
- Reduced use of system resources. An external drive does not eat up electrical power from the internal power supply, does not generate heat within the case, and does not make use of IRQs (Interrupts) or other system resources.
- Portability. An external hard drive can easily be moved from machine to machine to deliver a huge block of information without the need for a network. Or the drive can be used for backup purposes and stored in a locked, fireproof safe when not active.

You can attach an external hard drive to your system several ways, including:

- **USB.** The most common modern external I/O system allows as many as 127 devices to attach to a single external bus. Devices are hot-swappable, meaning they can be attached or detached while the computer is running.
- **E-SATA.** The Serial ATA interface that is becoming the standard on new modern machines is due to be joined by an external port

on many machines beginning in 2007 or 2008. E-SATA will function almost identically to a USB port although the number of devices that can be attached to a single port will be limited to just a handful. Devices are hot-swappable.

- **FireWire.** A relatively small number of external devices attach to the IEEE1394 or FireWire port found on some advanced machines. FireWire works in a similar manner to USB. Devices are hot-swappable.
- **SCSI.** A SCSI port can be extended to the outside from a motherboard controller or an adapter card in the bus. SCSI devices can be connected one to another but are not hot-swappable.

I discuss USB and FireWire technology and equipment in Chapter 15. An example of an external USB hard drive, a 300GB Maxtor One-Touch, can be seen in Figure 10-18.

FIGURE 10-18: *A 300GB external USB drive from Maxtor; the device can be the end of a USB connection, or be in the middle of a FireWire connection. The ports on the rear of the device shown here are, from left to right, USB, FireWire, FireWire, and external power supply.*

An older storage system in my office is a four-bay SCSI storage box I assembled myself from easily available components. One bay holds a 1GB Jaz cartridge drive for data backups, a second holds a CD-R, a third bay is used for a speedy Cheetah Wide SCSI drive from Seagate, and the fourth has a DVD-ROM. Each SCSI device is linked to the others by a short internal cable, with the single external cable snaking back from the box to the connector on a SCSI adapter in the PC. The entire subsystem can be transferred from one machine to another by moving just that one cable. It is also shared on the office's local area network.

The box, literally the size of a toaster, includes a small 65-watt power supply, SCSI ID switches and drive activity lights, and even a set of audio output plugs for use with a CD or DVD drive. The hard drive is used to create a mirror of the files to be installed onto the CD-R, enabling quick and uninterrupted transfer of data from one device to the other.

In Figure 10-19, you can see a two-bay SCSI enclosure about to meet a 10,000 RPM 4.5GB Seagate Cheetah SCSI ST34501 hard drive. The drive connects to power, data, SCSI ID, and drive access LEDs within the enclosure; CD-ROM drives also have a pair of audio jacks on the back with an internal connection.

This particular version of the Cheetah drive uses a relatively rare 80-pin SCA adapter that merges data, control, power, and LED connectors in a single attachment. This arrangement is intended for use in swappable hard drive cases, enabling the drive to be removed and transported, or locked away for security.

FIGURE 10-19: *An external SCSI enclosure during the assembly of the subsystem.*

Ch 10

I consulted the back pages of computer supply catalogs to find an adapter that broke out the SCA connectors to a more standard SCSI-3 adapter with a power input and a pin block for SCSI ID and LED wiring. Figure 10-20 shows the adapter.

Figure 10-20: *Installing an SCA converter on the 80-pin, all-in-one connector on the Seagate Cheetah SCSI drive.*

Troubleshooting Hard Drives

Try these solutions to common problems.

Problem: How do I access the CMOS system setup if I want to add information about the new drive?

Solution: The procedure to bring up the Setup screen varies from one ROM BIOS to another; consult your system's instruction manual. On most systems, Setup is available during system bootup. Common instructions call for pressing Esc or the F1 or F2 function keys during bootup. Some systems enable you to access Setup after the system has completed bootup; common instructions to access Setup for such systems include Ctrl + Alt + Esc, Alt + F2, or Ctrl + S.

Problem: The drive won't spin up, or it spins down after a few seconds.

Solution: Check to see that the drive is properly attached to a power cable from the power supply. If the power is good, this problem is probably a drive failure. Contact the manufacturer of the hard drive for assistance. (See the list of hard drive manufacturers in the previous section.)

Problem: A PATA (IDE) drive works as a slave but not as a master — or as a master but not as a slave.

Solution: Check the master/slave jumpers on the hard drive; consult your instruction manual for the proper settings. Different drive manufacturers use different jumper assignments. In some cases, mixing two drives with different speeds or timings can cause the system not to see one of the drives. It may be necessary to swap the assignment of the two drives. (SATA drives connect directly to a port on the motherboard or on an adapter card; with only one device per cable and port.)

Problem: The drive has been installed and the drive parameters have been entered in the CMOS, but the drive won't boot, or the system displays a message of an HDD controller failure or indicates that a drive cannot be accessed.

Solution: The drive must be partitioned and formatted under DOS before it can be accessed.

Problem: Can hard drives be mounted at any angle?

Solution: Consult your instruction manual or hard drive manufacturer. (See Table 10-4.) Most drives can be mounted right side up or on their sides without a problem; it is generally not good practice to mount a drive upside down.

Problem: A new ATA hard disk drive is not detected by the system BIOS.

Solution: Assuming your motherboard's BIOS is capable of working with the ATA standard, here are some steps to take:

- **Verify the cable connections.** Check that both the data cable and power supply cable are properly installed; check to see that the cables are fully seated in connectors and that no pins are bent. The stripe on one edge of the data cable should be matched up to pin #1 on the drive and pin #1 on the motherboard. To test the data cable, use a known-good cable or try the cable from the non-functioning drive on a known-working drive.

▪ **Verify the jumper settings.** If the drive is a master or a stand-alone drive (on a standard data/ribbon cable), the DS jumper needs to be installed, or the DS switch needs to be enabled. If the drive is a slave, the DS jumper must be removed, or the DS jumper must be disabled. If you're using an Ultra-ATA data cable that uses a Cable Select configuration, both master and slave drives must have their CS jumpers installed or the CS switch enabled. Check to see that the Ultra-ATA cables are properly installed — on most systems, the master drive is attached to the end connector, colored black; the slave is connected to the gray middle connector, and the blue connector is attached directly to the motherboard or to an ATA adapter card.

▪ **Swap the ATA adapter card or the drive.** To isolate a problem not solved by working with the cables, you can try swapping a known-good adapter card into your system to see if it will recognize your drive. Or, you can temporarily install a known-good hard drive (be sure to back up any irreplaceable data).

SUMMARY

Phew! That's a lot of hard drive information, but then again, there have been quite a few steps along the evolutionary path from the day of the dinosaurs to today. I examine one more class of hard drive — removable drives used for transfer, security, and expandability — in the next chapter.

Ch
10

Chapter 11

Removable Media Hard Drives

Throughout this book, I've preached the critical importance of backing up before you go forward.

The key to truly safe computing is to have copies of current data stored at a site away from the machine. I'm not just talking about the threats from hard disk failure or a complete PC meltdown. Theft can also be a serious problem. Your insurance probably covers the theft of your PC and may even repay you for the loss of your programs, but most of us are not covered for the theft of data.

You also have the problem of how to get your data from here to there. How do you easily transport a set of massive graphics files, a few hundred megabytes of downloaded music, a year's worth of department PowerPoint presentations, or a complete copy of your great American novel from one system to another if you don't have a network?

Of all the elements of the PC, data storage has gone through the most change during the evolution from dinosaur to modern machine. This chapter examines many of the most important backup and transport devices; in the next chapter I explore recordable CD and DVD drives, which have smaller capacities and are recorded and read back using non-magnetic technology.

Removable Storage Devices

In the early days of computing, the efforts of many engineers were directed at finding ways to make files smaller and in developing ways to compress (or Zip) files to a smaller size. After all, floppy disks could only hold (at first) a few hundred kilobytes and later topped out at 1.44MB. Hard disk drives were very expensive. And dial-up modems were very slow.

All of that has changed, of course, for two interrelated reasons:

- The cost of storage devices has tumbled to tiny fractions of what they once were. Two examples: 70GB Iomega Rev disks, which cost about 89 cents per gigabyte in 2006, and 4.7GB DVD + RW discs for about 10 cents per gigabyte.
- The graphically based Windows operating system and the applications that run under it no longer make much of an effort to keep file sizes in check. Some programs are a gigabyte or larger, and digital photos and sound files can easily require anywhere from a few gigabytes to dozens of gigabytes of space.

By this point in the book, you should certainly understand my professional aversion to putting all of my eggs in one electronic basket. I maintain live backups of important projects on secondary internal and external hard drives and regularly burn CDs or DVDs with backup copies that are stored outside the computer.

For your purposes in this book, I divide storage devices in this way:

- **Internal or fixed storage.** This is primarily a hard disk drive. These are very fast and easy to use and you always know where they are: right there inside your machine. That's the good news; the bad news is that if the machine is stolen, catches fire, or suffers cataclysmic damage all of the data on the internal drive can be lost. We've covered hard drives in Chapter 10.

■ **External storage.** These are devices that attach to a port on the computer or to an Ethernet hub or switch on your network. (The connection was typically a USB or FireWire port for current machines, with eSATA a developing option. Some older modern machines used a SCSI port.) These devices include one or more platters for storage as well as the mechanism to store them, electronics for encoding and decoding data, a power supply, a case, and a cable. In theory, these devices can be unplugged and locked away for safekeeping, although that is not the way most are used. Instead, external storage devices are popular because they are an easy way to add disk space without having to open the PC and play around with internal cables and settings. These devices are explored in Chapter 15.

■ **Removable media hard drives.** These are devices where the media can be taken out and a new recording package installed. The advantages are many. The media can be stored in a separate location for security or shipped to another location for transfer of its contents. And although the initial cost of a removable media device may be higher than that for a fixed external storage device, a removable media storage unit essentially has an *unlimited* capacity. When one platter or cartridge is filled, it can be replaced with another . . . as many times as you want. That's what we're talking about in this chapter.

I'll also make brief mention of a very simple alternative device for easy storage and transfer: a USB flash drive (also known as a thumb drive or a USB key). These little devices, smaller than a stick of gum, hold a block of flash memory that will hold data without the need for a continuous source of power. There are no moving parts, and like all of the other technology in this book, the direction of prices is unremittingly downward. They're included in this chapter because they are a close cousin to a hard disk (without the need for a spinning platter).

Over the history of personal computers there have been many attempts at producing the ultimate removable media storage device. The mix keeps changing, and a number of products (and manufacturers) have fallen by the wayside; as this book goes to press, the leading maker of removable media hard drives is Iomega and its main products are the Zip and Rev drives. Figure 11-1 shows a selection of some of the devices I've worked with.

FIGURE 11-1: *A cornucopia of large-capacity removable storage media, including outmoded but still workable SyQuest 44MB and 270MB cartridges, a CD-R write-once read-many times disc with a capacity of more than 600MB, an older streaming tape backup cartridge with a capacity of about 60MB, an Iomega Jaz cartridge that can hold 1GB of information, and a 100MB Zip disk, also from Iomega. Iomega has replaced the Jaz system with the much larger-capacity Rev system, while the relatively inexpensive and simple Zip family has been extended to 250MB and 750MB versions.*

CROSS-REFERENCE

I explore recordable and rewritable CD and DVD drives in detail in Chapter 12.

Mega-floppy disks: Zips, Revs, and SuperDisks

Iomega woke up the computer industry in 1995 with the introduction of the low-cost Zip drive, which stores an impressive 100MB of data on a special 3.5-inch floppy disk. Although not quite as fast as earlier technology, such as Bernoulli or SyQuest drives, it won converts based on its low price and simplicity of use. The Zip 100 has a data transfer rate of 1.4MB per second and an access time of 29 milliseconds (ms). At the time of this writing, you can purchase an internal Zip drive for as little as $50, an external parallel port or SCSI device for about $100, and a USB model for about $125. At the close of 2006 Zip cartridges for the 100MB drives cost less than $10 each, or about 10 cents per megabyte.

Zip drives suffered from an unusually high failure rate in early years, sometimes destroying disks as they failed. Current devices are more reliable. Most users employ Zips for data transfer from machine to machine, not as a backup device.

The Zip drive — widely used in graphics departments and other applications where it is necessary to transport or archive large files between clients or unrelated companies — is available in 100MB and 250MB versions. The larger-capacity drive also reads the smaller disks. Zips are sold with SCSI, USB, and parallel port connections in internal and external versions. Figure 11-2 shows an internal 100MB Zip drive. An external 250MB Zip drive is shown in Figure 11-3. Zip 250 followed the 1995 release of the Zip 100 in 1999. Zip 250 units are available in an internal version, plus FireWire, SCSI, and USB external models; a parallel port version was offered, but has been supplanted by USB technology.

In 2004, the family was expanded to include a 750MB drive, which also can read and write 250MB discs; it can read, but not write, to 100MB media. The latest incarnation of the decade-old technology added internal SATA to its connection options. Details of the Zip family are shown in Table 11-1. For the latest information on Iomega products, consult www.iomega.com.

FIGURE 11-2: *An internal 100MB Zip drive. This version of the drive attaches to a PATA (IDE) connector on the motherboard or in the bus of the computer. In the setup pictured, the 3.5-inch-wide Zip drive is mounted in an available 5.25-inch bay.*

Courtesy of Iomega Corporation

FIGURE 11-3: *An external 250MB Zip drive. Such devices are available in USB and FireWire versions. The latest member of the Zip family uses discs with a capacity of 750MB.*

TABLE 11-1: Iomega Zip Drives

	Zip 100	Zip 250	Zip 750
Capacity	100MB	250MB	750
Read/Write Compatibility	100MB discs	250, 100MB discs	750, 250MB discs
Read-only Compatibility			100MB discs
Average Seek Time	29 ms	29 ms to 40 ms*	<29 ms

USB model without separate power source is slightly slower than PATA model.

Ch 11

The Zip drive was the winner in a competition against the SuperDisk technology from Imation Corporation and its licensees. For details about SuperDisk drives, which can store 120MB or 240MB on a cartridge, see the appendix to this chapter.

Iomega also offered a device called the Jaz drive from 1995 through 2003. The system could store 1GB or 2GB of data on a removable cartridge. The original version operated at a respectable 6.6MB per second transfer rate and a 12 ms access time — just slightly slower than a typical hard drive. The later 2GB model was 30-percent faster. Most Jaz devices required use of a SCSI interface. The model line never caught on, and has been replaced by the Rev family. A would-be competitor, the Castlewood Orb drive, had even less success; you can read some of its details in the Chapter 10 appendix on the CD. Specifications for Jaz drives are shown in Table 11-2.

TABLE 11-2: Iomega Jaz Drives

	1GB	2GB
Capacity	1.07GB	2GB
Maximum Transfer Rate:		
SCSI	6.62MBps	8.7MBps
Average Seek Time	10 ms	10 ms
Disk Rotational Speed	5,400 rpm	5,400 rpm

External Hard Drives

Although they are not often thought of as a form of removable storage, external hard drives can also be used for that sort of purpose. Hard drives with capacities of 300GB or more are available in versions that use USB, FireWire, Ethernet or SCSI connections. These drives can be easily unplugged and moved from machine to machine or locked in a safe as a form of secure storage.

At the time of this writing, the best deals can be found on USB drives — devices that are capable of interfacing to your computer under the USB 2.0 standard that permits a transfer rate of 480MB per second, as much as 40 times faster than the original USB standard. At the end of 2006 drives with *eSATA (External SATA)* interfaces are appearing and I expect this interface to be widely available before the next version of this book arrives.

CROSS-REFERENCE

I discuss external USB drives in more detail in Chapter 15.

External drives are typically priced about $50 to $75 more than internal drives because of the cost of the necessary case, power supply, and cable.

Flash memory (USB Memory Keys)

Flash memory is a form of nonvolatile memory, similar to the SD, Memory Stick, SmartMedia, CompactFlash, and other, similar memory modules used in digital cameras and portable digital music players. The matchbook-sized memory cards are not in ordinary use on desktop PCs. You can, however, purchase a reader that allows you to download data from a camera or musical device to your PC; most of these readers use the USB port as an interface.

Another class of device is a portable plug-in block of non-volatile RAM, variously referred to as *flash key, USB key, thumb drive,* or *memory key.* One example of a flash memory key is shown in Figure 11-4.

Figure 11-4: *A block of non-volatile RAM resides in a Plug-and-Play container on a key ring in this flash memory key; the device attaches to a USB port.*

Just over two inches long and fashioned as a key fob, DiskOnKey includes its own intelligence and is capable of storing files, as well as running multiple applications directly from the product. It can be used to transport files from office to office, as a security device, and as an easy way to cross boundaries between a PC and an Apple Macintosh without making alterations to either operating system. The device is immediately recognized as a supplementary hard drive by the host computer when it is plugged into a USB port.

Currently the most common capacity is 1GB or 2GB, but much larger versions are available. As this book is written, key disks with 4GB capacity are arriving in the U.S., but the price hasn't dropped in line with the smaller-capacity devices. Key disks with 8GB capacity are available, mostly from foreign suppliers, but use caution if you feel drawn to one of these devices. During 2006 a spate of key disks imported from China and labeled as 8GB devices hit the U.S. market at very attractive prices, but turned out to contain only 32MB to 125MB of storage. Apparently, unscrupulous manufacturers were trying to unload supplies of old, low-capacity chips. During 2007 you likely will see true 8GB key disks in the U.S., but the prices per gigabyte will be higher than smaller units for some time.

Tape Backup Devices

The old reliable backup scheme for a great deal of information is a tape drive, a technology first developed for the early days of mainframe computing. Tape drives lay down information on a moving strip of tape held within a cartridge.

Modern tape drives are offered in internal versions and as stand-alone boxes with dedicated interfaces or parallel port connections. Today's basic units have capacities of 10 to 20GB, with advanced units capable of storing as much as 500GB. With compression of stored data, those 500GB tape drives are capable of holding as much as 1.6 *terabytes* of data. Tape backups are another area in which hardware prices have dropped precipitously in recent years.

Tape devices may be appropriate for huge storage systems, but they can be painfully slow to use for anything other than middle-of-the-night automated backups. The principal reason for their slowness is the fact that tapes store information in a serial fashion — one bit after another down the length of the tape. If the information that you want is located near the beginning of the tape, you can reach it fairly quickly; if it is near the end of the tape, you may have to wait several minutes before the drive is able to fast-forward its way to that location. Think of it as trying to find a particular scene on a VCR tape.

If you purchase a tape drive, I recommend that you choose one that will work with third-party backup software, as well as those offered by the hardware manufacturer. Without such standardization of the data organization and data-encoding scheme, if the built-in tape drive failed, the backup tapes could only be read by a drive of the identical type.

In addition, as with any backup scheme, test your ability to restore data before an emergency arises. I know many companies that have bet their business on tape backup or other technologies, only to discover that they couldn't restore the data when they most needed it. This unfortunate circumstance can occur because of easily corrected hardware or software settings, but you need to know that the settings are wrong before you lose that important data.

Helical-scan drives

DAT and 8mm drives use rotating heads mounted on a slight angle to the width of the tape. The head records a slanted magnetic trail of data across the width of the tape, thus enabling much higher data densities than the ordinary lengthwise track used on quarter-inch tape media. But the rotating heads and sophisticated tape advance mechanism used in helical-scan tape drives are expensive. You can see the difference in recording methods in Figure 11-5.

Ch 11

Q/C Tape

Helical Scan Tape

FIGURE 11-5: *QIC tape versus helical-scan tape. See the appendix for this chapter for information on the QIC tape format.*

These devices were developed in the late 1980s for high-end audio uses, hence the name *digital audiotape*, or DAT. Most DAT drives are SCSI devices, often using the high-speed SCSI-2 version of the standard.

Both 4mm DAT drives and 8mm helical-scan tapes generally hold far more data than quarter-inch tapes. You won't be surprised to learn that the 8mm tape holds roughly twice as much data as the 4mm tape and that 8mm tape drive systems are roughly twice as expensive as 4mm tape drive systems.

High-End Backup Devices

Large computer installations have broken ground with other high-speed, high-capacity backup devices, including magneto-optical recorders and transportable hard drives.

Magneto-optical recorders are similar to CD-ROM in operation. They use special, high-coercivity disks. *Coercivity* is a measure of the strength of the magnetic field needed to write data; the smaller data bits of high-capacity disks demand higher coercivity.

Transportable hard drives first came about as devices for use in high-security settings, including government agencies. At the end of the day, the entire hard drive mechanism was taken out of its holder and placed in a safe. These drives are declining in popularity, although some offices use lightweight versions with parallel interfaces as a high-capacity version of a sneaker net, picking up or delivering data to far-flung machines when carried on foot.

Troubleshooting a Removable Storage Device

The removable storage devices discussed in this chapter attach to your computer through an IDE connector; an SCSI, USB, or FireWire port, or a parallel port.

Too many types of devices and too many possible combinations of controllers, devices, and systems exist to go into step-by-step troubleshooting here. But the good news is that if you run into difficulties with a removable storage device, it is fairly easy to isolate which part of the whole package is the source of the problem.

I assume that your drive was working properly at one time, and now it doesn't. Ask yourself the following questions:

- What has changed since the last time it worked properly? (This is the first question you should ask.)
- Have you added any new hardware? Are all cables properly reinstalled and power cords attached? Are you certain that any new adapter cards are properly seated in the bus connector?
- Have you made changes to IRQs, I/O addresses, or DMA settings? Under Windows 95/98 and later versions, go to the Device Manager and check for conflicts. Change settings, if necessary, to avoid having two devices making the same demand on your PC.
- Have you installed new drivers that may have overwritten earlier ones? Try reinstalling the software and drivers for the hardware that has stopped working.
- Are you certain that the media — the disk, cartridge, or tape — has not failed? Try taking a copy to a coworker or friend with the same hardware and see if it works there; you may also be able to bring the media to a computer store and try it out on a machine there.
- Use a diagnostic program to check that the port is performing properly. Take the portable unit and install it on another machine to see if it works there.

SUMMARY

This chapter examined the growing category of high-capacity removable storage devices, which have moved from a somewhat exotic novelty to an essential add-on for the careful computer user. The next chapter covers another class of hardware that has moved from the fringes to the center of the PC market: CD and DVD devices.

Notes

Chapter 12

CD and DVD Drives

The designers of the first PC almost certainly never imagined that high-tech software programs would one day be stamped out on an assembly line alongside the latest release from Madonna. And they probably never considered the possibility that users would record their own plastic disks with hundreds and thousands of megabytes of data, or hours of music and video.

The still-expanding world of CD and DVD drives present some of the most exciting opportunities for computer owners, who can now do the following:

- Load huge operating systems and office suites from a single disc.
- Make backup disks of their essential data on a CD-R, CD-RW or a DVD recorder.
- Create their own movies and animations.
- Make compilations of music downloaded from the Internet, recorded from broadcast radio, or from their personal collection of CDs, cassettes, and records.

The first CD-ROM players for PCs offered little more than large-capacity platters of text, delivered at a snail's pace of 150K per second. These early drives required complex SCSI or proprietary connections to the system and sold at eye-popping prices. Today, a modern machine can have an inexpensive CD-ROM drive that reads data up to 72 times as fast (10,800K per second) and is capable of delivering movie-like video, high-fidelity audio, and nearly instant access to full encyclopedias of data.

Or, a machine can include a CD-R, which is a device that allows you to record your own disc, or a CD-RW that can write and then rewrite data to a disc multiple times. Today, nearly all modern machines offer a multifunction DVD device that can read and write gigabytes of data on a DVD and maintain compatibility with the older, slower, and less capacious CD design.

The CD Story

CD-ROMs are a computer adaptation of the CDs produced for audio systems, first introduced in 1982 at about the same time that PCs were first mass-marketed. Although the potential of CD-ROMs as a storage medium for computers was immediately obvious, it took a while before prices and capabilities reached acceptable levels.

When CD drives were first introduced for computer use, they were only capable of reading data or music from a CD-ROM (CD read-only memory.) Discs were manufactured by pressing a master into a soft plastic disc to imprint it with a pattern of pits and flat areas that denote the 0s and 1s of digital information.

To read the disc, a CD player focuses a narrow beam of laser light on a section of the spinning disc. Light reflects from the flat surfaces but doesn't reflect from the pits. Inside the CD drive, a photo detector converts these on/off light flashes to electric signals that are brought to your microprocessor across the bus.

Although you can still purchase a CD-ROM drive today, most users have adopted much-more-capable CD-R (CD recordable) or CD-RW (CD rewritable) devices. I discuss CD-Rs and CD-RWs shortly.

Today, a standard CD can hold 700MB or 800MB (some discs promise to accommodate as much as 900MB) of information on a platter that costs just pennies to manufacture. At the factory, CDs are very cheap to produce once the original master has been made. In other words, the first copy of a CD-ROM may cost several thousand dollars to make, but subsequent copies may cost only a few dimes. Obviously, a run of 10,000 copies brings the total price down substantially, but factory-manufactured CDs are not cost-effective for one or two copies.

Players are available in internal and external varieties, with USB, Parallel ATA (IDE), SCSI, and proprietary interfaces. In coming years, External SATA drives are expected on the market. Figure 12-1 shows a basic "bare" internal CD drive.

As I mentioned previously, CD-ROM drives are by definition read-only. The next step up in flexibility is the CD-recordable (CD-R) device, and the even-more-capable CD-rewritable (CD-RW) drives.

Figure 12-1: *A bare CD drive with supporting data and audio cables for a Parallel ATA interface.*

CD-Rs and CD-RWs use focused laser beams to melt pits or change the reflective properties of special CD blanks. They are very well suited to make a small number of copies of discs for personal use, including backups of data. CD-Rs can only be recorded once; CD-RWs can be recorded to, erased, and re-recorded much like a hard disk drive.

Most modern CD drives can read all types of discs: CDs, CD-Rs, and CD-RWs. Early CD-ROM and CD-R drives, though, do not work reliably with CD-RWs because there is less contrast between the reflective and the non-reflective areas on CD-RWs.

How CD-Rs and CD-RWs work

CD-Rs and CD-RWs have the same physical shape as a CD-ROM, but they are not designed to be pressed in a factory; instead they come blank but with a special recording layer.

On a CD-R, the recording layer is made with organic dyes. Depending on the manufacturer, these dyes typically include compounds of green cyanine, gold phthalocyanine, or silver-blue azo. Although some disc makers claim particular advantages to their particular chemical formula, most scientists say the differences among these three dyes are miniscule.

To create a pattern of pits, a CD-R uses a focused laser beam to heat the dye to about 200 degrees Celsius (about 400 degrees Fahrenheit) to melt a permanent gap in the dye. A plastic layer alongside the dye expands into the space to make a highly reflective area. When a CD attempts to read back information from a disc, the reflective area is interpreted by the drive's electronics as a bit of information. The melted area on a CD-R can't be reset to its original condition, and therefore, CD-R discs can't be re-recorded or erased.

On the other hand, a CD-RW disc can be reused hundreds or even thousands of times, depending on the quality of the disc; manufacturers have made great progress in efforts to improve the lifetime of these discs.

The recording layer of a CD-RW disc is typically made of an alloy of silver and other metals, including indium, antimony, and tellurium. The high-powered laser in a CD-RW heats pinpoint areas to 500 to 700 degrees Celsius (about 900 to 1,300 degrees Fahrenheit). This intense heat melts the crystals at the point of focus, changing them to a non-crystalline structure that reflects back less light than the surrounding area.

To erase a CD-RW, the laser heats the recording layer to about 200 degrees Celsius, which is just enough to return the alloy to a reflective crystalline form. Erasing an entire disc requires a sustained heating period; depending on the drive and disc maker, erasing can require twenty minutes to an hour.

Instead of erasing a CD-RW disc, the medium can instead be overwritten (the rewriting in the RW label) in a process that combines erasing and recording in one step. In rewriting, the drive's laser records a new decrystalized pattern on the disc for information and new crystallized areas between the pits by alternating between high-heat, high-energy pulses for recording and low-energy pulses for erasures. Rewriting typically occurs at a slower rate than writing to a virgin disc but faster than a full-disc erase process.

A CD-RW's hardware and electronics are more complex than those of a CD-R drive, and the discs are somewhat more expensive than write-once CD-R discs. In 2007, CD-Rs sold for as little as 10 to 25 cents apiece; CD-RWs were priced from 50 to 60 cents each.

CD disc speed ratings

In addition to a stated capacity, CD media are marketed with a speed rating. At the time of this writing, the highest commonly available speed rating was 52X. These ratings represent the manufacturer's certification of the fastest reliable recording speed for the media.

To get the best results, you should use media that matches the fastest recording speed of your CD-R or CD-RW drive. If you use a disc that is certified at a slower speed, you should adjust the recording speed of your CD-burning software accordingly unless you have determined through your own testing that the drive can record at a higher speed than the disc's rating. Some advanced drives are able to read an identification code on the blank disc and set their recording speed accordingly. A high-speed disc won't record any faster than the top speed of the drive.

Should you use a CD-R or a CD-RW?

First of all, it is becoming increasingly difficult to find a new CD-R in the market; manufacturers have changed over to producing only CD-RW devices. Again, as with other PC components, prices have continued to decline just as capabilities have improved. In 2006, high-speed internal CD-RW drives sold for as little as $40; external USB drives were priced as low as $60.

Current CD-RW drives are very flexible — they can be used to read manufactured CDs, to read and write (once) to a CD-R disc, or to read and write multiple times to a CD-RW disc.

CD-Rs are less expensive to manufacture than CD-RWs, although the price gap between the two types of media has narrowed considerably since each was introduced. In early 2007, I found no-name CD-Rs on sale for $6 for a spindle of 100 discs, which works out to 6 cents apiece; brand names — which may or may not be of higher quality — were selling for about $25 for a spindle of 100, or 25 cents apiece. (Before you invest heavily in either brand name discs or store brands, buy a small quantity of each and conduct your own tests.)

At the same time, bulk purchase prices for CD-RWs dropped to below 60 cents apiece, down from about $20 each when the devices were first introduced about 2000.

CD-R discs are particularly suitable for private archiving and permanent storage. Because CD-R discs are not erasable, they provide some level of audit trail that is useful for some types of data, such as recording financial transactions at a bank. Each day's information can be added to a backup CD-R, but you can't erase previously recorded data, thus preserving the integrity of the archival backup.

To decide which one makes more economic sense, think about the role that CD-Rs or CD-RWs will play in your office or home system. In my office, I use CD-Rs for deep storage and to send very large files to clients outside of my office. At 10 cents for a CD-R and 60 cents for a CD-RW, I would have to reuse the rewritable media at least six times before I'm ahead of the game. If the disc is going out of my office, or if I intend to keep it untouched as an archive, CD-Rs are much more economical. And I have to keep in mind the fact that some of my clients might not have drives capable of reliably reading some CD-RW discs.

CD-ROM, CD-R, and CD-RW discs are sturdy, with a much longer shelf life than tapes or ordinary disks. Because the data is stored physically, magnetic fields can't erase or damage the data, and the optically readable pits are covered with clear plastic, which reduces the chance of accidental damage by abrasion. Although no one has yet been able to test this empirically because the technology is still young, engineers estimate that CD-R and CD-RW discs will remain readable for more than 15 years after being written. You can extend their life by storing them in a stable environment such as a safe or a file cabinet in an air-conditioned office rather than leaving them out on a shelf and subject to direct sunlight and temperature variations.

Ch 12

CD-ROM, CD-R, CD-RW data specifications

As is discussed previously in the chapter, a manufactured CD-ROM is pressed one disc at a time from a mold at a factory while CD-Rs and CD-RWs are created one bit at a time in a recording drive. The end result is very similar.

Unlike most other disk media, the data on a CD-ROM is written in one long spiral track, like the groove on a record. (You do remember record albums, don't you?) But unlike records, early CD-ROM drives played CD-ROMs at a constant linear velocity (CLV). To maintain constant linear velocity (a constant number of inches per second passing the read/write head), these CD-ROM drives use sophisticated drive-spinning mechanisms that spin the drive more slowly as the head gets closer to the outer edge of the disc.

Other types of WORM (write once, read many times) drives and most magneto-optical (MO) disks record data in multiple concentric rings arranged like rows of seats in a stadium rather than a single long spiral. Most other disk media (such as floppy disks, hard disks, Bernoulli cartridges, and Floptical disks) also use this concentric track system. This type of media is read and written at a constant angular velocity (CAV).

Because the outermost edge of a CD is the hardest area to manufacture accurately and the most easily damaged, a CD data track starts at the inside of the disc and spirals out toward the outer edge. Ordinary magnetic disk media, including hard disks and floppy disks, record on the outer tracks first, gradually working their way in toward the crowded central tracks.

CD drive speed

Just as with a hard disk, a CD drive's speed is measured in several ways, but the sorts of demands put on a CD drive are different from those of a hard drive.

The most important measure of speed for a CD drive is its *data transfer rate,* also referred to as *throughput.* Throughput tells you how quickly a CD drive can transfer data from a CD to the computer's data bus.

On a hard drive, speed of access to a bit of information is very important because users typically pick one small data record from a huge database. Because a CD is typically used to supply a long stream of information, such as audio or video for a game or other multimedia

applications, data transfer rate is a more important consideration than speed of access.

When CD drives first arrived on the PC scene, the original data transfer rate standard was 150K per second, which is considerably slower than most other data storage devices. That speed was extremely limiting in multimedia applications, thus preventing PCs from displaying streaming video effectively and requiring more than an hour to record a full disc.

Several years later, a new generation of CD drives was introduced. They were capable of data transfer at 300K per second and became known as double-speed, or 2X, devices. Within a few years, triple-speed (450K per second) and quad-speed (600K per second) drives appeared, and then in short order, 6X-speed (900K per second), 8X-speed (1,200K per second), and 10X-speed (1,500K per second) drives arrived.

Today the top end of consumer CD drives run at speeds of up to 72X (10,800K per second), although a more realistic and reliable maximum speed is 52X. The most advanced CD-R and CD-RW drives are capable of writing at speeds of 52X and rewriting at 10X.

NOTE

Some exceptionally honest drive makers list their reading speeds as a range, such as 40X–52X. This is due to the fact that on a spinning disc, the grooves at or near the center move slower than the grooves toward the outer edge; more data is available at the outer tracks than on the inner ones. Unfortunately, because the data spiral begins on the inside and most CDs are not full, fast CD drives are rarely called upon to deliver data at their highest throughput. But, in general, faster is better.

Early designs for CD drives varied the speed of rotation so that all data passed under the head at the same speed. This required some extra electronics and put some strain on the motor. Modern CD drives, though, have added sophisticated electronics and memory buffers that allow the drive to run at a constant speed while dealing with differing rates of data acquisition in various parts of the disc.

Another reason for multiple spin or retrieval rates for CD drives is that computer data and audio data must be read at different rates on double-speed and faster drives. The standard speed for audio information was set at 153.6K per second (usually rounded to 150K per second) when the first CDs were created. Computer data was originally intended to be read at the same rate, but as CD technology advanced, the reading speed of data doubled, doubled again, and then doubled again. However, the standard for audio data transfer has remained unchanged. If you were to read a song at 600K per second, it would sound like Alvin the Chipmunk on helium. So when a CD drive needs to transfer audio information, the drive must slow down to 150K per second. When it goes back to data, it speeds up.

In Table 12-1 you find a guide to the meaning of X in CD drive speeds.

TABLE 12-1: The Meaning of X

Drive Speed	Data Transfer Rate	Access Time
1X	150KB/second	400 ms
2X	300KB/second	300 ms
3X	450KB/second	200 ms
4X	600KB/second	150 ms
6X	900KB/second	150 ms
8X to 12X	1.2MB/second to 1.8MB/second	100 ms
16X to 24X	2.4MB/second to 3.6MB/second	90 ms
32X to 52X	4.8MB/second to 7.8MB/second	85 ms

CD-R and CD-RW drives list their speeds for their various functions. The specifications for a CD-R tell you how fast they record and how fast they read a disc with data already in place. A CD-RW lists three speeds: recording on a write-once CD-R disc, recording on a multiple-write CD-RW, and reading a disc with data.

What does the writing speed of a CD-R mean in actual time? Data recorded to disc at 1X moves at about 150KBps, or about 9MB per minute. A fast CD-R drive will save you more than an hour per disc, as Table 12-2 shows.

TABLE 12-2: The Value of X

Recording Speed	Time Required
CD 1X recording 650MB of data	74 minutes
CD 2X recording 650MB of data	37 minutes
CD 4X recording 650MB of data	18.5 minutes
CD 8X recording 650MB of data	9.2 minutes

Recording Speed	Time Required
CD 12X recording 650MB of data	6 minutes
CD 16X recording 650MB of data	4.6 minutes
CD 24X recording 650MB of data	3 minutes
CD 32X recording 650MB of data	2.3 minutes

Access speed is the other critical indication of the meaningful speed of a CD drive. This specification tells you, on average, how long it takes the drive mechanism to locate a particular block of information and move its read head into position to begin data transfer.

Access speed is most important for applications, such as a database, in which you need to pick up a number of small blocks of data in rapid succession. It is generally less important in playing audio, video, and multimedia games because once the drive locates a particular section, all the CD has to do is unload a large section of contiguous video and audio.

The lower the access speed, the faster the CD drive responds to requests for information. Therefore, look for the best combination of high throughput and low access speed. Current consumer-grade CD drives have access speeds of about 100ms, which is slower than a hard drive but more than adequate when it comes to retrieving large blocks of information and to initiate the start of streaming audio or video.

Data buffer

In general, a bigger data buffer is better, assuming that the buffer is properly designed. Think of a buffer as a first-in, first-out staging area. When the system is momentarily busy and can't accept data, data read from the CD is held in the buffer. When the system is ready for the data, the information held in the memory chips that make up the buffer can be delivered many times faster than data that must be fetched from the CD. With a buffer, a CD drive does not have to stop and then resume delivering data as often as it does without a buffer. (The system does have other chores to attend to and can't always just serve the CD drive.)

Early CD drives had no buffer, but then moved to 64K and then 256K memory chips. Current models include buffers of 2MB or more.

Ch 12

CD capacity

The capacity of a CD disc depends on two factors: the data encoding specification used by the publisher of the disc, and how much of the available space the publisher actually uses. The range of maximum capacities for consumer products runs from about 540MB to 800MB.

The nature of the material recorded on the disc also can affect its capacity. Data that is intended to be read in a continuous stream — such as audio and video — may take up slightly less space than data that is intended to be taken in many small chunks, such as database entries.

Because CDs are written in a spiral, the amount of data that you can get on a disc is affected by how tightly spaced the "groove" is. A standard Red Book audio CD or Yellow Book CD permits recording as much as 74 minutes of data. An 80-minute disc has roughly 360,000 sectors instead of the usual 333,000, a theoretical increase in data capacity from 650MB to 703MB.

Of course, this doesn't guarantee that all CD devices will be able to read or write to an 80-minute disc reliably. In fact, you should expect some modern drives and most older devices to have difficulty with them. And consumer CD players in your stereo system or your car are all but certain to balk at playing back an expanded 80-minute disc.

One other issue: a 650MB CD disc actually has a capacity of about 747MB of audio; that's because audio sectors hold 2,352 bytes per sector, while data sectors hold only 2,048 bytes, using the remainder for error correction.

At the time of this writing, manufacturers are experimenting with 90-minute and 99-minute CD-R discs, with capacities of about 791MB and 870MB, respectively. This form of media is all but certain to be unreadable on most CD devices now in use.

Playing music CDs on a computer CD drive

Because computer CD drives are direct descendants of audio CDs, all of the mechanical and electronic elements to play music CDs exist. You need to add a proper device driver and software program that enables the selection of specific tracks.

Most modern CD units have an external jack for directly attaching a headphone; there is usually a volume control but no other facilities to adjust the quality of the sound.

Microsoft Windows users can play CD music tracks with the Windows Media Player that is part of the operating system. For more fancy options, including the capability to shuffle tracks, make random selections, or create a directory of songs by name, you can use a specialized music CD program starting with applications shipped as part of a package with sound cards from most makers.

An internal analog output connects the CD to your sound card, allowing you to use the sound card to drive speakers attached to your PC. You can also use the sound card to record tracks or samples from a CD onto your hard drive. Keep in mind that in doing so, you are sending the data on the original CD through two conversions: from digital information on the disc through a digital-to-analog converter on the CD and then through an analog-to-digital converter on the sound card. You are also giving up a lot of the precision that is part of a digitally recorded and stored music file.

Most modern CD drives also allow you to directly output the digital audio files from a disc, in what is called *digital audio extraction*. You can use this facility to directly record digital files on your hard drive, or output a signal to an advanced home stereo system with digital inputs.

High-Capacity DVDs

A DVD is just like a CD, only more so; much more so, actually. CDs record only on one side and have only a single layer of information, but DVDs can have two layers on one or both sides of the disc. And the spiral tracks of the disc are less than half the width used on a CD.

There were three types of DVDs (and associated readers and writers) in use by consumers in 2007:

- Single-sided, single-layer with a maximum capacity of 4.7GB
- Single-sided, double-layer with a maximum capacity of 8.5GB
- Double-sided, double-layer with a maximum capacity of 17GB

In general, DVD machines are *downwardly compatible,* meaning that the most advanced device (in this case, a double-sided double-layer model) can also work with the two lesser standards. Table 12-3 shows the evolution of modern DVD drive technology.

Ch 12

Table 12-3: DVD Technology Evolution

Description	Capacity	Comments
Single-sided, single layer	2.6GB	Not used in modern machines
Double-sided, single layer	5.2GB	Not used in modern machines
Single-sided, single-layer Version 2	4.7GB	—
Single-sided, double-layer Version 2	8.5GB	—
Double-sided, single-layer Version 2	9.4GB	—
Double-sided, double-layer Version 2	17GB	—

Comparing DVDs to CDs

DVDs pick up extra capacity in four physical ways and one logical way:

- The tracks are much closer together on a DVD as compared to a CD (about 740 nanometers versus 1,600 nanometers).
- The pits that are used as data markers on a DVD are about half the size of those on a CD (400 to 440 nanometers versus 830 nanometers).
- DVDs can be double-sided and/or double-layered (with two sets of data on one side of the disc).
- DVDs use slightly more of the real estate on the disc than CDs, starting closer to the spindle at the center and ending closer to the edge.
- Advanced encoding techniques and improvements in the laser mechanism allow DVDs to demand less overhead for error correction. CDs must devote more space to extra error-checking bits than DVDs.

Just as the CD-ROM was an outgrowth of a consumer audio disc system, DVD traces its roots back to a scheme for a consumer video delivery technology called *digital video disc*. Today, DVD officially stands for *digital versatile disc*, although the name that lies beneath the acronym is rarely used. The video part was dropped as the industry realized that this technology was, indeed, more versatile than just video. DVD is a fast-rising technology destined to change the way you store data on your computer and the way you entertain yourself in front of the tube.

This technology crosses the boundary between entertainment and data storage, promising the possibility of a single device that can work with your computer and your television for music, movies, and data. The original DVD standard was developed to link a special entertainment player to a television set. DVD-ROM is the computer industry's adaptation of that standard for use in PCs. DVD drives for televisions generally can't play computer-written DVD-ROMs, but DVD drives attached to a computer are capable of playing DVD video discs.

Recordable DVDs were introduced in 1998; the first DVD-RAM units could record 2.6GB per side. The high cost of these devices, though, prevented wide acceptance. A year later, the DVD Forum introduced the DVD-RAM 2.0 specification, which boosted capacity of the recordable drives to the same 4.7GB capacity as prerecorded discs. A subsequent DVD RAM 2.1 standard embraced 1.45GB per side mini discs for use in digital cameras and appliances. DVD-RAM drives and their associated discs have mostly fallen by the wayside, replaced by newer and incompatible standards.

As with CD drives, recording and playback speeds are measured as they relate to the speed of the original device in the class. The first generation of DVD-ROMs was able to read data from discs at about 1.3MB per second. Current technology allows DVD-ROMs to read at as much as 16 or 32 times that rate; they are referred to as 16X and 32X devices. As with CDs, several types of drives are in circulation. And as in the early days of the CD, several competing and not-fully-compatible versions of DVD recorders are available. Here are the three basic types of drives:

- **DVDs (also called DVD-Video)** are used for the playback of video on a television set, and are capable of holding an entire movie with added interactive features, including interviews with actors, directors, and critics. In general, this type of drive can only read a commercially produced DVD, not one created on a writer attached to a computer.
- **DVD-ROMs** in a computer can read prerecorded DVDs holding video, audio, and data. They can also read DVDs created by some types of DVD recorders.
- **DVD recorders** in a computer can create data, audio, and video discs.

The basic technology of DVDs is similar to that of CDs. Data is stored in the form of tiny bumps (called *lands*) and holes (called *pits*) recorded along a single spiral track that runs from the interior of the

Ch 12

disc to the outside. A laser beam focuses on the spiral as it spins; the lands reflect light while the pits do not. A converter in the drive converts the pulses into the 0s and 1s that make up the binary code used for data in a computer.

DVDs are able to store much more information than a CD because they use tracks that are much closer together: 0.74 microns wide, compared to 1.6 microns for a CD.

To record the data in a track that is less than half as wide as that found on a CD, DVDs use a different type of laser than employed by a CD. This same laser is unable to read the various types of CDs, and so modern DVD-ROM manufacturers put a second CD-only laser in the drive. The DVD's recording laser heats spots on special recordable discs to change a land into a pit.

Recording-capable DVD drives let you store data on special discs called *blanks*. When the recording laser in these drives hits the light-sensitive material on the disc surface, tiny reflective blocks become nonreflective, like the pits on commercially pressed DVDs.

Today's DVD represents an extraordinarily capable hodgepodge of sometimes conflicting aims and standards. The first DVD-R machines were priced at as much as $15,000. In 2006 they dropped below $1,000; at the time of this writing, DVD read-write devices sell for as little as $70.

The computer, consumer electronics, movie, and record industries embraced DVDs for various purposes. Many of the incompatible standards have been resolved; current DVD drives have set aside most differences and can work with DVD +R and DVD-R writable discs and DVD + RW and DVD-RW rewriteable discs. If you have an older drive it might only work with + or – versions of DVD standards. And DVD-RAM devices have mostly become islands unto themselves, unable to work with any other standard.

The following types of recording-capable DVD drives are available:

- **DVD-R** devices could initially read and write (just once) DVD-R discs at 3.95GB, later increased to 4.7GB. This class of machines can also read and write CD-R and CD-RW discs at 650MB. Single-sided DVD-R media take about half an hour to record at double speed.
- The **DVD-RAM** allows multiple writing and rewriting sessions on special discs loaded in cartridges; the original discs could hold as much as 2.6GB per side. Later versions of DVD-RAM devices advanced to 4.7GB in single-sided cartridges and 9.4GB in

double-sided holders. Developed by Panasonic, Toshiba, and Hitachi, the discs use a phase-change chemical allowing for multiple writing and rewriting. The resulting discs are not compatible with standard DVD-ROM drives.

In late 2006, manufacturers began preparing drives that work with a new specification, DVD-RAM2. Included under that label are 6X, 8X, 12X, and 16X formats in a protected cartridge. Developers were quick to point out that DVD-RAM2 discs may not work reliably — or at all — if installed in older DVD-RAM drives or other DVD designs. At best, the older drives may reject the media; at worst, they may grab hold of the disc and refuse to release it using ordinary eject procedures. Discs using this new technology are expected to be marketed using a RAM2 icon.

- **DVD-RW (DVD-Rewritable)** was first developed for use in consumer electronics devices, including DVD video recorders; it, too, has a capacity of 4.7GB. Developed by Pioneer, similar to CD-RW in design, it uses a phase-change chemical for multiple recording. Sold in Japan as a home video recorder.
- **DVD + RW (DVD Plus Rewritable)** was backed by the rival DVD + RW Alliance, which is primarily backed by Hewlett-Packard, Philips, Ricoh, and Thomson Multimedia. It can be used for data as well as video and consumer electronics applications, and as first released, supports storage of as much as 4.7GB on single-sided discs and 9.4GB on double-sided media. DVD + RW units are capable of reading and multiple writes to DVD + RW media, as well as the ability to record CD-R and CD-RW discs and read DVD-R and DVD-RW discs.

One potential advantage of DVD + RW is the ability to transparently switch between data and video modes, allowing use for interactive training and entertainment. A future enhancement of the standard will include support for DVD + R (write-once) media. Developed by Sony, HP, Yamaha, and Philips. Uses a phase-change chemical for multiple recording; high-frequency wobbled grooves allow discs to be used in DVD-ROM drives.

How DVD drives work

DVD drives and recorders work similarly to their CD equivalents. Data is written by using phase-change recording; the heat of a laser changes a spot from crystalline to a less-reflective form. When the disc is read, the laser detects differences between reflective and non-reflective areas and converts them to 0s and 1s. To erase or rewrite a block of data, a lower-powered laser reheats portions of the disc to change them back to crystalline form.

The main difference between the two types of systems is the density of data. A conventional CD platter has a single substrate on a 1.2mm-thick disc, while DVDs layer two 0.6mm substrates on the same 1.2mm platter. The DVD drives use a shorter wavelength of light as well. CD-ROM drive lasers operate at about 780 nanometers, in the infrared range, and DVD drives use a light source between 650 and 635 nanometers (red light).

On a single-layer DVD, the track starts at the inside of the disc (nearest to the spindle hole) and works its way out in a long spiral to the outside. (That single track, if stretched out in a straight line, would reach for nearly 7.5 miles.) A double-layer DVD can be set up with both tracks beginning at the inside, or the second layer can work from the outside in, allowing a seamless or near-seamless transition in the stream of data — especially important if the disc is used for audio or video.

The tracks are incredibly thin and close to each other; the pits and bumps are no more than 320 nanometers wide and the tracks are separated by a distance of just 740 nanometers. A nanometer is one-billionth of a meter; 740 nanometers is equal to about .00003 (three hundred-thousandths) of an inch. Just for comparison's sake, a typical human hair averages about 80 nanometers in width.

Nearly all designs for high-capacity double-sided DVDs require the discs to reside in cartridges or caddies, although (like early CD-ROM designs) this may change over time.

You can see Hollywood's influence on these specifications in the fact that early DVD drives were designed to accommodate a feature film's typical running length of about two hours. But the DVD-ROM specification goes beyond mere picture and sound.

With compression, a full-motion image requires about 3,500 kilobits per second to display. Stereo surround-sound demands an additional 384 kilobits per second. But the international entertainment industry lobbied for three additional sound tracks for foreign language dubbing, plus four tracks of information to enable the inclusion of a quartet of subtitles. Another use of the image storage space would be to offer different versions of the same film — perhaps a PG-13 and an R version, with a password protection device on the player so that parents can provide guidance. The total space envisioned for video and audio entertainment would then require about 4,692 kilobits per second; multiply that by two hours, and you have space for a full motion picture with bells and whistles on one side of a DVD disc.

DVD is also set up to display movies in three different ways, depending on personal preference and the artistic judgment of the director. The wide screen version yields an anamorphic video signal that can be used with a special wide-screen television set to fill the entire screen as if it were a movie screen. The pan and scan version uses current methodology to fill the screen of a traditional television with a specially edited version of the film that does not cut off the parts of the image that would otherwise appear off the edges of the screen. The letterbox mode displays the full image across the width of a traditional TV screen and fills the top and bottom with black bands.

The DVD-ROM specification includes MPEG-2 compression to pack as much image information as possible on the disc. MPEG is a form of differencing compression. A basic frame is stored, and then subsequent bits of information describe the difference between the reference frame and subsequent frames.

Playing audio CDs on a computer DVD drive

A DVD drive can play the sounds and music of a standard audio CD.

In addition, there is the potential to record and play back audio from a DVD at a much higher quality. The difference lies in a DVD's sampling rate and the fact that sounds are sampled with 24 bits of information rather than 16 bits. A 16-bit computer word can hold 65,535 values; a 24-bit word can contain 16,777,215 values.

That said, there are not yet many DVD discs that make use of the best possible specifications for purely audio discs; most merely emulate a CD. However, many DVD movies include surround-sound Dolby.

That situation may change in coming years. By lowering the sampling rate or depth of a DVD, as much as seven hours of CD-quality audio can be stored on a DVD.

In Table 12-4 you can see the possibilities for CD and DVD audio.

TABLE 12-4: CD and DVD Audio

	CD Audio	DVD Audio
Sampling Rate	Up to 44.1 kHz	Up to 192 kHz
Sample Depth	Up to 16 bits	Up to 24 bits
Minutes of audio at maximum quality	74 minutes	74 minutes
Minutes of audio at best CD quality	74 minutes	Up to seven hours

Ch
12

System requirements for a DVD

Nearly all current PCs come equipped with one or another form of CD or DVD; modern motherboards and operating systems are well suited to work with them. If you're working with an older machine and you are enticed into adding a CD/DVD or upgrading from a CD drive to a DVD drive, make sure you have the CPU horsepower required to make it work adequately.

Most consumer-grade DVD-ROMs use the computer's CPU to do the processing of MPEG-2 video for movies and multimedia applications; this is not a strain for computers with microprocessors running at about 300 MHz and faster. On slower computers, movies may drop frames or not run at all.

If you have a senior-citizen machine, you may be able to take the load off your CPU by installing an inexpensive MPEG-2 card, which has its own dedicated processor for video purposes.

When it comes to playing back a video DVD, your computer monitor offers better resolution than a television set. To get the best sound quality, connect the output of the DVD to an audio system that accepts digital audio input and can process Dolby Digital surround-sound (sometimes referred to as 5.1-channel sound).

Coming Attractions: Blu-ray and HD-DVD Discs

In 2006, the first of a new generation of high-capacity, high-definition but incompatible optical discs began arriving in the market. The Blu-ray disc, developed by a consortium of companies led by Sony, is capable of storing as much as 25GB of information per layer and 50GB on a dual-layer disk. In theory, the design could permit 100GB on each side of a double-sided disc. (TDK, Sony, and other leading digital media producers announced in 2006 that they had developed a 200GB Blu-Ray technology; products using the new discs were not yet available as this book was written.)

A competing standard, HD-DVD, can store "only" 15GB of data per layer in its initial design, but may be less expensive to produce.

Both new technologies are based around a blue laser for reading and writing. Blue lasers have a shorter wavelength (about 405 nanometers) than the red laser used in a current DVD (about 650 nanometers) or the infrared laser for a CD (about 780 nanometers). The shorter the wavelength, the greater the ability of the drive to work with tracks that are closer together and with smaller pits or markers on the disc.

Blu-ray and HD-DVD discs are not compatible with each other, and are also incompatible with previous DVD devices. As this book goes to press, the first Blu-ray read-write drives were arriving on the market, priced at about $1,000; unless you absolutely must have the capability to produce discs for that standard, you have no reason to be the first on your block to buy one. Just as with every other piece of hardware covered in the eight editions of this book, it is all but certain that prices will plunge — and capabilities will rise — in a relatively short period of time.

It seems likely that either Blu-ray or HD-DVD (but probably not both) will become a dominant product and make its way onto computers and that the other standard will fade away, like Betamax and VHS in the early days of VCRs.

CD and DVD Interfaces

Today, five common interface designs are used to connect CD and DVD drives to your PC: Parallel ATA (IDE), USB, FireWire, SCSI, and parallel port. A sixth and seventh means have been introduced: External SATA and SAS (Serial-Attached SCSI), with advanced products for those ports just beginning to make their way to market.

Today for internal CD or DVD drives, the vast majority of modern machines use the Parallel ATA (IDE) internal connector on the motherboard for data interchange. For external drives, the most common interface is a USB port.

By 2008, though, most, if not all, new machines are likely to use a Serial ATA port on the motherboard for inside mounting. External devices will likely be split between USB and External SATA ports.

A SCSI interface, which can be internal or external, can be extended to additional devices by adjustments to switches or jumpers on the drives and addition of necessary device drivers and other software to the system.

Internal devices

Making a connection to an internal Parallel ATA (IDE) or a Serial ATA port is relatively easy using standardized connectors. The process does require opening the computer's case and connecting cables and power supplies.

If you're dealing with a PATA port, each cable has three connectors: one for the motherboard and two for IDE devices. One of the devices is identified to the system as the primary (or master) drive and the other as the secondary (or slave) device. Some manufacturers strongly recommend that your CD drive not be installed on the same Parallel ATA interface with a hard drive, so that the hard drive is not slowed down because of the lower access and transfer speed of the CD drive.

Among the beauties of the SATA port is its use of a single cable for each device; there is no primary or secondary device and therefore no competition amongst devices for resources or supremacy. (Other advantages of SATA, which I explore in more detail in Chapter 10, is the fact that the data cable is also a thin and flexible set of wires instead of the cumbersome ribbon cable of a Parallel ATA system.)

External devices

The simplest way to add a CD or DVD drive is to attach an external device to a port (USB or FireWire) or to an External SATA connector. All three of these I/O ports are capable of recognizing a new device and working with the operating system to install any needed device drivers or other software. And all three have the advantage of being hot swappable, meaning that a device can be installed (or powered on) after the PC is up and running; you can turn them off or remove them without shutting down the machine. External devices typically cost about $25 to $50 more than an internal device; the drive itself is the same but the extra money pays for a case, cable, and power supply. Because of its power demands for reading and (especially) writing discs, the DVD-RW requires an external AC adapter.

A technology that is now relegated to the dinosaur bin is an EPP (enhanced parallel port). I worked with one such device, a Backpack portable CD-ROM drive, shown in Figure 12-2. These devices were made obsolete by the arrival of the USB port; however, if you are working with dinosaur hardware or software that predates USB you may be able to find a parallel port CD or CD-R for sale at Internet auction sites or on the dusty back shelves of a used computer equipment store. Parallel port CDs were not particularly fast, and some uses — including streaming video — are beyond their capabilities.

Similarly, although the first round of CD drives included many that used a SCSI interface, that design has also gone over to the dinosaur graveyard. Although these drives were capable for their time, they offer no advantage over a USB connection. Again, you may need to locate a used model if you must replace a failed SCSI drive. Figure 12-3 shows a CD-R unit that connects to an SCSI port.

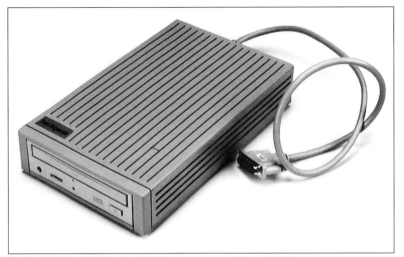

Figure 12-2: *This Backpack external CD-ROM drive was one solution to adding a drive to older modern machines, connecting to the parallel port, without the need to install internal adapters or cables.*

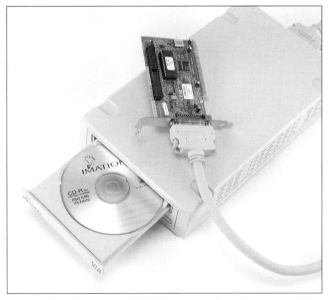

Figure 12-3: *An external CD-R from Imation that uses a SCSI connection to record at speeds up to 8X and play back at a respectable 20X rate.*

Ch 12

Installing an internal CD or DVD drive

On the hardware side, you install CD and DVD drives the same way.

Internal devices connect to a data stream from a controller on the motherboard. They also require a power cable, and in many older installations there is also a separate set of cables to bring the drive's audio output, or the audio input, to and from a sound card or sound circuitry integrated on the motherboard. Modern systems using Windows 2000, XP, or Vista commonly use a feature called *Compact Disc Digital Audio (CDDA)*, which sends a CD's or DVD's audio output over the data connection (either internal IDE, external USB, or SATA) onto the bus where it can be captured and used by the sound card. See Figure 12-4.

Windows XP and Vista are delivered with CDDA enabled as the default setting; users of Windows 2000 will have to enable it. To turn on CDDA, go to the Control Panel and double-click the System icon. In the System Properties dialog box, click the Hardware tab. Click the Device Manager button and then double-click the DVD/CD-ROM icon to display the list of installed and detected optical devices. Right-click the icon for the drive you want to work on; from the menu that appears click Properties. Locate the Digital CD Playback box and select the Enable Digital CD Audio for This CD-ROM Device check box.

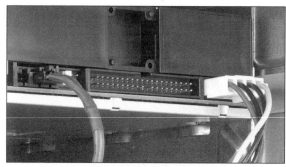

FIGURE 12-4: *The connectors on the back of this older internal CD-RW are, from left to right, an empty connector for Digital Audio output (SPDIF) for some advanced sound card functions; a CD Audio analog output for playing standard audio through a sound card; a set of jumpers for configuration adjustments; an open connector for an IDE data cable, and a power cable. Newer models make use of CDDA to send audio signals over the bus.*

Internal drives require access to the outside of the case for insertion and removal of discs; in most installations the drive is held in place in an internal bay with a set of metal or plastic rails. The rails may be secured with one or more screws, or click into place with a latch. A drive kit should include rails plus data and audio cables; many cases also come with extra rails in anticipation of upgrades.

NOTE

If you install a drive to an IDE controller, try installing it as a master on the secondary IDE connector (assuming it uses an IDE interface). Many of these drives may not work well as the slave drive on an IDE bus. They also may not work well if they share the same IDE connector as a hard disk drive. Here's a place to pay close attention to the instruction manual for the installation of the CD drive.

Installing an external CD or DVD drive

Most modern external CD and DVD drives plug in to an available USB port. In coming years, you can expect to see devices designed to attach to an External SATA port. (Another possibility is devices that connect to a FireWire port.) Modern operating systems are smart enough to detect the presence of a new device and will automatically install needed drivers and software or guide you through that process.

Any of these devices receive their data through the bidirectional port, and are able to send audio and video back to the motherboard and on to the audio and graphics subsystems without need for additional cabling. Most, though, require use of an external AC adapter for power. It is generally considered good practice not to place a CD or DVD device (internal or external) on the same port as a hard disk drive; the demands of the CD or DVD may overwhelm the channel in certain circumstances and, if you are burning an audio or video disc, the information stream from the hard drive may be interrupted, which could corrupt the disc.

Troubleshooting a CD or DVD Installation

If your CD or DVD drive doesn't work after installation, consider taking the following troubleshooting steps:

- Use the Device Properties reports of Windows 95/98 and later Windows versions to check for conflicts among IRQs, DMAs, and I/O ports that may have slipped through, despite the best efforts of the Plug-and-Play wizard. See Chapter 23 for details on troubleshooting Windows.
- Does the unit show up in the Device Manager display of Windows? If not, it may not be receiving electrical power or may not be properly connected to the data bus.
- To check if the drive is receiving power, press its eject button to see if the door will open or one of its front panel lights will flash.
- The next step is to disconnect the power from the PC and remove the covers. Confirm that the power connector is properly attached to the pins on the CD or DVD; most power connectors click into a holder and are unlikely to work themselves out of the socket, but they can be dislodged if they were not fully seated when installed.
- Next check the gray or beige IDE ribbon cable that carries data to and from the computer bus. On nearly all internal storage devices, the red stripe on the cable should be facing the power connector (but check to make sure the cable is properly aligned with the connector on the drive; the red stripe indicates pin one). Check to see that the cable is properly seated and that pins on the socket are not bent out of position.
- Follow the data cable from the CD or DVD to the connector on the motherboard (or in some cases, a connector on a plug-in IDE controller in the bus). Make sure that it is properly installed and that the pins on the socket are not bent out of position.
- If your CD or DVD is receiving power but the drive door won't open, the device may possibly have a mechanical problem. In some instances, a CD or DVD that is not centered properly in the drawer can jam the mechanism. Most devices have a small pinhole on the front to manually eject the drawer; insert a straightened paper clip or small screwdriver into the hole and push gently to open the drawer.
- On a newly installed drive, it is possible that mounting screws tightened too firmly on the mounting rails can block the movement of the drawer. Try loosening the screws slightly.

Problems recording a disc

When everything goes well, burning a CD-R, CD-RW, or DVD-R is more-or-less a point and click operation. However, a recording process can be disrupted or ruined in many, many ways. The main source of the problem is that the making of CDs or DVDs, especially audio or video discs, requires nearly all of the computer's attention. Any other process can interrupt the stream of data to the recorder, resulting in a corrupted disc or an aborted session.

CD and DVD recorders have a small block of memory that serves as a buffer to keep a constant supply of data. Think of the buffer as a bucket; new data comes into the top, while the recorder draws out stored data from the bottom. If the flow of data to the buffer is interrupted long enough to result in a gap, the recording session will stop because of a *buffer underrun*.

Here are some tips on safe recording:

- Make sure that you have enough free space on your hard drive. Most CD-recording software needs temporary space equivalent to the size of the CD that it will create, at least 700MB; DVD-recording software works in a similar manner, although files are typically divided into segments smaller than the total size of the drive, and recorded segment by segment.
- Use the facilities of your recording software to test the facilities of your recorder and the capabilities of your PC before you write your first disc and after any significant change to your setup.
- If your hard disk is more than 5 percent fragmented, run a defragmenter before burning a CD or DVD.
- Keep all discs clean, especially unrecorded ones. Smudges, fingerprints, or dust on a virgin disc can affect the recording process.
- Use a soft-tip marker to label a disc on the top or printed side of a CD or DVD. Don't write on the bottom where the data tracks of a CD are recorded. Never apply an ordinary paper label to a disc; sooner or later they will come off and jam inside your player or recorder.

If you still suffer from interrupted recording, here are some more radical additional steps:

- Disconnect from the Internet.
- Turn off screen savers.
- Disable antivirus software for the duration of the session.
- Turn off any other software that may come to life during the recording session. Note that if a recording session is interrupted, the CD-R is most likely unusable and should be thrown away. A CD-RW or DVD-R can most likely be reformatted and used again.

Ch 12

If you are concerned about the security of the data on a CD that you are throwing away, the best way to disable a disc is to cut it in half. But please be very careful in doing so: the disc can shatter into very sharp pieces. Use a heavy-duty paper cutter or shears, holding the disc at arms length and away from your eyes and face.

Changing the drive letter for a CD or DVD drive

When you install additional drives in a system, other drives may have their identifying drive letters changed. IDE hard drives will automatically occupy the lowest letters, beginning with C.

If you want to adjust the designation for other drives, you can change the Reserved Drive Letter for each. From the desktop, right-click on My Computer. From the menu, choose Properties, and select the Device Manager tab. Expand the listing for the drive that you want to adjust.

Under Windows XP, click Start, then right-click My Computer. From the menu, choose Properties. Select the Hardware tab and then choose Device Manager.

For example, to specify a setting for your CD drive, expand the listing for that class of device by clicking the + symbol. Select your particular device and click on the Properties button and then on the Settings tab.

At the bottom of the panel is the Reserved Drive Letters section. Here you can set a start and end for a range of letters, or you can specify a particular available letter by using the same character for both start and end.

Reboot the system after any change.

SUMMARY

This chapter completes my spin through the world of CDs and DVDS. In the next two chapters, I look at video adapters and computer monitors.

Ch 12

Notes

Chapter 13

Tools Needed:

- Phillips screwdriver

Video Display Adapters and Standards

The video monitor is your view into the computer. No matter how impressive the PC, no matter how dazzling the software, if your monitor is too fuzzy for you to view what's on the screen or too slow to keep up with your work pace, you're looking straight into frustration and aggravation.

Computer video uses different standards and specifications than the Panasonic in your family room. To begin with, your computer monitor receives only one channel—the signal coming from the video card of the PC. The adapter is responsible for converting the information within your computer into a stream of information that can be displayed on your monitor.

On the most basic of levels, all current video adapters (and integrated video circuitry built into some motherboards) are very similar. In theory, any of them will work with modern operating systems and applications including word processors, spreadsheets, databases, and entry-level graphics programs. And all of them will work with online tasks such as the Internet and e-mail. Put another way, if your computer is capable of running a program, any current video adapter can display the application and its data on a screen.

But there are many, many details—small and very large—that stand between the simplest video circuitry and the most advanced boards on the market. The easiest decision has been made by the market: for the consumer, all video cards are aimed at use with the SVGA standard, which demands output of at least 640 × 480 pixels and at least 256 colors; few cards offer just that low a resolution and color palette. After the video standard, though, here are the other variables:

- **The bus design.** On today's modern machines, you may an find old-school PCI bus, a more capable AGP bus dedicated solely to the use of a video adapter, and increasingly, a PCI Express bus with slots including an x16 version that is available for graphics cards. This is a physical specification: Cards designed for a PCI bus work only with slots of that shape and size; the same applies for AGP or PCI Express devices. (Video circuitry that is built onto the motherboard may use an integrated PCI, AGP, or PCI Express bus to communicate with the processor and memory.)
- **The amount of memory on the card.** The larger the amount of dedicated video memory on the card—up to a point—the higher the potential resolution of the image and the more colors and shadings the electronics can produce. Today's most modern cards typically come with 256MB of VRAM, with more advanced devices offering 512MB. Although you may see even larger blocks of memory in years to come, as of today there's not much use for more than 512MB in consumer systems. (Video circuitry integrated onto the motherboard usually does not have dedicated video memory; instead, designers typically "share" some of the system memory for video purposes. That is one of the major drawbacks of using integrated video circuitry. Although the electronics are often similar in capability to those on adapter cards, the fact that the chips have to go out on the bus to use slower and more distant system memory results in lesser performance.)
- **The power of the processor and associated chips.** Video adapters and integrated graphics systems are based around a dedicated microprocessor that oversees the creations of bitmaps

of images and characters. Over the years these processors have become faster and more capable; along with this has come greater demand for electrical power and, at the same time, a significant amount of heat in the case interior. The fastest of graphics processors now come equipped with heat sinks, fans, or both. The two leading manufacturers of name-brand graphics processors are ATI and nVidia; products are marketed directly by those companies as well as third-party boards based around processors from those makers. Graphics card manufacturers tend to release chips in families that offer the same basic features. Each successive (usually higher-numbered) chip in the family expands a bit on the capabilities of lesser processors.

- **The card's output configuration.** Today, current video adapters offer — at a minimum — a VGA connector for an analog CRT monitor or an analog LCD, and a DVI-I connector to provide a direct digital signal for a digital LCD. (The DVI-I connector can be converted with an adapter or specialized cable to work with an analog device.) You may find three other types of output connectors on a modern video adapter; these are related to signal use with a television set rather than a computer monitor. A round seven-receptacle female S-Video connector delivers an analog signal that is separated into brightness and color components, allowing a high-quality image on compatible television sets. Another form of output is a round composite video connector that combines brightness and color components in the same two-wire cable. The third form of television output is a screw-on connector for a CATV coaxial cable, like the one used in cable television systems; this also delivers a composite analog signal.

My philosophy on video cards is this: Head for the middle of the market. If you're going to run any programs that are especially demanding of the graphics subsystem (including editing very large digital images, playing video games, or engaging in simulations designed to take advantage of some particular facilities available on only a certain class of cards), your shopping list is going to be very specific, and probably very expensive. Otherwise, set your target on a video adapter that is a notch or two above the basic capabilities of the circuitry integrated into your motherboard.

This chapter concentrates on the current, ubiquitous SVGA standard. In the appendix on disc you'll also find help in understanding, troubleshooting, and upgrading from dinosaur standards, including VGA, MDA, CGA, and EGA as well as some truly arcane standards as 8514/A, XGA, and TIGA.

What Makes Good Video?

A good place to begin is with a quick description of how monitors work. When you look at a computer screen, as well as at a television, you are looking through the front glass at an image that is drawn on its backside. The image is made up of hundreds of thousands or even millions of little phosphor dots that glow when they are struck by a moving electron beam produced by the monitor's electronics, controlled by the video display adapter, and based on data produced by the computer.

Why am I beginning a discussion of video display adapters by describing how a monitor works? Because a good display is a function of the highest capabilities of the display adapter and the monitor. Today's PCs have all but abandoned text-mode displays, so I'm concentrating on graphics. The next sections describe the elements of monitors.

 CROSS-REFERENCE

Chapter 14 goes into more detail on how monitors work.

Pixels

A *pixel* (the term comes from *picture element*) is an individually controllable set of dot triads on a traditional monitor screen. Each triad consists of one red dot, one green dot, and one blue dot. The number of dot triads in one pixel depends on the size of the pixel and on how close together the dots are located. The video display adapter tells the monitor what color each pixel should be, and the monitor's electronics energize each pixel's red, green, and blue dots to produce the desired color. A pixel on a monitor using Sony's Trinitron technology, which covers the screen with thousands of thin vertical stripes of red, green, and blue phosphor, consists of a short vertical portion of three adjacent stripes.

Another monitor, NEC's ChromaClear, blends dot triads and Trinitron features by using vertical oval phosphors. When combined with a slot mask, the phosphors appear elliptical in shape, compared to round phosphors of dot triads and stripes of a Trinitron.

Resolution

Resolution is a measure of the number of individually controllable pixels on a monitor screen. The higher the stated resolution, the more information can theoretically be displayed, but this is just one part of the sharpness equation. Maximum resolution is determined by the highest capability of the video display adapter and the monitor. A monitor can't display more pixels than a video adapter is capable of describing, and a video display adapter can't command a monitor to use more pixels than the monitor was designed to use.

Resolution is generally described in terms of the number of horizontal dots and the number of vertical dots that a screen can hold. The basic PC resolution is expressed as 640 × 480 pixels, meaning 640 pixels horizontally and 480 pixels vertically. Modern display adapter and monitor combinations routinely display 1,024 × 768 pixels or 1,280 × 1,024 pixels. On current larger monitor screens, resolution generally reaches as much as 1,920 × 1,440 pixels.

Dot pitch

Dot pitch is a monitor specification that tells you how closely together the dots are located. The finer the dot pitch (the lower the number), theoretically, the finer the image. Today's better monitors have a dot pitch of 0.28 mm or less, and as fine as 0.24 mm on some consumer-grade devices. Sometimes monitors are measured in *mask pitch*, which gives a slightly smaller measurement than the monitor's dot pitch, but is otherwise comparable. One exception to dot or mask pitch measurement comes from monitors that use Sony's Trinitron technology; these screens use a grille of fine vertical wires that keep electrons from unintentionally striking neighboring stripes. Specifications for Trinitron devices are measured in *aperture grille pitch*, and 0.24 mm is considered quite good. Another exception is NEC's ChromaClear technology and other dot-mask/Trinitron hybrids, which express the fineness of their screens in mask or *slot pitch*, and like the Trinitron, 0.24 mm is quite good.

Refresh rate

Also called vertical scanning rate, *refresh rate* is a measure of how often the monitor rewrites the screen. The higher the refresh rate, the more stable the image appears and the less chance of apparent flicker. Motion on your computer display or monitor employs the same fool-the-mind trick employed by motion pictures: displaying a changing series of still frames at a rate faster than the human brain can detect the individual images.

Up to a point, the faster the video adapter's refresh rate, the more stable the image appear. And in certain situations, such as a very advanced video game paired with a fast video adapter, there can be situations where the computer's hardware is producing frames at a speed faster than the monitor to display them. The result is a change to the image part of the way through a refresh, resulting in *tearing* of the image or *artifacts* that show parts of the previous frame mixed in with the current one.

Proper hardware or software design calls for *V-Sync (vertical synchronization)*, which requires that the video adapter and computer system match the number of frames produced per second to the maximum ability of the monitor. Today's hardware typically uses refresh rates of between 60 and 120 times per second.

Image quality

Some monitors are simply higher quality than others, using better and brighter phosphors or better electronics that can produce whiter whites and more brilliant colors. On monochrome monitors, the best displays are capable of producing a wide range of grayscale hues that improve the quality of graphics and text. Image quality is mostly in the eye of the beholder, although reviews of monitors can measure brightness and color intensity.

In my opinion, one of the most important and telling measures of image quality is the whiteness of whites and the blackness of blacks, even on a color monitor. Open a word processor application, for example, and set the background color to paper white if it isn't already the default. If black text on this white background doesn't have a crisp black-on-white, printed appearance, the rest of the monitor may not be up to par. Some low-end monitors tend to produce a gray-cast white and black that isn't sharp and distinct.

Number of colors

The more colors a monitor produces, the more apparent depth and realism an onscreen image has. Think of colors as information. The capability of a display to show 30 variations of forest green, for example, makes it possible to have much more detail in a wildlife scene. The number of colors that a monitor can produce is dependent upon the video display adapter. To use more colors, a display adapter needs a great deal of video memory.

Ch
13

Like resolution, the number of colors that an adapter displays affects overall image quality, as well as user acceptability — particularly with today's graphical operating systems and software applications.

Way back when, the most basic display adapters displayed just 16 colors; you'll have a hard time finding an adapter today that is so limited. A 16-color range is enough to determine that color is present on the screen, but you won't be happy with that limited selection after you've had a look at your neighbor's machine, or at a television screen, for that matter. The next step up is 256 colors, which is still much less than what we have come to expect on a modern computer, especially if you use your machine to watch multimedia, play games, or edit photographs. (Just as a point of comparison, a current low-end cell phone with a color screen usually draws its image with a palette of 65,536 [64K] colors.) After you've seen screens capable of displaying thousands or millions of colors, however, you'll set your goals higher.

Just as with screen resolution, the ability of a video adapter or integrated graphics chip to display hundreds, thousands, or millions of colors is related to the amount of video memory it can use to construct an image in the millisecond before it appears on your monitor or LCD.

Most display adapters delivered with today's modern machines hold at least 64MB of dedicated video RAM on the card, and we are not far from when the minimum will be 256MB. Video adapters that are integrated onto the motherboard typically do not have memory of their own, but instead use a portion of the system memory; this is usually done on a *dynamic* basis, meaning that if the adapter needs only 8MB to draw a screen of text, that is all it will grab, but if it needs more for a complex graphic image, it can increase its demand. A typical integrated video system today can use as much as 96MB of system RAM.

To see what your computer is using in current versions of Windows, right-click anywhere on the desktop and choose Properties. When the Display Properties screen appears, click the Settings tab. Here you will see the screen resolution and the color quality in use by your video adapter. You can pull down a list of settings for each of these components by clicking the down arrow to the right.

If you have properly installed your video adapter and its drivers, the Display Properties screen offers only settings that are within your adapter's capabilities. On the most modern of adapters, you may see only a choice of Highest (32 bit) or Medium (16 bit); older adapters may offer settings that identify the number of colors, beginning as low

as 16 or 256, moving on to true color (16 bit for 65K colors) at the minimum, and true color (32 bit for over 4 billion colors).

Speed

The speed at which a video display adapter can construct graphic images and send them to the monitor for display becomes an important measure for graphics programs and graphical user interfaces, such as Windows. The more colors and the greater the resolution, the harder the video display adapter has to work to produce images. Modern adapters, especially those connected to the local bus of the CPU and/or equipped with a graphics accelerator, work much faster than earlier adapters. For any adapter working at its top speed, however, the more information (resolution and/or colors) it displays onscreen, the slower those scenes are constructed and displayed (refresh rate).

Designers boost the speed of video adapters in several ways:

- By tightly integrating the circuitry into a chipset
- By using specialized high-speed memory
- By widening the video bus width on the card

The video bus width is the highway between the chipset and the memory. The top end of video adapters offer a 64-bit or 128-bit bus; the video bus width still has to meet up with and work with the 32-bit or 64-bit PCI or AGP bus on the computer's motherboard.

The Video Display Adapter

The video display adapter has most of the brains of the team; the monitor mostly follows orders. The adapter controls the resolution, the scan rate, and the colors or shades of gray available on a particular monitor. Of course, the adapter can't order color on a monochrome monitor, nor can it ask for a screen resolution greater than the physical capability of the display. By the same token, a monitor with extraordinary facilities is underutilized by working with a low-end display adapter or one with insufficient memory to display a full range of colors.

In the early days of the PC, video standards were based on a *digital signal* — a redirection of the internal bit map within the computer. This delivered a high-quality signal, but one that had to precisely describe every color; until recent years, the cost of memory limited the ability of adapters to work with thousands and millions of colors. With the arrival of the VGA specification, adapters changed over to an analog design that converted the bitmap from digital to analog and opened the door to more colors and gradations. Today, improved electronics and the sharp drop in the cost of memory are fueling a return to digital adapters; they are already used for many LCDs, and in coming years you may see a complete switch to digital output from a video adapter.

NOTE

Current video adapters generally offer both a standard analog VGA connector and a digital DVI-I connector. The analog signal will work with most CRT monitors and many LCD screens that accept that sort of signal. The digital signal can be used without alteration by many LCD screens. And it is easy to add an adapter plug or specialized cable that converts analog to digital, or digital to analog.

In the original design of the PC and on many modern machines, the display adapter is a card that fits into a slot on the expansion bus or — in a local bus or accelerated-graphics-port design — into a slot that connects more or less directly to the CPU.

Nearly all current machines use one of two designs: Entry-level machines often provide video circuitry on the motherboard itself, saving money on components and sharing RAM with the system, while more advanced systems make allowances for the installation of a video adapter, with its own block of memory, in a specialized high-speed bus slot.

Beginning in 2005, motherboard manufacturers almost universally made the changeover to the PCI Express technology. Today, nearly all new research and production of video adapters is directed toward producing devices that plug into a PCI Express x16 slot.

Video adapter interfaces

Think of the video processor in a modern machine as a high-powered image factory, capable of producing huge amounts of pictures (including pictures of letters, words, and numbers) in incredible variations of colors, textures, and motions. But like any other factory, its production is only as good as the ability of its parts supplier to get raw materials in the door, and its trucking system to deliver the product to the user.

To expand a bit on that analogy, a video processor's parts supplier is the computer's microprocessor and system memory, which brings instructions and data. And the trucking system is the computer's data bus, which carries completed product to the display or monitor and keeps the product fresh on a millisecond by millisecond basis.

If the computer produces more data than a video adapter can process, there will be a backup going into the video processor. If the video adapter can generate more information than the system bus can carry in a particular period of time, the jam will occur at the adapter's exit port. The solution is to continue expanding the capabilities of the bus and the processor and design systems.

Today's modern machines use one of three types of graphics interfaces: PCI, AGP, and PCI Express. I discuss these buses in more detail in Chapter 4, but here's a recap:

- **PCI.** The Peripheral Components Interconnect is the oldest and slowest computer bus still in use on older modern machines. It is capable enough for many types of adapters, including those used for sound, network, and low-end I/O functions, including some hard disk and optical disk interfaces. Although video graphics cards are available for the PCI slot, these devices have been much surpassed by more modern graphics systems developed for special-purpose bus designs.
- **AGP.** The Accelerated Graphics Port was designed to provide a direct connection between a graphics adapter and the system processor. AGP, produced in its original specification and then quickly superseded by 2X, 4X, and then 8X designs, has been exclusively used by video adapters. The principal advantage of the AGP design is that it provides a dedicated path between the processor and the adapter, allowing for faster communication. Other advances include the availability to directly read a graphical texture for system memory; PCI Cards had to copy the texture into its own memory first, which slows down response. Motherboard designers typically added a single AGP slot to a motherboard, which also provided a handful of PCI slots for other purposes.
- **PCI Express.** The latest and fastest internal bus design for modern computers, this is a distant cousin to the original PCI specification and design. The biggest change is that PCI Express is a high-speed *serial* communications pathway. The slots offer varying number of links or lanes that can be used separately or

combined for the greatest bandwidth. For example, a PCI Express x16 slot — the most advanced specification as this book goes to press — brings together 16 lanes. Most current video adapters are designed for the x16 slot.

Each specification involves a different and incompatible electrical and physical design. Devices produced for a PCI bus will only install in a PCI slot and not in an older ISA slot or a newer PCI Express slot. AGP devices will only install in AGP slots and must match exactly the speed specification: An AGP 8X slot is larger and incompatible with an AGP 4X slot. PCI Express devices offer interchangeability within the family, but only in what engineers call *downward compatibility*: a PCI Express x1 device will plug into and work with a PCI Express x8 or x16 slot, but not the other way around.

As this book goes to press, there is a virtual tie in the capabilities of an AGP 8X graphics slot and a PCI Express x16 slot. But PCI Express devices are less expensive to produce, and the next round of video adapters is almost certain to open a wide gap between PCI Express and AGP.

Until 1997, nearly all modern machines used a PCI slot for the video display adapter. In the period from 1997 through 2005, most motherboards came equipped with an AGP slot and that was generally the home of the video adapter. In recent years, highly integrated PC motherboards that included onboard video chips were delivered in two styles: with an unfilled AGP slot that is available to upgrade the video capabilities (or add a second card to drive additional monitors), or with only a set of PCI slots. That was the situation with Dell's inexpensive Dimension B110 or near-twin Dimension 1100 machines; the onboard video chips could only be upgraded through installation of a PCI video card, which delivers only a tiny improvement over the integrated electronics. An older PCI card is shown in Figure 13-1.

Beginning with the advent of ATX-design motherboards, most modern machines were built around a motherboard that featured a high-speed, *accelerated graphics port (AGP)* connector for video display adapters that meet its specifications. An example of an AGP card is shown in Figure 13-2.

FIGURE 13-1: *An ATI Radeon 7000 graphics adapter designed for use in a PCI slot. This card was close to the top end of consumer-grade graphics when it was introduced in 2002; it came with 64MB of DDR memory and its onboard processor ran at 300MHz. Its performance is about equal to a modern integrated video chipset, although integrated graphics may have access to a larger amount of system memory for its purposes.*

Although new products are aimed at PCI Express, because of the huge installed base of machines that have AGP slots and the still significant number of machines that only offer PCI slots, you'll still find AGP and PCI cards available for sale as upgrade and replacement modules — and for use as a second adapter in a system that will be used with a pair of monitors; however, little or no new research and development is going into cards that use the older bus connections.

FIGURE 13-2: *This older 4X AGP card is also produced by ATI and based on the same Radeon 7000 processor used in the PCI example shown in Figure 13-1. This particular version offered just 32MB of memory and only a single analog VGA port; thus it was intended for use with a single monitor. A more modern AGP card is typically aimed at installation in a faster 8X AGP slot, and would include at least 256MB of DDR RAM.*

FIGURE 13-3: *A highly capable mid-range PCI Express card, the ATI Radeon X1600 Pro includes 512MB of DDR memory and its processor is certified as supporting all Windows Vista features.*

Today, the major manufacturers of video cards include ATI Technologies and Nvidia, with smaller market shares from companies including Diamond and PNY. Specialized adapters are offered by Matrox. There are also many adapters from less-well-known companies that are based around chips purchased from or licensed by Nvidia and ATI. A modern PCI Express video adapter is shown in Figure 13-3.

This class of high-speed adapter requires fans, heat sinks, or other cooling technologies to remove heat buildup. A failure of the fan can result in the burnout of the video processor or damage to other components within the case. At the low end of the market, many modern machines place the display adapter circuitry on the motherboard itself; among manufacturers of chipsets that deliver video in this way are Intel and Via Technologies. Built-in video circuitry is less expensive than devices that reside on an adapter card because there is no need for a separate card with all of its hardware and electronic components and because the chipsets are designed to share the system memory for graphic purposes, rather than use its own RAM. (If you're shopping for a new machine, the tip-off that the motherboard is home to the video circuitry is a specification that tells you of "shared" RAM.) If the integrated graphics chip is permitted to grab as much as 96MB of RAM—a typical specification for current hardware—that means the amount of memory available to the PC for the operating system and applications is reduced by that amount.

Although there is no slot involved with a built-in video chipset, electrically these devices usually offer the equivalent of an AGP connection. Built-in video circuitry is generally acceptable for most office and Internet tasks, but systems will lag behind in speed and capability when it comes to applications that make heavy demands on graphics such as games and image editing.

In most designs, you can upgrade built-in video circuitry or work around a failed set of chips by plugging a video adapter into a PCI Express, AGP, or PCI slot. (Consult the manufacturer's instruction manual or online resources to see if the built-in circuitry needs to be disabled by the setting of pins on a jumper or through a designation in the CMOS System Setup screen.)

However, you don't have to use an AGP card on a system with an AGP port or a PCI Express card on a machine with a PCI Express slot; you can still plug a video adapter into the PCI bus. (And if you plan on using two monitors, you'll need a second video adapter in the PCI bus.) On the other hand, if you have an older industry-standard architecture (ISA) bus machine, you may find it difficult to obtain state-of-the-art video display adapters; you may have to search sources for used computer parts, or specialty computer suppliers.

All modern video display adapters require installation of device drivers that are added to your operating system to let your operating system know about the capabilities of the card. The instruction manual for the card should give details on installation of the drivers.

Keep in touch with the maker of your display adapter, especially if you have purchased a state-of-the-art device or if your operating system goes through any significant changes. Most display adapter makers regularly post updated or improved versions of their device drivers on the Internet, or will send them to registered users. Newer drivers can improve speed, add features, or fix bugs in previous releases.

In any case, it pays to have a fully capable display adapter and as good a monitor as you can justify buying. If you're upgrading in stages, buy the display adapter first. As noted previously, if the monitor's capabilities are greater than those of the adapter, you won't be able to take advantage of the monitor's capabilities.

You should also realize that many dinosaur PCs can't be upgraded to VGA and SVGA because of limitations in their ROM BIOS. Check with the PC manufacturer or the maker of the video display adapter to be sure. In some cases, you may be able to upgrade the BIOS of an old machine.

Getting Graphics Off the Bus: PCI Express and AGP

For most of the PC's first two decades, graphics information moved along the bus along with other types of data. In the beginning, this was not a problem because graphics were relatively simple and the overall system speed was relatively slow; other slowdowns — including processing power and memory transfer — were more of a bottleneck than was bus congestion.

This all began to change with the arrival of Windows, which used graphics for its user interface. And vast amounts of data began to move along the system bus as users loaded video games, the Internet, and image editors. The solution was the development of direct connections between the graphics adapter and the processor. Clunky early attempts included the *VESA Local Bus (VL Bus)* that extended the original PC bus with a secondary set of connections. In 1997, though, Intel introduced the *AGP (accelerated graphics port),* which was a dedicated superhighway for graphics.

Today, all modern machines use either AGP or the more recent PCI Express as a means of communication between graphics chips and the processor. On machines where the graphics processor is integrated onto the motherboard, the connection follows the same design as AGP or PCI Express without the physical slot and connector.

PCI Express

PCI Express, PCIe, or *PCI-E* (not to be mistaken for PCI-X) is an implementation of the PCI computer bus that uses existing PCI programming concepts, but bases it on a completely different and much faster physical communications protocol. Once again, this is an example of current PCs stepping back from parallel pathways to speedy serial wiring.

The connection between any pair of PCIe devices, or between a PCIe device and the controller on the motherboard, is called a *link.* The specification allows designers to build up links from one or more lanes: the minimum is x1, while today's current motherboards generally offer an x16 slot for using a graphics card. Less demanding devices can work in more advanced slots, but not the other way around — for example, an x1 or x8 device will work in an x16 slot, but an x16 device cannot physically fit or electronically work in an x1 or x8 slot. For more details about PCI Express, see Chapter 4.

PCI Express offers a pair of significant advantages to users. The first is the high bandwidth available in x16 slots, as much as 8GBps, which can be split by the computer as needed for upward or downward communication. The second advantage of the design is its ability to deliver as much as 150 watts of power to adapters, with 75 watts coming from each of two available electrical connections. (By comparison, AGP 8X could only provide about 43 watts in its original form, and about 110 watts in versions that required the use of two power connections from the motherboard.) Table 13-1 shows a comparison of PCI Express (in its currently available x16 specification and the proposed x32 version), AGP, and the PCI bus.

The increased power allows for faster processors and more memory on current video adapters. On the downside, this much power generates a great deal of heat on the card.

When PCI Express was introduced, many graphics adapter makers were able to convert existing AGP designs, which may result in some minor drop in speed; the most modern of graphics adapters are *native* PCI Express devices, meaning they were designed from the ground up to use the new interface.

The PCI Express example shown in Figure 13-3, an ATI Radeon X1600 Pro, incorporates a number of new technologies. For people who have an extreme need for speed, the Radeon X1 series works with a certain class of motherboards that include two (or more) PCI Express x16 slots and a special CrossFire Xpress chipset; the CrossFire specification allows the computer to chain together the functions of two or more adapters.

For the rest of us, it's enough to point to the Radeon's facilities including 3-D imaging and its support for coming enhancements to video output to support high-definition video formats. The Pro version of the card includes 512MB of DDR memory. The processor has 157 million transistors, providing for twelve pixel-shader processors and five vertex-shader processors.

Another advantage of using an advanced card such as ATI's Radeon X1600 Pro or competitive products sold by nVidia is the availability of sophisticated control software for the card. ATI's Catalyst Control Center driver software offers 3-D acceleration control coupled with high-quality graphics and image quality. ATI claims the software uses "safe GPU overclocking" to achieve better performance than competitors. User-oriented features such as programmable hot keys

and custom profiles help you customize the look and feel of your video display.

Multi-card video processing

For some people, with certain needs, one high-speed wide-bandwidth video adapter card is not enough: They need two of them in one computer. Applications that might need such extreme graphics horsepower include commercial simulators, graphic rendering for animation, and the most demanding of video games (or the users of video games who are most demanding).

Today, two solutions allow chaining together the output of multiple video cards. One is SLI from Nvidia, and the other is Crossfire from ATI. With either technology, you need two or more video adapters designed for multi-card processing and a motherboard capable of supporting them.

This is also an area of rapid changes in technology. Consult Nvidia, ATI, or the maker of your motherboard and system for current details and requirements.

As far as performance, linking two graphic cards does not guarantee a doubling in output; with current hardware you can expect to see performance ratings of about 125 to 150 percent greater than one card can deliver. And you have to take into account the high electrical demand of multiple modern video cards and the resulting heat they produce; make certain that your system has sufficient power for such a configuration and that the cooling system is up to the task.

Accelerated Graphics Port (AGP)

The increased demands of graphics programs, and especially 3-D gaming and design applications, moved well beyond the capabilities of the PCI bus in the late 1990s, and in response Intel introduced the *accelerated graphics port (AGP)* design on motherboards in 1997. Although still a capable technical answer to moving vast amounts of graphics data quickly, AGP is in the process of being supplanted by PCI Express.

AGP is not a replacement for the PCI bus as a general I/O interface. AGP is physically, logically, and electrically independent of the PCI bus; it is designed solely for the use of a graphics controller.

Ch 13

TABLE 13-1: Video Bus Comparison	
Bus	**Maximum Theoretical Throughput**
PCI	132MBps on 66MHz system bus
	200MBps on 100MHz system bus
AGP	266MBps
AGP2X	533MBps
AGP4X	1.06GBps
AGP8X	2.12GBps
PCI Express x16	4GBps
PCI Express x32**	8GBps

"Proposed.

The original AGP bus extension ran at 66 MHz, which was twice the speed of the PCI bus at the time of its introduction. The next step was AGP2X, which ran at 133 MHz. Today, modern systems offer AGP4X ports; AGP8X technology is on its way. Like AGP4X, AGP8X implements a 32-bit-wide bus, but the new specification allows a doubling of speed to 533 MHz and supports a data rate of 2GBps.

NOTE

Different sources report data throughput in different ways. Don't be confused. You may see, for example, 4,000 MBps (*megabytes* per second) or 4,000 Mbps (*megabits* per second).

Among the ways AGP speeds video processing is to use main PC memory to hold large 3-D images and their associated complex texture data — in effect, giving the AGP video card an unlimited amount of video memory (or at least up to the limits of available main PC memory). Accordingly, the AGP was intended to be accompanied by a large amount of system memory; happily for PC users, the price of most forms of RAM has dropped precipitously just as the need for more memory has increased.

To speed up data transfer, Intel designed the port as a direct path to the PC's main memory by using a design called *Direct Memory Execute (DIME)*. AGP uses a 32-bit connector, like a PCI device, but the video bus connector has 64 contacts and a 64-bit-wide data path between the graphics chipset on the card and the specialized graphics memory nearby. On an ATX-format motherboard, the AGP slot is positioned between the CPU's support chipsets and the graphics controller. This enables rapid data transfer between the PC's graphics controller and system memory. Conventional technology uses the PCI bus (or whatever expansion bus is part of the design) to pre-fetch graphics data from system memory and deliver it to the graphics controller's RAM; AGP uses a separate high-speed bus for this memory-to-controller data interchange.

With AGP, the graphics controller can execute texture maps directly from system memory rather than caching them in the controller's local RAM. AGP also facilitates transfer and display of motion video, an increasing part of the online and desktop computing experience.

The AGP design enables main system memory to be allocated to support 3-D facilities, enabling high-speed image creation and transport. This sort of design has been previously used in graphics workstations, but not in PCs.

AGP enables 3-D textures to be stored in the computer's memory and transferred to the graphics accelerator at high speed. Because memory in the PC itself can be used to supplement onboard graphics memory, there is less need for more costly specialized graphics memory on the card.

Remember that you need both a motherboard with an AGP slot and an operating system that supports its facilities. Windows 95 does not fully support AGP, and in many cases, Device Manager will report device conflict errors if you attempt to use such a card. If the card works despite the error message, you can continue to use the older operating system; if not, you need to update to Windows 98 or a later version.

Cooling off a hot video card

A modern video card — especially one designed for an AGP8X slot — can draw as much as 150 watts of power. Put your hand above a lit lightbulb of that wattage; it's hot enough to hurt or even to set a piece of thin paper aflame. (Of course the lightbulb is an inefficient user of its power, designed to produce light of a specified output without regard to the resulting heat.)

Newer video adapters made to work with PCI Express slots are more efficient in their electrical design, but still can demand 60 to 100 watts or more. And some users chain together the output of two video cards for advanced graphics effects; in doing so they double the electrical draw. And, while a computer chip is more efficient than a lightbulb, more power consumption translates to more heat.

The generation of that much heat within a closed PC box can be dangerous to the video adapter as well as to other components, including the microprocessor. For that reason, an essential element of a modern machine is a proper cooling system. As I've already discussed in the chapter on case design, heat is removed from a modern machine through a combination of elements: a heat sink or active cooling device on the video adapter and microprocessor, a fan to move cooler air into the case and out an exhaust opening, and a proper design within the case to channel the air over the hottest components.

The cooling system has to be reliable. Its failure could lead to flaky performance of the graphics chips, the destruction of the video processor itself, or the production of too much heat for the rest of the system to handle. It's also nice if the fans within the PC are quiet and the surrounding parts are properly isolated from vibration. One of the machines in my office causes an annoying whine that has eluded three years of troubleshooting; it's not the fan itself but instead a poor design for the cooling cowling tunnel that encases the processor and there is no solution short of replacing the tunnel . . . or keeping the office stereo system at a professional background-music level.

A *heat sink* is a passive device that works by drawing heat away from the surface of whatever device to which it is attached; most dissipate the heat by sending it into a set of fins or folded or coiled surfaces that expand the area wicking away elevated temperatures. A specialized extension to a heat sink is called a *heat pipe,* a system that draws heat away from the chip surface to a larger heat sink located nearby. This works in two ways: It takes the heat off the processor and it allows the heat sink to be moved directly into the path of air moving through the PC. A second design combines a passive heat sink with an active fan. The heat sink draws the heat up and off the chip, and the fan pushes the heated air toward the exit.

Some specialized PCs, especially those used in high-end graphics processing tasks such as rendering animation, use active cooling devices that are like tiny electronic refrigerating units.

Connectors on Current Video Cards

Desktop by desktop, LCD screens are beginning to displace CRT monitors. They take up less real estate, produce brighter, more stable images, generate much less heat, and have come down in price to provide real competition to older monitors. (And computer manufacturers have arrived at the point where the slightly higher cost of an LCD is offset by the lower cost of shipping it to the buyer.)

Most current video adapters, therefore, take into account the possibility that the user will have either, or both, types of displays. A common design offers one high-density DB-15 connector for CRT monitors and one *DVI (digital video interface)* connector for LCD displays. Or you may have two DVI connectors.

The DVI design is available in three versions: DVI-D (digital only), DVI-A (analog only), and DVI-I (digital and analog). In the best case scenario, a modern LCD can work with a cable that delivers both analog and digital signals and select the one that it needs (or allow the user to specify whether to work with the analog or digital information). Otherwise, you need to match an analog cable to an analog display or a digital cable to a digital display. Finally, most video cards can work with a cable adapter that converts DVI-A or DVI-I to an analog signal and cable that will drive a CRT monitor. This flexibility allows most current video cards to work with one or two monitors at the same time.

The next step in the evolution of video interfaces is expected to be HDMI, developed for use with high-definition television sets and other consumer entertainment devices. It provides high-definition video information as well as audio signals in the same cable.

Step by Step: How a Video Display Adapter Works

When an application or the operating system calls for the display of an image on your monitor, it sends a request to an element of the operating system, the *graphics driver interface (GDI).* The GDI hooks into the *API (application programming interface),* which is a component of the graphics driver designed specifically for your particular video display adapter. The graphics driver translates the request from the operating system into instructions that can be executed by the video display adapter.

NOTE

An outdated or corrupted driver is a common cause for problems with video display adapters, sometimes spilling over to cause problems with other devices, including a mouse or other pointing device. Take the time to check for updates to drivers on the web site of the manufacturer of your card and on the Windows Update page offered by Microsoft.

Ch
13

Next, the PC moves data from memory across the bus to the video display adapter. As I have noted, within modern PCs the data travels from a special PCI Express or AGP slot on the motherboard. On older PCs, video display adapters plug into PCI or ISA slots.

The board's specialized processor, the *graphics processing unit*, converts the digital data into pixels. Drawing two-dimensional characters or lines is a very simple task — basically a matter of connecting two points on a map. But to produce a complex 3-D image, the graphics processor makes use of the computer's *dumb strength* (very fast repetition of simple tasks); like a cartoonist, the system begins by laying out a wire frame of straight lines. To this simple outline, it then adds texture, color, and lighting effects. And then, to create the illusion of movement, the processor creates many slightly varying versions that can be streamed, one after another.

At a screen resolution of 1,024 × 768, the processing unit calculates the colors and then creates 786,432 pixels, updating the data 30 to 90 times each second. And here is where all of that extra memory on a modern video card comes into play: The video RAM stores the constructed images and there is no need to send pixels back to the system memory for storage. (Here, too, you can see the disadvantage of an integrated graphics chip on the motherboard; in this design there is no dedicated memory associated with the graphics processor and instead the data must be moved to system RAM and then out of the machine to a display.)

The data in the video RAM is divided between an index that describes each pixel, including its location and other attributes, and a section devoted to storage of fully drawn images, called a *frame buffer.* Before the image can be displayed on a CRT monitor or an analog LCD, the data has to be converted from digital to analog form — changed from precise numerical values to a set of red, green, and blue rising and falling wave signals. The conversion is performed by the video display adapter's random access memory digital-to-analog converter, or *RAMDAC.* The faster the RAMDAC, the higher the potential resolution of the video display adapter and the faster it can refresh the image.

For use with a digital LCD, the card output is sent to a *DVI-I (Digital Video Interface)* port. A DVI-I port includes digital and analog signals, allowing you to choose which form of information you want to use. A direct connection to an LCD uses the digital signal; a small converter plug or a specialized cable picks up just the analog signal and can be used with an analog LCD or monitor. A total of 29 pins are on the DVI-I connector; five are used only for an analog signal and the other 24 are used in various combinations for analog and digital signals.

Two other designs for DVI ports have been designed, but are not in common use today. DVI-D delivers only the digital signal and may be implemented some day when analog signals are no longer in common use. DVI-A provides only the analog signal, using the larger connector design of DVI instead of the older VGA connector.

The speed at which the board paints pixels is called the *fill rate;* a typical current card can spit out information at about one gigapixel (more than one billion pixels) per second. The screen is painted one line at a time; a fast fill rate permits a fast *frame rate,* also called a *screen refresh rate,* which is a measurement of how many times per second the entire screen is redrawn. Computer video uses a frame rate of at least 30 frames per second, which creates the illusion of movement.

The higher the resolution, the more pixels the video display adapter must produce per frame. The greater the *color depth* (the number of potential colors), the more information the card must process. Today's fastest graphics processors, together with the large amount of video RAM on modern cards, has greatly reduced slowdowns in frame rates caused by an overload in the GPU and RAMDAC.

Video processor clock speed

Just as it is with a computer's microprocessor, the clock speed of a video processor is the drumbeat that moves data forward. If you were to compare two video graphics adapters with the same architecture but different clock speeds, the card with the faster beat will outperform the other. In that situation, for example, a 500-MHz processor will result in a 25 percent boost in performance over a 400-MHz chip.

Where things become complicated is with different mixes of bus speeds or PCI Express lanes. A roadblock on data entering or exiting a processor can nullify its potential speed advantage over a more basic processor.

Video display memory

Display adapters define how many colors your monitor can use to display an image. The more colors the card uses, the more bits of information are necessary to describe each color. The images your computer displays are first constructed in the graphics memory that is associated with the video adapter.

On low-end modern machines, manufacturers can save money by placing the video processor on the motherboard itself and having it share a piece of the system's RAM. This is called *shared video memory,* and it is slower and less capable than dedicated video memory, but is without doubt less expensive. It's quite acceptable for a machine that is dedicated to basic operations (office tasks, Web browsing, and simple games), but it will not satisfy a hard-core gamer or digital illustrator.

A better solution is to have a block of video memory, sometimes called *local graphics memory,* just for the use of the video processor. Designers place the memory as close as possible to the processor itself to reduce even the tiny delays that are caused by long wires (or motherboard traces) between components.

Today's current modern video adapters for AGP or PCI Express slots typically come with a minimum of 128MB of local memory; an upgraded card offers 256MB or perhaps 512MB of memory. In theory, more video memory is better than less. More memory permits the processor to produce more data and store it close at hand. However, it is also possible to have a situation in which the video adapter produces and seeks to move on to the bus more information than can be handled, resulting in a bottleneck that slows down the system.

A low-end video card may only offer a 64-bit-wide bus which is about half or one-quarter as capable as a card with a 128-bit or 256-bit bus. (Today's most advanced memory cards offer a 512MB-wide bus.) Given a choice between a card with a lot of memory and a lesser bus, or a card with a fast bus and less memory, go for the faster bus. Put another way, the optimal choice is a card with a 128- or 256-bit-wide bus and a substantial amount of memory: I specified a 256MB model for the dream machine in this edition.

The next issue in video adapter ratings is the memory clock speed; just as in the PC's main system, this refers to the electronic beat of the drum that marks each push of data from one place to another. Faster clock speed is better than slower clock speed, although I have already noted that the adapter has to have a wide enough gate (the external bus) to handle the data trying to squeeze through. As an example, a block of 1.2-GHz memory meeting a 64-bit bus performs slower than 700-MHz memory and a 128-bit bus.

Color depth

Cards are sometimes categorized by the following color depths: 8 bit (capable of describing as many as 256 colors because $2^8 = 256$), 16 bit (65,536 or 65K), or 24 bit (16,777,216 or 16.8 million).

You will also find some cards described as being 32-bit devices; in theory, this could allow as many as 4,294, 967,296 or 4.3 billion colors. In actuality, however, this is a special graphics mode used by certain games and digital video applications for special effects. In this scheme, 24 bits are used for 16.8 million possible colors, and the other 8 bits are used as a separate layer to represent levels of translucency in an object or image.

Just to make things complex, some cards can also simulate 12 bit and other unusual sizes for computing power. Table 13-2 summarizes common color depths.

TABLE 13-2: Color Depths

Bit Depth	Binary Math	Number of Colors
1	2^1	2 (monochrome)
2	2^2	4 (CGA)
4	2^4	16 (EGA)
8	2^8	256 (VGA)
16	2^{16}	65,536 (High color, XGA)
24	2^{24}	16,777,216 (True color, SVGA)
32	2^{32}	16,777,216 (True color plus alpha channel)

How much memory do you need?

Not sure how much memory you need? As I have noted, more memory is generally better than less. More important are the speed of the video processor, the memory bus width, and the memory clock speed.

Dinosaur and senior-citizen video cards, developed at a time when memory was relatively expensive, had as little as 64K of video RAM. Today the price of memory has dropped and the demands on video graphics systems has risen to the point where a current modern machine typically uses at least 64MB of video memory, with 128MB most common. And it is usually only a small step up in price to 256MB.

In terms of performance, a card with 256MB is nearly identical in speed to one with 128MB. The difference lies in the card's ability to produce textures and other image elements of greater complexity or resolution.

As Table 13-3 demonstrates, all you need to display 16.8 million colors at $1,280 \times 1,024$ pixel resolution is 4MB of video RAM. But if you do so, your card has no room left over for advanced graphics manipulation. You really don't want to run most of today's applications with a 2MB to 4MB display memory that was common just a few years ago.

Ch
13

TABLE 13-3: Minimum Video Memory Requirements for a Display Adapter

Video RAM	Available Resolutions	Color Depth	Number of Colors
512KB	640 × 480	4, 8	16, 256
	800 × 600	4, 8	16, 256
	1024 × 768	4	16
1MB	640 × 480	4, 8, 16, 24	16, 256, 65,536, 1,677,216
	800 × 600	4, 8, 16	16, 256, 65,536
	1024 × 768	4, 8	16, 256
	1280 × 1024	4	16
2MB	640 × 480	4, 8, 16, 24	16, 256, 65,536, 1,677,216
	800 × 600	4, 8, 16, 24	16, 256, 65,536, 1,677,216
	1024 × 768	4, 8, 16	16, 256, 65,536
	1280 × 1024	4, 8	16, 256
4MB	640 × 480	4, 8, 16, 24	16, 256, 65,536, 1,677,216
	800 × 600	4, 8, 16, 24	16, 256, 65,536, 1,677,216
	1024 × 768	4, 8, 16, 24	16, 256, 65,536, 1,677,216
	1152 × 864	4, 8, 16, 24	16, 256, 65,536, 1,677,216
	1280 × 1024	4, 8, 16, 24	16, 256, 65,536, 1,677,216
	1600 × 1200	4, 8, 16, 24	16, 256, 65,536, 1,677,216
8MB	640 × 480	4, 8, 16, 24, 32	16, 256, 65,536, 1,677,216
	800 × 600	4, 8, 16, 24, 32	16, 256, 65,536, 1,677,216
	1024 × 768	4, 8, 16, 24, 32	16, 256, 65,536, 1,677,216
	1152 × 864	4, 8, 16, 24, 32	16, 256, 65,536, 1,677,216
	1280 × 1024	4, 8, 16, 24, 32	16, 256, 65,536, 1,677,216
	1600 × 1200	4, 8, 16, 24, 32	16, 256, 65,536, 1,677,216

Ch
13

Here's how the memory minimums are calculated: Multiply horizontal resolution by vertical resolution to get the total number of pixels and then multiply this figure by the number of bytes of color. (Remember, 256 possible colors is 8-bit color, which equals 1 byte; 65,536 colors is 16-bit color or 2 bytes; 16.8 million colors is 24-bit color, or true color, and uses 24 bits or 3 bytes.)

For example, the basic 640 × 480 pixel resolution requires about 600K of RAM at 16 bits, just under 1MB of RAM at 24-bit color, and about 1.23MB of RAM for 32-bit color. If you're working with a larger monitor and want to use the higher 800 × 600 pixel resolution, you need about 1MB for 16-bit color, almost 1.4MB for 24 bits, and around 2MB for 32 bits of color depth. Of course, PC RAM, including that on a display adapter, comes only in sizes that are a power of 2. Therefore, the display adapter has 2MB of RAM to support display needs of 1.4MB.

Now, forget about the formula: The needs of a modern graphics adapter have gone well past mere considerations of color depth and resolution. Today, designers look for huge blocks of memory to construct images before they need to be displayed and to be able to produce incredibly complex manipulations including shading, textures, 3-D effects, and specialized lighting effects. That's the reason the example of a current PCI Express adapter in this chapter, the ATI Radeon X1600 Pro, comes delivered with 512MB of memory. All that extra memory is not devoted to creating billions and quadrillions of shades of blue, but instead to allowing the preparation of images that can be cascaded, one after another, in the playback of a high-resolution DVD video image or a video game.

The good news is that the plummeting price of RAM has made video memory inexpensive; this is especially so when manufacturers are able (or choose) to use standard DDR2 memory on their cards—the same memory used for the system processor. Some video card manufacturers have announced plans to populate their cards with various types of specialized video memory, but because of the relatively small market for these designs, this results in sharply increased costs for a small increase in speed and a decrease in power demands.

As this edition goes to press, basic brand-name video cards with 64MB or 128MB of memory sell for as little as $40, and high-end boards with 512MB of special video RAM are priced as high as $600. The sweet spot (for those of us who perform ordinary office functions, digital editing, and Internet use) is a card with 256MB or 512MB of DDR2 RAM, priced in the range of $100 to $200.

Types of memory

Memory on a video card is the electronic scratch pad used by the computer to construct images. The higher the resolution, and the more colors in the palette, the more information that must be stored and then transmitted to the display. Add to this the element of *refresh rate*—the number of times per second the image on the display is redrawn. The combination of all these factors puts a tremendous demand on memory.

Basic video memory from dinosaur days is called DRAM (dynamic RAM) and is the same as the DRAM popularly used for system memory. Either the digital-to-analog converter (called a RAMDAC) or the graphics controller can access DRAM on a display adapter, but they can't access it at the same time. DRAM is too slow to deliver high-resolution, high-color, and a high refresh rate for a modern machine.

In the evolution of PC display adapters, the next form of memory was VRAM (video RAM, an unfortunate name because any kind of display adapter RAM is also called video RAM). VRAM is *dual ported,* meaning that two devices can access it simultaneously, thus allowing the processor to write to memory at the same time that it is refreshing the image on the display. Dual-ported RAM enables the display adapter to perform faster because the graphics controller and the RAMDAC don't have to take turns. The faster performance enables higher refresh rates for a given resolution.

Next up the line were forms of EDO memory. EDO stands for *extended data out*, an indication of an expanded bandwidth for its data. DRAM and VRAM versions of EDO chips were about 10 to 25 percent faster than equivalent standard chips. EDO memory improves speed by enabling the next cycle of memory to begin before the previous cycle finishes its job. On the downside, EDO RAM can cause slowdowns any time you use color depths of more than 8 bits per pixel.

A slight improvement over VRAM was WRAM (Window RAM), which is specifically intended for systems running graphical user interfaces, such as Windows. WRAM is dual ported (like VRAM) and includes logic that speeds bit-block transfers and pattern fills.

SGRAM (synchronous graphics RAM) is clock-synchronized, single-ported RAM designed for video memory, aimed for use in low-cost adapters. The technology uses *masked write*, which enables selected data to be modified in a single operation rather than as a sequence of read, update, and write operations.

Current video adapters almost all use *DDR2 (double data rate)* memory, very similar or identical to the chips that are employed in system memory. DDR2 transfers twice as much data per clock cycle as previous designs retroactively renamed *SDR (single data rate).* DDR memory is rated at its effective data throughput; RAM that is advertised as 4.2-GHz DDR memory actually functions at 2.1 GHz, but does it twice in each cycle.

Some cards use newer technology called GDDR3 or GDDR4, which are specialized Graphics Double Data Rate modules. They are very similar to DDR2, but require a bit less power and thus produce a bit less heat. GDDR3 transfers four bits of data per pin on each of two clock cycles. GDDR4 can transfer twice that amount of memory per cycle. It remains to be seen whether these forms of specialized video memory will become widely used.

Older modern designs were based on single data rate SDRAM. For a brief moment in time—before economics trumped technology—some adapters employed *RDRAM (rambus dynamic RAM),* a system that used a proprietary bus that speeds up the data flow between video RAM and the frame buffer.

Video display resolution

The more individually controllable pixels are on a monitor screen, the crisper the image. Resolution is indicated as horizontal pixels times vertical pixels on the screen. Whatever the capability of the monitor, though, it is still up to the video display adapter to produce the signal that drives it. All of the video modes are the result of a partnership between the display adapter and the monitor.

Ch
13

Table 13-4 shows many of the video modes available throughout the history of the PC. Early adapters had a text and a graphics mode. The text mode was based around predefined character sets; characters were drawn within a specified character box of a particular number of pixels in width and height. Today, nearly every modern PC uses the SVGA standard in one or another of its advanced modes.

The more memory in your card and the more capable the processor, the more flexible the device is in producing a wide range of resolutions at various color modes at various frequencies that match the needs of monitors or LCDs. And because the Apple Macintosh architecture has become very close to that of the PC (now offering Intel processors, PCI Express slots, USB, and other familiar technologies on the hardware side), you'll also find that modern video adapters offer some unusual resolutions that match the slightly different standards in a Macintosh.

Table 13-4: Video Standards

Resolution	Colors	Mode	Character Box	Vertical Frequency	Horizontal Frequency	Compatible Hardware
MDA Monochrome Display Adapter (1981)						
720 × 350	1	Text	9 × 14	50	18.43	None
CGA Color Graphics Adapter (1981)						
640 × 200	16	Text	8 × 8	60	15.75	None
320 × 200	16	Text	8 × 8	60	15.75	None
160 × 200	16	Graphics	N/A	60	15.75	None
320 × 200	4	Graphics	N/A	60	15.75	None
640 × 200	2	Graphics	N/A	60	15.75	None
HGC Hercules Graphics Card (1982)						
720 × 350	1	Text	9 × 14	50	18.1	MDA
720 × 348	2	Graphics	N/A	50	18.1	MDA
EGA Enhanced Graphics Adapter (1984)						
640 × 350	16	Text	8 × 14	60	21.85	CGA, MDA
720 × 350	4	Text	9 × 14	60	21.85	CGA, MDA
640 × 350	16	Graphics	N/A	60	21.85	CGA, MDA
320 × 200	16	Graphics	N/A	60	21.85	CGA, MDA
640 × 200	16	Graphics	N/A	60	21.85	CGA, MDA
640 × 350	16	Graphics	N/A	60	21.85	CGA, MDA
PGA Professional Graphics Adapter (1984)						
640 × 480	256	Graphics	N/A	60	30.5	CGA

Resolution	Colors	Mode	Character Box	Vertical Frequency	Horizontal Frequency	Compatible Hardware
VGA Video Graphics Array (1987)						
720 × 400	16	Text	9 × 16	70	31.5	CGA, EGA
360 × 400	16	Text	9 × 16	70	31.5	CGA, EGA
640 × 480	2, 16	Graphics	N/A	60	31.5	CGA, EGA
320 × 200	256	Graphics	N/A	70	31.5	CGA, EGA
MCGA Memory Controller Gate Array (1987)						
320 × 400	4	Text	8 × 16	70	31.5	CGA, EGA
640 × 400	2	Text	8 × 16	70	31.5	CGA, EGA
640 × 480	2	Graphics	N/A	60	31.5	CGA, EGA
320 × 200	256	Graphics	N/A	70	31.5	CGA, EGA
8514/A (1987)						
1,024 × 768	16, 256	Graphics	N/A	43–48	35–52	VGA passthrough
640 × 480	256	Graphics	N/A	43–48	35–52	VGA passthrough
XGA Extended Graphics Array (1990)						
640 × 480	256	Graphics	N/A	43–48	35–52	VGA
1,024 × 768	256	Graphics	N/A	43–48	35–52	VGA
640 × 480	65, 536	Graphics	N/A	43–48	35–52	VGA
1,056 × 400	16	Text	8 × 16	43–48	35–52	VGA
SVGA Super VGA or VESA Specification (1989 and subsequent expansions)						
640 × 480	256–16.8 million	Graphics	N/A	50– 120	24–86	VGA, CGA, EGA
800 × 600	16–16.8 million	Graphics	N/A	50–120	25–86	None
1,024 × 768	16–16.8 million	Graphics	N/A	60–100	24–86	None
1,152 × 864	256–16.8 million	Graphics	N/A	60–100	24–86	None
1,280 × 720	256–16.8 million	Graphics	N/A	60–100	24–86	None
1,280 × 800	256–16.8 million	Graphics	N/A	60–100	24–86	None
1,280 × 1,024	16–16.8 million	Graphics	N/A	60–100	24–86	None
1,360 × 768	256–16.8 million	Graphics	N/A	60–100	24–86	None
1,280 × 1,200	256–16.8 million	Graphics	N/A	60–100	24–86	None
1,600 × 1,200	256–16.8 million	Graphics	N/A	60–100	24–86	None
1,600 × 1,280	16–16.8 million	Graphics	N/A	75–150	24–86	None
1,680 × 1,050	256–16.8 million	Graphics	N/A	60–100	24–86	None
1,800 × 1,440	256–16.8 million	Graphics	N/A	72–100	24–86	None
1,920 × 1,200	256–16.8 million	Graphics	N/A	60–100	24–86	None

Ch 13

In the end, it doesn't really matter if you're sending a signal to a capable multifrequency video display; the display can work with a very wide range of settings. On the other hand, if you're using an LCD, you may have to be more selective in your choice of a resolution because most such displays have a single hard-wired resolution and can only work with other specifications with the assistance of a software conversion.

Each step along the way from CGA to today's amazing SVGA adapters brought dramatic change. It is almost comical how crude and unimpressive a CGA screen looks in comparison to a multimedia screen from SVGA today. Everything has changed: resolution, number of colors, and speed. In addition, prices have plummeted.

Resolving resolution issues

Using a monitor at a 1,280 × 1,024 pixel resolution gives you more than four times as much viewable information as can be presented on a standard 640 × 480 pixel setting — four times as many cells in a spreadsheet, four windows with four word processing documents, or any other wide-screen or ultra-sharp use you can conjure. That's the good news. The bad news is that individual elements on the screen are less than one-fourth as large.

Although high resolution may be essential in certain applications, such as desktop publishing and graphic arts work, for many users, text may be simply too small for comfortable writing and editing. However, you should be able to adjust the "view" of a screen from within many applications, including word processors, to adjust what you see on the screen to a comfortable size. Another solution is to use a zoom feature that may be an element of the driver for your particular graphics adapter or available as a separate graphics utility software package. Using a zoom or a view is a compromise, adding some extra keystrokes or mouse clicks to views of the screen and giving up some of the advantage of high resolution in the first place.

When you enable higher resolutions, you can improve readability of text by turning on large fonts. To do this, right-click on the desktop and choose Properties. From the Properties dialog box, choose Settings and click on Advanced. In the Display group, choose Large Fonts. Click OK twice to close the Advanced and Properties dialogs. Older versions of Windows may ask you to re-boot your computer before the new display settings become effective.

You can also adjust the size of characters in Web pages using current editions of Microsoft's Internet Explorer and other browsers, or temporarily zoom the display to enlarge a portion of the screen.

Of course, the higher resolutions of modern graphics adapters have been accompanied by an increase in the size of the monitors on the desk. At one time, a 13-inch monitor was considered large. Today, a 14- or 15-inch screen is considered hopelessly small. Budget-priced computers may be offered with 17-inch screens, but the plummeting price of monitors has made 19-inch models the basic size if you're going to stay with the older CRT technology. In 2006, computer makers began shipping 19-inch LCDs as the standard for their machines and larger displays are expected to become more common. As you explore in Chapter 14, the fact that LCDs have to give up less of their viewable surface to the supporting frame makes a 19-inch flat screen equal to or larger than the usable surface of a 20-inch CRT monitor.

The Still-Expanding Universe of SVGA

At the consumer level, computers have been offering one or another version of SVGA (Super Video Graphics Array) since 1989. This standard, expanded over the years by an industry group called the Video Electronics Standards Association (VESA), is an extension of the VGA standard developed by third-party manufacturers and is in common use on nearly every modern machine.

SVGA was originally defined as a small improvement over standard VGA, with resolutions of as high as 800 × 600 pixels. As it turned out, that particular resolution level was considered insufficient by many Windows users, and the SVGA definition was expanded and improved to include specifications of 1,024 × 768 pixels, or 1,280 × 1,024 pixels, or higher. SVGA also extends down, including a superset of all VGA modes and specifications, which included most of the earlier EGA and CGA modes.

The standard is not a law, and some display adapters may support select elements of the SVGA definition or may offer some features that go beyond its official limits. Similarly, you will find SVGA-capable monitors with a wide range of available resolutions, frequencies, and other specifications. Spend the time to research both ends of the connection — the adapter and the monitor or display — before you make a purchase.

NOTE

A number of other definitions for extended graphics standards have arisen over the years, but are not in wide use. IBM put forth the XGA as its own improvement on the standard. Another term, *Ultra VGA (UVGA),* is sometimes used for displays with resolution of 1,024 × 768 pixels or greater.

3-D SVGA graphics adapters

Are you ready to enter the PC third dimension? Hot and flashy 3-D graphics accelerators are yet another extension to the flexible SVGA standard; several years ago this facility was only offered on high-end graphic cards or on systems built for special purposes.

All of the new cards offer impressive gains in speed and visual quality on 3-D software. You can also reasonably expect speed improvements of 25 percent or more over 2-D graphics accelerators that run equivalent applications.

However, you must understand one thing right up front: What you see onscreen is not really 3-D, at least not in the special-glasses, reach-out-and-touch-the-butterfly-hovering-in-front-of-your-nose kind of way. Instead, think of 3-D graphics as the difference between an old Road Runner cartoon and the modern state of cartoon art in computer animation movies, such as *Toy Story.*

When designers and marketers speak of 3-D today, they are talking about the capability of a video display adapter to produce and manipulate 3-D objects — mathematical representations of width, height, and depth of a shape. The addition of depth opens the door to the next great advance in graphics.

Add this new term to your PC lexicon: *texels.* Texels are pixels with a third layer of information defining the pixel's texture.

Anisotropic filtering is an element of 3-D graphics aimed at improving the quality of textures on surfaces that are far away and at high angles with respect to an image's view. A related feature is *mipmapping,* which allows a program to use precalculated and optimized bitmap images that accompany a main texture; for example, a computer game might draw one highly detailed image of a soldier and then reproduce hundreds of thousands of others (sometimes with minor alterations in color, size, or perspective) elsewhere on the screen. The result is a significant boost in speed as opposed to individually drawing each figure.

In most cases, you want to leave the decisionmaking on advanced features of a modern video card to the engineers and the programmers. However, you can adjust your own with the use of the driver and control software provided with these cards. An example of a technical adjustment of mipmap detail level using the Catalyst controls of an ATI Radeon card is shown in Figure 13-4.

FIGURE 13-4: *Advanced settings within the ATI Catalyst software allows adjustment of anti-aliasing, anisotropic filtering, and mipmap detail level.*

The role of DirectX and OpenGL

As graphics adapters began to offer greater levels of sophistication, some makers got so far ahead of the crowd that certain games and applications were designed only to work with particular hardware. That situation, of course, could pose serious problems for users who have a mix of advanced software on their systems.

The solution came in the development of a set of common *API (application programming interface)* codes that stand between the hardware and the operating system; these are, in effect, specialized device drivers that allow software makers to issue commands for what they would like to see onscreen and for hardware companies to respond using advanced features that may differ from one brand of graphics card to another.

The two principal APIs are:

- DirectX, a proprietary set of multimedia instructions for graphics, audio, and input devices developed by Microsoft, and widely used in computer games for current versions of Microsoft Windows, as well as the Xbox 360, the company's gaming machine. Components of DirectX, including Direct3D, are also used in many high-end computer-aided design and manufacturing programs and other professional applications requiring 3-D graphics.
- OpenGL (Open Graphics Library), an open-source definition developed by Silicon Graphics and adopted by a wide range of software makers.

Nearly all drivers for modern graphics adapters include support for both DirectX and OpenGL. And when you install new software, you may be instructed to obtain the latest update of necessary APIs.

As this book goes to press, the most current versions of DirectX are 9.0c for Windows XP and 10.0 for Windows Vista. (The initial release of DirectX 10.0 is compatible only with Windows Vista, while 9.0C works with all versions of the Microsoft operating system from Windows 98 through XP.)

If you are not certain which version of DirectX is installed as a component of your operating system, you can run the DirectX Diagnostic Tool. Click Start ➪ Run. Enter **dxdiag** in the Open box and click OK. The report, in its Windows XP version, is shown in Figure 13-5.

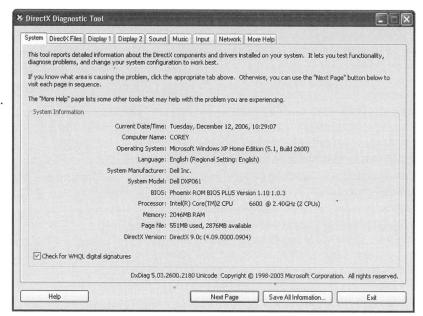

FIGURE 13-5: *The opening screen of the detailed DirectX Diagnostic Tool. Among important information found here is the version of DirectX installed. This is also a quick way to determine the current BIOS on the system board and double-check installed RAM.*

What are 3-D graphics?

Three-dimensional cards bring together a combination of specialized graphics processing, high-speed dedicated memory, and advanced software schemes. It all comes down to the addition of depth to graphics images. In mathematical terms, width and height are called X and Y dimensions, while depth is the sought-after Z dimension.

To achieve this addition of depth on the software side, you can use half a dozen impressive extensions to the graphics capabilities of the PC. At the heart of the improvements are texture mapping, Gouraud shading, and z-buffering. The first two improvements are ways to use a computer to apply realistic textures, color shadings, and light shadings to the basic shapes that constitute images; the effect is to enable the complex simulation of perspective and shadow.

Texture mapping gives the most eye-popping effects. Textures, with variations for perspective and changing atmospheric conditions, are applied to a shape and modified as action demands. Texture mapping is much slower to produce and manage than flat or Gouraud shading because it adds one full, additional level of information to be generated, manipulated, and stored in a new block of memory called the z-buffer.

Gouraud shading is a step up from flat shading, which assigns a single shade and intensity to fill the interior of a computer-generated shape. Although flat shading is fast, it robs an image of the variations that give the appearance of depth and reality. Gouraud interpolates color or gray shades across an object to make it seem to have depth.

Z-buffering is a scheme that assigns the computer the task of keeping track of the depth of each shape, including hidden surfaces that can't be seen in the current view, and managing the shape's appearance as the view changes. Most graphics chips use information in the z-buffer to determine whether pixels in an object are in front of (and thus displayed) or behind (and thus hidden) another object.

In a 3-D world, the entire database representing the modeled world is processed for every frame displayed, with the relative position and orientation of every object recalculated in every frame. Just as in the real world, you may be looking at just the portion of an object that is in direct view, but the rest of the object — its depth and mass — exists nevertheless.

How 3-D video display adapters work

Three-dimensional images are created in what designers call the 3-D graphics pipeline, a connection that starts at the computer's CPU and passes through the graphics adapter en route to your monitor. Despite the impressive raw power of a current CPU, most users would not be satisfied with the slowdown in image creation that would result if the CPU rendered advanced 3-D graphics all alone.

To accomplish their magic without bringing your PC to a halt, most 3-D video display adapters offload some of the intensive number-crunching assignments from the computer's CPU to a specialized chip on the video display adapter itself. Not only does this reduce the load on the CPU, it also makes it possible for tasks to take place simultaneously. While the rendering engine produces the current frame using the dedicated processor on the 3-D card, the Pentium's CPU is calculating the geometries of the next frame.

The operating system is the highest-level control for your PC, controlling the disk and system memory operations of your computer. An API (application program interface) stands between your operating system and your 3-D graphics accelerator to translate specific demands of the software to the capabilities of your graphics hardware.

The next element in the production of 3-D images is the *geometry engine*, which translates descriptions of an image into smaller polygons — triangles and other vector graphics (geometric forms that are drawn from point to point, much like the way you draw a triangle on a piece of paper). Generating the polygons and rotating them in a scene to support the 30-frames-per-second imagery of an advanced game is a calculation-intensive assignment, a task that is well suited to floating-point unit CPUs like all current microprocessors.

The third element in the production of 3-D images is the *rendering engine*, which has the assignment of pixel processing. These tasks include rendering polygons with shading; attaching textures; overlaying atmospheric effects, such as fog or lighting; correcting perspective; and removing hidden surfaces. The end result is a pixel-by-pixel description for an image, ready to be transmitted to the monitor.

Each board works with a driver that stands between the operating system and the card, directing appropriate calls from the operating system directly to the hardware. The controller converts information into a pixel-by-pixel description of the image.

From the controller, the graphics information is sent to the memory on the card itself, a so-called frame buffer that prepares the image as a grid. Finally, a chip or chipset called the RAMDAC (random access memory digital-analog converter) changes the digital pixels to the analog signal required by nearly all monitors.

CROSS-REFERENCE

For a wealth of information on video display adapters and other technology, point your Web browser to `http://developer.intel.com/technology`.

TV Output

So, you'd like to be the next David Letterman with your own television studio? The time may also come when you want to get your fancy PC-based presentation from the computer to a large-screen television or projection TV. Or perhaps you want to make your own training tape for a sales meeting or scan in a collection of photos to produce a nifty electronic photo album.

Modern PCs can work with a variety of hardware and software products that enable you to edit moving images onscreen. Once you've made your own movie, you can choose between:

- Outputting to media such as a hard disk, removable disk, videotape, or DVD. You can also upload your work to the Internet.
- Sending a signal directly from your computer to a television set, projector, or VCR.

You have two relatively simple solutions. One is to work with a video adapter card that includes a TV-out port. The very modern ATI Radeon X1600 Pro used as an example in this chapter also offers internal circuitry to produce a high-quality video signal. The Radeon's S-video output that can be directly connected to some TVs or converted (with cables supplied by ATI) to separate composite cable signals accepted by VCRs and some television sets.

Another way to accomplish the same task is to use a converter that takes the output of a standard computer video card and splits off a television signal. I worked with one such solution from AITech; the company's line of MultiPro Plus PC-to-TV digital converters change over a PC signal to NTSC or PAL television standards. NTSC is used in the United States, Canada, and parts of Asia and Latin America, while the slightly higher-resolution PAL system is used in Europe and parts of Asia. For information, consult `www.aitech.com`.

Installing Multiple Video Display Adapters

Among the advanced features of Windows 98 and later versions of Windows is the ability to run multiple display adapters and monitors on the same system. You can use the monitors to display a different program on each, or you can use the facilities of some applications to display some elements of the program on one monitor and other elements on another.

For example, if you perform intensive graphics editing using a program such as Photoshop, you can display the image on one monitor and all of the menus and control panels on the other. Look for some advanced games to display one view on one screen and another view on a second screen.

For high-end graphics developers and gamers, there is also a special class of video cards that allow you to install two or more adapters in a modern machine bus and electronically chain them together to bring a tremendous amount of horsepower to the images displayed on a single monitor. Among products that work in this way are ATI's CrossFire cards and Nvidia's SLI.

Multiple monitors under Windows XP and Windows Vista

The most current versions of Windows — Windows Vista and Windows XP — are even more accommodating to set up with more than one monitor — in fact, it can work with as many as ten monitors displaying the same or different programs or windows. You can open a different file on each monitor, or you can stretch one item across several monitors, such as a massive Excel spreadsheet. The operating system allows you to choose which of the monitors to use as the primary device for log in and to start programs.

If you want to work with multiple monitors under Windows Vista or XP, take the following steps:

1. Install a video adapter that supports multiple monitors. The system will detect the new video adapter and monitor and install appropriate drivers.
2. After drivers are installed, open Display in the Control Panel and go to the Settings tab of the Display Properties screen. There, click the icon for the monitor that you want to use as a secondary monitor. The Windows XP screen is shown in Figure 13-6.
3. Select the check box Extend My Windows Desktop onto This Monitor to permit dragging items across your screen onto alternate monitors.
4. To adjust the relative position of one monitor to another, click the monitor icons and place them alongside each other, or one above the other as you prefer.

The ATI Catalyst Control Center, the software component of that company's advanced graphics boards, offers its own set of screens for the configuration of multiple monitors. The advanced displays manager for the ATI Radeon X1600 Pro, shown in Figure 13-7, supplements the basic controls that are part of current Microsoft Windows versions. Details about the display positioning are shown as an element of the step-by-step wizard, shown in Figure 13-8, available within the Catalyst center.

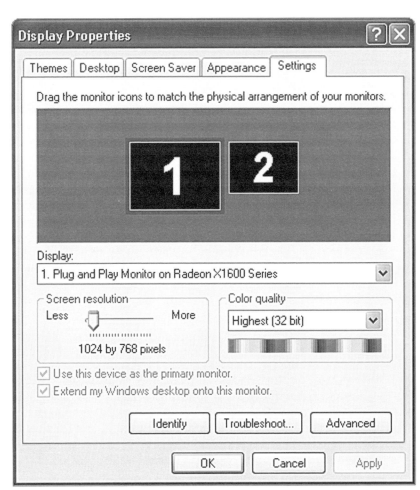

FIGURE 13-6: *The Windows XP Display Properties screen is a standalone component of the Control Panel. To make further adjustments, you need to burrow deeper into the Advanced tab.*

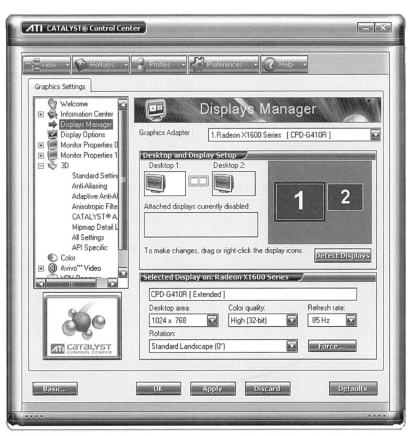

FIGURE 13-7: *The Displays Manager screen of the ATI Catalyst Control Center brings together the ability to assign multiple displays to one or more adapter, position the displays in logical space, and set the resolution, number of colors, and refresh rate.*

Ch
13

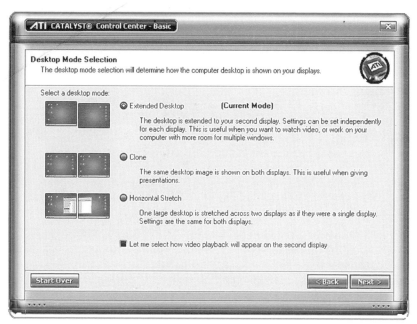

FIGURE 13-8: *The basic mode of the ATI Catalyst controls explains in detail the three most common settings for multiple monitors: extended desktop, clone, or horizontal stretch.*

Using two monitors under Windows 98

Windows 98 permits use of two display adapters and two monitors. You can set the two display adapters to the same or different resolutions and color depths. Begin by installing and configuring one video adapter and monitor, and make sure that both are functioning properly. Then simply install the second card in an available slot. Windows automatically designates one of the cards as the primary graphics controller and the other card as secondary. Certain 3D and multimedia features may be available only on the primary card.

If you install both a PCI and an AGP display card in the same system, in most cases, the PCI card is designated as the primary and the AGP as the secondary controller. Some motherboards may have a BIOS that allows you to override this automatic selection and choose the much faster AGP as the primary.

If you install two PCI cards, the primary video display adapter is usually the one installed in the PCI slot with the lowest number. On most motherboards, this is the PCI slot farthest from the ISA slots.

Troubleshooting VGA or SVGA Cards

To troubleshoot a video card and monitor, follow these steps:

1. Before you do anything rash, such as taking apart your computer, make sure that the display adapter is properly connected by cable to the monitor. Is the cable firmly attached at both ends and not partially connected?
2. Check that the monitor is plugged into a source of wall current. It may be plugged into a special outlet on the back panel of some dinosaur machines, or it may connect directly to the wall outlet.
3. Make sure that the monitor is turned on. Do you see an indicator light on the monitor? If not, check to see if a fuse is present on the monitor and that the wall outlet is live. Notice also that many modern monitors include multicolor indicator lights that show yellow when they are receiving power but not receiving a signal from the CPU. They show a green light when power is present and they are receiving a signal from the computer.
4. Finally, check that the contrast and brightness settings on the monitor are not turned all the way off.

Here are some common software issues to check before you suspect the hardware:

- **Windows won't permit a setting better than basic video VGA resolution of 640 × 480 with 16 colors.** If your card is capable of more (as most are), check the level of hardware acceleration that Windows has set. Go to Control Panel, and Display, and then click the Settings tab. Click Advanced, and then click the Performance tab. Drag the Hardware acceleration slider to None. Click OK.
- **Certain display setting options are missing in the Display Properties dialog box.** Make sure that Windows has properly detected your specific monitor manufacturer and model. An incorrect or generic setting may limit your available choices. Windows includes listings for most major manufacturers; newer monitors come with disks or CDs with hardware information for Windows.

Testing SVGA or VGA cards

The display adapter, the monitor, or a multitude of difficulties in the computer system unit can produce a display problem. The troubleshooting charts in Appendix A on the CD provide a plan to help you identify the culprit.

Before you go too far in diagnosing a display problem, try out an extra monitor (if you have one) on the troublesome system. You can plug a monitor that you know is good into a questionable PC system or try the suspect monitor on a PC that you know is good. If the suspect monitor comes to life on another machine, the problem is likely with the display adapter or internal chips of the original PC. If the good monitor fails on the suspect machine, you have the same clues.

If you are running Windows 98, the first thing to check for is conflicts with the system resource settings for your card. Of course, this raises a question: How can you see the settings if your display adapter is not working?

If you have absolutely no video signal on the display, then you must open the system and explore for hardware problems. In many cases, Windows 95/98 and later versions are capable of booting up in Safe Mode, which makes minimal demands on the system, usually as a generic VGA mode using ordinary Windows drivers.

If you can get into the operating system this way, the problem probably lies with an improper display card driver or a conflict of resources. Go to the Device Manager and use its facilities to look for the source of the problem. Try resetting the video display adapter to a basic configuration, such as 640 × 480 and 256 colors, and then rebooting to Windows; if you are able to proceed from there, you can make other adjustments within Windows.

One other software option is to attempt to reinstall the drivers for your card from the floppy disk or CD-ROM provided by the manufacturer.

If you need to check out the hardware, first unplug the cables from the back of the PC, including the power cord, and then remove the cover.

NOTE

A class of all-in-one senior citizens and low-level modern machines had video circuitry on the motherboard. In these systems, the video adapter can't be repaired, but in most systems, a replacement card can be installed in the expansion bus. Check your instruction manual for details.

Because the monitor is attached to the display adapter card, look on the back of the system unit to find the 15-pin female connector that your monitor's data cable plugs into. The 15-pin connector, called a DB-15, is the video port located on the display card or located on the

motherboard. The first thing to check is that the card is firmly seated in the bus.

Many SVGA or VGA cards come packaged with diagnostic software. This software is helpful if the display card is working but misbehaving. CheckIt or another diagnostics package also can test a card for subtle malfunctions.

If you can, try installing the suspect display card into a computer that you know to be good and that is configured for the same type of card. If you have one or two incorrect characters on an otherwise good screen, the video memory located on the display card is likely at fault.

Note also that an older monitor may not be capable of the higher refresh rates delivered by modern cards, including AGP adapters. You should be able to continue to use an older monitor if you instruct Windows to install and work with generic SVGA drivers, but you will lose the advanced functions of the AGP card.

Removing and installing video cards

Before you remove a video card, you must turn off the computer and the monitor. Disconnect the data cable (it runs from the video card to the monitor) at the video card end. You will probably have to remove two small screws that are used to hold the cable connector tight to the card. Remove the system unit cover. The card itself is secured to the back wall of the system unit chassis with a single screw. Remove and save the screw. Remove the card. Lift the card straight up; it should require only moderate force.

Installation is the reverse of removal. As already noted, nearly all SVGA cards are designed to plug into a PCI slot, moving toward AGP slots over time. You may have difficulty finding a state-of-the-art card for an ISA slot, although older models may be offered at a full-line dealer or mail-order house.

Line up the slot connector on the card with the slot on the motherboard and then press down firmly. When the card is in place, the screw hole on the card lines up with the screw hole in the back of the chassis. Reinstall the screw and test the machine.

If you are installing a different type of display card — for example, if you're replacing the original VGA card with a new SVGA card — be sure to consult your PC's instruction manual to see if you need to set any switches or jumpers on the motherboard to reflect the new display adapter.

If you have a modern machine, you may need to run the Setup program to store the new hardware information in CMOS on the motherboard. Windows 95/98 and later versions should recognize a Plug-and-Play card. Owners of senior citizens may need to check with the manufacturer of their motherboard or system to determine if they need to upgrade the system BIOS.

Nearly all newly installed modern display cards will initially power up in basic VGA mode of 640 × 480 resolution and 16 colors. Plug-and-Play under Windows 98 and later versions should identify most new adapters and install drivers that are part of Windows or prompt you to install drivers from a disk or CD provided by the manufacturer. Be sure to consult the instruction manual for the new card.

If you are installing a new card in an older system, or one running Windows 95 or earlier, change the display adapter setting to the generic Standard Display Adapter (VGA) before removing the old card and installing the new one. After the machine is up and running, use the new driver to change resolution and color settings.

SUMMARY

This chapter explored the transmitter to your PC's monitor. I also spent a good deal of time discussing various older display adapter technologies. You can see from the specifications on these older devices that using them for anything but the most basic computer tasks would be difficult or impossible. Nevertheless, I know a fair number of people who continue to use older computer hardware. Several years ago they purchased PCs on which they installed basic word-processing or accounting software that continues to do what they want done. After you decide to move beyond early versions of Windows, or move up from DOS to Windows, you'll want to install newer display technology. The next chapter moves from the adapter to the monitor itself.

Ch 13

Notes

Chapter 14

Monitors and LCD Displays

You may not know much about the electronics of video monitors, but you almost certainly know what you like. Modern displays are Rembrandts compared to the cave scrawls of dinosaur systems. The current state-of-the-art for modern machines is a high-resolution SVGA *cathode ray tube (CRT)* monitor or a flat liquid crystal display (better known by the acronym *LCD*).

Although both types of devices could interchange their names and still be correct, for the purposes of this book I will call a CRT a *monitor* or *CRT* and a liquid crystal display an *LCD*.

Today many PC users consider a 17-inch CRT monitor to be the basic minimum for a desktop; that's up from 15 inches just a few years ago. And prices for 17-inch monitors have never been lower: In 2006, a capable brand-name monitor sold for about $115, with occasional sales that drop the price below $100. If you think about it, that means that Asian factories are producing these screens for well under $50 and still making a profit after a 10,000-mile trip to your store.

The next step up, very valuable for graphics work and multitasking assignments, is a 19-inch monitor and in 2006 these were only slightly more expensive than 17-inch screens. Also available were 19- and 21-inch CRTs, although buyers were asked to pay a steep price for ordering something that is much less popular much heavier.

In fact, in coming years it will become harder and harder to find CRT monitors of any size. We have entered the era of the LCD.

Cool, thin, sharp, and energy-efficient LCD screens have come down in price tremendously. A 17-inch LCD — which costs as much as $1,000 in 2002 — had dropped to as little as $150 in 2006. It will not be long before LCDs are less expensive than CRTs, and at that point there will likely be no reason to buy . . . or sell . . . old-fashioned cathode ray tube monitors to consumers.

Already, many PC manufacturers who offer a "free" monitor along with a system unit have made the changeover to 15- and 17-inch LCDs. (If you think about it, the cost of shipping the heavier CRT probably negates any supposed price difference between the LCDs and CRTs.)

As a user, a good LCD — and most current models are well made — offers many advantages. The LCD takes up much less space on your desktop, especially in depth. And they are much more energy efficient.

The Sony 19-inch CRT in front of my keyboard as I write these words is about 18 inches wide and 15 inches tall at the front and extends back about 18 inches, or about 2.8 cubic feet of space. It also weighs 56 pounds and 3 ounces. It draws about 135 watts of electrical power per hour and generates a noticeable amount of heat. For comparison's sake, I looked up the specifications for a modern 19-inch LCD from Sony. The SDM-HS93's dimensions are 18.9 inches wide, 17 inches tall, and 10 inches deep (about 1.8 cubic feet in total). It weighs 15.7 pounds, and consumes no more than 36 watts of electricity per hour, producing a negligible amount of heat.

Any modern machine should readily work with high-resolution SVGA monitors or an analog LCD. (Another class of LCDs works directly with a digital signal from a video card; you may need to change or adapt your video card to use one of these displays.)

Some senior citizens may require new video display adapters and, possibly, upgrades to ROM BIOS chips to work with high-resolution monitors or LCDs. The oldest of the dinosaurs may not have BIOS fixes or motherboard circuitry to enable them to work with advanced video systems.

If you intend to use high-resolution settings on your monitor, make sure that the display device and your graphics adapter are a good match for each other. You can't view more pixels than your monitor can display, and you can't ask a graphics adapter to address more pixels than it is capable of rendering in memory.

After you've chosen your monitor, maintaining it becomes the focus. For the most part, monitors are not repairable — at least not by anyone other than a highly skilled technician. That's the bad news; the good news is that monitors are generally very reliable.

NOTE

With prices for CRTs hovering around the $100 mark, it probably does not make sense to repair a monitor that is no longer covered by a warranty. Although it may hurt to throw away a monitor (carefully and in accordance with your state or local laws about disposal of hazardous items) that is generally the route you will follow once a monitor has reached its typical end after about five or so years of regular use. Some manufacturers and government entities have instituted recycling programs that can recapture some of the components of a monitor and prevent poisoning of the earth with some of the chemicals and metals within.

As with most every piece of high technology, monitors have two periods of high mortality. A monitor may fail in its first few months of use after enough on-off cycles put stress on any manufacturing defects. After then, a monitor is likely to provide consistent service for a number of years and then reach its end of life. The warning signs of impending failure include dimming of maximum brightness, shrinking in the size of the image, and buzzing or humming noises that persist after the monitor has warmed up.

You can, and should, defend your monitor against some threats by making sure to use a surge protector between it and the wall outlet. This will protect against spikes in voltage. If your home or office is regularly subjected to "brownouts" or low-voltage — a common condition in some areas during periods of high electrical demand — you might want to purchase a UPS (uninterruptible power supply) which powers the monitor with a consistent level of voltage from its own internal battery source; the battery is in turn constantly recharged from the wall outlet.

LCDs are simpler devices than CRTs, and some of their components can be repaired. But once again, the cost (including parts and labor) may approach or surpass the price for a replacement. When you first start using an LCD, look closely for any *dead* pixels. Display a blank white screen and look for black or colored spots; display a black screen and look for white spots. In theory, there should be no dead areas, but most LCD manufacturers consider a display with no more than 10 such spots to be "perfect." If there are many problems with a new screen, return it to the place where you bought it immediately.

One sign of an LCD's decline is an increase in the number of dead spots. And a more certain indicator of impending failure is the arrival of black or white bands across the screen. Although you can repair a failed LCD (including replacing the backlight that illuminates the screen), it often does not make economic sense to do so; your best defense is to purchase a display with a repair or replacement warranty that gives you at least a year of protection.

Here are four things that you can do to help your monitor or LCD have a long and healthy life:

- Make sure to plug it into a good-quality surge protector. (This is the best thing you can do to protect the life of your monitor.)
- Make sure that the cable between the monitor and the video card is firmly attached at each end and not crimped or pinched.
- Be sure that the monitor is safely installed on a sturdy desk with its cable properly out of tripping range of passersby.
- Keep your workplace tidy: Don't place any papers on top of the ventilating holes on the back and side of the monitor. Periodically use a new paintbrush or the brush end of a vacuum cleaner to remove accumulated dust from the monitor's ventilation holes. (If the brush end of the vacuum cleaner is dirtier than the monitor ventilation holes, clean the brush first!) And I don't have to warn you about placing cups of coffee or soda anywhere in the vicinity, right?

Choosing the right monitor or LCD and understanding it are the topics at issue in this chapter.

How a CRT Monitor Works

Amateurs — including this author — should not attempt to repair a monitor. High voltage, delicate glass, and toxic chemicals are inside. Confine your troubleshooting to the outside of the box, please, and if you think it makes economic sense to pay for a repair, take your monitor to a professional shop.

To help you troubleshoot, though, let's work on a basic understanding of the way a monitor works.

A monitor is, at heart, a very high-quality television set that is tuned to just one channel: the signal coming out of the PC's video adapter. The inside of the glass front of the monitor is coated with phosphor compounds that glow whenever an electron beam strikes them. The monitor's electronics view the screen as a grid of dots to be painted with light. Each group of red, green, and blue dots is called a *pixel*, which stands for picture element.

A color monitor creates color display by combining the three primary colors of light: red, green, and blue. Black is the absence of any color. Combining green light and blue light creates yellow. Combining all three light sources creates white.

Inside a monitor, an electron beam is aimed toward a phosphor-coated screen. The phosphor glows whenever the electrons hit it, producing lighted images on the screen. When the monitor is plugged into a video adapter card, it receives a signal called the *scan frequency*. The monitor must lock in on the scan signal; in other words, the electron beam must cross the screen in synchronization with the scan signal.

The electron beam starts at the top left of the screen. It scans across the screen from left to right, exciting some dots of phosphor and bypassing others. When the beam reaches the right side of the screen, it quickly returns to the left and scans another line directly beneath the first one. An ordinary monochrome monitor has 350 of these scan lines per screen.

When the electron beam reaches the bottom right of the screen, it leaps up to the top-left corner and traces the 350 scan lines from the top again. This set of 350 scan lines — often visible when the brightness control is turned up too high — is called the *raster pattern* (or *raster*).

A basic SVGA monitor refreshes the screen (rescans the complete raster) 60 to 75 times a second. The refresh or vertical scan rate is, therefore, 60 to 75 Hz. By comparison, the horizontal scan rate is 31,500 to 60,000 times per second (31.5 to 60 KHz).

The video adapter, located as a card in the computer's bus or as a set of chips on the motherboard, provides explicit directions to the electron gun in the monitor. As the electron beam scans across the screen, the video card calls for a burst of electrons here to excite this pixel or a burst of electrons there to excite that pixel. A match must

exist between the capabilities of the video card and the monitor or else the monitor may not be able to work at its optimum resolution or other settings.

The higher the resolution you select, the faster the horizontal scan rate that the video card must produce. Table 14-1 contains the requirements for the most common video standards; in Chapter 12, you can find a more detailed listing of standards and their requirements.

TABLE 14-1: Horizontal and Vertical Scan Rates

Machine Class	Video Standard	Horizontal Resolution	Vertical Scan Scan Rate (KHz)	(Refresh) Rate (Hz)
Dinosaur	CGA	640 × 200	15.75 KHz	60 Hz
Dinosaur	EGA	640 × 350	21.5 KHz	60 Hz
Dinosaur	VGA	640 × 480	31.5 KHz	60 Hz
Dinosaur	VESA	640 × 480	37.5 KHz	75 Hz
Modern	SVGA	800 × 600	37.5 KHz	60 Hz
Modern	VESA	800 × 600	48 KHz	72 Hz
Modern	XGA	1,024 × 768	56.6 KHz (interlaced)	44 Hz
Modern	SVGA	1,024 × 768	48.3 KHz	60 Hz
Modern	VESA	1,024 × 768	60 KHz	75 Hz
Modern	VESA	1,280 × 1,024	80 KHz	75 Hz

Most computers include basic VGA video output as part of the motherboard; this allows the display of bootup messages and the BIOS Setup Screen before the more-capable video adapter is recognized and initialized by the operating system.

Nearly all modern monitors deliver SVGA specifications, an extension of the VGA standard that is one of the demarcation lines between dinosaurs and senior citizens. Dinosaur RGB monitors are no longer supported by modern machines, and EGA screens have very limited utility today.

Each monitor must be paired with an appropriate video display adapter card located in the computer system unit. *Multiscanning* circuitry — nearly ubiquitous today — allows monitors to lock onto multiple vertical and horizontal scanning frequencies, so a single multiscanning monitor is compatible with many different video cards.

Ch 14

Monitor components

The main internal components of a monitor are as follows:

- **CRT.** The cathode ray tube (CRT) is a sealed glass vacuum tube. Within it is an electron gun that emits a beam of electrons. A deflection yoke moves the beam horizontally and vertically as it strikes the phosphor-coated screen on the inside of the tube's front. Each of the points struck by the electron beam emits a red, blue, or green light for a fraction of a second.
- **Flyback transformer.** This component generates the high voltage needed to produce the electron beam within the CRT.
- **Power supply.** Circuitry within the CRT changes the incoming alternating voltage into necessary direct current.
- **Video amplifier.** The incoming video signal from the computer, usually about 0.7 volts, must be amplified to a level needed by the CRT to generate an image, usually above 40 volts.
- **Degaussing coil.** Circuitry here removes from the CRT any stray magnetic field, which can cause signal impurities.
- **Microprocessor.** Modern monitors have their own brain to manage special features, including screen adjustments.

How a monitor draws an image

Monitors use one of three ways to draw an image or a character on the screen:

- One way uses simple instructions from the CPU that tell the video card and the monitor to display the letter J at position 12,180. The card needs to have a definition for each letter and a particular style for that letter; the description is then communicated to the monitor in the form of instructions about which individual dots to illuminate. The original monochrome display adapter for the first IBM PC used such a scheme. Although very few modern users work in "text mode," all subsequent improvements to graphics modes maintain this facility as part of their repertoire.
- Another means of drawing images uses a video display adapter that maintains a library of shapes and colors that are then communicated to the monitor.

- Modern *graphical user interfaces (GUIs)* such as Windows produce the entire screen as a bitmap in memory, drawing all characters and graphics. The video card transfers this bitmap to the monitor for display as a series of illuminated dots. Bitmaps are not nearly as fast as direct display of characters, but offer other significant advantages, such as the ability to draw any type of imaginable image and to use an unlimited number of type styles and sizes.

One additional, essential element of monitor quality is *resolution,* which is a measurement of the size of the pixels. On two monitors of the same size, the one that displays more pixels is the one with higher resolution because the pixels must be smaller to fit in the same space. A set of tiny pixels on a small screen yields a high-resolution display; those same pixels on a huge room-sized screen won't yield as sharp an image.

Types of Monitors

Inexpensive monochrome monitors, the kind that were standard on PCs through the 1980s, are capable of displaying only one color — usually white, green, or amber against a black background.

Some very capable monochrome displays exist for modern machines. Higher-priced monochrome monitors are available with very high resolution and multiple shades of gray. Ultra-high-resolution monochrome monitors with proprietary video systems, intended for desktop publishing and computer-aided design, usually have extra-large screens designed to show two facing pages or a vertical page in true proportions. Some monitors used in medical procedures also present high-contrast, ultra-high-resolution images in a single color.

But today's computers generally offer high-resolution color video; the most common standard is SVGA color, with resolutions of up to 1,600 × 1,280 pixels on home machines. In fact, the designation of monitor specifications by labels such as SVGA, VGA, and other tags is declining; manufacturers instead market primarily on the basis of resolution.

Microsoft Windows, large spreadsheet, and desktop publishing users appreciate a full-page view of their work. In addition, high-level graphics users are choosing to manipulate photos, video, and animation with 32-bit color video cards capable of displaying millions of subtle color shades.

How an LCD Display Works

LCDs produce images on a flat surface by shining or reflecting light through changeable liquid crystals and colored filters. LCDs offer a number of advantages over a traditional cathode ray tube, including:

- They take up less space.
- They consume much less power, perhaps 30 to 50 watts compared to a video display tube's need for 100 to 150 watts.
- They produce much less heat.
- They don't flicker or strobe, thus reducing eyestrain.
- Screen surfaces produce little or no glare.
- LCD screens require a much smaller frame around their edges, yielding more usable display space than a cathode ray tube of the same nominal size. The viewable area of a typical 15-inch LCD is about the same as that of a typical 17-inch CRT.

The disadvantages of LCDs are relatively few:

- As this book goes to press, an LCD costs a bit more than a CRT of equivalent size. Until recently, that statement would have read "much more," but like almost every other part of the modern PC, LCDs have plummeted in price. By about 2008, there will probably be no difference in price between a CRT and an LCD, and CRT monitors may be difficult to find, except for special uses.
- Some LCD devices may not have as wide a viewing angle as a conventional CRT monitor. Early LCD displays had to be viewed at close to a head-on angle. Moving more than about 10 degrees to the left or right, or sitting at a chair too high or low could result in a dimmed or distorted image. Today, however, the situation is much better, with viewing angles from 130 degrees or so to as high as 175 degrees in more expensive high-end devices.
- Good-quality LCDs are very sharp and easy to read, but even the best models can't display colors as brightly or as well-defined as a good CRT can. Because each pixel can be addressed individually, LCDs are capable of creating sharper text than CRTs, which depend on a moving beam of electrons that must be kept in focus and controlled properly. Those same sharp edges, however, make graphics a bit less lifelike than those shown on a CRT, where various tricks can be used to create subtle gradations of color and brightness.

- When you compare specifications among various LCDs, pay attention to the *contrast ratio;* the higher the number, the greater the difference between black and white. As this book goes to press, the low end was about 400:1 and the best machines promised as much as a 1000:1 ratio. Another difference between models is the refresh rate, measured in milliseconds; the lower the rate, the faster the image reacts to changes and the less likely you'll see momentary blurring (or *artifacts*) when part of the screen lags behind the newest information. As this book is written, refresh rates ranged from a high of about 16ms to a low of about 4ms; lower is better.
- LCDs are capable of working with only one physical, or *native,* resolution, limited by the number of pixels built into the display; in general, that's the setting that delivers the best quality. However, nearly all current models have ways of converting an input to simulate a range of other resolutions. A typical standard resolution was 1280×1024, with some consumer models offering 1600×1200 resolution.

The technology behind LCDs goes back to experiments with liquid crystals as early as 1888. Scientists found that certain liquid chemicals can be made to align precisely when they are subjected to electrical current; think of the way metal shavings will align at the poles of a magnet.

An LCD works by energizing or de-energizing liquid crystals to act like shutters to block or permit the passage of light. Early LCDs, still used in inexpensive calculators, some cell phone screens, and some of the first laptops, depended on light penetrating through the screen to reach a reflective surface and then to be bounced back at the viewer. Modern LCDs typically use a powered fluorescent backlight to shine through the crystals. Light from the backlight passes through one or more polarizing filters and then through a layer that contains many thousands of tiny spots of liquid crystal arrayed in tiny cells.

The frame of the LCD screen contains thousands of tiny electrical paths that connect to tracings that extend across the rows of cells. When the display's controller sends an electric current to a particular row and column, the liquid crystals at that cell twist into a position that permits the polarized light to pass through. Modern LCDs, like the one shown in Figure 14-1, use a *thin-film transistor* to deliver current to individual cells; these active-matrix systems are much improved over earlier passive-matrix systems.

Ch 14

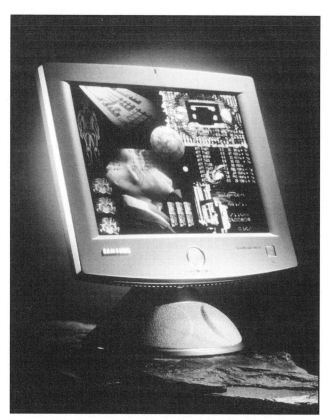

FIGURE 14-1: *A monitor without a video display tube, the Samsung SyncMaster is a flat-panel LCD display.*

On a monochrome screen like the one you may have on a desktop calculator, the crystals block the passage of light to display black. Color LCDs use similar technology. Each pixel is made up of three cells of liquid crystal; each of these cells has a red, green, or blue filter allowing creation of almost every hue by the additive color process.

Within an LCD, the addressing of the pixels is done digitally. Although the PC itself manipulates a graphics bitmap digitally, a standard video adapter then converts the information to an analog signal. Nearly all early LCDs converted this analog signal back to digital form, adding circuitry that minimizes ghosting and fluttering that can be caused by the conversion from digital to analog and back to digital.

The best quality, though, comes with designs that stay digital all the way, working with specialized digital video adapters. Today, many LCD designs use the *Digital Visual Interface (DVI)* standard, ending several years of incompatible digital standards between the Digital Flat Panel standard, put forth by the Video Electronics Association, and the DVI standard promulgated by the Digital Display Working Group. The standard regularizes connectors and electrical signals for digital video controllers. If you've got an older LCD, probably one built before 2002, you may need to mate it with a specific display adapter and cable to work properly.

The LCD difference

An LCD has many things in common with a CRT monitor, and a few that are distinctly its own. The basics of resolution, brightness, and contrast ratio are very similar. Here are a few areas in which an LCD is different:

- **Aspect ratio.** A standard CRT monitor has a rectangular proportion of width to height of 4:3. For example, the 19-inch monitor on my desktop is 14.5 inches wide and 11 inches tall, which matches that ratio very closely. However, many LCDs are now offered in widescreen designs that enhance viewing of movies and also make it easier to have multiple windows open on the desktop. Nearby, I have a widescreen 17-inch LCD with a viewable screen that is 13 inches wide and 8.25 inches tall for a ratio of 16:10.

- **Digital and analog signals.** LCDs are designed to work with digital signals — strings of 0s and 1s — rather than the rise and fall information of the analog signal used by most CRT monitors. LCDs today are offered in three versions: displays that accept a standard analog signal and perform the conversion to digital, models that can work with either an analog or digital signal, and one that expects a pure digital (DVI) signal from the card.

- **Pixel response rate.** On an LCD, this is somewhat similar to the refresh rate on a CRT monitor. The faster the response rate, the less likely a moving image will smear, streak, or ghost on the screen. To view a movie or computer game, you should have a pixel response rate of no more than 15ms; the best of modern LCDs have dropped below 6ms and are moving to near-instant reaction.

Ch **14**

■ **Viewing angle.** Less of an issue for current LCDs than first-generation models, a wide viewing angle is better than a narrow one.

■ **Screen mode.** An LCD screen can easily be rotated from the standard horizontal view (wider than tall, called landscape mode) to a vertical one (called portrait mode). A special device driver for the display handles the rotation of the image. Portrait mode is valuable for some specialized uses, including spreadsheet work and some desktop publishing tasks.

NOTE

Because LCDs don't require a wide supporting frame around the display, a 15-inch LCD presents nearly the same viewable surface as a 17-inch cathode ray tube monitor.

How Big Is 17 Inches?

What exactly is a 17-inch CRT monitor or a 17-inch LCD? In theory, screen size is measured as the diagonal distance from top-left to bottom-right corners, or top-right to bottom-left corners. However, not all screens are shaped the same, and in any case, the plastic frame around the screen (called a *bezel*) can crop as much as an inch on all sides of the tube.

Partly as the result of some consumer lawsuits, monitor makers now are a bit more careful in their claims. Look for the manufacturer's specification of maximum viewable image size. Often, a 15-inch screen has viewable sizes in the range of 13.5 to 13.9 inches; 17-inch screens are usually in the range of 15.5 to 16 inches.

Probably more important is the difference in square inches of screen real estate offered by monitors of various sizes. Going from a 14-inch monitor to a 15-inch box yields about a 12 percent boost in size, from 84 square inches to 94 square inches. Going from a 15-inch monitor to a 21-inch behemoth doubles the view, from about 94 square inches to about 185 square inches. All of these numbers are rough because no two monitor makers frame their tubes with the same width of plastic bezel.

Also consider the fact that very few monitors actually send electrons all the way to the edges of the tube. Additionally, those that are capable of doing so may deliver a distorted picture at the edges. You need to adjust the picture to deliver the best view, usually resulting in a frame of about a quarter-inch on all sides. Note also that on some monitors, each time you adjust the resolution, the side-to-side and diagonal measurements of the image may change.

On my desktop, I use a 19-inch monitor that delivers a diagonal viewable image size of about 18 inches; it is capable of displaying a clean and crisp image at 1,024 × 768 resolution. Table 14-2 compares real estate for monitors from 14 to 21 inches diagonal measure.

TABLE 14-2: Monitor Real Estate Comparison

Monitor Size*	Typical Viable Image Size*	Typical Square Inches	CRT Real Estate Index**	Typical Maximum Resolution
14 inches	13.2 inches	84	100	1,024___768
15 inches	13.7 inches	94	112	1,024___768
17 inches	15.7 inches	108	129	1,280___1,024
19 inches	18 inches	146	174	1,280___1,024 to 1,600___1,280
20 inches	19 inches	168 inches	200	1,280___1,024 to 1,600___1,280
21 inches	19.8 inches	185 inches	220	1,280___1,024 to 1,600___1,280

*Measured diagonally.
**Fix Your Own PC CRT Real Estate Index: Square-inch measurements of viewable image size are compared to a 14-inch CRT monitor. For example, the 21-inch monitor listed here is approximately 2.2 times larger than a 14-inch monitor.

The fact that a monitor is technically capable of operating at a high resolution does not mean that it will present a usable image. For example, a 14-inch monitor looks best at a 640 × 480 resolution and will give you an electronic headache at 1,280 × 1,024 or higher. By the same token, some very large monitors are optimized for use at higher resolutions and may look too blocky at lower resolutions. It all comes down to personal preference; some users like to use large characters on a large screen, while others prefer to see more information.

TABLE 14-3: LCD Real Estate Comparison

LCD Size*	Typical Viewable Image Size*	Typical Square Inches	CRT Real Estate Index**	Equivalent CRT Size	LCD Real Estate Index***	Typical Resolution
15 inches	15 inches	108	129	17 inches	100	1,024 × 768
17 inches	17 inches	142	169	19 inches	131	1,280 × 1,024
19 inches	19 inches	176	209	20 inches	163	1,280 × 1,024
20 inches	20 inches	194	231	22 inches	180	1,280 × 1,024

*Measured diagonally.

**Fix Your Own PC CRT Real Estate Index: Square-inch measurements of viewable image size are compared to a 14-inch CRT as shown in Table 14-2. For example, the 20-inch LCD listed here is approximately 2.19 times larger than a 14-inch LCD.

***Fix Your Own PC LCD Real Estate Index: Square-inch measurements of viewable image size are compared to a 15-inch LCD as shown in Table 14-3. For example, the 20-inch LCD listed here is approximately 1.8 times larger than a 15-inch LCD.

LCD monitors have a very narrow frame around their screens; for all intents and purposes, the entire screen is viewable. For that reason, LCDs yield more viewable area; a typical 17-inch LCD gives you about as much screen as a 19-inch CRT monitor. Table 14-3 contains a comparison of available real estate on LCDs. More displayable real estate is available at every size.

Table 14-4 is a chart of typical best settings for a CRT monitor. However, what is best in any given situation depends to some degree on the application that you are running. Highly graphical applications certainly will do better at higher resolutions, but you won't see much difference if you are using text-only applications all the time.

The Elements of a High-Quality CRT Monitor or LCD Screen

Five important specifications make up the elements of a high-quality CRT monitor:

- Dot pitch
- Refresh or scan rate
- Brightness and contrast
- Interlace or noninterlace scan
- CRT screen shape

The following sections describe each element in detail.

Table 14-4: Best Resolution by CRT Monitor Size

Display Size (Nominal Size)	640 × 480	800 × 600	1,024 × 768	1,280 × 1,024	1,600 × 1,200
14 inches	Best	Good	Fair	Poor	Poor
15 inches	Good	Good	Best	Poor	Poor
17 inches	Fair–Good	Good	Best	Fair	Poor
19 inches	Fair	Fair	Good	Best	Fair
21 inches	Poor	Fair	Good	Best	Good

Dot pitch

The first element that most monitor buyers consider is the *dot pitch,* a measurement of how close together the dots of phosphor are placed to make up a video monitor's image. The finer the dot pitch (the lower the number), the finer the image — theoretically. Today's better monitors have a dot pitch of 0.28mm or less.

On traditional monitors using dot masks, dot pitch is measured as the diagonal or vertical distance between two dots of the same color. The smaller the dot pitch, the finer the image. I wouldn't choose to strain my eyes with anything coarser than 0.28mm for a video monitor or LCD panel. (Dot pitch is sometimes called *pixel pitch* in LCD specs.)

As with everything else in personal computing, specs are getting better. Although CRT technology may have reached its peak as far as computer users are concerned (television sets have moved on to HDTV models and many monitor makers have switched over to LCD screens), there have been some remarkable improvements in quality over the years. You'll find some 21-inch CRT monitors with dot pitches of 0.24mm or better. Trinitron and similar tubes are measured by stripe pitch, mask pitch, or slot pitch. These represent the horizontal distance between two stripes of the same color. Look for pitches of 0.25mm or less for desktop monitors, and 0.24mm or less for 20- and 21-inch models.

One specialized class of monitors is large presentation devices used in instructional settings and as part of a family room PC/entertainment center system. These monitors are big, even by television standards — up to 42 or 48 inches in size — and are intended to be viewed at some distance from the screen. Typical dot pitches for these room-size monitors can be in the 0.75mm to 0.90mm range and larger. One design uses a smaller dot pitch at the center and a larger dot pitch at the corners, where information is presumably less important.

Someday, the prices of another type of monitor — the plasma display — may drop to a reasonable range. Plasma displays use charged gas to create separate light sources for each pixel, like a tiny neon light. Displays are as perfectly flat as an LCD, and much brighter than a video display tube or an LCD. For example, a 42-inch plasma in 2006 offered a 10,000:1 contrast ratio and a brightness (measured in candelas per square meter or cd/m^2, or in a similar measure called *nits*) of 1,200. (A good-quality LCD might have a contrast ratio of 800:1 and a brightness reading of 500.) These devices — just a few inches thick — can be produced in giant sizes. Like all great technologies, prices have plummeted over time, although plasma screens are still much more expensive than CRTs or LCDs. In 2001, a 50-inch plasma display sold for just under $10,000; in 2006, an improved model of the same size sold for about $3,200.

Refresh or scan rate

Refresh rate, also called *vertical frequency* or *vertical scan rate,* tells you how many times per second the monitor redraws the image on screen. Most current users find that refresh rates below 75 Hz (75 refreshes per second) cause visible and annoying flicker. Slow scan rates produce flicker because of the decay of phosphor illumination between passes of the beam. High scan rates produce a rock-solid image, but monitors capable of high scan rates are more expensive. A scan rate that is adequate on a 14-inch monitor will seem to flicker on a big 17- or 20-inch monitor because the high-resolution video modes often used on these large monitors need a higher scan rate.

For most CRT monitors, the refresh rate declines as the resolution increases. In other words, a monitor may be capable of 100 to 150 Hz at 640 × 480 resolution, but only 75 to 85 Hz at the 1,280 × 1,024 setting. Put another way, when you see a high refresh rate advertised for a monitor, it almost always refers to the display's capability at its lowest resolution. Pay attention to its specifications at the resolution you intend to use most often.

The original IBM PC's monochrome card rewrote the monitor screen 50 times per second. A vertical scan rate of 50 Hz is too slow for most people's eyes, so IBM specified long-persistence phosphor compounds on the monitor screen. Once excited, these phosphors continue to glow for a while even after the electron beam has moved on to another part of the screen. This cures the flickering, but the monitor displays annoying ghosts when the user scrolls text.

Modern monitors adjust refresh rate according to the display resolution. You may see specs for a 21-inch monitor for example, that show a 130 Hz refresh rate at 640 × 480 resolution, and an 85 Hz refresh rate at 1,600 × 1,200 resolution.

An RGB color monitor, the color monitor paired with the CGA video card on the early IBM PC, refreshes the screen 60 times per second. High-resolution VGA and multiscanning monitors refresh at rates of as much as 80 times per second.

Do you see a pattern in these numbers? A high vertical scan rate is better. Monitors that can handle Super VGA (800 × 600) screen resolutions at 70 or 72 refreshes per second look good. The same Super VGA resolution on a lower-quality Super VGA monitor that refreshes the screen 56 times per second will look jumpy and appear to flicker.

Brightness and contrast

What you see is what you get, and not all monitors or LCDs (or eyes) are created equal. Most users prefer a bright screen, and a bright screen is enhanced by a high contrast ratio between black and white. (This is especially important for word processing and many web sites that present text as black on white.)

The best way to judge whether a monitor is right for you is to spend some time using it, preferably in the same sort of lighting you use in your home or office — not under a ceiling full of fluorescent bulbs in a computer store.

Another way to consider the light values for a screen is to read the manufacturer's specifications very carefully. You're looking for two numbers:

- **Contrast ratio.** The higher the number, the better. A ratio of 400:1 is near the low end of modern screens, and 1,000:1 near the top for an LCD. (Pricey plasma screens can have contrast ratios as high as 10,000:1.)
- **Brightness.** Manufacturers measure the maximum brightness of their screens in cd/m^2, which is the number of candelas per square meter, sometimes using a similar measure called *nits*. As a measurement of light intensity, candelas go all the way back to the day of the candle. The modern definition has moved beyond a flickering flame; a candela is now defined as the intensity of a light source producing single-frequency light of 540 terahertz (THz) with a power of 1/683 watt per steradian, That's a rather complex calculation, and one that is meaningless to most of us; suffice it to say, the higher the number of candelas per square meter, the brighter the display or monitor. Most modern LCDs deliver about 250 to 500 cd/m^2, and CRTs about half that level, generally in the range of about 100 to 125 cd/m^2. Given a choice between a lower contrast ratio and a higher one, and a lower brightness level and a higher level, go for the brighter, more contrasty display. If you can't have it both ways, choose a higher brightness level.

Interlaced versus noninterlaced monitors

In the high-tech equivalent of the search for a free lunch, monitor designers came up with interlaced monitors, displays that refresh only the odd-numbered rows of pixels in one pass, and then refresh the even-numbered rows of pixels in a second pass. Interlaced monitors can display *high-resolution video* (many rows of pixels on the screen), yet at the time they were introduced, they cost much less than noninterlaced monitors.

It's a subjective decision — some viewers don't mind the flicker inherent in the design; others can't abide interlaced monitors, especially if they spend many hours in front of the screen. Because the overall price of monitors has gone down at the same time that quality has gone up, interlaced monitors are now relatively rare and really not worth buying.

CRT screen shape

The sheet of paper in the book that you are reading is more or less flat. So, too, are LCD screens.

CRT monitors, on the other hand, are more or less curved. Designers add curvature to television and computer monitor screens to deal with the fact that the edges of the screen are farther away from the electron gun than the center of the screen. Think of it this way: at the center of the screen, the angle between the electron gun and the front face of the tube is flat. However, to illuminate a pixel in the upper-right corner, for example, the electron gun has to point up and to the right. A pixel located at the exact center of the tube, therefore, may be perfectly round, while a pixel in one of the corners receives a relatively oblique pulse that results in an oblong or *astigmatic* illumination. Therefore, the larger the screen, the wider the angle between the electron gun and the corners.

Some of that physics problem has been solved by modern electronics, but nearly all tubes still have a bit of curve today. Tube designs include spherical, cylindrical, and flat.

- **Spherical tubes** present a face like a slice of a ball, with curves at the top, bottom, and sides. They are generally the least expensive, but often the least pleasing to critical eyes. They are usually seen on 14-inch models; some 20-inch monitors use spherical tubes to present a lower-cost alternative to 21-inch behemoths.
- **Cylindrical screens** are like a slice taken from the side of a large barrel, resulting in a nearly flat vertical and a slightly curved horizontal shape. Cylindrical tubes are well suited to Trinitron designs. (Sony's original design has since been licensed and adapted by Mitsubishi and other manufacturers.)

Ch
14

- **Flat screens**, for the most part, are close enough to claim the name but are still deserving of quotation marks. These designs are a slice of a very large sphere, so large that the curves are barely perceptible. Some of these designs sacrifice a bit of sharpness at the edges. Flat screens are very common now, although some less-expensive monitors still throw users a bit of a curve.

Color and shades of gray

The number of colors offered on a monitor is determined by the capabilities of the video adapter. More color does not make the monitor display any sharper, but it does make it easier to read or easier to pick out details in an image, which may make additional colors the functional equivalent of sharpness.

A total of 16 colors was once the standard for text work and simple graphics, and was considered adequate for those tasks. Today, I don't think anybody with a modern machine would be satisfied with a 16-color display. A 256-color display was once considered the minimum for multimedia work, but today's users want more than that even for text displays. Even the most basic graphics display card — if you can still find one — is capable of 65K colors (16-bit color) and most can go to 16.7 million colors (24-bit color) or more (32-bit color). If you perform any graphics editing, including retouching and manipulation of photographs, you need a high-resolution video card and monitor.

WARNING

Higher color counts come at a price, though, and I'm not merely referring to purchase cost. The more colors the system has to draw with and transfer, the slower the screen redraws and the slower the general video response.

A high number of colors and high resolutions place a great demand on video display adapters. Just a few years ago entry-level graphic cards offered as little as 4MB of RAM on board; today the minimum is 64 to 128MB and the most capable machines offer 256MB to 512MB and more.

CROSS-REFERENCE

See Chapter 12 for more about the specifications and capabilities of video display adapters.

A monochrome monitor — almost impossible to find in a consumer model anymore — substitutes shades of gray for colors. The more shades of gray, the more detail the monitor can impart in graphics. A high number of gray shades can make the display seem much sharper, even though you are still working with the original number of pixels per screen. Clever font designers use gray shades strategically on the edges of characters to fool the eye, a technique called *antialiasing*. The user perceives noticeably crisper fonts with cleaner, smoother curves.

Antiglare

One not-so-minor issue for monitor owners is dealing with glare from office lighting and open windows. The cheapest CRT monitors can be so shiny that you can comb your hair in the reflected glare. LCD screens are much less prone to glare; part of the manufacturing process involves installing a protective (and antiglare) plastic covering over the screen itself.

You can do a number of things to reduce interference from outside light sources. The first issue is often to deal with the lighting situation at your workplace. Some users find a good solution in turning off overhead lights and replacing them with smaller, focused task lights on or alongside your desk. You can also install light-filtering shades or curtains to reduce glare from outside sources. Monitor makers can mount their devices on a tilt-and-pivot stand that allows for adjustment.

The lowest level of glare protection is a coating that is sprayed onto the outside or inside of the glass that faces the user. Another technique, called *spin coating,* involves applying a very thin, optically clear protection. Some makers offer *microfilter CRTs.* In this scheme, a tiny, colored filter over each phosphor dot absorbs light bouncing off the filter. An added plus for this design is that the tubes can be made of clear instead of tinted glass, allowing the monitors to be slightly brighter than standard devices.

The importance of maintaining control

No two offices or rec rooms have the same lighting conditions, your eyes may be different from mine, and two models of the same monitor may have different brightness, contrast, or color levels. And finally, everything is subject to change over time.

For that reason, shop for a CRT monitor that offers a full set of controls. The best location for these controls is on the front side of the monitor; you want to be looking at the screen at a standard reading distance as you make adjustments.

The original design for computer monitors used knobs or wheels to make analog adjustments; lower-priced (and mostly outdated) models still offer these controls. The problem with knobs is that the settings you make affect only the current resolution. Any time you change resolution — which includes bouncing out of Windows to DOS — the image size, centering, brightness, contrast, and other settings may bounce around.

Modern monitors use digital controls with digital memories that store the precise settings you make for each resolution or graphics mode. The monitor senses changes and uses stored settings automatically. Other advanced features include onscreen menus that display instructions for making settings on the monitor, and in some cases, produce test patterns for adjustment purposes.

The monitor should at least include controls for brightness, contrast, vertical size, horizontal size, and position. Some less-expensive monitors may offer a switch to turn overscan on or off, which expands the image vertically and horizontally, but gives you less flexibility than separate controls. You may have a situation where text is placed off the displayable face of the monitor.

Better monitors include a degaussing circuit that clears up color and convergence problems caused by magnetic fields. The process can take place automatically each time you turn the monitor on, or you can initiate it by pressing a button among the controls. If you hear a *brief* buzz each time you turn on your monitor, that's the sound of an automatic degausser at work.

An advanced color adjustment, offered in addition to color level, lets you set a monitor's white balance. Photographers sometimes refer to this sort of adjustment as *color temperature*. A white balance setting can add a slight pink (warm) tint or a slight blue (cool) tint to what may otherwise be pure white. This sort of feature is valuable if the particular monitor has a warm or cool tint as delivered.

Other advanced image controls are intended to compensate for distortions such as pincushioning in which vertical lines bow outward or barrel distortion in which the lines bow inward. A trapezoid control can improve trapezoidal distortion that gives an image varying widths at top and bottom.

Why bad things happen to good monitors

Why does the CRT monitor that got such good reviews in a computer magazine, or the one that shone with uncommon excellence on the shelf at the dealer, look like a 1956 Philco when you plug it in at home or at your office?

The fact is that monitors are subject to variations in assembly and are also vulnerable to mishandling in shipping or setup. Because a bit of hand work is involved in finishing display tubes and in placing and adjusting the electromagnets that aim electrons at the screen, a minor misplacement or a location shift after a monitor leaves the factory can throw a monitor out of focus, shift its image off-center, or otherwise affect image quality.

Another possible cause of less-than-expected brightness or contrast, or an image that does not fill the screen properly, is low voltage. This could be the result of a temporary brownout caused by a house, neighborhood, or city full of air conditioners on a summer afternoon (or there may be a problem with the voltage you receive all the time). You can check the voltage with a multitester; some UPS devices (see Chapter 24) can also generate a report that tells you about the incoming juice.

WARNING

Over time, power supplies age and change characteristics, and the stress and strain a monitor undergoes as it is turned on and off can have an effect. One indicator of a failing power supply is a shrunken display that no longer can extend to the corners of the screen; another indicator is a reduction in the intensity of the whitest whites or other bright colors.

Be sure to test your monitor meticulously when you first plug it in. And don't be afraid to reject a monitor that doesn't live up to your expectations. For that reason, be sure to buy the screen from a reputable dealer willing to give you a money-back guarantee that will be in effect for a reasonable period of time after purchase. Compare the potential savings you may obtain from a mail-order house to the cost of returning a bad display if necessary.

Also, go back and make adjustments to the controls for your monitor every six months or so to tune it up in that way.

Green monitors

Green monitors can display hundreds of colors — not just the color of the forests or money. The term *green* refers to a standard intended to reduce electrical usage by devices. These monitors have their own internal hardware that reduces power draw or even shuts down the device entirely if the user ceases activity for a particular period of time. Green monitors often also work with software and BIOS-based controls.

Look for compliance with the Energy Star standards for consumption in sleep modes and the *Display Power Management Signaling (DPMS)* standard that allows a DPMS-compliant graphics card to initiate sleep modes. Some monitors support the Swedish Nutek standards, which are even more stringent in power consumption controls.

If you are concerned about electromagnetic emissions from monitors, look for compliance with the current MPR-II specifications or the even more stringent TCO standard. Your best defense against electromagnetic emissions is to sit at a proper distance from your monitor, generally about an arm's length, and never to operate a monitor with its cover off or with a crack or other opening in the shielding.

Plug-and-Play monitors

With the arrival of the Plug-and-Play standard came monitors that can communicate with the PC when they are plugged in.

Nearly all monitors now offered for sale support this standard. These monitors use an adaptation of the common DB-15 VGA cable and connector to send information about the monitor's capabilities to the graphics adapter in the PC and vice versa. The biggest problem addressed by this new intelligent connection is avoiding refresh rate mismatches between monitor and adapter.

The cables use four rarely used data lines in the cable for this purpose, but the monitor and adapter must subscribe to the VESA *Display Data Channel (DDC)* protocol. Some monitors indicate compliance with DDC by coloring their cable connectors bright blue.

The original standard here was DDC1, which has Plug-and-Play monitors continuously sending information back up the wire to the graphics adapter. The more advanced DDC2B specification has the monitor send information to the PC only when it is requested to do so by the graphics adapter. Monitors must support both DDC versions 1 and 2B, while the adapter can support either specification.

NOTE

A DDC monitor will work without problem on a PC that doesn't have Plug-and-Play capabilities and with an adapter that does not support DDC. The system will simply be as dumb as it always was before the new specification.

Even further advanced is the DDC2AB specification that allows software control of monitor features, including color settings and size and distortion adjustments.

The Universal Serial Bus can offer the same facilities, and can also permit daisy-chaining of peripherals including mice, keyboards, and printers. Although it was envisioned that someday monitors would connect to a PC through the USB port, consumer models of that design have not been brought to market. However, some models that use a standard SVGA connector also attach to a computer's USB port so that the monitor can offer a convenient desktop USB hub for various devices.

In mid-2006, manufacturers in the Video Electronics Standards Association (VESA) approved the specifications for the DisplayPort interface standard. The high-bandwidth interface allows high-definition digital audio to be available to the display device over the same cable as the digital video signal. The standard was released to the industry as an open specification, which will encourage wide usage.

Monitor Prices

Here's another area where your computer dollar goes further than ever before. In recent years, the prices of monitors began to drop sharply at the same time that buyers became more demanding of quality, resolution, and size.

Table 14-5 contains the price range from discount sources for a selected group of high-quality monitors, updated in early 2006. I compare the prices to 2002 and 2000 levels. In this book's previous edition, this chart began with 15-inch CRTs; in 2007, the dwindling offerings of monitor manufacturers began at 17-inch models.

Based on today's prices, I recommend a 17-inch monitor to get the most for your money, and a 19-inch monitor if you can spare a few dollars more. If you spend your entire day in front of a monitor, consider an investment in a 21-inch screen.

Table 14-6 presents similar information for LCDs, with prices as they were in early 2007 and as they were in 2002 as these models first arrived on the market in large quantities.

Ch 14

TABLE 14-5: Monitor Prices

Consumer-Quality CRT Monitor	Price Range in 2007	Price Range in 2002	Price Range in 2000
15-inch SVGA 0.28mm dot pitch, 1,280 × 1,024	$50 to $90	$140–$150	$140 to $160
17-inch SVGA 0.28mm dot pitch, 1,280 × 1,024	$50 to $150	$170–$220	$210-$300
19-inch SVGA 0.26mm dot pitch, 1,600 × 1,200	$99 to $200	$220–$260	$300 to $600
21-inch SVGA 0.28mm dot pitch, 1,600 × 1,280	$150 to $250	$560	$740 to $1,400

Table 14-6: LCD Prices

Consumer-Quality LCD Display	Price Range in 2007	Price Range in 2002
15-inch, 1,024 × 768	$120 to $160	$339 to $639
17-inch, 1,280 × 1,024	$120 to $300	$599 to $1,299
19-inch, 1,280 × 1,024	$165 to $330	$1,999 to $2,499
21-inch, 1,680 × 1,050	$500 to $900	$1,999 to $2,499

Testing a Monitor

If your CRT monitor or LCD screen has no video, it's best to start with a quick switch and cable check. Are both the computer and the monitor plugged in and turned on? Look for an indicator light to tell you that the monitor is receiving power. For a cruder but more interesting way to test whether your monitor is powering up, you can try the following manual test. Monitors develop a big electrostatic field in the first couple of seconds after they are turned on, so turn off the power to the monitor, and then hold the back of your hand to the monitor screen and power it back on. The hair on the back of your hand will stand up as the electrostatic field develops.

Check the video data cable from the video card to the monitor. It must be plugged in tight and screwed down at the video card end.

If your monitor suddenly seems to have lost the ability to think in more than one color, the problem could be serious — the failure of the electron gun or the tube itself in a CRT monitor or a problem with some of the internal electronics of an LCD screen — or it could be no more than a loose connection.

Just hope that the problem is simple: Make sure that the cable that runs between the PC and the monitor is properly seated at both ends; look for misaligned pins; see whether the cable has been crimped or cut. If you have another working graphics cable, try substituting it to see if the problem goes away. You can also try another working monitor to see if the problem lies in the original cable.

Are you certain that your monitor is plugged into a working electrical outlet or surge protector, and that the switch on the monitor (and on the surge protector) is turned on? If your monitor is old enough to have a rotary dial to adjust brightness or contrast, make sure that the setting has not been inadvertently rotated to a dark setting.

Have you changed your computer's video settings under Windows? If you ask Windows to switch to a resolution, color depth, or refresh rate that is not supported by your graphics card or your monitor, you might end up with Windows not displaying a visible image. (The solution here is to reboot and choose Windows Safe Mode, which automatically uses a very basic video setting; once you have the operating system loaded, you can go to the Control Panel and change the video settings back to an acceptable set of parameters. I discuss this fix in Chapter 12.)

 CROSS-REFERENCE

The video card, the monitor, or a multitude of problems in the computer system unit can cause an absence of video. The troubleshooting charts in Appendix A (on the CD) provide a plan to help you identify the culprit.

Before jumping into the troubleshooting charts, try a couple of quick swaps if you have duplicate monitors or comparably equipped computers available. Try attaching the suspect monitor to a computer that you know works. If the monitor works on the comparable computer (one that has the same video adapter card), then test the suspect computer and the video card. For testing ideas, check the troubleshooting charts in Appendix A on the CD.

If you have *snow* (a fuzzy, random-dot effect) on your monitor, the most likely problem is a video card that is incompatible with your monitor; a modern machine and current video card are compatible with almost any current monitor, but not with dinosaur-era monitors. Going the other direction, a dinosaur-era video card is not likely to work with an advanced current display.

Monitor diagnostics

Most diagnostic programs include a set of test screens that allow you to explore the capabilities of your monitor and video card; some card or monitor makers include a few specialized demo programs with their products.

For more precise adjustment and testing of your CRT monitor or LCD, you can check out the DisplayMate products from DisplayMate Technologies (www.displaymate.com). DisplayMate for Windows is an end-user video utility for setting up and tuning up a display for optimum image and picture quality. The program walks you through more than a dozen detailed exercises using the monitor's adjustments to display as much detail in as sharp a presentation as possible. An example of a DisplayMate adjustment screen is shown in Figure 14-2.

The program supports modes from 16 colors to 24- or 32-bit, 16.7-million colors; all resolutions up to 4,096 × 4,096; and all screen shapes and aspect ratios including landscape, portrait, and HDTV. It runs under any video board and monitor supported by Windows. You can use the program's all-purpose diagnostic screen as your Windows opening screen for a daily checkup.

Removing and installing a monitor

Turn off the monitor and the computer. It is not good practice to attach a cable to a computer that is powered up — a slight misalignment of the plug can result in a short that can damage the video adapter, the monitor, the motherboard, or all three.

Undo the screws that hold the monitor data cable to the video connector on the back of the computer. If you're working with older cables, there may be tiny screws on the shoulders of the connector end; on modern models, you're likely to find inch-long extended posts that make it easier to attach or detach cables without a tiny tool. Disconnect the video cable and power cables, and then replace the malfunctioning monitor with an equivalent good one.

SUMMARY

Now that you understand how your computer visually displays its operations and results, it's time to move on to the mechanics behind communications with devices outside of the box. In the next chapter, I explore serial communication, including asynchronous serial, USB, and FireWire specifications for use with modems, certain printers, external storage devices, and high-bandwidth digital video cameras and other accessories.

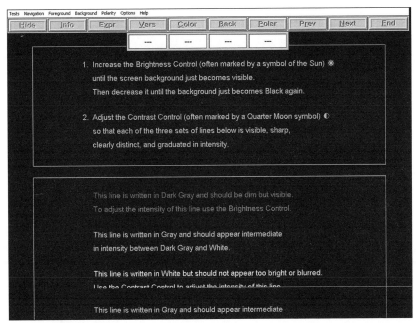

Figure 14-2: *A DisplayMate adjustment screen for contrast and brightness.*

Chapter 15

Tools Needed:

- Phillips or flat-blade screwdriver

Working Outside the Box: External Serial, USB, eSATA, and FireWire Connections

Everything old is new again, in a high-tech computer sort of way. That's the story of serial communications, which were the original form of I/O data interchange for large computers and the first personal computers.

It's the morning commute, and thousands of cars, trucks, and buses speed along in a thick river on an eight-lane limited-access superhighway. Then the entire column comes to a single tollbooth with a gate at the entrance to a two-lane tunnel. This scenario is pretty close to the situation inside your computer when data is forced to switch over from the 8-, 16-, or 32-bit-wide parallel superhighway that connects the CPU, memory, and most internal devices to the local road that exits to most modems and some other external peripherals.

The two-lane roads are called *serial lines* because the data is forced to march one bit behind the other. One road runs from the computer to a device, and the other from the device back to the computer. The PC adds marker signals to indicate the beginning and end of each word of data and, in many cases, also adds error-detecting codes so that it has a reasonable chance to correct errors in transmission.

In theory, a parallel interface is much faster than a serial interface, just as an 8- or 16-lane superhighway can carry more vehicles than a two-lane back road. Within a computer, a short parallel pathway — like the computer bus — is indeed the fastest way to communicate information. When you take the parallel path out of the PC, a parallel cable is also relatively fast when it is in direct connection to a device that is very close.

However, as computer microprocessors and buses got faster and faster, parallel pathways ran into the limitations of physics: Although 8 or 16 bits of information may be sent from the interface at the exact same moment, various problems — including interference, crosstalk, and flaws in the wire or the metal itself — can result in tiny delays at the receiving end. Technicians call this *skew* and the more the delay, or the more information being forced down the wire, the more problems skew can engender. Problems with parallel communications increase with the clock speed, the drumbeat that paces the transmission of packets of information across the wires.

Designers were able to push parallel communication along by using more robust construction of the cables and by adding shielding between wires and in the connectors. SCSI interfaces, which were a form of very high-speed parallel communication in their original design, require especially heavy-duty components.

Serial cables are much simpler, essentially using just two wires for carrying information. Although data must be converted from its parallel form as it exists on the computer bus, high-speed circuits and specialized memory caches are able to keep up with that task. Also, because only two data wires are present, the chance of interference is much less. It is therefore easier to boost the clock speed of communication on a serial cable than on a parallel cable.

Serial connections were a holdover from the early days of computerdom, when the massive room-sized machines were so relatively slow that forcing data into a single line didn't have that much effect on overall speed. With the debut of the PC, most machines switched to parallel ports to communicate with printers; serial ports were used with devices such as modems that move data in serial fashion.

Today, though, the pendulum has very much swung back in the direction of serial communications. Within the computer, almost all current modern machines have made the transition from ATA or IDE interfaces (now renamed by the industry as Parallel ATA) in favor of a simple but very fast technology called Serial ATA. The first devices for SATA were internal hard drives; by mid-2007, internal CD and DVD drives that connect to SATA should be common.

The state of the art in external communication interfaces for consumer products from printers to modems to just about anything else is the Universal Serial Bus 2.0 (USB 2.0). Very close in capability, but not in as wide use, is IEEE 1394, better known by its Apple marketing name of FireWire. But as this book goes to press, we are beginning to see the SATA system make its way to outside of the box with the External SATA port, also known as eSATA.

In this chapter, I look at serial communications in its modern state and trace its history and tips and tricks back to the original design.

Universal Serial Bus

For the first decade and a half of the PC age, the typical computer had one parallel port, a serial port, a keyboard connector, and a mouse port. If you attached a printer, a mouse, a keyboard, and an external modem, you would have used up all your standard external connections. To add more devices — such as video cameras, touchpads, secondary printers, external CD-ROMs or hard drives — you would have had to install a new I/O card. And then you'd have to tangle with reallocating IRQs, DMA channels, and memory resources; all of this was made even more complex if your system also included a needful sound card or network interface card. This process became much simpler with the arrival of the Universal Serial Bus (USB).

This all-in-one connector allows as many as 127 devices to share a single high-speed port; more realistically, the design permits a modern computer to have multiple, independent USB ports (current motherboards typically offer six or eight) and each port is generally used for several devices.

USB is a bus, meaning that devices can share a common interface for interconnection and data transfer. In theory, you can hook almost anything to a USB — a keyboard, mouse, modem, plotter, printer, camera, joystick, and so on. Like a FireWire or SCSI port, USB allows multiple devices to share a single port in a daisy-chain connection. USB is what technical types call *PC-centric* or *managed*. The PC is the host, and all peripherals are slaves to it; in this scheme, the PC manages transfers, and peripherals can only respond. Inside the four-wire cable, two wires send and receive data,, another provides as much as five volts of power to peripherals, and the fourth wire is an electrical ground. The small connectors to the USB, as shown in Figure 15-1, are flat rectangles. USB cables have an up- and a downside: Connectors don't allow cables to be inserted incorrectly. Although parallel and serial ports send data in the form of individual pulses of data, USB operates in a manner more like a network or the Internet. Data is gathered into *packets* — packages with a beginning, an end, and a destination and return address. The technology employs *non-return to zero invert* encoding; simply put, this means that a USB interface sends out an efficient signal that does not require a return to a particular voltage level between bits. High voltage means 1, and low voltage means 0, and a continued high voltage level can be interpreted by the system to mean a string of 1s.

Beyond its speed, though, one of the principal advantages of USB is its simplicity of use. You can daisy chain together as many as 127 devices through a single connection. The USB adapter in the PC creates what is called the root hub. Outside of the PC, the USB chain can be further split off into smaller branches with hubs. The hubs split off pieces of bandwidth as well as subdivide available electrical current to operate devices. All attached devices are designed to be recognized automatically by the Plug-and-Play components of the hardware and the operating system. In addition, all of the devices on the chain communicate through a single USB port that demands only one of the computer's limited supply of IRQs. Also, one of the advantages of USB is the ability to hot swap devices, which means you don't have to turn off your computer to add new devices.

On many modern machines, a group of two to six USB ports exit from the rear panel of current motherboards, including motherboards that follow ATX specification, as shown in Figure 15-2. Some designers run cables from the motherboard to one or two additional USB ports on the front of the machine, making it easier to attach devices for short-time use. If you add a USB hub, you can place that connector on your desktop or in another convenient location to allow for quick connection.

FIGURE 15-1: *A standard element of current modern motherboards is a set of Universal Serial Bus (USB) ports.*

FIGURE 15-2: *The rectangular USB connectors are stacked like a pizza oven at the rear of an ATX motherboard.*

USB development

An industry group finalized the first specification for USB in 1996; two years later, the specification was refined. USB 1.0 and 1.1 run at a top speed of 12 megabits per second. In other words, if the chain contains one device, it could theoretically take all that available bandwidth for itself. If two devices were attached, they would have to split the capacity. A system packed with 127 devices would have to divide the bandwidth into tiny fractions. However, even though several or dozens of devices may be plugged into a USB chain, they will very rarely make demands at the same time.

In its original release, Windows 95 did not recognize USB devices; Windows 95 OSR 2.1 adapted the operating system to add support, but not all peripherals will work under that adaptation. Full support for USB 1.1 did not arrive until Windows 98. Today, current operating systems (including Windows XP and Windows Vista) offer full support for the original and subsequent improved versions of USB.

The original version, USB 1.0, and the slightly improved USB 1.1 were designed to handle data transfer at a minimum of 1.5 Mbps (about the speed of a T1 high-speed data communication line) to a maximum rate of 12 Mbps.

USB 2.0, marketed as High-Speed USB, arrived in 2001, offering a possible top speed of 480 Mbps — 40 times faster than the original USB standard. This specification allows use of the USB for external hard drives, CD and DVD drives, digital cameras, and other devices that demand a great deal of bandwidth.

Very few current devices are capable of working at or near that speed limit of 480 Mbps. A more typical situation is an external hard disk drive, like Maxtor's One Touch III, that promises a *sustained* data transfer rate of 33 Mbps and a *burst* transfer rate of 480 Mbps. Data that is in the drive's data buffer and ready to go can move at USB 2.0's fastest possible speed; but if the drive has to seek out and pick up data from a corner of the disk, the sustained rate falls off to a very fast, but well below the maximum speed.

Today, then, three data rates are part of the USB 2.0 specification:

- The **low speed** rate is 1.5 Mbps. It is used for devices that do not require the exchange of a great deal of data but otherwise benefit from the flexibility of the USB system. Devices that commonly use this speed include keyboards and mice; in Microsoft-speak, these are called *Human Interface Devices*.
- The **full speed** rate is 12 Mbps; this was the former top end for USB 1.1. Devices capable of working at this speed divide the

total USB bandwidth on a first-come first-served basis and it is possible to overwhelm a chain with too high a demand.

- The **hi speed** rate, introduced with USB 2.0, offers a potential maximum speed of 480 Mbps. Not all USB 2.0 devices are capable of working at that speed; check the specifications for details.

If you have a modern machine running USB 2.0, your machine can maintain backward compatibility with USB 1.0, meaning older devices will operate (at their original slower speed) when connected to either a 2.0 or 1.0 USB system. Going the other direction, though, a USB 2.0 device will only operate at the earlier, slower speed if connected to a PC that offers only USB 1.1 or 1.0 ports.

Under the USB standard, the PC actively manages the assignment of bandwidth, querying attached devices to identify them and dividing them into those with the need for high-speed and those (like keyboards and mice) that can work well with a smaller pipe. Each time a device is attached to the bus, the PC reconfigures the bandwidth and assigns each device its own identification number that is used to label the packets of data.

Nearly every current modern motherboard comes equipped with chipsets and ports that support USB 2.0; you can upgrade older modern motherboards by installing an adapter that brings the new functionality. An example of a USB 2.0 card is shown in Figure 15-3. You also can use adapter cards to add USB to a system that doesn't include circuitry on the motherboard; you can also use the card to add USB ports. After the operating system recognizes the presence of a USB 2.0 port, you need to update drivers for the operating system. On the software side, you need to have an operating system that works with USB 2.0 and appropriate drivers for this class of device. Microsoft added drivers for USB 2.0 to Windows XP in 2002; without support for USB 2.0, devices automatically revert to the earlier USB 1.1 specification. Windows Vista offers full support for USB 2.0. Make sure you keep your operating system updated to receive all current benefits.

Cables designed to be fully compliant with USB 1.1 should work properly at USB 2.0 speeds. If you are uncertain about the quality or design of a hub or cable, however, you may want to consider replacing them with current connectors specifically labeled as appropriate for USB 2.0.

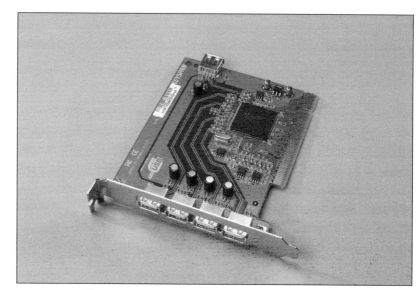

FIGURE 15-3: *This adapter card, from Keyspan, is a Plug-and-Play update that delivers four USB 2.0 ports to an older modern machine.*

Although USB storage and recording devices have been available since the arrival of the standard's first version, the introduction of 40-times-faster USB 2.0 has brought a broad and capable crop of valuable products.

I have augmented my office systems with a number of external USB storage devices: a 40GB Maxtor drive for current project backups (shown in Figure 15-4), a 300GB Maxtor drive for long-term file storage, and an external HP DVD read-write drive. The prices of external USB storage devices have plummeted in recent years, tracking the drop in cost for the drives themselves; you can expect an external unit to sell for about $20 to $50 more than a bare drive intended for internal installation.

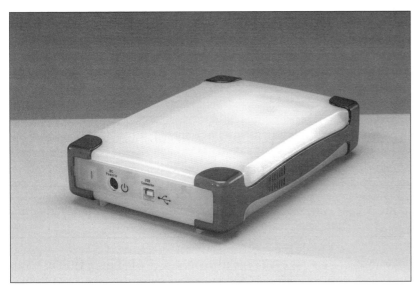

FIGURE 15-4: *This Maxtor 40GB USB drive can be hot plugged into a running system, an unusual feature for a storage device.*

The next USB standard

The next step in the development of USB standards will cut the cord: Certified Wireless USB is expected to pick up where USB 2.0 leaves off. The wireless system is planned to allow communication between a PC and a device at 480 Mbps at a distance of 3 meters (just under 10 feet) and 110 Mbps at 10 meters (about 32 feet).

Wireless USB will utilize a radio specification called the common WiMedia MB-OFDM Ultra-wideband (UWB) platform. The specification is intended to preserve the functionality of wired USB devices, while extending it to a new class of wireless devices. The first chipsets and motherboards supporting Wireless USB, along with the first devices to work with the standard, are expected to arrive on the market in 2007.

USB hubs and peripherals

Devices plugged into a USB port draw both data signals and electrical power from the computer's bus. That works perfectly well for low-power devices like mice and keyboards. Other devices, such as hard

disk drives, CD or DVD drives, amplified speakers, video cameras, and printers generally need to connect to an external power supply.

To connect more than one device to a USB port, you'll need to split the signal from the port. To do that, you'll use a device called a *hub*, which connects on one side to the USB port on the computer and commonly offers two, four, or seven connectors for devices. Typical hubs sell for about $20 to $50. Figure 15-5 shows a basic USB hub. Figure 15-6 shows an unusual mini-hub that can be used with a portable PC or a desktop.

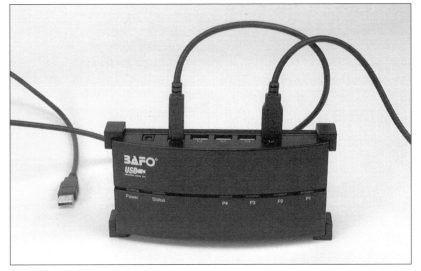

FIGURE 15-5: *A USB hub that splits one port on the computer into four ports on the desktop or floor.*

Note that you will need a USB 2.0 hub to maintain compatibility with a USB 2.0 port; if you use a hub that meets only the 1.1 specification, devices attached to that hub will operate at the original standard's slower speed. Some USB devices, including keyboards and hard drives, have built-in ports that allow easy desktop connection of more peripherals without the need for a separate hub.

NOTE

If devices plugged into your USB port sometimes operate but sometimes fail, the most common problem is insufficient power.

Hubs are available in two types: an unpowered hub that merely splits the signals and power, and a powered hub that connects to an electrical outlet and boosts the current available to devices. Hubs without their own power source, or those with insufficient power, can restrict the number of peripherals you can use on a USB channel or can cause intermittent failures. I suggest that you use self-powered USB hubs with at least 500 milliamps per channel. Another important feature to look for when considering hubs is per-port switching, which prevents the failure of one device from shutting down all devices attached to a hub.

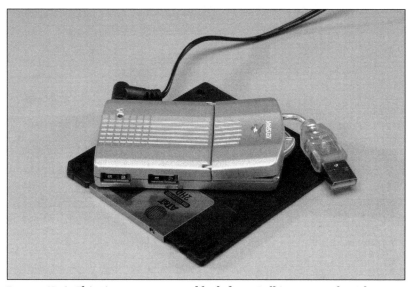

FIGURE 15-6: *This tiny non-powered hub from Belkin can work with a desktop or go on the road with a portable.*

 NOTE

Don't use cables longer than necessary because signals and electrical power can be degraded. In most cases, the cable length should be no more than 15 feet or 5 meters.

Some older modern motherboards offered USB circuitry, but not a USB port. If you have one of these older motherboards, you need to connect an adapter cable and bracket like the one shown in Figure 15-7.

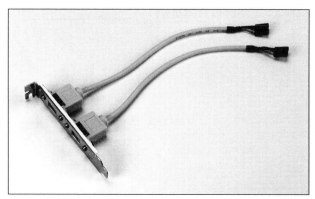

FIGURE 15-7: *An external Universal Serial Board adapter for motherboards that don't include attached USB ports.*

Manufacturers now offer nearly every peripheral in a USB version. You'll find printers, mice, keyboards, scanners, CD and DVD drives, and flash memory card readers designed to use the port. Some PC makers, with the encouragement of Intel and Microsoft, have begun to offer "legacy-free" computers that dispense with built-in serial and parallel ports, replacing them with USB circuitry. If you have older peripherals that you want to connect to a USB port, you may be able to work with adapters such as the USB-to-parallel converter cable, shown in Figure 15-8. This simple device requires no settings; it simply takes in USB at the computer or hub and outputs bidirectional parallel signals at the other end. On the PC, Windows printer drivers believe that they are communicating with a USB device; at the printer end, the device believes that it is working with a standard parallel port.

Another interesting product that helps keep alive older external devices is Keyspan's USB Serial Adapter, a short cable that plugs into a USB port at one end and terminates in a DB9 serial connector at the other. The Plug-and-Play installation gives you a serial port that is capable of communication at rates of as much as 230 Kbps, twice the speed of a standard serial port. The adapter is shown in Figure 15-9.

Nearly all current keyboards now use the USB port to connect with a PC's motherboard. If you have an older keyboard with a PS/2 connector, you can obtain an inexpensive adapter plug that converts a PS/2 connector to a USB connector.

FIGURE 15-8: *USB to IEEE-1284 parallel printer converter.*

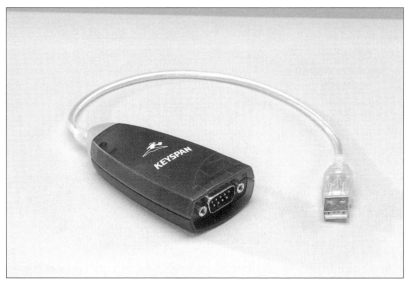

FIGURE 15-9: *Keyspan's USB Serial Adapter is compatible with serial modems, tablets, cameras, and other devices.*

Similarly, if you have an older modern machine with a PS/2 connector and need to use a current keyboard with a USB connector, the cable can be adapted from one standard and shape to another.

In my office, my main production PC has a pair of external hard drives, an external DVD+/-RW drive, a keyboard, and a flash card reader attached to several USB ports. Over the years, other devices I have worked with in the laboratory have included:

- USB color PC camera from SIIG, shown in Figure 15-10
- USB wheel mouse from Logitech, shown in Figure 15-11
- USB 56K data/fax/voice modem, shown in Figure 15-12

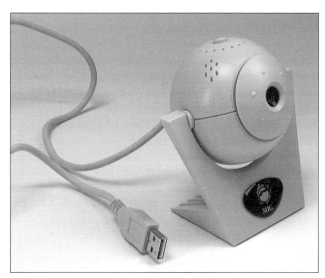

FIGURE 15-10: *This USB PC camera from SIIG includes a 350-pixel CCD (charge couple device) sensor that can create snapshots for e-mail or for live video conferencing.*

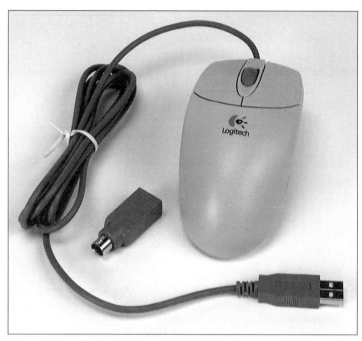

FIGURE 15-11: *The Logitech USB Wheel Mouse connects to a USB port or to a PS/2 port with the included adapter. The scroll wheel enables you to move screen displays without having to click the scroll bar in an application or a web page.*

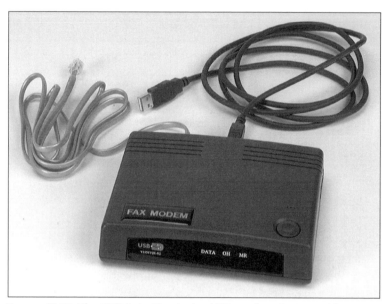

FIGURE 15-12: *The 56K data/fax/voice USB modem is a capable, generic device to add a dial-up modem to a machine.*

Flash memory drives

Although *flash memory* — a form of non-volatile computer memory that can be electrically erased and reprogrammed — is not commonly used in PCs for large blocks of RAM, it is an essential element of many personal electronic devices. Your music player, your cell phone, and your digital camera (you are a very unusual consumer if you don't have at least one of these devices, if not all three) are made possible because of this form of memory.

Flash memory's greatest asset is the fact that it does not require a continuous source of power to retain information. That's what allows it to substitute for camera film, for example. Flash memory is also used in *memory keys* (also called *flash drives*) that hold large blocks of data on a temporary basis; in many ways, flash drives have come to replace floppy disk drives on current computers.

(In a computer, volatile RAM is used because it is faster at writing or reading information. Many computers, though, use non-volatile memory to hold the settings made for the system setup, which is associated with the BIOS. Several new technologies, though, may result in the use of new variations of non-volatile memory for system RAM in coming years.)

You can transfer the contents of flash memory from an external device to a PC one of three ways:

- By direct connection between the device and a port on the computer, usually a USB connection
- By wireless communication between the device and the computer, usually WiFi or Bluetooth interchange
- By removing the flash memory from the device and installing it into a reader attached to the computer

Each method has advantages and disadvantages.

Removing the media from the device increases the chance that the memory will be damaged or that contacts on the memory or within the device will corrode or become dirty; however, transferring files in this way does not use the battery power of the camera or audio player, does not require installation of any supporting software or drivers on the PC, and may be more convenient for photographers who own multiple memory cards.

A direct connection is an easy way to transfer files (and for certain types of devices including some music players, a convenient way to recharge the battery using the power that comes along with the data through a USB port). This method requires installation of software or drivers on the PC, and in my experience the tinier the device and its connectors the more likely that the hardware will become a point of failure.

Wireless communication is convenient, but generally not quite as fast as a USB 2.0 connection or a direct uploading from a reader. For some users, wireless is suspect because of the possibility of unauthorized eavesdropping, although you have to decide whether your pictures of Spot chasing Felix in the backyard are worthy of theft.

You can see an example of an extremely versatile flash memory drive in Figure 15-13. The Addonics Mini Digidrive II works with ten different formats for memory cards, adding a few more variations. The palm-sized device is powered by a USB port, and in a system that supports USB 2.0 it can transfer data in either direction at speeds of as much as 480 Mbps. The next step in the evolution of the flash memory

key may be the U3 standard, which is intended to allow use of a memory key as a means to carry applications, settings, and data from one computer to another. In theory, you could plug an U3-compliant memory key into any machine anywhere, and it will operate and look very much like the one you have at home or at your office. Software makers are in the process of developing U3 versions of their programs that will be sold as separate versions, or as components of the desktop package.

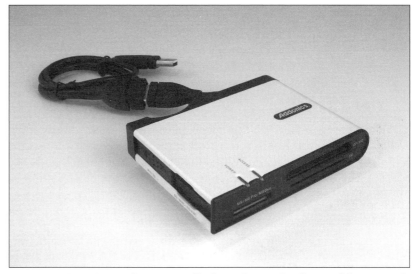

Figure 15-13: *A tiny multipurpose flash media reader from Addonics, with five slots that can work with ten different devices: MMC, SD, Mini SD, SmartMedia, xD, CompactFlash, Micro Drive, Memory Stick, Memory Stick Duo, or Memory Stick Pro.*

IEEE 1394 FireWire

FireWire (also known as i.Link or IEEE 1394) is another high-speed serial interface. Introduced at roughly the same time as USB, and with similar capabilities for ordinary tasks such as communicating with external hard drives and optical drives, it is much more widely used in specialized applications such as uploading or downloading digital audio or video. On many advanced systems, FireWire has replaced SCSI. If you intend to use your PC in direct connection with a digital camcorder, an advanced analog camcorder, or a digital audio device, you'll likely find that the external device is designed to work with FireWire.

In the view of some experts, USB was designed with an eye on simplicity and cost, while FireWire offers the potential of greater performance at a slightly higher cost.

NOTE

Let me stop here for a moment and explain the triple set of names for this standard. The specification was defined by the *IEEE (Institute of Electrical and Electronics Engineers)* as a standard with the numerical title of 1394, later modified to 1394a and 1395b versions. Apple introduced the product commercially in 2003, calling the port FireWire. And Sony applied the label of iLink to its implementation on video equipment; the iLink uses a different cable and connector but is otherwise the same standard. In this book, I use the more recognizable FireWire brand name.

The latest versions of the specification are FireWire 400 (IEEE 1394a), capable of transfer rates of approximately 100 Mbps, 200 Mbps, or 400 Mbps, and FireWire 800 (IEEE 1394b), which adds 800 Mbps to the offerings of the previous standard. Technologies are near introduction that can bring the 1394b version of FireWire all the way to 3.2 Gbps. (And as with USB, specifications are being developed for a wireless version of FireWire/IEEE 1394.)

Like USB, the lowest speeds are for devices that do not require a huge amount of back-and-forth data exchange and the highest speed is expected to be used for burst transmission of small amounts of data. In between is very high-speed communication for streaming audio or video.

One potential advantage of FireWire is that it is a peer-to-peer architecture, which allows devices to communicate directly with each other as well as with the computer; USB is a client-server or star-topology technology, which means that all communication goes to the device at the center of the system and back out to attached devices. For example, on a FireWire system a digital camcorder can send and receive data directly to a hard drive or CD recorder, while on a USB system the data goes from the camera, past the storage device, to the PC, and then back to the drive.

On a FireWire 400 system, the total length of an individual cable can be no more than about 15 feet, although as many as 16 cables can be connected to each other through repeaters or hubs (up to a maximum length of about 230 feet).

Windows XP supports 1394a, and Microsoft plans full support for the IEEE 1394b (FireWire 800) standard in Windows Vista.

The FireWire bus uses a six-wire cable for most computer devices; two lines deliver power, and two pairs of lines are used for clock and data signals. The iLink implementation uses a four-wire version of the cable and is used with self-powered devices such as camcorders.

FireWire is not a standard component of all current modern machines, but is easily added with an adapter card in the bus or (in some designs) with an internal converter that makes a USB port act as if it were an IEEE 1394 port. One example is shown in Figure 15-14.

FIGURE 15-14: *This PCI adapter from Belkin is a Plug-and-Play upgrade that adds three FireWire ports to a modern machine. It includes an optional connection to the PC's power supply to provide additional power to FireWire devices.*

The IEEE 1394 standard theoretically can be expanded to thousands of devices. I'm having a hard time picturing exactly what sort of a network would have tens of thousands of nodes — perhaps some future manufacturing line — but the basic point is that FireWire is very flexible in its organizational structure. Devices created for the 1394b standard can be designed either to support only that standard or also to work with the original version of FireWire by using "bilingual" chips.

Data is broken into packets encased within a block that includes identification of the sender and receiver. The design of the cable includes shielding for the wires that reduces noise and interference. FireWire cables are not supposed to be more than 4.5 meters (just under 15 feet) long.

As with USB, one FireWire device can be daisy-chained to the next. As I have noted, FireWire is a peer-to-peer network between and among the devices on the node without active control by the PC at its heart; devices can even communicate with each other without management by the computer. The design also permits two computers to share a single peripheral. An example of a FireWire hub is shown in Figure 15-15.

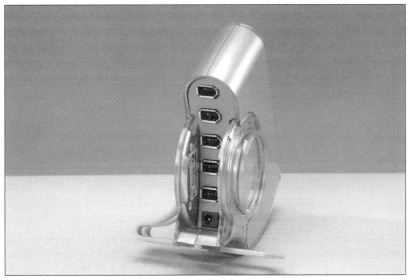

FIGURE 15-15: *Belkin's elegant FireWire six-port hub operates as a bus-powered or self-powered repeater; the rear panel contains five ports and another is hidden behind a panel on the front. A docking ring on the side allows you to attach multiple hubs, routers, and other Belkin devices.*

Like USB, FireWire can divide the available bandwidth *isochronously*, dedicating a particular slice of the spectrum to particular devices — useful in such applications as streaming video. FireWire also can operate *asynchronously*, a more flexible means of communication for devices that can accept information broken into packets and able to deal with sometimes-changing conditions along the shared cable as other devices request access to the stream of data.

Finally, like USB devices, FireWire devices are hot-pluggable, allowing them to be attached or disconnected to a PC without rebooting. Devices broadcast their unique identification number to other devices on the network and obtain a place on the network.

To obtain all of the facilities of FireWire, you need a current version of Windows: Windows 98 SE or later versions of Windows, including Windows 2000, Windows Me, Windows XP, or Windows Vista. Windows 95 and the original version of Windows 98 deliver only limited functionality.

NOTE

For more information on FireWire, you can consult the trade association's page at www.1394ta.org.

External SATA Port

The speedy and simple Serial ATA technology began taking over the internal connections for most hard disk drives in 2005, displacing the IDE (now renamed Parallel ATA) system that had been in place for more than a decade. Manufacturers also are bringing to market CD and DVD drives that connect to the SATA ports on the motherboard.

The next step is External SATA, also called eSATA. This system extends the SATA pathways on the motherboard to a connector on the case. In theory, eSATA is much faster than USB 2.0 and FireWire (IEEE 1394b) and can work with a slightly longer external cable (as much as 6 meters or more than 19 feet in length). As with the other standards, devices are *hot swappable*, meaning they can be installed, turned on, turned off, or disconnected while the machine is running.

eSATA picks up its speed advantage because it has a much lower overhead than USB and FireWire; those other interfaces require the system to encapsulate data and then de-encapsulate it after it is received. While USB 1.1 or 2.0 has to devote as much as 33 to 50 percent of its data to start-stop bits and error checking, and FireWire about 25 percent, in its internal and external form SATA has an overhead close to 0.

As this edition goes to press, motherboards with eSATA connectors are not widely available but that is likely to change quickly. Modern machines without eSATA can add the feature with an adapter card in the bus or a converter that extends an internal SATA port to a bracket on the back panel of the PC.

In Figure 15-16 you can see an example of a plug-in adapter that changes a USB 2.0 port into a standard eSATA port. This device, from Addonics, provides an instant conversion to eSATA facilities as defined in SATA 1.0A specifications.

External drives that use USB or FireWire are almost all adaptations of Parallel ATA (IDE) drives with the addition of a conversion chip that changes the ATA protocol from the motherboard as needed; the same conversion happens when data is retrieved from the drive. This adds overhead (which is the same as subtracting throughput). And USB or FireWire drives also require an external source of power, usually from an AC adapter.

Drives designed specifically for SATA, whether internal or external, require lower voltage signals, thinner cables, and smaller connectors. And as a newer specification, SATA is intended to be made faster and more flexible in coming years.

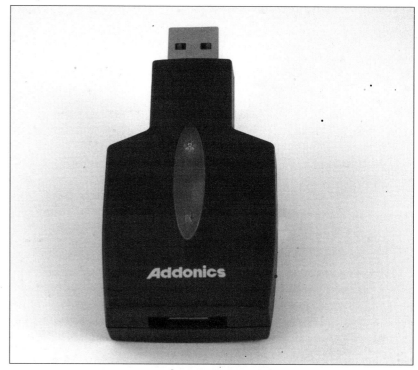

FIGURE 15-16: *This USB 2.0 to eSATA 1.0 adapter from Addonics installed automatically under current versions of Windows.*

SUMMARY

In this chapter, I explored serial communications, including USB, FireWire, and the developing eSATA technologies. In the next chapter, I examine a class of devices which once were the primary users of serial communication: modems.

Notes

Chapter 16

Modem Telecommunications

Amodem is your entrance ramp to the global information superhighway. The original purpose of a modem was to *mo*dulate the digital signals of your PC so they can be sent in analog fashion over a telephone wire; incoming analog signals are then *dem*odulated to become digital. Modern modems serve to alter one form of digital signal on a cable television wire or a fiber optic line to a digital electrical signal that can be used by a computer.

In the early days of personal computing, modems were true peripherals; a relatively small number of users attached them to their machines and they were for very narrow purposes including direct transfer of files from machine to machine, early e-mail store-and-forward services (like the almost-forgotten MCI Mail), and exchange of messages and information of cumbersome "bulletin board" services.

Modems changed from an optional and occasionally used accessory with the birth of the first virtual communities, including CompuServe and AOL Online. And then came the arrival (for individual users) of the Internet. What began as a military/educational institution in the late 1960s and through the 1970s began to open up to the general public; the Internet made major inroads into homes and businesses in the 1990s, and by 2006 nearly 70 percent of the population in North America had access.

NOTE

Just for the record, the Internet still has a long way to go in places other than in the developed nations. Worldwide, just under 16 percent of the planet's 6.5 billion people could find a way to get on the Web in 2006. That's a lot of people — more than a billion — but not close to universal.

Modems in homes and small- to medium-sized businesses are available in several forms:

- Dial-up devices that use standard telephone lines
- Moderate-to-high–speed broadband satellite links for download, in combination with dial-up links for upload
- Moderate-to-high–speed broadband DSL modems that use special telephone circuits
- High-speed broadband cable modems that use coaxial and fiber-optic links through cable television providers
- Ultra-speed fiber optic cable modems attach to new networks put into service by former telephone providers

In 2003, nearly every home and most business users found their way to the Internet using a dial-up connection through local or national *Internet service providers (ISPs)*. Dial-up used standard telephone services to connect from point to point. And though telephone modems were greatly improved over the years — a 56K modem was nearly 180 times faster than the 300-baud devices that were first used in many homes — dial-up was (and is) too slow to take full advantage of streaming video and audio as well as other complex elements that are now common on the Internet.

By 2006, the percentage of American users still connecting over standard telephone lines had dropped to about 34 percent; the other 66 percent of PC users with Internet links had made the shift to broadband technologies. The two most common means of broadband, or high-speed, connection are over a cable television link (using a *cable modem* at the PC end) or over a DSL system that employs specialized technologies to make use of different frequencies on existing telephone wires. A small percentage of users reach the Internet through satellite/telephone combinations or through dedicated special facilities offered by phone companies and others.

And a growing number of users make wireless connections from their laptop or desktop to a WiFi network; I discuss that technology in Chapter 20.

Modems attach to your computer in four ways:

- As internal cards that attach to the bus as a serial device
- As a chipset built in to the motherboard of your computer
- As external devices that connect to a serial port, a USB port, or a parallel port
- As external devices that connect to an Ethernet port on your computer

Dial-up modems are still offered in both internal and external versions and each style has certain advantages. High-speed broadband modems are almost exclusively an external device.

In this chapter, you explore cable modems and DSL modems first, and then move on to a review of older, slower, dial-up communication. For most home and small office users, the fastest Internet connection is a cable modem. Depending on the provider and your local conditions, this sort of system was capable in 2007 of speeds of as much as 6 or 7 Mbps. DSL can deliver about half that speeds.

In early 2007, Verizon and a few other "telephone" providers began turning on the switches to a new form of broadband based on *fiber optic cables* that carry information in the form of digital pulses of light; at the connection to your computer or home network, the pulses of light go through a special modem that converts the information into an electrical signal. Verizon's FIOS claimed possible download speeds

of as much as 30 Mbps, with uploads as fast as 5 Mbps; most early adopters will be offered services with speeds of 10 to 15 Mbps into your home or office and 2 to 5 Mbps going the other way. And just as cable television operators have managed to pack their wire with TV, Internet, and telephone services, Verizon and other telephone companies plan to use their fiber optic cable to carry the same trio.

Check out Table 16-1 for a comparison of typical modem speeds.

TABLE 16-1: A Comparison of Typical Modem Communication Speed (Download)

Type of Connection	Description
Dial-up modem V.92	Up to 53 Kbps
Satellite	500 to 700 Kbps downstream/50 Kbps upstream
DSL basic	Up to 768 Kbps downstream/128 Kbps upstream
DSL advanced	Up to 3 Mbps downstream/768 Kbps upstream
DSL premium	Up to 7.1 Mbps downstream/768 Kbps upstream
Cable modem	3 Mbps to 7 Mbps downstream/300 to 400 Kbps upstream
Enhanced cable modem	10 to 16 Mbps downstream/1 Mbps upstream
Fiber optic cable	5 Mbps to 30 Mbps downstream/2 to 10 Mbps upstream

Why Modems Are Necessary

Your computer stores information in the form of 0s and 1s. This stream of digits is assembled into a stream of information by the PC's *universal asynchronous receiver/transmitter (UART)* and sent as a serial signal to a modem. There the modem's electronics change the bits into a signal that can be sent over the particular medium that connects your computer to the Internet or to another computer.

Modems designed to use standard telephone lines had to deal with the fact that the system was designed (by Alexander Graham Bell and other great minds of the 1860s and 1870s) solely for the purpose of carrying a version of the human voice from place to place. The two-wire copper cabling carried the rising and falling signal as an analog of the human voice that could be recreated at the other end on a speaker.

More than a century later, when the first computer modems were designed, they had to work with Bell's system. And so the basic dial-up modem had to convert the discrete digital 0s and 1s of the computer into an analog signal that could be sent over the phone lines; the solution was a warbling sound wave that indicates 1s with its peaks and 0s with its valleys. At the other end of the connection, another modem receives the wave and converts the peaks and valleys back into 1s and 0s for the recipient.

For a decade in the early days of personal computing, this annoying warble and screech was music to the ears of adventuresome users. Most learned to detect when a signal was good or bad, and celebrated the sound of the successful connection of two machines.

Cable modems are similar in concept to telephone modems since most cable TV systems send downstream and upstream Internet traffic as analog signals; some cable systems, though, have converted to all-digital signaling. Fiber optic systems, like Verizon's FIOS, are all digital. However, both cable and fiber optic systems require a device to convert the signal they provide to one that can be used in your computer or local area network; for want of a new name for the device, they're all called *modems* whether they modulate and demodulate a signal or merely convert the signal from one technology to another.

Consumer modems, like those I write about in this book, are considered *asynchronous* devices in that the data stream is not tied to timing; rather, it is defined by the start and stop bits of each byte. Specialized modems used in direct connection or leased-line communication are sometimes *synchronous,* moving to the beat of a clock.

Cable Modems

From the same people who bring you *American Idol,* Red Sox baseball games, and the Home Shopping Network: high-speed, broadband Internet. It's a concept that is miles beyond the original intention of cable television, but a reality that has taken a huge share of the consumer market in the 21st century.

Cable television was introduced in the hills of Pennsylvania in the 1940s as a way to bring TV to people who lived too remote from a broadcast tower to use an antenna; the original acronym was CATV for Community Antenna Television. This will only make sense to you if you are old enough to remember rabbit ears (the TV kind). At first, the cable was only able to deliver a dozen or so channels, but improvements over the years expanded the number (if not the quality) to hundreds.

The flexibility of cable television is based on the fact that it was built around a fat and fast pipe—a coaxial cable—that was much more capable than the century-old pair of copper wires that is at the local end of a telephone connection. A coaxial cable is capable of carrying hundreds of television channels; each standard channel occupies just a 6-MHz slice of the spectrum. And when the cable television company offers digital channels, this information is compressed into a smaller segment.

The Internet signals don't interfere with your cable television reception. When a cable television company offers Internet service, it generally devotes a slice of about 2 MHz at the low end of the spectrum for upstream communication from the user to the ISP and 6 MHz (the same as a television channel) at the high end of the cable's spectrum for downstream data. In the most modern cable television systems, the main trunks that serve a neighborhood may be very-high-capacity high-speed fiber optic cables; the branches off the fiber are transformed from pulses of light to an electrical signal for the final stretch to your home or office.

The necessary piece of hardware for this sort of system is a *cable modem,* which is similar in concept and operation to a dial-up modem; in most designs it converts an analog signal on the cable to a digital signal for the computer or the other way around for information and commands sent upstream to a *cable modem termination system* at the provider's equipment center. One additional piece of essential equipment is a *tuner* that can pick out the specific frequencies used for upstream and downstream communications. Figure 16-1 shows a Toshiba PCX1100 cable modem.

An advantage of a cable modem is the fact that speed and quality of service do not degrade based on the distance between your home or office and the cable company's switching equipment. On the other hand, if you are sharing a particular cable with many other users, you may see a significant drop in performance; a well-run cable company deals with problems like that by adding more channels for Internet use and subdividing users into smaller groups.

Cable modems (and DSL modems) offer the advantage of being available all the time. Once your computer connects to either type of modem at bootup, the link is active and very quick to respond. The constantly connected nature of the cable or DSL modem makes an attractive target for malicious and mischievous hackers who troll the Internet for ways to break into computers. I absolutely recommend that you install a firewall to protect your system from intruders — either a hardware firewall that is part of a router for a small network, or a software firewall. And you will also want to install and keep current an antivirus program to scan e-mail and incoming files.

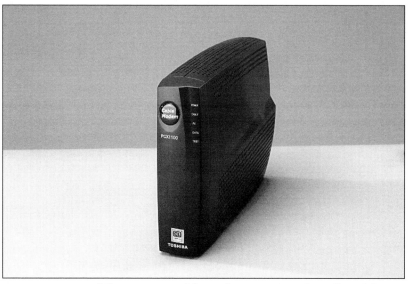

FIGURE 16-1: *A Toshiba PCX1100 cable modem, a DOCSIS broadband device in wide use.*

In general, you will have to use your cable company's ISP once you're online. This doesn't mean that you can't connect to any web page or check your mail from other sources. However, you may end up with redundant mail accounts and Web hosting accounts if you want to hold on to existing addresses you had before the cable company wired your PC.

Most cable modems connect to the PC through an Ethernet network interface card; a smaller number of cable modems connect to a USB port on the PC. Modems sell for about $75 to $100, although many cable companies will rebate the cost for new customers. Or you can rent a modem; my local cable company charges $3 per month. Renters also have the security of knowing that if the modem fails or if the provider upgrades to a new protocol or hardware, you can arrange for a quick swap at no additional cost. I choose to pay rent, and I'm now on my third-generation modem.

Several protocols are available for cable modems, but in 2000, the industry came to an agreement to use a standard called the *Data Over Cable Service Interface Specification (DOCSIS)*. In 2005, DOCSIS 2.0 was made standard.

Before you sign up, though, be sure you are satisfied with the quality of the cable television signal you see on your TV sets. If you have a weak, snowy picture on the Sony in your bedroom, chances are the signal to your PC will be slow or unreliable.

When the technician came to my office to wire my system, I asked him to measure the signal strength on the incoming cable. He found that the signal was unacceptably weak; I asked for, and received, a new incoming cable from the road. The technician ran the new cable directly to my PC, splitting it off to the televisions just short of the computer.

Fiber Optic Modems

Systems based on fiber optic cables operate similarly to that used by cable TV Internet providers. A fiber optic link comes from the street, to your home or office, to a router and splitter that send the signal to computer, telephone, and television systems.

This is still very new technology, so various companies may use different equipment combinations. In the initial Verizon's FIOS network rollout, most subscribers received a combined modem and wireless router for Internet use. The modem converts the digital light pulses from the fiber optic cable to an electrical digital signal the computer can use. You can connect the supplied router to an existing wired router that interconnects the computers in your home or office, and its wireless feature can extend the network to other parts of your home or office.

For information on Verizon's offerings, consult `www.verizonfios.com`. Other former telephone companies and other providers are expected to offer their own similar service in coming years.

DSL Modems

A *Digital Subscriber Line (DSL)*, sometimes called an *ADSL* to indicate that it operates asymmetrically, also follows the same general design as a dial-up modem. This sort of service is offered by phone companies and some ISPs and can usually use the same old double copper wires of regular phone lines; the difference lies in the technology that sends a signal that lies outside of the relatively narrow band reserved for voice.

Voice communication is confined to a narrow frequency range of about 0 to 3,400 Hertz (cycles per second), well below the top end of human hearing which — depending on the ear — may be up around 20,000 Hz. DSL takes over at frequencies above that; the copper wire can handle frequencies of as much as several million Hertz. DSL moves its data at a higher frequency in a much broader bandwidth between 25 KHz and 1 MHz. This allows transmission of much more information without interfering with voice calls.

The signal is asymmetric, meaning that there is a larger segment of the frequency devoted to downloading than uploading. At the provider's office, a *Digital Subscriber Line Access Multiplexer (DSLAM)* brings together all of the various customers into a single stream that goes out onto the Internet.

DSL modems permit simultaneous use of the phone line for voice and data communication and each user has a dedicated line back to the main office so there is no loss of performance if there are a great many users in your neighborhood. On the downside, DSL service is limited by the fact that quality and speed declines the further a home or office is from the provider's headquarters. In 2006, many phone companies only offered DSL to customers within three miles of a central office.

And if your local telephone service is not very good to begin with, the quality of DSL is not going to be great. If your phone lines regularly fail or if the signal quality is poor, you can expect slow or poor DSL service. (In my rural neighborhood, our fiber-optic cable television system is many decades younger than the copper telephone wires, and DSL does not seem like a good choice.)

Another type of DSL service is *Rate Adaptive Digital Subscriber Line (RADSL)*, a system that continuously samples the quality of the phone line and then automatically adjusts the access speed based upon its condition.

As with cable modems, the DSL provider may give subscribers a free modem at the time service is contracted. Or the modem may be available for rental. After you are certain that DSL works well for you, and that your provider seems to be well established, you can consider purchasing your own modem.

Dial-up Modems

Up until recently, the majority of PC users connected to the Internet and other communications services through "old" technology. Dial-up modems attempt to eke every possible bit of capability from technology that is more than a century old: a pair of copper wires that stretch from your home or office to a central telephone switch. (Sometime in the next few years, though, broadband cable and DSL modems — discussed later in this chapter — are expected to predominate.)

Throughout the history of the PC, dozens of modem manufacturers have been on the scene, some claiming higher speed, better quality, or improved features while others have marketed on the basis of price alone. Today, though, dial-up modems have reached a technological wall at 56K and a marketing chasm: Modems are now mostly a commodity — nearly all modems perform comparably. All modems have to go through the same computer gateway — a serial, parallel, or USB port at one end and the antique two-wire copper telephone line at the other — and none of them can perform better than the facilities on either side of them.

CROSS-REFERENCE

I discuss UARTs in detail in Chapter 15. If you are working with a senior-citizen or dinosaur machine, be sure you know the capabilities of your system before you purchase an external modem so that you don't buy one that's beyond the capabilities of your PC. Modern machines are all capable of working with current modem devices.

Even the most capable modem still has to deal with the quality of the phone line between your home or office and the telephone company's central office. From there, it still has to travel to the central office nearest the call's destination, and then over the local lines to the destination. The very best modem will be slow and problematic if it uses phone lines of poor quality. (From my very rural office, the best we can expect to get from a 56 Kbps modem is about 40K, and then only when the weather does not interfere with the signal to and from the phone company's microwave tower.)

Only a limited number of primary manufacturers produce the chipsets used in most modern modems. The brain of nearly every modem comes from Rockwell International, Texas Instruments, Motorola, Lucent, or IBM. Literally dozens of modems are on the market, with tremendous change from month to month in price and capabilities. Over time, the trend has been falling prices and increasing functionality.

Many current modems include sophisticated voice facilities for a few dollars more. You can use the modem to answer your telephone, for example, and the software provided with the hardware lets you set up multiple voicemail boxes. Some modems even support simultaneous voice and data connections on the same phone line — a real plus when you have only a single line and you need help troubleshooting your Internet connection. The state of the art for dial-up modems in terms of speed and capability today are 56 Kbps devices built to adhere to the V.92 standard. I discuss real and potential speed later in this chapter.

Dial-up modem quality

Two factors have combined to bring about the near-end of new designs for dial-up modems: firstly, the rapid shift toward high-speed broadband modems in the home and office, and secondly the fact that dial-up standards seem to have reached the limits of their speed and capability. Today, nearly all dial-up modems are based on V.92 standard and incorporate the same essential design with the same basic chipsets.

What we have now is a commodity market. Companies are mostly competing on the basis of price, and to a lesser extent, on quality or support.

In 2006, you could purchase an internal dial-up modem for about the cost of one or two double espresso French Roasts (as little as $5 for a no-name PCI card and as much as $20 for a very similar brand name). External modems cost a bit more because of the cost of a case, a few connectors, and a power supply; expect to pay between $20 and $50.

How do you judge the quality or support on a commodity product? I would start by judging the seller: What kind of a return policy is offered? Then I would check the manufacturer to see what sort of support they offer: Is there a web site with device drivers and troubleshooting? Is there a phone number for technical support?

My favorite technique is this: Make a phone call to the support department with a pre-purchase question. My theory is that if the company is uncooperative before you make a purchase, there is no reason to expect cooperation once they have your money. Be a wise consumer.

If you are purchasing an internal serial card, you are almost certain to find only those built for installation in a PCI slot, the most common bus design for modern and senior-citizen machines. If you are seeking to upgrade or replace a modem in a dinosaur, you are not likely to find an ISA bus card at a retail store, but they may be available through used computer part stores or on auction sites. Similarly, external modems are mostly intended for connection to a USB port; old machines do not support that form of I/O; you can shop for a used serial modem on the Internet.

PCI slots allow Plug-and-Play ease of configuration. These modems may also include connections to link to a sound card for answering machine facilities, although that facility is not commonly used. A relative handful of computers have a specialized internal slot called an *Audio Modem Riser (AMR)* and can accept modem cards in that format without giving up a bus slot.

Today, the easiest way to attach an external dial-up modem is through the use of a USB port; the self-configuring nature of USB makes setting up these modems a breeze.

CROSS-REFERENCE

I show an example of a USB modem in Figure 15-12, which is in Chapter 15.

Before the arrival of the USB, some manufacturers introduced devices that connected to the parallel port of the PC, avoiding problems with outmoded UART chips and also leaving existing serial ports untouched. One example was the Deskporte line, originally offered by Microcom (now part of Compaq) and still available from the back bins of some dealers. These devices use a special device driver that redirects communications to the parallel port.

Dial-up modem speed

It would be perfectly logical to think that a 56K modem is capable of receiving and transmitting data at 56,000 bits per second, and twice the speed of a 28.8 Kbps, but the truth is a little bit short of that.

Technical and regulatory speed limits set the maximum download speed for a V.90 and V.92 modem at about 53,000 bits per second (bps). The upload speed — from your computer to the Internet — is notably slower: V.90 sends data up the line at as much as 33,600 bps, while the newer V.92 standard theoretically is capable of transmitting at as much as 48,000 bps.

To begin with, 56K technology only works if there is no more than one analog/digital conversion present along the way. If you work or live in a big city with a good telephone company, you may have part of the equation in place — a good connection from your PC to the central office and a digital line from there.

If you are unable to connect at 56 Kbps, a current modem can downshift to slower speeds covered under earlier standards.

There is no good reason to save a few dollars by buying a used modem that is slower than 56K. The small amount of money you save would quickly be eaten up in lost productivity. The latest widely accepted modem standards, V.90 and V.92, not only offer the possibility of supporting 53 Kbps, but have other desirable connectivity features that will provide a better online experience at any connection speed. A no-name internal modem is shown in Figure 16-2.

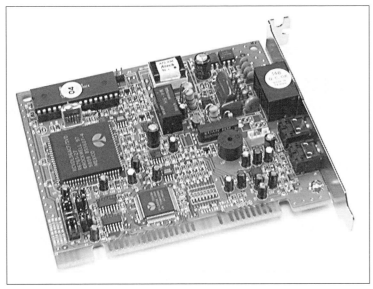

FIGURE 16-2: *A generic 56 Kbps internal modem awaits installation in a PCI slot.*

External versus internal modems

External modems have LEDs or other indicators that make it easier to diagnose problems, and you can turn off external modems to reset them without having to shut down the computer. They also don't draw power from the PC bus, produce heat under the covers, or use one of the computer's limited bus slots. Figure 16-3 shows an external modem.

Internal modems are a bit less expensive because they don't require a case, power supply, and cable. And though they use one of the internal slots, they don't necessarily use up one of the PC's two standard COM ports. With the proper software, you can set them to COM 3 or COM 4.

Table 16-2 compares external with internal devices.

FIGURE 16-3: *An external modem connects to a serial or USB port, without demanding an internal slot. External modems also provide visible indicators of telecommunication status.*

TABLE 16-2: A Comparison of External and Internal Dial-up Modems

	External Serial Modem	External USB Modem	Internal Modem
Slots	+ Does not occupy an internal slot	+ Does not occupy an internal slot	− Requires an internal slot
Ports	− Uses a serial port	+ Shares a USB port with other devices	+ Usually supplies own serial port
Power, Heat	+ Does not draw on PC's power supply; does not add to internal heat; can be turned off	−/+ Draws small amount of power from USB bus or hub but does not add heat within case; can be turned off	− Draws power from internal supply and adds some heat within case; generally cannot be turned off
Indicators	+ Usually offers range of indicator lights to show progress of session	+ Usually offers range of indicator lights to show progress of session	− Some models offer an onscreen display of the progression of the session
High speed with old UART?	− No. UART must be upgraded, or a separate serial adapter must be installed, requiring a slot in bus	+ Yes; provides its own high-speed UART	+ Yes; provides its own high-speed UART installed
Reset	+ Can be reset by turning off power switch or unplugging	+ Can be reset by turning off power switch or unplugging	− In some situations, lock-up of modem can only be cured by resetting entire computer
Cost	− More expensive because of case, power supply, cable	−/+ Slightly higher price than internal, but may not require power supply	+ Least expensive form

WinModems: Minimalist technology

A modem consists of certain basic components to enable the necessary send-and-receive data conversion and to conduct transmission and reception of information over the telephone line. Recall that the UART is one necessary component for the serial communications part of the modem. The other devices are part of a fairly standardized chipset supplied by one of several manufacturers. Each of these chipsets has its own features, but they all work pretty much the same and are all quite good.

The least expensive means of adding dial-up modem capability to a modern modem is to add a few chips to the motherboard and make use of a scheme that offloads some of the processing of data to the PC's microprocessor. Some modem manufacturers save money during construction by cutting redundancy, by using lower-cost support components, and so on, but all hardware modem manufacturers must start with one of these core chipsets. The fact is that hardware costs money. In a competitive computer marketplace, where consumers pretty much expect a modem as part of the computer hardware package, manufacturers are always looking for ways to reduce the cost of the package to the consumer.

Manufacturers have found one way in what is sometimes referred to as a *soft modem* or *WinModem*. These devices are meant to operate under Windows 95/98 and later. Soft modems work by offloading some of the work normally done by modem chips to a modern computer's main CPU; this means that the microprocessor is taking on other duties normally handled elsewhere, and that information must travel along the PCI bus to and from the modem to get the work done.

Windows-only modems (sometimes called WinModems) are internal Plug-and-Play devices that usually share system memory and are dependent on drivers in the Windows operating system to function properly. As an internal device, WinModems use system resources including an I/O address and IRQ. In addition, many WinModems also use a DMA channel. If the modem attempts to use the same resources as another device, there is a resource conflict and either or both devices may not work.

Some implementations of a WinModem, including a design by 3COM, eliminates one hardware component—the controller—but still has a hardware data pump, the modem piece that takes care of the basic modulation/demodulation tasks. The controller handles protocols for error correction, data transfer, and so on. I suppose that this model could be called a "half-soft modem."

Other designs replace both the controller and the data pump with software running on the host computer (HSP modems, for host signal processor). These are more difficult to configure and, in my experience, the least likely to provide reliable service.

NOTE

A number of manufacturers supply software modems. The 3COM WinModem is one example, and the 3COM chips are supplied to a number of other vendors as an OEM product. The designation *WinModem* is a certain sign that the modem is at least partly based on software. If a modem is advertised for Windows only, it probably is a soft modem. If the manufacturer calls it a *controllerless modem*, it certainly isn't playing with all the hardware it really needs. Rockwell's RPI modem series were software-based modems, as were Lucent's LT WinModems.

I'm not saying you can't get satisfactory performance out of a software-driven modem. Many designs are available, and some units work better than others. Some use more hardware and less software, and some locations accept a software modem better than others. However, if you're having trouble getting online or having problems getting the kind of speed your modem was designed to deliver, consider upgrading to a better, hardware-based modem. It can save a lot of troubleshooting headaches and, in the end, save you money.

You can check on resource conflicts from the Device Manager. Click Start ⇨ Settings ⇨ Control Panel. Double-click System, and then click the Device Manager tab. In most cases, a resource conflict or other problem with a device is indicated by an exclamation point in a yellow circle.

Fax Modems

The fax modem is another technology that is beginning to fade away because of lack of use. By the early 1990s, the fax machine was an essential component of nearly every office and began to arrive in many homes; it was a quick and easy way to send copies of paper documents from place to place over the phone lines; it required roughly 20 to 60 seconds per page.

With the rise of the PC, developers realized that computers could send and receive the same sort of facsimile information. The first round of hardware to accomplish this included dedicated communication adapter cards and external boxes; these were followed by the integration of faxing facilities as part of internal and external data modems.

The first computer fax cards were only capable of transmitting at 9600 bps; later versions doubled the speed to 19.2 Kbps to match the capabilities of office fax machines.

You can prepare a document for faxing by computer two ways. One way is to use a scanner to convert a piece of paper into an image file and then send that from the fax modem. The second way is to prepare a file on the computer—using almost any software application, including a word processor, spreadsheet, or image editor—and then "print" the output of that program to the fax modem.

Today, though, the fax machine in the office and the fax capabilities of a modem have been mostly replaced by e-mail. You can send an entire document—not a facsimile snapshot of it—from one machine to another at blazing speeds over the Internet. And if it is absolutely essential that the recipient see a picture of a piece of paper, that can also be accomplished by scanning it and sending it as an image file over the Internet.

That said, almost all current fax boards and soft modems include the ability to send faxes. You'll also find a relatively easy-to-use software application to control the preparation of files and a cover sheet and the management of the transmission. But I'll bet that 99 out of 100 PC users don't even know the facility is there.

To use your fax modem to receive incoming faxes, you have to leave the modem and PC on all the time, with the modem set to auto answer.

If you're like me, you've switched to a broadband cable or DSL modem for direct connection to the Internet; your ability to send and receive faxes with your PC takes a different route. You either need to keep a dial-up modem available just for faxing, or subscribe to one of several Internet-based fax services that link your Internet address to a phone line at their end.

If you have only a single telephone line in your home or small office, you may want to look for a modem that includes support for distinctive-ring services offered by most telephone companies. With such a setup, you can obtain a second telephone number for the same single line and devote that number to incoming faxes or telecommunications. The second number, which costs less to install and use than a separate phone line, has a different ring sound or pattern, and you can instruct a sophisticated modem to automatically answer calls to the second number only.

Dial-up Modem Standards

Over the years, modem designers had succeeded in pushing communication in exciting but relatively small increments: from 300 bps when the IBM PC first arrived to 1,200, and then 2,400; 4,800; 9,600; 14,400; 28,800; and then up to 33,600. When modem manufacturers developed and introduced several competitive standards for communication at 56,000 bps in 1998, there came a warning that technology was nearing the maximum speed limit for a simple pair of copper wires.

The competing standards for 56K communication have been resolved, but dial-up modems have not surpassed that 1998 speed limit since. And actually, the true speed of devices that claim 56K compatibility is generally a bit less than advertised. Although these modems are capable of working at 56,000 bits per second, technical restrictions limit download to no more than 53,000 bps.

For top speed, it is also essential that only one analog segment be present in the communication path from your PC to its destination or the other direction. Remember that the purpose of a dial-up modem is to convert the digital information within your PC to an analog wave signal that can travel the simple two-wire telephone circuit from your home or office to the phone company's nearest central switching office. After the signal arrives at the phone company facility, in most cases, it is converted to digital form. If the signal has to be reconverted from digital to analog at the central office nearest the destination of your Internet communication (and then back from analog to digital at the receiving computer) the throughput will be reduced markedly.

When 56K modems were introduced, the two most common (and incompatible) standards were X2 and K56Flex. If you had a modem that used one of these standards, you were only be able to connect at 56 Kbps if your modem found a like-minded device at the other end of the phone line.

In 1998, the industry came together behind a single standard called V.90. Some modems supported at least two and sometimes three of these standards, automatically switching to the correct one depending on the kind of hardware they encountered on the other end. A V.90 modem that includes X2 in its name, for example, adheres to the V.90 standard, but can also communicate with devices that are capable of using only X2 on the other end. Likewise, a V.90/K56 modem supports those two standards.

Two standards introduced after 1998 offer the possibility of squeezing out a bit more data from the effective dial-up speed limit of 56 Kbps modems.

V.92 ekes out a bit more speed, allowing uploads at as much as 48 Kbps, up from V.90's theoretical maximum of 33 Kbps. Modems using this standard can work with call-waiting services on your telephone to put the Internet on hold, in order to allow you to answer an incoming voice call. And V.92 promises to perform its "handshaking" connection to an Internet provider faster than previous standards.

The second new standard, V.44, provides an improved means of data compression. Systems using V.44 can compress Web pages at the ISP and decompress them at the receiving modem. In some situations, use of V.44 can double or even triple the speed of download of Web pages. The compression, though, won't speed up streaming video or audio data.

As with many other previous modem standards, there is one important gotcha: To make use of its advanced features, a compatible modem must be present at both ends of the connection. If you have a V.92 modem but the machine or the ISP at the other end has a lesser device, your communication can be no better than the slowest modem of the two.

One technology that held some promise but was not widely accepted was *multimodem* or *shotgun* setups, which combined two modems over a pair of phone lines, yielding a theoretical throughput of up to 112 Kbps. Of course, there had to be another shotgun marriage at the other end of the connection. Data was split in two and sent down both pipelines to be recombined at the receiving end.

CCITT/ITU standards

For much of the history of modern electronic devices (from about 1960), global standards for telecommunication were kept orderly by the International Telephone and Telegraph Consultative Committee (known by the French acronym CCITT for its full name, Comité Consultatif International Téléphonique et Télégraphique). The group is now known as the ITU Telecommunications Standardization Sector (ITU-T), an agency of the United Nations.

CCITT and now ITU standards begin with the letter V and are followed by a numeric code.

Table 16-3 gives a listing of dial-up modem standards, from dinosaur to modern machines.

TABLE 16-3: ITU Dial-up Modem Standards	
Standard	**Description**
V.22	1,200 bps. Synchronous or asynchronous data transmission with full-duplex operations over two-wire leased or dial-up lines. Comparable to Bell 212A.
V.22bis	2,400 bps.
V.32	9,600 bps, fallback to 4,800 bps. The first universal standard for 9,600 bps modems on dial-up or leased lines.
V.32bis	14,400 bps. Includes the ability to retrain connected modems to reduce transmission speed to deal with line noise, if necessary.
V.34	28,800 to 33,600 bps. This standard began at 28.8 Kbps, but firmware improvements allowed modems to eke out a bit of extra speed, moving from 28.8 Kbps to 33.6 Kbps in good conditions.
V.90	56,000 bps. Download at as much as 53 Kbps; upload at as much as 33.6 Kbps in good conditions. Most designs are backward compatible to allow communications with earlier devices, and many support the other 56K protocols, 56KFlex, and X2.
V.92	56,000 bps. Download at as much as 53 Kbps; upload at as much as 48 Kbps in good conditions.

Error correction and data compression

After the transmission speed for the bits of information has been set, you can add protocols that help ensure error-free transmission of data, or that compress data so that the effective rate of transmission is even greater. Data compression is one way to increase the speed of the modem without having to deal with the physical limitations of the wiring used. A compression ratio of 6:1 (the ultimate potential rate of V.44) effectively converts a 56 Kbps modem to nearly 200,000 bps in throughput. Two caveats: you must have the same protocols installed at both ends of the modem connection for the information to be properly encoded and decoded, and not all data can be compressed. Some data is already shrunk by application software and some types of information don't lend themselves to high ratios of compression.

Table 16-4 shows a listing of current telecommunication protocols.

TABLE 16-4: Current Dial-up Telecommunication Protocols	
Protocol	**Description**
MNP Levels 1-4	The Microcom Networking Protocols permit error-free asynchronous transmission of data.
MNP Level 5	This protocol adds a data compression algorithm to the error-correction code. Data is compressed by a factor of about 2:1.
MNP-10	Includes previous levels and adds features to support cellular data connections.
V.42, V.42bis	The CCITT definition for a protocol that is comparable to MNP Level 5. The V.42 protocol offers error correction with MNP levels 2-4 and LAPM (link access procedure for modems), while V.42bis adds compression.
V.44	Improved data compression; systems using V.44 can compress Web pages at the ISP and decompress them at the receiving modem.

Ch
16

NOTE

Although current modems from different manufacturers are generally fully compatible with each other, you may need exactly matched modems to take advantage of some highly specialized features. For example, if a modem uses an optional data-compression standard, such as MNP, you need another MNP modem to get the benefits of the data compression. Some very fast proprietary modems speak only to another identical model.

Troubleshooting an External Modem

When it comes to troubleshooting an external modem, you should test the following separate components:

- **Port:** Test the port by using a diagnostic program, such as AMI Diags. By examining Device Manager from within Windows, you can check whether the port is disabled because of a resource conflict. Older external modems connected to a PC using a serial port; a handful made use of a parallel port. Modern external modems generally connect to computers through a USB port.
- **Modem:** Is the modem plugged in and turned on? Do the modem lights turn on when power is applied? Some modems have a self-test that should generate an OK or other message after you turn on the device.
- **Software settings in your telecommunications program:** Check the settings in your software program. Is it set to use the proper COM (serial) or USB port?
- **The cable to the PC:** Check the cable running from the serial port to the modem by substituting a new or replacement cable that you know to be good.
- **The cable to the telephone socket:** Test the connection from the computer to the modem by going into the Hyper Terminal program that is available from within Windows. By default, this little-used program is part of the Communications subgroup in the Accessories group of Windows. Load the terminal emulation program. Type **AT** and press the Enter key. If your modem is working and is properly attached to a working serial port through a working cable, the software program should report an OK message onscreen.

- **The phone line:** Is the modem properly plugged into the phone jack? Swap a phone cable that you know to be good for the one in use. Try plugging a telephone into the jack to confirm that there us a dial tone on the line. If the jack itself is dead, you may have to troubleshoot the phone line within your home or office. If the problem lies at the network interface between your building and the phone company's incoming line, it's time to call the phone repairman. You can also purchase an inexpensive telephone line tester that will tell you whether the line is active, and if the + or – wires are reversed; a telephone will generally work with the lines reversed, but some high-tech devices, including answering machines and modems, may not. An example of a line tester is shown in Figure 16-4.

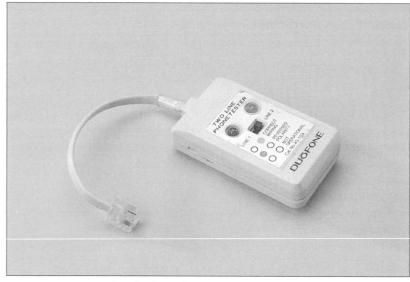

Figure 16-4: *A simple telephone line tester reveals whether the line is live and whether the internal wiring is properly installed.*

Modem Cables

You can have the speediest PC in town, equipped with a state-of-the-art dial-up, cable, or DSL modem and a subscription to the best Internet provider in town—and still end up with bad connections, disconnects, and corrupted files.

The problem may lie in the easy-to-overlook, inexpensive cables that hook it all together.

A dial-up modem is most susceptible to this kind of problem, since the phone cord that connects to a wall outlet is often all but ignored. It's very easy to think that these cables will last forever and always perform as if new. This is simply not true. Here are a few ways that a simple phone cable can go bad:

- It can be pinched beneath a desk or chair, causing a short circuit or break in the wires.
- It can be made fragile by proximity to a radiator or heater or direct sunlight. Repeated heating and cooling can cause the wire to shrink, or damage the insulation around the wire.
- Wires can be stretched or connectors damaged if they are pulled when a computer or desk is moved.

Any time you experience problems with a modem, I suggest that you carefully examine phone wires for damage. Try replacing the cables to see if a fresh wire will fix the problem.

It is also possible that a problem with a cable, telephone, or wall jack elsewhere in your home or office can short out the phone line throughout your operation. To attempt to solve a mystery phone or modem problem, start by confirming that your phone line is operating properly. Do so by plugging a working telephone into the Network Interface installed by the phone company at the point where it enters your home or office. A phone that does not work properly indicates that the problem lies in telephone company wiring and equipment. A phone that's working properly indicates that problems exist between the incoming phone line and the various devices plugged into the system in your home and office.

To find problems on your side of the network interface, start by unplugging every phone device. Then plug them in one at a time, checking for problems one at a time. If your modem operates well until a particular phone, answering machine, or other device is plugged into the phone line, you can assume that the problem is with the last device you attached.

Although modern devices are pretty well shielded against interference, you may be able to fix problems with modems by eliminating radio frequency interference from monitors, modems, and other peripherals. Some of these devices come with small iron rings, called *ferrite chokes*, that reduce interference when attached to cables; if you can't find a set in your kit of leftover bits and pieces of equipment, you can purchase ferrite chokes from most electronics stores.

If you're using a cable or DSL modem, the connections are a bit more robust, but the possibility of failure is still there. A cable modem generally uses an Ethernet or USB cable to connect to the PC, and a coaxial cable to connect to the incoming and outgoing signal. A DSL modem also uses an Ethernet or USB cable on the PC side, and a slightly larger, thicker version of a standard phone cable to connect to the phone network.

Both cable modems and DSL modems may attach to a router or gateway to allow their broadband facilities to be shared by multiple PCs in your home or office. If your modem is showing signs of problems, you need to check all of its connections — on the PC side and on the path that leads to the incoming signal.

Troubleshooting an Internal Dial-up Modem

In theory, the Plug-and-Play facility of current versions of Windows (from Windows 95/98 through Windows XP and Windows Vista) will set up an internal PCI bus modem to avoid conflicts with IRQ and I/O port addresses. Follow the instructions that come with the modem.

Older cards, including all ISA bus devices, require you to physically make these settings by using jumpers or switches. Here's the procedure for most of them: Examine the Device Manager to look for available IRQs and I/O port addresses and then change the jumpers on the board if necessary. Then install the modem and go to the Modems Setup screen of Windows to assign IRQs and I/O port addresses.

Test the machine before reinstalling the cover — it's easy to make a mistake here. The I/O port address must be unique — it must not interfere with another device already installed in the machine. If your telecommunications software supports COM 3 and/or COM 4, set the modem to COM 3. You are unlikely to have another serial device set to COM 3. Be sure to set the IRQ for the I/O port address that you are using (each I/O port address is paired, by tradition, with a particular interrupt).

CROSS-REFERENCE

See Appendix D on the CD for a list of common I/O port addresses and their associated interrupts.

Ch
16

Then check the phone line. Is the modem properly plugged into the phone jack? Swap a phone cable that you know to be good for the one in use. Try plugging a telephone into the jack to confirm that a dial tone is on the line. If the jack itself is dead, you may have to troubleshoot the phone line within your home or office; if the problem lies at the network interface between your building and the phone company's incoming line, it's time to call the phone repairman.

Telecom Problems

Whether you use an external or internal modem, your telecommunications software must be set up correctly. A minor baud rate error or the incorrect I/O port address will make your perfectly good modem appear to be stone-cold dead. Modems are just that way; they either work fine or they don't work at all. Some pieces of communications software are very picky about the brand of telecommunications hardware in your system.

The call-waiting headache

The call-waiting tone unfortunately can disrupt modem communications. The result can be a simple loss of characters, a corruption of a file that you're transmitting, or a complete loss of the connection.

On most phone networks, you can disable call waiting by manually entering *70 from the dialing pad of a telephone before you place the call. As soon as you hang up, though, call waiting goes back into effect.

Some telecommunications programs have a setting for automatically including the disable signal before any call is dialed. For other applications, type *70, (include the comma) at the end of the dialing prefix.

Dial-up modem troubleshooting

Here are some suggestions to determine the source of your modem's ills.

Modem is recognized but cuts off before connecting

If your modem seems to be working properly but cuts off before a connection is successfully negotiated, try instructing Windows to be a bit more patient.

1. Click Start ➪ Settings ➪ Control Panel, and then double-click Modems.
2. On the General tab, click the name of the modem you are using and then click Properties ➪ Connection tab.
3. Add 15 seconds to the value for Cancel the Call if Not Connected Within xx Secs Value. Click OK, and then click Close.
4. Try the call again. If the problem recurs, repeat the steps until you are at the Properties tab, and turn off the waiting period entirely. Clear the Cancel the Call If Not Connected Within xx Secs check box. Click OK, and then click Close. Try the call again.

Another important modem checkup: Make sure you are using the most current device driver.

1. To update a modem driver, click Start ➪ Settings ➪ Control Panel, and then double-click System.
2. Click the Device Manager tab. If a Modem branch is displayed, double-click to expand it. Double-click your modem, click the Driver tab, and then click Update Driver.
3. If you have an updated driver on a disk, you can specify a location. If you're using Windows 98, you can launch the Update Device Driver Wizard to search for a driver on a Web page maintained by Microsoft.

Modem does not connect at its full speed

Check these possibilities if your modem is going slowly.

- Consider the quality of your phone line. If your voice telephone is regularly scratchy or disconnects by itself, your data modem is going to do no better.

- In most homes and offices, telephone companies have installed a box called the *network interface*; it may be located on the outside of the house, in the basement, or in a utility closet. The incoming telephone line comes into the box and from there it is split off to serve your home or office.

- The first task in checking a telephone line is to determine whether the problem lies in the phone company's connection to your home or office, or in the wiring that you own. Go to the network interface and plug a telephone directly into the interface and make a call. If the connection is clear and clean, your problem is probably on your side of the interface; if the line is bad, contact your telephone company and have them test the line.

- You can also call your telephone company and request a report on the possible top data connection speed for your line.

- In most cases, a problem on the telephone company's side of the interface is the responsibility of the utility. You will have to repair a problem within your home or office, or you can pay the phone company or a communications specialist to do the repair. Check the telephone directory supplied by your phone company — not one of the independent directories — for details about network interfaces and repair policies.

- If the phone line seems okay on both sides of the network interface and Windows finds the modem and does not report a resource conflict, the problem may lie in the settings that you have made for the Internet connection or the dial-up line you are using. Here you should enlist the assistance of your Internet Service Provider if possible; call customer service and go through all the settings you have made. Make certain your modem is compatible with the ISP's modem.

Testing your line for 56K capability

The only sure way to test whether your phone line is capable of connecting at 56K is to install a 56K modem and try it out. See if you can borrow a high-speed modem from a friend or colleague or a demo model from a store.

Dial into an ISP or a modem link that promises 56K compatibility, but make certain that your model matches the protocol used by that service. Today, that's probably V.90, but some earlier 56K devices may still be out there.

If the connection is successful at anything above 40K, you're all set — that is, unless line conditions change. Remember that most phone companies don't guarantee high-speed or digital connections unless you pay extra for a specific type of service. If you want to find out how fast your connection actually is, contact your modem manufacturer or visit the manufacturer's Web page. Many companies offer a dial-in testing service that can verify whether your modem is operating correctly. Software utilities available on the Internet can show you how fast you are exchanging data with other hosts.

SUMMARY

I've explored the current state of modems for telecommunications into and out of a PC. In the next chapter, I move on to a different form of mass transport within the PC: the parallel interface, used primarily for printers but also for devices including scanners, external storage devices, and a specialized category of modems.

Chapter 17

Tools Needed:
- Phillips or flat-blade screwdriver

The Parallel Interface

In the earliest days of computing, the idea of *parallel* communication seemed as obvious a solution to gridlock as the difference between an eight-lane superhighway and a two-lane country road. In PC terms, it was a choice between sending eight bits of information (one byte) all at once along eight wires marching to the beat of a clock, or stacking up those eight bits, one behind the other, and sending them along a single wire from place to place surrounding them with start, stop, error-checking, and identification codes.

In those first days, when the speed of the computer's microprocessor, memory, and the interconnecting bus were relatively slow, the parallel port was the clear winner in the communications race. The fastest printers, scanners, and a number of other devices were all designed to attach to what was first called the printer or LPT (line printer) port and later became known as the *parallel port*.

NOTE

You may also see references to a *Centronics* port because a company of the same name was among the first to offer desktop printers for the PC market. It designed a 36-pin connection scheme for parallel ports called the Centronics connector.

Serial communication — where bits followed one behind another — was used for devices where the computer was faster than the medium: dial-up modems (limited by the ability of phone wires to carry data) and hard disk drives, as well as devices that required only a relatively small amount of attention, including the mouse and keyboard.

But technology has trumped logic. Here's what happened: As parallel communication was pushed to become faster and faster, engineers ran into problems with the laws of physics. An electrical signal running through a wire is not much different from water running through a pipe; it can be slowed down by resistance along the way. If the wire has any impurities, or if one wire is just a bit longer than its neighbor, or if the wire is forced to make a sharp turn, the signal may be slowed down by a millisecond or so.

As I discuss in Chapter 15, when the beat of the computer clock was slow, this didn't make much of a difference; the system had more than enough time to wait for all eight bits to arrive. But with the advent of high-speed buses, there began a collision of data like a backup at the top of an escalator. If the system had to discard a byte because it was corrupted or the pieces arrived too far apart, the replacement byte (or a whole segment of data) had to be re-sent while the processor twiddled its electronic thumbs.

The advance of technology came on the serial side. Though the data has be changed from parallel to serial at the starting line and then reassembled into bytes at the receiver, designers have managed to turn up the speed (and improve the flexibility) to the point where serial circuits are now the champions of the computer test track.

For peripherals, nearly all modern PCs have shifted over to using a USB port; a small number of devices is intended for use with a FireWire port. The most modern of machines no longer offer a standard parallel or serial port, although they can be adapted (most simply with an external cable that attaches to a USB port, or with an adapter card installed in a PCI slot) to give this facility.

This chapter, then, concentrates on troubleshooting and replacing parallel port hardware on senior-citizen and dinosaur PCs, or on modern machines that have been adapted to make them capable of working with older peripherals such as printers not blessed with a USB connection.

Parallel Port Designs

The original PC parallel port had one basic function: to send data in one direction, from computer to printer. An adapter called a parallel card collected data from the computer bus and sent it 8 bits at a time to the printer.

For years, the PC's parallel port was called the *printer port* or LPT (line printer) port, which was an appropriate name because very few parallel devices existed other than printers. Devices that, at the time, were considered very sophisticated were capable of sending a small amount of data back up the wire to communicate from the printer to the PC. For example, the computer could receive an out-of-paper or printer-busy signal from the printer, but that signal held up data transmission.

Senior-citizen machines and some modern machines have true two-way parallel ports (also called *enhanced parallel port,* or *enhanced capabilities port*) so data can flow freely into and out of the computer. At its peak in the 1990s, the two-way parallel port spawned a whole raft of parallel-interface peripherals including modems, network adapters, CD-ROM drives, backup drives, and even external hard disks and tape backup units that communicated with the host computer through a parallel port. Figure 17-1 shows a D-shaped, 25-pin, female parallel connector on a PC.

Over the years, four basic types of parallel ports were available on PCs; each had differing speeds and capabilities. By the time that the parallel port was mature — just before the arrival of the USB port — computers offered ports that included all four modes. Here are the elements:

- **Unidirectional.** The original definition for the port, enabling one-way flow of data from a PC to a printer and occasionally to other devices. The top speed under this mode is about 50 Kbps.
- **Bidirectional.** In addition to the potential for two-way communication, this protocol boosts the possible transfer rate to as much as 300 Kbps. The bidirectional signal is mostly used to communicate status back from the device to the PC. Such information can include an out-of-paper signal from a printer.

- **EPP (enhanced parallel port).** An expansion of the protocol to speeds from 500 Kbps to more than 2 Mbps. The EPP was widely used by a new class of external devices that include hard drives, removable storage devices, and network adapters.
- **ECP (extended capabilities port).** A further extension of the EPP to improve two-way communications between peripherals and the PC.

Your best bet to avoid confusion is to follow carefully the advice in instruction manuals for your PC and devices attached to it. If your PC and peripherals support ECP, you have no reason not to use this most current and fastest implementation of the parallel port. Device drivers and setup programs should automatically prepare your machine for use with new hardware. You can also make changes using the Device Manager under Windows. You may also need to enter your computer's ROM BIOS to configure some types of new hardware. If Plug-and-Play doesn't catch your hardware, try configuring it from inside the BIOS.

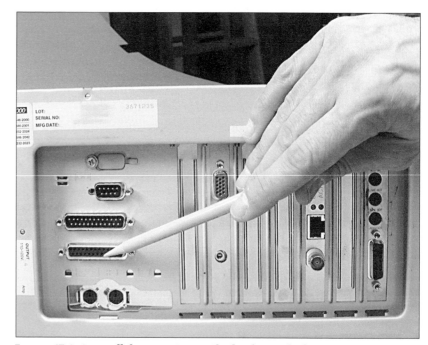

FIGURE 17-1: *A parallel connector on the back panel of a PC.*

How a Parallel Port Works

Because computers store information in 8-bit bytes, the simplest way to send a byte of information to a printer is to use eight separate wires from computer to printer. Each of the 8 bits is sent on its own wire, parallel to other wires within the cable.

Older modern machines typically offered only a single parallel port, although a standard motherboard is capable of having as many as three parallel ports, numbered as LPT 1 through LPT 3. Under Windows 98 and later versions, the Plug-and-Play function should assign IRQs, I/O port addresses, and DMA channels automatically, although the occasional conflict still slips by. If you have more than one LPT port in your system, they should have resource settings that are unique to each other, as well as different from those of other devices in the PC.

Table 17-1 shows the standard resource settings for parallel ports. Note that the standard settings for LPT 1 and LPT 2 both use IRQ 7. One or the other (preferably LPT 2) should be given a different IRQ to avoid conflicts.

TABLE 17-1: Standard Resource Settings for Parallel Ports

Port Name	IRQ	I/O Port Address
LPT 1	IRQ 7	3BC-3BFh
LPT 2	IRQ 7	378-37Ah
LPT 3	IRQ 5	278-27Ah

Many modern parallel port devices include a pass-through cabling system that enables you to daisy-chain at least one more peripheral. For example, you can use a parallel port to communicate with an external CD-ROM drive and plug a printer cable into the back of the CD-ROM case to serve a printer. In theory, this is another Plug-and-Play solution, but in practice you may find occasional conflicts if both devices seek the attention of the PC at the same time. In the case cited here, for example, you may have problems printing information from the CD-ROM to the printer that is daisy-chained through it. One solution is to print to a file on your hard disk, and then resend the file to the printer.

Three signal lines on early parallel ports were assigned to the printer to send out-of-paper, printer-busy, and data-acknowledgment signals back to the computer. The parallel port could transmit signals on the eight data lines, but not receive them. New parallel ports can send and receive on all lines.

A standard parallel printer cable — sometimes called a Centronics cable for the 36-pin Centronics connector at the printer end — connects the parallel card to the printer. (Some of the most modern devices have begun to use a smaller, high-density 36-pin connector at the printer end; the specification is called IEEE 1284-C.)

NOTE

Unlike serial ports, all parallel ports send the same signals on each particular pin, so no custom parallel cables are needed.

If you are going to use an ECP or EPP parallel device, though, your hardware may demand a high-quality bidirectional cable. Some devices use high-density connectors that are smaller than the traditional DB-25 connector used on earlier PCs.

Extended Capabilities Port/Enhanced Parallel Port

ECP and EPP ports offer improved throughput for some peripherals and add to the number of ports that you can have on your PC. This high-speed parallel specification (also referred to as IEEE 1284) can transfer data in parallel fashion up to 50 to 100 times faster than traditional parallel (Centronics) interfaces.

The 1284 specification provides for five basic port modes:

- **Compatibility.** A one-way mode that sends data only from the host to a peripheral. Sometimes called Centronics or standard mode, this is the way parallel ports worked in the beginning.
- **Nybble.** A 4-bit bidirectional mode, but somewhat limited, and most often used to get information back from a printer, such as out-of-paper, offline, or other status information. A peripheral can send a full byte of information to the host, but it takes two 4-bit transmissions to do it.
- **Byte.** The bidirectional port mode. Eight bits at a time are transferred bidirectionally.

- **EPP.** A bidirectional, 8-bit mode. This is a fast data-transfer mode that can achieve transfer rates from 500K to 2MB per second. Transfer requires only a single ISA bus cycle. With this data rate, the parallel port peripheral can operate at about the same speed as an ISA bus card.
- **ECP.** Also a high-speed data interchange mode, designed for host-peripheral data transfer with printers, scanners, and other peripherals.

Although ECP/EPP ports offer much faster transfer and bidirectionality, they also maintain compatibility with older peripherals, so you can upgrade your PC with a new parallel port board and still hook up your older printer or other parallel device.

On the other hand, don't expect to see dramatic changes in printer speed (or the speed of other peripherals) just because you have installed an IEEE 1284-compliant interface. You must have the proper drivers to support the port and the applications that you want to use with it, and, of course, your peripheral must be designed to handle the faster host communications.

Table 17-2 describes the signals that take ownership of each of the lines in a 25-wire parallel connector.

Unfortunately, parallel cables are only guaranteed to be accurate for short runs of 12 to 15 feet, though users sometimes successfully use cables as long as 25 feet. Each case is different. If it works, it works.

If a longer run does not function reliably, several solutions may help. One involves the use of a *parallel line booster*, which is a specialized amplifier that can extend the useful transmission distance of a parallel signal as much as 2,000 feet. These relatively inexpensive devices (costing less than $100 from mail-order sources) essentially convert the parallel signal into a specialized high-speed serial signal and send it over a standard telephone cable to a receiver where the signal is changed back to a parallel signal.

TABLE 17-2: Signals on a 25-Pin Parallel Port Connector

Pin	Name	Direction
1	− Strobe	Out
2	+ Data bit 0	Out
3	+ Data bit 1	Out
4	+ Data bit 2	Out
5	+ Data bit 3	Out
6	+ Data bit 4	Out
7	+ Data bit 5	Out
8	+ Data bit 6	Out
9	+ Data bit 7	Out
10	− Acknowledge	In
11	+ Busy	In
12	+ Paper out	In
13	+ Select	In
14	− Auto line feed	Out
15	− Error	In
16	− Initialize printer	Out
17	− Select input	Out
18	− Data bit 0 Return (Ground)	In
19	− Data bit 1 Return (Ground)	In
20	− Data bit 2 Return (Ground)	In
21	− Data bit 3 Return (Ground)	In
22	− Data bit 4 Return (Ground)	In
23	− Data bit 5 Return (Ground)	In
24	− Data bit 6 Return (Ground)	In
25	− Data bit 7 Return (Ground)	In

Finding a Parallel Port

If you have a printer, follow the printer cable to the back of your computer and examine that connector first. Nearly all parallel ports use 25-pin connectors (called *DB-25 connectors*). The parallel port on the computer system is a female DB-25 socket. The cable to the printer has a male DB-25 connector for the computer end of the link. (Male DB-25 connectors have protruding pins; female DB-25 connectors have openings to accept the pins.)

Just to make things interesting, serial ports can also use a DB-25 connector, although modern machines that have parallel ports also changed over to smaller DB-9 connectors. For users of the oldest PCs, serious confusion often occurred because some serial ports used female DB-25 sockets identical to the parallel port socket. All modern machines and most PCs manufactured after that period of initial confusion use male connectors for serial ports.

The DB-9 connector on an older modern machine is male. You may still find a second DB-25 socket on the back of your PC for a second serial port, but it will have a male socket — with protruding pins — to differentiate it from the parallel printer port. IBM, which has almost always marched to its own drummer, reintroduced the confusion with some of its PS/2 computers in the early 1990s. If you're lucky, your machine has labels identifying the nature of all connectors on the back panel. Consult the PC's instruction manual if you have any doubts. Among dinosaurs, you will also find parallel ports on some video cards, multifunction cards, and on separate I/O (input/output) cards.

Figure 17-2 shows an add-on parallel port card that can be used to upgrade an older machine or to replace failed circuitry on a more current machine.

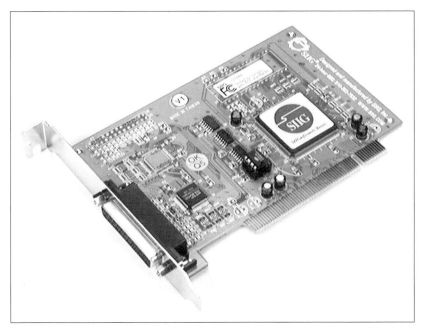

FIGURE 17-2: *You can add an enhanced parallel port card, such as this CyberParallel PCI card from SIIG, Inc., to an older machine to get the benefits of bidirectional parallel communication.*

Testing a Parallel Port

Parallel ports seldom fail. If you have a problem, it is more likely that the cable has worked loose, been crimped, or shorted out, or that a change to a software setting or a driver has caused it to stop responding. In my experience, however, the most likely cause is a failed cable. I recommend that you keep replacement parallel and serial cables in your supply cabinet. Here are some logical steps for troubleshooting parallel port problems:

1. Check the power cable to the printer. Most printers have a self-test capability; check the instruction manual to run the self-test. If the printer is plugged in and the self-test does not work, your printer has a problem.
2. Next, check the data cable connections between the parallel port and the printer. Is the cable firmly attached at both ends? Try using your new cable or a spare cable that you know to be good. If changing the cable fixes the problem, throw away the old cable.
3. Take the printer and the cable to another machine that has a working parallel port. If the printer and the cable work, then you can assume that the parallel port on the original PC has either failed or has an improper setting.
4. Try printing from another application. I have experienced printer failure from within application software many times. The software simply doesn't recognize the printer for some reason, even if it has worked properly before. (Okay, it shouldn't be that way, but these are computers, after all. Stuff happens!)
5. Try re-installing the printer driver software. For reasons probably nobody understands, printer drivers that worked fine yesterday can stop working today. Under Windows versions through Windows 98, use Start ➪ Settings ➪ Printers to display the printer dialog box, then right-click the icon that represents the printer that is not functioning properly and select remove or delete from the pop-up menu. Then choose Add a printer from this dialog box and follow instructions for re-installing the printer driver. This may, indeed, correct your printer errors. Under Windows 2000 and Windows XP, go to Start ➪ Printers and Faxes.

CROSS-REFERENCE

Reference the troubleshooting charts in Appendix A on the CD for more hints on how to test a parallel port. See Chapter 18 for additional information on printers and printer configuration.

If the printer and the cable are good, and changing applications and printer drivers doesn't fix the problem, use a diagnostic disk to see what parallel ports the computer thinks are installed. If you have two physical parallel ports, but your Windows System Information utility or a troubleshooting utility such as Norton's System Information shows only one, the switches and interrupts on one of the ports are probably not set correctly.

The earliest versions of video with parallel port cards have a port enable/disable jumper. Check the manual for such a jumper. In addition, the physical port address and the interrupt assigned to the card are set with jumpers on some parallel cards. Again, check the manual.

As with serial ports, you must be careful to give each parallel port a unique hardware address. The operating system refers to these different addresses as LPT 1, LPT 2, and LPT 3, as I mentioned previously. Be sure that your software is set up correctly to send information to the appropriate parallel port. The printer cabled to LPT 1 won't print your document if the word processor is sending the text to LPT 2.

If you find no obvious problems, investigate the parallel port further. Try the CheckIt printer port tests. They require a wrap plug (also called a *loopback plug*). Wrap plugs sometimes come with the software, you can purchase one from an electronics supplier, or you can construct one out of a spare male RS232 plug (also available at an electronics supplier).

If you want to make your own wrap plug, you can short out the pins of a DB-25 connector with solder or connect the wires in a short parallel cable. Use short jumper wires or clean solder bridges to connect the pins electrically. You must make five solder connections. Details are shown in Table 17-3.

If the parallel port passes the wrap plug test, the port is probably good. Check again for a mismatched LPT port and interrupt and for mismatched word processor output parameters. If you still can't find the problem, try the troubleshooting charts in Appendix G, which have complete, step-by-step, parallel port diagnostic/repair procedures.

TABLE 17-3: Parallel Loopback Plug Combinations

Solder Pin	To Pin
2	15
3	13
4	12
5	10
6	11

Removing and Installing a Parallel Port

Older but still capable modern machines have serial and parallel circuitry built into the motherboard, with the ports extending out the back of the chassis. If a problem occurs with the parallel adapter on the motherboard, or if you want to upgrade to a better system, you may need to disable the adapter with a jumper or switch; older-generation modern machines usually allow you to turn off a parallel port on the motherboard through a setting on the CMOS Setup screen. Consult your PC's instruction manual or the manufacturer for details.

The following instructions apply to parallel ports on an add-in card plugged into the bus:

1. Before you remove a parallel port, turn off the computer and unplug it from the wall. Remove the cables and computer cover. Disconnect the printer cable (the cable from computer to printer) at the parallel port end. The cable may have two long, threaded knobs on the card end or a pair of narrow, thin screws to hold the cable connector tight to the card. Unscrew the knobs or screws by turning them counterclockwise. If the parallel port is part of the video card (a dinosaur-era design), remove the video cable, too. After you disconnect the cables, remove the system cover.

2. Remove the old card. The card is secured to the back wall of the system unit chassis with a single screw. Remove this screw and save it. Lift the card straight up; it shouldn't require too much force.

3. Install the new card. Installation is the reverse of removal. Old-style parallel, video-with-parallel, and multifunction cards are 8-bit cards that used the ISA bus. Modern add-in cards use PCI slots. Carefully line up the edge connector on the card with the slot on the motherboard and press down firmly. When the card is in place, the screw hole on the card lines up with the screw hole in the back of the chassis. Re-install the screw and test the machine.

Adding a New Parallel Port

You can upgrade your modern machine with a new ECC/EPP parallel port or add a second port to a PC with add-on cards, such as the CyberParallel PCI card from SIIG. This Plug-and-Play PCI card gives you an IEEE 1284-1994 parallel port that supports all current types of devices, including printers, removable cartridge drives, CD-ROM drives, scanners, and more. The board includes an intelligent IRQ-sharing feature to eliminate conflicts, and it works with Windows 95/98 and later to automatically assign the next available I/O port address.

Today, a much easier solution is to use a USB-to-parallel conversion cable. The special electronics in the cable store up the incoming serial data from the computer and put them out the other end through a parallel plug. One example of this sort of converter is shown in Figure 17-3.

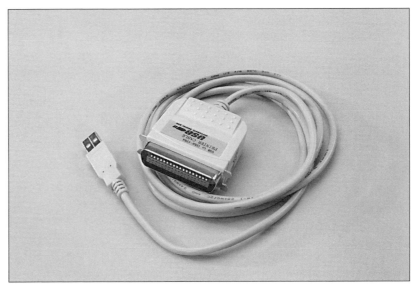

FIGURE 17-3: *This specialized printer cable connects to a computer's USB port and converts serial data to output through a standard Centronics connector.*

SUMMARY

In this chapter, I completed the exploration of the parallel port. In the next chapter, I move on to the process of using a printer to produce hard-copy printouts.

Chapter 18

Hard Copy

In the early days of computers, printers were expensive, large, slow, and loud mechanical devices, falling somewhere between a lawnmower and a Smith Corona typewriter. The most common design used a mechanism with a spinning "daisywheel" that had typewriter-like molds for each character. (IBM's hugely successful variant was the Selectric ball.) A hammer struck the character through a ribbon and onto the paper. These devices were called *character* printers.

Computer mainframes used huge printers that had a set of wheels or a metal band a full page in width, allowing them to print a line at a time. These devices were called *line printers*, and that name lives on in the official name for the parallel port on personal computers, LPT1.

All of these devices were *character-oriented*. The computer sent a signal that told the printer to hit the letter J mold against the ribbon. If you wanted to type an italic J, you had to change the type wheel or ball to one that had an italic J.

Both line printers and character printers also carry another designation: impact printers. The reason for this moniker should be obvious: A mechanical mechanism causes whatever device that holds the characters to move quickly against a ribbon and strike the paper, causing ink in the shape of the selected character or characters to be deposited on the paper.

Soon after personal computers arrived on the scene, printer manufacturers introduced a whole new type of design. These devices are called *dot-matrix* printers. Nearly every printer now sold for use with PCs uses this technology, which is cheaper, smaller, faster, and quieter than character printers.

Early dot-matrix printers used the impact of tiny pins or wires inside a movable print head. Instead of slamming fully formed characters against a ribbon and then into the paper, dot-matrix printers created each character by forming a character from a set of dots. As technology improved, the grid of dots was made denser and the quality of character output and simple graphics improved.

Very few modern dot-matrix printers are impact printers, though; instead, the ubiquitous laser and ink jet printers use electrostatic charges or tiny spray nozzles to paint characters onto papers. The characters or images are still made up of dots, but the points are tiny and they lie on the surface of the paper.

This chapter examines all the major technologies for printers and offers advice on tracking down the source of problems with hard-copy output devices.

Types of Printers

Modern machines use three major types of printers: impact, ink jet, and laser. All three are dot-matrix printers.

Keep in mind that the recipient of a letter you send, a report you prepare, or a graphic that you produce knows little about all that went into its preparation; they do, however, make a judgment about the quality of your work based on the quality of the page in front of them.

As with every other component of a personal computer, printer prices have fallen as quality, speed, and capability have increased. At the time of this writing, you can purchase a capable inkjet printer for as little as $20, a color inkjet for as low as $35, or a high-resolution color photo printer for about $80. There's not much of a step up to the next level: You could purchase a personal laser printer for as little as $99, a color laser printer for about $300, or a high-end office laser for about $700. If those prices don't impress you, perhaps you would be interested in buying one of half a dozen old machines in my closet, each of which cost more than $1,000 when new.

As I explain in the next section, most printer manufacturers have come to realize that it makes sense to all but give away the machine itself and hope for profit from the sale of ink cartridges for inkjets, and toner cartridges and replacement drums for lasers. Over the past decade, there have been relatively few significant changes in technology other than improvements in reliability and drops in price. Nearly all current modern printers offer USB connections to a computer; advanced models may also connect to an Ethernet for direct sharing among multiple machines. A small percentage of machines also retain a parallel port to maintain compatibility with older computers.

The principal difference between machines at the high and low end of the price spectrum today is speed and what manufacturers call a *duty cycle*. An inexpensive machine is generally not intended to be in constant, heavy use; parts may wear down, and the cost of consumables — ink, toner, ribbons, or drums — may be unacceptable.

For most modern users, the machines of choice are laser (and closely-related LED) printers, and inkjet printers. I discuss all of these in this chapter.

Inkjet printers

Inkjet printers squirt tiny droplets of ink in programmable patterns. They are similar in concept to dot-matrix impact printers, except that they replace hammers and pins with ink nozzles. Characters, however, are still made up of dots. Current models can work with a wide range of types of paper, including ordinary office copy paper. Inkjet printers are every bit as impressive as a low-end laser printer — with the same 600-dot-per-inch resolution — at least when you first take them out of the box. Quality can fall off slightly if you don't keep the nozzles clean, if you use poor quality paper, or if you operate the printer in extremely humid conditions.

As with conventional impact dot-matrix printers, most common machines today electronically emulate a few common designs. Look for Hewlett-Packard Ink Jet or Canon emulation to be sure of compatibility with a wide range of software packages.

Before you buy an inkjet printer, check the price and availability of ink cartridges for the printer. You should also compare the per-page cost for inkjet devices. The printers' specifications should give you the information that you need. In other words, some printer manufacturers have embraced an old theory of American marketing: Give away the razor to sell the blades. Some low-cost printers require expensive cartridges or other supplies, making their total cost of operation comparable to printers that may have a higher initial price tag.

You can obtain third-party replacement supplies for the most widely sold machines, including those from HP, Canon, Brother, and Epson. On the other hand, you may find private-label machines (including those sold online by Dell or under the name of a retailer) that, though they may be manufactured by one of the major makers, are modified so that it is difficult or impossible to obtain supplies except from the original seller.

Color inkjet printers use three or four reservoirs of ink, creating pictures by overlaying color in an additive process. Simple color inkjets for business presentations will work with most smooth papers; sophisticated devices intended to print out photo-quality images usually require specialized expensive coated paper.

Color printers have one additional cost issue: the sometimes-inefficient use of ink reservoirs. The worst design, from the standpoint of economics, is an all-in-one cartridge that includes black and several color inks. If you use up one color, you have to replace the entire cartridge. A better design uses separate ink cartridges for each color. A good compromise is a design that uses a separate black cartridge and a multicolor cartridge.

Laser and LED printers

Laser printers have become as commonplace in the office as copy machines. The differences between the two are not as great as you may think. You can think of a laser printer as a computerized copy machine, requiring the same kind of care.

The creation of this class of printers begins with a dot matrix of characters or graphics in a bank of memory. When the full page is ready to be printed, electronics in the device control the output of a tiny laser beam that pulses out flashes of light. In most such devices, the laser beam is moved around on a metallic drum by a system of tiny moving mirrors and lenses.

A light-sensitive drum within the laser printer is given a positive electrical charge by a *corona wire* or *corona roller*. As the drum rolls, the tiny focused dot of light from the laser beam strikes it at certain points; each place touched by the light loses its positive electrical charge. The result is an electrostatic image of the entire page to be printed.

Next, the drum is coated with positively charged toner. If you can remember back to high school physics, you will recall that opposite charges attract each other while same charges repel each other. The toner sticks only in the places where the laser has created a negative charge.

The drum then meets up with a sheet of paper that is moved into position by the printer mechanism. The paper is given a stronger negative charge than the drum, which forces the toner to move across to it.

Finally, the paper is passed through a set of heated rollers, called a *fuser*, which melts the toner. Meanwhile, the drum is exposed to a bright discharge lamp that erases the electrostatic image and readies it for another use.

An LED printer uses the same drum and toner concept, but uses a light emitting diode printhead as a light source within the imaging device. The printhead is solid-state and has no moving parts; it pulse-flashes across the entire page width and creates the image on the print drum as it moves down. As far as the user is concerned, the operation is identical to that of a laser printer. In general, LED printers are a bit slower but less expensive than an equivalent laser device. Some manufacturers claim that they have a longer service life because they have fewer moving parts.

The important specifications for a printer are resolution (with 600 dots per inch a reasonable current minimum, and 1,200 dpi increasingly common), pages per minute (based on the output of simple text pages, and usually starting at about 4 or 6 ppm), and printer memory (original lasers were shipped with as little as 1MB of internal memory, which put a great deal of demand on the computer's resources; modern machines typically come with at least 16MB of memory, and the most advanced machines can be expanded to as much as 320MB). The more memory in the printer, the quicker it will respond when you ask it to produce a page with complex graphics. You will also find differences related to the particular page description language in use: For example, PostScript generally requires more memory to construct a page than does PCL.

 NOTE

Bear in mind that the page-per-minute rating is based on plain text pages. It can take quite a while—sometimes several minutes—for the computer to compose a complex bitmap and send it to your printer for output. In such a case, a 4 ppm printer is just as fast as a 20 ppm device—they both put out only a single page at a time. Also, some printer manufacturers quote page-per-minute rates based on printing the same page over and over again. Copier manufacturers use this same scheme. It takes longer to send a succession of different pages to the printer because the printer electronics have to accept and digest the new data before putting it onto paper. Assume page-per-minute specifications are the maximum that your printer can do. Actual throughput will fall off under a variety of conditions.

Insufficient memory can slow down printing, or cause the device to refuse to work at all with complex pages that contain graphics or multiple fonts. Some printers accept standard memory in SIMM format, making it easy and inexpensive to upgrade the device; other printers demand proprietary memory modules, raising the cost for consumers. You should check the memory design and default memory size before making a purchase.

Another critical difference among laser printers involves the quality of construction and the cost of consumables. You can often gauge the quality of construction by looking at the length of warranty offered by the manufacturer and checking the reviews in computer magazines.

Many laser printer makers put many of the mechanical elements, including the light-sensitive drum, in a removable cartridge that also contains a supply of toner; typical prices for one of these all-inclusive cartridges is about $100. You replace the cartridge after printing a certain number of pages. Another design uses inexpensive toner cartridges and more expensive separate drum packages; you replace an image drum after every dozen or so toner cartridges. Both schemes work, and in many cases work out to about the same cost per page.

One note about toner: You can save some money by purchasing refilled cartridges from companies other than the original manufacturer. Exercise caution when doing so, however, for the following reasons:

- The cartridges for many printers include the image drum and other moving parts, and you have no idea of the condition of those parts in a used package.

- The replacement toner is usually a generic formula that may not be a perfect match for the material sold by the original equipment manufacturer.

For these reasons, I stay away from "garage" refillers, but I have had success with refills from national brand name office supply houses. If you want to experiment here, buy one replacement cartridge and test it in your machine before filling your supply closet with third-party units.

Page description languages

Laser, LED, and most inkjet printers are page printers that assemble a full page in memory — either within the printer or in the computer — before producing an image on paper. Early printers used a scheme called escape codes to communicate commands; these specialized characters instruct the printer to produce a limited set of features.

The two most prevalent modern page description languages are *Printer Control Language (PCL)*, developed by Hewlett-Packard and sometimes called Printer Command Language, and PostScript from Adobe. For most users, all that matters is that your printer comes with a driver that interprets commands from your application — a word processor, a spreadsheet, an Internet browser, and the like — and applies a proper set of instructions for your printer. Some printers are also capable of directly working with PDF documents, which grew out of PostScript; PDF files embed text, art, fonts, and instructions in a package that can be reproduced on a wide variety of devices.

At one time, PostScript was the leading printer language for high-quality desktop publishing and graphics. PostScript is an *object-oriented language*, meaning that pages are created using the assembly of geometric shapes rather than as bitmaps or individual characters. Fonts are described as an outline, and the printer generates images based on this mathematical description. As such, fonts are scalable in size and alterable to versions such as italic and bold forms. Because the printer is generating the shapes, quality of output is dependent on the resolution of the printer; for example, a 600 dpi laser printer will be a noticeable improvement over a 300 dpi model, while a 2,400 dpi device used in a print shop will be good enough for publication. PostScript exists in several versions; at the time of this writing, the current version is PostScript 3.

Adobe has licensed PostScript to many printer manufacturers. You will also find several "PostScript emulators" offered with hardware; in general, this sort of clone software will work well with most applications. If you are preparing work to be sent to a service bureau for professional purposes, make certain that the emulator is exactly equivalent to the software that will be used for the final product. Check with the service provider for details.

Hewlett-Packard's PCL was developed for use with the company's well-respected DeskJet, LaserJet, and other printers; a number of other makers have since licensed the code for their own drivers. Current versions of PCL deliver most of the functionality of PostScript, even surpassing it in some ways.

Networking Printers

Networks used to be found only in office settings, and usually were the province of a technically trained systems administrator. Today, though, current Windows operating systems and modern machines are preconfigured for quick setup of a network anywhere. There's a real benefit for offices and homes: not only can you share files, but you can also share hardware including printers.

You can share a piece of hardware over a network two ways:

- By making available to other PCs a printer that is directly attached to another machine on the network
- By installing a printer that includes its own Ethernet interface and is directly accessible by any machine on the network.

Attaching a printer to a network connection instead of directly to a PC gives you the following advantages:

- You may be able to free up a USB port (or a parallel port on an older PC) for something else.
- You will gain flexibility in placing the printer almost anywhere you want; an Ethernet cable can be much longer than a parallel cable.
- A direct connection to a network relieves the need to use a PC as a printer server, which requires memory and CPU resources.

Although, as I note earlier, attaching a printer to one of the computers does tax some of the resources of that computer, this is still the simplest (and usually the least expensive) way to share a device. Another disadvantage of this arrangement, though, is that the sending and receiving computers must be turned on and functioning as part of the network to permit printing.

If you are already working with networked computers, then attaching a networked printer is an easy task. The printer simply becomes one more device on your network, like another computer. Software spoofs applications into believing that they are printing to a local printer attached to a computer. Once this is set up, the printer works the same as a device connected directly to another PC on your network.

Determining the Source of a Printer Problem

A parallel or serial printer port, a USB port, or an Ethernet port rarely breaks. The most common sources of problems for hard-copy output are cables, switches, and the printers themselves. A functioning port of any type can be knocked out of commission by resource conflicts.

To identify the source of a problem, first run the printer's self-test. Consult your instruction manual or call the manufacturer to learn how to test the machine. If the self-test fails, your printer needs servicing. If the self-test works, move on to test your printer interface and cable.

To send a test page to the printer from within Windows, start by turning on the printer and continue by following these steps:

1. Click Start ⇨ Settings ⇨ Printers. (Under Windows XP, click Start ⇨ Printers and Faxes.)
2. Highlight the printer that you want to test, and then right-click it.
3. Choose Properties.
4. Select the General tab, and then click Print Test Page.

If the printer delivers the test page, your problem is most likely a setting within an application, such as your word processor or office suite. Try resetting printer options from within that application.

If the printer does not work, test to see whether the problem may lie in the Windows operating system. Go to DOS. One way to do this is to choose Start ⇨ Programs, and then click the MS-DOS prompt. Another route to the DOS prompt is to restart the system; click Start ⇨ Shutdown and then select Restart in MS-DOS mode.

Under Windows XP, you can reach a version of the operating system prompt by clicking Start ⇨ All Programs ⇨ Accessories ⇨ Command Prompt.

Turn on the printer. From the prompt, type **DIR > LPT1** to send a copy of the folder directory to be printed. The printer should produce

the directory. Some devices may require you to turn the printer from On Line to Off Line and then press Form Feed to manually eject a page from the printer. If the printer works in this test, your problem is probably related to a setting in your operating system or in the printer driver.

If the printer fails both tests, try substituting a data cable that you know to be good and running the same test. If the printer now works, the original cable has failed and should be replaced.

If the cable is not the problem, try hooking up the printer to another computer. Try the printer from an application and from DOS, as described previously. If the printer doesn't work, take it in for service. If it works properly, your problem lies with the original computer.

Test the serial or parallel port of your computer as appropriate, using a diagnostic software program. If your printer attaches to a USB port, you probably can test the port simply by plugging in another USB device such as an external disk drive, memory key, camera, or an MP3 player. If your computer recognizes one of these devices and it works as expected, the problem is not with the physical hardware port.

If you have a very old printer, you may have a nonstandard serial cable. Consult the instruction manual for details. Chapter 15 discusses one almost-foolproof solution to serial cable problems—a magical device called the Smart Cable. The Smart Cable can adjust to match the needs of either end of the connection.

 CROSS-REFERENCE

See Chapter 15 for more serial connection troubleshooting tips.

Hardware checks for parallel port printers

The first hardware question you should ask yourself: "Is the printer turned on and connected by cable to the parallel port of my PC?"

If the answer to that question is "Yes," then start by making sure that the printer itself is functioning by performing a self-test. Each printer has its own way to produce a test page; consult your instruction manual for details.

Next, check the connection from your PC to the printer by sending a simple file from DOS. You can open a prompt window—choose Start ⇨ Programs ⇨ MS-DOS Prompt from within Windows 95/98, or exit Windows to the DOS prompt. From Windows XP, choose Start ⇨ All Programs ⇨ Accessories ⇨ Command Prompt.

Type the following two commands and then press Enter. The first creates a small file consisting of a copy of the directory of the subfolder; the second sends a copy to the printer.

```
Dir > dir
COPY C:\dir LPT1
```

If C: is not your boot drive, or if your printer is not connected to LPT 1 — the standard parallel port designation — then make the appropriate changes to the command. You can send any file to the printer.

You may need to manually eject a page from your printer to see the results. On most devices, press the On Line button (to set the printer offline) and then the Form Feed button. If the printer produces a copy of your file, you have established that the printer, its cable, and the PC's parallel port are all functioning properly.

> **NOTE**
>
> If you have more than one printer and therefore more than one logical printer port configured under Windows, this test may not work because DOS may not be able to identify your printer hardware correctly. If you suspect a problem with your computer hardware, use the Printers utility in the Control Panel to remove all printers except the one you are testing. Reboot your computer and try this DOS-level test again.

Next, eliminate problems with any advanced text-processing application. If you are running Windows 95/98 or XP, click Start ➪ Programs ➪ Accessories ➪ Notepad (or WordPad). Type some text on the screen, and then attempt to print.

If you can't print from either of the accessories, check the settings for the printer port by using Device Manager. (Choose Start ➪ Settings ➪ Control Panel ➪ System.) Scroll down to Ports (COM & LPT), click its plus sign, and then double-click the port for your printer — usually Printer Port (LPT 1).

Click the Resources tab and check that the conflicting devices list does not indicate a conflict. Examine the settings for the port. The usual input/output range for a standard LPT 1 port is 0378-037A. If a second parallel port is installed, LPT 2 is ordinarily assigned to 0278.

If there appears to be a conflict or if the port settings are incorrect, use the Device Manager program to remove the printer port from the system and then restart the computer. When Windows is running

again, click Start ➪ Settings ➪ Control Panel. Then double-click Add New Hardware to enable Windows to detect the hardware again.

Windows also includes a printer test facility that you can access from the Properties dialog box of most printers. Click Start ➪ Settings ➪ Printers to display the Printers dialog box. Right-click the printer that you're having problems with and choose Properties. At the bottom of the General tab, you should see a button labeled Send Test Page to Printer. Click this button. Windows then asks if everything printed normally. If it did not print normally, choose "No," and then follow the onscreen instructions for testing your printer.

Printer software issues

If you can print from a DOS command prompt but not from within Windows-based programs, and you have already examined port settings, you may have a problem with spool settings or bidirectional communication. A print spool holds information prepared by the PC for printing. Copying information to the spooler enables the computer to get back to other tasks and leave output as a background function.

Experiment to see if the problem lies in the spool settings. Click Start ➪ Settings ➪ Printers; then point to the printer that you're attempting to use and right-click it to bring up a submenu. Click Properties, and then click Details and the Spool Settings button. Finally, click the Print Directly to the Printer option button to turn off spooling.

If the Details tab indicates that the printer is set up to support bidirectional communication, try turning off that advanced facility. Click the Disable Bidirectional Support for this Printer button. Click OK, and then try to print from Notepad or WordPad. If the printer now functions properly, experiment with other settings for the spooler in combination with the bidirectional printing option.

Bidirectional printing requires an improved parallel printer cable, one that conforms to the IEEE 1284 specification. You may need to replace your printer cable to use its facilities. Bidirectional printing may also fail if the cable is too long. And you may lose bidirectionality if the parallel cable goes through a switch box or line extender.

Printer drivers

Printers vary in the way they handle hard returns and line feeds and the way they interpret escape codes for fonts and print size. To accommodate these differences, you must install a software program called a printer driver.

The most common reason for printer problems is an incorrect printer driver installation. This doesn't mean that you've installed the printer incorrectly, but that you've installed the wrong printer driver while setting up the software. The result can be some truly odd characters that appear when you print bold or underlined words. When you first use the software, you must select the correct printer driver to copy into the program. If you don't see the exact model number and guess wrong, or if you inadvertently type the wrong choice, you will install the wrong printer driver.

Application settings

Too many applications exist and too many combinations of problems are possible to address here. However, you can explore a few basic questions before you call the software maker.

First, determine the nature of the printing problem. Are you able to produce text, but not graphics? Will text print, but not in proper fonts? Does the problem only occur in one document?

NOTE

One interesting test is to attempt to print a blank page to the printer. If the empty page goes through the printer, this may indicate a problem with memory or fonts.

You may need to reinstall the applications, or you may have a problem with the System Registry (used for 32-bit applications) or an .INI file (an initialization file used for a 16-bit program).

If you're trying to use an application written for an older operating system, consult the maker to see whether any updates or patches are available.

Finally, you may have a problem with the printer driver for your hardware. Windows supports more than a thousand printers directly. When you install Windows on a system with a connected printer, Windows will use the printer driver it has for that printer. Contact the maker of the printer to see whether an updated driver is available. You almost always can download the latest printer driver from a web site.

Printer speed

Printers, like hard disk drives and CPUs, sometimes exist in an Alice-in-Wonderland world when it comes to measures of speed. A dot-matrix printer may, in fact, be capable of zipping along at 192 characters per second (cps) on a small-sized font, but may slow to 160 cps on a larger font. And dot-matrix printers usually make a distinction between draft and letter-quality printing. The difference in characters per second can be significant; the same printer in the preceding example may be able to produce its best type at a relatively slow 45 cps. A truer measure is the number of hammer strikes per second, but by itself this won't tell you how long your resumé will take to exit from the printer. And neither specification will easily inform you how long it will take to print out a graphic.

Here's a real-world appraisal: A typical single-spaced page of manuscript for this book contains 381 words or 1,762 characters. (In the English language, the average word length is about 5 characters.) At 192 cps, a dot-matrix printer would require about 9.2 seconds to spit out a draft-quality copy of the page. At the (near) letter-quality speed of 45 cps, the page would require a fairly slow 39 seconds.

Similarly, a laser printer may be advertised as an 8 ppm device. However, laser printers are page printers in that they form the entire page in their internal memory (or in some designs, in the memory of the PC) and then produce the page in a single pass. The 8 ppm specification refers to the speed of continuous pieces of paper through the printer after the pages have been formed in memory. Each page requires 7.5 seconds, which works out to something like 235 cps. However, creating the first page of a text document typically requires 20 to 30 seconds. A more reasonable ppm rating for an eight-page document is about 6.6. Remember, though, that a laser printer is *always* producing letter-quality pages.

NOTE

Modern laser printers may have settings that let you adjust the dpi settings and darkness levels of printed pages. These settings work similar to the way the draft and letter-quality settings on older impact printers work, except that for text output on a laser printer, you can rarely see the difference. By choosing an economy or draft setting in your printer's control panel, you may improve throughput and almost certainly will save toner, allowing you to get more pages out of a single toner cartridge. Save the high-quality output for graphics or photographs.

Creating a complex graphic image can slow a laser printer to a crawl, sometimes requiring a minute or more to create the page. After that page is completed, it will be spit out at the ppm rate—7.5 seconds in the supposed 8 ppm example.

What can you do to improve printer speed? A laser printer will benefit from the addition of RAM. The memory will either speed the creation of the page being printed or enable creation of the next page in the background as the current one is being produced.

One device that improves your computing environment is a hardware printer cache or a software printer buffer. Either one will enable you to move on to new tasks while pages are created and stored in the background. Neither solution speeds up the production of the pages themselves, but they do improve your personal productivity.

Printing speed in Windows

In some cases, you can improve the performance of your printers under Windows 95/98 and later editions by adjusting the spool file setting. When you print a document from an application, Windows creates a temporary spool file on your hard disk and copies the document to that file using a special format. After the spool file has been created, Windows returns control to your application and then manages the printing of the document in the background.

You can use one of several routes to the Printers folder, where you can make changes to the settings for the spool file. Here's the most direct. Under Windows 95/98:

1. Click Start ⇨ Settings ⇨ Printers.
2. Right-click the icon for the active printer, and click Properties.
3. On the Details tab, click the Spool Settings button to display the Spool Settings dialog box. An example is shown in Figure 18-1. By default, the settings are intended to allow you to get back to work as quickly as possible.

The first option — Spool Print Jobs so Program Finishes Printing Faster — turns on spooling, returning control to your application while printing goes on in the background.

The next two options present an either/or choice. The default choice is Start printing after first page is spooled, which gets the printer to work as soon as the first page has been copied to the spool; additional pages are put in the temporary storage while printing continues. The other option makes the printer wait until the last page has been spooled. This speeds up the spooling process but slows down the return of control to Windows; it also requires more hard disk space for the spooled pages.

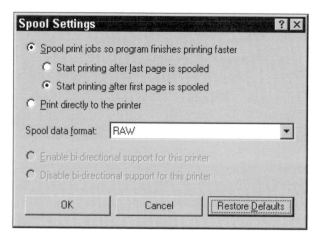

FIGURE 18-1: *The Spool Settings screen of Windows 95 and 98.*

Depending on the model of printer you have installed, you may also be able to select Print Directly to the Printer. With this option, Windows devotes all of its attention to sending pages to the printer; the printer responds as fast as it is able to do so, but you won't be able to perform other tasks until the last page has been sent.

Another option available only with certain printers is a choice of Spool Data Format. If available on the printer, Windows will try to work with a file format called *enhanced metafile format* (EMF), which is smaller than a RAW format, which takes a bit longer to load but is customized for each printer.

Windows 2000 and XP work in a similar fashion:

1. Choose Start ⇨ Printers and Faxes, and then right-click the printer you want to adjust.
2. On the Advanced tab, make changes to the spool settings. Note that the screen you see is specific to the type of printer you have installed on your system. And if you are working with a machine located on a network, the network administrator may have disabled some options or preselected settings.

An example of the Windows XP spool setting configuration screen on a printer's Advanced tab is shown in Figure 18-2.

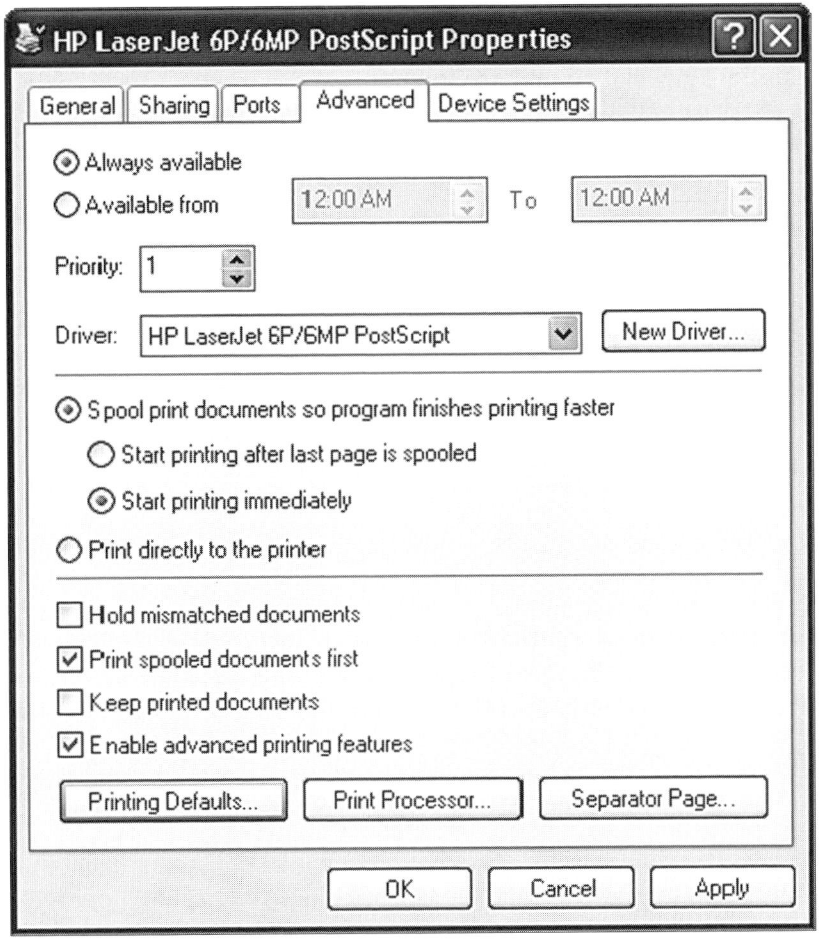

HP LaserJet 6P/6MP PostScript Properties

General | Sharing | Ports | Advanced | Device Settings

⦿ Always available
◯ Available from   [12:00 AM] ⇕ To [12:00 AM] ⇕

Priority: [1] ⇕

Driver: [HP LaserJet 6P/6MP PostScript ▾]   [New Driver...]

⦿ Spool print documents so program finishes printing faster
  ◯ Start printing after last page is spooled
  ⦿ Start printing immediately
◯ Print directly to the printer

☐ Hold mismatched documents
☑ Print spooled documents first
☐ Keep printed documents
☑ Enable advanced printing features

[Printing Defaults...] [Print Processor...] [Separator Page...]

[OK] [Cancel] [Apply]

FIGURE 18-2: *The Advanced tab of the properties screen for a printer, under Windows XP, shows how to configure spool settings within that operating system.*

Troubleshooting a troubled printer

Ask yourself the following questions when troubleshooting your printer:

Am I using an appropriate printer driver? A printer can freeze, or produce garbled output, if you use an incorrect, outdated, or corrupted printer driver.

To check printer properties: Click Start ⇨ Settings ⇨ Printers. Right-click the icon that represents the printer that you want to use, click Properties, and then click the Details tab. Check that the driver settings are correct and that an appropriate driver is being used. Under Windows 98, the Driver tab offers the option to check the Windows Update Web site for an updated driver. Under Windows 2000 and XP, the driver update is accomplished through the Advanced tab.

Are my printer driver graphics settings correct? Consult your printer documentation to determine the correct settings for your printer. Click Start ⇨ Settings ⇨ Printers. Right-click your printer icon, and then click Properties.

Depending on the particular driver for your printer, you may see a Graphics tab, a Device Options tab, or an Advanced button. Start by changing any settings back to the recommended defaults for your printer; consult the device's instruction manual for suggestions on changes.

Do I have enough paper, toner, or ink? Some printers are smart enough to stop the job when you run out of supplies, but may not be communicative enough to tell you why. Study the printer's instruction manual to learn the meaning of error codes on the printer or messages that may be displayed on your PC.

Has the quality of output degraded? Uneven darkness across a page is often an indication of low toner on a laser printer. You can usually eke out a few dozen more pages from a cartridge by removing it and gently shaking it from side to side and back and forth to redistribute the toner. Another possible cause for uneven printing is damage to the photoreceptor, or a light leak into the receptor from a nearby lamp or window.

Dark lines down the length of a laser-printed page may be caused by a scratch or other damage on the drum; the drum is usually part of the laser cartridge that is replaced when toner is depleted. White gaps or lines down the length of the page may be caused by damage to the toner cartridge or debris in the path between the cartridge and the drum. It may be possible to remove obstacles; otherwise, the cartridge will need to be replaced.

Blotches of black or white on the paper may indicate contamination of the drum or the fusing roller. The drum is not easily cleaned; if your cartridge includes a drum, the problem will be fixed when you replace it. Most printers include a small brush and sometimes a cleaning solution for the fusing roller. Consult the printer's instruction manual for advice.

An inkjet printer is prone to clogs in the print head that can result in loss of resolution, or dropouts in text or graphics. Many modern printers include a utility to clean the inkjet head; consult the instruction manual for details. On most machines, the manufacturer recommends removal of the ink cartridge if a printer is left unused for a lengthy period of time.

Am I using an inappropriate grade of paper? Different printing technologies and resolutions require various paper qualities. To get the most out of a laser printer, you want to use a good quality copy paper certified for a laser printer or copying machine. Inkjet printers generally require an even smoother paper surface because the ink is applied wet and the text or image can become fuzzy if the ink is absorbed into the paper; photorealistic inkjet printers work best with glossy or coated stock.

Does paper jam in the printer regularly? Paper jams are usually caused by one of three conditions: debris (including pieces of paper) stuck in the paper path; high humidity causing paper to stick together or to rollers; or inappropriate paper. Consult the instruction manual for advice on cleaning the paper path; use a vacuum with a soft brush to remove debris. One way to deal with high humidity is to store your paper in a sealed box, installing only as much as you need to print a job. Finally, check the specifications for your printer for acceptable weights and grades of paper; stock that is too thin, too thick, or too glossy can jam a printer.

Does my printer have enough memory? Try printing a small, simple document from the same program. If it works properly, the problem may lie in the printer's memory. You can also run any self-test routine that is part of the printer to check for error messages.

You can adjust printer settings to minimize the amount of memory that the document requires. If that doesn't work, or results in unacceptable print quality, your choice may come down to reducing the complexity of the document or adding more memory to your printer. Consult the instruction manual for your printer for specifics on how to adjust settings.

Are my printer time-out settings long enough? A very complex printing job — or a slow printer — may take longer to be ready to print than the time allotted under Windows.

To lengthen the time-out settings for the printer, click Start ⇨ Settings ⇨ Printers. Right-click your printer icon, click Properties, and then click the Details tab. Increase all of the values under Timeout settings. Under Windows XP, go to Start ⇨ Printers and Faxes ⇨ Device Settings.

NOTE

You can adjust time-out settings only for printers that are local to your PC; devices on a network are under the control of network settings.

Do I have enough free space on my hard disk? If you have enabled a printer spooler under Windows, the operating system will need space to prepare pages for printing; your system will likely grind to a halt if you have less than 10MB of available space.

You may be able to free up some space by emptying the Recycle Bin, deleting unneeded temporary files, removing programs that are not needed, and defragmenting the drive. And, of course, you can install an additional hard drive or upgrade to a new larger storage device.

SUMMARY

Now you've completed the exploration of hard-copy output devices — better known as printers. In the next chapter, you explore how mice and scanners bring hands and eyes to your PC.

Notes

Chapter 19

Tools Needed:

- Phillips or flat-blade screwdriver

Your Computer's Hands, Eyes, and Ears

Your fabulously capable, high-speed personal computer would be no better than a high-tech boat anchor if not for its capability to communicate with the outside world. The key to that interchange is your PC's ability to respond to input that it receives from the outside world through devices such as keyboards, mice, scanners, laboratory control equipment, and other devices.

For the first decade of the history of the PC, input devices generally connected to the computer through the serial port. For a short period at the start of the modern PC era, a number of devices found a bit more speed and flexibility by connecting through the parallel port or through a specialized SCSI adapter. Today, though, most external devices have completed a migration back to serial communication, using the high-speed, nearly limitless USB system.

In this chapter, I discuss important input and output devices — a hand, an eye, and a set of ears for the computer. I explore various species of keyboards — the computer mouse, game controllers, scanners, Web cameras, and sound cards.

The Keyboard

It's easy to overlook the keyboard, but don't do that. The device that sits beneath your fingers is critical to the operation of your computer, and it's also essential that it fit your style of work like a glove.

Keyboards have two basic types of feel — soft and click. The original IBM PC came with Big Blue's computer equivalent of its famed Selectric typewriter keyboard; each press of the keys was a smooth passage to a firm bottom, accompanied by a solid click. Soon thereafter, though, many PC clone makers began adopting a soft-touch keyboard, on which the key presses did not necessarily reach a bottom and the click was gone. Both types of keyboards work, and some users barely notice the difference between the two types of feel. Some people are strong partisans of one style or another.

Across the history of the PC, there have been three commonly used types of keyboard connections. All three use a serial connection to the motherboard, which works fine for all concerned; keyboards produce a relatively tiny amount of data per millisecond and are predominately one way in their communication.

The original attachment point was a dime-sized PC-AT connector that mated with a large DIN plug. That was followed by a pencil-sized port and connector called a PS/2 design (named after the IBM model that introduced it); you can see a PS/2 port in Figure 19-1. Today, nearly all keyboards connect to the flexible USB port. Most computer stores offer adapters that upsize or downsize between PS/2 and PC-AT connectors, or between PS/2 and USB ports. No software conversion is needed for any of the adapters.

Some users prefer to cut (or rather, avoid) the wire between a keyboard and the computer by employing a wireless device that uses a small infrared or radio transmitter to communicate. At the computer, the machine requires an infrared, WiFi, or BlueTooth receiver; these common laptop components are generally an add-on for a desktop PC.

Wireless keyboards (and mice) are of special value for lecturers who want to control a PC from a lectern. One technology uses digital spread-spectrum radio with frequency-hopping technology (similar to the system used by portable phones in your home) to communicate at distances of as much as three meters (about ten feet). Another design uses the BlueTooth specification, another design for radio communication. RF-based systems don't require a direct line of sight to the PC or the base station.

Infrared wireless keyboards use the same sort of technology employed by the remote controller for your television set, with a range of as much as 25 feet. These keyboards must have a clear line of sight between the transmitter and receiver, or have the lucky coincidence of walls or ceilings that bounce the signal in the right direction.

FIGURE 19-1: *A small PS/2-style keyboard connector on the back panel of an older modern PC. Some senior citizens and most dinosaurs employed a larger AT-style connector. Current modern machines use the USB port. Adapter plugs are available to convert any of the three designs to match the connector found on your PC.*

After you have decided the keyboard feel you want and the type of connection you want to use, you need to choose a keyboard maker. Dozens of keyboard makers — most of them in Asia — proliferate the market. Two schools of thought exist on buying strategies. One is to search high and low for the highest quality keyboard you can find. The other idea is to go for low price and consider the keyboard an expendable part of the system — like tires on a car. I generally place myself in the latter group; I look for a comfortable, inexpensive keyboard and plan on replacing it once a year or so.

Some folks, however, prefer the solid, heavy-duty feel of the original IBM PC keyboard, a sturdy click-style device that was derived from the famed IBM Selectric keyboard. IBM moved on to light, mushier keyboards for most of its systems. The company spun off its keyboard and printer division to a separate company called Lexmark, and in 1996, that company sold off its technology to Unicomp. Today you can purchase several derivatives of the IBM/Lexmark click keyboards directly from Unicomp and through distributors.

In technical terms, the IBM click design is called "buckling spring key" technology. I experimented with Unicomp's EnduraPro, which is a power tool of a keyboard. The keyboard is shown in Figure 19-2. The 104-key device, which weighs in at nearly six pounds, includes an integrated pressure-sensitive pointing stick that can substitute for a mouse, as well as a port for an external PS/2 mouse on the board.

Table 19-1 contains a listing of major keyboard manufacturers. Several no-name makers in Asia will sell directly to computer makers and retailers.

 NOTE

There is absolutely no reason why you can't select the keyboard of your choice to work with your old or new PC. With only a few exceptions, all keyboards are interchangeable. You may have to purchase conversion plugs to adapt a keyboard with one sort of connector to the appropriate port on your PC.

FIGURE 19-2: *The Unicomp EnduraPro keeps alive the heavy-duty design and click feel of the original IBM keyboard along with a versatile pointing stick that substitutes for a mouse.*

TABLE 19-1: Major Replacement Keyboard Manufacturers

Manufacturer	How Sold	Web Site
Belkin	Retailers and direct	www.belkin.com
Cherry	Retailers	www.cherrycorp.com
Chicony	Retailers	www.chicony.com
Kensington	Retailers and direct	www.kensington.com
Key Tronics	Retailers and direct	www.keytronic.com
Logitech	Retailers and direct	www.logitech.com
Microsoft	Retailers and direct	www.microsoft.com/hardware/mouseandkeyboard
SIIG	Retailers and direct	www.siig.com
Unicomp	Retailers and direct	www.pckeyboard.com

The next issue in choosing your keyboard involves the layout of the board. Some keyboards are available full-sized with 101 to 105 keys including numeric keypads, separate cursor-movement keys, and 12 function keys; others are 80- to 84-key small footprint models that give you just the basics. Again, they all work; I prefer full-size models, like the one shown in Figures 19-3 and 19-4, because I spend hours at the keyboard, but the choice is yours.

In addition to the basic keyboard, you may also see some variations that are aimed at making use a bit easier on human shoulders, wrists, and elbows.

One design uses a tiny round button set into the middle of the keys that is used as the controller for the mouse cursor. Slight pressure on the button in any direction moves the cursor just as sliding a mouse on a desktop does. The built-in controller began as a space-saving solution for laptop computers, but has also been made available in some desktop models. It's an acquired taste, but for some users it is faster and less fatiguing than removing a hand to operate the mouse.

Ch 19

FIGURE 19-3: *A modern replacement keyboard with a few special keys for Windows. This model was manufactured for one line of Dell computers; similar boards are available for other brands and generic PCs.*

Figure 19-4: *The extra keys on a Windows keyboard bring up the Start menu and can be programmed to bring up a specific menu within an application. On this Dell keyboard, four extra buttons are recessed into the board: above F8, a button to open the default mail program; above F10, a button to summon the home page you have set for your Internet browser; above F12, a button to call for the default search engine for the browser, and above the backspace key, a button to put the PC into sleep mode.*

Ergonomic keyboards reject the rectangular, straight-line layout of the keyboard in favor of one that is said to be more like the shape of the human hands. One design, the Microsoft Natural Keyboard, splits the left and right sides of the keyboard along a curved shape and adds an extended wrist support in front, intended to help avoid strains in the hands.

In my experience, though, long-time users of traditional keyboards have a long and sometimes difficult adjustment period to ergonomic keyboards. In my case, I never became comfortable with the split design.

Finally, keyboards that offer Windows-specific keys include a button that summons a popup Start menu and another that duplicates the context-sensitive effect of pressing the right mouse button. The

advantage of the Windows keyboard is that it allows users to keep their hands on the board to initiate many common commands.

Most such keyboards include two Windows logo keys, one to the left of the left Alt key and the other to the right of the right Alt key. A special Application key is located between the right Windows logo key and the right Ctrl key. Pressing the Application key generally brings up the same context-sensitive menu that you see by clicking the right mouse button within a program; press the Esc key to remove the menu. However, software programmers can assign special functions to that key; check instruction manuals for your applications.

Pressing and releasing either one of the Windows logo keys opens the Start menu. If you press the Windows key and hold it and then press additional keys, you can initiate operating systems commands, as shown in Table 19-2.

Table 19-2: Windows Keyboard Special Commands	
Key or Combination	**Function**
Application key	Display context-sensitive menu
Windows key	Open Start menu
Windows key+F1	Display Help menu
Windows key+Tab	Activate next taskbar button
Windows key+D	Show Desktop or undo minimize all
Windows key+E	Explore My Computer
Windows key+F	Find files or folder
Windows key+Ctrl+F	Find computer
Windows key+L	Lock computer on network domain
Windows key+M	Minimize all
Windows key+Shift+M	Undo minimize all
Windows key+Pause/Break	Display System Properties
Windows key+R	Display Run dialog box
Windows key+U	Open Utility Manager (Windows XP)

How the keyboard works

A keyboard is essentially a box full of switches. When you press or release a keyboard key, the keyboard sends a signal to the computer over a cable (or through a wireless link in a few models) to a keyboard port on the motherboard. Various designs keep the two halves of the switch apart with springs, rubber domes, and spongy foam.

Ch
19

Beneath the keys on the keyboard is a grid of circuits. When you press a key, two wires on the grid are connected. These wires send a signal to the keyboard microprocessor, which converts the grid signals to standard scan codes (signals identifying which key you pressed or released). The scan codes are sent through the keyboard cable to the motherboard.

Preventive maintenance for keyboards

You'll most likely know there is a problem with your keyboard without the need for special diagnostic programs: It may refuse to transmit a particular letter or double up on the character when you only want one to appear. The two most likely fixes here are cleaning the contact or replacing the keyboard.

What if the keyboard completely stops responding? Before you panic, see if the device is properly connected at the computer end and look for any cuts or crimps in the cable. Try rebooting the system to see if the keyboard comes back to life; if you're lucky, you might be experiencing a once-in-a-blue-moon system lockup. If the keyboard (or other components) freeze more frequently than a blue moon, or if the intervals between freeze-ups begins to shorten, you may be seeing the early symptoms of an impending failure of a major component such as the motherboard or the power supply.

If you want to be especially conscientious, every few months run the keyboard test that is part of most diagnostic programs to test the electronic logic of the keyboard and the motherboard's keyboard controller. The test also forces you to run through all the keys on the board, including a few you may not ordinarily use.

NOTE

Keeping your keyboard clean and dry is essential to its health. You shouldn't have a cup of coffee, a can of soda, or anything else liquid or sticky anywhere near your keyboard—or your PC, for that matter. Although it may be possible to clean a keyboard that has been doused with a soda, this is a problem you don't need. If your keyboard is bound to be in a wet or sloppy environment—in a kitchen or a restaurant, for example—you should look into purchasing a keyboard skin that covers all the keys with an impervious plastic that you can peck through. You can also purchase an industrialized keyboard that comes sealed within a waterproof or water-resistant membrane.

To clean a keyboard, turn off the power to the PC, unplug the keyboard, and turn it over to shake out dust and dirt. For an even better cleaning, use a can of compressed air to blow between individual keys or a vacuum to suck it clean.

You can use a cloth dampened with a weak plastic cleaner or a small amount of isopropyl alcohol to polish the keys and the surrounding case; the most fastidious among us may want to use a cotton-tipped stick to clean between the keys. If it is absolutely necessary, you can also remove individual keys using a special tool that is supplied with many keyboards; a technician's tweezers with hooked ends will also work. Do so very carefully to avoid breaking the plastic keycaps or the somewhat delicate switches beneath.

NOTE

An excellent tool for cleaning the keyboard, the screen, and other parts of the computer is a soft, unused paintbrush. I keep a couple of different sizes on or near my desk at all times. The soft bristles won't scratch hardware or screen surfaces, and they can reach down between keys and into other cracks and crevices to remove dust and other undesirable debris.

In some keyboard designs, it is reasonable to remove all keys for extended cleaning except the spacebar. In newer keyboards, construction may be too delicate to permit the safe removal of key caps.

In some PC repair and maintenance books you find amazing stories of rescuing a polluted keyboard by rinsing it under a faucet or even putting it through the rinse cycle of a dishwasher (no soap, cool water). Although it is possible that the keyboard *may* still be usable after such treatment, I have two important words of advice here: Get real!

Capable basic replacement keyboards cost as little as $10 to $20; more robust and special-purpose keyboards may cost as much as $100. There is little reason to devote a large amount of time to attempting to fix a sticky or stuck board.

I recommend that you always have a replacement keyboard on hand. Like hard drives and other mechanical elements of the PC, keyboards are bound to fail sooner or later. A keyboard in the closet can save you time and aggravation. To remove the keyboard, turn off the PC, and simply unplug it from the system unit. To install a keyboard, do this in reverse. Rotate the new keyboard's plug until the pins fit into the connector on the motherboard and then push it in firmly. USB keyboards can be unplugged or attached while the system is running. The flat USB connector has a top and bottom; be sure not to force the connector in place in the wrong orientation.

 WARNING

It is not a good practice to attach or remove a keyboard while the PC power is on. It is possible to generate a short or static surge that could damage the PC or the keyboard. The exception: keyboards that use the USB port for connection. Devices attached to the USB can safely be connected or disconnected while the system is running.

Testing the keyboard

Before you try to correct a keyboard problem, analyze the situation. Does the problem involve just one or two keys? If so, try cleaning the bad keys with compressed air or with a good quality, noncorrosive electronic circuit cleaner to clean out the contamination.

If you have a whole row or column of nonworking keys while other keys are working properly, the grid beneath the keys has failed because of a broken wire or short. This is not worth repairing; you have to replace the whole keyboard.

Sometimes no portion of the keyboard works properly. It's possible that a bad microprocessor chip is in the keyboard, but before you discard the keyboard, check that the keyboard is tightly plugged in at the system motherboard. On a dinosaur system, see that the XT/AT switch is properly set. On a system that uses PS/2-style connectors, check that the keyboard is plugged into the keyboard port and not into the nearby mouse port, which is the same size.

Also don't forget to check for a stuck key. If you can't fix the problem at the plug or through the keys, it's time for a new keyboard.

Mice and Trackballs

A mouse gives your computer a hand. This electronic rodent changes small hand motions into pointer motions onscreen. Although the general concept has been around for many years, it was with the arrival and acceptance of graphical user interfaces, such as Microsoft Windows, that mice went from an option to a necessity on most modern machines. A close relative of the mouse is the trackball, which places a large ball on top of a stationary pointing device.

Five types of connections enable a mouse to communicate with the computer:

- A *serial mouse* uses a standard serial port.
- A *bus mouse* uses a dedicated controller card that plugs into the bus and has a unique port address of its own.
- A *PS/2-compatible mouse port* is a special connection that does not use one of the system's standard serial ports.
- A *USB mouse* attaches to the system's USB port or a hub. This is the most common form of connection for current modern machines.
- An *infrared mouse* or a *wireless mouse* uses an infrared or wireless receiver to communicate with the computer.

All five are still serial devices, but PS/2, bus, infrared, and USB mice don't use the system's standard serial ports, their port addresses, or their interrupts — leaving these system resources free for other purposes.

PS/2 ports ordinarily use IRQ 12 and I/O (input/output) port addresses 60h and 64h, usually free on standard PCs. Figure 19-5 shows a PS/2 connector.

Nearly every modern PC comes with a mouse; in most cases, these are basic, inexpensive models. If you're a power user, you'll want to consider an upgrade to a sturdier or more comfortable device. Like keyboards, mice have a finite life and will eventually need replacement. I always keep a replacement model in my supply closet in anticipation of the day when my mouse won't skitter anymore.

The two most significant manufacturers of mice are Microsoft and Logitech; each offers mechanical and optical models of mice and trackballs. You'll also find many other manufacturers offering either very inexpensive simple replacement models or advanced special-purpose devices. Kensington is a leading maker of trackballs.

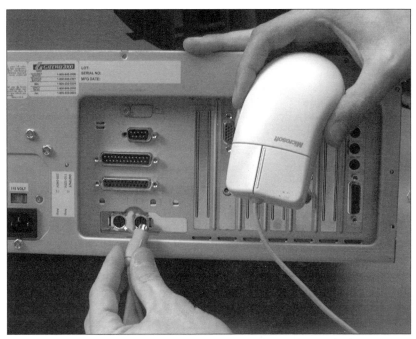

FIGURE 19-5: *A PS/2-style mouse connector on the back panel of an older PC. Older modern ATX motherboards may cluster the mouse and keyboard connector with the serial and parallel ports; current modern machines may dispense with PS/2, serial, and parallel ports in favor of a set of USB ports.*

How a mouse works

When you slide a mouse across the desktop or a mouse pad, the mouse detects this motion in horizontal and in vertical directions. The mouse sends this information to the computer along a cable attached to the computer's motherboard through one of its ports. Inside the computer, a *device driver* (a software program designed to interface the mouse to the computer) translates the mouse signal into instructions the computer can read.

Mice can detect hand motion in many ways. Some mice use a ball that rolls as your hand slides the mouse across a flat surface; most mice today are optical, detecting motion through LED senders and receptors on the bottom of the case. In all, four types of mice are available, and three related devices are worth considering:

- Mechanical mice
- Optical mice
- Optomechanical mice
- Wheel mice
- Pointing sticks
- Trackballs
- Joysticks

Common to all mouse designs are one or more microswitches that lie beneath the buttons on the mice. Pressing the button closes the switch and sends a signal (a click). The mouse software interprets the signals to determine whether the user has double-clicked the button.

Mechanical mice have a hard rubber ball inside that rests loosely in a chamber surrounded by sensing rollers. As you move the mouse along a desktop or a mouse pad, the ball rolls, and the rolling ball moves the rollers (Microsoft calls its internal parts *shafts*), causing copper contacts or brushes to sweep across a segmented conductor. In function, the arrangement is somewhat like the brushes of an electric motor, except that the rotating contacts within the mouse are circuit board lands. As an electric circuit makes and breaks contact, electronics in the mouse can count the number of clicks electrically. By knowing the distance between each electrical contact, the diameter of the shafts, and so on, it is fairly easy to calculate where the mouse is moving — how far and how fast.

The conducting strips are attached to a circular board in a spoke-like arrangement. The conducting wheel is called an *encoder*. As the moving conductor goes across the segmented contacts, electrical impulses are generated and the signals are counted in the attached electronic circuitry.

The impulses can be either negative or positive, depending on the direction of rotation. The polarity of the pulses tells the electronics the direction the mouse is moving, and the speed of the pulses shows how fast the mouse is moving.

In most designs, the two rollers inside the mouse ball cavity are opposed at 90 degrees to each other, enabling them to differentiate between horizontal and vertical movement. If both rollers turn, the movement is interpreted as oblique, and the electronics of the mouse interpret the relative speed and polarity of the pulses to compute a precise direction of movement.

Optical mice have no moving parts and offer very high resolution. They are used in applications requiring very fine motions, such as certain art and graphics programs. Optical mice may use a special grid pad with a reflective surface, or they may use a high-intensity, light-emitting diode (LED) that bounces off of a desk or other surface and is picked up by an optical receiver inside the body of the mouse. Sensitive electronics inside these newer designs can find enough texture on virtually any surface to judge mouse movement through the reflected light. When the user moves the mouse on this surface, an LED shines light onto the pad, and photosensors in the mouse detect motion from the streaks of light reflected back. After the pulses are received and counted, the optical mouse functions similarly to mechanical and optomechanical designs. However, because the optical mouse has no mechanical components, to the user it feels very different from a mechanical device, and little — if any — mechanical maintenance is required.

Optomechanical mice use a hybrid design that lies between mechanical and optical devices. With this device, the movement of the ball is translated into an electrical signal by an optical device. The mechanical ball turns rollers, just as with a mechanical mouse, but instead of using mechanical electrical contacts, the optomechanical design rotates slotted or perforated wheels. An LED shines through the openings on the wheel, and optical sensors on the other side count the resulting pulses.

Wheel mice (Microsoft's name for this type of device is IntelliMouse) are the standard for a current modern machine. This two-button mouse, like the one shown in Figure 19-6, has a small wheel mounted between the buttons. You can easily spin this wheel forward and backward with your index finger while you manipulate the mouse. Beneath the wheel is a microswitch that serves as a third button. The default setting is for the wheel to control document or page scrolling. Rotate the wheel forward (away from you) and the current page of information moves down to reveal data farther up in the document; pull the wheel towards you and the page of information scrolls up to display data farther down in the document. The wheel performs the same function as the up and down arrows on the vertical scroll bar displayed in many applications and dialog boxes.

Although the microswitch beneath the wheel is programmed by default to enable a fixed scrolling function, you can use included utility software to program the function of the wheel and switch. When these mice first started to appear, some applications wouldn't work with them. Today I find that virtually every display that supports scroll bars recognizes the wheel. You do have to install supplemental driver software to support the wheel function in Windows 95 and in early versions of Windows 98. A wheel mouse can be either mechanical, optical, or optomechanical for its basic functions; the wheel just adds additional convenience and functionality.

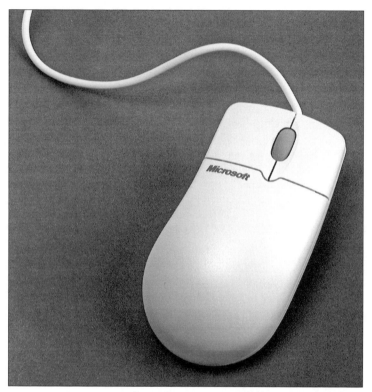

Figure 19-6: *A Microsoft IntelliMouse. You can use the wheel between the buttons to scroll onscreen displays.*

A *pointing stick* is a specialized version of a mouse, a pencil-eraser-like nub that sits on the keyboard, usually centered in the lower third of the keys above the letter B. (IBM, which patented one design for this sort of pointer, calls its product the TrackPoint.) The little stick interprets finger pressure as it is pushed in one direction or another; the harder the stick is pressed, the faster the onscreen cursor moves. Keyboards that employ this system have one connector that runs to the PS/2 port on the PC and a second connector that attaches to a PS/2 mouse port. For some users, a pointing stick is a great way to avoid having to remove their hands from the keyboard to make mouse movements. An example of a modern keyboard with a pointing stick is seen earlier in this chapter in Figure 19-2. Some users love this sort of design, while others can never quite master moving the cursor with their index finger; I would suggest you take one of these keyboards for a test drive before making a commitment. Pointing sticks require no special maintenance, although the little rubber nub usually wears down with use; most keyboard makers provide a package of replacement nubs.

Trackballs are upside-down mechanical mice. The ball rests loosely in a cavity and sensors track horizontal and vertical movement. Instead of moving the hardware across the desk, you use your hand to spin the ball in place.

Trackballs have three advantages. The first is that you can place them on a desktop and they take up just a small amount of valuable real estate. The second advantage is that a trackball can be incorporated into a keyboard. And finally, an ergonomic advantage for some users (including me) is the fact it puts less strain on the shoulder and wrist because a trackball is stationary on the desk. Two rather different interpretations of a trackball are shown in Figure 19-7.

Joysticks work in a manner similar to the pointer devices. Instead of rollers, joysticks use pressure-sensitive electronics or mechanical potentiometers that vary voltage by changing resistance in an electronic circuit.

Mouse tracking resolution

Mice and other pointing devices can differ in their capability to read very small movements. Older mice were usually able to discern differences in location as small as $1/200$ of an inch; this capability is called resolution. High-resolution models send more motion signals to the computer per inch of hand motion, with resolution as great as 1/1200 inch. Some specialty pointing devices for artists and designers have even finer resolution.

With an optical mouse, resolution is determined by the ability of the mouse electronics to read motion from the reflected light. With a mechanical or optomechanical mouse, higher resolution requires more holes in the light wheel or more physical segments for the mechanical brush to pass over.

FIGURE 19-7: *At left, a Kensington Orbit trackball. A right-hander would use the thumb for the left-click, the index or middle finger to move the trackball, and the ring finger for the right-click; the trackball can easily be used with the left hand. At right, Microsoft's Trackball Optical, which uses the thumb for the trackball with the rest of the right hand draped around its curved body. Be sure to test-drive a trackball before making a commitment.*

Some designers improve effective resolution by sophisticated software routines. By counting the actual pulses and then interpolating what would fall between the physical pulses, higher-resolution performance can be simulated.

NOTE

For most desktop applications, including moving the onscreen pointer under Microsoft Windows, the difference between 200 points per inch (ppi) and 400 or 1,200 ppi may not matter enough to be worth the extra expense. If you are using the mouse for drawing or other fine graphics manipulation, though, higher resolution may be worthwhile.

One other difference between high- and low-resolution pointing devices is the speed of onscreen movement. Most high-resolution devices seem much faster.

Many input devices enable you to vary the *sensitivity* — the relationship between the distance moved on the desktop and the distance moved on the screen. Similarly, you often can control acceleration with a software setting. Acceleration is the relationship between the speed and distance of mouse movement and the speed and distance of cursor movement. As you move the physical mouse faster, the onscreen pointer or cursor picks up speed and moves farther than when you move the mouse at slower speeds.

Connecting the mouse

USB mice use the facilities of a modern machine's USB port. As with all USB devices, they offer the benefit of not requiring their own system resources, and they can be part of a long daisy chain of devices attached to the port. Finally, USB devices are *hot swappable,* meaning they can be attached or removed while the system is running.

PS/2 mice, used on older modern machines and senior citizens, attach directly to a port on the motherboard. (The port received its name because IBM first introduced it as a component of its PS/2 systems; the connection became a generic element of most subsequent motherboards.) The PS/2 connector is wired to the motherboard's keyboard controller, which converts the mouse signals to a form that the computer can interpret; as such, it does not require the assignment of a separate port and IRQ for the mouse. Most such mouse port devices use IRQ 12. Note that the mouse connector is identical in size and shape to the keyboard connector; you should avoid mistakes here, although reversed plugs will probably not damage the computer — the mouse or keyboard will not work, however, if attached incorrectly.

Serial mice, used on dinosaurs and senior citizens, don't require system resources of their own; instead, they use the I/O port address and assigned IRQ interrupt of an existing serial port. A serial mouse, shown in Figure 19-8, requires a unique port address because it gets control signals from the bus. The microprocessor speaks to a device by sending a port address down the bus. All the devices are looking at the bus, waiting for their distinctive port address. When a device recognizes its own port address on the bus, it pays attention to the subsequent data signals.

FIGURE 19-8: *This older three-button serial mouse connects to a standard serial port on a PC.*

Most of the time, the mouse is trying to send, not receive, information. When a mouse is ready to transmit data, it sends an interrupt to the microprocessor. The microprocessor looks up the interrupt number in the interrupt vector table, which tells the microprocessor to start using mouse-specific routines to accept the incoming data.

Bus mice need a unique port address and a unique interrupt, attaching to special-purpose serial adapters that plug into the expansion bus. This design was used for a period of time during the late senior-citizen era, but they were replaced by PS/2 and then USB models. The mouse card required its own interrupt, and mouse cards can conflict with the other hardware installed in the computer if they demand the same IRQ.

As with keyboards, there is a wide range of converter plugs. For example, you can attach a dinosaur DB-9 serial plug to a PS/2 connector, with an adapter like the one shown in Figure 19-9. Adapters also are available to convert a USB mouse to a PS/2 or serial mouse connection, or the other way around.

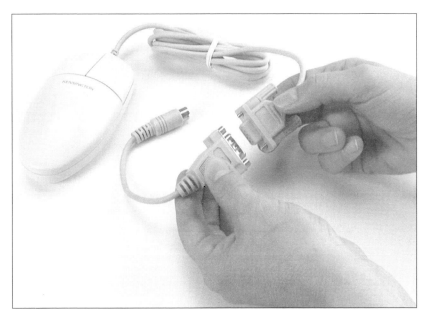

FIGURE 19-9: *This adapter converts a DB-9 serial connector to a PS/2 connector.*

Most modern mice come with a control program to set up special features; the same program usually offers a basic test of the mouse's capabilities. You should also consult the web site of the manufacturer to see if updated or corrected device drivers have been released for your mouse.

MOUSE SKITTERS

If your mouse pointer no longer seems to follow your commands—especially if you've recently made a change in screen resolution or color depth—the problem may be related to a conflict between the device drivers for the mouse and the display driver.

To check for a conflict, go to the desktop and right-click My Computer. Click Properties, and then select the Performance tab. Click the Graphics button and slide the Hardware acceleration pointer one notch to the left. If your mouse now works properly, this is an indication of a driver conflict. Contact the manufacturer of your mouse and display adapter for more current drivers and bug fixes.

Basic mice will work with the built-in drivers that are supplied with current editions of Windows. However, any special features—including Microsoft's IntelliMouse facilities—require the installation of drivers that are supplied with the pointer, or available over the Internet. Spend the time to keep your drivers up to date, especially if you update or change your operating system. Check the web site for the mouse manufacturer or the Windows Update facility of www.microsoft.com. In some cases, conflicts can occur between the drivers for video adapters and mice; check the instruction manuals for both devices or the manufacturer's web site for assistance in resolving problems.

Testing a mouse

If you have trouble with a mouse, the first thing to do is to make sure it is properly connected to the computer. If it is, go to the Windows Control Panel to see if the operating system reports a failure of a serial port, a PS/2 port, or a USB port. If you see no port problems, check the mouse setup in the Control Panel for conflicts or problems with device drivers.

Installing a mouse

Mice come packaged with mouse device drivers and test software; many current models don't even require driver installation, instead taking advantage of advanced built-in Windows XP and Windows Vista facilities. Be sure to follow the instructions provided by the manufacturer, including checking the Internet for updated or corrected drivers that might have been posted after the plastic packaging was placed around your mouse at the factory.

If you are running Windows, the operating system comes with a driver that works with most pointing devices. If you have an unusual device, you should expect to receive a custom driver from the manufacturer, along with instructions for installing it in Windows.

Under older operating systems, including DOS and Windows 3.1, you need to install the mouse driver in the `config.sys` or `autoexec.bat` file. Most mice are shipped with two drivers, one suitable for the `config.sys` file and one for the `autoexec.bat` file. You can use either. Read the installation manual for your mouse.

Good mousekeeping

Your mouse travels miles and miles, sliding back and forth on your desktop. Along the way, it's likely to pick up dust, cookie crumbs, oils, and whatever else is floating around in your office. Sooner or later, the going is going to get a bit sticky.

The solution is to practice good mousekeeping — keep your desk as clean as possible and every few months take apart the mouse, as shown in Figure 19-10, and clean the roller or ball. To do so, unplug the mouse from the computer. You can get to the roller ball in most mouse designs by rotating a ring to release it. Clean the ball (and rollers, if there are any) with alcohol and a lint-free cloth. Check the instruction manual for your mouse for details.

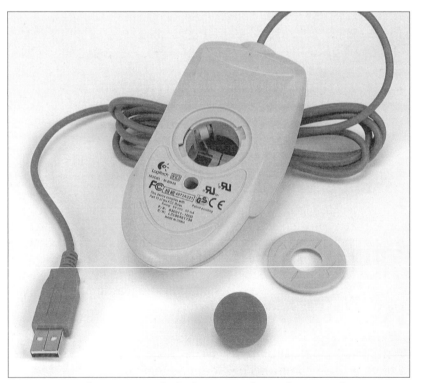

Figure 19-10: *If your mouse finds the going a bit sticky, it may be worthwhile to remove the mouse roller and clean it with soap and water or alcohol. In most designs, a simple twist-release mechanism on the bottom of the mouse frees the ball.*

If an optomechanical or a mechanical mouse works but seems jerky and less fluid than it should be, check the roller ball and associated shafts for contamination.

Cleaning an optical mouse is simpler because it contains no moving parts. Use an alcohol cleaner or a small spray of window cleaner to remove any buildup from the sensor on its bottom.

To be truly fastidious about your mouse's personal hygiene, you can purchase a mouse cleaning kit from specialty computer stores. The fully equipped office also includes a vacuum cleaner to remove dirt from crevices, an air cleaner to remove dust from the air, and even antistatic mats and sprays to reduce dust-collection charges from the carpeting and other surfaces.

Game Controllers

Advanced gamers will want to give their computer a hand with a joystick or other game controllers including roller balls, video-game-like pads, and even specialized simulations of airplane yokes for flight simulators and steering wheels for driving games. All of these devices work by transmitting to the computer a set of X and Y coordinates representing a position on the screen, which itself is a display of a bitmap in memory.

The most modern of game controllers use the USB port, allowing for easily changeable, advanced devices that are specific to particular types of games. USB also operates much faster than an original serial port, allowing more responsive controllers.

Older game controllers require you to add a game port to your system. Most modern sound cards include a DB15 game port among their features; in some cases the game port performs double duty as a MIDI breakout port. The game port, a large DB15 connector that will work with a MIDI device, is at the left end of the Sound Blaster Live! card (shown later in this chapter in Figure 19-16).

You may also find a game port as part of a multi-I/O card that adds enhanced serial, parallel, and IDE ports to an older machine.

Owners of dinosaurs and senior citizens can also add an inexpensive game port card to their systems. Figure 19-11 shows an example of a simple ISA bus game port card.

FIGURE 19-11: *On older machines, serious gamers will want to install a game port card to enable use of joysticks or other controllers. Modern machines use devices that attach to the flexible USB port.*

Scanners

A scanner gives your computer eyes. You can use a scanner to capture drawings and photographs for use in your printed or onscreen work. I use a scanner as a replacement for a copying machine in my office; I can send scanned images through an image-editing program to a printer. A scanner can also work in conjunction with an optical character recognition (OCR) program to convert typed or printed text into computer files that you can edit and change.

How a scanner works

Scanners bounce light off a target — which may be either a picture or text — and measure the amount of reflected light. Most of this light is reflected from white paper, less from halftones in a photograph, and almost none from black text characters. The scanner sends this information to a scanner interface card in the computer, where either OCR or graphics software takes over. The software processes the light level measurements. You can save the resulting file as a standard bitmap file for further manipulation by the computer.

Color scanners shine three separate lights (red, green, and blue) on the image or use a single light with a set of red, green, and blue filters.

These are the two essential elements of a high-quality scanner:

- **Resolution.** The scanner converts an analog image to a digital representation, presented as a series of tiny dots. The finer the dots, the sharper the image. Modern scanners for graphics work start at 300 dots per inch (dpi) and progress upward from there. Devices at that resolution are more than sufficient for Web-page images, but may be less than optimal for a high-resolution printer.
- **Bit depth.** This is a measure of how many samples of colors or grays the scanner records. The higher the bit depth, the more lifelike the representation of colors. For desktop users, a 24-bit depth is a minimal level with 30 bits an up-and-coming standard.

NOTE

Scanners and OCRs work with any computer, although both make very heavy demands upon the microprocessor, video, and hard disk systems. This is not the sort of work you would want to perform using a dinosaur or senior citizen.

OCR software converts light gray shades to white and dark gray to black. Then, using this two-color image, the OCR software tries to identify the letter written on the paper. Character recognition software uses one of two techniques: font matching and feature recognition. Font matching compares the character against all memorized fonts, similar to using tracing paper to match an unknown shape against stored standard patterns. Feature recognition uses logic and piece-by-piece analysis of a character to deduce what letter it really is. Feature recognition relies on questions such as, "Does an extender protrude below the line of type?" (The letters *p, q, g, y,* and *j* all share this characteristic feature.) By asking itself successive questions, the software is able to systematically eliminate characters. Pattern recognition software is more flexible because proportional spacing and new fonts are less likely to throw it off stride. It is also more expensive.

Graphics software retains the middle range of signal values — the ones that represent gray tones in an image. Some scanners convert the intermediate gray tones to dithered patterns (prepared patterns of black and white dots that match the approximate light/dark ratio of the gray tone). Other scanners retain up to 64 levels of gray in the stored image (called *grayscaling*).

Scanner interfaces

Consumer-level scanning devices commonly use one of four high-speed, high-bandwidth interface connections:

- A modern machine's USB port; nearly all current scanners take this easy and quick route to the computer
- A SCSI card installed in an internal slot, with the scanner capable of being one of seven devices in a chain
- A proprietary interface card specific to the scanner that in many cases is an adaptation of SCSI, but does not enable other devices to be used with the specialized card
- An older PC's parallel port

The simplest connection is through a USB port, a Plug-and-Play installation. Parallel port devices are also easy to install and use, but their throughput is generally slower than using a dedicated SCSI card or a USB port. Each scanner comes with its own device driver to identify itself and its capabilities to the Windows operating system on your PC.

CROSS-REFERENCE

For the details on parallel port connections, see Chapter 17. For the details on the USB, see Chapter 15.

Web Cameras

A Web camera turns your desktop into a broadcast studio — not quite up to network standards, but quite acceptable for such tasks as making Internet video phone calls and producing e-mail postcards.

A simple PC camera perches atop your computer, linked to digital capture software with a link to an Internet chat, mail, or other program. Figure 19-12 shows two examples of inexpensive, capable cameras from Intel and Logitech.

Basic PC cameras offer CCD sensors capable of VGA (640 × 480) resolution, 24-bit (16.8 million) color, and automatic exposure over a wide range of lighting conditions. The cameras can be used to capture individual images or as much as 30 frames per second of video.

Cameras attach to a USB port. You'll need an Internet connection to make video phone calls. For a listing of Intel's offerings, consult `www.intel.com/support/createshare/camerapack`.

Another leading maker is Logitech, which offers products of similar capability; the company's inexpensive QuickCam Express uses a CMOS sensor, which generally yields slightly lower-quality results compared to a CCD sensor. For information, consult `www.logitech.com`.

Most cameras come packaged with software for basic capture and editing.

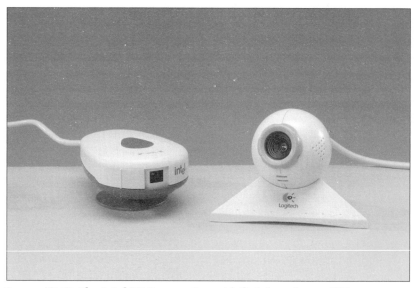

FIGURE 19-12: *The Intel PC Camera Pro, at left, is based on a CCD sensor. The simple and less expensive Logitech QuickCam Express uses a CMOS sensor.*

Film Scanners

Another way to bring photographs into your PC is with a film scanner. These devices use a high-resolution scanner to produce a bitmap of negatives or slides that you can store and manipulate on the computer.

A film scanner represents a good compromise for many photographers. You can continue to use your existing traditional film cameras and lenses (many of which are capable of producing higher-quality images than consumer-grade digital cameras), and you can also have access to a lifetime's worth of old negatives or slides stored under your bed.

Among major manufacturers of film scanners are the electronics divisions of photographic equipment makers Canon, Minolta, and Nikon, and computer peripheral makers Acer, Microtek, and Plustek. In Figure 19-13 you can see an older but still capable scanner from our laboratory, an Olympus ES-10. This device can scan 35mm and *Advanced Photo System (APS)* negatives and slides at a maximum resolution of 1,770 dpi. The resulting image files at top resolution are about 11MB in size, more than sufficient for printing an 8 × 10-inch print or larger. Compare this to a 2.1 megapixel camera that yields an image file of about 6MB at its highest resolution setting. Once you scan images, you can adjust them using most image-editing software, including Adobe Photoshop.

As with most other peripherals, current scanner models now make use of the USB port for data transfer. Older models required either a SCSI interface or attachment to a bidirectional parallel port.

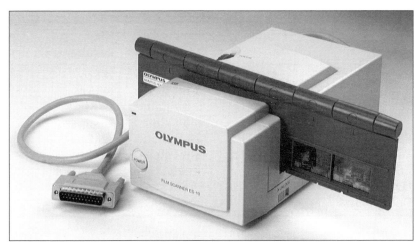

Figure 19-13: *This film scanner bridges the worlds of traditional film photography and digital computer image editing.*

Sound Adapters and Cards

A sound card or adapter gives your computer a voice and a set of ears.

The first PC had a silver dollar-sized speaker capable of producing little more than annoying beeps and pathetic squawks. Today, a modern machine can have a symphony orchestra within its covers, with rich sound booming forth from tabletop speakers with powered subwoofers.

Today, nearly all modern machines have special circuitry on the motherboard or on a plug-in adapter card that bring advanced audio features. The PC can speak to you by playing back recorded digital speech or through a text-to-speech program. The PC can listen to you with voice recording and voice recognition features. A sound card or adapter can also play audio from a music CD or produce a wide range of sounds for business, education, and gaming applications. Music, sound effects, and speech are essential parts of the multimedia revolution.

In this section I generally refer to sound circuitry as a *sound adapter*. This includes audio circuitry chips built into a modern machine's motherboard, those which exist on an adapter card that plugs into a PCI slot on a modern machine (or into an ISA slot on a dinosaur). A third variant, very valuable for laptop computers as well as modern machines with limited internal slots, is an external sound adapter that connects via the USB port. You get the best quality from the second and third options: a plug-in card or an external box.

The other part of the equation is a set of external speakers to play the sounds and voices; the best solution for most users is a pair of small desktop speakers plus a small subwoofer that sits on the floor. The *subwoofer* produces the bass sound that underlays music and other audio; unlike the left and right stereo speakers, though, the bass sound does not have to be positioned in front of your ears. Other options include attaching a headphone to the sound adapter's audio output, or connecting the audio circuitry's output to a stereo amplifier and speaker in your home or office.

Other advanced features include the ability to record audio to the hard disk through a microphone input or a line input that can accept a signal from a tape recorder, radio, television set, or CD player. Top-of-the-line sound boards provide multiple interfaces, such as CD-ROM drive, CD player, microphone, joystick, portable speakers, AUX jack on your stereo, and MIDI.

Ch 19

To some users, the quality of a sound card is a critical element of their entire computer system. These folks are the high-tech cousins of audiophiles who claim to be able to distinguish between pairs of $5,000 speakers for their home stereo systems. I guess if you really can hear the difference, it's worth the effort.

For the rest of us, though, follow these hard-and-fast specifications that tell a great deal about the quality of a sound card.

- Modern machines should use a 16-bit or (even better) 24-bit adapter for recording and playing back music; an older-technology 8-bit card or adapter will disappoint. When I talk about bits here, I'm referring to the bit depth of the audio sample. Think of this as equivalent to the number of colors used by a video adapter to draw a picture; a picture or a sound will be recognizable in 8-bit form but richer and more subtly shaded using 16 bits of information. An 8-bit card describes sounds in 256 steps, while a 16-bit card is capable of 65,536 gradations and a 24-bit device 16,777,216 shades of difference in sound. Be sure that the card offers a reasonable range of frequencies. Most humans can hear sounds from as low as a deep rumble at about 20 Hz to a high-pitch squeal around 20 KHz. Just for perspective, consider that a standard piano has a range from 27 Hz to 4.2 KHz; the voice frequency band on a telephone runs from 300 Hz to 3400 Hz. Sound purists will tell you that even subaudible frequencies or those slightly above the ordinary hearing range have an effect on the quality of the sound we perceive from a speaker. I suggest that you look for a sound card capable of producing signals from 20 Hz to 20 KHz or better.
- Consider the signal-to-noise ratio, a measurement of the strength of the signal in comparison to background or underlying noise. The greater the S/N ratio, the cleaner the sound. Look for a ratio of at least 95dB for good quality. Current top-of-the-line cards offer as much as 116dB for left-and-right stereo signals as well as front and rear and subwoofer channels.
- Another indicator of quality is total harmonic distortion, a measurement of undesirable harmonics present in an audio signal. Expressed as a percentage, the lower the THD, the better; the best consumer devices claim THD of 0.0008 percent or lower. Most modern cards give users a range of options for the quality of sound file. Just as you can choose the resolution of a digital camera file or the screen resolution of a picture displayed on your monitor, the higher the quality of sound file you select the larger its size. The quality of a sound file is related to the *frequency* (the number of samples taken per second) and the *bandwidth* (the amount of information collected). And, of course, the quality of the computer file is related to the quality of sound you are recording; garbage in, garbage out . . . at least until you use some of the facilities of advanced sound editing programs to repair problems.

Sound files are stored as digital representations of the waveforms of an analog sound. The most common file format is WAV, used by Microsoft for many sounds within Windows as well as for extended recordings of music; most users call them "wave" files. At CD-quality recording, a five-minute song recorded as a stereo WAV file occupies about 50MB on your hard disk. In Table 19-3, I present some of the most common sound file settings.

Nearly all modern sound cards also include *data compression* facilities that can be used to reduce the size of a recorded file by a factor of as much as 4:1. Specialized adapters can use even more powerful compression schemes such as the MPEG standard that can compress a file as much as 30:1.

TABLE 19-3: Sound File Resolution

Type	Frequency	Bandwidth	File Requirements
Basic	7,418 Hz	8-bit mono	7KBps
Basic	7,418 Hz	8-bit stereo	14KBps
Telephone quality	11,025 Hz	8-bit mono	11KBps
Telephone quality	11,025 Hz	8-bit stereo	22KBps
Radio quality	22,050 Hz	8-bit mono	22KBps
Radio quality	22,050 Hz	8-bit stereo	44KBps
CD quality	44,100 Hz	16-bit stereo	172KBps
DVD audio/ Dolby Digital 5.1	48,000 Hz	16-bit stereo	188KBps

Compression does not come without a price. In general, the higher the compression rate, the more information is lost. Most begin by chopping off sounds at frequencies most humans cannot hear; audio purists, though, will tell you they believe that even inaudible sounds have an effect on the overall quality of a piece of music or recorded voice. Then a scheme may play with the phrasing of music, trimming off parts of notes that are longer than a standard beat. The bottom line: if you have the space on your hard drive and a desire for the highest quality sound reproduction, avoid data compression and use a CD-quality sampling rate.

Here are two other noteworthy forms of files for music:

- MIDI (musical instrument digital interface) files contain digital notations of instructions for special types of hardware; the notations may call for the playing of a sampled sound, or for a particular frequency and volume. As such you are not playing back a recording, but rather a set of instructions for a device to create sound using its own facilities. MIDI devices include synthesizers; many capable sound cards include small synthesizers for creation of music for games and multimedia purposes. Note that MIDI files are not intended to reproduce voices, or at least not ones that are very close to real ones. MIDI files are much smaller than waveforms. A five-minute selection of music in MIDI form might occupy 42K of storage.
- Another form of digital-only file format is MP3, most commonly used in portable music players. A high-quality MP3 file records at 128 kilobits per second, near the resolution of a CD-quality waveform. The recording is "ripped" (converted to digital form) and then compressed; a typical five-minute song occupies about 4MB of space. Microsoft pushes WMA, which is capable of producing CD-quality sound with a recording rate of 64 kilobits per second, half that of MP3.

The sound card de facto standard are cards in the Sound Blaster family from Creative Labs. That doesn't necessarily mean that the Sound Blaster provides the best quality or the most features — although Creative Labs' cards have led the industry almost from the start. However, if you buy a card from another maker, be certain that it promises full Sound Blaster compatibility. Without it, you cannot be sure that all multimedia software will work properly with your card. Though third-party cards may perform quite well, and even surpass Sound Blaster in some capabilities, they may occupy different memory addresses or interrupts and may confuse some games and multimedia programs. Be sure to insist on a full explanation of the meaning of compatibility from any card maker. One example of a compatible card from another maker is the SIIG card, shown in Figure 19-14.

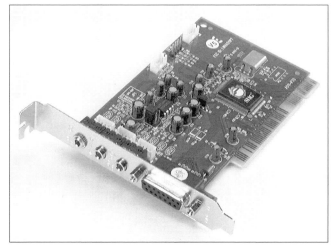

FIGURE 19-14: *This example of a third-party Sound Blaster-compatible sound card is from SIIG. The card, which plugs into a PCI slot, includes 64-voice stereo channels, true hardware wave table synthesis, and a digital signal processor that delivers 3-D positional sound effects.*

Some motherboards come with integrated sound facilities that are an element of the chipset or otherwise installed on the board. This sort of setup should deliver acceptable basic performance, but rarely equal the quality or breadth of features offered by a plug-in card. You should be able to upgrade to a plug-in sound card; depending on the BIOS, the motherboard will either automatically disable the onboard sound facilities or you will have to turn off the built-in chips from the Setup screen or (less commonly now) physically disable them by moving a jumper or a switch on the motherboard.

In recent years, Microsoft has simplified life for multimedia developers and users by interposing the DirectX suite of Application Program Interfaces between hardware and applications. Before the arrival of DirectX, software writers had to choose which design of hardware to support, or attempt (usually with only limited success) to work with many different standards. Today developers of hardware and software write to the requirements of DirectX. As a user, your responsibility is to make sure you have the latest most appropriate version of DirectX installed on your machine under Windows; the easiest way to do this is to use the facilities of Windows Update (a component of Windows 98 and later versions) or to visit www.microsoft.com every month or so and allow Microsoft to probe your system to make certain components are current. In late 2006, the most current release of DirectX was version 10.

You should also devote the effort to keep your drivers up to date, especially if you have upgraded the PC's operating system. Check the web site for the manufacturer of the sound card as well as the Windows Update page.

About MP3

MP3, which draws its name from the standard it is based on, MPEG-1, Layer 3, is a compression standard that creates relatively small high-quality digital audio files for playback on a computer or a specialty portable music player.

A typical uncompressed .wav file under Windows can require about 10MB of hard disk space for each minute of CD-quality sound. An MP3 file of the same minute of sound compressed at 128 kilobits per second needs only about one-tenth that space.

MP3 encoders perform their magic by getting rid of unnecessary audio information. Part of the conversion is the filtering out of audio signals that are above or below the average human's range of hearing; in theory, this shouldn't be noticeable, except perhaps by your pet sheepdog, but audio purists maintain that even inaudible frequencies have an effect on the sound we do hear.

In any case, because some of the data is thrown away, MP3 is considered *lossy compression.*

MP3 files can be compressed at several settings. Most files are encoded at 128 kilobits per second. At a setting of 96 kilobits per second the files are smaller still but often include discernible distortion and unwanted noise; a higher-quality setting of 160 kilobits per second is usually regarded as nearly equivalent to a CD, at least for those of us with untrained, less picky, or aging eardrums. Uncompressed audio on a CD is usually stored at a bit rate of 1411.2 kilobits per second. You can download files encoded as MP3s; some advanced audio programs include encoders to create your own files. You'll also need an MP3 decoder to play back the files. A number of decoders are available as free files on the Internet.

Future refinements of MP3 may include an adaptation of MPEG-2 Advanced Audio Coding, which can compress files at 96 kilobits per second at a higher quality.

Setting up a sound adapter

When recording sound, the adapter feeds audio from the in jack (microphone, CD player, whatever) through an analog-to-digital converter (ADC). To play sound, the sound board converts digitized audio or digital descriptions of sounds to an analog signal that enables a speaker to reproduce sound.

A modern sound card is a jack-of-all-trades when it comes to multimedia. State-of-the-art Sound Blaster cards and external adapters include as many as a dozen connectors for various functions; the primary connection to the computer itself is through a PCI slot (for an internal device) or through a USB port (for an external device).

Many problems in using a sound card are related to inserting the wrong plug into connectors on the card. Card manufacturers, prodded by Intel and Microsoft with the PC99 Design Specifications, have begun color-coding the connectors on the hardware; the connectors are also marked with (tiny) symbols or descriptions of their intended use. I list a modern sound card's connectors in Table 19-4. You can find a full listing of the color assignments of PC99 in Chapter 1 of this book. Figure 19-15 shows the external panel of a current card.

Some advanced sound cards have so many available facilities that they end up being forced to share connectors for more than one purpose. They may use a breakout box that expands available connectors to an external box. In Figure 19-16 is a fully featured current card.

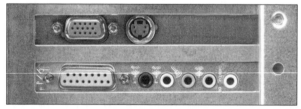

FIGURE 19-15: *On the external panel of this Creative Labs Sound Blaster Live! card you find, from left to right, the DB15 game controller/MIDI connector, rear out, line out, microphone in, line in, and digital out. Above the sound card is an AGP video adapter with a DB9 for a monitor and an S-VHS connector for use with a television.*

FIGURE 19-16: *Sound cards have become among the most highly integrated devices of a modern PC. In addition to the six connectors on the rear panel of this current Creative Labs Sound Blaster Live! card, it also includes seven more connectors for internal devices.*

Sound cards have gone through a great deal of change in the course of a few years on the scene, always in the direction of improved capabilities. The biggest points of difference are between 16- and 32-bit cards and FM synthesis versus wave table synthesis.

In general, 16-bit cards are capable of using more memory to describe and prepare notes than a dinosaur 8-bit card; a 32-bit card offers still more definition and produces better sound.

FM synthesis creates sounds by using algorithms to produce mixed sine waves that are analogs of real instruments. Depending on the capabilities of the card, the quality of output can range from Game Boy-like beeps and squawks to decent, but artificial, sound. Wave table synthesis is based on actual recorded instrument samples that can be called upon and manipulated by MIDI commands.

When you record music or sound from an outside source, such as a tape deck, video recorder, or the analog output of a CD player, the information travels to the sound card as an analog audio signal that plugs into an input jack on the back of the sound card.

However, if you want to play the digital audio output of a CD-ROM player installed internally, you may need to connect an audio cable inside the PC between the sound card and the digital output of the CD-ROM.

Other features to look for include the power of the sound adapter's amplifier. Many sound cards produce as little as 1 watt per channel, which is barely enough power for use with external speakers that have their own amplifiers. More modern cards generate as much as 4 watts per channel, but this is still insufficient for clean sound — they are likely to produce noise along with the signal. If you are a sound purist, look for a card that adds a low-level (unamplified) line-out connector that you can attach to a more generous external amplifier or to a set of powered (amplified) speakers.

WARNING

On many sound cards, it is very important to disable the onboard audio amplifier if you will be using the card with an active or powered external speaker system. On some cards, the onboard amplifier is shipped already disabled and you must turn it on if you want to use it. Consult the instruction manual for more information.

Prices for sound cards, like most everything else related to computers, have come down sharply. You can get pretty good sound — good enough for games, audio response to your application programs, and even music CD playback — for $10 to $20 at online computer parts suppliers. If you want a name brand, like SoundBlaster, Diamond, or Turtle Beach, the price rises to the mid-$40 range for a basic card and as much as $150 to $300 for state-of-the-art cards with (literally) all of the bells and whistles.

You also face the problem brought about by all of the possible functions of a fully featured card: too many choices to easily control. One interesting solution is a remote control, similar to the multifunction remote for your VCR and cable box. Keyspan offers a Digital Media Remote that offers wireless access to PowerPoint, QuickTime, DVD, CD, and MP3 software. The device is shown in Figure 19-17.

Ch 19

TABLE 19-4: Jacks and Connectors on a Modern Sound Card

Type	Color Code	Location	Purpose
Line In	Blue	Rear bracket	An analog connection to the output of an amplified external device such as a cassette recorder, CD player, DAT, or MiniDisc player, or the direct output of a musical synthesizer.
Microphone In	Red	Rear bracket	Connects to the output of an external microphone for recording voice or other audio, or to the microphone output of an unamplified musical instrument such as a guitar. Most cards record from microphone in monaural only.
Line Out	Green	Rear bracket	Connects to powered speakers, headphones, or an external amplifier for playback.
Digital Out	White	Rear bracket	Connects to an external digital device, such as a Digital Audio Tape (DAT) or MiniDisc recorder that uses the SPDIF digital device specification.
Rear Out	Black	Rear bracket	Provides an amplified signal to basic speakers, or for rear speakers in a four-speaker setup. Avoid using this connector with powered speakers unless the sound card's amplifier is turned off.
Joystick/MIDI	Yellow	Rear bracket or built-in jack	DB15 connector for a joystick or a MIDI music device; can be adapted to work with both at the same time.
SB1394 port	—		Connects to IEEE 1394 (FireWire) devices such as digital audio players, camcorders, webcams, and digital cameras. Also used for interconnection of certain network games.
PCI	—	Internal base of card	Provides electrical power for the card, plus data interchange with hard drive, and carries instructions from the microprocessor.
AUX	White	Internal	Links the card to internal audio sources including a TV tuner, MPEG converter, and other devices.
Analog CD Audio	Black	Internal	Connects to the analog audio output of an internal CD or DVD, using a CD audio cable.
Digital CD Audio	—	Internal	Connects to the digital audio output of an internal CD or DVD using a digital audio cable.
Telephone Answering Device (TAD)	Green	Internal	Monaural connection of audio to and from an internal voice modem.
Modem	—	Internal	A pin header that connects to certain classes of modem cards.
PC Speaker	—	Internal	Connects to the internal speaker on the motherboard.
CD SPDIF	—	Internal	Connects to a SPDIF (digital audio) output of an internal CD-ROM or DVD-ROM.
Audio Extension (Digital I/O)	—	Internal	A pin header that connects to a specialized digital I/O card.

Ch
19

A neat solution for modern machines is an external USB sound adapter. Prices as this book went to press began at about $75 for a capable box, and rose to about twice that amount for the latest and fanciest device. A USB adapter does not make demands on the computer's internal resources and does not require you to open the case and use a PCI slot; the box may also have more — or easier to access — connectors than can be crammed on an internal card.

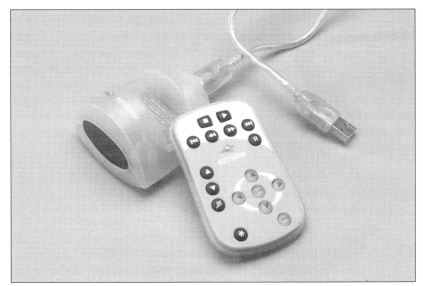

Figure 19-17: *Keyspan's Digital Media Remote includes a receiver that plugs into a USB port and a matchbook-sized wireless infrared remote. Included software allows users to customize commands for multimedia software.*

Built-in sound facilities on motherboards

Many modern motherboards — especially those intended for use in budget systems or in office settings where computer games and audio editing are not standard assignments — offer built-in sound facilities. The chipsets are more than capable of basic stereo sound production and connect to standard line-in, microphone-in, line-out, and speaker-out connectors on the computer's backplane.

The advantages of built-in sound chips include reduced cost because they do not need to be mounted on an adapter card and because they can share system memory. The disadvantages include the fact that the chipsets generally lack advanced features and cannot be repaired if they fail.

In the unlikely case of a failure, you should be able to instruct the system setup to disable the sound facilities. (Some systems may require physical disabling through the use of a jumper across pins on the motherboard.) You can work around a failed sound system — or upgrade one — by installing a sound card in a PCI slot or using an external sound adapter that connects through the USB port.

Installing and testing a sound board

Although CD-ROM drives, DVD-ROM drives, and sound cards are individually very different types of peripherals — the first two are storage devices and the last is an electronic orchestra and sound effects generator — they are very much linked in modern machines in that they are essential elements of the burgeoning multimedia explosion.

Many sound cards are electronically linked to CD-ROM drives as interfaces to the bus and as amplifiers for CD- and DVD-based audio.

Most modern internal adapter cards require a PCI slot; in fact, you'll have a hard time finding an older, less-capable card that uses the ISA slot of a senior citizen or dinosaur unless you shop the used computer stores or online auction sites. On a modern machine, Plug and Play should do most or all of the heavy thinking when it comes to configuring a PCI card. Most PCI sound cards use IRQ5 and DMA 5 for all native and emulated modes.

In most cases, you'll need to attach an analog audio cable from your internal CD-ROM to the sound card's CD Audio In connector. A number of different designs are available for this cable; this is one reason to use an industry card like those offered by Creative Labs or a card that adheres closely to the Sound Blaster standard.

Advanced CD-ROMs and DVD-ROMs also offer a digital audio connector that attaches to the sound card's S/PDIF or digital audio input, allowing you to play digital audio CDs.

You also have to install device drivers to Windows and DOS to inform your operating system of the presence of the sound card. Consult the instruction manual for the card for details. Most sound cards include their own diagnostic programs to test their settings and performance.

Troubleshooting a sound card

Before you curse the silence, check the most obvious sources of problems.

Speak to me. First of all, are your speakers plugged into the output of the sound card? If the speakers have a power amplifier, check to see that they are turned on and that they are connected to a power source — usually a DC transformer. Some speakers use batteries, and these must be in place and holding sufficient power.

Next, check to see that the sound card is enabled, and configured as the active preferred device.

- **Verify that your sound card is enabled**. Click Start ⇨ Settings ⇨ Control Panel. Double-click System, and then click the Device Manager tab. Double-click Sound, Video and Game Controllers, and then click your sound card. Click Properties. If the Disable In This Hardware Profile check box is selected, click the check box to clear that choice and enable the card. Click OK, and then click OK again. Restart your computer if the system requests you to do so.
- **Verify that your sound card is the preferred device.** Click Start ⇨ Settings ⇨ Control Panel, and then double-click Multimedia. In the Preferred Device boxes under Playback and Recording, click your sound card. Click OK.
- **Verify that Windows is configured to use the audio features of your sound card**. Click Start ⇨ Settings ⇨ Control Panel, and then double-click Multimedia. Click the Devices tab, and then double-click Audio Devices. Click your sound card, and then click Properties ⇨ Use Audio Features on This Device. Click OK to return to the Control Panel window. Restart your computer.
- **Check for corrupt sound files.** If you are having a problem playing a particular .wav or .mid sound file, try playing another similar file to see if it is the file itself that is causing the problem. You'll find wave (*.wav) files in the Windows System folder. You can locate other wave or MIDI files on your computer by clicking Start ⇨ Find ⇨ Files or Folders and type in *.**wav** or *.**mid**.
- **Verify you are using current sound drivers.** Update the driver from within Windows if possible, go to the manufacturer's web site, or call the manufacturer to obtain a current driver.
- **Check for hardware conflicts**. Click Start ⇨ Settings ⇨ Control Panel. Double-click System, and then click the Device Manager tab. Double-click Sound, Video and Game Controllers, and check

to see that your sound card is listed; if it is not there, it has not been recognized by Windows. It may not be physically installed properly or may have failed. If you see your sound card listed, check for an exclamation point in a yellow circle; if you see this symbol, Windows is reporting a problem with the device. The source of the problem can include a resource conflict, a corrupted or absent driver, or a hardware problem with the device itself. To attempt to resolve the problem, double-click the sound card, and then click the Resources tab. Check the panel that displays the Conflicting device list. If Windows reports a conflict here, you have to reconfigure the sound card or one or more other conflicting devices to use different IRQ or memory resources. Check instruction manuals or contact the manufacturer for information on suggestions to end the conflict.

NOTE

In all Windows versions — at least since late Windows 98 — you may have success letting Windows reconfigure things for you. Open the Device manager as described earlier and right-click your sound card listing and choose Remove. Now reboot Windows. The operating system should locate this new hardware and attempt to reinstall it for you. The previous driver software you used should be on the hard drive, where Windows will find it and set up your sound card again. If Plug-and-Play works properly, the previous resource conflict should be cleared automatically.

More sound card fix-its

After you have dealt with issues of resource conflict, you may run into some other problems to be fixed. Here are some common issues for sound cards, with typical solutions.

No sound or low volume

Are the speakers plugged into the proper output of the sound card; double-check that they use the line-out or speaker jack. If the speakers have an amplifier, is it plugged into the wall current and turned on? Is the volume control of the speakers set to a middle or high position for testing?

Check the settings of the Windows sound mixer. See that the mixer doesn't mute the output of the sound card, and that volume settings are at a middle or high position for testing.

Try using a different application to generate sound. For example, try the Windows sounds, configurable and testable from the Control Panel. If you hear sounds from another source, the problem is likely with whatever software you first tried.

Scratchy or weak sound

Poor quality sound may be the result of the device's DMA setting not matching the DMA setting under Windows; Plug-and-Play should prevent this situation, but problems still occur. (This is a potential problem only for devices that install in a PCI or ISA slot, not for those that use the USB port.) Follow these steps to determine if the DMA settings are correct:

1. Right-click My Computer and then click Properties.
2. On the Device Manager tab, click Sound, Video and Game Controllers. Then click Remove.
3. Restart the computer. Once Windows is up and running again, click Start ⇨ Settings ⇨ Control Panel.
4. Then double-click the Add New Hardware icon and reinstall the sound card.

Be sure to let Windows search for new hardware first. If it finds it, you'll stand a better chance of getting the right driver installed. If this doesn't work, choose manual and try to point to the right driver on the manufacturer's disk or CD-ROM included with the product.

Another possible cause for poor sound performance is an attempt to mix wave file formats. For example, you cannot play a 16-bit wave file on an 8-bit sound card.

Monaural sound or one channel

If you hear sound through only one side of the speaker pair, or if you can determine that the sound you hear is monaural and not stereo, check to see that you are using a stereo jack in the sound card's speaker output. A mono jack combines the left and right signals into a single stream; as you look at a jack, you will see three segments for a stereo unit and two segments on a mono unit. Check the sound card's drivers and support software for any configuration errors, including a manual assignment of monaural sound. Check, too, that

the Windows sound mixer is not set up to mute one of the two channels of a stereo signal. If you are replaying the output of an external device, check to see that its balance setting is not turning off one channel and that switches are not set to produce a mono signal.

Hum or distortion in the signal

Tracking down the source of a hum can be very tricky. One common source of the problem is placement of the speakers too close to the monitor, or to a poorly shielded television or FM receiver. The problem can also be caused by a pinch in the cable or damage to one of the connectors. Check to be sure the plug is fully inserted into the connector. In some instances, the sound card itself may be receiving interference from another component within the PC; if possible, move the card to another slot away from other adapters.

Overpowered speakers

If you overpower the speakers with too much power, sound will be distorted. It is best to adjust the volume from within Windows or on the sound card before the signal travels to the sound card. Adjust the volume control on the speakers to a middle position. If your sound card has a volume control, adjust it to a middle position. Then adjust the volume within any audio control panel put in your system by the sound card; look for a volume control icon on the desktop. Or, check for a volume control within Windows. Click Start ⇨ Programs ⇨ Accessories ⇨ Entertainment ⇨ Volume Control, and then adjust the volume.

Speakers

Consider the quality of the speakers you use to reproduce sound. A great sound card coupled with a tinny pair of speakers will sound tinny, just as a superior set of speakers used with an inadequate sound card won't satisfy most ears.

The choice of speakers includes two variables: price and personal preference. The cheapest of speakers almost always sound tinny and . . . cheap. But for most of us there is no need to go all the way to the other extreme and purchase very expensive speakers. You may be able to audition speakers at a retail store; I appreciate setups that allow me to switch a recorded sound sample between a shelf full of speakers. Moderately priced speaker kits, with a subwoofer, sell for $25 to $100; I can't recommend spending more than that for a *computer's* speakers.

In most cases it is not a good idea to use ordinary home stereo speakers directly connected to your PC for two reasons: Their magnetic coils are not shielded and can cause disturbances to your monitor or damage to floppy disks, and they may require greater wattage than is produced by the tiny amplifiers of sound cards. A good compromise, and a very appropriate choice for users who don't want to disturb others, is a quality set of headphones instead of speakers.

Computer speakers are generally lightweight and small. A proper design shields the magnetic coil on the speaker to prevent distortion of the image on a computer monitor and distortion of the audio because of leaking magnetic waves and radio frequency radiation.

The best quality speakers have their own small amplifiers; even better than a simple two-speaker setup is a system that uses a third speaker called a *subwoofer*. Subwoofers deliver clean, resonant bass; because low frequency sounds are relatively non-directional, this sort of speaker can be placed on the floor or corner in the general area of the left and right speakers. Amplified speakers obviously require a source of power; tiny and tinny speakers may use batteries, while more impressive models require power from an AC to DC adapter; some smaller (and less impressive) speakers draw power from the USB system (or a powered USB hub) in modern PCs.

To judge the quality of speakers, you should pay attention to the frequency range and the total harmonic distortion, just as you do for the sound card. The third most important element is the wattage of the built-in amplifier. Within reason, the more wattage the better; most consumer-grade speaker systems offer amplifiers yielding from 10 to 100 watts.

You'll also want to use connecting cables of decent quality. Cheap wire or connectors can result in distortion.

The current ultimate in computer audio is 7.1 Surround Sound. This scheme, similar to that used in a high-end home theater, uses eight speakers. Two speakers are located in "front" of the user, usually on either side of the monitor. A third front speaker delivers a computer-derived "middle" channel that fills in the sound between left and right. Two more speakers are placed behind the user. A subwoofer is placed on the floor. Up to this point, what you have is called 5.1 Surround Sound, which pretty impressive.

To go the extra step to 7.1 Surround Sound, you'll add two more speakers that sit a few feet to the immediate right and left of your ears.

These speakers are used in some action games to enhance the sensation of something moving from one side of the screen to the other; think of a race car cutting across the room or a jet plane swooping by. It's neat stuff, and a lot of fun for gamers and people who watch DVD-based movies on their computer; for the moment, though, 7.1 is major overkill for ordinary audio assignments like listening to music or Internet entertainment. Your audio adapter card or external sound box has to support 7.1. Creative Sound Blaster Audigy 4 Pro is one such product.

After your speaker system is in place, use the facilities of the sound card's software to define the sound setup. Most applications can make adjustments to the sound to adjust it to the size of room, type of music, and number of speakers.

Microphones

To record voice or to use a voice-recognition or dictation system with a PC, you'll need a microphone. The price and quality of mikes varies tremendously, but if you're planning on basic tasks, an inexpensive model should suffice. If you're planning on recording music, you'll need a more professional model and you may want to invest in a specialized sound card and an external mixer.

To judge the quality of a microphone, look at the same specifications you consulted for a speaker: frequency range, signal-to-noise ratio, and total harmonic distortion. You want a wide frequency range, a high signal-to-noise ratio, and a miniscule level of distortion.

Be sure to plug the microphone into the correct connector on the sound card, and check to make sure the cable does not become crimped or damaged. Some microphones include a small battery-powered amplifier; be sure the batteries are fresh and that an on-off switch is in the proper position.

SUMMARY

This chapter concludes the hardware tour of PCs, from dinosaurs to modern machines. In the next few chapters, I look at some good software and operating system practices that help you keep your hardware working properly and protect you against losing your data when hardware fails.

Ch
19

Notes

Chapter 20

Networks, Gateways, Routers, and WiFi Wireless

The days when personal computers were islands unto themselves are long gone. Sooner or later, nearly every home or office ends up with more than one computer: one in the den and one in the home office, or one in the front office and another on the desk of the sales manager. In many situations, you can find more than just a handful; very few offices are without a computer on each desk, and many families end up with PCs for each child in school and one or more for mom and dad. It has always been possible for a PC to stand on its own without a network to other machines. The low-tech solution to sharing information is to make copies of files on floppy disks or other portable media and move them from machine to machine by hand. Wags dubbed this solution a *sneaker net*.

Files and programs can be stored on local disks, and you can equip the computer with its own modem, printer, and other peripherals. Each computer can be linked to its own telephone line or high-speed connection to use the Internet. However, equipping each computer with its own peripherals and Internet account is generally not a sound financial decision. Printers are rarely in constant use and can be shared easily. And one of the greatest ways to save money with a network is to share a single broadband Internet connection (either cable or DSL) with several linked computers.

A much better solution is the creation of a *local area network (LAN)*, a system that links multiple machines to allow users to exchange files and programs and share devices. In the early days of the PC, establishing a LAN was a black-magic task left to the technicians. Today, a basic office or home network is close to a Plug-and-Play application. And one of the greatest ways to save money with a network is to share a single broadband Internet connection (either cable or DSL) with several linked computers.

In this chapter, I explore the hardware side of networking including network interfaces, hubs, switches, routers, and gateways. And I explain how it is becoming easier and easier to cut the cord: wireless networks are a great solution to interconnecting machines and sharing services and peripherals without the bother of stringing wire along the floor, through the walls, or into the floor.

I also touch on some of the basics of software protocols. Microsoft Windows includes extensive information on configuring a network after the hardware is in place. You can also obtain assistance from makers of network cards and other devices. Additionally, I discuss a related critical security issue for networks connected to the Internet with an introduction to hardware and software firewalls.

Network Components

To become part of a local area network each computer needs three principal components:

- A network interface. This is a computer I/O subsystem that bundles data into packets to be sent out onto the network and collects packets addressed to it from other devices. On modern machines, chips built into the motherboard and connected to a port at the back of the computer usually provide network connectivity. You can also use a network interface adapter card that plugs into an internal slot (hence the device's original name, a *network interface card,* or *NIC),* or an external adapter that connects to the computer through a USB port.

- A system of wires (or a wireless equivalent) to link one computer to another, usually in conjunction with a central device that is located (in logical terms) in a position like the hub of a wheel. In a hub-and-spoke design, a central switch or router accepts incoming data from any device linked to it and then re-routes it to the proper destination amongst other devices in the network. (Among possible linked devices in a network: computers, printers, modems, and wired or wireless bridges that connect multiple networks to each other.)
- A software protocol to manage the network operation; in the early days of personal computing, this was an add-on to the operating system and was extremely complex in its implementation. Today, networking is built into all current versions of the Windows operating system.

For most of today's personal computers, networks are based around the Ethernet specification, which defines the hardware and the communications protocol that encases chunks of data between a sender's address and a receiver's address and other information.

Currently, Ethernet has many varieties that vary in speed and physical medium used. Perhaps the most common forms used are 10BASE-T, 100BASE-TX, and 1000BASE-T. All three use twisted-pair cables and 8P8C modular connectors (often incorrectly called RJ45). They run at 10 Mbps, 100 Mbps, and 1 Gbps, respectively. However, each version has become steadily more selective about the cable it runs on, and some installers have avoided 1000BASE-T.

Gigabit Ethernet (GbE) describes various technologies for transmitting Ethernet packets at a rate of a gigabit per second, as defined by the IEEE 802.3-2005 standard. (A gigabit is equal to 1,000 megabits.) The current state-of-the-art in Ethernet is Gigabit Ethernet, also called 1000Base-T, although that specification is not yet in wide use because of the preponderance of older, slower hardware already in place in homes and offices. Already in development and testing are 10- and 100-gbps versions.

Today the most common standard is 100Base-T, or Fast Ethernet, which is capable of passing as much as 100 megabits of data per second. Fast Ethernet superseded 10Base-T, which could move at 10 megabits per second.

NOTE

Ethernet is by far the most common *topology* (the geometric shape) for networks. Less commonly used transport mechanisms include token ring and ArcNet. These technologies are virtually a thing of the past, with the exception of existing installations.

The Ethernet interface uses a protocol called Carrier Sense Multiple Access With Collision Detection, which means that the network interface card monitors the stream of traffic moving past on the network and looks for an opening. Think of merging your car onto a crowded expressway. You can't just plow ahead blindly. You must wait for an opening at least as large as your car and within the capabilities of your engine's ability to catch up with it.

In an Ethernet system, each computer listens in on the network in search of a gap in the stream of data and then transmits its short packet; if two devices happen to send a packet at the same moment, there will be a collision and both computers will be instructed to resend the packet after a randomly assigned wait.

Ethernet was originally envisioned for use for PCs located near each other in a LAN. However, the system has been expanded into use across wider groups and as the mechanism behind connections between a PC and such devices as a cable modem network and shared printers.

Within a network, packets flow along cables arranged in a particular *topology.* The most common design is a *hub and spoke* or *star* topology that connects each of the computers in the network to a central hub. The hub reroutes the packets out to the other computers in the network.

A *passive hub* sends every incoming packet out on the network where it passes all of the computers until it comes to the proper address. A *switched hub* sends packets only to the particular hub to which it has been addressed; as such, it operates considerably faster than a passive hub.

Another design for a network is a *bus* topology in which all computers branch off of a single main line.

Wireless networks mimic hardware cable designs. Data is transmitted by each computer to a receiver that functions as the hub of the network. The receiver retransmits data to the addressed computer.

Note that an Ethernet is only capable of working at the speed of its slowest component. For example, if you have 100Base-T network interface cards but a 10Base-T hub, the network will move no faster than 10 megabits per second. If you have a 100Base-T hub that connects to a 10Base-T NIC in a computer on the network, you'll also be limited to that slower speed.

For that reason, purchasing a 10/100Base-T hub or switch capable of working at both speeds, or a Gigabit/100/10Base-T device may make sense for buyers with an eye on the future.

Network Topologies

The physical design of the connections between network components is called its *topology*. Several designs are commonly used, including bus, star, and ring. Most simple networks — including virtually every wired and wireless system in the home and small office — use the hub-and-spoke design.

Hub-and-spoke topology

A *hub-and-spoke* design, also known as a *star topology,* is centered around a server, a hub, or a switch. A cable to the hub or server connects each computer; the path from one computer to another passes through the central device.

The principal advantage of this design is that the failure of any spoke — a computer or a networked device such as a printer or broadband modem — does not bring down the entire network. A star topology typically requires much more cabling than a bus, because machines that may sit next to each other do not connect directly to each other but instead must be linked to the central device.

If the server — an active PC — or the hub or switch fails, the network will not operate but individual machines can work independently.

Bus topology

A *bus topology* uses a single cable with workstations and peripheral devices connected anywhere along the way. In a typical setup where Windows is the only networking software you are using, the system is a *peer-to-peer* network in which each PC on the network is essentially equal to every other one.

The bus must remain unbroken from one end to the other with hardware termination at each end. The network won't work if the cable is damaged, a connector comes undone, or a network interface fails.

Again, because each member of the network is a computer capable of functioning on its own, the individual network components can still work in the event of a failure, but they won't be able to communicate with each other. Data can be shared via floppy disk or other removable media, but there will be no direct connection.

Ring topology

A *ring topology* is a closed system, a form of bus without any termination. Each PC or other network component attaches to the continuous network wiring, with the ends of the loop connected to each other to form a ring.

All of the components — cables, connectors, and interfaces — must be working properly for the network to operate. (Think of a Christmas tree light set with the lamps wired in serial form; the failure of one lamp brings down the entire string.) Unlike the Christmas tree light example, however, individual components — because they are intelligent entities in their own right — can still function, but without network communications.

Network Interface

The *network interface* is the hardware that provides the physical connection between your computer and the network. It works with the networking software to establish and manage the protocol that chops up data into packets and adds a destination address to each piece.

Although the device is commonly referred to as a bus adapter card, network interface card, or a NIC, it can also exist as a set of chips on the motherboard or as a plug-in module that attaches to the USB port of a modern machine. Portable computers can use a USB device or a network interface on a PC Card.

Within current modern machines, the network interface is tightly integrated with the chipset and the motherboard. If you must install an adapter card, all modern versions work well with Plug-and-Play, allocating hardware resources automatically. External USB adapters function without configuration, although you may need to install a device driver.

It is always best to have a system where all the components have the same specifications and follow the same standards, but that is not essential to network operation. However, as I have noted, a 100Base-T NIC connected to a 10Base-T hub, or a 100Base-T hub linked to a

10Base-T NIC will operate at the slower speed. If you have a mixed system, nearly all current hardware offers an *autonegotiating* feature that can adjust to the network's speed. Such devices are sometimes advertised as 10/100 devices or 1000/100 devices.

Figures 20-1 through 20-3 show a selection of network interfaces, in a PCI bus version, an external USB adapter, and a PC card for use in portables.

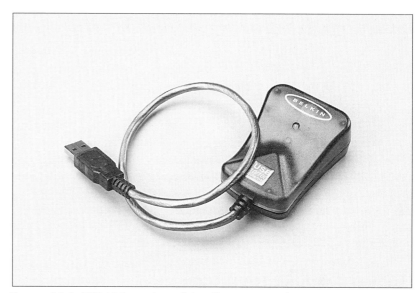

FIGURE 20-2: *USB NICs, such as this Belkin 10/100 Ethernet Adapter, do not require any system resources other than those already claimed by the USB chain.*

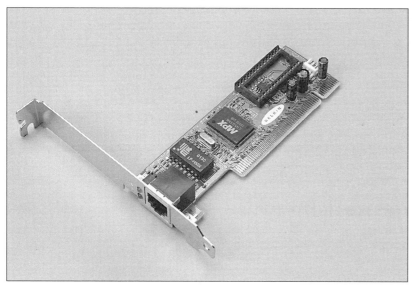

FIGURE 20-1: *The Belkin Network PCI Card is an example of a basic plug-and-play NIC for modern machines. It includes support for 10 Mbps and 100 Mbps networking.*

FIGURE 20-3: *A 32-bit CardBus or PC Card network adapter like this model from Belkin allows attachment of a portable computer to a home or office network, and to broadband modems.*

Hubs, Switches, and Gateway/Routers

A *hub* (known to some techies as a *concentrator*) is an external hardware device that serves as a central connection point for cables from PCs and other devices; to connect from one to another, the cable goes to the hub and then back out.

You also can use a hub to convert one type of cable to another, such as linking a section of a network using older (mostly commercial or industrial) 10Base-2 coaxial to a device or network segment that requires a 10Base-T or 100Base-T connection more commonly used in homes and offices today. And it can merge together segments that are based on differing speeds, such as 10Base-T and 100Base-T. As I've noted: a slower device will continue to operate at its base speed, and a slow hub will reduce all segments to its speed limit.

Hubs are a bit like an unguarded highway intersection, with as many as 24 lanes of traffic on some models. Packets of information are brought together from sending devices to join the stream of data that visits every machine on the network.

In today's market, it is hard to find a mere hub anymore. Hubs were at first replaced by intelligent switches, and switches have subsequently been supplanted or supported by routers. Let me explain the distinctions.

A switch works by reading the distinct address of an incoming packet and then selecting a path to send it directly to the intended recipient instead of sending it out on the network to every attached device. As such, each sender and receiver has access to the full bandwidth of the network rather than having to share it with all of the other traffic. The direct path also reduces the chances for collisions between the packets, resulting in a greater efficiency rate.

Today, most network switches are available in versions with four to eight ports; autonegotiating RJ45 ports capable of working with 10Base-T, 100Base-T, or Gigabit segments; LEDs on the front indicate the speed of each port. An uplink port allows connection to additional switches or to a router to extend the system. (Although many modern switches have electronically configured ports that can serve as a regular network port or an uplink port without the need for special wiring for connecting other devices.)

A more capable device is a combination gateway and router, sometimes called a residential gateway. These devices combine a switch to link together the devices on a network with a gateway router that permits an entire network to share a single cable or DSL

modem Internet account. All modern versions of a gateway router also include a hardware firewall to protect against unwanted intrusion by hackers.

Most routers use a version of *Network Address Translation (NAT)* to convert multiple IP addresses on a private local area network to a single public address that is sent out on the Internet or other wide area network. This adds security to your operations because the addresses of PCs on the local network are not transmitted onto the potentially public wide area network.

A typical home or small office setup uses a switch and gateway that includes a broad range of firewall and security facilities including packet filtering. In Figure 20-4 you can see a basic combination broadband router intended to connect to a cable or DSL modem, as well as to seven other computers or devices on the network.

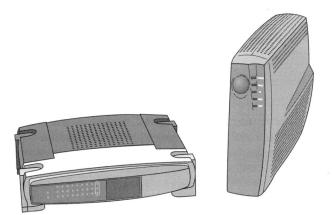

FIGURE 20-4: *An eight-port cable/DSL router, alongside a cable modem. The router is set up and managed from a Web page accessed through the browser of an attached computer on the network.*

Cabling

The simplest type of cable for use in home and small office PC networks is twisted pair wiring, a more robust version of the familiar two- or four-wire telephone cable. Networking cable uses eight wires, configured in pairs of wires, twisted together to reduce interference. Twisted-pair cables use a slightly larger version of the familiar plastic snap-in connector of a telephone, too, and in an office installation can be wired to connection boxes in the wall. Cables are rated by quality and capacity; Category 5E (Cat 5E is the common designation) is the most common high-quality design, and is designed to support network speeds up to one gigabit per second (1 Gbps, "gigabit networks").

However, the demand for faster and faster networks has spawned two new wiring standards, Category 6 (and 6A) and Category 7. These wiring standards are similar in that they use twisted-pair cabling, but each progressive one is made to higher quality and technical standards to support faster communication. Cat 5E is better than Cat 5, Cat 6 is better than Cat 5E, and Cat 7 is better than Cat 6. Category 6 cables use a plug and jack system designed to higher standards than Category 5. Category 6 cables can plug into a Category 5 panel but, by definition, the resulting connection conforms to Cat 5, not to Cat 6. Category 7 (not yet fully accepted as a recognized standard) adds shielding around individual pairs in the cable and also has an outside shield around all pairs. Category 7 uses a different connector than the RJ45 plug used with previous twisted-pair wiring and is designed for communication speeds up to six times faster than current designs. As this book is written, Cat 6 is being recommend for all new commercial and office wiring, and I expect Cat 6 to be used increasingly within the home.

In larger offices, coaxial cable was once the standard transport mechanism. Coaxial cable is made up of a center connector surrounded by a plastic dielectric (insulator). A copper braid is woven around the dielectric sheath and is covered by a thin plastic outer layer. This cable is similar to the wiring used by cable television providers; on computer networks, the wire attaches to network interfaces and hubs with a twist-on BNC connector. Coaxial cables are sturdier than twisted-pair and may be required by some fire codes for in-wall installation. But in most cases, the coaxial backbone will be converted to twisted pair before connecting the network to individual PCs.

Coaxial networks using Ethernet can extend for about 2,000 feet in total; a twisted pair network is limited to about 300 feet. Some hub designs can improve on — or reduce — total distances.

Today, where longer distance and faster speed are important, fiber optic cable offers greater security and speed; it is, however, difficult to install and more expensive than other technologies. And because few PCs have the ability to connect directly to a fiber backbone, you need adapters to convert fiber to copper before attaching it to your computer. Fiber cable, connectors, and converters once were prohibitively expensive for all but the largest of installations, but fiber is becoming more common and more cost effective.

In this book, I'll concentrate on twisted-pair protocols, 10Base-T, 100Base-T, and the developing 1000Base-T. In Table 20-1 you can see some of the various industry categories for twisted-pair cables that have been used or proposed for Ethernet networks and for other office communication purposes.

TABLE 20-1: Twisted-Pair Wiring Types

Category	Industry Standard	Computer Use
Cat 1	None	Copper telephone wiring, ISDN
Cat 2	None	Outdated 4 Mbps token ring networks
Cat 3	10Base-T	Older 10 Mbps Ethernet
Cat 4	Not in current use	Older 16 Mbps token ring networks
Cat 5	100Base-T	100Base-T Ethernet installations
Cat 5E	100Base-T, 1000Base-T	Current 100 Mbps and 1000 Mbps Ethernet
Cat 6/6A	100Base-T, 1000Base-T	100 Mbps and 1000 Mbps Ethernet*

Although the throughput specifications for Cat 5E and Cat 6 are the same, Cat 6 reduces crosstalk (interference) between pairs and therefore theoretically offers greater actual throughput.

Network Software and Protocols

On the software side, you need a driver to connect your NIC to the operating system and a network-capable operating system. All current versions of Windows (beginning with Windows 95) provide both software components. Windows includes drivers for most current network interfaces; some manufacturers supply customized drivers along with their hardware.

Consult the Help screens and the capable built-in wizards of current versions of Windows for advice on configuring your network. In Figures 20-5 through 20-7 are some Windows XP components; similar facilities are offered in Windows Vista.

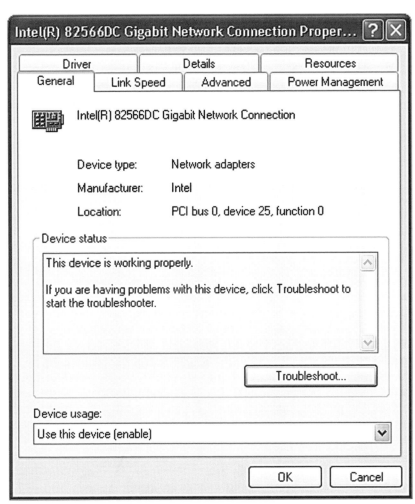

FIGURE 20-5: *The properties screen for the built-in 1000Base-T (Gigabit Ethernet) chips on a modern machine.*

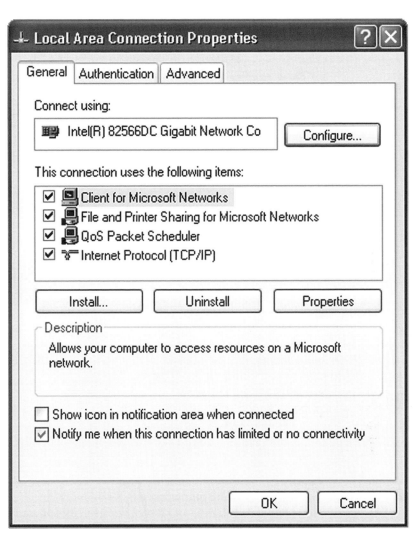

FIGURE 20-6: *Configuration options for a local area network. Much of the decisionmaking here is automated through use of either the Windows Networking Wizard or a networking utility you may receive along with hardware such as NICs or routers.*

Ch
20

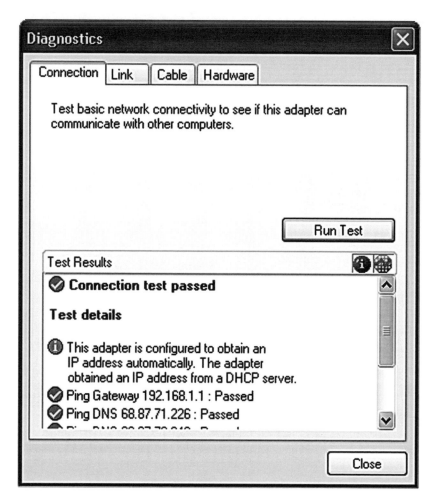

FIGURE 20-7: *Built-in troubleshooting and information screens of Windows can help you determine the characteristics of your networking hardware and perform basic tests such as Ping which sends an "Are you there?" message to known locations on a local or wide area network or on the Internet.*

hardware architectures and operating systems, including the Internet and Unix-based hosts. Under Windows XP, this protocol is recommended for a local area network.

- **Microsoft NetBEUI.** The native networking protocol for Windows through Windows 98, NetBEUI is a NETBIOS-compatible (**NET**work **B**asic **I**nput/**O**utput **S**ystem) protocol — pronounced by techies as "net-buoy" — that facilitates communication with other NETBIOS machines, including Windows for Workgroups and Windows NT server.
- **Microsoft IPX/SPX.** A Novell NetWare-compatible protocol that you can use with an existing Novell network; Novell also offers its own version of the protocol that may offer some advantages to users.

Wireless Networks

A wireless LAN is similar to a wired Ethernet, except without the wires. Data is transmitted over radio waves, with information broken up into packets that identify the address of the sender and recipient.

For many users, the best thing about wireless computing (often called *WiFi*) is the ability to surf the Web and check e-mail as you travel with laptops. You'll find wireless *hotspots* (designated areas where users can latch onto a signal) in airports, hotels, coffee shops, and many other public and private places. Some hotspots are free and open to the public, some require payment of a daily or monthly fee, and some are private networks available only to employees or clients with an account and password.

But you have some good reasons to add a wireless network to serve the PCs in your home or office. For example, you may have a wired network that connects two or more machines in an office or den, and you may want to move a laptop from place to place for occasional use. Or there may be a physical (or fiscal) impediment to adding another machine to your network: In an office setting it may be necessary to hire an electrician to install wiring that meets the fire code. At home you may not be willing or able to drill holes in floors, ceilings, or walls to string cables.

The solution may be the creation of a wireless network, either as the principal means to connect multiple computers and peripherals or as an adjunct to a wired network. There are two parts to the process:

The **hardware.** You need some or all of the following components:

Windows can support multiple protocols on the same system. The operating system includes these built-in network protocols:

- **Microsoft TCP/IP.** The Transmission Control Protocol/Internet Protocol is well suited to link computers with a mix of

- A **wireless adapter** in your PC or laptop. This can be in the form of a built-in chipset and antenna on the motherboard or an adapter card that plugs into a PC's internal slot, or an adapter that connects to a USB port on a PC or laptop. (Some older laptops used an adapter card that plugged into a PC Card slot.)
- A **wireless access point (WAP)** that serves as a receiver and transmitter for data and connects to a wired Ethernet hub or switch that links other computers and usually a broadband Internet cable or DSL modem. The WAP can also be part of a **wireless router** that also serves as a hub for wired devices and a link to the Internet. The advantages of using a wireless router include the fact that the configuration for the wired and wireless sides of the network can be accomplished with a single utility.
- In certain setups, you may need to add a **wireless range extender** (also called a **wireless repeater**) to extend the reach of your network. For example, if you find that your WiFi network will reach about 200 feet and you need to connect with a machine that is 250 feet away, you can place a repeater somewhere in between. Another situation could look like this: A home has a signal that has to bend around a corner; the signal is not strong enough to go through walls in a direct line. An extender or repeater picks up a signal, amplifies it, and retransmits it.
- Another way to improve performance is to add a high-gain **external antenna** to a router or to the adapter installed in the PC. In theory, a larger well-designed antenna can significantly improve a wireless system's range, improve the signal quality (boost the signal-to-noise ratio), or both. Sometimes an external antenna's greatest gain is the ability to move its away from a location blocked by metal cases or shielding, and out where it has a better chance at a line-of-sight connection to devices.

The **software.**

- Users of current versions of Windows need only to enable built-in support for wireless networking and make choices on settings for included firewall and other security settings. Some devices may require installation of a device driver. And you may need to communicate with a router to make settings; in most cases you are directed by the manufacturer to use your Web browser to navigate to a specified address that is not out on the Internet, but within the local hardware. An example of the built-in wizard for setup of a wireless network that is part of Windows XP is shown in Figure 20-8.

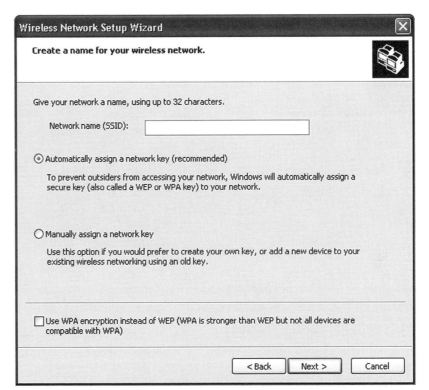

FIGURE 20-8: *The Windows wireless setup, used together with utilities provided by makers of wireless hardware, automates most of the work involved in setting up a network. Some manufacturers supply their own utility that works around Microsoft's suggestions.*

Windows Vista Network Center

The improved facilities of Vista include the Network Center, which includes reports on how your machine is functioning as a member of a *local area network (LAN)*. A feature called Network Map displays the various links graphically, and if one of the PCs in your LAN loses its link, you can see the problem and use Network Diagnostics in search of a solution.

The center is also the entryway to adding connections to other available networks or the creation of a new one. The Network Setup Wizard allows you to set up wired or wireless networks by identifying unconfigured network devices and adding them to the network. Also included are features to lock down some of the network settings to protect against intrusion and damage.

Under Windows Vista, network settings can be saved to a USB flash drive to allow quick and easy configuration of additional PCs not yet connected. Windows Vista automatically tunes itself to receive more data at any given time by detecting your Internet connection speed and the amount of bandwidth available to you.

A new feature called Network Explorer simplifies the process of sharing files and peripherals, presenting a view of all PCs and devices (including printers and modems) on the network; it replaces My Network Places from Windows XP. Among its advances: the ability to directly interact with certain devices. For example, you may be able to adjust settings or control music playback of current hardware.

The Network Awareness feature in Windows Vista can adjust applications based on changing network elements. Among uses of this technology are a home-office machine that switches between personal use and connection to a corporate network; the Network Awareness utility recognizes the change and can adjust firewall settings to open or close ports as needed for IT management tools.

And Microsoft promises to keep data more secure with enhanced support for the latest wireless security protocols, including WPA2. Safeguards in the operating system are intended to help users stay away from fraudulent wireless networks that appear to be legitimate wireless hotspots but are instead intended to capture keystrokes or steal personal information.

About WiFi wireless

The most commonly used technology for wireless communication in homes and offices is one or another (or more than one) flavor of what is called the 802.11 standard. This technology's specification was developed by several committees of the IEEE, an international association for electrical engineers and manufacturers.

Each network adapter has its own ID number that serves as an address. Transmitters monitor the stream of traffic on the network, waiting for a break in which to send out a packet of information. In a peer-to-peer network, each PC has its own transmitter and receiver capable of communication with other devices within the same network and within its operating range. In a hub-and-spoke network, each PC has its own adapter that communicates with a fixed access point transceiver with its own antenna. In this design, the transmitter can send packets to other devices or link to a wired Ethernet network.

As a user, there's not a great deal you need to know about the technical details of the various standards. On the practical side, bear in mind two points: The most current specifications (802.11g and the 802.11n) have advantages over the earlier designs, and the specifications are *downwardly compatible*, which means that an 802.11n device also works with the earlier a, b, and g designs. However, you cannot expect an 802.11g device — just as an example — to deliver the performance of the more advanced 802.11n standard.

As this book goes to press, the most capable specification is 802.11n, which permits transmission of data as fast as 540 Mbps at a distance of as much as 200 feet; it is also less likely to suffer from interference from other household or office devices. It will take a number of years, though, before 802.11n becomes predominant because of the installed base of millions of older pieces of hardware; the most common specifications in use in 2007 are 802.11g and a still-large, but gradually diminishing, base of 802.11b devices

The biggest problem with wireless devices one or two steps behind the current specification is that they rely on the 2.4-GHz frequency band, an unregulated slice of the radio spectrum that unfortunately is also commonly used by many cordless telephones, Bluetooth devices, and even microwave ovens and other appliances. If it is not annoying, then it has to be funny to consider the fact that your ability to conduct business or research over the Internet with a WiFi connection may be slowed or interfered with by someone chatting on a cordless phone (not a cell phone) or nuking a slice of pizza.

For engineers, the selection of a radio frequency is not a simple matter. To begin with, whole segments of the radio spectrum are regulated for particular purposes, such as commercial broadcasting, emergency services, and the military. And in so-called *unregulated* frequencies that do not require a license or other forms of permission, there can be interference. For example, millions of garage door openers use a frequency (lower than that employed in WiFi) that is also occasionally used by military and Homeland Security forces, which brings all sorts of potential comical or frightening situations in a national emergency or test.

A higher frequency is not necessarily better; in general, lower frequency signals of 2.4 GHz can reach through walls or around corners better than 5-GHz devices, which work better in line-of-sight situations.

As you can see in Table 20-2, the older 802.11b standard had the greatest potential indoor range, at 400 feet. But it (and the faster 802.11g specification) use the same frequency range as the pizza heater. The design for 802.11n allows use of 5 GHz, which removes microwaves and most cordless telephones as possible sources of interference. You can improve even more on the efficiency of a WiFi connection by employing special features such as MIMO, special antennas, or repeaters; I explain each of these in the next section.

TABLE 20-2: WiFi Standards				
Protocol	Operational Frequency	Data Rate (Maximum)	Data Rate (Typical)	Approximate Indoor Range
Legacy	2.4 to 2.5 GHz	2 Mbps	1 Mbps	Variable
802.11a	5 GHz	54 Mbps	25 Mbps	100 feet
802.11b	2.4 to 2.5 GHz	11 Mbps	6.5 Mbps	400 feet
802.11g	2.4 to 2.5 GHz	54 Mbps	25 Mbps	100 feet
802.11n	2.4 or 5 GHz	540 Mbps	200 Mbps	200 feet

Extensions to the standards

The good thing about a standard is that it assures uniformity amongst products. Assuming manufacturers follow all the rules, any 802.11g device should be able to communicate with another that follows the same specifications; the only difference between the devices may be the hardware quality and the level of technical support and warranty offered by the maker. But that also presents problems or opportunities for manufacturers seeking to distinguish their product from those from their competitors.

For that reason, the marketplace has products that incorporate IEEE standards and add special features. The 802.11n standard began as an unofficial extension before being ratified by the industry. In 2007, among other extensions to the standard are Super-G and MIMO.

Super G harnesses a pair of 802.11g channels to yield something close to a maximum signal rate of 108 Mbps. To achieve that level of performance, you need a Super G device at both ends: adapter and router. The concept was developed by Atheros, and among hardware makers that license the technology for consumer products are D-Link and Netgear.

Another current technology aimed at improving the performance of existing transceivers is *MIMO*, which is an acronym for *multiple-input multiple-output*. This design allows use of multiple antennas on the same device for receiving and transmitting signals. The result, in the proper conditions, is an increase in the connection efficiency — getting the most from the potential top speed of the specification in use.

MIMO is mostly used with 802.11g and 802.11n systems. Engineers can use any or all of a number of enhancements that are part of the MIMO design. These include *beamforming*, which adapts and focuses the antenna signal based on ambient conditions; *spatial multiplexing*, which is the simultaneous streaming of separate data signals from more than one transmit antenna at the same time, multiplying the amount of information sent, and *space-time coding*, which calls on the transmitter to send multiple copies of the same data packets at the same time over multiple antennas to lessen the chances that data will have to be re-sent. An example of a MIMO system, from peripheral maker Belkin, is shown in Figure 20-9.

FIGURE 20-9: *Belkin's Super G MIMO router offers a pair of antennas that can work together or separately to improve connectivity in an 802.11g system.*

Linksys put forth the *SRX (Speed and Range Extension)* technology for some of its wireless devices beginning with 802.11b and 802.11g models. When both ends of a connection use SRX, the router can use twice as much of the available radio band, yielding throughput of as much as ten times a standard G network. According to Linksys, the technology also checks for other wireless devices in the area to avoid interference that might be caused by grabbing too much of the available radio spectrum.

Setting up a WiFi router

As with most modern electronic enhancements, in theory adding a WiFi router is an exercise in Plug-and-Play technology. That may be true for the simplest of installations, but it certainly is not the case for more common, more complex arrangements.

Belkin's Super G MIMO router came with an "automatic" installation CD. The ports on the back of the router were blocked with a piece of yellow tape that advised: "Wait! Do not connect your Router until instructed to do so. Please read the instructions first." Fair enough, except that the instructions only dealt with the use of this particular router as if it were the only piece of network sharing equipment in my office: The instructions said to connect the output of the broadband modem (in my case a cable modem, although it could also have been a DSL modem) to the router, and then attach any wired computers to one of the four ports on Belkin's little box.

Alas, my system is much more complex: I have a cable modem, a VoIP telephone adapter, and an eight-port wired router that serves the needs of six computers and a printer. I wanted to add Belkin's WiFi device as an extension of the wired router to permit use of laptops anywhere in the office.

The bad news was that the simple and attractive step-by-step CD-ROM supplied with the Belkin router did not address this possibility. The good news was that Belkin's customer support desk was very good about guiding me through the manual configuration of the router as an *access point* branching off the wired router. To make the settings, I had to temporarily attach the Belkin router directly to a computer in my office and make changes to the Setup screen using a Web browser.

This is an example of the value of investigating the customer support offerings of a company *before* you make a purchase. Call the company or consult its online facilities. Ask questions about the installation; if they won't help you before you own their product, will they likely be of assistance after they've got your money? (If you make your purchases from a retail store, do the same sort of investigation: Find out what sort of technical support you can expect from the seller.)

Once the router was configured, I had to find the best location for the device. In general, a WiFi antenna should be as close as possible to the center of the set of devices that will use it. There is no point in broadcasting your signal out the window toward your neighbor — unless you are planning to make your network available across the property line. Avoid obstacles and interference, including large metal objects like filing cabinets and appliances.

Whenever possible, avoid placing a wireless router near a 2.4-GHz cordless phone. And in any case, use the configuration panel on the router and any switches on the phone to have them use widely separated channels: Belkin recommended setting its router at 11 and any phone at 1. If you live in an apartment building or near another home with its own wireless system, you may need to experiment with various channel pairs to avoid interference.

Finally, don't forget to enable security on your WiFi system to prevent unauthorized eavesdroppers from using your network. It's not just an issue of blocking freeloaders; you also don't want to allow unauthorized persons to read your e-mail, monitor your Web browsing, or break into the files on machines that are connected to the router by a wireless or wired link.

You must perform several steps to establish a proper level of security for a wireless device. The first step is to create your own *SSID (Service Set Identifier),* which is the name of the router-managed network. Most manufacturers ship their device with a default name, which can lead to confusion and security lapses: If you leave your laptop's WiFi transceiver on as you travel, you're sure to find any number of SSIDs called Linksys, Belkin, D-Link, or another hardware maker.

Make the SSID your own, but don't make it too obvious. Give it a name with personal meaning but not one that would be obvious to a casual eavesdropper. On most routers, you change the SSID by visiting the device's internal Setup screen. You can provide an additional level of security by turning off broadcasting of the SSID. Your *wireless access point (WAP)* will broadcast its SSID by default, so roaming users can find it. If you turn off broadcasting and change the name, it is unlikely that neighbors or potential hackers will find your wireless system.

The next step is to enable one of the various encryption and security standards including the current *WiFi Protected Access (WPA)* standards and the older, less-capable *Wired Equivalent Privacy (WEP).* By default, most wireless routers come with security disabled; don't let it be.

For most home and small office users, the WPA2 security standard is capable of protecting your network and the attached machines when it is used in conjunction with an antivirus program. WPA2 is supported by Windows XP in Service Pack 2 and in Windows Vista. If you are running a system with a different operating system, you may need to obtain a patch to add WPA2 capability or use a different encryption and security standard.

NOTE

If you are running Windows XP without Service Pack 2 installed, you can get a patch from Microsoft that adds WPA2. Visit http://support.microsoft.com/?kbid=826942 for the free update. Better yet, upgrade your operating system with the full suite of tools included in Windows XP Service Pack 2.

You'll need to add a password (for some reason called a *passphrase* on WiFi setup screens.) You can choose between 64-bit or 128-bit codes; unless you have a particular concern about hackers within a few hundred feet of your home or office, 64-bit codes is probably sufficient. One nice thing about 64-bit codes: They are ten digits or letters in length. That happens to coincide with the size of an American or Canadian telephone number (without the preceding 1). Do not use your home or office phone number, but I don't see anything wrong in using a phone number that has some meaning to you but cannot be directly traced to your name. For example, use the phone number of a distant relative or friend, or use the phone number for a business you deal with but that would not be obvious to a hacker.

More secure 128-bit numbers require 26 digits, which is more than I can easily remember.

Bluetooth wireless

At one point, proponents of another wireless standard called Bluetooth claimed that it would be their technology, not 802.11, that would take over the workplace and home. Bluetooth was developed in 1994 at Ericsson labs, where researchers were working on new cell phone technologies. Several years later, an Intel technician and amateur historian gave the standard its unusual name in remembrance of Harald Bluetooth, a Scandinavian king who brought together the two warring communities of Denmark and Norway in the tenth century. The technology has been championed by companies in that region, including Ericsson and Nokia, as well as other manufacturers.

Bluetooth — which operates in the same 2.4-GHz band that is used by 802.11 in its b and g flavors — requires less power than WiFi equivalents. It has not been widely adopted in homes and offices to connect PCs, but it has found a use in small, battery-powered devices, such as cell phones and PDAs. The wireless headsets favored by many cell phone users communicate to the phone with Bluetooth, and you can use a Bluetooth link to sync a Blackberry or Motorola Q with your laptop email and calendar. The maximum distance between a Bluetooth device and an access point is 30 feet.

The 2.4-GHz band is considered an industrial, scientific, and medical band, open to unlicensed devices for short-range communication. Other devices in that band include garage door openers, recent cordless phones, and baby monitors. Bluetooth employs several high-tech solutions to attempt to avoid interference, including frequency hopping. It is possible for both WiFi and Bluetooth to coexist in the same environment.

In a Bluetooth world, computers would meet and greet cell phones and PDAs as their owners entered a room; laptops and handhelds could surf the Web in airports, hotel lobbies, and meeting rooms; and eventually nearly every consumer appliance — microwaves, refrigerators, and televisions, to name a few — could communicate with other devices about needs and wants.

The market, though, responded with a very cautious wait-and-see attitude. In its first version, the technology proved prone to interference and incompatibility; that problem has been mostly fixed, although like any 2.4-GHz device, it can suffer from problems caused by microwave ovens and other consumer devices. Microsoft chose to have it both ways, at least at first, backing both Bluetooth and WiFi, but then supporting only WiFi in Windows XP.

Today, there are a number of Bluetooth keyboards and pointing devices, and some portable music players and cell phones can connect to a Bluetooth receiver on a computer to upload or download settings, information, and data.

Future tech: Wireless USB

The next great thing, for some users, may be the arrival of Wireless USB (WUSB). Though not technically a network, I've included it in this section because it shares many of the same facilities as WiFi.

WUSB is expected to initially allow use of peripherals including hard disk drives, CD/DVD drives, modems, printers, digital cameras, LCD projectors, and just about any other device at speeds of about

480 Mbps, which is comparable to real-world throughput on wired USB 2.0. Plans are already underway for doubling WUSB to at least 1 Gbps by about 2010.

WUSB will be logically organized as a hub-and-spoke topology with devices communicating with a central host. As with wired USB, the host will theoretically be able to connect to as many as 127 devices. Since the devices will not be physically connected to a computer or a USB hub, each will have its own power source, which lessens the electrical draw on computers and allows for more robust devices, such as wireless printers. WUSB will use a technology called Ultra Wideband radio. Devices should be able to communicate at distances of about 10 meters (39 feet) within a home or office.

The first systems will likely be offered in the form of adapter cards that install within a PC or boxes that attach to a wired USB port on a computer. Some or all future motherboards will likely offer wireless USB as a standard feature.

Internet Security

As I have noted, cable modem and DSL connections are especially vulnerable to attacks because they are connected to the Internet anytime they are turned on; they receive an IP (Internet Protocol) address from the service provider and hold on to that address for as long as they are powered on and connected to the cable or telephone line. In addition, in most cases, that IP address is assigned from a particular range that belongs to major ISPs, making it that much easier for a malevolent hacker to troll through a group of addresses in search of an open door. And the high bandwidth of a cable or DSL mode — the capacity behind the term broadband — makes it easier for some hackers to pump a huge amount of code through an open machine in a very short period of time.

By contrast, a dial-up telephone connection to the Internet is usually transitory, existing only for the length of a session and using a new IP address each time.

Many broadband connections attach to a computer through an Ethernet connection. Further, many broadband links are shared over a network. For that reason, I'll deal with Internet security here as a network issue.

About TCP/IP ports

To understand a bit about the security vulnerability of a PC connected to the Internet, it's worthwhile to learn about the "ports" that a computer opens to the world under the TCP/IP scheme. There are thousands of possible open doors to your computer; the first thing a security program or a firewall does is close as many as possible and restrict access to those that remain open or accessible.

For example, to connect as a client to an e-mail application running on a remote server your computer connects to the port associated with the Simple Mail Transfer Protocol (SMTP), typically assigned to port 25. Similarly, the Hypertext Transfer Protocol (HTTP), the key to the World Wide Web, uses TCP port 80. A list of some of the most common assigned TCP ports is in Table 20-3.

TABLE 20-3: Common TCP/IP Services with Assigned Port Numbers	
PING (also called ECHO)	7
FTP	20 and 21
Telnet	23
HTTP (World Wide Web)	80
SMTP (E-mail)	25
Windows file and print sharing	137–139
Registered ports	1024–49151
Dynamic or private ports	49152–65535

When a computer opens a port, it monitors that location for appropriately addressed packets; a packet arriving at port 25, for example, is sent to the computer's e-mail application.

A hacker looks for open ports. In addition to doorways for the Web and e-mail, one of the most commonly attacked ports on client computers is 137, used by Windows for file and print sharing over a local area network (LAN). Microsoft — the creator of this vulnerability — and many security experts recommend that sharing be disabled on the Internet connection of any computer directly connected to the Internet. Of course, that could disrupt the facilities of a LAN; in practice, a hardware firewall should provide sufficient protection from intrusion, especially in combination with a software equivalent.

Other areas of particular danger include open FTP ports, personal Web sites, and remote-access programs, such as pcAnywhere.

Some virus programs, including so-called Trojan horse programs, sneak into machines as attachments to e-mail or downloaded programs; some of these programs open a port to the Internet without the user's knowledge.

I recommend that you check the status of your computer's ports — and their ability to hide behind a hardware or software firewall — by visiting a port-checking site. One such site is Shields Up at www.grc.com, operated by longtime utility programmer Steve Gibson and Gibson Research Corporation.

Internet firewalls

A firewall is intended to stop the spread of damage. Cars have a firewall between the engine and the interior of the passenger cabin. Big buildings and cruise ships have them in strategic locations.

In personal computer terms, a firewall is a barrier against intrusion and leakage by outsiders trying to gain access to your data or cause mischief on your system.

Every Internet user, especially those using broadband connections, such as cable modems and DSL links, needs to pay attention to security. Broadband links are usually on all the time, making them especially attractive targets for malevolent snoops trolling the Internet.

The Internet is a fast-moving stream of billions of small snippets of information, called packets. When your PC is connected, it is sticking an electronic toe into the stream looking for packets that are addressed to you. Going the other way, when you click an Internet link or send a page of information, your machine is creating a packet with your return address and a recipient.

Hackers and snoops let loose on the Internet packets that are like skeleton keys, jiggling the doors of millions of PCs until they find one they can open. The odds of one of these packets breaking into a specific machine in this way are very low; however, the fact that so many millions of machines are connected to the Internet makes it likely that sooner or later some machine somewhere is going to be attacked.

A firewall works by standing between your computer and the Internet, examining every data packet sent to or from your PC. Based on a set of criteria established by the manufacturer and updated and adjusted by the user, the firewall decides whether to block a packet or let it pass.

The most common type of device is called an application gateway firewall, also known as a *proxy*. The rules for the firewall can be set to check packets against a particular list of addresses or to set specific limits on the actions of particular applications. For example, the proxy could block downloads or prevent a packet from initiating a deletion or change of a file.

Other firewall designs include *packet filters*, which only allow entrance to packets from specified addresses, and *circuit-level* firewalls that only permit communication with specific computers and Internet service providers.

The newest and most advanced design is stateful inspection firewalls; these devices actually read the contents of packets and block those that are determined to be harmful or an unauthorized threat to privacy.

Software firewalls

A slightly less expensive alternative is a software-based personal firewall.

These programs run within your PC, so they are much closer to your data than is an external hardware firewall. But a properly designed and maintained software firewall is able to monitor against intrusion attempts and block most assaults. It can also provide security settings that protect your private information.

I worked with Norton Internet Security from Symantec (www.symantec.com), which includes a firewall, antivirus software, and other utilities including the ability to block or control pop-up ads and cookies. Other well-regarded utilities are BlackIce Defender from Internet Security Systems (www.networkice.com), ZoneAlarm from Zone Labs (www.zonelabs.com), and McAfee.com Personal Firewall (www.mcafee.com).

How a firewall works

The two most common designs for software firewalls are *packet-filtering routers* and *proxy servers*.

Packet filters exist at the network level of the seven-layer Open System Interconnection (OSI) model or the equivalent IP level of the TCP/IP model. They work by examining the source and destination addresses and ports in individual IP packets and comparing them against known threats and suspected sources. They work quickly and do not affect network performance greatly.

Proxy servers offer a higher level of security, monitoring Internet traffic at the highest, application level of the OSI or TCP/IP model. Users can specify which applications can access the Internet, and which types of incoming packets can get past the firewall. The price for the extra safety is a more significant effect on network performance.

Firewalls also set up machines to block intrusions at specific ports unless you allow them; for example, port 7 would otherwise respond to "pinging" by port scanners in search of open ports. A ping utility sends a packet to a particular address and measures the time it takes for a reply from that site to arrive; the name comes from a utility called Packet Internet Groper.

Hardware firewalls often use a technique called Network Address Translation (NAT), acting as a physical gateway between the Internet and a local area network. The entire LAN appears as a single IP address on the Internet; on the network side, each client PC receives its own private IP address, and that information is not available to the Internet. Intruders cannot find open ports on attached computers because the Internet appears to end at the gateway.

An expansion of NAT is called *stateful* port inspection; in this design the firewall also examines all inbound packets to make sure that they match the source of an earlier outbound request. Inbound traffic from the Internet is only allowed to the computers on the network when the firewall finds a matching entry in its internal records that shows that the communication exchange began on your side of the firewall.

Yet another firewall design is a piece of software that makes the PC emulate a hardware gateway, acting as a "proxy" for a computer. Examples of this include WinProxy. Microsoft Windows 98SE, Windows 2000, Windows Me, and Windows XP allow Internet Connection Sharing, a form of proxy software. Experts recommend the addition of a software firewall to proxy software to fully protect the system.

Windows XP includes a basic personal firewall called Internet Connection Firewall (ICF). The built-in firewall is intended to work in conjunction with Internet Connection Sharing (ICS), a software component of current versions of Windows that allows multiple PCs to work with a single Internet connection. Microsoft recommends enabling ICF on the Internet connection of any computer directly connected to the Internet. ICF should not be enabled on other computers on the network because it will interfere with some network functions; the other computers will be protected by the firewall on the PC with

the direct connection. The built-in Windows XP firewall is shown in Figure 20-10; you can also add more extensive protection from third-party software makers.

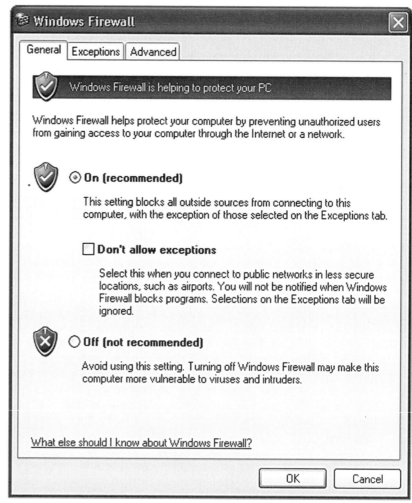

FIGURE 20-10: *The Setup screen for the built-in firewall provided with Windows XP; Windows Vista has a more extensive facility, and you can also extend either operating system with programs from other companies.*

ICF can also be enabled on a single computer connected to the Internet through a dial-up, DSL, or cable modem; however, it should not be used on a virtual private network because it will interfere with file sharing. As a stateful firewall, it will block any incoming traffic that was not initiated by one of the computers on your network; you can allow specific inbound traffic by making an entry in the Services tab.

And ICF is not needed and can cause some problems if your network already has a hardware or software firewall or a proxy server in place.

WARNING

If you have a network in which computers share an Internet connection but also have the ability to make a direct dial-up connection using a modem, you should enable ICF for the dial-up connection. If you don't, your entire network will be vulnerable through that unprotected connection.

A belt-and-suspenders solution

On my office network, eight PCs are connected to the Internet through a cable modem.

When I first installed the cable modem, I experimented by having just a single PC connected to the broadband link. On that machine, I installed Norton Internet Security as a software firewall.

The good news is that my machine was never successfully violated, and my personal data did not leak out on the Internet without my permission.

The bad news was the discovery that my system was under regular attack. The firewall reported an average of three attempts at breaking into my machine each day.

The next step was the installation of a Linksys EtherFast 8-port Cable/DSL Router. This device combines an eight-port Ethernet switch to bring together the PCs in my office with a hardware firewall.

I kept the Norton Internet Security in place on the machine at the hub of the network. With both hardware and software firewalls in place, the software firewall has not reported a single attempted intrusion.

Does this mean that you can get by with either a software or a hardware firewall? Probably. If I had to choose between the two, I would take the hardware device because it sits physically outside of my computer rather than on the hard drive within. But being a cautious user, I'm very happy with my inside-and-out, belt-and-suspenders solution. The Linksys hardware device stands guard between the cable modem and my PC, while the Norton Internet Security software sits between Windows and the Internet, receiving regular updates from the Symantec web site.

SUMMARY

In this chapter, you learned about networks, gateways, and routers. In the next chapter, I explore the rules of backing up regularly.

Ch
20

Chapter 21

Backup Strategies

When it comes to the safety of the data on my machine, I choose to adopt a belt-and-suspenders philosophy. They may not make for the most stylish wardrobe, but your pants won't ever fall down — and your computer data will never completely disappear.

My goal in computer life is to strive toward a fail-safe world where a hardware failure, a software error, or a slip of the fingers at the keyboard is a mere annoyance and not a job-threatening disaster.

Remember that if you're lucky, your hard drive will have a full, healthy, and productive life. And then it will die. It may be tomorrow, or it may be in 10 years, but it will fail. It's up to you to be prepared for the hereafter.

In this chapter, I explore the best methods for protecting your data before a problem occurs, and some utilities to recover data from a system that has failed.

CROSS-REFERENCE

In Chapter 11, I discuss some of the hardware devices that can be employed for backup.

A Basic Data Protection Strategy

To protect your data, follow these steps:

1. Make backups of essential data onto removable media, such as CDs, DVDs, Zip disks, tapes. Or, make copies on an external hard disk drive or leave copies on a secure hard disk you access across a local area network or over the Internet.
2. Install and keep current a disk diagnostic and maintenance utility.
3. Run defragmenting and surface analyzer utilities regularly.
4. Enable the Windows Recycle Bin (or an enhanced version of the recycle bin offered by third-party utility makers) to allow you to undelete files that were mistakenly trashed.
5. Conduct regular tests of your backup data on the original machine and on another machine.
6. Perform Step 1 regularly.

You can prevent most data loss with good backup habits. If you keep copies of your data that are only a few hours old, the worst thing that can happen if the computer or one of its disk drives fails is the loss of a few hours' worth of work. I describe the three levels of backup in the following sections.

Current document backup

The first level is current document backup, a feature common to many advanced application programs.

This book was written using Microsoft Word. In all current versions of that program — and most other major word processors — you can instruct the application to make backups of your files as you work on them. In the latest version of Word, the facility is called AutoRecover. Other programs refer to the same sort of function as Automatic Save or Timed Document Backup.

In my office, I ask Word to update its temporary backup file every five minutes. So if Word, Windows, the operating system, or a piece of hardware causes the PC to lock up, I have a copy of the file that is no more than roughly 3 minutes and 59 seconds old and usually younger. In Word, you enable AutoRecover from the Options menu, selecting the Save tab. The Microsoft Word Options menu is shown in Figure 21-1.

A current document backup, however, does not protect against the failure of the storage media. If the hard drive fails, you may lose any work since the last time a copy was stored on different media.

Version backup

The second type of backup is version backup.

Microsoft Word has an option called Always Create Backup Copy, and other programs have similar facilities. With this option enabled, any time you save a file, the program makes a copy of the previous version of the file. (The standard filename for the backup under Word is `Backup of {filename}.wbk`.) If you decide that the changes or additions you have made to the current version are not what you want to keep, you can revert to the previous version.

Again, version backup does not protect against the failure of the storage media. If the hard drive fails, you may lose any work since the last time a copy was stored on different media.

Ch 21

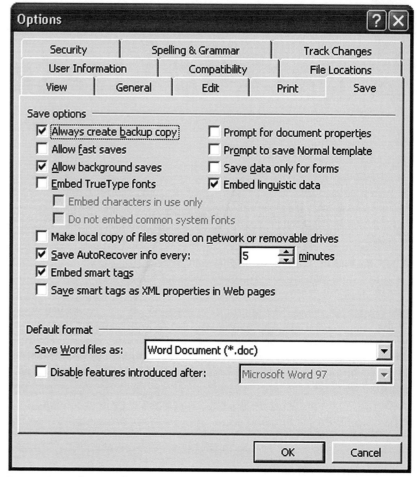

FIGURE 21-1: *The Word Save tab includes several important settings that can guard against the loss of a file because of a momentary electrical failure or system lockup. I recommend enabling Always Create Backup Copy and setting Save AutoRecover Info to a short interval of three to five minutes. The backup copy saves the previous version of the file any time you issue the Save command; the AutoRecover feature makes temporary copies of work in progress between Save commands.*

Deep storage backups

The third type of backup is what I call "deep storage." These are copies of all your important data files that you maintain on some sort of removable media and keep on a shelf, in a fireproof safe, or in a safe deposit box inside a bank's fireproof vault. Another way to make this sort of copy is to use an external hard drive, or to use a hard disk you reach across a local area network or over the Internet.

Deep storage guards against the failure of the hard drive in the original machine, and depending on the situation, protects against the theft of the machine. (If you're using an external hard drive, you can unplug the drive and lock it up each night.)

Removable media include floppy disks (or their current common substitute, a USB flash memory key) for individual files, high-capacity Zip or Rev drives, tape backups, and recordable CDs or DVDs.

What files should be backed up?

Concentrate on the data. Everything else can be reconstructed, and a good renovation may be healthy for your system every once in a while.

Here's what I include in my data backups:

- Every data file from my applications, including those from the word processor, spreadsheet, personal finance, and the calendar and address book from my personal data assistant
- Personalized dictionaries and customized Windows desktop and sound themes
- All of the downloaded image files from my digital camera
- Copies of e-mails sent and received
- The address book from my e-mail program

Beyond the data, your operating system also contains hundreds of settings for appearance and actions. Your Internet browser and e-mail program are also customized for appearance, security and privacy, subscriptions, and accounts. If you're a heavy user of the Internet, you may have dozens or even hundreds of favorites grouped and stored for easy access. All of this information can be copied to backup storage for retrieval in case of a hardware failure.

Although you can choose to make a full-mirrored backup of your entire hard drive, including the operating system and applications, you should know some good reasons not to do so. To begin with, you may have difficulty reinstalling an image back to a new or reformatted hard drive. Also, if your operating system or one of its applications was the cause of your system crash — because of a corrupted file or a virus, for example — reinstalling a mirror of the hard drive will simply give you a new copy of the original problem.

A much better plan of action is this: Set up a safe and secure storage place for original installation CDs or diskettes for your Windows operating system and all applications and device drivers. Keep a notebook nearby in which you list every program, update, and upgrade that you make to your system. If you download a program or a driver over the Internet, make a copy of the pre-installation file and store it with your other originals.

Making deep-storage backups of valuable data presents a logical and procedural dilemma for most users. The whole goal is to make copies that are as current as possible and yet are physically separated from your main computer so that a failure (or theft) does not take away irreplaceable information.

How Should You Back Up?

How often is enough? Answer this question immediately after your hard drive dies.

Every user can come up with his or her best answer. Some users make a backup an unvarying assignment at the end of every day: In my office, I perform backups each night before I straggle out of the office, and I have been known to do an extra backup in the middle of the day any time I've been working on an especially important project.

If I suspect that my machine is tottering on the edge of collapse, I make more frequent backups. Similarly, if Windows is going through one of its occasional hiccups where it crashes regularly, I step up the pace for backups.

Over the course of two decades of personal computing, I've used half a dozen different backup devices — beginning with a stack of floppy disks, moving on to a few designs of removable platter hard drives, a tape drive, and most recently, a combination of a recordable CD/DVD drive and a large external hard drive.

Ch 21

Floppy disk backups

Once upon a time, floppy disks were a viable option for backups, back when an IBM PC-AT came equipped with a 20MB hard drive. The entire disk could be backed up to a stack of about 15 floppies.

Today, though, it is ridiculous to consider storing the contents of a 20GB hard drive on a set of 15,000 or so disks.

However, some users use floppy disks to make copies of individual files they worked on over the course of a day to serve as a short-term repository between full backups. The downside: Files can't be larger than 1.44MB (or about 2.8MB if you use a disk-doubling utility). Also, floppy disks are fragile and easily misplaced, which can be a threat to the security of your files.

USB memory key backups

Flash memory keys, which encase a block of non-volatile RAM in a package about the size of a stick of gum, have become a very useful device to store files on a short-term basis or as one quick, easy way to make a copy of a file on a machine that is not linked to your main PC by a local area network or the Internet.

As this book goes to press, flash memory keys are available with capacities of as much as 8GB, with larger blocks of memory on the horizon. As with other computer products, prices have tumbled as size and speed have improved; as this book went to press, 2GB flash memory keys were available for as little as $50 and devices with 8GB (four times as large) sold for double that price, or about $100. (But as I have mentioned, select low-priced, high-capacity flash drives carefully, as there have been a spate of professional-looking fake drives on the market that turn out to hold 100MB or less.)

Among the many beauties of the flash memory key is the ability to quickly store and transport a huge amount of information in a device that slips easily into your pocket or briefcase; for example, the entire text and art for this book could fit on a 2GB block of memory. Of course, this makes some businesses and government installations very nervous; in some situations, IT departments disable USB ports or modify the operating system to prevent use of USB flash keys to prevent inadvertent or intentional removal of sensitive information.

Removable storage backups

Removable storage media, including recordable CDs or DVDs, are excellent ways to create backups of your files. In large business and institutional settings, tape backups are used to make copies of huge amounts of data, often reflecting all transactions from start to completion of an order or a job.

> **CROSS-REFERENCE**
>
> I discuss many of the available storage devices in Chapter 11.

As previously discussed, most users don't need to store the entire contents of a drive in backup. Also, very few users will ever create more than a gigabyte or two per day. In fact, unless you're working with graphics, video, or audio files, the chances are your daily output of new and changed files is only a few tens of megabytes or less.

With today's large hard drives I consider a CD-R as the smallest reasonable size for a backup device. Recordable CDs can store as much as 800MB of data per disk, and they offer a reasonable recording speed. DVD-Rs can store as much as 4.7GB and have become very attractive for backup purposes as the price of the drives and media have come very close to that of a CD-R. Recordable CDs and DVDs are not reusable, but they are inexpensive, thus allowing users to maintain an archive of the day-by-day or week-by-week status of their files. Rewritable CDs and DVDs are a bit more expensive, but still worthy of consideration.

Another easy-to-use backup device is an external hard drive. Modern machines can connect to these standalone drives through a USB, FireWire, or eSATA port or over an Ethernet network. The drives can remain in place atop the PC, or they can be disconnected and stored in a fireproof safe, in a briefcase that you take with you, or anywhere else away from the machine that they back up. I use a couple of Ethernet-based hard drives for backup by installing them in different locations (one even in a different building in a locked closet) and making regular copies of data to them. The beauty of this scheme is these drives don't need a PC, and they are small, relatively inexpensive, remain out of the way, and are always available.

For huge hard drives and commercial operations where it is important to maintain a continuous stream of transaction-by-transaction changes to a database, the solution often involves tape drives, capable of storing hundreds of gigabytes of data. Tape drives, however, are slow and data is not stored in a random-access form; the tape must be fast-forwarded or rewound to particular locations to yield a particular block. In addition, different tape backup designs use different storage technology; that technology usually requires proprietary software to store and retrieve data. It is important with any backup to practice restoring the data periodically, but with tape systems this admonition is especially important.

A Real-Life Backup Policy

Analyze the patterns of work in your own office to see what scheme makes the most sense for you. In my office, my backup procedure in 2007 works like this:

- **Daily.** As I write them, all files are backed up elsewhere on the hard drive every five minutes by Microsoft Word. At the end of each day, I use a CD-R to burn a disc that contains the folders for the projects I worked on that day.
- **Every other day.** I make a copy of the changed files from the My Documents folder of my machine on a large external USB 2.0 hard drive.
- **Every Friday.** I send a complete image of the My Documents folder across my office Ethernet to an external hard drive on a file server machine.
- **On the last business day of the month.** I make a fresh DVD copy of all of the data files I have created or modified in the past month. I place that DVD in a fireproof safe in another room of my office.

WARNING

Remember that backup media will eventually fail, just like any floppy disk or hard drive. Plan on retiring backup tapes or removable disks at least once a year. Most recordable CDs and DVDs are expected to have a shelf life of five to ten years.

I routinely practice one special backup task: If I am going to be out of the office on a long trip, I create a CD or DVD with a complete image of my document subdirectory on a CD-ROM and throw it in my briefcase. This is a protection against a catastrophe while I am away and a most valuable emergency disk in case I absolutely must get into one of my files while I am on the road. Sometimes I also copy active files to my laptop computer for the same reason.

Backup Utilities

If you are careful and consistent in organizing your hard drive and understand the types of files in your system, it is possible to manually identify files to be backed up by using the facilities of Windows Explorer.

However, the Windows operating system offers some niceties that allow you to make automated, selective backups. The operating system can distinguish between new files and those that have already been archived (backed up). This allows you to make incremental backups that make copies of just those files that are not already in storage.

You can also purchase third-party backup programs that include many customizable settings and advanced features.

Windows XP Backup Utility

The ever-engulfing Microsoft maw added a file backup program to Windows 95/98, adding new features in later versions, including Windows XP and Windows Vista.

As delivered in Windows XP, the Backup Utility can copy the entire contents of your hard disk or specific files; as part of a program of regular backups, it can also manage the archiving of just those files that have been changed since the last backup operation was performed.

As is the case with most of the utilities that have been added to Windows over the years, Backup performs well and reliably but lacks some of the features and polish of third-party equivalents.

To start Backup, go to the Start menu and point to Programs, then Accessories, and then System Tools. Then click on Backup.

Note that Backup is not automatically a part of Windows 98 or Windows XP Home Edition; if the utility is not listed in System Tools, you'll have to add it from the Windows installation disk. Under Windows XP Professional, you must sign in as an administrator or backup operator to perform backup tasks.

The Windows XP version includes an option to back up all data plus the System State, which includes essential configuration information in the registry and the Active Directory database, if used. (System State can be backed only on a local computer, and not on a remote device.)

Windows XP and 2000 users also need to note that although it is possible to back up and restore data on FAT16, FAT32, or NTFS volumes, if your original data is held on an NTFS volume, it is possible to lose data and some file and folder features if the backup file is later restored to FAT16 or FAT32.

By default, Backup files are given the filename extension of .bkf, although you can choose any extension.

Windows Vista Backup

The enhanced Windows Backup included with Vista adds more choices for location of backup files, including CD or DVD drives, an external hard disk drive attached through a USB or FireWire port, another hard disk within your computer, or another PC or server connected to your network.

Vista includes the ability to schedule backups, based on settings you choose with a simple wizard. Restoring from backup files also begins by the invoking of a wizard. The Previous Version feature allows you to recover a file accidentally lost or changed. This component automatically creates time-stamped copies of files as you work and any version saved can be restored.

Third-party backup utilities

You may find some specialized backup products more convenient than Microsoft's offerings. Many of these programs use compression and speed-up routines.

Many hardware vendors offer a backup utility along with removable drive devices. For example, Iomega includes a set of Windows utilities with the company's Zip drives.

Norton Ghost from Symantec provides high-performance utilities for system upgrading, backup, and recovery. It writes disk images directly to many popular CD-R/CD-RW drives. Facilities include fast PC-to-PC cloning by using high-speed parallel, USB, or network connections.

You can add files to previously created images, thus eliminating the need to reclone the entire disk to back up new contents. The program can automatically size destination partitions to help streamline the cloning process. Norton Ghost is sold as a standalone product and is also included as a component of the Norton SystemWorks suite. For more information, consult www.symantec.com.

Another Norton product is intended for more selective backup of files in a small business or home office setting. Norton Save & Restore includes most of the features of Norton Ghost, adding tools more suited to non-technical users.

Backing Up Outlook Express E-mail Files

For many users, your e-mail correspondence makes up an important part of your business or personal life. Ask yourself this question: Would it be a problem if one day you turned on your machine and all of the mail you have received and sent for the past year or so had disappeared?

It's good practice to make backup copies of your e-mail files on a regular basis, so in case of disaster you can reconstruct them. And when you upgrade to a new computer or a new hard drive, you can also bring your old e-mail files with you.

Windows XP and Windows Vista include a Files and Settings Transfer Wizard that will bring over e-mail as well as preferences and settings for your Internet connection and other applications. You can also purchase utility programs from third parties that will do the same for earlier versions of Windows.

Your e-mail files are stored in special file formats, stored away in a less-than-obvious location on your hard drive.

Here are the steps to back up your e-mail in Outlook Express; other mail programs are organized similarly.

1. Minimize or close all applications.
2. Right-click an empty section of the desktop, and select New and then click Folder.
3. Right-click the new folder and select Rename; type a name for the folder, such as **OE_BACKUP**.
4. Open Outlook Express and click the Inbox that you want to back up.

5. Click Edit and then Select All; all mail in the box should be highlighted.
6. Right-click the selected e-mail and drag it into the new folder on your desktop; release the mouse button and click Copy Here.

To back up your Address Book from Outlook Express:

1. Minimize or close all applications.
2. Right-click an empty section of the desktop, and select New and then click Folder.
3. Right-click the new folder and select Rename; type a name for the folder, such as **OE_ADDRESS**.
4. Open Outlook Express and click Address on the toolbar.
5. Click one of the Addresses in the Address Book to highlight it, and then click Edit and Select All to highlight all of the contacts.
6. Right-click the highlighted items and select Copy.
7. Double-click the new folder to open it; right-click anywhere inside the folder and select Paste.

Testing Your Backups

I know from personal experience that a good backup policy carried out according to plan is only part of what you need to help ensure against data loss. I know of at least two fairly large companies who learned this lesson the hard way. One particular company was storing many gigabytes of company and customer data in a RAID assembly across multiple computers and hard drives. The RAID configuration by itself should have been enough to ensure against losing any data. After all, the information was automatically mirrored across multiple computers on the network, using multiple disk drives. Even so, this company conducted daily, automatic backup to high-capacity streaming tape. The backup tapes were removed from the office each morning and a full weekly set was stored onsite, as well as at a remote location.

Foolproof, right?

Wrong!

Something went wrong with the RAID system one day and the data couldn't be recovered. No one was particularly worried. A new, high-speed computer was positioned on the network, a very large capacity hard drive was installed, and the current backup tape (only hours old) was put in the tape drive. After a full day's work and despite receiving help from the manufacturers of the tape drive, the backup software, and the computer, this company's backup files could not be restored. Though employees had religiously made backups, they had never tried to restore files from them. The tapes were useless.

The lesson: You should regularly take one of your backup disks or tapes and restore the data to a hard drive that you aren't using for live data, an extra drive on the network, or a spare drive or directory on your primary computer. If you can restore and read the data satisfactorily, then your backup plan really is complete. Otherwise, you need to find out what is causing problems and fix it before you really need this backup information.

SUMMARY

This chapter discussed ways to protect and recover your data. After making copies to protect against disaster, the careful computer user does everything possible to guard against them ever being needed. In the next chapter, I explore some capable electronic physician's assistants that give your system a checkup and help repair small problems before they become major headaches.

Ch
21

Chapter 22

In This Chapter:

- The Modern Plague: Viruses and Worms
- Diagnostic Utilities
- Diagnostic and Data Recovery Utilities
- Disk Analyzers
- Defragmenting Utilities

Antivirus, Utility, and Diagnostic Programs

Alas, there always seems to be someone who is determined to draw graffiti on the wall, vandalize mailboxes, or commit more serious crimes against public or private property. In most cases, they seem to perform these acts out of boredom . . . and because they can. So, too, it is with the authors of various forms of what has become known as *malware:* computer viruses, worms, unwanted adware, and phishing attacks.

It's all very unfortunate, and as a computer user you should constantly be on the lookout for assaults on your machine and the information contained on it. Even if you manage to avoid having your personal details stolen, any of these types of programs can degrade your computer's performance and cause problems with legitimate software and operating system components.

The bottom line: Never connect to the Internet or load a file or program onto your system without having a capable and current antivirus program in place, and consider expanding the scope of your protection to include utilities that seek out and remove adware and spyware.

NOTE

In those rare instances where you need to disable the antivirus program—during installation of certain other software, or updates of the security program itself—scan your system afterwards to assure that nothing nasty snuck in when the door was open. Some security programs even allow you to set a timer so that the antivirus component automatically re-enables itself after a period of time if you manage to forget to turn it back on yourself.

Despite all of our best efforts, sooner or later many computers become infected and damaged by malware, or hurt by inadvertent mishaps including power spikes, controller errors, and conflicts amongst legitimate programs. When the ship's doctor of a Federation starship needs to find out what's going on inside an injured or ill Star Trek crewmember, he or she waves a tricorder over the patient's body. When you're on your own trek to figure out what ails your PC, the best thing you've got is a good diagnostic program.

When it comes time to fix whatever the diagnostic has found, the best tool may be a specialized utility program.

This chapter examines the various types of diagnostic programs available, plus configuration utilities used to prevent hardware conflicts when you are installing new boards. In the next chapter of this book, I explore some of the very useful utilities that are part of current editions of Windows.

The Modern Plague: Viruses, Worms, Adware, Spyware, and Phishers

A *virus* is a self-replicating piece of computer code that can attach itself to files or applications with the intent of making your computer do something that you don't want it to do.

A *worm* is a self-replicating program that insinuates itself into computers and out through network connections to infect any machine on the network, taking storage space and slowing down the computer but not altering or deleting other files.

And then there are those who seek to invade your computer for illegal — or legal — espionage purposes. Legitimate businesses may seek to place ads on your machine with or without your permission; that's called *adware.* Then there is *spyware,* which is software that gets onto your computer and then collects personal and financial information about you without your permission and sends it to a person or organization; at best, the information is used to target you for advertising, and at worst this could be a criminal enterprise seeking to steal your passwords and information and move on to stealing your money and identity.

Another form of nastiness is *phishing,* often delivered as e-mail or instant messages but sometimes contained within the body of a web page; phishers commit fraud by masquerading as a legitimate business or a person you know and try to trick you into revealing personal and financial details including bank account numbers, credit card numbers, login names, and passwords. In years past, this sort of unwanted gift was also called a *Trojan Horse.*

Whatever they are called, these malicious codes are sometimes annoyances and sometimes major disruptions to the way we run our businesses and our personal lives. Several times in the past few years a new virus has swept around the world, spread over the burgeoning links of the Internet. Thousands of other times, minor outbreaks have infected clusters of computers in offices or on networks.

You must understand two things to protect your machine and fix your PC when it becomes infected: how viruses spread, and how you can inoculate and doctor your machine.

Malicious code can enter a PC through almost any connection that it has to the outside: The most common ways are through an infected floppy disk, e-mail, or a downloaded file. A hacker coming in through an unprotected Internet connection can also plant an infection.

Viruses are generally classified into five major types:

- **Boot Sector Virus.** A piece of code that hides in the boot sector — the place on a hard drive or floppy disk that the operating system goes to first to boot up the machine. This sort of virus can make it impossible to boot the disk, or can damage the essential file attribute table that keeps track of the location of files on the drive. At one time this was the most prevalent form of virus and the most difficult to guard against; today, though, current operating systems are designed to inspect the boot sector before it is loaded and antivirus programs have been adapted to form a second line of defense against this sort of sneak attack.

- **File Virus.** Sometimes called a *parasitic virus,* this is a piece of code that attaches itself to executable applications. As such, it may lay dormant for a period of time before the infected program is run.
- **Macro Virus.** A simple but effective code that hides within a data file, including word processor and spreadsheet files, and modifies a common embedded command to do something else, usually malicious. A related form of malware is a *worm,* which is a piece of software that hitchhikes a ride within an otherwise legitimate file and uses it to make copies of itself wherever it can.
- **Multipartite Virus.** A hybrid code that infects executable files and the boot sector, allowing it to spread quickly and reinfect your system repeatedly. The code may come from an outside source, such as a file received over the Internet or an office network, and enter into computer memory; from there it seeks an opportunity to change the boot sector to suit its purposes. Modern antivirus programs include components that are constantly on the lookout for attempts to modify the boot sector, and operating systems are designed to inspect that section of the disk before it loads.
- **Polymorphic Virus.** A code that changes some of its elements each time it replicates in an attempt to defeat antivirus scanners.

Adding a security program

The good news is that capable antivirus software can detect nearly all types of known viruses and sniff out new ones as they are released into the wild, but it is absolutely essential that the software be updated regularly to keep it current. The products offered by the leading makers are each backed by a staff of programmers who are ready to react to any new outbreak of viruses or any change in the nature of malicious software; if your computer is connected to an always-on broadband Internet connection, the security program will automatically be updated on a regular or emergency basis.

NOTE

If your machine is only connected to the Internet occasionally, it's up to you to make sure that the utility seeks out and obtains updates. A machine that is not linked to the Internet or to an internal local area network by cable or wireless connection cannot "catch" a virus from those sources, but it is still at risk if you load a piece of infected software or a data file from a disk.

Even with antivirus software in place, you also need to practice safe computing. Your antivirus program should be set to scan all incoming e-mail. If you are adding a new program to your computer, use the antivirus scanner to check the program's safety before you install it, and make sure you never leave a floppy disk or other bootable external media in a device attached to your computer when you turn off the machine unless doing so is part of a legitimate installation or update process. Remember that, depending on the settings you made in the Setup or Configuration screen, the machine may look at devices other than the hard drive as the source of boot files; if the machine reads from a floppy or CD before it loads Windows, a virus can get into the PC before the antivirus program is running. Be very wary of any e-mail with attachments, especially if they are from people you don't know. Delete any suspect e-mails without opening them; send messages (or make a phone call) to people you know to confirm that they sent you a file and that they believe it to be virus free. (And make sure your antivirus software scans your e-mail anyway.)

Choosing antivirus and security software

Antivirus software generally works in two ways: by scanning for known viruses in search of signatures (identified blocks of code), and by employing heuristic intelligence that looks for virus-like activity by any program.

Either way, set up your software to automatically stop the progress of a virus or virus-like program and confirm with you whether you want to zap the bug or let the innocent program proceed. Any security program that includes an antivirus component is better than none at all. At least half a dozen companies offer products in this area. However, most experts (and this author) put their faith in two industry leaders: the Norton series of products sold by Symantec and the McAfee VirusScan line. Beginning in late 2006, both companies are also facing a strong challenge from Microsoft, which has launched its own online protection service.

(Some people argue that buying protective service from Microsoft is rewarding the maker of a faulty product; it is Microsoft, of course, that makes the Windows operating system that is the object of near-constant attack by virus and malware writers. However, in all fairness, I think Microsoft does try pretty hard to plug all of the many holes that virus writers seek to exploit. Windows is simply a very large and attractive target for miscreants.)

Here are some of the best programs intended for loading onto your system and run from there:

▪ **Norton Antivirus.** Available as a standalone product, or as part of a utilities suite such as Norton SystemWorks or Norton Internet Security. The package includes a one-year (renewable at a fee) subscription to an automatic updating service with the latest virus definitions, as well as protection for incoming and outgoing e-mail and a guard against malicious Internet scripts. The main control screen for Norton SystemWorks is shown in Figure 22-1, and the antivirus and spyware component of that program in Figure 22-2. An additional product, Norton Confidential, was introduced in 2006, adding security features to block fake web sites, authenticate popular banking and shopping web sites, and keep passwords encrypted on your site. For more information, consult www.symantec.com.

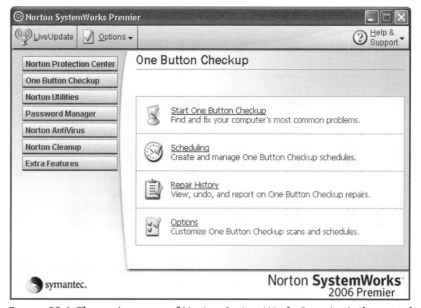

Figure 22-1: *The main screen of Norton SystemWorks Premier is the portal to antivirus, system security, and other utilities. The program's One Button Checkup scans the Windows registry for errors and checks on other system components and also serves as a reminder to download necessary updates and perform scans; the checkup can be scheduled to perform its task daily, weekly, or other intervals. A good practice is to have the checkup performed during lunch hour when you can hope to be away from your keyboard.*

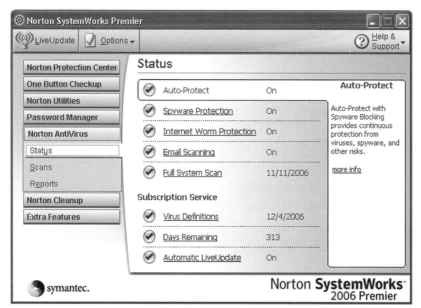

FIGURE 22-2: *A quick glance at the antivirus screen within Norton SystemWorks Premier tells the user the status of the program's various security components and also advises the dates of the last full system scan and when new virus definitions were most recently downloaded.*

- **McAfee VirusScan.** This capable antivirus program with a renewable annual subscription service also includes an integrated personal firewall. For more information, consult www.mcafeeathome.com/products/virusscan.
- **PC-cillin Internet Security 2006.** Another worthy competitor with claims of greater speed and smaller memory demands. For more information, consult www.trendmicro.com.

Most of the security suites also include protection against spyware and some will also help removed unwanted adware; if the product you have does not offer that level of protection you can add it with a standalone package. Among the best is:

- **Ad-Aware SE Personal.** This capable program sniffs out adware and spyware based on its own list of known programs and also looks for suspect snippets of code that behave in the same way. This is an after-the-fact cleanup tool; it does not monitor your

machine while you are out on the Internet like some of the more capable products from Symantec, McAfee, and Microsoft do, but it also sometimes finds snippets of code that sneak past the continuous monitoring product, as seen in Figure 22-3. There is a free personal version of the program as well as several levels of more advanced software sold for a reasonable charge. You can download Ad-Aware from www.lavasoftusa.com/software/adaware.

- **Spybot Search and Destroy.** Another adware and spyware detector, Spybot can be a good addition to Ad-Aware. Again, no single program can detect everything unscrupulous folk throw at your PC. I run both of these programs to help ensure against unwanted software lurkers. You can configure Spybot to run automatically to scan, find, and remove spyware programs on your system. Learn more and download your own copy of this utility at www.safer-networking.org.

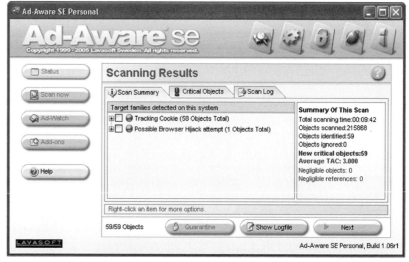

FIGURE 22-3: *A scan by Ad-Aware turned up a piece of software that was capable of attempting a browser hijack on one of the systems in my office; this is an attempt to redirect a Web command so that a page other than the one requested is displayed. This might be done to attempt to sell you something, or it might be done in hopes of fooling you into revealing personal or financial information to a would-be thief.*

An essential feature of any security program is regular updates with the latest response to viruses and other malware; if you buy a piece of software and merely install it, you are at great risk of falling victim to nasty work that is specifically designed to fool older antivirus programs. All of the major makers — including Symantec, Trend Micro, and McAfee — promise to be constantly on guard against new assaults and to update your software for as long as you hold a valid license. A one-year subscription is usually included with a new program and you can usually purchase additional years of coverage. Eventually, though, the basic engine of some security programs becomes too old for update and the maker discontinues updates; at that point you need to purchase a more current version.

If you have a broadband Internet connection, I recommend setting your security software to automatically make contact with the manufacturer each time the machine is turned on (or at a regular time of day for machines that are left running continuously) to check for updates. If you are still using a dial-up modem, set the security software to check for updates anytime the Internet is connected to your machine. An example of an update service, from Norton SystemWorks, is shown in Figure 22-4.

Online security protection

As I've noted, Microsoft launched its own service in late 2006. Windows Live OneCare software includes antivirus protection as well as PC-tuning and backup utilities. As first introduced, Microsoft offered a package that included three licenses for multiple machines in a home or office.

A small basic component of the Windows Live OneCare system runs on your machine to guard against unwanted behavior, while other elements are delivered and updated as needed over the Internet. The elements include Protection Plus, which offers antivirus and anti-spyware scanners, and a managed, two-way firewall; the utility runs continuously in the background, but you can scan individual files and folders for viruses on demand by right-clicking them.

Performance Plus automatically defragments the system's hard disks to make them run more efficiently and also helps manage the installation of Windows security updates from Microsoft. You can instruct the Backup and Restore utility to regularly copy important files and settings to CD, DVD, or external hard disk.

FIGURE 22-4: *The LiveUpdate component of Norton SystemWorks checks for updates to all of its components on a regular basis.*

In response, Symantec announced it would offer an online service of its own in 2007. Norton 360 offers protection from viruses and other malware, a personal firewall, PC tune-up utilities, identity theft protection for online shopping, and the security of data on the hard disk drive. Also part of the package is an automated local and online backup service for data files. A report screen from the beta version of the program is shown in Figure 22-5.

The advanced features of Norton 360 include continuous monitoring of any files that are opened or executed to prevent viruses or malicious codes from infecting PCs. The firewall extends to monitoring of incoming e-mail and instant messages. Background Scheduler allows Norton 360 to work on threats, backups, and tune-ups when users are not engaged with their computers.

FIGURE 22-5: *The status screen of Norton 360 (from a beta version) shows configuration of PC security, online transaction protection, settings for backup of essential data files, and a report on automated performance tune-ups.*

Users will also be able to instruct the utility to automatically make backups of files on local drives or send them as encrypted files over a broadband connection to servers maintained by Symantec; files can be restored using a built-in wizard. The initial allotment of storage space included with an annual Norton 360 license was expected to be about 2GB, and users will be allowed to purchase additional online space to store essential files.

Diagnostic Utilities

Diagnostic programs can give your machine a checkup and help you with treatment, but they're not much good at autopsies. Here's what I mean: In most situations, your PC has to be able to start up and boot from a floppy or hard disk to run a software-based diagnostic program. If all you hear when you flick the switch is stony silence, you're going to have to figure out what is wrong by yourself (with the help of this book, of course).

Some diagnostic programs are useful only after Windows is loaded and running. Others are capable of being loaded from a floppy disk drive (if your machine still has one) or from a CD or DVD drive, running off their own special-purpose mini-operating system. Yet another variant allows you to create your own emergency boot disk (on a floppy disk or a CD). The fourth design, used by some PC manufacturers, offers a full set of diagnostic programs stored in a hidden partition on a new machine's hard disk; at bootup, you can instruct the machine to load the diagnostics instead of Windows or another operating system. Even the very best diagnostic program requires a capable supercomputer to interpret its findings. That supercomputer is your brain.

No matter how good the diagnostic program, none can test every last modular element of your PC. Here are a few examples of real-world problems that are generally beneath a diagnostic program's radar:

- **The health of your power supply.** I've heard the story of one inexperienced technician who replaced four or five hard drives in a row because his diagnostic disk kept reporting sector read/write errors on the drive. A new drive would function well when first installed and then report increasing errors during the all-night read/write testing that the technician conducted to confirm that the repair was done correctly. Each morning, he examined the error log, saw the new read/write errors, and assumed that the hard disk replacement that he had installed the previous day was defective. Many hard drives later, the true cause was discovered: a bad power supply. One solution: the most up-to-date motherboards now include a set of monitors that can check heat buildup and certain voltage readings.

- **Intermittent hardware problems.** This problem can take the form of a transitory short in a card that happens only when the system is hot, for example. You may be able to deal with the situation by putting a diagnostic program into a repetitive loop and running the machine all night.

- **An interrupt or memory conflict for a device that appears to be turned off or is electrically malfunctioning.** This category includes problems in external cables. For example, a parallel port may be functioning perfectly, but the cable that runs from it to a printer may have a short or may be only partially attached. Once again, the path to diagnostic joy here involves using your own logic — swapping with cables you know to be good or changing printers, for example.

Whole machine, disk/data diagnostics, and system snoopers

I'm going to divide the world of diagnostic programs into the following three categories:

- **Whole machine diagnostics.** These products attempt to test the entire machine. They test memory, the microprocessor, the DMA chips, the numeric coprocessor, the floppy and hard drives, the serial and parallel ports, the video, the mouse, and the keyboard. They also provide full system configuration information, including the interrupt, input/output (I/O) port settings, and memory addresses used by each piece of hardware.

- **Disk/data diagnostics.** These products concentrate on the disk drives and the data structures of the hard disk and/or the floppy disk, painstakingly reading each sector in search of corrupted data. These programs usually include sophisticated data recovery utilities. A typical disk/data diagnostic program provides intensive testing routines, bad sector lockout, file-moving utilities, and a sector-by-sector hard disk editor.

- **System snoopers.** These products report on the hardware and software installed in the computer plus the interrupts, I/O port settings, and addresses used by that hardware; however, they don't attempt to test them. You must know which interrupts, I/O port settings, and memory addresses are in use when you install new cards — especially network, MIDI, fax, and other exotic hardware items. Each expansion card needs its own exclusive interrupt and I/O port setting; a card with a ROM may need a unique memory address range as well. Products in this class are sometimes called *configuration utilities* or *system information utilities*.

Windows includes its own detailed report on hardware and resources used. Go to the Control Panel and select System ➪ Hardware Tab ➪ Device Manager. From the View pull-down menu, you can choose to look at devices by type or resources used. I show an example from a modern machine in Figure 22-6.

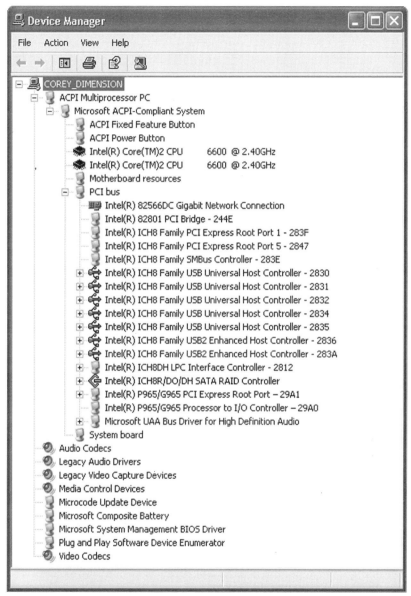

FIGURE 22-6: *You can instruct the Windows Device Manager to display the names and some of the details of all devices in the system, viewed by the nature of their connection to the processor, motherboard, or bus.*

Diagnostic programs can't tell you everything, but they are very useful. Because each of these diagnostic programs uncovers slightly different types of problems, you are probably best off investing in one of the disk/data diagnostic programs as well as a whole-machine diagnostic. These diagnostic programs are good, but always remember that your brain, especially if you are an experienced technician, is better. And nothing beats the eyeball when troubleshooting installation problems such as cables, switches, and jumpers. Use the diagnostics and consider their repair recommendations, but don't follow them blindly.

Imagine that your computer is a patient in the hospital. Diagnostic programs are excellent at testing one limb at a time — the serial port, extended memory, or keyboard, for example. The patient must be conscious, though, to report to the doctor, or the tests are useless.

Pre-boot diagnostics

Some computer manufacturers (or the makers of their motherboards) offer buyers access to diagnostic programs that do not require the full operating system to be working and may offer some extended or specialized testing particular to your computer. As an example, the modern Dimension 9200 that is the test machine in this chapter includes a diagnostic that is invoked during bootup of the machine before Windows is loaded.

In this example, the program is resident on the boot hard drive that comes with the computer, in a hidden or utility partition that is separate from the operating system and other files on the drive. When I ran the test, it began by displaying the machine's Service Tag, a code that Dell uses to track machines that have been configured and shipped to consumers.

The test includes full exercise of the processor, its cache, system memory, the motherboard, and attached devices. It also exercises the adjustable-speed front and rear fans, checks for the presence of motherboard jumpers and cables, and tests USB and other ports. The video adapter test goes all the way back to the oldest and lowest resolution graphics modes and then pushes the adapter to go to as high a resolution as it is capable of supporting.

An express test option runs the hardware through a 10- to 20-minute quick exam; the full extended test can take nearly an hour. And if you are dealing with a troublesome intermittent error — a maddening problem that appears every once in a while but cannot be made to occur on demand — you can instruct the diagnostic program to run multiple iterations of most of the tests (those that do not require keyboard or mouse confirmation by the user).

There's more detail in this test than you'll find in most other consumer-grade diagnostic programs. And if any errors are found, a test message and an error code appear; that information can be used in troubleshooting the problem yourself or to communicate the nature of the failure to a technician at the manufacturer.

As with any other diagnostic program, if the failure is too severe to allow the system board to function and read the utility partition of the hard disk drive, the test cannot be conducted. If the video adapter has failed, you may be able to conduct only the most basic tests using the low-level graphics functions that are built into the motherboard's chipset. And although the test does examine the basic functioning of any installed hard disk drives, the test does not examine the state of the files on the disk (that test must be conducted under Windows). And similarly, there is no test for the Windows components.

Finally, the built-in diagnostics offers a set of specialized tests that are keyed to specific problems. The System Tree brings together some specific set of tests — down to the individual chip level where appropriate — for problems with audio, video, keyboard, and pointing device. Other test groups offer information to help with a noisy machine, an overheated case, system lockups, hard drive errors, and Windows blue screen errors that are likely caused by memory, motherboard, or chipset problems.

Limitations inherent in the testing process

Suppose that your diagnostic disk tells you that something in a particular system — the sound card or the floppy drive, for example — is malfunctioning. Is this true? Maybe.

One thing you can be sure of is that something is wrong. It may not be exactly what the diagnostic program is reporting, though. Diagnostics often don't identify which part is bad, only that a particular subsystem is bad. Because any one of several components may cause a given symptom, it is often impossible to know from the diagnostic report exactly which component is to blame. Instead, use the report as your starting point in exploring the system by using the techniques described in this book and in the troubleshooting flowcharts in Appendix A, on the CD.

System reporting utilities

In many instances, the key to resolving problems in a Windows-based system is the ability to let the operating system count its fingers and toes and tell you what it finds — and what it can't find.

CROSS-REFERENCE

In Chapter 23, I discuss Device Manager and other essential utilities in current versions of Windows.

Diagnostic and Data Recovery Utilities

Hard disk diagnosis and data recovery are closely allied. You may choose to buy separate programs to perform each function, or you can look for products that combine all features. This section includes descriptions of some of the best products; be sure to check the utilities shelf of your computer retailer or a mail-order catalog for the latest and greatest.

Some manufacturers of the most modern of computers now provide advanced diagnostic programs as part of their machines; for example, Dell offers a powerful set of utilities that are stored in a hidden partition on the main hard disk and can be brought to life before the operating system is loaded. This allows testing of all of the hardware components without the sometimes confusing extra layer that is added by Windows.

This sort of pre-boot diagnostic program is best used in conjunction with a second utility program that tests the machine once Windows and applications have been loaded. This can help identify problems caused by errors in the System Registry and missing or corrupted DLL, drivers, and other pieces of software. Diagnostic program error messages, your computer's BIOS ROM error messages, and DOS error messages are all based on educated guesses. Use the information that these error messages give you, but remember that they are not infallible. I've listed common error messages in Appendix B, along with suggestions for approaches to try if one of these messages appears on your screen.

Among worthy products in this class are CheckIt Diagnostics from Smith Micro Software (www.smithmicro.com/checkit) as shown in Figure 22-7, and System Mechanic Professional from Iolo Technologies (www.iolo.com). CheckIt is also offered as a component of Norton SystemWorks. Both CheckIt and System Mechanic Professional are capable of putting almost every element of your machine and all of its

internal and attached components through detailed tests. In my office, I use these tools as the first line of inquiry any time I experience problems that may be related to memory, video adapters, and sound cards.

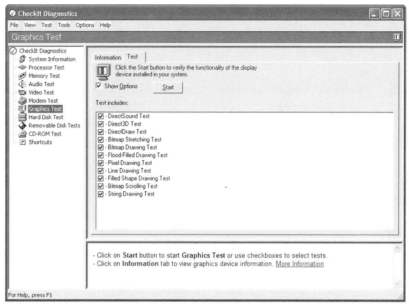

FIGURE 22-7: *The detailed graphics test of CheckIt Diagnostics puts your video adapter through all of its paces. Other available tests are shown in the left pane of the screen.*

American Megatrends, maker of the AMI BIOS as well as a range of utilities and special-purpose hardware, offers AMIDiag, one of the more complete sets of generic hardware diagnostics for consumers. The program detects and checks CPUs from Intel, AMD, Cyrix, SGS Thompson, and Texas Instruments. Component tests examine the processor, memory, floppy and hard drives, CD and DVD drives, video, USB, serial and parallel ports, sound cards, network interfaces, and more. For more information, consult www.amidiag.com.

Because almost all diagnostic tests require a living, breathing patient (a functioning computer) to run the test and to communicate with the diagnostic software, this sort of software is ideal for torture-testing a running computer. If you must certify that a particular computer is good, you can't beat a good diagnostic program that can be set to test all day or all night without any supervision.

Even this sort of extensive automated checkup has a flaw. The diagnostics programs can test the machine longer, in greater depth, and more creatively than any user ever could — except by using the machine — and therein lies the potential problem. Many technicians run 72 hours of sophisticated diagnostics on a particular machine and then hand the machine to the user, swearing that everything is perfect. Within five minutes of normal use, the machine breaks, and the technician looks like a fool. Nothing is wrong with the diagnostic program, nothing is wrong with the technician, and nothing is wrong with the user. It's just that the user may be asking the computer to do something that the diagnostic program didn't check.

Peter Norton began his empire selling a rather simple unerase utility to computer enthusiasts and clubs when the IBM PC was first introduced. Other products may have some individual elements that are better or offer some specific bells and whistles that may hold special appeal, but overall, the various Norton Utilities (now owned and produced by Symantec) offers a very complete and well-polished package.

I've already discussed Norton SystemWorks in a discussion of antivirus and security programs, but it is also worth noting the very powerful and capable disk and Windows repair utilities that are part of the package.

At the heart of the utility are Norton Disk Doctor and Norton System Doctor, which operate in the background to search out disk and system problems and can launch utilities to repair many problems. System Watch monitors system resources under Windows and alerts you to potential and real problems. For more information, consult www.symantec.com.

And as I also have previously noted, many of these same system repair and maintenance utilities are included in a new generation of Web-based services including Microsoft's Windows Live OneCare and Symantec's Norton 360.

Disk Analyzers

Surface analysis programs analyze your hard drive by performing a read/write test to see whether the entire surface can reliably hold data. Using ingenious data-repair algorithms, they reconstruct the data in the suspect areas that DOS can't read.

If the boot cluster is damaged, the operating system won't be able to recognize the disk and will display a message such as Non-System Disk, if it can give any message at all. Usually, the machine just locks up. If the FAT is slightly damaged, the DOS command CHKDSK, the improved DOS program SCANDISK, or a data-recovery program may be able to reconstruct the *pointers* (the directions to the next cluster in the chain). If the FAT is unreadable, the pointer information and whatever data the disk contains are lost. Even though the information is actually still on the disk, there is no way to access it in any meaningful form.

CHKDSK, which dates back to the very early versions of DOS, has been in place in the underlying system for Windows from the very start. Under Windows 95/98, Microsoft recommended use of the enhanced SCANDISK program. With the arrival of Windows XP, Microsoft updated CHKDSK, including facilities that make repairs and display information about partitions that use the NTFS system.

Third-party surface analyzers include more complex and thorough tests. Such products include Norton Utilities and SpinRite (from Gibson Research Corporation, available through www.grc.com). You can count on any of these programs to find bad spots, move the data to a safe part of the disk, and mark the bad spots so that they won't be reused. These programs are easy to use and take less than an hour to run on an average-size drive. Their value is in catching bad spots before you lose data.

The best thing about third-party programs like Norton SystemWorks and Norton Utilities is their ability to reconstruct data from a drive that suffers from a corrupted file attribute table or other problems. If the problem seems to be one-of-a-kind, you can thank your foresight in installing the program; if the hard drive is failing, you should make a backup to another drive and replace the failing drive.

If the disk has been damaged by fire or water or if the disk surface has been damaged by the actual crash of the read/write head into the surface, I recommend that you use a commercial data recovery service. You can find listings of such companies in the back pages of many of the major computer magazines and on the Web.

Aside from physical damage to a disk, probably the trickiest data recovery problem is a bad sector in the middle of a long file. If the sector is totally unreadable, the rest of the file may be lost. For example, a tiny error equivalent to an inkblot covering two bad characters on page 13 can make the hard disk lose the rest of this book. DOS and Windows can correct small errors — the equivalent of one bad character — on their own. But no consumer-level program can correct more than 11 bad bits (that's about one-and-a-half 8-bit characters). You did remember to make backups to your data files, right?

Defragmenting Utilities

When you store a file on disk, the operating system puts the file in an available space on the disk. On a freshly formatted disk, the file is stored in a contiguous fashion—one sector after another from the beginning to the end. When you store your next file, it may well begin right at the end of the previous file and continue from there.

Fragmentation occurs when you reopen an existing file and expand it. The operating system may not be able to place the additional sectors of the file immediately after the end of the original file. In fact, for files that you open and change regularly—and most data files are altered many times between creation and completion—the data may be scattered across several places on the disk.

The file attribute table keeps track of where the pieces of each file are and tells the hard drive how to attach the pieces when you ask it to read the file.

However, fragmented files take a bit longer for the hard drive to read and present a danger if the file attribute table is ever damaged. The solution is to defragment files from time to time as part of your regular maintenance duties.

Under Windows, you can initiate a defragmenting process by going to My Computer and highlighting a drive. Right-click and choose Properties and then go to the Tools Tab and choose Defragmentation.

The Windows defrag program will do the job just fine, although on a large drive it can take hours to complete—this is a job I usually leave running overnight.

Several third-party programs do the same work faster and with some additional bells and whistles. Norton Utilities and Norton SystemWorks include Norton Disk Doctor that monitors the status and health of your drives and can manage a faster version of a defragmentation utility. For more information, consult `www.symantec.com`.

My preference for a specialized tool is Diskeeper, which is significantly faster and more efficient than Microsoft's built-in utilities, and also includes a technology called InvisiTasker, which allows the utility to run invisibly in the background. Diskeeper can also prioritize defragmentation to concentrate on essential system files. The product is available in basic, Professional, and Pro Premier versions, each with more features and greater flexibility. An example of a report screen is shown in Figure 22-8. For more information, consult `www.diskeeper.com`.

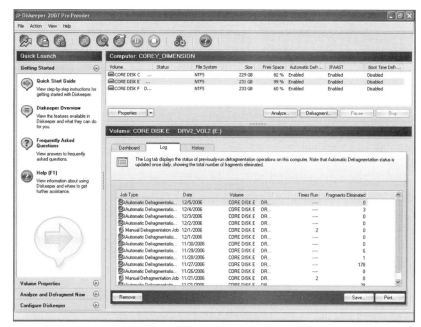

Figure 22-8: *A report from Diskeeper shows the status of installed drives on a modern machine along with information on automatic defragmentation performed without user intervention.*

Summary

The next chapter examines the extensive troubleshooting and configuration utilities that are built into current versions of Windows.

Chapter 23

Windows Troubleshooting and Repairs

Someday, operating systems will meet up with science fiction dreams. "Good morning, Corey," my machine will declare. "I've been feeling a bit slow lately, and I really feel bad about the work you lost yesterday when I had a system crash. I've figured it out, though: That new sound card you installed the other day was arguing with my network interface card. I've rearranged the interrupts, and all is well. While I was at it, I now understand why the Microsoft Office taskbar was hanging up; the driver was corrupted, so I downloaded an updated version. The hard drive was also very badly fragmented so I ran a utility during the night so I'd be ready to fly this morning. Would you like me to compose a symphony in your honor?"

Actually, we are almost there: Modern operating systems, beginning with Windows 95/98 and accelerating with the arrival of Windows XP and continuing with the improved facilities of Windows Vista, include a broad range of tools that allow them to self-configure, make repairs, and help the most complex and capable brain in your office or home — that would be you — troubleshoot more complex problems and make repairs.

Three interrelated components give current operating systems the ability to actively partner with the user when it comes to installing hardware and associated drivers, overseeing the proper functioning of both, and assisting in troubleshooting most of the components of the computer. The pieces are:

- A set of intelligent buses and adapter cards that are capable of communicating with each other so that the system can detect when a new piece of hardware has been installed at startup or in a hot install of a USB, eSATA, or IEEE1394 (FireWire) device. If necessary, the computer searches for available drivers already in place on the machine or requests the location of needed drivers on a disc or on the Internet. The concept was first introduced under the label Plug-and-Play with Windows 95, although it did not fully function as advertised until the arrival of Windows XP and Windows Vista.
- Advanced features of current operating systems, such as the Device Manager, Device Driver Rollback, and System Restore. These utilities can help you check on the status of installed devices, make changes to device drivers, or go back in time to a previous condition in the event of a problem with settings or configuration.
- The ability to boot the operating system into a special state known as a *safe boot*, which allows you to make changes to settings to a computer that might otherwise not start properly. An associated feature is the ability to instruct the computer to load the Last Known Good Configuration.

Plug-and-Play interlinks the system BIOS, hardware devices, and the operating system in a way that allows the computer to configure new hardware components automatically by assigning interrupts, DMA channels, and memory resources without conflicts, and to manage the installation, monitoring, and update of device drivers.

Plug-and-Play began with features incorporated into nearly every PCI adapter; these cards needed to be able to announce their presence to the PC and to be flexible in their demands for system resources. The computer's BIOS was then able to work its way through the various devices installed in the bus and choose the best combination of settings. Most ISA cards are not capable of negotiating with a Plug-and-Play system.

Included in the specification is a wide range of external devices that can identify themselves to the system and work out the kinks of configuration. Plug-and-Play equipment includes intelligent monitors and printers.

In current machines, Plug-and-Play extends to include devices attached to internal and external buses including PCI, PCI Express, AGP, USB, IEEE1394 (FireWire), eSATA, bidirectional parallel ports, and storage devices attached to PATA, SATA, and SCSI interfaces.

USB, FireWire, and eSATA devices are generally *hot-pluggable,* which means that they can be attached to a computer that is running and will be automatically configured. SCSI devices that are certified for Plug-and-Play use permit automatic configuration of device ID and termination settings as well as dynamic changes to the adapter. One way to assure that any of your devices are properly recognized by the system is to keep all of your device drivers up to date and also to update Windows regularly.

Identifying the process associated with a program

Each application running under Windows is identified to and managed by the system through a specific process or group of processes. A *process* is a running instance of a program, containing whatever instructions the operating system needs to be able to interface with the application's actions.

In some cases, troubleshooting a system crash or the failure of a program to load and run can be helped by identifying which process or combination of processes is running. To learn about current processes, open the Task Manager by right-clicking the Windows taskbar and clicking Task Manager, or by pressing and releasing the Ctrl + Alt + Del key combination and then selecting the Task Manager tab.

Once the manager is displayed, click the Applications tab, then right-click the program for which you want to identify the process. Then click Go to Process. The process associated with the program is highlighted on the Processes tab.

You can learn the percentage of CPU resources or the amount of RAM used by the process. To close a stalled process, or to end an unnecessary process (and its associated program), click a process and choose End Process.

WARNING

Ending a process associated with an open program will close that application without further notice and in most instances will cause the loss of any unsaved data. And if you end a process that is part of the operating system itself, some features may not work properly or the entire system may come to a crashing halt.

Exiting a program that is not responding

To end a program that has stopped responding, go to the Task Manager. (You can use either of the methods outlined under "Identifying the process associated with a program.") On the Applications tab, click the program that is not responding, and then choose End Task.

Sometimes ending a program is quick and easy, and sometimes it requires you to go through the preceding steps more than once. The difference is generally related to the program's complexity and how deeply entwined its processes are in the system.

Using the Event Viewer

Event Viewer, available under Windows XP and Vista, displays detailed information about significant events performed by or that happen to your computer; it can be helpful in performing a postmortem after a crash or in determining the likely source of problems with Windows as well as programs that run under the operating system.

Depending on how your machine was initially configured, you may need to enter an administrator password or load an administrator account.

To open the Event Viewer, click the Start button, then choose Control Panel/System and Maintenance/Administrative Tools. Finally, double-click Event Viewer.

The report you see is called an *Event Log.* Information recorded within includes the date and time when a user logs on to the computer as well as any time a program encounters an error. Global Logs include:

- **Application (program) events.** The events are classified as error, warning, or information. An *error* is a significant problem, such as a crash or the loss of data. A *warning* is an indication of the possibility of a future problem. An *information event* is a record of the successful operation of a program, driver, or service.

- **Security-related events.** Called *audits* by the system, these are reports of the successful or unsuccessful completion of system events such as a user's Windows log-on or a shutdown.
- **System events.** System events are logged by Windows and Windows system services, and are classified as error, warning, or information.

Other types of events, generated by programs that run on the computer and by certain Windows services, are recorded as Application Logs.

The Device Manager

Current versions of Windows do a pretty good job of spotting many problems with drivers, system resources, some hardware devices, and the operating system itself. The Device Manager, a key component of the System utility on the Control Panel, does much of the snooping and reporting.

As I noted previously in this chapter, the most complex and capable brain in your home or office is not the computer — it's you — at least for the foreseeable future. The Device Manager facility allows users to deal with problems beyond the abilities of the computer to fix, and to make the occasional manual assignment of resources or to force the use of a different device driver.

To display the Device Manager, go to the Control Panel and choose System.

Device Manager is a report card on nearly every piece of hardware in your system, as well as hardware settings, device drivers, and resource allocations.

The facilities of Device Manager allow you to do the following:

- See at a glance an indication of whether Windows believes the hardware on your computer is working properly.
- Disable, enable, and uninstall devices.
- Determine major hardware configuration settings and properties, and make changes to them.
- Learn the identity of device drivers for each device, and see information including the maker of the driver and its version.
- Install updated device drivers, and (in the most current versions of Windows) roll back to the previous version of the driver to undo problems caused by updates.
- Print a summary report of the devices that are installed on your computer; with your permission, (usually) the same information can be supplied over the Internet to support desks or registration systems.

Note that under Windows Vista, XP, or 2000, you must have administrator status to manage device drivers and make certain changes to configurations and settings if the machine was configured to require an administrator login.

You can take several routes to open the Device Manager; the most commonly used is to click Start ➪ Control Panel, then double-click System, then on the Hardware tab click Device Manager.

The goal of the software engineers at Microsoft, in conjunction with Intel and other hardware makers, is an unalloyed world of Plug-and-Play devices, with Windows automatically configuring every device so that it will work without conflicts with other devices when assigning IRQ lines, DMA channels, I/O port addresses, and memory address ranges.

A modern motherboard, in conjunction with current adapters and a current Windows operating system, should allow automatic configuration of almost every device. I say *almost* every device because you can make almost an infinite number of different combinations of devices, chipsets, resources, and configurations; sooner or later, most users run into some sort of conflict. In theory, the chances of conflicts should be less and less over time — we can hope.

If two devices require the same resources, the result is a *device conflict*. Sometimes this causes one or both devices to stop functioning or to act unpredictably. In the worst case, the operating system or the system itself may come to a halt — often displaying the "blue screen of death."

If you use an older adapter card that does not support Plug-and-Play, the system won't be able to set resources automatically. You may have to live with the default setting that the card's designers have assigned or (if permitted) make changes to those settings by moving jumpers or setting switches on the card. For assistance, consult the instruction manual and web sites for card makers.

The other alternative is to use the facilities of Device Manager to manually assign resources.

By setting the resources on a non-Plug-and-Play adapter or assigning them under Device Manager, you may solve one problem but cause another, because Windows will end up with less flexibility when it comes to dynamically allocating resources to other devices.

The XP version of System Properties is shown in Figure 23-1; under that operating system, the Device Manager is accessible through the Hardware tab of System Properties. Figure 23-2 shows the General tab of the display under Windows 98; tabs behind it open the way to the Device Manager as well as other controls.

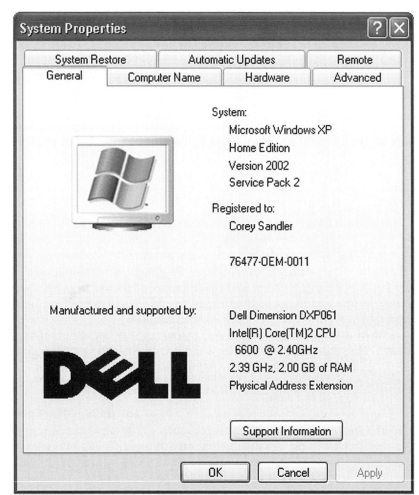

FIGURE 23-1: *The General tab of the System Properties screen in Windows XP offers access to reports on hardware as well as settings for System Restore and Automatic Updates. It's also a quick way to check on the type and speed of processor and the amount of installed system RAM. Similar facilities are also available under Windows Vista.*

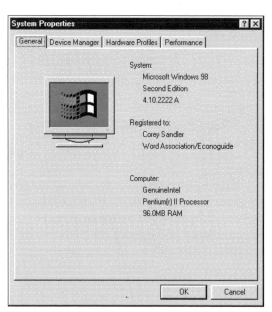

FIGURE 23-2: *The General tab of the System Properties dialog box in Windows 98.*

FIGURE 23-3: *The available System Properties screen tabs in Windows XP include access to the Device Manager, Drivers, and Hardware Profiles from the Hardware Tab.*

Under Windows XP, you can reach the Device Manager by clicking on the Hardware tab of System Properties, as shown in Figure 23-3.

Once System Properties has been displayed, click the Hardware Tab to burrow a layer down to view available options, as shown in Figure 23-4.

FIGURE 23-4: *Click the Device Manager to examine all of the hardware devices that your computer is able to detect through Plug-and-Play. Other options include an examination of installed drivers, settings for automatic or manual updates of the Windows operating system, and the ability to create more than one hardware profile that enables, disables, or configures particular sets of equipment for special purposes.*

When you've arrived at the Device Manager, you can instruct the system whether to show devices by type or by connection; you can see an example in Figure 23-5. Check the hardware tree list for devices where the computer is reporting a problem. An exclamation point (!) in a yellow circle indicates a potential or actual conflict; an X in a red circle tells you that an ill-behaved device has been disabled.

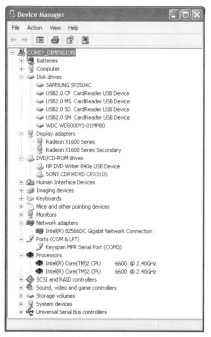

FIGURE 23-5: *You can expand Device Manager's tree layout by clicking the plus sign (+) to the left of the device name. Click the minus sign (–) to collapse the tree.*

Double-click a device to check its properties; Device Manager tells you a bit about the hardware itself and whether it appears to be working properly. Actually, the report only tells you whether the device is communicating clearly with the system. Figure 23-6 shows a typical General tab of system properties; the Windows XP version shown here includes a link to troubleshooting scripts for many important devices.

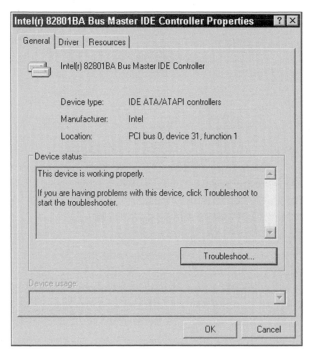

FIGURE 23-6: *Double-clicking a device brings up its Properties dialog box. Here, in the General tab of the Windows XP version, you learn whether the hardware appears to be working properly and have access to a troubleshooter.*

Click the View Devices by Connection radio button to sort the device list differently. Sometimes during Plug-and-Play installation, the system gives unfamiliar names to some devices that you have installed. Changing the way you look at this information can help you to understand what's installed and what each device does.

Located under the Resources tab is a window indicating which resources are available for the selected device. The scroll box at the bottom of the page shows a Conflicting Device list. With the information in the two windows, you should be able to figure out the source of the conflict and a solution.

If you're having problems with a sound card, CD-ROM drive, or another device that could be classified as a multimedia device, simply open Multimedia from the Control Panel to display the Multimedia Properties dialog box. Click the Devices tab of this dialog box to see a list similar to the System list.

For Windows to successfully assign resources to a detected device, the Use Automatic Settings check box on the Resources tab of the Device Manager has to be checked. Depending on the device and the associated driver, you may be able to uncheck the automatic configuration to manually adjust elements of the resource settings. Figure 23-7 shows the Resources tab.

You can scroll through available interrupts or memory addresses using the arrow keys. Pay attention to the report of possible conflicts with other hardware. A dialog box can help you choose an interrupt that does not conflict with other devices.

If you believe a problem lies with an incorrect or corrupted device driver, restart Windows in Safe Mode and remove the conflicting drivers under Device Manager. Then restart Windows normally and start the Add New Hardware Wizard from the Control Panel. To completely disable a device in Device Manager but leave it in place in the system — one step in an advanced troubleshooting process — click the Original Configuration (Current) check box on the General tab to clear it. You can later enable the check box after you've cleared up the conflict.

Checking the status of a device

Open Device Manager and double-click the type of device that you want to view. Right-click on the specific device and then click Properties. Go to the General tab; under Device status is a report on the functioning of the device.

If the device is not working properly or has a potential conflict, the status box will display the problem. Depending on the device and manufacturer, additional information may include a problem code or number and a suggested fix.

Under Windows XP and Vista, many devices are also linked to a hardware troubleshooter.

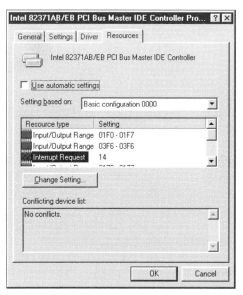

FIGURE 23-7: *The Resources tab reports the I/O range, interrupt, DMA (if used), and other information for a particular piece of hardware. Look in the lower section to see whether Windows reports that the device is conflicting with the resources used by another device.*

Uninstalling or disabling devices

Another advantage offered by the Plug-and-Play design is that it allows you to uninstall most devices by merely removing them from the system when it is turned off; when the system is next powered on, the operating system should be able to note the absence of the device and adjust the allocation of resources if necessary. Be sure to consult the instruction manual for your device for details.

If it is a hot swappable USB or FireWire device, you can merely detach it from the port. For devices installed in the bus, turn off the computer, unplug it, and remove the cover. Remove the adapter from the bus.

NOTE

For any FireWire or USB device — but particularly a storage device such as a key disk (flash memory) — there is a slight possibility of losing data if you just unplug it. It is safer to use the Windows Safely Remove Device utility, which you access through a small icon on the System Tray normally located at the lower right of your screen.

For a non-Plug-and-Play device, you may need to go to Device Manager and uninstall the device. Then turn off the machine and physically remove the adapter or device from the system or from an attached port. Again, check the instruction manual for the device for any specific additional recommendations.

In some situations — such as an attempt to identify the source of a conflict — you can use Device Manager to temporarily disable a Plug-and-Play device. The device remains in place in the bus or attached to a port, but the Windows Registry is changed so that device drivers are not loaded when the computer is started. If the device is later re-enabled, the Registry is changed again and the device drivers load at startup.

To disable a device driver (and thus turn off the device itself) without removing the driver, go to its Drivers tab under Device Manager and choose the disable box. (The option to disable differs slightly in wording across the various versions of Windows, but the effect is the same.)

To enable a device, open Device Manager and double-click on the type of device that you want to enable. Right-click on a specific device and then click Enable.

Hardware profiles

Device Manager also allows creation of multiple hardware profiles, allowing you to choose from two or more user profiles that might have different sets of devices enabled or disabled.

Windows sets up Profile 1 to include all devices installed in the computer when the operating system is first set up, or when you first set up a second profile. You can instruct Windows to ask which profile to use when you start the computer, or you can swap profiles from a running system and reboot to enable the differing devices.

NOTE

Current versions of Windows, including XP and Vista, extend the concept of Plug-and-Play with Universal Plug-and-Play, which allows a PC to look beyond its own bus and ports to locate and control networked devices and services, including network-attached printers, Internet gateways, and consumer electronics equipment. This scheme allows the PC to join an up-and-running network, obtain an IP address, announce itself to the other devices on the network, and find out about—and connect to—everything else on the network.

With Universal Plug-and-Play, a user can add a new printer or a storage device to a system and it will immediately be made available to any other PCs on the network at that time or in the future. Be sure to keep your system current with Windows Update from the Microsoft web site and protect your system behind a firewall and antivirus software.

Windows System Information Utility

Current versions of Windows offer another utility that may prove useful if you try to diagnose system problems caused by non-Plug-and-Play hardware or by unknown sources. Use the System Information utility—also accessible from the System Tools menu under Accessories—to display a variety of data about your system configuration, as shown in Figure 23-8.

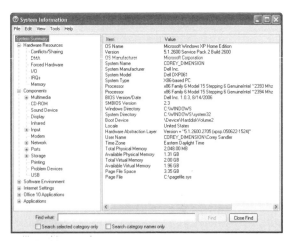

FIGURE 23-8: *A Windows XP System Information Window.*

The left pane of the System Information display allows you to select various types of hardware and system resources; each category can be expanded by clicking a plus sign (+) beside any entry that includes additional information. Click the plus signs to expand the display and show information about the selected topic. You can browse system settings through this facility to determine IRQ settings for various devices, to see which devices are using what memory segments, and to learn about other hardware settings. Double-clicking a particular component reveals details including the name of the device, details of some of its capabilities, the driver version in use, and much more. An example of a System Information report on the video adapter in the current machine profiled in this book is shown in Figure 23-9.

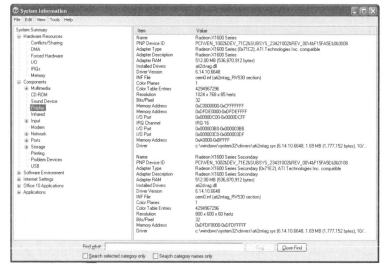

FIGURE 23-9: *A Windows XP report on what the system knows about the installed ATI Radeon X1600 Pro video adapter.*

Under current versions of Windows, you can open a software window that shows which drivers are loaded and whether they are 16-bit or 32-bit, as shown in Figure 23-10.

Windows XP and Vista offer other details about drivers, including details of *digital signing* — a security measure that assures that drivers have passed Microsoft compatibility tests and to help alert users to corruption or tampering. Figure 23-11 shows a Windows XP report on signed drivers. An associated tool within System Information is File Signature Verification, which checks to see which system files and device driver files are digitally signed; if you enable logging, the search results are also written to a log file.

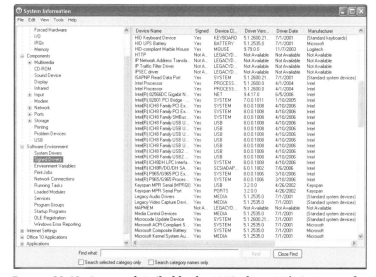

FIGURE 23-10: *A more detailed look at Windows XP's System Information window reveals details about device drivers.*

The Registry Checker — available in Windows 98 only — scans your current Registry for errors and then gives you an opportunity to back up the registry if you want.

The Version Conflict Manager, another Windows 98 facility, may be useful if you're having software problems. It displays a list of file versions that are different from the versions Windows would have installed. You can back up these files and restore the Windows originals, a move that sometimes can fix flaky Windows operation. If it doesn't solve your current problem, then copy the newer files back to where they belong.

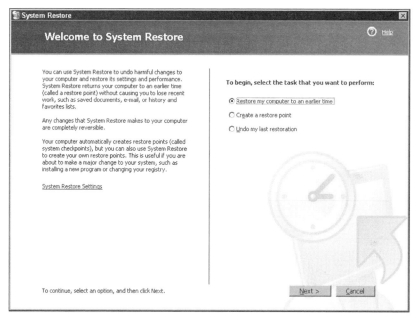

FIGURE 23-11: *Windows XP includes a detailed report on the provenance of device drivers.*

Device Driver Roll Back (Windows XP and Vista)

Another safety net within Windows XP and Vista is the Device Driver Roll Back, which does exactly what its name promises. If you install a device driver and later find that the system has become unusable or a piece of hardware becomes unreliable, you can reinstall the driver previously in use and restore any driver settings that were changed when the new driver was installed. No other files or settings are altered.

This specialized form of a system restore utility does not work with printer drivers. Check the Properties for hardware to see if a Device Driver Roll Back is offered; an example is shown in Figure 23-12.

You'll find Device Driver Roll Back on the same Drivers tab of Device Manager in Windows XP.

FIGURE 23-12: *The Driver tab of the Properties screen for a CD drive in a modern machine; this piece of hardware offers the option for a rollback to an earlier version of the device driver.*

Last Known Good Configuration (Windows XP and Vista)

What happens if your computer won't come to life at all? Assuming that the machine's hardware — the hard drive, CPU, memory, video adapter, and BIOS chips as a minimum — is performing properly, the problem may be due to a change to the configuration.

Windows XP and Vista include a feature called Last Known Good Configuration that restores Registry settings and drivers that were in effect the last time the computer successfully started. This is not quite the same as System Restore, which can be invoked days or weeks later to reset a system to a previous configuration; however, System Restore can only be used on a PC that is up and running.

This tool instructs Windows to locate and use a file that recorded the most recent system settings that allowed the machine to start properly. As part of its self-preservation, Windows makes a record of essential system settings each time the machine shuts down successfully. (That's the main reason you should try to never shut off the power to your computer before the operating system has completed its orderly shut down.)

This should be your first line of defense if you have installed a new piece of hardware or software and find that the system will not restart properly. It may be a faulty driver or registry setting associated with the new component or a driver that's incompatible with your operating system.

This utility should be used in the following situation: The computer started and ran properly the last time you turned it on, but now it will not load and run Windows. The Last Known Good Configuration allows you to recover from improper newly added drivers; it won't, however, solve problems caused by corrupted or missing drivers or files.

On the other hand, if Windows is up and running and the system is behaving improperly, your better option is often a different utility: System Restore. This tool allows you to return system settings to one of a number of saved configurations in recent days, weeks, or months. (The number of saved configurations depends on the instructions you gave to the utility during installation of the operating system or alterations to those instructions made later on.)

To run System Restore, go to System Tools and select the utility. Follow instructions to choose a restore date you believe to be before your computer began to exhibit problems. When you select a date, the computer shuts down and restarts using those settings. If the restoration is successful, you can test the machine and decide if the problem has been fixed; if the computer is unable to use the previous settings (usually because of other changes made to the system files), it restarts using the same settings that were in effect before you ran the utility.

The advantage to using System Restore is that changes made by selecting a particular point in time as the settings source can be undone by repeating the process. Changes made through Last Known Good Configuration are permanent.

Either utility only records system settings, and a restoration does not delete or change data files, e-mail, or applications. And neither utility repairs or replaces a deleted or corrupted driver or program; to make that sort of fix you need to reinstall the driver or program from the original source or from an online source.

To use the configuration tool under Windows Vista, do the following:

1. Remove any disks from the CD, DVD, and floppy disk drives that may be part of the system.
2. Restart the system.
   - If the computer has just one operating system installed, repeatedly press and release the F8 function key as the

machine restarts, before the Windows logo appears. If the logo appears, wait until Windows has fully loaded, then shut down and restart the machine to try again.

- If the computer has more than one operating system available for booting, use the arrow keys to highlight the operating system you want to start in Safe Mode, and then press F8.

3. When the Windows Advanced Options Menu screen is displayed, you'll see the following options:
   - Safe Mode
   - Safe Mode with Networking
   - Safe Mode with Command Prompt
   - Enable Boot Logging
   - Enable VGA Mode
   - Last Known Good Configuration (Your most recent settings that worked)
   - Directory Services Restore Mode (Windows domain controllers only)
   - Debugging Mode
   - Start Windows Normally
   - Reboot
   - Return to OS Choices Menu

4. Use the arrow keys to highlight Last Known Good Configuration, and then press Enter.

   If there is more than one operating system installed, your options include configurations for each of them; choose the option for the operating system you want to restart using the Last Known Good Configuration.

System Restore (Windows XP and Vista)

Most computer users have come to dread installing a new application or even updating a device driver, knowing that many times the latest "improvement" may end up causing all sorts of new problems or even bringing everything to a complete halt. It seems that too many combinations of hardware, software, and settings are available for developers to anticipate every possible conflict that may arise.

One of the most useful facilities of Windows XP and Vista is System Restore, a utility that takes an electronic snapshot of your system settings and many application files. If you run into a problem, you can instruct System Restore to reset the computer to a previous, properly

operating state. Personal data files, such as word processor files, e-mail, and other application files, are not affected by the rollback.

The opening screen of the utility allows you to create a restore point before you perform an action, or restore the computer to the settings in effect at an earlier time. If you've just performed a system restore, a third option gives you the opportunity to undo the last restoration.

System Restore automatically creates *restore points* — identified by a time and date — anytime you install a new application or install a new or updated driver. You can also instruct the utility to automatically take snapshots at specific intervals, and you can manually create a restore point anytime before making a change to your system.

As you step through the available restoration points (look for bold-faced dates on the calendar) you'll see whether a saved point was an automatic action or one related to the installation or removal of a piece of software or hardware, as seen in Figure 23-13.

The utility requires a minimum of 200MB of space within the system partition; the program automatically manages the space, purging the oldest restore points to make room for new ones, thus creating what Microsoft calls a "rolling safety net" under the user.

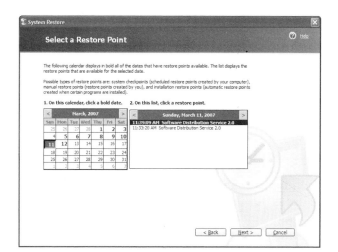

FIGURE 23-13: *The calendar screen of System Restore in Windows XP, showing several saved data sets, including an automatic checkpoint, the installation of a utility, and its later removal. Depending on other actions that might have been taken subsequently, it may be possible to restore the system to any of these three previous configurations.*

The Windows XP version of System Restore was based on a filter that watched the system for changes made to a predetermined group of file extensions; it made copies of the files before they were changed and overwritten. Windows Vista designers changed the approach to add the possibility of recovery from a wider rage of changes; under Vista, when a restore point is requested or automatically generated, a shadow copy of a file or an entire folder is created. The *shadow copy* is a compressed version of settings as well as files and folders; if this sounds to you like Microsoft has adopted some of the features of third-party automatic backup programs, you're correct.

When you ask Vista's version of System Restore to recover from a restore point, files and settings are copied from the shadow version to the live volume used by the operating system.

Running Windows in Safe Mode for Troubleshooting and Repair (Windows XP, Vista, and 98)

Safe Mode is an excellent way to determine the source of problems or to undo changes made to trouble-causing configurations. The utility is available in current versions of Windows including XP, Vista, and 98.

Under Safe Mode, you have access to basic files and drives, including those for the mouse, monitor, keyboard, hard drives, and basic VGA video. If your system is performing properly after you start the system in Safe Mode, default settings and minimum device drivers are not the cause; instead, this should point you toward settings or configurations that you have recently made or to new drivers or devices recently added to the system.

A number of other tools are available to you at startup, including the ability to boot the operating system in a Safe Mode that loads just the basic set of drivers and services; doing so generally permits you to get to the Control Panel to change settings or make other system adjustments that would otherwise be impossible because of conflicts, inappropriate settings, or corrupted files.

Using Safe Mode allows you to isolate the problem between the basic components of Windows and add-on drivers and configurations. If the system loads and runs properly under Safe Mode, there is a problem with modifications you have made; if the system does not run under Safe Mode, you have a problem with basic hardware or the basic elements of Windows.

If your machine starts in Safe Mode all by itself, some component of your machine is preventing a normal startup. If you have just installed a new component — software, driver, or hardware — it's a reasonable assumption that this is the cause of the problem. Under Safe Mode, uninstall any new drivers or software; shut down the machine and uninstall any new hardware. If the problem goes away, you've isolated its source; at that point I suggest contacting the manufacturer of the new hardware or software and seek their assistance.

If Windows does not come to life at all, then the basic operating system files are likely damaged beyond repair; your best bet is to attempt to restart using the Windows boot disk that you should have created when the operating system was installed. You may also be able to bring the system back to life by booting from the Windows installation disc or from a specialized recovery CD provided by some computer manufacturers.

Under Windows XP and Vista you can also use the Recovery Console to restore many corrupted or damaged Windows facilities.

Starting the computer in Safe Mode

To manually start your computer in Safe Mode, do the following:

1. Remove any disks from the CD, DVD, and floppy disk drives that may be part of the system.
2. Restart the system.
   - If the computer has just one operating system installed, repeatedly press and release the F8 function key as the machine restarts, before the Windows logo appears. If the logo appears, wait until Windows has fully loaded, then shut down and restart the machine to try again.
   - If the computer has more than one operating system available for booting, use the arrow keys to highlight the operating system you want to start in Safe Mode, and then press F8.
3. When the Windows Advanced Options Menu screen is displayed, use the arrow keys to highlight the Safe Mode option you want to use, and then press Enter. You see a set of options, including the following:
   - **Safe Mode.** Loads Windows with a minimal set of drivers and services, permitting access to the Control Panel and certain other utilities.
   - **Safe Mode with Networking.** Loads Windows in Safe Mode and includes the standard set of networking drivers and

services needed to access the Internet or other computers on your network.

- **Safe Mode with Command Prompt.** Loads Windows in Safe Mode but displays the command prompt window instead of the usual Windows interface, permitting direct execution of utilities that run outside of Windows.
- **Enable Boot Logging.** During the startup process, this option creates a file that lists all the drivers that load during startup. Examining the file, ntbtlog.txt, may offer clues for advanced troubleshooting.
- **Enable VGA Mode.** Loads Windows with the current video driver but using low-resolution, minimal color-set, and slow refresh-rate settings. This option allows you to reset the display settings if they were intentionally or accidentally set outside of the acceptable range for your hardware.
- **Last Known Good Configuration.** Described in an earlier section, this option loads Windows with the last registry and driver configuration that worked successfully.
- **Directory Services Restore Mode.** Loads the Windows domain controller running Active Directory so that the directory service can be restored; this is an option for system administrators and advanced users; a support professional might direct you to choose this option.
- **Debugging Mode.** Another advanced troubleshooting mode that lets you make changes to certain elements of the Windows code itself; you might be directed to use this option by a support professional.
- **Disable Automatic Restart on System Failure.** This option allows you to specify whether Windows will automatically restart if an error causes Windows to fail. Microsoft recommends that you disable automatic restart if Windows is stuck in a loop where Windows fails, attempts to restart, and fails again repeatedly.
- **Start Windows Normally.** Starts Windows in Normal Mode instead of any of the other options.
- **Disable Driver Signature Enforcement.** This option allows drivers containing improper or unverified signatures to be loaded.
- **View System Recovery Options.** Choosing this option displays a menu of recovery options that can help solve startup-related problems; this option is available only if Startup Repair is installed on the computer's hard disk.

4. Log on to your computer with a user account that has administrator privileges.

   When the computer has loaded in Safe Mode, you see a basic Windows screen (probably using a lower number of colors than you are used to seeing, and possibly at a lower resolution; the words Safe Mode appear in each of the corners of the screen.).

5. To exit Safe Mode, restart the computer and allow Windows to load normally.

Devices, drivers, and services that start in Safe Mode

Here is the standard set of hardware devices and drivers that are enabled under the Windows Safe Mode:

- Floppy disk drives (internal, USB)
- Internal optical (CD or DVD) drives (PATA, SATA)
- External optical (CD or DVD) drives (USB, eSATA)
- Internal hard disk drives (PATA, SATA, SCSI)
- External hard disk drives (USB, eSATA)
- Keyboard (USB, PS/2, serial)
- Mouse (USB, PS/2, serial)
- VGA display card (PCI Express, PCI, AGP)

   The following Windows services are loaded under Safe Mode:

- Event log
- Logical disk manager
- Plug-and-Play
- Remote procedure calls
- Help and Support
- System Restore
- WMI (Windows Management Instrumentation)

Diagnostic tools available in Safe Mode

Once you have restarted a troublesome machine in Safe Mode, you can use a number of diagnostic and repair tools to attempt a fix. Here are some of the best offered under Windows Vista. Most are similar to their predecessors in Windows XP:

Ch 23

- **System Restore.** Allows you to restore the state of the computer's system to a previous point in time. Try to find a time and date just before the computer began to exhibit problems; if you reach too far back in time you may lose updates and configuration changes that you have to redo. System Restore is invoked from Accessories/System Tools.
- **Device Manager.** Allows you to update device drivers and configure hardware. To load Device Manager, click Control Panel/System and Maintenance/System/Hardware and Device Settings/Device Manager.
- **Command Prompt.** In certain circumstances you may want to reach the command prompt to run a program that resides outside of Windows; a support professional may tell you to do so. To display the prompt, click Accessories/Command Prompt.
- **Registry Editor.** Not for the uninformed amateur: You may be directed by a support professional to make changes to your Windows Registry files by using the Registry Editor. Do not make changes without backing up the previous set of files and without specific instructions about changes. A mistake in a critical section of the Registry can render your Windows system unusable, requiring a reinstallation.

NOTE

Under Windows 95/98, your machine won't be able to access a connected network. Windows XP and Vista, though, offer an additional startup option of Safe Mode with Networking, which adds essential services and drivers to join an existing network. Another XP and Vista option available is to restart to the Last Known Good Configuration, which starts the computer by using Registry information saved at the last orderly shutdown.

Recovery Console

If you are unable to use Last Known Good Configuration, or if you can't start the computer in Safe Mode, you can use the advanced facilities of the Recovery Console. The Recovery Console, available in Windows 2000 and Windows XP, is essentially an enhanced version of a DOS system prompt.

From the Recovery Console, you can access FAT, FAT32, and NTFS volumes on the drives of your computer without starting Windows. You can also enable or disable device drivers, copy files from the Windows installation disc for the operating system or from a hardware installation disk, or create a new boot sector and master boot record to repair damage to the file organization of a hard drive.

You can start Windows Recovery in two ways:

- Load the console from the Windows installation disk. At the Welcome to Setup screen, press F10 or type **R** to repair, and then type **C** to initiate the console.
- Add the Windows Recovery Console to the Windows Startup folder. Consult the Windows help screens for assistance on installation. If you go this route, the console will be readily available any time you boot up without need for the Windows installation disk.

Automated System Recovery

If you are unable to restart your computer by other means, or if you have had to replace a damaged system hard drive, you can use a previously created Windows Backup file that includes an Automated System Recovery set.

This facility is available only in Windows XP Professional; it replaces the Emergency Repair Disk option of Windows 2000 and Windows NT 4.0.

Automated System Recovery restores all disk signatures, volumes, and partitions on the disks required to start the computer, plus a basic version of Windows capable of restoring the backup file that you created.

Performing a Clean Boot

One of the most valuable diagnostic and repair tools in current Windows systems is the ability to restart the system with a Clean Boot. In other words, you will load the operating system with only the drivers and startup programs you choose to have running. This amounts to a selective version of a Safe Mode restart.

The key to this power tool is the System Configuration Utility, available in Windows 98 and Windows XP. Under Windows 98, you can launch the utility in two ways:

- From within Windows 98 or Windows 2000, choose Start ⇨ Programs ⇨ Accessories ⇨ System Tools ⇨ System Information. On the Tools menu, click System Configuration Utility.
- To run the same program from a command prompt under Windows 98, choose Start ⇨ Run. Type **msconfig.exe** in the Open box, and then click OK.

After the program is displayed, go to the General tab and then click Selective Startup. From here you can click to clear or restore the following check boxes: Process Config.sys File, Process Autoexec.bat File, Process Winstart.bat File (if available), Process System.ini File, Process Win.ini File, and Load Startup Group Items. Click OK, then restart your computer when you are prompted to do so.

To perform a clean boot in Windows XP, you must be logged on as an administrator. Choose Start ⇨ Run, type **msconfig** in the Open box, and then click OK. On the General tab, click Selective Startup, and then clear the check boxes that are available to you. Click OK, and then click Restart to restart your computer.

After Windows 98 or XP has restarted, you can check whether you are still having problems. If all is well, you can then selectively turn on drivers and configuration files — one at a time. Go back to the System Configuration Utility and enable an item by checking its box.

Your goal is to keep adding more back to the ordinary startup group until the problem recurs; when it does, you can hone in your detective work on the contents of that file or driver.

If all of this sounds time-consuming and tedious, that's because it is. However, it may be the only way to determine the source of a problem caused by an unusual combination of programs, drivers, or settings on your machine. Many technical support desks — including Microsoft — will point you in this direction when your problem does not match one of the usual suspects in their knowledge base.

Note, though, that Microsoft strongly recommends against using System Configuration Utility to modify the Boot.ini file on your computer unless you are doing so with the assistance of one of their support staffers.

To return from a clean boot state, load the System Configuration Utility one more time and go to the General tab. Click Normal Startup (Load all Device Drivers and Services). Click OK and then Restart.

Creating a Boot Disk

If your primary hard drive sustains damage to the outermost tracks where the system keeps its all-important bootup information — or if your operating system files are somehow damaged — your computer is going to be unable to start.

Depending on your system's configuration, you should be able to bring the computer to life by using a *bootable floppy disk* or another medium, such as a CD-ROM or Zip disk.

With current versions of the operating system (Windows 98, Windows NT 4, and later), you can boot from the installation copy of Windows. Doing so will automatically begin the process of reinstalling your operating system.

If you just want to reboot your system to examine the contents of the hard drive or to make repairs, the best way is to use a bootable floppy disk created under Windows or with the assistance of a Windows utility available in Windows 95/98, ME, and NT. Under Windows XP, the installation CD includes the Recovery Console that can be used for this purpose.

To make a floppy bootable, the computer's system files need to be copied to the floppy disk from a properly functioning system. You'll be offered the opportunity to create a bootable floppy as part of the Windows installation process; you can also create one later from within Windows.

To create a boot disk from within Windows 95/98:

1. Choose Start ⇨ Settings, and then choose the Control Panel.
2. Click on Add/Remove Programs and then choose the Startup Disk tab.
3. Insert a disk into your computer's floppy disk drive and then click on Create Disk. The process will automatically create a bootable disk with necessary system files.

You can also choose to manually create a startup disk from within Windows:

1. Insert a disk in the floppy disk drive. Go to the desktop and double-click on the My Computer icon.
2. Click once on the A: drive to select it, and then right-click to bring up a pop-up menu. Under Format Type, choose Full.
3. Under Other Options, choose Copy System Files. Click the Start button.

4. When Windows is finished formatting the disk, close the format window. Now you will need to manually copy some additional system files to the floppy. Use Windows Explorer to identify and copy the following files to the floppy drive: from within the Command folder, copy `Fdisk.exe` and `Format.exe`.

Several Windows utility programs, including Norton Utilities, Norton SystemWorks, and other applications, can also create a bootable floppy and in some systems a bootable CD or DVD. These disks will usually also include antivirus cleanup files and access to a CD-ROM if one is installed in your system.

Whichever way you create your bootup floppy, be sure to conduct a test to make sure that the system will boot from it. Install the floppy in the floppy disk drive and restart Windows; the disk should bring the system to life and allow you access to your hard drive.

Booting from a CD or DVD

To boot from a CD, restart the computer with the Windows CD in the CD-ROM drive.

If you are unable to boot, your PC may not be set up to look for a bootable disk in the CD or DVD drive. You may need to instruct the BIOS to check the CD or DVD as well as the floppy disk drive (if present) and the hard drive.

Restart the computer and go to the system BIOS before the PC begins to load Windows. When the BIOS menu is displayed, locate the section that lists available boot devices; this is often an element of Advanced Features in the BIOS.

On this screen, you can instruct the computer where to look for bootable disks, and the order in which to search. If you want to force the system to go to the CD or DVD drive first, change the setting for Boot Device 1 to CD/DVD.

If you want to have the system attempt to boot from the hard drive first, and if it is unsuccessful there to look at the CD/DVD next, set Boot Device 1 to the hard drive (usually identified by connection such as SATA1 or IDE1) and Boot Device 2 to CD/DVD. Most modern machine BIOS systems allow selection of three or four boot devices.

On dinosaur machines, you may have to set switches on the motherboard or run a configuration disk to instruct the system to check a drive other than C: first. If your dinosaur machine uses a SCSI interface for the CD drive — common when CD drives first became popular — you may not be able to get the machine to boot from the CD drive because Windows needs a special SCSI driver to use the SCSI interface. When you set up a boot floppy disk (see the later discussion on this process), you may have the option to install SCSI drivers when you copy the operating system software to the floppy disk. That still won't let you boot from the CD drive, but it does let you access the drive once you have booted from the floppy drive.

To make a CD-ROM drive accessible in Safe Mode under Windows 95/98, restart the computer to Safe Mode and choose Command Prompt Only. At the command prompt, type **win /d:m** and press Enter.

Emergency boot disk

You can bring any version of Windows back to some semblance of life by using an emergency boot disk. This is a disk that you can install in a bootable drive on your machine to bring the PC to life if your hard drive refuses to do the job. (Users of Windows 2000 and XP can use the Recovery Console for the same purpose.)

Depending on the components of your PC system, the bootable drive may be a floppy drive, a CD-ROM, a Zip drive, or an external SCSI hard drive. The concept is the same: This is another drive that your system can be instructed to check for boot files and then the operating system and hardware drivers.

Windows 95/98, Windows ME, and Windows 2000 give you the option to create a startup disk as part of their installation or upgrade process. To create the disk, go to Control Panel, then Add/Remove Programs. Select the Startup Disk panel and follow the instructions. Be sure to look for the option to install special drivers (such as a driver to support a SCSI CD drive) during this process.

A number of PC utility programs, including Symantec's Norton Utilities and McAfee Antivirus, automate the process of making an emergency or rescue disk for the same purpose.

You want your emergency disk to include the low-level boot tracks and as much of the operating system as necessary to bring the system to life. It should also include any necessary device drivers to enable the BIOS to recognize the presence of a hard drive and CD-ROM drive. On most systems, you also need `config.sys` and autoexec.bat files that refer to those drivers on the emergency disk.

Installing Multiple Operating Systems Under Windows XP or Vista

Sometimes one operating system is just not enough . . . not just for the sheer technological accomplishment, but sometimes because you specifically need to run a particular application or perform a task that is only available in an older (or newer) version of Windows.

Windows XP supports multiple booting with MS-DOS, Windows 3.1, Windows 95, Windows 98, Windows NT 3.51, Windows NT 4.0, and Windows 2000. Windows Vista adds Windows XP to that mix.

To set up a multiboot system, you need a hard disk set up with a separate partition for each operating system, or you'll need multiple hard disks. The process is easiest done with a clean install on a new drive or drives, but can also be done by reformatting and repartitioning an existing drive or drives.

WARNING

Reformatting erases all programs and data, as well as the previous operating system.

The partition or disk where Windows Vista is to be installed must be formatted under the NTFS file system; other operating systems may function under older or different protocols.

You find full details on setting up a multiboot system in online or printed instructions from Microsoft. If you are already running Windows Vista or XP, you can find instructions on establishing a multiboot system in the Help screens of the operating system.

Changing the default operating system for startup in a multiboot system

You can use a third-party utility to enable multibooting (selecting from more than one possible operating system at startup) with any current version of Windows. And you can even do it yourself from within Windows XP, although the process is a bit complex. (See the Help screens within XP or consult the knowledge base at www.microsoft.com for assistance.)

With the arrival of Windows Vista, though, Microsoft has incorporated its own utility to set up and change multiboot options. Here's how to change the default operating system for machines that include Windows Vista:

1. Click the Start button, Control Panel ⇨ System and Maintenance ⇨ System. If you are prompted for an administrator password or confirmation, type the password or provide confirmation.
2. Click Advanced System Settings ⇨ Advanced tab. Locate Startup and Recovery and click Settings.
3. Under System startup, in the Default operating system list, click the operating system that you want to use when you turn on or restart your computer.

    If, instead, you want to be able to select which operating system to use each time you turn on the computer, select the Time to Display List of Operating Systems check box, and then choose the number of seconds you want the list of available operating systems to be displayed at startup before the default operating system is automatically loaded.

Repartitioning a formatted hard disk

You can repartition a hard disk that is already in use one of two ways; repartitioning changes the subdivision of the disk into logical volumes.

The official Microsoft method requires you to reformat the disk and, in doing so, delete all of the data, settings, applications, and the operating system. To do this, use the installation disk for Windows or the Disk Management tools available as part of Windows XP and Vista. Earlier versions of Windows used the Fdisk command-line tool, which can create FAT32 and other FAT file systems, but not the NTFS system that is commonly used in Windows XP and Vista.

The unofficial method is to use one of a number of third-party utilities that allow you to repartition without deleting all files. Most of these programs work by temporarily relocating files to clear space for new partitions; because of that, they may not be available to you if your hard disk has little or no unused space.

Windows Vista Advanced Utilities

Windows Vista offers nearly all the utilities that have made Windows XP the most stable and (when necessary) most easily repaired Microsoft operating system. The carryovers have been improved in places, and a number of new tools have been added.

Among the new features of Windows Vista is Startup Repair, a recovery tool that can fix certain problems related to missing or damaged system files that may cause the operating system not to open or to start incorrectly. Startup Repair scans the boot disk in search of problems and then seeks to repair or replace files as needed. Microsoft offers the utility as part of the off-the-shelf version of Windows Vista sold to computer manufacturers; some computer makers who bundle Vista with their hardware may customize or even replace that tool; manufacturers may also choose to install the utility on the hard disk and enable it to automatically run if there are problems at startup.

As delivered by Microsoft, the utility is located on the Windows installation disc. If Windows fails to start, or if you are seeking to fix an improper startup configuration, do the following:

1. Insert the Windows installation disc in the CD or DVD drive as appropriate.
2. Restart the computer.
3. When the Startup Repair utility is loaded, click View System Recovery Options (Advanced).
   If your computer is set up with multiple accounts or passwords, you are asked to enter a user name and password.
4. From the list of recovery tools, click Startup Repair.

The utility may find the problem (often a corrupted or inadvertently deleted system file) by itself. In other situations, you may be asked to make choices based on the tool's recommendations. Startup Repair cannot fix hardware failures and cannot remove viruses (although it may detect and repair files corrupted by viruses). If the utility is unable to make a repair, it displays information about any problems it detected and offer links to support options.

If the computer manufacturer has installed System Startup on the hard disk, you can configure it to start automatically and attempt to repair a problem detected during the startup process. If it is installed on your hard disk, you can also manually invoke the recovery options menu by going to the Windows Advanced Options menu.

Checking for memory problems (Windows Vista)

Memory issues — especially inconsistent (*flaky*) failures or freezes — can be some of the most vexing problems for computer users. Windows Vista includes a facility that automatically detects certain types of problems with RAM, and offers you the opportunity to run the Memory Diagnostics Tool.

If you receive such a notification, you can choose to restart your computer and run the tool immediately or defer the test until later. I suggest that you immediately save any work in progress, close any open programs, and restart the machine to run the test now . . . before the next crash causes you to lose work or make it difficult to retrieve files.

If the Windows Memory Diagnostics tool does not run automatically, you can instruct the system to run it manually. Click the Start button, then click Control Panel ⇨ System and Maintenance ⇨ Administrative Tools ⇨ Memory Diagnostics Tool. You can choose to run the tool immediately (after a shutdown and restart) or instruct the system to run the tool the next time the computer is started.

When the Memory Diagnostic Tool is running, you'll see a progress bar indicating the status of the test. When it is completed, Windows restarts automatically.

If the test does not find any errors, that's a bit of good news/bad news. The good news is that there is apparently not a permanent RAM failure. The bad news is that some sort of transient event or condition caused the system to suspect a problem with the memory — possibilities include a power spike or undervoltage, overheating, corrosion on contacts, and other conditions — and you may not be able to determine the cause. The best you can hope for is that such problems are infrequent; if the memory fails once every few months, you are probably better off living with the problem; if the failure occurs every few hours, it's time to test the modules and make replacements as necessary.

To test memory modules, turn off the machine and remove the power cord. Open the case and remove all of the memory modules. Check for dirt or corrosion on the contacts. Reinstall the modules one by one (or in pairs, if your machine's motherboard requires this) and try to determine which one is causing the problem. This involves installing the minimum amount of memory — one or two modules — powering up the machine, rebooting it, and testing the memory. If the first test doesn't uncover memory problems, remove the module(s) you just tested (following proper procedures to shut down the machine and remove power) and install another module or modules. Repeat this process until you determine which memory module is giving problems, and then replace the troublesome hardware.

You can also bring the modules to some computer shops for testing, although you may find it less expensive to merely replace them.

Obtaining computer speed and performance information (Windows Vista)

The Windows Vista Performance Rating and Tools utility shows information about the performance and overall capability of your computer's hardware. To run the tool, click the Start button, then click Control Panel ➪ System ➪ Maintenance ➪ Performance Rating ➪ Tools.

The Windows System Performance Rating is a number that indicates the relative speed and power of your computer in running Windows and other applications. The number takes into account your computer's motherboard, CPU, memory, hard disk, video adapter, gaming hardware, and other components. A higher performance rating means the computer can be expected to operate faster and more efficiently than a computer with a lower number; many new software programs produced for Windows Vista will include the minimum or recommended Software Rating for that application.

The utility also provides details about the computer's hardware, and may make suggestions about performance issues that you can address. For more details about these suggestions, click Advanced Tools ➪ View Performance Problems.

Using the System Configuration Utility (Windows Vista)

Under Windows Vista, the System Configuration Utility is an advanced tool that can help identify problems that might prevent Windows from starting correctly; the program is similar to one available under Windows XP. To start the utility, click Start ➪ Run; type **msconfig** into the command box and click OK.

System Configuration is intended to find and isolate problems, but not as a startup management program. Once you have determined the offending program or service, you have to uninstall it or change it from the Control Panel or a special uninstall utility associated with it.

Use System Configuration by turning off all non-essential services and startup programs and then turning them back on, one at a time, restarting the system each time a possibly troublesome program or service is enabled. If Windows works properly until a particular program is added to the startup package, you have identified the likely source of the problem. Contact the maker of the program for advice on whether to replace, update, or remove the offending piece of code.

System Configuration has three startup modes:

- **Diagnostic.** Starts Windows with basic services and drivers only. If the computer runs properly here, you know that the foundation of Windows is solid and problems likely lie with Windows extensions or third-party additions to the startup files.
- **Selective.** Starts Windows with basic services and drivers, adding other services and startup programs that you can individually select.
- **Normal.** Return Windows to its standard startup package. Choose this option after you have completed your troubleshooting.

Problems that slow down startup or shutdown (Windows Vista)

Some programs are set to automatically start each time Windows is loaded. That's exactly what you want for certain utilities, including antivirus and antispam programs, but some companies seem to have a highly inflated concept of the importance of other programs that you may or may not consider essential tools. Remember that the more programs and utilities Windows must load at startup, the slower the entire process will be. (This can become especially annoying if you are troubleshooting a problem with Windows and have to shut down and restart Windows repeatedly with various settings.)

To disable specific programs from the startup process, Windows Vista works with the Windows Defender utility.

The sophisticated power-saving modes that are part of Windows Vista serve an important purpose: Saving watts reduces power demand, which reduces global warming . . . and PC warming, too.

A problem with device drivers and settings on some programs may interfere with the way Windows shuts down or makes use of power-saving modes. The Power Rating and Tools utility in the Control Panel displays programs it has determined to be interfering with the power settings of Windows.

Here are ways to deal with a problematic program or driver:

- Check with the manufacturer of the program or driver for an update.
- Close programs before shutting down. Some programs are just obstinate that way; you might find your machine behaves better if you close down some or all running programs before shutting down Windows.

General Windows Troubleshooting and Repair Tips

Here are some common problems that arise in Windows-based systems, with some suggestions for troubleshooting or repair based on current tools in Windows Vista; similar tools are available in Windows XP.

- **After a new program is installed, Windows no longer works properly.** The first possibility is that the new program might be incompatible with your current version of Windows; that may well happen with a number of applications developed for Windows 98 or Windows XP and installed in Windows Vista. Restart Windows in Safe Mode and uninstall the program. Then contact the manufacturer by phone or over the Internet to see if there is a later version of the program available, or a patch to the earlier one.
- **After a new piece of hardware is installed, Windows no longer works properly.** The most likely culprit is a device driver that is incompatible with your version of Windows. Try uninstalling and reinstalling the driver and check for a new version that may be more compatible with your particular system configuration.
- **The machine no longer connects to the Internet.** Begin by making sure that your Internet connection is still active; if you have a cable modem or a DSL modem, an indicator light should tell you if the service is active; if it is not, first try turning off or unplugging the modem (unplug the power cord and the DSL or cable connection as well). After waiting half a minute or so, reconnect everything, repower it, and restart your PC to see if Internet service is restored. That process will often get you past an occasional modem lockup. If the indicator light is still showing problems, call the ISP to see if there is a problem with the network.

(If you're using *VoIP [Voice over Internet]* for your phone service, here's why you need a second line of some sort: a cell phone or a basic-service land line. If the Internet goes down, there's no way to use an Internet phone to call for assistance.) If the indicator lights tell you that the Internet is available to your modem, try restarting your machine using Safe Mode with Networking. This allows you to use Device Manager to check on the status of your networking hardware and to communicate with your modem and router (if using one). Seek the assistance of your ISP in troubleshooting your particular setup.

Recovering from an accidental deletion or format

Deleting a file or reformatting a disk full of data sounds like capital punishment, but in the world of personal computing, reprieves are available. However, the reprieves only work if you act quickly after performing the offending act. This section explores some critical life-saving utilities.

Undeleting

When you erase or delete a file, the operating system doesn't actually remove the file from the disk. Instead, it first changes the name of the file in the directory by writing hex code E5 (written E5H in computer-speak) over the name's first character. The old file and the details of its size and date and time of creation are still on the disk, but the DOS or Windows directory doesn't display this information because it has been programmed to ignore any filename that begins with E5H.

After completing this first step, DOS zeroes out the FAT entries of the clusters that still contain the deleted file to indicate to the system that those clusters are now available for a new file. When DOS examines the FAT, it now sees the zeroed-out entries as permission to use the associated clusters for new data.

As long as you have a reasonable amount of space available on your hard drive, it's likely to take a while before the system overwrites the space held by the "deleted" file.

Soon after the birth of the PC and its first DOS, several utilities were offered that could "undelete" these files — they located filenames that began with E5H and allowed users to change that first letter back to an allowable character, and made necessary changes to the FAT. The entire Norton Utilities empire — now part of Symantec — was born from such a program.

Microsoft Undelete became part of DOS and was offered through early versions of Windows.

Today, Windows 95/98 and all subsequent versions of Windows include a Recycle Bin that holds the contents of recently deleted files. You can open the bin and restore a deleted file with a few clicks of the mouse. You can adjust the size of the bin — the larger it is, the longer it will take for the oldest file in the bin to be overwritten by new materials.

Some utility programs, including Norton SystemWorks, expand the facilities of the Recycle Bin with new features including configurable data protection. An example of an enhanced recycle bin is shown in Figure 23-14.

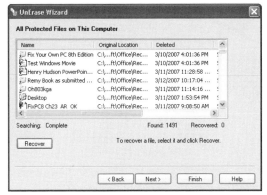

FIGURE 23-14: *The Norton Protected Recycle Bin, part of the Norton Utilities from Symantec, allows quick recovery of files using a wizard.*

Unformatting

In certain circumstances, it is possible to unformat a disk that has been reformatted. Windows versions from Windows 95/98 through Windows ME extend a DOS command to UNFORMAT a disk, although you can only recover an accidentally erased drive if new files have not written over the older ones. The utility was not continued into Windows XP.

Some third-party utilities, including Norton Utilities and Norton SystemWorks, include enhanced versions of the Unformat command. Most are based around a data-loss prevention program that makes copies of the FAT and root directory. If your FAT or root directory gets corrupted, the second part of the program uses these copies to recover data from the disk.

Repairing a damaged hard disk

In certain situations you may be able to recover from damage done to the software side of a hard disk drive: the file attribute table and other indexes that help the system locate a file, as well as problems that crop up in the file name and other file identification information.

There are three ways to make repairs. One, which I'm not going to describe in all of its gruesome detail, involves manually editing the machine code; I've done it, way back in the dinosaur era, and my hair still hurts when I think about the process. The second option is to use the limited facilities that are part of the Windows operating system. And the third choice is to allow a capable system utility program, such as Norton Utilities (in its standalone version or as part of Norton SystemWorks) to do the drudge work for you.

To use the built-in Windows tools follow these steps:

1. Open My Computer and then click the local disk you want to check.
   It becomes highlighted on the screen.
2. Right-click the disk name (or go to the File menu and click Properties).
3. Choose the Tools tab.
4. In the Error-checking section, click Check Now.
5. Finally, in the Check Disk Options, select Scan for Attempted Recovery of Bad Sectors.

NOTE

You must close all open files on the drive you are seeking to repair; the only elements that can still be running are those associated with the operating system itself. If you are unable to close the files, you can instruct Windows to automatically perform the disk check the next time the system is restarted.

If you have a third-party utility installed on your machine, it will most likely alter the displayed options on the Properties page to include its own facilities. For example, in Figure 23-15 you can see the display for a drive in my system that is under the guardianship of Norton Utilities.

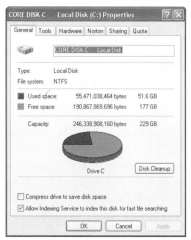

FIGURE 23-15: *The Properties screen for this drive includes a Tools tab that offers standard Windows error-checking as well as a Norton tab that is the entryway to the more capable Disk Doctor program.*

Seeking remote assistance

Advanced Windows Vista and Windows XP features, together with an Internet connection (preferably a high-speed broadband link), allow you to hand over control of your machine to a support technician anywhere in the world. Obviously, you want to make sure that this is only done with your permission and only with a person or company you trust.

Under Windows XP, Remote Assistance was initiated from within the Help program (search for Remote Assistance) and users could send an invitation to a technician by e-mail or instant message. Windows Vista greatly enhanced the process, offering faster performance and less network bandwidth; the program in Vista is a stand-alone utility that you can invoke from outside Windows if necessary. Consult the Help screens of your Windows version or seek the assistance of a technician who will guide you in a remote session.

Recovering a lost setup

On many modern machines and senior citizens, an unwelcome visitor is a bootup error message of "Invalid Configuration Information" followed by "Hard Disk Failure."

Among the possibilities in this case is an accidental trashing of the PC's setup information, something that can happen as the result of a power spike or that can occasionally be caused by a poorly behaved piece of software. On the other hand, the problem may be as simple as dead batteries.

Begin by rebooting the machine and go to the setup or configuration screen. Check the entries against the copy of settings you maintain in a notebook alongside your computer. If that advice catches you by surprise, run out, get a notebook, and write down the settings now. On many setup screens for modern machines, you can ask the computer to autodetect your hard drives and make its own settings. Save your changes (the method varies based on the BIOS maker and version of setup provided, but you should find instructions on the screen) and then reboot the system to see whether it now comes to life.

If this fails, or if setup holds the configuration only for a while until it loses it again, you may have a dead battery connected to the clock-calendar chip that holds the setup information. Check the instruction manual for your motherboard or call the manufacturer for advice.

Open the case, replace the batteries with fresh ones, and run the setup program.

Missing device drivers

The symptoms of a missing device driver are usually something like this: Your computer boots, but Drive D: has disappeared, the scanner has stopped scanning, or you can't get back on the network.

If you are working under Windows 95/98, go to the Device Manager (discussed previously in this chapter) and check for the presence of proper drivers for your devices. You can update a driver from the properties page for a hardware device.

Under Windows XP and Vista, Microsoft has made several valuable improvements. First of all, Windows device drivers and operating system files are now digitally signed by Microsoft to ensure their quality to indicate they have passed compatibility testing and that the file has not been altered or overwritten by another program's installation process.

The operating system also includes a facility to roll back a driver when a driver upgrade doesn't work properly or causes interference with other components of the PC. When you update a driver, Windows XP stores information about the previous driver, and choosing "Roll Back Driver" from the properties page for a piece of hardware will revert to the earlier version.

Repairing or updating a driver

Device drivers — small pieces of code that help the operating system adapt its general commands to the specific capabilities of various pieces of hardware — sometimes become corrupted or accidentally deleted. And over time, many hardware manufacturers issue updates to their drivers to deal with errors or to adapt to new versions or features of the operating system.

You can instruct Windows to look for newer versions of device drivers by connecting to the Windows Update web site maintained by Microsoft. You can also manually install a new driver or an update that is provided to you by the device manufacturer on a web site or on a disk.

To update driver software using Windows Update, your machine needs to have Internet access.

1. Open Windows Update by clicking Start ➪ All Programs ➪ Windows Update.
2. On the left pane of the screen, click Check for Updates.
3. If updates are available for the devices installed in your machine, click View Available Updates.
4. Click the name of any driver software you want to install, and then click Install.

To manually update driver software, follow these steps:

1. Open Device Manager by clicking Start ➪ Control Panel ➪ System. ➪ System/Hardware and Device Settings/Device Manager.
2. Double-click the device you want to update.
3. Click the Driver tab, and then click Update Driver.

NOTE

Recovering a Lost Driver under a dinosaur operating system is, on the one hand, more direct and simple; on the other hand you won't have much in the way of assistance from the system. If you are working under DOS or Windows 3.1, you should first direct your attention to the config.sys and autoexec.bat files to check for a problem with the driver references located there.

Have drivers been removed, renamed, or moved? When you check your config.sys file, see that it includes all the DEVICE= statements required to load all your device drivers. Add-on peripherals and boards are often shipped with installation disks that make alterations

to the autoexec.bat and config.sys files. Before you install an add-on, first copy your files to autoexec.old and config.old. Then rewrite the originals or run the installation program to add the necessary DEVICE= statements. The lines required by the device driver are now in your config.sys file, but you have the backup files in case something goes wrong and you want to look at the old instructions.

A corresponding problem crops up in the Windows 3.1 win.ini file, which contains specific instructions about the Windows setup. New software writes additional lines into win.ini. Well-mannered software makes a copy of the old file in case you uninstall or need to make other changes. If you get strange symptoms, something may have zapped your win.ini file.

Fixing problems with display quality

Assuming that your LCD screen, CRT monitor, or associated video adapter are not exhibiting hardware problems (check the Device Manager or run a diagnostic program to confirm), reduced video performance may be caused by too many programs running at the same time or by improper system settings you made. You may improve your system's capabilities by installing a more powerful video card with a high-speed processor, coupled with faster and more abundant video memory.

Here are some suggestions to reduce the demands on the system:

- **Reduce the number of open programs or windows.** The more programs open, the higher the demand on system resources. Close any programs that are not necessary.
- **Avoid running too many graphics-intensive programs at the same time.** Certain graphics-intensive program combinations may overwhelm your system and its video adapter. Among very demanding programs are digital-image or video editors and games. The image you see may respond slowly, skip frames, or appear jittery. Close any programs that are not necessary.
- **Reduce the monitor's resolution.** In general, the highest resolutions and the highest number of colors in the palette require the most system resources. Try reducing the resolution to see if problems go away.
- **Choose a simpler desktop theme.** Some supplied desktop themes, as well as custom configurations, may be too demanding on your particular video adapter.

Troubleshooting the video adapter driver

If your video adapter is demonstrating odd behavior but you can still see the screen, the best way to troubleshoot the device is through built-in Windows troubleshooting tools. Find the video adapter in the Device Manager; here's how:

1. Click Start ⇨ Settings ⇨ Control Panel.
2. Double-click System ⇨ Hardware ⇨ Device Manager.
3. Locate the Display Adapters listing, and click the + sign to its left.
4. Look at the listing to see if it is marked with a yellow question mark (indicating possible trouble) or a red exclamation mark (telling you the system has detected a definite problem).
   You can also double-click the video adapter driver to display its Properties screen. Select the General tab and read the Device Status box to see if the system reports a problem.
5. To run the display troubleshooter, click the Troubleshoot button. Follow the instructions offered by the system.

Updating, rolling back, or uninstalling the video adapter driver

To make a change to the video driver, follow the preceding steps to reach the adapter's Properties screen. Then click the Driver tab, and choose the appropriate button from these options:

- **Driver Details.** Click to display details about the driver files in use.
- **Update Driver.** Follow the instructions to update the driver from a supplied disk or from a file you have downloaded from the manufacturer's web site.
- **Roll Back Driver.** If the device fails to operate properly after installation of an updated driver, you can choose this option to uninstall the new driver and replace it with the previous one.
- **Uninstall.** Choose this option for removal of the existing driver without installing a replacement.

WARNING

If you choose the Uninstall option for your default video adapter, you may be unable to view the screen since the adapter will be unable to communicate with Windows.

Checking the status of a video adapter in Safe Mode

If you suspect a problem with the device driver for your video adapter and are unable to examine its status under Windows, you are caught in a conundrum, a computer Catch-22. How do you troubleshoot a device when you need to use the device to see the screen?

A related question: if you make an error in settings for a video adapter (choosing a resolution or refresh rate it cannot support, for example) how can you fix the problem if the screen is garbled and unreadable?

The solution in most cases is to restart the system in Safe Mode, which automatically sets the video adapter to its most basic group of settings.

System Crashes: Rounding Up the Usual Suspects

At the heart of the Windows operating system is its ability to work with many programs open at the same time; the microprocessor is able to shift its attention from one to the other as needed, dividing up jobs as needed to give the appearance of everything happening at once.

That's the good news; the bad news is that the number of programs running in the background can begin to grow to unmanageable size, and even worse, may cause minor to major problems without you even being aware that they were loaded.

To see how many programs are running on your PC at startup, load Windows. After it is running, hit the Ctrl + Alt + Del key combination once to bring up the Close Program box. (Under Windows XP, the more capable equivalent is the Windows Task Manager, which includes information about Processes running in the background and also gives access to CPU and network usage reports.)

Be careful not to press the keys a second time to avoid resetting the computer.

Each of the programs that you see listed is currently active and demanding a bit of your CPU's attention. Among the programs that you are likely to see are utilities to support your mouse, keyboard, advanced graphics card, and other hardware. If you're running an antivirus program (and you should) you'll see one or more components of that application monitoring the activities of your computer.

All of these programs are part of your startup group. After you load an application, such as Microsoft Word, Internet Explorer, or Quicken, they will be added to the list of open programs.

If you suspect problems caused by one of the startup programs, you'll need to put on your sleuth's hat and try disabling the programs one at a time to try to isolate the one at fault.

If you are running Windows 95, you'll have to do all of the work by yourself; identify each program and look for a menu command to disable it. Keep track of all changes you make so that you can track your progress and undo the process later.

Under current versions of Windows, you can use the included System Configuration Utility to disable and enable programs one at a time. To launch the utility, click Start ➪ Run. Type **MSCONFIG** and press Enter. An example of the General Tab of the utility, in its Windows XP version, is shown in Figure 23-16.

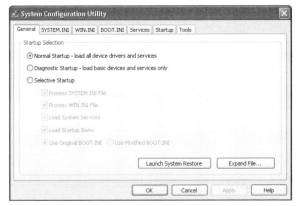

FIGURE 23-16: *The System Configuration Utility includes options for startup, as well as more specific adjustments and an entry to the System Restore utility.*

Before you test each program individually, a process that can take a while, find out if the problem is in one of your startup programs. From the System Configuration Utility, go to the General tab and remove the check mark in front of "Load startup group items."

Now reboot the system. Your computer will come to life without any of the startup programs running. If the problem persists, it is very likely that it is not caused by one of the programs in the startup list. If the problem goes away, go back to the General tab and put the check mark back.

At this point, your assignment is to disable all of the startup programs and then enable them one at a time until the problem comes

back. You'll have to reboot the computer each time you re-enable a startup item.

With the System Configuration Utility panel displayed, click on the Startup tab to see the list of programs that automatically start each time the system is booted. Check or uncheck the boxes alongside the program names to include or disable programs from the startup process.

Remember that deselecting a program here does not remove it from your system. You can later return it to the startup list by checking its box.

With luck, you'll find the offending program. When you do, decide if you really need to have it running. Check with the manufacturer for an updated version or for a bug fix.

And while you're in the neighborhood, disable any startup items that you don't need. Each slows down the loading of Windows and uses system resources.

Resetting a Windows XP Password

If you plan ahead, you can recover from a forgotten password using the aptly named Forgotten Password Wizard of Windows XP.

The utility lets you create a password reset disk that you can use to recover your user account and personalized computer settings.

Open User Accounts from the Control Panel and click on your account name. Under Related Tasks, click "Prevent a forgotten password." Follow the instructions to create a floppy disk with a back door into your system; store the disk with your Windows CD. If you don't have a floppy disk drive . . . you're out of luck.

Under Windows XP or Vista, you should take advantage of the option to provide a hint to help you remember the password. Please don't list the actual password as a hint; anyone turning on the machine can read the hint. Instead, choose a password with particular meaning to you and then list a hint that will jog your memory but no one else's. For example, if your password is the year and model of your first car (in my case, a rattletrap 1970 Plymouth Duster) I might choose 1970duster. For the hint, I would type *year first car.* The fact that I listed the hint in lowercase reminds me not to use capital letters.

If your Windows XP machine is on a domain, press Ctrl + Alt + Delete to open the Windows Security dialog box. Click Change Password ➪ Backup to open the Forgotten Password Wizard. Follow the instructions on the screen.

Ch 23

Operating System Housecleaning

This book concentrates on the hardware side of the computer equation, but it is a basic fact of PC life that the hardware and the operating system are inextricable. Each can cause the other trouble, and determining the source of the problem is sometimes as easy as herding cats.

In this section, you'll find a few operating system tips and tricks that will help you keep the software side of your system healthy.

Cleaning up the System Tray

Too many programs on the System Tray (known as the Notification Area in Windows XP) of the taskbar can slow down startup and steal clock cycles from your CPU, slowing down the system.

You can remove or disable some of the programs you find there by right-clicking on each icon; look for an option to disable or remove the program.

Under Windows 95, you can remove any program from the Startup folder in this way: Open Windows Explorer and click on Windows ⇨ Start Menu ⇨ Programs ⇨ Startup folder.

Under Windows 98, run the Microsoft System Configuration utility. Click Start/Run and open MSCONFIG. Open the Startup tab and unclick the box next to any program that you don't want to start with Windows. (Note that this does not remove the program from your system; your action merely disables it as part of the startup process.)

Under Windows XP, right-click on the Notification Area and then choose the Customize button. You can then choose to hide, or hide when inactive, components of the tray. Windows Vista has a similar procedure.

Emptying the Temp folder

Windows stores working files and placemarkers in a file folder at C:\Windows\Temp and other locations.

Depending on the sort of programs you run and your working practices, this folder can rapidly fill with hundreds or even thousands of files. Some programs will clean out entries they place in the folder, and others create tiny or even empty files there. In some cases, the swelling folder can waste space on your hard drive and even slow down the start-up process.

You can check the contents of the folder by clicking on Start ⇨ Find ⇨ Files or Folders. Under Named, enter *.tmp and Look in the C: drive.

You can individually delete files here, or select all files for deletion. Either way, the best practice is to reboot your system after deletions.

Under Windows 98 and later versions, including Windows XP, you can also clear out temporary files by going to a Windows utility. Choose Start ⇨ All Programs ⇨ Accessories ⇨ System Tools and Disk Cleanup. Open the Select Drive box and choose a drive to clean up, and then click OK to open the Disk Cleanup box.

You can also rely on the services of a system utility such as Norton SystemWorks from Symantec to clean up the clutter as part of regularly scheduled maintenance.

Dinosaur sweepups

Windows 95/98 users can also add a command to the Autoexec.bat file that is executed by the operating system each time you boot up.

Under Windows 95 and earlier operating systems, find the Autoexec.bat file in the root directory of the C: drive and open it for editing in Windows Notepad.

Under Windows 98 and XP, run the Microsoft System Configuration utility. Click Start ⇨ Run and open MSCONFIG. Click on the Autoexec tab and add a new line. Enter the following new command: `del C:\Windows\Temp\*.tmp > nul`.

With this command in place, your operating system will sweep out the contents of the Temp folder each time you start your machine. Unless you're very comfortable with this sort of do-it-yourself programming, though, I recommend using a third-party maintenance utility to automate the process.

Safely shutting down Windows

You should always follow official procedure when you shut down Windows; click on Start and then Shut Down under Windows 95, 98, and 2000. Under Windows XP, click on Start and then Turn Off Computer; Windows Vista operates in a similar fashion.

While Windows operates, it stores information about configuration and settings in temporary files. If you merely turn off the power, these files may be left in place or corrupted.

Of course, if your machine freezes and you can't perform an orderly shutdown, you'll have to turn off the power or press the reset button on the case and hope that Windows can (as it usually does) repair problems caused by the shutdown.

Senior-citizen tech

One common annoying problem with Windows 98 is a hangup during shutdown. The good news is that this is a fairly common problem, and well known to Microsoft. The bad news is that it can have many causes and is not easily fixed.

In many cases, you can solve the problem by disabling a Windows feature called "fast shutdown." This facility reduces the time Windows requires to close down files it has opened for its own needs. However, there may be some incompatibilities between fast shutdown and some hardware devices.

To disable fast shutdown, click Start ➪ Run, and type **MSCONFIG**. Press Enter to run the utility program. After it is displayed, click on the Advanced button (on the General tab) and click the check box to disable fast shutdown. Restart your computer and test again for proper shutdown.

NOTE

Some older BIOS systems may not offer fast shutdown.

If the problem persists, visit Microsoft's Knowledge Base at sup-port.microsoft.com on the Internet and follow the steps in article Q202633 for Windows 98 or Q238096 for Windows 98 SE. Among the files that Microsoft suggests you check is the Windows shutdown sound.

Other usual suspects include devices that require a great deal of system resources, such as sound cards and network interface cards: You can experiment by disabling devices one by one to see if the problem goes away. When you identify the problematic device, you should contact its manufacturer for assistance.

To temporarily disable a device, right-click My Computer, and then click Properties. Click the Device Manager tab, and then double-click a class of devices.

For sound cards, choose Sound ➪ Video and game controllers. For network cards, double-click Network adapters. Click the first device in the list, and then click Properties. Select the Disable in this hardware profile check box, and then click OK. Restart the computer and check for the effect of your changes.

If the problem does not go away, repeat these steps and choose another device.

You should also investigate whether Advanced Power Management (APM) is causing the problem. This feature is intended to help reduce the use of electrical power by the computer, shutting down hard drives, monitors, and other devices, but it may not be fully compatible with all devices installed in your system.

To determine whether APM is causing a problem at shutdown, try disabling it. To do so, click Start ➪ Settings ➪ Control Panel, and then double-click System. Click the Device Manager tab, and then double-click System Devices. (In Windows 2000, click the Hardware tab of the System dialog box, and then click on the Device Manager button on this dialog box.) Double-click Advanced Power Management in the device list, then click the Settings tab. Clear the check box in front of Enable Power Management. Restart your computer and test shut-down. If disabling APM seems to fix your problem, keep it shut off.

NOTE

Some BIOS systems don't offer this feature, and Advanced Power Management won't be listed.

Uninstalling programs properly

When you install a program under Windows, elements of the application are typically spread across a number of different folders on your hard drive, and changes are made to the System Registry and other configuration files. For that reason, it is not a proper — or safe — procedure to attempt to remove a program by merely deleting its main executable file.

If you want to remove a program, check whether it has its own uninstall option by looking in the application's Start Menu group or within Add/Remove Programs in the Control Panel. This will usually get rid of the program.

If the program does not have an entry in Add/Remove Programs, go to the Programs listing from the Start menu and see if the application has its own uninstall utility.

Internet Troubleshooting

If your Internet connection slows down markedly, begin with this basic question: Have you changed any settings or added any programs or software since the last time it functioned properly? If so, you should double-check your work, and consider reinstalling software.

If you have made no changes to your system, check with your Internet Service Provider. If you can get online to the ISP's home page,

Ch 23

look for reports of technical problems or scheduled maintenance; some companies, including cable and DSL services, offer utility programs that monitor the condition of your connection and deliver messages.

Another way to gauge the performance of your system is to use Ping, a DOS utility that is included in most versions of Windows. Ping sends a small packet of data from your PC to a web site of your choice and then reports how long it takes for a response.

To run Ping, you need to be running Windows and have an Internet connection open.

Under Windows 95/98, click Start ➪ Programs ➪ MS-DOS Prompt, and then open a DOS window. Under Windows XP or Vista, click Start ➪ Programs ➪ Accessories ➪ Command Prompt.

You will be greeted with a command prompt from the operating system that underlines Windows. Type **Ping** followed by the name of a web site you want to test, and press Enter.

If the Ping is successful in reaching the web site, you will receive a report. For example, here's a report I received using my high-speed cable modem broadband connection:

```
C:\WINDOWS>ping Econoguide.com
Pinging Econoguide.com [82.165.195.76] with 32 bytes of data
Reply from 82.165.195.76: bytes = 32, time = 19ms, TTL = 45
Reply from 82.165.195.76: bytes = 32, time = 19ms, TTL = 45
Reply from 82.165.195.76: bytes = 32, time = 21ms, TTL = 45
Reply from 82.165.195.76: bytes = 32, time = 19ms, TTL = 45
Ping statistics for 82.165.195.76:
    Packets: Sent = 4, Received = 4, Lost = 0 (0% loss)
Approximate round trip times in milli-seconds:
    Minimum = 19ms, Maximum = 21ms, Average = 19 ms
```

From this report, I learned that my web site, www.econoguide.com, was reachable and that the average roundtrip time for the transmission of 32 bytes of data and a response was about 19ms, a zippy response for a busy time of day on the Internet.

One other test: Ping 127.0.0.1 to check your system's TCP/IP settings. You should receive an almost instant response — an average response near 0ms — if not, your TCP/IP settings are probably incorrect. Check with your Internet service provider for assistance.

Tracking the Registry

When you install new hardware and software, Windows keeps track of it in a special database file called the Registry. The Registry is a crucial component of any Windows installation because it stores configuration information about everything you have on your machine. Unfortunately, not all third-party programs (or even Windows itself, if the truth be known) always do a good job of keeping the Registry current with the real world. If your computer starts acting flaky and you've eliminated a virus as the problem, chances are you have a corrupted Registry.

The Registry can become corrupted by a number of causes, but the most common are hardware problems that physically damage data in the Registry database, or software that you install or remove that doesn't properly update the Registry. Remember that uninstalling is different from simply deleting software. Uninstalling cleans up all the parts of a software program that may exist on your system. If you simply delete a file or program, you may not be aware of related files that should also be deleted. You'll certainly encounter Registry problems if you just delete a program directory without uninstalling the software. Deleting leaves instructions and configuration information in the Registry about software that no longer exists.

You can use a built-in Windows utility called RegEdit to view Registry information and change it. However, I recommend that you stay away from this editor unless you are working under the direct supervision of a technician at a support desk. It is simply too easy to cause more problems than you fix unless you have experience in this area. If you want a peek at just how complex the entries are, there's a sample of just one category in Figure 23-17.

You can use a number of commercial utilities to help track or repair the Registry. Microsoft offered its own utility, RegClean, for systems from Windows 95 through Windows 2000; that product was withdrawn in 2001.

For users of Windows XP, the best solution is to become a regular user of System Restore. Set up that utility to record regular snapshots of your Registry and other system settings. Then before you make any major change to your system, including installation of new software or hardware, manually instruct System Restore to create a restore point. If your system does not perform properly after a change, go back to System Restore and revert to one of the saved points in time.

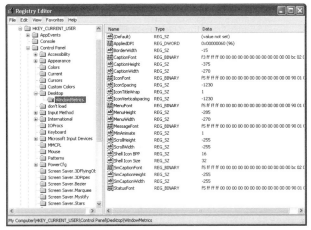

FIGURE 23-17: *The Registry Editor available to users of current versions of Windows should be approached only by advanced users or under the guidance of a technical support desk.*

Users of earlier versions of Windows may need to consider occasionally reinstalling Windows. If you notice software problems, you can try reinstalling Windows in the same directory where it currently resides. This preserves all of your installed software and data files that reside in the Windows directory. If this doesn't correct the problem, then consider a fresh installation.

Run the Windows setup program and specify a different directory for your Windows software. Doing this ensures that you start with a clean Registry and that all extraneous DLL files are removed. Of course, it also means that you have to reinstall all of the software that you want to use.

If you decide to reinstall Windows in this way, make sure to back up any data files that you need before you erase the files in the original directory.

A last-ditch repair

And finally, here's a tip for the not-of-faint-heart. If your system seems to have slowed down to a crawl or has become what seems to be hopelessly disorganized, consider a major housekeeping. Think of it as the ultimate step in system tuning. Here are the steps:

1. Back up all of your data files to an external or secondary hard disk, or to one or more DVDs.

2. Back up copies of your Internet favorites and settings. Consult the Help section of your browser for instructions on exporting this information.
3. Back up copies of your e-mail settings and saved mail.
4. Collect copies of all of your installation discs for applications (or registration confirmations for downloaded programs).
5. Make sure you have a bootable copy of your Windows operating system.
   If you have an upgrade disk rather than a full retail version, you also need your older version of the operating system to be inserted at the proper time during the reinstallation.
6. Double-check the preceding steps and calls or consult online resources to answer any questions you have about reinstallation of programs, settings, and Windows.
   Ready?
7. Use a disk utility to reformat your hard drive and then reinstall Windows.
8. Once it is up and running (installation usually takes about two hours), reinstall your applications and utilities.
9. From within your Internet browser, reinstall settings and favorites. Do the same within your e-mail program.
10. Finally, reinstall data files from their backup locations on an external or secondary disk or from DVDs.
11. Run the Windows Update program over the Internet to install security and feature updates. Do the same for all of your applications.

Sound drastic? It is, but you'd be amazed at how clean and fast your system will become after you do this. An additional benefit is that this tactic forces you to organize and store what you need and to throw away what you don't. I usually end up with several hundred megabytes of free space after a format because I don't put back everything I took off. Think of it as cleaning out the garage: You don't like to do it, you don't do it often enough, but after it's done, you feel really good about having a clean, clear space to park your car.

SUMMARY

The advanced utilities of Windows offer valuable tools to help you figure out the source of many problems with your system. In the next chapter, I explore some hard-won hints and tips from long-time users.

Chapter 24

Common-Sense Solutions to Hardware Headaches

Throughout this book, you've explored some very technical solutions to computer problems. At the same time, many users also know that one way to get a balky hard drive to start spinning is to whack the side of the case in just the right spot, that the solution to a noisy cooling fan may be to put an old floppy disk under the front of the case to change its position slightly, or that an aging monitor may work best at a refresh rate other than its original recommended setting. These are the sorts of lessons that come with experience; they are common-sense solutions to common problems.

In this chapter, I disclose some of the best tips and techniques that you can use to solve many problems that cause big headaches.

Top Ten Crimes against Your Computer

Don't go looking for trouble; trouble will find you. But you can do some things to make yourself less of a target. Here are the top ten crimes a user can commit against his or her computer. (Let's be careful out there, people.)

1. **Failing to back up your files.** You can do dozens of things to try to keep your PC's hardware and software in good working order, and you should do as many of them as you possibly can. However, the most foolproof preventative measure is having a good set of backup files of all of your essential data in case of disaster.

   Analyze your work habits and consider the amount of data that you create each day. Depending on the size of your files, you should back up copies to some form of removable storage:

a Zip or Rev disk, a CD-R, a tape cartridge, or a superfloppy among them.

2. **Not inoculating against infection.** Computer viruses are out there; it's a crime to operate a computer that is any way connected to the outside world without having a proper antivirus program in place. This includes nearly every PC: if your machine is connected to the Internet, to AOL, or to a home or office network, it is at risk. And, if you load software or data files from a floppy disk, you risk infection in that way.

   At the very least, install a capable antivirus program. Even better, add a software or hardware firewall.

   And once you have an antivirus program installed, you've got to make the effort to keep its definitions up to date; most programs, such as those sold under the Norton or McAfee brand, are meant to check online regularly for updates to combat the latest threats. You need to renew subscriptions for this service annually, or install new software with a fresh subscription.

   You should also install and use protection against spyware and other programs that attempt to steal information from your computer or track your travels on the Internet. Microsoft introduced Windows Defender in 2006; other programs from third parties include Ad-Aware (`www.lavasoft.de`) and Spybot (`www.safer-networking.org`). You can obtain free personal-use licenses for such programs, or pay a fee for more capable versions aimed at business use. Search the Internet for download sites.

Ch
24

Microsoft Windows XP and Vista come with their own software firewall. You can also purchase third-party versions from companies including Symantec, and there are also hardware firewalls. Each of these works by establishing a set of rules about which sites and users, and which types of files or programs are allowed to enter your system. They can also be set up to prevent your computer from sending malicious software to other computers as the result of an infection that has somehow made its way onto your machine.

3. **Playing with unfinished software.** Many software companies — including Microsoft — offer individuals and companies the "opportunity" to work with pre-release, or *beta,* software. In a way, users who agree to do so become unpaid testers for the software companies. Unless you have a very good reason to do so, I advise against trying these products. They are considered beta versions because they may cause problems with your system. Having stated that, I regularly try out beta versions of operating systems and applications for my books. However, I do so on a machine separate from my mission-critical systems, and I fully expect the need to reformat and reinstall operating systems on that machine regularly. I never mix beta software with my irreplaceable data files.

A related issue: *Acting cautiously,* keep your finished software current by installing appropriate updates when they are made available by the manufacturer. Software makers regularly ship minor revisions of their software to address bugs and incompatibilities discovered after the product was shipped, and sometimes offer new features to registered users between release of completely new versions. Check with your software maker to see if there is a means for automatic notification or download of updates.

4. **Rushing into updates.** When I say "act cautiously" regarding updates, here's what I mean: Unless your program is broken or a specific issue that needs addressing, try not to be the first person on the block to apply an upgrade. Sometimes the best policy is to wait a few weeks or months before upgrading to allow other users to be the guinea pigs for the software maker. Not that it happens all that often, but occasionally a cure proves worse than the disease . . . at least at the start.

5. **Performing improper housecleaning.** Life as a PC user would be so much easier if the process of adding or removing a piece of software was as simple as copying the application onto your hard drive. Alas, although the original DOS more or less worked like that, the arrival of the multitasking Windows environment and the concept of the interlinked office suite put an end to that.

Under Windows, components of an application are typically spread across many places in the computer, and additions or alterations are made to numerous components of the operating system, including the System Registry.

However, you can cause damage to your operating environment by installing or uninstalling software without regard to the proper procedure. Follow all instructions at installation, including shutting down any other unnecessary Windows applications while new programs are put in place.

If you choose to uninstall a program, use the facilities of the Add/Remove Programs option that is part of the Control Panel. Or, use the program's own uninstaller, or a third-party program *sweeper.*

6. **Not playing doctor with your drives.** Even the largest hard drive will eventually become cluttered with fragmented files, wasted clusters, and errors, such as crosslinked files.

The prudent user regularly employs ScanDisk (built into Microsoft Windows), or a third-party disk utility, such as Norton SystemWorks from Symantec or Diskeeper from Executive Software.

There is nothing magical about the work that these programs perform — the creation of fragmented files and wasted clusters is an ordinary consequence of the way the file attribute table works. In an ordinary home or office, it is good practice to defragment your hard drive anytime more than 10 percent of the files are inefficiently scattered.

7. **Failing to keep your system high and dry.** Put most simply: Don't drink and compute. And eating around the keyboard is not such a great idea, either.

Speaking just for myself, I figure I drop a glass or spill a can of soda once every few months. It's no big deal if that happens on the beach or in my kitchen. But if I spill a can into my PC or monitor, the consequences can be catastrophic. Later in this chapter, I present some common-sense solutions that *might* undo the damage. But the only way to be sure food and drink don't damage any of your components is to simply keep them away from your system.

8. **Not keeping your cool.** Heat is one of the principal enemies of your computer and your monitor.

Never block the inflow and outflow openings on your PC's case. A well-designed case is part of the cooling system for your computer, and most systems don't cool properly without the case in place.

Never operate a PC without its cooling fan properly operating. Monitors produce a great deal of heat that is normally vented through its top. Never place papers or other objects on top of the case. One of the dumbest office products I have ever seen is a set of plastic shelves intended to encase your monitor and allow you to place a telephone and books above it. This sort of device is almost guaranteed to cause the monitor to overheat and shorten its life; in the worst case, it could cause a fire.

9. **Mispowering your system.** Electricity is a flowing river, but like a waterway, it sometimes surges and wanes.

A power surge or spike can fry your PC. A brownout can shut down your system or cause damage. Don't connect your PC directly to the wall outlet. Every system should have a surge protector in place on the power line. Even better is an uninterruptible power supply that isolates the system from the power line; a UPS powers the PC from a large battery, all the while recharging the storage device.

10. **Not keeping your system clean.** Cigarettes, hair spray, pet hair, dirt, and dust are unfriendly neighbors for a PC. They can cause a hard drive to crash, make it difficult to read an optical CD-ROM, and block the air vents for cooling. Vacuum your office or workspace regularly, and consider using an air cleaner in especially dirty environments.

Getting Good Technical Support

As part of any purchase decision, include an assessment of the quality and availability of technical support. If you're considering making a major purchase of an application, make a call to the support desk with a question about configuration or system requirements; if you're not satisfied with the quality of the response you get before you buy the product, you have no reason to expect good service after your check has been cashed.

Here are some more tips:

1. Make a record of error messages. Keep a notepad by your computer, and write down any error messages that you receive.
2. Make notes on what you were doing before the error occurred. Which programs were open? What key combinations or mouse clicks had you just entered? How long had the machine been powered on?
3. Keep copies of every instruction manual, program installation disk, and driver file. I keep all of these materials in large envelopes on one level of the bookshelf in my office, organized by type of device. If you have multiple machines, be sure to attach a note indicating in which machine the device is installed, and the date of installation.
4. Prepare for your technical support call. Know the system specifications for your machine, including the operating system and version, the type of processor, and internal devices. Have your machine running, and call from a telephone near the keyboard so that you can perform any actions asked of you by a technician. Keep a notebook to keep track of actions that you are asked to make.
5. If possible, call when support desks are least busy. In general, it's not a good idea to call on Monday morning after a weekend's pent-up problems, or late in the afternoon when a day's issues are before them. When does that leave? I've had the best luck calling early in the day during the week.
6. Write down the name of the technician you speak with, and see whether you can obtain a direct telephone number or an e-mail address for follow-up questions. Find out whether the support desk assigns a case number that documents your interaction with the support desk, and be sure to record that information. If you call back another time, a technician can read the entire history of your case.
7. Be polite, but firm. There's no point to losing your cool. But if you feel you are not getting good advice, politely ask whether you can speak to another technician or a supervisor who may be able to help.

Ch
24

Secrets of the Hardware Gurus

There is hardware and then there is hardware: The lack of a simple machine screw — about a penny's worth of metal — can cause an adapter card not to seat properly in the system bus and cause your $2,000 PC to resemble an electric paperweight. Or a sudden spike in electricity — caused by a lightning storm or your kid opening the refrigerator — can fry your PC in an instant.

The following sections give some hard-won solutions to knotty problems that computer manufacturers — and the writers of instruction manuals — somehow seem to ignore year after year.

Resetting a system password

Many modern BIOS systems offer the chance to set a system password that must be entered before the PC begins to load an operating system. This is a good way to protect a machine from mischief, but can be a danger if you happen to forget the password or if the CMOS memory for the BIOS becomes corrupted.

If you are unable to get past a system password, your options are limited; the password is not stored in a file, but rather in a small segment of specialized memory on the CMOS.

Consult the instruction manual for the BIOS or contact the manufacturer of your system to determine whether there is a default password that supercedes your private entry. Ask also whether there is a reset button on the motherboard or a jumper that can be changed to reset all of the entries in the CMOS. One last step is to find out whether the battery that keeps the CMOS memory alive can be disconnected or removed to cancel all settings for the BIOS.

If you end up clearing the BIOS, you will need to enter new settings, including those that allow your system to recognize the hard drive and other peripherals. It's a good idea when you first purchase a machine to walk through the BIOS settings and write down critical entries, including hard drive type and all of the specifications that accompany it, memory and display settings, and anything else that the system may not be able to determine automatically if this data is lost during a hardware problem.

Just as an example — because different motherboard manufacturers handle the process differently — current Intel motherboards have a pair of jumpers near the backplane where connections are made to the outside world. One jumper is called CLRPSWD, and as its name suggests, it is used to clear the password.

Intel motherboards are used by a number of computer manufacturers, including Dell. Other makers usually offer similar facilities. Consult the instruction manual or online resources for your computer.

A typical password reset works like this:

1. Unplug your computer, ground yourself, and open the case to expose the motherboard.
2. Locate the password jumper. (As delivered, the jumper is enabled, meaning that it is in place across the two pins to complete a circuit.)
3. Remove the jumper to disable the system password feature; carefully set aside the jumpers.
4. Close the cover and reattach the power cord and any other cables that were removed.
5. Power up the computer and load Windows. Once the operating system is running, use the standard method to shut down the computer from within Windows.
6. Unplug your computer, ground yourself, and open the case to expose the motherboard.
7. Locate the password jumpers and replace the jumper across pins 1 and 2 to reenable the password feature.
8. Close the cover and reattach the power cord and any other cables that were removed.
9. Power up the computer and load Windows. You will be given the option to assign a new password, or you can skip over the password screen, which enables the machine to load without that security feature.

Clearing the CMOS settings

If you have altered the default settings for the system setup and the machine does not function properly, your best bet may be to reset the CMOS system memory to its default condition — the settings that were assigned to it by the manufacturer.

There are three ways to do this:

- The CMOS Setup screen has a command that will change all settings back to their default condition. Consult the instruction manual if you cannot find the command.
- Most current motherboards offer a jumper you can remove, causing the system memory to reset to its default configuration.
- Depending on the motherboard's design, you may be able to remove the battery that backs up the memory to effect a reset.

One jumper is called CLRCMOS, and as its name suggests, it is used to Clear the CMOS memory.

Intel motherboards are used by a number of computer manufacturers, including Dell. Other makers usually offer similar facilities. Consult the instruction manual or online resources for your computer.

A typical CMOS reset works like this:

1. Unplug your computer, ground yourself, and open the case to expose the motherboard.
2. Locate the CMOS Reset jumper. (As delivered, the jumper is disabled, meaning that the jumper does not connect across the two pins to complete a circuit.)
3. Remove the jumper from the nearby system password pins and connect it across the two open pins for the CMOS Reset; leave it in place for ten seconds.
4. Remove the jumper from the CMOS Reset and return it to its former location on the system password pins.
5. Close the cover and reattach the power cord and any other cables that were removed.
6. Power up the computer and load Windows. Once the operating system is running, use the standard method to shut down the computer from within Windows.
7. If you need to make adjustments to the CMOS system memory, restart the computer and go to the Setup screen.

Check the cables first

Before you think I'm trying to embarrass you with a problem I haven't had myself, let me assure you that sooner or later every computer owner — including authors of PC repair books — has a moment of sheer panic caused by something as simple as an unplugged PC or monitor or a blown fuse caused by a disagreement between the vacuum cleaner and the color TV.

Always check the electrical connection first if your computer appears to be dead. Is the PC plugged into the wall and is the other end of the power cable properly attached to the PC? Check the power outlet by plugging a lamp or radio into the socket. If your computer is plugged into a spike protector, line conditioner, or uninterruptible power supply (something I highly recommend), check that one of these protective devices hasn't blown a fuse.

The next thing to check is the jumble of cables worming out of the back of the computer. It's easy for one of them to get unplugged by a vacuum cleaner, your cat, or a tug from the other end of the cable.

Check all the connections to make sure that they are firmly seated on their sockets. Screw cables into connectors where possible, making certain that the plugs go into place evenly without one side off-center.

A loosely connected video cable, for example, can sometimes cause blurred characters or a color shift. A wobbly printer cable can make "Now is the time for all good men to come to the aid of the party" come out as "Mpe od yjr yo,r gpt s;; hppf ,rm yp vp,r yp yje sof pg yjr [sryu."

Power supply

Your computer, depending on the design of its power supply, has the right to expect a steady and reliable source of electricity in the range of 110 to 120 volts at 50 to 60 cycles per second. (Your power supply may also be able to work with foreign current sources of 240 volts.)

Modern machine power supplies are pretty good at dealing with current that dips slightly below that range momentarily or that surges a bit above the top end for a few milliseconds. Power supplies are not designed to work with long-term overvoltage or undervoltage situations, however. Severe spikes can pass through some power supplies and travel through the low-voltage DC lines to the chips. Long-term overvoltage conditions stress every motor and every chip in the computer.

Chronic undervoltage produces its own set of symptoms. A hard disk that is getting less than 12 volts, for example, may not come up to speed the first three times you turn on the computer in the morning. The fourth time, though, it may work fine and seem okay all day. Low voltage can also cause mysterious intermittent computer lockups.

If you are constantly replacing parts, I suggest that you buy or borrow a voltmeter or other line voltage-testing device and plug it into your wall socket. If the meter reads outside the expected range (about 100 to 120 volts) for no good reason, call the electric company or an electrician.

What can cause power fluctuations? The reasons run from the ordinary — a brownout on the hottest day of the summer or power line interference by major appliances — to just plain bad electrical service. When an air conditioner or a refrigerator turns on, the draw caused by its motor may produce a momentary dip in the line voltage, followed by a spike as the power comes back up. Thunderstorms are also notorious for the voltage spikes that they cause.

A momentary dip in current can cause the voltage to drop so low that the memory chips start to forget things. When this happens, the computer locks up. Perhaps you didn't see the lights brown out for an instant during the voltage drop. It doesn't matter, because a voltage drop lasting only a thousandth of a second can lock up an older computer.

Similarly, a momentary voltage spike to the hard disk head may write gibberish in the middle of a file, or, much worse, to the boot sector or the FAT (file allocation table). You won't notice this problem until you go back and try to read the file or boot from the hard disk. This is where routine use of disk maintenance programs can pay off. Run a disk utility such as Norton Utilities on a regular basis so it can catch and repair these problems. If the boot sector is trashed, these utilities may be able to repair the boot sector or help you recover the FAT and files.

Every system in any home or office should, at the very least, be plugged into a *spike protector*. These units, which sell for $10 to $50, are electronic sacrificial lambs. They are intended to blow a fuse or even blow up themselves to shut down the line to your computer if a dangerous spike is headed its way. A *line conditioner* is a device (priced less than $100) that boosts the power during momentary drops and acts as a surge protector as well.

Uninterruptible power supply (UPS) systems are electronic guarantors of a reliable source of power in brownouts, overvoltage situations, and even power failures. They generally include line-conditioning circuitry, as well as a large internal battery and a regulator. UPSs come in two designs: a standby style that includes a very fast switch that can jump into the fray to substitute battery power for line current in an emergency, and a true uninterruptible style that constantly feeds your computer from its battery at the same time that it uses line current to keep the battery charged. UPS systems sell for about $100 to $300 for units intended to work with single PCs.

In my very rural office, the electrical system is rather unreliable. Undervoltage is common, storms bring the occasional spike, and brief — and sometimes extended — outages pop up regularly. All of the computers in my office are plugged into uninterruptible power supply (UPS) boxes, and electric spike protectors or line conditioners protect every other major device. The UPSs protect from under- and overvoltage incidents and provide about 15 minutes of battery power in the case of a complete outage — enough time to conduct an orderly shutdown. I also have all of my major applications programs, including my word processor, configured to automatically save files in progress every five minutes. This means that the most I could lose in the event of an unexpected shutdown (or system crash) is whatever work I have done in the last 4 minutes and 59 seconds.

After the power gets past the surge protector, line conditioner, or UPS, the computer's power supply is in charge of converting AC to DC and stepping down the voltage. In general, power supplies are usually good for many years of use; the entire PC will typically be out of date before the supply will fail.

But power supplies can fail, especially if they are not well-protected from over- or undervoltage. They can also break down if the cooling fan does not work or if vents are blocked. Here are some signs of the failure of a power supply:

- A completely dead system with no cooling fans running on the power supply or elsewhere in the case
- Repeated failure of the system to bootup
- Unexpected rebooting or shutdown of an operating machine
- Repeated parity check or other memory errors

You can test the output of a power supply with a voltmeter. As with floppy drives, it does not make economic sense to repair a faulty power supply within your PC. Replacement units sell for about $30 to $100 and installation is simple. Be sure to match the same physical size and design; you can, though, increase the wattage of the replacement unit.

Hard disk or hard disk controller problem?

Before you consider replacing a dead hard drive, ask yourself the basic troubleshooting question: What has changed since the last time the system worked properly?

If you have been recently working under the covers of the PC, go back in (unplug the PC and turn off the power first) and see whether you accidentally dislodged or failed to reconnect a power or data cable at the hard drive or at the controller end on the motherboard or in the bus.

A diagnostic program can tell you whether the hard disk controller is functioning properly; it can also give information about any problems it finds on the drive itself. The utility can't, however, give information about a dead controller or a dead hard drive.

Check the BIOS Setup screen to make sure it has not become corrupted and that it properly identifies hard drives and controllers in your system.

The next step is to try substituting a replacement hard drive that you know to be good in your system or testing your suspect hard drive in a properly functioning PC.

CROSS-REFERENCE

Other sources of hard disk problems are a damaged boot track, damaged system files, or a failure of the disk mechanism itself. Explore those possibilities in Chapter 10.

Floppy drives

Floppy disk drives are cheaper, smaller, and more reliable than they ever used to be. They're also used a lot less now than in the early pre-hard-disk days of PCs.

Therefore, floppy disk alignment problems and outright failures are uncommon now. When one occurs, it generally makes much more sense to replace the drive — about a 15-minute and a $25 investment — than to attempt to make a repair.

CROSS-REFERENCE

See Chapter 9 for more details on floppy drives.

The most common problems with floppy drives are failures of mechanical parts, such as latches and springs. I've also lost a few drives to human failure: An insistent shove of an upside-down or backwards floppy disk into a slot will chew up a drive.

Before you replace the drive, however, you can check a few things. If you've recently been working inside the computer, go back inside to see whether you dislodged or disconnected the data or power cable to the floppy drive.

You can purchase diagnostic programs that include drive alignment tests and a factory-formatted floppy test disk that is certified as correct. However, the cost of the software and the cost of a repair — if you can find someone who will take the job — is much more than the cost of a replacement unit.

You don't need specialized tools, though, to figure out whether your floppy disk drive has lost its will to store and retrieve data reliably. Create a disk using a floppy drive that you believe to be working properly — if you don't have another PC, ask a friend or business acquaintance or a computer retailer for 30 seconds of their machine's time. Format the disk and copy a few files of varying sizes to the floppy.

Try the good floppy on the suspect drive, and try a disk created with the suspect drive on a PC that you know to be functioning properly. If the suspected drive can't work reliably with the good diskette, or a good drive can't reliably read the suspect disk, it is reasonable to assume that the drive is out of alignment or working improperly. Although it may pain you to do so, the best solution is to throw away the drive and replace it with a new one.

Although I don't recommend repairing broken floppy disk drives, you can take a couple steps to help your floppy drives live long and prosper:

- Keep the disk drives clean. Use a vacuum cleaner to suck out the dust that may have worked its way into the drives. Don't use floppy disks with broken covers, sticky labels, or other damage.
- If you make heavy use of the floppy disk drive — not all that common anymore — you can purchase a disk-cleaning kit to treat dirty drive heads. Follow the manufacturer's directions carefully and be sure not to overdo the amount of solution or frequency of cleanings.

NOTE

A noisy floppy disk drive is not always an indication of trouble. The poor thing may have been born that way. The only real test is whether it reads and writes to its own diskettes and those produced by other machines.

Solving printer problems

The good news about printer problems is that you can usually isolate the hardware from the software. Most printers have self-tests that can tell you whether they are working properly, and you can also try plugging them into another PC to see whether they work with a different machine. Don't forget to rule out the cable as the source of the problem.

After you are satisfied that the printer is working, you can turn your attention to the operating system and software.

The causes of a printer malfunction can range from a broken or disconnected cable (most likely) to a bad printer port (the least likely). The printer itself can fail to operate properly because of paper jams — from huge wads of crumpled paper to tiny shards stuck at critical sections of the paper path. Ink or toner cartridges can also gum up the process.

Test the possible causes, in this order:

- Cables and power
- Switch box or parallel pass-through device (if you have one)
- Printer
- System configuration

Cables and power

See whether the data cables are properly attached at each end; a cable that is not squarely seated on its connector may result in garbled or unreliable operation. Be sure that the printer is receiving electrical power; check any suspect wall outlet by plugging in a radio or lamp.

Test the cable by substituting one you know to be good. That's one good reason to stock your closet with a few extra pieces of hardware — mine includes cables, connectors, and keyboards.

Switch box

If you use a switch box to share a printer between two computers or to share the use of a single parallel or serial port, test the setup by removing the box from the circuit and attaching the cable directly to the computer and printer. If the printer works now, you either have a failed switch or a problem with one of the extension cables used with the box.

Many switch boxes don't fully support bidirectional cables; they may be able to transmit data to the printer but not report back on paper supply, ink or toner, or other information.

If you have a parallel pass-through device, like a scanner, cabled between the PC and the printer, make sure that it's on and the cables connected to it are seated properly. If your printer still has a problem, remove the device from the circuit and attach the cable directly to the computer and printer. If the printer works now, you either have a failed pass-through device or a problem with one of the extension cables used with it.

Note that this does not apply to modern printers that use a USB port for connection. Devices connecting to USB either have their own port or are able to daisy chain one behind the other without the need for a switch.

Printer

Run your printer's self-test. If the printer appears to be working properly, test it by hooking it up to another computer in your office or take it to a friend's setup. If you purchased the printer from a retail store, you may be able to take it to the shop to test it there. That option may or may not be possible if you bought the printer or your computer from an electronics superstore.

System configuration

Before you break out your screwdriver, take a moment to check whether your computer has done anything to disable or redirect the parallel, serial, or USB port used by the printer. Have you installed a new operating system, utility, or application since the last time the program worked?

Go to the Windows Device Manager and check to see whether the port is operating properly without any system resource conflicts. If there are any conflicts with IRQs, DMAs, or memory resources, they need to be fixed.

To test the port, use a diagnostics software package. The best utilities require use of a loopback plug that attaches to the parallel and serial ports and simulates an attached device for the purposes of the test.

 CROSS-REFERENCE

For more information about troubleshooting printers, consult Chapter 18.

Monitors

Make sure that your monitor is properly connected to the video adapter of the PC and plugged into a working wall circuit. Check the brightness and contrast settings on the monitor; an accidental turn of a knob may make the screen dark and unreadable.

CROSS-REFERENCE

You can find more information about monitors in Chapter 13.

Windows should be able to identify current monitors as Plug-and-Play devices and install proper device drivers — either from the ones provided by Microsoft as part of Windows or from an installation disk that comes from the monitor manufacturer. If Windows has not recognized your monitor, or if somehow the driver has become corrupted, the system may be attempting to communicate with your monitor at a resolution or refresh rate that it does not support.

Reboot the system into Safe Mode, which will load generic VGA monitor drivers. Go to the Display item of Control Panel and make appropriate adjustments there.

Some older or special-purpose monitors have an external fuse. Unplug the unit and remove the fuse. Examine it carefully and replace it if it has blown. If it appears to be good, the fuse may have come unseated because of heat or vibration. Reinstall the fuse and try the monitor again.

WARNING

If your monitor has failed, do not attempt to make internal repairs yourself. The video circuitry can retain deadly high voltage, even when off and unplugged, and any adjustments require specialized training and equipment. It probably does not make sense to repair a basic monitor; new models will likely cost less than the repair bill. On the other hand, I have had good luck in getting monitors repaired at old-fashioned TV repair shops. If you use a lot of computers and monitors — as I do — it might make sense to establish a relationship with the proprietor of such a shop if you can find one. An older, 15-inch monitor can be thrown away, but a new 19-inch device that quits working may be worth fixing if you can find someone who really knows their way around the inside of the thing. Chances are you won't find anybody at a computer store or computer repair facility with these qualifications.

Liquid on the computer

As mentioned previously, your computer and liquids are a dangerous combination, so your best bet is to keep the two of them apart.

However, accidents do happen, so consider the following information if a spill does occur on your system.

If a can of soda or a cup of coffee has spilled on your keyboard, you may be out of luck. After all, water and electricity don't get along well, and soda and coffee are corrosive. However, replacement keyboards sell for as little as $10 for a cheap model to about $125 for a deluxe replacement.

Water or soda on a keyboard may be something that can be cleaned up. First of all, unplug the board. Next, you have a couple of choices:

1. Try to clean off the liquid
2. Throw it away and buy an inexpensive ($10 to $25) new one

If you've spilled water, your best bet is to let the keyboard dry off. For other liquids, consider popping the keys off the board, taking care to keep track of springs and plastic parts that underlay each key. After the caps are removed, you can attempt to clean up the spill with a damp cloth; some fixer-uppers wash the board under running water and dry it with a hair dryer. As far as I am concerned, I would rather buy a new board.

If you do spill something onto your computer, shut it down immediately and let it dry off completely. To be very safe, remove or at least disconnect your hard drive; in case your computer is fried, you should be able to install the hard drive in a new PC and recover the data that it held.

A spill into an electrified monitor is almost always a fatal event; if it were my display, I wouldn't even try to find out if it worked anymore. If the monitor is worth the fee that a service department will charge, bring it to a technician for testing.

Page fault errors

Most computer users are unhappily familiar with the dreaded Page Fault Error, one of the blue screens of death that from time to time crashes Windows 98 and earlier operating systems. (Current versions of Windows, including XP and Vista, have mostly kept Microsoft's promise to be less likely to crash, and to be able to isolate the death of a particular application so that it does not bring down the entire computer.) A page fault is generated when a virtual address established by an application points to a page that is not in physical memory. When that happens, the Virtual Memory Manager attempts to load the page from the hard disk or other storage medium into memory. If there is not enough free memory to hold the page, or if it can't be found, an error occurs.

You have several solutions to prevent future page fault errors:

- Add more RAM to the system
- Work with fewer programs open at the same time
- Make any available setting within the offending program so that it uses less memory

Slow display

Windows applications make heavy demands on the computer, especially the video card. Waiting for the screen to catch up can drive you nuts, especially in graphics-intensive programs such as drawing or image-editing software.

Before you make a change to the hardware, check to see if you are running too many graphics-intensive programs at the same time. Do you really need to have four browser windows, a digital image-editing program, and an animated cursor running at the same time? Sometimes the easiest cure to slow display action is to cut down on the system resources drain.

Graphics and publishing packages can use as fast a video card as you can afford. The plummeting price of memory has made it reasonable to consider 128MB of RAM a minimal level of memory for a new graphics card, and 256MB a very worthwhile upgrade. The additional memory enables greater resolution levels and a larger number of colors.

If you've got a current machine, the best place for a graphics card is in a PCI Express x16 slot. On older modern machines, be sure to take advantage of any special-purpose bus extensions your PC may offer, including AGP, or VESA local (VL) bus on a senior citizen. Graphics cards can pick up significant speed boosts by direct connection to the CPU through these slots.

Nearly all modern graphics cards lay claim to an accelerated graphics label. Computer magazine reviews of the latest crop of cards show their rankings on standardized benchmark tests.

I recommend that you stay away from no-name video cards at the bottom of the price lists. Some storefront PC makers who concentrate entirely on price use these cards in their systems. The price difference between brand X and an established name is usually not all that much, and for the extra money, you can expect more current and advanced technology, better technical support and warranty, and availability of software driver and hardware upgrades.

As soon as you install a new graphics card, contact the card's manufacturer to determine whether you have received and installed the latest device driver. Companies often produce new drivers after boxes of hardware are in the sales channel and often update drivers to improve speed and fix bugs. You can find the new drivers on the web sites of many display adapter manufacturers.

Memory

With today's prices on RAM, you have no good reason to scrimp on memory for Windows; you'll pay a lot more in lost time and system crashes. For current machines running Windows, a realistic minimum amount of RAM is 256MB, with 512MB or 1GB highly worthwhile and not all that expensive. More memory is probably the best upgrade you can make to a computer.

Consult the instruction manual for your motherboard or contact the maker of your PC to determine the type of RAM, its module design (RIMM, DIMM, SIMM, SIP), its speed, and the upgrade path.

CROSS-REFERENCE

For more information about considering types of memory and troubleshooting the memory in your system, check out Chapter 8.

Some motherboards require you to upgrade in blocks of a particular amount. Other PCs cheat their owners by inefficient use of the motherboard; these designs may require you to throw away perfectly good SIMMs or DIMMs of small capacity and replace them with larger blocks of memory. But do you really have to throw away perfectly good memory? No. Check the ads in the back pages of computer magazines for memory specialists who may buy used memory or accept it in trade for new, larger blocks of memory.

Memory prices are sometimes very volatile; the best price for RAM can shift from one source to another based on supply. In general, you can find good prices at mail-order companies that specialize in memory during times when RAM is plentiful. These companies usually buy on the spot market and can take advantage of downturns quickly. When RAM is scarce, you may find better prices through major manufacturers who have long-term contracts with memory makers that may predate current price increases.

Bigger hard drives

Don't bother to upgrade from a 1GB drive to a 2GB device; the prices of hard drives have dropped so steeply in recent years and the storage demands of modern applications have grown so sharply that it makes no sense to skimp here. In fact, you'll have a hard time finding new hard drives smaller than 20GB anymore.

CROSS-REFERENCE

Chapter 10 shows you how to replace a hard drive and controller.

Take the opportunity to upgrade to a drive of at least 80GB; as this book goes to press that size drive represents entry-level storage priced at as little as $50. Most of that cost goes for the case and packaging. It costs relatively little to go up a few notches to even larger drives.

In years (and editions) past, I have given qualified recommendation to data compression software programs such as Microsoft's DoubleSpace or DriveSpace or third-party products including Stacker. These products compress the size of many programs and data files by as much as half, effectively doubling the capacity of a drive (including floppy disks and some backup storage devices).

The products perform their magic by using codes to represent blocks of repeated data and interposing a device driver between the output of the disk controller and memory that expands information back to its real size. They also create a compressed drive that occupies a partition on your physical drive; it is not directly readable without the use of the disk compression program.

Some users swear by disk-doubling software, while others swear at them. In the early days of these products, users did encounter some problems with corrupted data, but current versions seem stable. With a fast processor, the small amount of extra CPU time required to deal with doubled disks is hardly noticeable.

Today, the sharp drop in cost of hard disk drives makes disk-doubling software an unnecessary complication on a modern machine.

SUMMARY

This chapter covered some basic troubleshooting solutions. See the troubleshooting flowcharts in Appendix A on the CD for even more help in determining the proper steps to walk through a series of common problems.

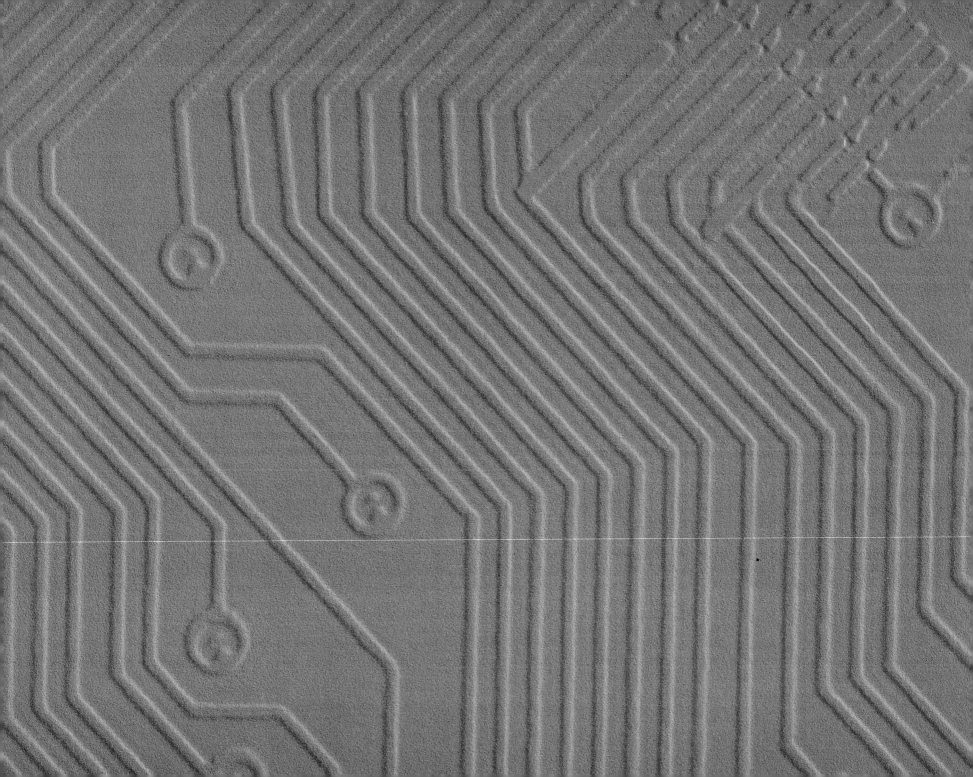

Glossary

10Base-T The standard for a local area network that uses simple twisted-pair cable and operates at a maximum of 10 Mbps. The definition uses "baseband signaling," meaning that only Ethernet information is carried on the circuit, and no other signals. Also called *twisted-pair Ethernet*.

100Base-T A current local area network standard that expands on 10Base-T to work at speeds of up to 100 Mbps. Also called *Fast Ethernet*. Depending on the type of wire, or medium, the standard may be expressed as 100Base-T4, 100-Base-TX, or 100-Base-Fx.

accelerated graphics port *See* AGP.

access time The time required to read or write data to a storage device, including RAM or a disk drive. The nature of the device, as well as the operating system settings, can affect the time.

ACPI Advanced Configuration and Power Interface. An open specification for operating system control of power and thermal management on motherboards, jointly developed by Intel, Microsoft, Hewlett-Packard, Phoenix, and Toshiba and used in current modern machines.

adapter ROM Read-only memory on an adapter card installed in the computer's bus. The ROM contains code to control the adapter device, such as a disk drive adapter, a video card, or a memory card.

ADC On a sound card, an Analog-to-Digital Converter that takes in analog signals from a microphone or other nondigital source, and then outputs digital signals (computer bits) that can be held in computer memory or recorded on a storage device, such as a hard drive, for playback or manipulation.

address A specific location in memory.

address bus The lines from the microprocessor to other parts of the system that are used to specify a location in memory.

AGP Accelerated Graphics Port. A high-speed graphics expansion bus on certain modern motherboards that directly connects the display adapter and system memory. AGP operates independent of the PCI bus and normally runs at 66 MHz, which is twice that of PCI at 33 MHz. The original AGP standard makes a single transfer per cycle for a maximum data-transfer rate of 266 megabytes per second. AGP 2X makes two transfers per cycle (533 MBps), and AGP 4X makes four transfers per second (1.06GBps). In the most modern of machines, AGP has given way to PCI Express slots, which can handle multiple types of cards, including graphics adapters.

allocation unit *See* cluster.

amplitude The height of a wave. This can represent the loudness of sound, brightness, or other measures.

analog A means of recording values by use of the fall and rise of a continuously variable signal. Analog signals are used, for example, to carry signals over standard phone lines. Contrast with digital, which represents values with discrete numbers.

analog loopback A modem test in which data is sent to the modem's transmitter, where it is modulated into analog form and then looped back to the receiver and demodulated into digital form.

anti-aliasing Technology incorporated in advanced graphics cards to smooth jagged edges associated with display graphics. Anti-aliasing technology makes images appear smoother by reducing the intensity of pixels on the edges of the shapes. Despite how it appears from a short distance, your computer screen is made up of a straight vertical and horizontal alignment of tiny, identically sized rectangles. There are no real circles or diagonals. Instead, the graphics adapter draws shapes by stair stepping up and over, or down and across. The stair-stepping Etch-a-Sketch-like effect is called aliasing or jaggies. Anti-aliasing technology reduces this jagged appearance.

API Application program interface. A set of subprograms and tools used to build software applications; APIs are behind the common look and feel of operating systems such as Windows. APIs provide a programmable interface between different applications.

application software The program your computer uses to do work, such as a word processing or a spreadsheet program.

arbitration A technique that permits devices to compete for possession of the bus. Devices are assigned levels of priority and can seize control from a lower-valued unit.

ARQ Automatic Repeat Request. A form of error control protocols that use error detection to trigger automatic retransmission of defective blocks of data.

ASCII code American Standard Code for Information Interchange. A definition for numerical codes that represent controls and characters used by many computers.

ASIC Application-Specific Integrated Circuit. A chip designed to perform a specific function. The chip starts out as a nonspecific collection, or array, of logic gates. In the manufacturing process, a layer is added to connect specific gates so that the final product will perform a specific function. By changing the design of the connection layer, the chipmaker produces ASICs for different purposes.

ASL Adaptive Speed Leveling. A protocol for modems that enables the devices to monitor line conditions and adjust transmission speed up or down if conditions affecting veracity change while connected.

ASPI Advanced SCSI Programming Interface defines a common language between SCSI host adapters and peripheral devices. It enables SCSI peripherals from many vendors to be used easily on a single SCSI chain.

asynchronous Not tied to a particular time frame or clockbeat. Asynchronous communication uses start and stop bits to mark computer words in the stream of data. Synchronous communication, mostly used in specialized terminal applications, uses time to separate the words.

ATA Advanced Technology Attachment, also known as IDE. A bus interface commonly used to connect to storage devices.

ATA/33, ATA/66, ATA/100, ATA133 (Ultra ATA/33) A set of current transfer protocols for hard disks and other devices, with a potential top transfer rate of 33MB, 66MB, 100MB, or 133MB per second. Also known as *Ultra ATA*.

AT bus The 16-bit data bus first used in IBM's PC AT computer, which was based on the Intel 80286 processor. The basic AT bus was adopted by other PC manufacturers, and it is now called the ISA (Industry Standard Architecture) bus.

AT command set A set of commands to control modems, originally developed by Hayes Microcomputer Products. Commands begin with the letters AT, which stand for attention.

Athlon A microprocessor family from AMD that is roughly comparable, in its various versions, to the Intel Pentium family.

ATX motherboard A specification for a motherboard, I/O connectors, and power supplies widely used in modern machines, with subclasses including MicroATX for small-footprint PCs. The most modern PCs have begun moving to the newer BTX form factor which, among other things, offers improved cooling for high-speed components and processors.

autodetection A process that enables an IDE device to inform a system BIOS about proper settings for hard disks and other devices.

backside bus A dedicated bus that connects a microprocessor to a Level 2 (L2) cache to eliminate performance bottlenecks. No other system device shares the backside bus.

bandwidth The amount of data that can be transmitted over an electronic line in a fixed amount of time. For digital devices, bandwidth is usually expressed in bits per second or bytes per second. For analog devices, bandwidth is expressed in cycles per second, or Hertz (Hz).

bank A set of memory chips divided into segments for easy access. Most modern-machine motherboards have two banks for memory.

bank switching A technology to expand available system memory by switching between banks of memory as needed. The off bank retains its memory when not in use but is not immediately available.

base memory The amount of available memory for programs in the first megabyte of memory in a PC. A holdover from the original design of the IBM PC, which held the top 384KB of memory (called *high memory*) for system use, leaving 640KB of base, or *conventional* memory. Modern machines can work with huge amounts of memory, but technically everything above 1MB is considered *extended* or *expanded* memory.

baud A measure of the number of voltage transitions in one second in a communications link. Each of the transitions can transmit several bits of information. It is often incorrectly interchanged with bits per second.

BBS Bulletin Board System. A computer equipped with a modem and attached to a phone line that can be contacted by other computers for the exchange of information. BBS systems have been mostly supplanted by chat rooms and user groups on the Internet.

benchmark A utility program that calculates the speed of completion of a particular task. It can be used to compare the performance of systems or system components.

bezel A frame that holds a device in place or covers an opening on a PC. Also used by monitor manufacturers to describe the frame around the glass tube that makes up the screen.

binary A base-two numbering system used by computers. All numbers are composed of 0s and 1s.

BIOS Basic Input/Output System. Code that controls the lowest, most basic functions of a PC: get a keystroke, read a sector of a floppy disk, how to boot, and so on. The BIOS generally acts as the interface between hardware and the operating system. The system BIOS is stored in ROM, so it does not need to be loaded every time the PC is turned on. This ROM also contains a power-on self-test (POST) routine and the capability to search for other ROMs. Most modern video cards, hard disk controllers, and other internal devices have ROMs that contain code (firmware) for controlling their functions.

bit The smallest piece of information in a computer represented as a 1 or a 0. A bit can represent a number or a state, such as ON or OFF, or TRUE or FALSE. A *byte* has eight bits.

bit depth The number of bits that lie behind the description of a color on a display. The more bits, the more gradations of color. A 1-bit pixel is monochrome; 24-bit or true-color allows for as many as 16.7 million shades for each pixel.

bitmap A representation of an image or font as a binary file. For two-color images (such as black and white), each bit in the map indicates whether the corresponding screen pixel is on or off. For images of more colors, every so many bits (depending on the number of colors) correspond to each successive pixel in the image.

bits per second bps. The number of binary digits that can be transmitted in one second. A more accurate means of measuring the potential speed of a modem.

boot The process the computer goes through to set itself up and load its operating system. Two kinds of boot exist: hard (or cold) and soft (or warm). When you turn on the computer or press the reset button, the system performs a hard boot. A hard boot forces the PC to set itself up from scratch. It performs a check of all hardware and creates a table of devices on the machine (such as number and type of floppy drives, the presence and size of the hard disk, and so on) before it loads the operating system. If you press Ctrl + Alt + Del, the computer performs a soft boot and only reloads the operating system.

boot drive The disk drive from where the operating system is loaded.

boot sector The first sector of the active (bootable) partition. It contains code for loading the operating system. When the computer starts, the BIOS looks for the first hard drive and loads the hard drive's first sector, the Master Boot Record (MBR). The MBR contains a table describing the hard drive's partitions and code for loading the boot sector. Reviewing the table, the boot sector loader determines the location of the active partition and loads the boot sector.

bps *See* bits per second.

broadband A high-speed means of connection to the Internet, such as cable modem or DSL telephone wiring.

BTX motherboard An Intel-backed specification for a motherboard, I/O connectors, and power supply introduced in 2006. The design offers improved cooling for high-speed components and processors.

buffer An area of system memory or other memory used to facilitate I/O (input/output) transfers, allowing a constant stream of data even when data transfer to the I/O port is coming in discontinuous chunks.

Burn The act of recording information onto an optical storage medium such as a CD-R or DVD-R. The device's unit burns pits, or markings, on the disc to indicate the 0s and 1s of digital data.

burst mode A scheme for data transfer that permits a device to remain inactive, as far as the bus is concerned, and then send large amounts of data in a rapid burst. This design is used for DMA transfers on the EISA bus.

bus A parallel set of wires on which multiple devices can reside and use to communicate. Many buses exist inside a PC, including several within the CPU itself. When used generically, bus usually refers to a PC's expansion bus, the place in a PC where devices on printed circuit cards are added. The structure of the expansion bus determines what sort of devices can be added to a computer and how fast the PC can perform certain types of functions. PCs using ISA (the original AT bus), EISA (the extended ISA bus), or Micro Channel (IBM's proprietary PS/2 bus) run slower than the microprocessor and offer narrower data paths than modern CPUs can handle. Intel's PCI (peripheral component interconnect) bus, used in Pentium-class systems, is capable of operating at full processor speed. *See also* bus board and bus connector.

bus board Also called a *backplane*. Some manufacturers of older modern machines chose to put the bus and bus connectors on one board and the rest of the motherboard chips on a separate processor board. In theory, this configuration enables easier upgrades, although proprietary designs sometimes make this unrealistic.

bus connector Expansion cards are connected to the bus through bus connectors on the motherboard. Modern machines use a PCI bus, which branches off the IBM AT-style industry standard architecture (ISA) bus.

bus mastering An architecture that permits add-in boards to perform complex tasks, including managing the bus independent of the CPU and thus demanding less processor time. Among devices that take advantage of this facility are some graphics accelerator cards and network adapters.

byte Eight bits, the smallest unit of data moved about in a personal computer.

cache Memory used to store multiple pieces of data that the computer can reasonably guess it will need soon. It is a bridge between a slow device and a fast device — for example, a hard disk (slow) and main memory (fast). When data is needed from a slow device, nearby data is also retrieved and stored in the cache on the assumption it is likely to be needed soon. When a sector of data from a hard disk is requested, for example, a hard disk controller with cache memory will read and store the sector's entire track in the cache (reading a whole track is faster than reading multiple sectors one at a time). If the PC then soon needs data from that track, it can get it from the cache, which is far faster than reading data from the disk. In the same way, main memory, which is slow by comparison to the CPU (microprocessor chip), can benefit from a memory cache. Cache performance (how much it speeds up your work) depends on several factors, including the speed of the cache chips, the size of the cache, and most importantly, the intelligence of the cache controller.

CAS Column Address Strobe. A signal sent by the memory controller that tells the memory that it can read the column address signal.

CAS Latency The amount of time it takes memory to respond to a command. Specifically, the time between receiving a command to read data and the first piece of data being output from memory.

Latency is measured in clock cycles, as in CL2 (two clock cycles) or CL3 (three clock cycles). If you mix memory of differing CAS Latency, your system will run at the speed of the slowest module.

CAT5, CAT7 Among the numerous categories of media used for Ethernet cabling. CAT5 permits data transfers of as much as 100 mbps while CAT7 permits a theoretical top speed of one gigabit per second.

CAV Constant angular velocity. A mechanism for disk storage in which the drive rotates at a constant speed, resulting in variations in data transfer rates between the inner and outer tracks. Compare to CLV (*constant linear velocity*).

CCITT An international organization that defined standards for telegraphic and telephone equipment, part of the International Telecommunication Union, which draws its acronym from the French title International Telephone and Telegraph Consultative Committee.

CD-Audio Also known as Compact Disc-Audio, or Compact Disc-Digital Audio (CD-DA). The original format for music CDs, established in 1980.

CD-Bridge A CD with additional information on the CD-ROM/XA track that enables the CD to play on a CD-I player used with a television or a PC. An example is the Photo CD.

CD-R Compact Disc-Recordable. A family of devices that can write a permanent record to a special type of CD, which can then be read on a standard CD-ROM drive or another CD-R device. Also known as *Compact Disc-Writable*.

CD-ROM Compact Disc Read-Only Memory. An adaptation of music CD technology that stores large amounts of data. A CD-ROM is fairly slow in transferring information, but can hold 650MB to 900MB of data depending on format. Most common are 700MB or 800MB devices.

CD-ROM/XA, CD-ROM/extended architecture An extended CD-ROM format that improves synchronization of data and audio, and adds hardware for the compression and decompression of audio information. Once a separate feature, it is now included as part of the capabilities of most modern CD drives.

CD-RW Compact Disc-Rewritable. A family of devices that can write a record to a special type of CD; the information can later be erased or changed. Although early CD-RW discs could only be read in a CD-RW device, newer CD-RW drives can create disks that can be read in newer CD-ROM players.

Celeron Intel's "value" version of the Pentium II or III, equipped with a smaller amount of L2 cache. *See also* Duron.

Centronics interface A link between a printer (or a few other devices including some scanners) and a PC's parallel port, using a 36-pin connector. A 50-pin version is used for SCSI devices. It provides eight parallel data lines, plus additional lines for control and status information.

CGA Color Graphics Adapter. A dinosaur display standard, introduced soon after the arrival of the IBM PC. By modern standards, it is extremely limited in number of colors and resolution.

checksum An algorithm for error checking. The CPU mathematically manipulates the bits in a block of data to create a checksum value. The value is compared with a checksum computed by another device or by a computer that has received the block of data.

chip A casual name for an integrated circuit. A chip is a silicon wafer that has layers of circuits photoetched into its silicon surface. Chip also refers to the ceramic or plastic packages in which chips come.

chipset An integrated set of chips that performs the functions of a larger number of discrete logical devices on a PC.

CISC Complex Instruction Set Computing. One design for a micro-processor. CISC uses complex assembly language instructions that usually require many clock cycles to execute. Compare to *RISC*.

clock multiplier A CPU design that improves processor performance by running internal processing at a multiple of the speed at which it communicates to the rest of the system outside of the chip. Intel's DX2 series of chips includes the popular 486DX2/66, which runs at an internal speed of 66 MHz while it communicates with the system bus and memory at 33 MHz. Intel's DX4 series triples the processor's internal throughput; for example, the 486DX4/100 runs at 100 MHz internally and 33 MHz externally. Also referred to as *clock doubling* or *clock tripling*.

clock speed The rate at which a computer's clock oscillates, usually stated in MHz (one million cycles per second). A motherboard uses the ticks of the clock to synchronize the movement of information in the CPU and the rest of the system.

clone A generic equivalent to an original design. By definition, all AT-class machines other than IBM's are clones of the original Big Blue PC.

cluster A group of sectors treated by the operating system as a unit. The operating system controls the number of sectors in a cluster. Also called *allocation unit*.

CLV Constant linear velocity. A design for storage on a rotating disk that spaces data in equal sized physical blocks. Because there is more space available at the outside of the disk than near its center, a CLV drive varies the speed of rotation so that data flows evenly. The disk spins faster for tracks near the center and slower in the more densely packed outer tracks. CLV is used on most CD drives and in Macintosh floppy disk drives. Hard disk drives and some newer CD drives use a scheme called CAV (*constant angular velocity*) in which the drive rotational speed does not vary. CAV CD drives thus yield differing transfer rates depending on the location of blocks of data; these drives usually advertise their speed as a range or list a "maximum" transfer rate.

CMOS Complementary Metal Oxide Semiconductor chips require little electricity and, therefore, are used to store information using battery power. On most modern PCs, a block of CMOS memory is used to store critical system setup information, including drive type (a number that refers to a table listing its characteristics), memory settings, date, and time. CMOS memory must be edited when drives or memory, and certain other elements of the system, are added or changed.

CMYK The four-color process used in printers. *See* RGB.

coaxial A form of cable with a central core surrounded by insulation and a grounding sheath; coaxial cable is used for cable television wiring and was employed in the outmoded 10Base2 Ethernet specification. Also known as *coax*.

CODEC COmpression/DECompression hardware or software used to compress or decompress digitized audio or video information.

cold boot Starting or restarting a computer by removing all power to the system or pressing the reset button. Compare to *warm boot*. In certain situations, a cold boot is necessary to reset some hardware devices.

COM port A serial communications port, as defined by the RS-232C standard. PCs usually have two serial ports and can support as many as four. The ports are numbered COM1, COM2, COM3, and COM4.

COMMAND.COM The command processor program of DOS, a basic element of the operating system.

command overhead In a storage device interface, such as ATA, the time devoted to sending commands to a device instead of moving actual data.

command prompt A screen symbol from the operating system that indicates the system is awaiting input from the user — for example, C: > .

CompactFlash A form of flash memory used in many digital cameras and audio devices. They include circuitry that mimics an IDE disk controller, allowing them to appear to the system as if they were a disk driver. CompactFlash cards can be installed in readers attached to PCs for the download of information and can also be mounted in special PC Cards for the same purpose. *See also* SmartMedia card.

compression *See* CODEC and disk compression.

CONFIG.SYS The DOS configuration file that is part of the boot sector of a disk. It is used to instruct the operating system about device drivers to be loaded, and it provides settings for system variables, such as memory. It is an element of operating systems from DOS through Windows ME.

configuration The group of parameters and settings that controls communication between the system, major system components, adapter cards, and peripheral devices. Configurations are established from the setup screen on a modern machine and through choices made in some shells, such as Windows.

conventional memory Memory located between 0 and 640K, separated by IBM PC convention from addresses above 640K to 1MB, and intended for use by the OS (operating system) and applications. *See also* base memory, expanded memory, and extended memory.

coprocessor A chip that performs a function in parallel with the processor. It has no responsibility for control of the machine. The usual example is the x87 (8087, 80287, and so forth) math coprocessor that handles floating-point calculations for the microprocessor at a faster speed than the general-purpose CPU. The 80486 DX and Pentium CPUs contain an integrated math coprocessor. *See also* floating-point unit.

corruption When data becomes scrambled, changed, or otherwise damaged.

CPU The *Central Processing Unit* is the part of the computer that executes instructions and manipulates information. PCs are based on Intel or compatible CPUs, including the original 8088 and later chips, such as the 80286, 80386, 486, Pentium, Pentium MMX, Pentium II, Celeron, Pentium III, and Pentium 4.

crossover cable A specialized form of cable (including Ethernet and serial communication) in which the outbound send wire is connected to the incoming receive wire and the outbound receive wire is connected to the incoming send wire. A crossover cable permits direct connection of one computer to another for data exchange without a network or other specialized hardware.

cycle time The amount of time it takes to read from or write to a memory cell. Cycle time includes the precharge, when the cell is prepared to accept information, and the actual access, when data is moved between the memory and the bus or directly to the CPU.

cyclic redundancy check CRC. A form of error checking that uses checksums.

cylinder Part of the computer's addressing scheme, used to locate data on a high-capacity hard disk. Data on a hard disk is stored on both sides of the disk in concentric circles, called tracks. Large hard drives have multiple platters with separate read/write heads for each surface of each platter. A cylinder is composed of all of the tracks that are located in the same place, and on both sides, on their respective platters. Each track on one surface of a platter belongs to a different cylinder. (If you were to center a cylindrical

cookie cutter over a hard disk and cut all the platters of the hard disk, you would cut through the tracks of one cylinder.) Large files are recorded on consecutive tracks of one cylinder, one file at a time (instead of consecutive tracks on one platter) to minimize the amount of movement and, therefore, minimize the time the heads need to read/write data.

DAC Digital-to-Analog Converter. On a modern video adapter, this circuitry is used to convert digital information into an analog signal that can be used by an analog monitor.

daisy chain Connecting one attached device (internal or external) to another in a string of devices instead of having each device connect directly to a port or connector on the computer. USB, FireWire, and SCSI devices can be daisy chained in this manner.

data pre-fetch A scheme that instructs some advanced processors to "look ahead" and fetch data from memory before the processor needs it. Modern systems using an L2 data cache usually employ a form of data pre-fetch.

data separation circuit The circuit in the path between the controller and the heads on the hard disk that extracts data from signals that were read from the media surface. *See* encoding scheme.

DDR SDRAM Double Data Rate Synchronous Dynamic Random Access Memory. An advanced version of SDRAM that doubles the memory bandwidth. Normal SDRAM provides data bandwidth up to 1.1 gigabytes per second (GB/sec) while DDR SDRAM doubles the rate to 2.1GB/sec. DDR SDRAM was developed for graphics cards but has been adapted for use as a faster alternative to SDRAM in desktops. The most modern of machines use an adapted version called DDR-2.

debug The process of finding and removing bugs, or errors, in a piece of software. From the very first PC through modern machines, the operating system has included a utility called *DEBUG* that allows advanced users to directly alter bytes of data in memory or in storage.

default A value, setting, or option that is preassigned by a program or system. Most configuration programs permit the user to drop back to the default settings, which are usually a good place to start when the user-selected configuration seems to be causing problems.

density The number of bits or characters that can be recorded in a specified space.

device driver A set of instructions to the computer that explains the commands a particular device understands. An extension of the BIOS, a device driver enables the operating system to access specific hardware in a hardware-blind fashion. The operating system doesn't need to know about the hardware details of a device to access the device driver that controls it.

DIMM Dual In-Line Memory Module. A high-capacity, high-speed memory carrier used in many current modern machines. The printed circuit board within the model allows dual channels to be used in a single interface. DIMM modules for desktops use 168 pins providing a pair of 32-bit memory paths forming a single 64-bit memory path. Laptops and printers commonly use 144-pin or 100-pin DIMMs. The predecessor to DIMMs was SIMM technology. (Direct Rambus DRAM uses a proprietary module, called a RIMM, for the same purpose as a DIMM.)

DIN connector A European-developed round plug and socket system, used on many PCs to connect keyboards and mice.

DIP switch Dual Inline Package switch. A little module containing several tiny switches. It is designed as a dual inline package (two rows of little legs) so that it can be mounted on a circuit board exactly like a DIP chip.

Direct Memory Access *See* DMA.

disk cache A segment of RAM set aside to temporarily hold data read from disks, which helps speed the movement of information.

disk compression A system that reduces the size of data files stored on disks by applying an algorithm that substitutes codes for repeated characters. The efficiency is measured by the compression ratio, which compares the original size of the file to its compressed size. For example, a 2:1 ratio means the original file was twice as large as its compressed version.

display adapter Hardware, on an adapter card or in circuitry on the motherboard, that controls the display of images on a monitor.

DLL Dynamic Link Library programs are executable elements of many Windows applications.

DMA Direct Memory Access. Data is transferred inside a computer through the DMA chip, not through the microprocessor, thus freeing the CPU to perform other tasks. For example, the hard disk controller uses DMA to read data from the hard disk and store it directly into RAM. PCs have eight available DMA channels.

DMF Distribution Media Format. A special format developed by Microsoft for installation disks in the dinosaur era. It enables the disk to hold 1.8MB of data rather than the standard 1.4MB. DMF formatted disks cannot be copied with DOS or Windows disk-copy commands. Today, most applications are distributed on CDs or DVDs.

DOCSIS Data Over Cable Service Interface Specification. A specification for use of a modem that employs a cable TV connection for data transfer.

dongle Specialized hardware used to prevent unauthorized use of a piece of software. The device (named after its inventor, Don Gill) includes an embedded serial number and typically attaches to a computer's parallel port. The software only works if it finds the dongle in place. Dongles are not commonly used anymore, except for certain expensive or custom software packages.

DOS Disk Operating System. The operating system originally provided by Microsoft to IBM in 1979, it has also underlaid all versions of Windows through Windows ME. Like all operating systems, it is an extension of the BIOS. It enables simple access to peripherals by higher (hardware-blind) programs. *See also* COMMAND.COM.

dot pitch The horizontal spacing between picture elements (pixels) on a monitor or LCD. The smaller the dot pitch, the higher the screen resolution.

double buffering A scheme used by 3-D graphics cards that uses separate blocks of memory for the finished image and for another image that is in the process of being rendered. This enables smooth transitions from one scene to another or film-like animation.

DRAM Dynamic Random Access Memory. Memory chips that need to be refreshed regularly. DRAM temporarily stores data in a cell made up of a tiny capacitor and transistor. Cells are accessed by row addresses and column addresses. While being refreshed, a DRAM chip cannot be read by the microprocessor. Therefore, slow DRAM read and write accesses often require CPU wait states. *See also* SRAM.

DRDRAM Direct Rambus DRAM. *See* RDRAM.

Driver *See* device driver.

DS/DD Double-sided/double-density. The most common disk form for older PCs. It includes 5.25-inch 360K and 3.5-inch 720K disks. The original IBM PC was shipped with single-sided, double-density, 160K floppy disk drives (that later read 180K disks), but these dinosaurs with only one read/write head quickly became extinct.

DS/HD Double-sided/high-density. A floppy disk form used in modern PCs that still use floppy disks. Currently, 3.5-inch 1.44MB disks are used in some PCs but CD and DVD drives rapidly are replacing floppy technology in today's computer systems.

DSL Digital subscriber line. A DSL is a form of communication offered by telephone companies and third parties that permits broadband Internet connection. Although fast, DSL lines are usually surpassed by cable modem connections.

DSP An element of a sound card, a modem, and other devices, the Digital Signal Processor chip is used to compress, filter, regenerate, and otherwise process signals and images.

dual boot A configuration that enables a computer to be loaded with more than one operating system, with the user able to choose among them at boot.

dual-core processor *See* multi-core processor.

duplex A communications channel capable of carrying signals in both directions.

Duron A "value" version of AMD's Athlon processor, equipped with a smaller amount of L2 cache. *See also* Celeron.

DVD Digital Video Disc or Digital Versatile Disc. A standard for high-density data, audio, and video. DVD is stored on a media the size of a compact disc. Drives and media are offered in a variety of designs, including a pair of specifications for writable discs: *DVD-R* and *DVD + R*. For rewritable discs that can be recorded and then edited or erased, standards include *DVD-RW* and *DVD + RW*. Drives that can read but not write or rewrite are called *DVD-ROM* or *DVD drives.*

DX2 *See* clock doubling and clock tripling.

DX4 *See* clock doubling and clock tripling.

ECC Memory Error Checking and Correcting Memory A form of memory that uses algorithms to detect errors. When data is stored in memory, the systematic code creates a check bit that is stored along with the data byte; when the data is later retrieved, the chip consults a reference table to check the validity of the data. ECC memory can detect single and double bit errors, and correct single bit errors.

ECP Enhanced capabilities port. A form of improved, bidirectional parallel port interface.

EDO RAM Extended Data-Out RAM. A faster form of DRAM that improved memory access time by allowing two blocks of data to be accessed at the same time. One block of data is sent to the CPU while another is prepared for access. Modern machines use even-faster SDRAM, which uses a similar scheme.

EEPROM Electrically Erasable Programmable Read-Only Memory. A special type of integrated circuit that can be used to store BIOS and other programming; it can be erased and reprogrammed by a special device. Flash memory is a form of EEPROM that can be updated in place within a PC by using special programs.

EGA The Enhanced Graphics Adapter was a relatively short-lived display standard that was used between the CGA and VGA eras. It can display resolutions as high as 640 × 350 pixels with 16 colors from a palette of 64. EGA uses a digital (TTL) signal.

EISA Extended Industry Standard Architecture. An improvement over the 16-bit AT (ISA) bus, it includes a 32-bit path and bus mastering. It still runs at a slow 8 MHz, and it has been surpassed by local bus and PCI designs.

embedded controller Circuitry built into an IDE or SCSI driver that handles the management of the drive, as opposed to earlier designs that had a hard disk controller in the bus of the motherboard.

EMI Electromagnetic interface. On a power supply, electromagnetic interference is noise generated by switching action. Conducted EMI is interference reflected back into the power line; it can usually be cleaned up by a line filter. Radiated EMI, interference radiated into the air, can be blocked by proper shielding, including a metal case.

EMS Expanded Memory Specification. Also known as Lotus/Intel/ Microsoft (LIM) EMS, named after the vendors that defined that standard in response to Quarterdeck's Expanded Memory Manager. Known as bank-switched memory, as well. *See* expanded memory.

encoding scheme Used to process data before it is stored on floppy disks, hard disks, tape, or other media. The encoding scheme massages raw data and turns it into a stream of signals, which makes error detection easier. Encoding schemes are also used to compress data.

Energy Star A specification for power-saving designs.

enhanced IDE An improvement to the IDE specification for disk drives and other devices, permitting data transfer rates up to 13MB per second.

EPP The Enhanced Parallel Port is an improved standard that permits data transfers of as much as 500K per second, more than triple the 150K speed of the original PC parallel interface.

EPROM Erasable Programmable Read-Only Memory. ROMs that are erased by a burst of ultraviolet light. *See* EEPROM.

ESDI The Enhanced Small Device Interface is an interface for hard drives in which the data separation circuit is in the hard drive, supporting a maximum transfer rate of 3MB per second. The cabling scheme is the same as the ST412/ST506 interface, but in ST412/ST506 the data separation circuits are on the hard drive controller. ESDI enables the manufacturer of the hard drive to use any encoding scheme it wishes, so the manufacturer can pack more data onto the physical drive surface.

Ethernet A local area network specification that uses a bus or star topology. In its basic design, sometimes referred to as *10Base-T*, it permits data transfer rates of 10 Mbps. *Fast Ethernet*, or 100Base-T allows transfer rates of 100 Mbps.

exabyte 1,000,000,000,000,000,000 bytes, or 1,024 petabytes. Abbreviated as *EB*.

expanded memory The memory used by an Expanded Memory Manager (*see* EMS) or bank-switched memory. This memory management scheme was designed to get around the 1MB memory barrier in 8088 CPU chips. It enables specially written applications to address as much as 32MB of memory, originally on a special memory

board, by switching multiple 64K banks. EMS exploits a window of available address space above 640K, but below the 1MB barrier. Banks of memory are switched into and out of up to four consecutive 16K windows as needed, which provides effective access to as much as 8MB of additional memory. Many application programs have been written to use expanded memory to store data or to store programs until they are needed.

expansion slot A connector on the motherboard that allows an *expansion card* to electrically become part of the bus.

extended memory The memory in a modern machine with an address above 1MB. It can be used under DOS by programs that throw the 286, 386, or 486 CPU chip — and advanced CPUs that emulate earlier microprocessors — into protected mode, where the CPU and associated programs can take advantage of this memory. Can be used to provide *expanded memory*.

external drive A storage device that exists outside of the case of the PC, connected to it by a cable. Common interfaces for external devices include FireWire, parallel, SCSI, and USB.

fan rating Airflow measured in cubic feet per minute. Designers say a 100 percent increase in airflow reduces system operating temperatures by 50 percent relative to the ambient.

Fast Page Mode DRAM A DRAM that speeds data access by identifying sections of memory as pages once they have been accessed; subsequent requests for the same block of memory can be retrieved by a single row address.

FAT The File Allocation Table is a listing created by DOS that tracks the use of hard disk space, noting which cluster(s) a file occupies and in what order the clusters should be read. The FAT also notes which clusters are available (unused) and unavailable (currently in use or bad).

FAT16 A variation of the File Allocation Table that uses a 16-bit field to address clusters in a logical partition. FAT16 is limited to approximately 2.1GB and 65,000 clusters. FAT16 is compatible with DOS, Windows 3.1, Windows 95A, Windows NT 3.5 and 4.0, and OS/2.

FAT32 An advanced version of the File Allocation Table based on a 32-bit field, allowing partitions larger than 2.1GB with millions of clusters. FAT32 is compatible with Windows 95 SR2, Windows 98, Windows 2000, and Windows XP.

fax mode On a modem, the mode used to send and receive files in a facsimile format.

FCB File Control Block. The operating system maintains information about the status of every open file in this section of memory.

FDD Computerspeak for floppy disk drive. *HDD* stands for hard disk drive.

FDISK An operating system utility program used to partition a hard disk drive.

feature connector A means to add capabilities to certain adapters including display adapters and sound cards.

firewall A piece of software or a hardware device intended to block intruders from accessing computers attached to a local area network or the Internet.

FireWire A fast and flexible external bus standard originally developed as the IEEE 1394 specification and later renamed by Apple as FireWire. In its current version it permits data transfer rates of as much as 400 Mbps, with faster versions expected.

fixed-frequency monitor A display monitor that is designed to work with only one signal frequency and that must be matched to the proper display adapter. Compare to *multifrequency monitor*.

flash disk A storage device using *flash memory*. Examples include PC Card memory, *CompactFlash*, and *Smart Media* cards.

flash memory Special memory chips that can hold their contents without power and can be erased and reprogrammed.

floating-point unit The technical term for *math coprocessor*, used in parallel with some dinosaur and senior-citizen microprocessors.

Floppy 3 Mode In Japan, the original standard for high-density floppy disks stored 1.2MB on a 3.5-inch diskette, instead of 1.44MB as is used elsewhere. In most systems, Floppy 3 Mode Support should be disabled in the BIOS to avoid problems.

floppy disk A storage device that uses flexible, Mylar disks coated with a medium that can hold a magnetic charge (similar to audio tape). The most commonly used disk on modern machines is the 3.5-inch disk, which adds a semirigid carrier and is capable of storing 1.44MB of data. Older machines used 5.25-inch floppy disks, with a top capacity of 1.2MB.

FM synthesis A technology of mixing sine waves that was used by older and lower-cost sound cards to simulate musical instruments, voice, and other sounds. A more advanced technology is wave table synthesis, which stores actual samples of musical instruments.

format (high-level) The process of preparing the media (disk or tape) for addressing by the operating system. Before formatting, the operating system checks the media for defects and creates certain tables. These tables enable the system to find the stored data.

format (low-level) The process of placing marks on the media so that data stored on the media can be found again.

FPU *See* floating-point unit and coprocessor.

frame In data communications, a block of data with header and trailer bits before and after the information. The added information is used for error-checking codes and start/end indicators.

Front-side Bus (FSB) Another name for the processor bus, the high-speed main highway that connects a microprocessor to other system devices.

FSB *See* Front-side Bus.

FTP File transfer protocol. A mechanism for transferring files over the Internet.

full-duplex A communications protocol permitting the sending and receiving of data signals at the same time. *See also* duplex and half-duplex.

function keys The set of extra keys on a computer keyboard, usually labeled F1 through F12, that can be programmed to perform special functions.

gas plasma display A specialized form of flat-screen display that uses a glass envelope filled with an excitable gas; application of electrical current to a particular point where horizontal and vertical electrodes intersect causes the gas to glow.

GB *See* Gigabyte.

Gb *See* Gigabit.

gender A description of the form of a connector, specifically whether it has protruding pins (male) or corresponding receptacles (female). To convert a connector from one form to another you can use a *gender bender*.

general MIDI A set of 128 standard sounds used in MIDI sound cards and output devices. *See* MIDI.

GIF Graphics Interchange Format. A compressed digital image format defined by CompuServe, commonly used on CompuServe and the Internet for transferring images. *See also* JPEG and PNG.

giga One billion.

gigabit Used informally to mean one billion bits of storage in hard drives and other storage media. For RAM, the actual size of a gigabit is 1,024 megabits, or 1,073,741,824 bits. Abbreviated as *Gb*.

gigabyte Used informally to mean one billion bytes of storage in hard drives and other storage media. For RAM, the actual size of a gigabyte is 1,024 megabytes, or 1,073,741,824 bytes. Abbreviated as *GB*.

Gouraud shading An advanced method for shading colors within a shape that works by averaging the color values at the edges of a shape and then adjusting the color values to evenly blend them across the shape. Without Gouraud shading, most graphics schemes fill shapes with flat shading—a color or gray scale that does not vary within polygonal elements of an image.

GPF General Protection Fault. A system crash in some versions of Windows.

GPU Graphics Processing Unit. The processor on an video adapter.

graphics adapter *See* display adapter.

GUI Graphical user interface. An operating system or program that allows the user to execute commands and move objects by pointing to icons, links, and pictures with the use of a keyboard or a pointing device such as a mouse. Microsoft Windows is the best-known example of a GUI. Technical types pronounce the term as "gooey."

half-duplex A communications protocol that permits only sending or receiving at one time. *See also* duplex and full-duplex.

hard disk A large-capacity storage medium that uses spinning platters coated with magnetic material.

hard reset Instructing a running system to reboot by pressing a reset button on the hardware. Also known as a cold boot. Compare to *warm boot*.

HDD Hard disk drive.

head The electromagnetic component of a floppy or hard disk drive that reads or writes data.

head actuator The mechanism the moves a read/write head to the center or back to the edge of a rotating disk.

head crash A disastrous failure of a hard disk that occurs when the read/write head that ordinarily hovers a few millionths of an inch above the platter comes to rest on the disk. In most cases, the hard disk is damaged beyond repair, although some data recovery services are able to extract data from the disk.

head load time On a floppy disk drive, the amount of time required for the drive head to settle after it is lowered onto the drive surface.

head settle time On a floppy disk drive, the amount of time required for the heads to settle after a seek operation.

head unload time On a floppy disk drive, the amount of time required for the drive head to settle after it is lifted from the drive surface.

heat sink A metallic (often aluminum) structure with vanes that radiate heat away from a hot component, helping to prevent failure of electronic devices. Modern microprocessors require a heat sink, cooling fan, or both because of the amount of heat they produce.

helical scan A technique to record more data on a moving tape storage device. A rotating read/write head is mounted at an angle to the moving tape, writing bands of data on the tape.

Hercules standard A dinosaur monochrome text and graphics display standard that produced a 720-x-348-pixel screen.

Hertz A measurement of the frequency of information; one hertz is one cycle per second. Abbreviated as *Hz*. A MHz (megahertz) is equal to one million cycles per second. The term is named after physicist Heinrich Hertz.

hexadecimal A base-16 numbering system. Digits are represented by the numbers 0 through 9 and the characters A through F.

high memory Memory of a DOS-based computer between 1MB plus 16 bytes to 1MB plus 65,536 bytes, or basically, the first 64K of extended memory. *See* conventional memory, upper memory, expanded memory, and extended memory.

HIMEM.SYS A device driver that manages extended memory in DOS; Windows provides an equivalent as part of its internal code.

HMA High memory area. *See* high memory.

host In a SCSI system, the computer in which a host adapter is installed. The host adapter card permits connection of SCSI devices to the bus.

hot swapping The ability to attach or detach a device to a computer while it is running, a feature that is one of the advantages of USB and FireWire systems.

HTML Hypertext Markup Language. The authoring language behind the pages of a web site on the Internet. It is up to the browser on the PC to interpret the generic HTML language for the needs of a specific computer and its display.

HTTP Hypertext Transfer Protocol. The mechanism behind the transfer of messages and web pages over the Internet.

hub A common connection point for components attached to a network or an expandable subsystem. An Ethernet hub brings together the cables from PCs in a hub-and-spoke topology. A USB or FireWire hub expands the number of connectors and amplifies available electrical power for devices on the chain.

HyperTransport A specification supported by AMD as a replacement for the PCI bus. An earlier name for the design was *Lightning Data Transport.*

Hypertext A means to link objects and files to one another. On a Web page, hypertext links allow you to jump to other pages or documents.

Hz *See* hertz.

IBM clone A computer that is functionally the same as an IBM PC, XT, or AT. After the Phoenix and AMIBIOSs came on the market, the terms clone and compatible came to mean the same thing. Some earlier IBM-compatible machines were unable to run standard software unless the software was modified.

IDE Integrated Device Electronics. A disk drive interface in which the electronic circuitry for the controller resides on the drive itself, eliminating the need for a separate controller card. The extended IDE (EIDE) interface is also used for some CD-ROM drives and other devices. *See also* ATA.

IEEE 802.x The underlying technical standard for network access control, the basis for Ethernets and other networks.

IEEE 1394 The technical standard behind FireWire. *See* FireWire.

INF file Windows drivers and information files use the .INF file description in their name.

initiator On a SCSI system, the device that requests an operation be performed by another SCSI device (the target).

inkjet printer A printing device that creates text or images by spraying tiny dots onto a page.

interleave Data is loaded onto the hard disk one sector at a time, but not necessarily in physically contiguous sectors. An interleave of two uses every other sector. An interleave of three uses one sector, skips two, loads one, skips two, and so on. Slow CPUs require higher interleave numbers to read from and write to a hard disk as quickly as possible. Some hard disk diagnostics find your computer's ideal interleave number and set up the hard disk for maximum access speed.

interleaved memory A method to reduce CPU wait states for slower RAM chips by placing odd-numbered and even-numbered bytes of memory in separate chips. Because the processor alternates the chips it accesses, each chip has more time to prepare for its next access. Therefore, slower RAM can be used.

internal drive A storage device that mounts within the case of a PC. A floppy disk, CD-ROM, Zip drive, and other forms of removable media require access to the outside of the case, while internal hard drives can be mounted anywhere in the case that is within reach of data and power cables. *See also* external drive.

interrupt For hardware, a call for the attention of a CPU. A PC is called an interrupt-driven system because every keystroke from the keyboard and every other event generates an interrupt to the processor. Unless two devices are designed to cooperate, they cannot share the same interrupt request line (IRQ). Current PCs have 16 IRQ channels. Hardware interrupts break in on a CPU's internal meditations and ask for attention from the CPU. Nonmaskable interrupts (NMIs) are hardware interrupts that demand immediate attention. The CPU must suspend operations for a NMI. Most hardware interrupts are maskable, though. They are mediated by an interrupt controller chip, which queues up the interrupts and asks the CPU to service each interrupt in its order of priority. Software interrupts are a jump to a subroutine. The subroutine locations and the interrupt numbers assigned to each subroutine are stored in the interrupt vector table.

Interrupt 13 and Interrupt 13 Extensions The BIOS routine that handles hard disk commands and data. The original routine, Interrupt 13, supported capacities up to 8.4GB. Extensions on newer BIOS chip sets add support for larger drives.

interrupt vector table A table of 256 interrupts, located in the first kilobyte of memory, that contains the subroutine address assigned to each interrupt.

I/O Input/output. The name for the process by which a computer communicates with the external world. Input comes from keyboards, mice, scanners, modems, and digital tablets. Output goes to printers, monitors, modems, and so forth. The term I/O is context-dependent. For example, data that is output from one program may become input for another program.

I/O port address A number assigned to a particular device (such as a disk drive, port, mouse, or other component) that is used to tell the device that data about to be sent down the bus is meant for that device. No two devices can be assigned the same I/O port address.

IO.SYS An element of MSDOS.SYS. *See* MSDOS.SYS.

IP address The Internet Protocol address is expressed as an identifying number for sites, devices, or users on an Internet (or on a TCP/IP network used to connect local computers together).

IRQ Interrupt ReQuest Line. Hardware lines over which devices can send interrupts to the CPU. IRQs are assigned different priority levels to enable the processor to determine the comparative importance of requests for service. *See also* interrupt.

ISA The Industry Standard Architecture is the original IBM PC-AT bus architecture adopted by compatible-PC manufacturers. It permits exchange of information between the motherboard and attached devices of as much as 16 bits at a time.

ISO International Standards Organization. An international association of standard-setting organizations.

ISP Internet service provider. A company or organization that sells access to the Internet to users.

Itanium Intel's 64-bit CPU aimed at servers and workstations.

joystick A pointing or controlling device based on an upright lever. Used in many arcade games and some specialty applications.

JPEG A graphics storage protocol developed by the Joint Photographic Experts Group that uses a compression scheme, which reduces the size of an image while preserving image quality. *See also* GIF and PNG.

jumper A small metal clip within a plastic block that is placed on metal pins to turn on or off a specific function or to make a particular setting.

K Kilo, as in 1,000. In reference to memory, K means one kilobyte (1,024 bytes), because memory — and other computer values — are based on the binary number system (2 to a power). Therefore, one kilobyte of memory is actually 210, or 1,024.

Kb Kilobit; 1,024 bits.

KB Kilobyte; 1,024 bytes.

Kbps Kilobits per second.

KBps Kilobytes per second.

kernel The most basic, essential element of the operating system, loaded first and kept in memory.

keyboard buffer A block of memory that can store a particular number of keystrokes that have not yet been processed by the computer.

keyboard controller A special-purpose microprocessor in the keyboard that interprets keyboard presses, relieving the PC's main processor from this task. The keyboard controller BIOS, located on the motherboard, manages the interface between the keyboard and the system.

KHz Kilohertz stands for 1,000 hertz (Hz), used to measure the sampling rate of audio.

kilo One thousand.

KVM Switch A controller that allows multiple keyboards, video displays, and mouse devices to share the same computer, or for multiple computers to share the same or multiple keyboards, video displays, and mouse devices.

L1 cache Level one cache is a small amount of SRAM memory integrated or packaged within the same module as the processor and used as a cache. L1 cache runs at the same clock speed as the processor. L1 cache is used to temporarily store instructions and data, keeping the processor supplied with data even if memory lags behind.

L2 cache Level two cache is SRAM memory near the processor or integrated into a processor. Also known as secondary cache, this is the second-fastest memory available to a microprocessor, second only to L1 cache.

LAN Local area network. A connection between two or more computers at a location.

landing zone On a hard disk drive, a particular cylinder where the read/write heads can safely park after power is shut off. Data is not stored in the landing zone.

laser printer A printer that produces pages based on electronic signals from a computer. The dots of an image are converted into a laser beam that imparts a charge to paper that attracts dry ink that is later fused in place by heat.

latency Generally, the amount of time a device has to wait to be served data from another. In terms of storage, latency is the average amount of time the drive has to wait for a particular sector to rotate into place beneath a read/write head. In networking, latency is the time it takes for a packet of information to travel from sender to destination. *See also* CAS Latency.

LBA Logical Block Addressing. A mode of accessing a location of a hard drive based on sequential numbering for the sectors of a disk, eliminating a slower and more complex calculation of cylinder, head, and sector coordinates.

LCD Liquid Crystal Display. A display, used on most laptop PCs and flat-screen monitors, that produces images by changing the polarity of light passing through individual pixels of a polarized filter in response to an electrical signal.

LED Light-Emitting Diode. A highly efficient semiconductor that converts electrical energy into light.

LIM Lotus-Intel-Microsoft (named for the vendors who developed the standard). A dinosaur-technology technique for expanding the amount of memory that a computer can use for data. This method only works with special LIM or EMS cards and programs designed to use this memory. *See* expanded memory.

local area network *See* LAN.

local bus A data bus that connects directly to the microprocessor, capable of operating at the transfer speed of the CPU.

logic Name for the internal parts of a computer that perform functions defined by the rules of logic, as in philosophy.

logical unit In a SCSI system, a physical or virtual device addressed through a target. Each logical unit of a device has a logical unit number (LUN) by which it is addressed.

Low-level format The electronic markings placed on a hard drive that mark the start of each sector. The operating system further refines the indexing of a disk when it formats a drive's sectors.

LPT1 A computer's name for its first parallel port. The term comes from the days of mainframes, when LPT was an abbreviation for line printer.

magneto-optical disk drive A data storage device that combines a laser and a magnetic medium for storing information.

mainframe A large computer intended to serve the needs of dozens or hundreds of users at the same time. The definition of a mainframe has changed considerably over the course of the history of computers; today's PCs have more power than early mainframes.

main memory Another term for conventional memory.

master The first addressed drive (device 0) on an ATA/IDE chain.

master boot record An essential element of the operating system, it contains the information needed to identify the location of the boot components for the PC. By definition, it is located within the first sector of the hard disk. If the MBR is corrupted or lost, the system will not operate until it is repaired or re-created. One of the most damaging types of viruses infects the MBR, taking control of the system before any other program — including antivirus software — can protect it.

math coprocessor *See* coprocessor.

Mb *See* megabit.

MB *See* megabyte.

Mbps Megabits per second. The number of bits, in millions, moved in one second.

MBps Megabytes per second. The number of bytes, in millions, moved in one second.

MBR *See* Master Boot Record.

MCA Micro Channel Architecture. A dinosaur technology used in IBM PS/2 Model 50s and later machines in that series. MCA buses are not compatible with ISA or PCI cards. The MCA bus supports multiple bus masters. On any bus, only one processor at a time can have control, but the MCA design enables any one of the processors in the machine to be in control. By comparison, ISA enables only the CPU to have control of the computer; all other processors are slaves to the CPU. EISA is a 32-bit bus and, like Micro Channel, enables other processors to control the bus. *See also* EISA, ISA, and PS/2.

MDA Monochrome Display Adapter. The original display standard for the IBM PC, it can produce only text at a screen resolution of 720 × 350 pixels.

media A physical device that stores computer-generated data. Floppy disks and hard disks are magnetic media. CD-ROMs are optical media.

mega A million. In reference to memory, equals 1,048,576 bytes, or 1,020.

megabit A million bits. In reference to memory, equals 1,048,576 bits. Expressed as *Mb*.

megabyte A million bytes. In reference to memory, equals 1,048,576 bytes. Expressed as *MB*.

megaflops A measure, in millions, of the number of floating-point operations per second of a CPU.

megahertz One million cycles per second. Expressed as *MHz*.

memory The part of a computer that remembers 0s and 1s. Unlike human memory, it cannot remember any context. *See also* expanded memory, extended memory, RAM, refresh, ROM, and system memory.

memory management unit Hardware that supports the mapping of virtual memory addresses to physical memory addresses.

memory refresh *See* refresh.

MFM Modified Frequency Modulation. One of many possible encoding schemes. MFM uses clock bits interspersed with data. The ST412/ST506 standard for MFM was the most common hard disk controller-encoding scheme for years. *See also* ESDI, RLL, and SCSI, all of which are competing hard disk controller designs.

MGA Monochrome Graphics Array. A dinosaur video display standard.

MHz *See* megahertz.

micro One millionth. Sometimes represented by the Greek character μ.

Micro Channel Architecture *See* MCA.

micron One millionth of a meter; one-thousandth of a millimeter.

microprocessor The part of the computer that processes. In microcomputers, the chip that actually executes instructions and manipulates information. Also called the CPU or the processor.

MIDI The Musical Instrument Digital Interface protocol is a specification for the interchange of music data. MIDI consists of a set of instructions to be executed by a MIDI output device. Because MIDI devices do not store the sound itself, MIDI files are small.

milli One thousandth.

minicomputer A computer smaller than a mainframe in both power and cost. Minicomputers were widely used as servers for groups of terminals and then groups of PCs in the early years of the PC. They have been largely supplanted by high-end PCs.

MIPS Million Instructions Per Second. A measure of the speed at which a computer executes instructions.

MMX A set of multimedia extensions added to the Pentium instruction set and introduced in new Intel Pentium chips in 1997 and incorporated within later CPUs.

modem Modulator/demodulator. A device that converts digital data from a computer into analog data for transmission over telephone lines by modulating it into waves. A related device is a cable modem, which converts data for transmission over cable television cables. At the other end, a modem converts the analog data back into digital form by demodulating it.

modified frequency modulation An older method for recording data on a hard disk drive by varying the amplitude and frequency of a signal. *See* MFM.

monitor A video display.

motherboard The main board of the PC, holding the microprocessor, system BIOS, expansion slots, and other critical components.

mouse A device used to control the location of an onscreen pointer that identifies data or issues commands to the processor.

MPC The Multimedia PC specifications were set by a consortium of hardware manufacturers and identify the minimum requirements for hardware that support multimedia applications. The senior-citizen era specifications and the association have been surpassed and superseded by modern technologies.

MPEG A video image-compression scheme developed by the Motion Picture Expert Group.

MSCDEX The Microsoft CD-ROM Extensions is a device driver that controls management of CD-ROM drives that are attached to DOS and most early versions of Windows.

MSDOS.SYS A file that is the essential element of the boot files for Microsoft operating systems from DOS through Windows 98. (In IBM's version of DOS, a similar file is called IBMDOS.COM.)

MTBF Mean Time Between Failure. A measure by hardware manufacturers that purports to show the average time a component can be expected to work before it fails.

multicore processor A microprocessor that includes two or more independent processors within the same physical chip, permitting certain applications to execute multiple processes at the same time. The first processors of this sort were dual-core, followed quickly by quad-core microprocessors.

multifrequency monitor A display that is capable of adapting itself to different display adapters' output frequencies, also called a multisynchronous monitor.

multitasking Performing multiple jobs simultaneously.

multiuser An operating system that enables many users to perform different tasks on the same computer.

nano (n) One billionth. A nanosecond is abbreviated as *ns*.

NIC Network Interface Card. An adapter that permits a device to connect to an Ethernet for the exchange of information and commands.

NLX form factor A specification for motherboards and power supplies used in low-profile cases.

NMI Nonmaskable Interrupt. An interrupt generated by hardware that cannot be turned off. An error message usually indicates a serious memory or I/O problem.

node A device attached to a network, such as a computer, printer, or gateway.

noise Engineers measure the acoustical noise of a fan or other system devices in dB(A) at 1 meter. dB is expressed on a logarithmic scale, with each reduction of 3dB representing 50 percent less noise.

noise interference Noise from any source that interferes with your computer. Examples include erratic electric, magnetic, or radio waves. Likely causes are an electric clock (magnetic), a thunderstorm (electric), or a local radio station (radio waves).

nonvolatile memory Memory that does not need to be refreshed. Therefore, it doesn't require much power. CMOS RAM is a form of nonvolatile memory.

north bridge A memory controller hub that is part of a modern PC's chipset. The processor communicates through the north bridge to close-in cache memory, main memory, and on to the peripheral bus (including PCI on a modern machine) and special-purpose buses such as AGP for a modern class of graphics cards. Some north bridge chipsets also include some integrated functions such as video and audio controllers. *See also* South Bridge.

NTSC The television standard used in the United States and some other countries, developed by the National Television Standards Committee. The format specifies a frame rate of 30 frames per second and a resolution of 485 visible lines.

null modem cable A specialized serial cable used to connect two serial devices directly, without the use of a modem.

numeric coprocessor For the PC, originally a special chip (8087, 80287, and 80387) designed to perform floating-point calculations, logarithms, and trigonometry. Today, numeric coprocessor circuitry is usually incorporated within a CPU.

OCR Optical character recognition. Software that converts scanned images of text back into files that can be edited with a word processor.

OEM Original Equipment Manufacturer. A company that produces equipment that is sold by another company under the other company's brand name. For example, Intel and Micron are OEMs of motherboards to many PC manufacturers.

offset A way to address memory, using a numbering system that indicates the relative distance (offset) from the beginning of a memory segment.

operating range On a power supply, the minimum and maximum input voltage sufficient to allow the device to deliver proper DC voltage to the system. The more uneven your local electrical service, the more you need a power supply with a wide operating range.

operating system (OS) A program that enables a computer to load programs and that controls the screen, the drives, and other devices. Microsoft's DOS was used in early systems through Windows 95/98 and ME; Windows 2000 and Windows XP use new code that performs the same functions.

operating temperature The range of ambient temperatures within which a device can be safely operated.

OS/2 Operating System 2, by IBM/Microsoft. (Operating System 1 is DOS.) IBM originally intended this operating system for the 80286, but released it for PS/2s.

output current In a power supply, the maximum current that can be continuously drawn.

overclocking Running a processor at a speed faster than its manufacturer certifies as its top speed. Usually accomplished by adjusting the *clock multiplier*. The processor may work fine, or it may crash and burn.

OverDrive CPU An add-on chip from Intel for upgrading a PC with a faster and/or more powerful CPU.

overvoltage protection In a power supply, a circuit that shuts down the device if the output voltage exceeds a specified limit.

paged memory *See* expanded memory and LIM.

page frame A range of physical memory addresses in which a page of virtual memory can be mapped.

page mode memory access A means by which the computer accesses data in RAM. In an ordinary scheme, the CPU activates a RAS (row address strobe) and a CAS (column address strobe) signal to specify the row and column of the data. In page mode memory access, the CPU assumes the data is located in the same page as the initial data and, therefore, the CPU can obtain information more rapidly.

PAL The television standard used in Europe and other locations. The Phase Alternate Line format specifies a frame rate of 50 frames per second and a resolution of 575 visible lines. Compare to *NTSC*.

parallel A means of transmitting data with the bits that make up a computer word traveling alongside each other on adjacent wires, like the lanes of a superhighway. Compare to *serial*.

parallel port The I/O channel to a parallel device, such as a printer.

parity A system used to check each byte of data for errors. The parity bit plus the 8 bits in the byte must add up correctly. For even parity, the number of 1s in the byte plus the parity bit must add up to an even number. If they don't, the computer knows there has been an error in transmitting the signal. For odd parity, they must add up to an odd number.

partition A disk can be divided into several partitions, each of which can act as if it were a separate disk. Using multiple partitions is one way to deal with a hard drive that is larger than DOS will recognize, a problem more common with earlier versions of the operating system. Some users prefer to divide their disks into separate partitions for organizational reasons.

password check option A feature of some ROM BIOS systems, it can be used to prevent unauthorized use of the system or alterations to the setup.

PB *See* petabyte.

PC100 SDRAM An Intel specification for SDRAM memory devices and modules that can operate at a 100 MHz Front Side Bus (FSB) frequency. PC-100 SDRAM memory is backward compatible with systems that use PC-66 SDRAM memory.

PC133 SDRAM An Intel Specification for SDRAM memory devices and modules that can operate at a 133 MHz Front Side Bus (FSB) frequency. PC-133 SDRAM memory is backward compatible with systems that use either PC-100 or PC-66 SDRAM memory.

PC1600 DDR A form of DDR SDRAM memory that provides 1.6 GBps throughput.

PC2100 DDR A form of DDR SDRAM memory that provides 2.1 GBps throughput of data.

PC Card The Personal Computer Memory Card International Association specification for a credit-card-sized addition to PCs, most often used in portable computers. In 1995, the group dropped the forgettable acronym of PCMCIA in favor of PC Card. The original Type I card is primarily used in handheld personal assistants. Type II cards are principally used for memory, network adapters, and modems. Type III cards are thick enough to hold miniaturized disk drives and other devices.

PCI The Peripheral Component Interconnect is a high-performance peripheral bus designed by Intel that runs at 33 MHz and supports 32-bit and 64-bit-wide data paths and bus mastering capability.

PCMCIA *See* PC Card.

peer-to-peer A networking design in which any node on the network can be the source (server) of information or the client. A basic Ethernet using a hub-and-spoke design is a peer-to-peer network.

Pentium The fifth major generation of Intel CPUs used in PCs. Intel has produced the Pentium II, Pentium III, and Pentium 4 microprocessor families.

peripheral A hardware device connected to a computer. Typical peripherals include keyboards, monitors, printers, disk drives, and more.

petabyte 1,000,000,000,000,000 bytes, or 1,024 terabytes. Abbreviated as *PB*.

PGA Pin Grid Array. One method of mounting chips on a circuit board, used by devices with a large number of lines to connect. Pins stick out of the bottom of the chip and are meant to mate with holes in a socket. PGAs are used for most microprocessors, for example.

Photo CD A technology, developed by Eastman Kodak in the senior-citizen era, that permits the storage and retrieval of photographs on a CD-ROM for display on home TVs or a personal computer.

physical address An actual memory address.

picosecond One-trillionth of a second.

PIF A Program Information File is an element of Windows that contains instructions on how to run non-Windows DOS applications.

pinout A drawing or table that lists the nature of the signals that use particular pins of a chip or connector.

pixel A picture element is the smallest addressable area of a computer image. Screen resolutions are expressed as pixels, such as the 640-X-480-pixel VGA specification.

platter The rotating disk within a hard disk drive used to hold data.

Plug-and-Play A component for a PC's BIOS jointly developed by Intel and Microsoft, with support incorporated within Windows 95/98 and subsequent versions, intended to make peripherals self-configuring. A new device plugged into such a system would be able to set its own IRQ, DMA channel, I/O port setting, and memory addresses while avoiding conflicts with other peripherals' settings.

PNG Portable Network Graphics. A compressed digital-image format designed as a patent-free alternative to CompuServe's GIF format for the transfer of images on the Web. *See also* JPEG and GIF.

POST Power-On Self-Test. The BIOS ROM contains a series of hardware tests that runs each time a computer is turned on. If hardware errors are found, POST either beeps or displays error messages.

PostScript A page description language for printing documents and producing images on other devices; it was developed by Adobe Systems.

power good signal In a power supply, a delay circuit used to initialize the computer and provide a logic signal.

power supply A critical element of the PC that converts AC wall current to DC current. Electronic circuits run at 3.5 or 5 volts, while most disk drive and CD or DVD motors draw 12 volts.

primary The first ATA/IDE channel of a computer. Each channel supports a chain of one or two devices, configured as master and slave. *See also* secondary.

processor The part of the computer that executes instructions and manipulates information. In microcomputers, this is a single chip. It is also called a CPU or a microprocessor.

processor interrupt An interrupt generated by the microprocessor, also known as a logical interrupt. One example is a divide-by-zero logical error.

PROM Programmable Read-Only Memory. A special type of memory that can be custom-produced to hold information or programming. A PROM cannot be rewritten. *See also* EEPROM and EPROM.

protected mode The mode of an 80286 or later microprocessor in which the processor can address extended memory and protect OS memory from direct manipulation by applications. 80286 and later CPUs are capable of operating either in real mode (basically, no extended memory) or in protected mode. The 80386 and later CPUs also have a virtual mode, which lets them run multiple virtual real-mode segments. *See also* virtual memory.

PS/2 Personal System 2. This 1987 IBM family of microcomputers originally incorporated a patented bus called MCA (Micro Channel Architecture). Classic-bus partisans feel that IBM designed this line to thwart cloning. As sales declined, later PS/2s reverted to the ISA bus. *See also* MCA.

quad-core processor *See* multi-core processor.

RAID Redundant Array of Independent Disks. A group of disk drives used for backup.

RAM Random Access Memory. Any part of this memory can be used by the microprocessor. Each storage location in RAM has a unique address, and each address can be either written to or read by the processor. In DOS, conventional memory, maximum 640K, is the area used to hold DOS, applications, and data. Expanded memory and extended memory are also RAM. When people use the term RAM casually (as in "How much RAM does your computer have?"), they're usually talking about conventional memory, plus expanded and extended memory. Windows, unlike DOS, uses both conventional memory and extended memory. *See* expanded memory and extended memory. *See also* DRAM, ROM, refresh, and SRAM.

RAMDAC Random Access Memory to Digital Analog Converter. A chip on video adapters used to convert the computer's digital output to an analog signal that can be displayed on a monitor.

RDRAM A type of memory, developed by Rambus, used to support some Intel CPUs beginning with the Pentium 4. Like DDR SDRAM, it transfers data on the rising and falling edges of the clock cycle. The memory device uses two data channels to improve transfer rates. Also known as *DRDRAM*.

read/write head The component of a storage device that reads recorded data and writes new information. Hard drives, floppy drives, and tape backup devices use magnetism to read and write; CD-Rs, CD-RWs, and DVD-RAMs use a laser to melt meaningful pits on a plastic disc.

real mode The 80286 and later microprocessors can operate in two memory addressing modes: real mode, which basically means no extended memory (such as an 8088 or 8086); and protected mode, which includes extended memory. The 80386 and later microprocessors also have a virtual mode that runs multiple virtual real-mode segments. These processors operate in real mode when running DOS. They operate in protected mode when running Windows.

reboot To restart the computer. *See* boot, cold boot, and warm boot.

refresh Dynamic memory (DRAM) forgets the information it holds unless it is rewritten regularly. Memory with a faster *refresh rate* responds quicker. Refresh rate also is another term for the vertical scan frequency of a monitor.

register One of several cells in a processor that is used to manipulate data. For example, a CPU can load a value from memory into a register, load another value into another register, add the two values together and put the result in a third register, and then copy the third register's value to a location in memory. The width of the register is measured by the number of bits it can hold, which, in turn, determines the range of values it can hold. The larger the register width, the more powerful the computer. Therefore, register width is used to describe CPUs. The 8088 is an 8-bit CPU, the 80286 and 386SX are 16-bit CPUs, and the 486 and Pentium CPUs are 32-bit CPUs. Numeric coprocessors usually have 80-bit registers. Many popular high-end graphics cards have dedicated 128-bit processors, meaning the processors use 128-bit registers to manipulate graphics data.

registry An essential component of Windows 95/98 and later versions holding the system configuration files including settings, preferences, and information about installed hardware and software.

resolution A measure of the sharpness or granularity of an image or monitor, usually expressed as a number of horizontal pixels multiplied by a number of vertical pixels.

RF interference Most electrical devices produce high frequency radio signals that can interfere with other devices, from your monitor to your neighbor's garage door opener. PC designers seek to shield cases so that RF does not escape.

RGB The red-green-blue specification describes one way in which colors are displayed on a monitor. This is an additive scheme; if all three colors are displayed at full intensity, the screen is white. *CMYK* (cyan, magenta, yellow, black) is a subtractive technology used in many color printers, which mixes colors to produce other hues.

ribbon cable A flat multiconductor cable used primarily under the covers of the computer to connect peripheral devices, such as disk drives to controllers.

RIMM A module for Rambus memory.

RISC Reduced Instruction Set Computing. A design for microprocessor logic that concentrates on rapid and efficient processing of a relatively small and simple set of instructions that can be executed in a minimum number of instruction cycles. *See also* CISC.

RJ-11 The male connector on a telephone cable, usually with four wires, that mates with a wall port or the input port on a telephone modem.

RJ-45 The male connector on an Ethernet cable, with as many as eight wires. It is similar in appearance to an RJ-11, but slightly larger and incompatible.

RLL Run Length Limited. This is a method of encoding data on hard disk surfaces that can record more data in the same amount of space than MFM can record. It is similar to MFM, but does not require clock bits. Instead, it uses a rule about the number of consecutive zeroes written in any data stream. IBM developed the method for use in mainframes. It is as reliable as MFM for recording data, but the recording surface must be very good. If the hard disk is not RLL-certified by the manufacturer of the drive, don't use an RLL controller on the drive. *See also* ESDI, MFM, and SCSI.

ROM Read Only Memory. Recorded once, at the factory, ROM is the ideal way to hold instructions that should never change, such as the instructions your computer requires to access the disk drive. *See also* BIOS and RAM.

ROM address The memory address location within a ROM chip, often used to mean the first address. When a computer boots, its BIOS ROM searches for any additional ROM chips in its system, reading the setup information from each ROM chip that it finds. A typical ROM is 8K, 16K, or 32K long. Therefore, it uses an 8K, 16K, or 32K block of memory addresses, beginning at the ROM address (the starting address). No two ROMs can be at the same starting address, and their blocks of memory cannot overlap. ROMs are on your video card (EGA and above), hard drive controller and/or SCSI host adapter, and many other expansion cards. No ROMs exist for parallel or serial ports, game ports, or ordinary floppy controllers because the computer already knows how to use these simple devices; the instructions are stored in the computer's BIOS ROM.

ROM BIOS *See* BIOS.

ROM shadow A technique — used in systems with CPUs that can virtualize memory addresses — in which BIOS code is copied from slower ROM to faster RAM at boot. The RAM addresses are virtualized to impersonate the ROM addresses, and the BIOS is then executed from RAM.

router A device that connects network hubs together. A valuable modern router includes a firewall to prevent unwanted intrusion by hackers.

RS-232C One recommended standard set by the electronics industry for serial data transmission. *See* COM port.

sampling rate The number of times per second a sound card grabs a sample of an analog sound in order to create a digitized version or image of the sound. The higher the sampling rate, the better the sound.

scanner A device that converts printed or written text or illustrations into a digital file that can be manipulated by the computer. A modern *optical character recognition* application can convert text in the digital image into characters than can be worked with by a word processor.

SCSI Small Computer System Interface. An intelligent interface that exchanges data. A 50-pin connector is used in SCSI devices. Up to seven devices, including the SCSI controller itself, can be attached to the SCSI bus via a single SCSI connection. The interface lets the drive manufacturer use any encoding scheme it chooses. However, SCSI is not supported in a standard way by the BIOS in PCs, often posing interesting installation problems.

SDRAM Synchronous Dynamic Random Access Memory. An advanced form of dynamic RAM memory that can be synchronized with the processor's clock, eliminating wait states and latency. Unlike DRAM, SDRAM uses flowing current instead of a stored charge, eliminating the need for continual refreshing. SDRAM permits up to 1.1 GBps data transfer while DDR SDRAM (Double Data Rate SDRAM) doubles the rate to 2.1 GBps.

secondary The second ATA/IDE channel of a computer. Each channel supports a chain of one or two devices, configured as master and slave. *See also* primary.

sector The smallest unit of storage that can be allocated by a hard disk — usually 512 bytes.

seek time The length of time for a hard disk head to find a track, expressed in milliseconds (ms). Although fast seek times are often touted as an indication of a fast hard disk, seek time alone is rather useless as an expression of hard disk speed. Transfer rate is more meaningful. *See also* settle time.

segment An element of the processor's addressing scheme. A segment is a unit of contiguous, position-independent space.

serial Connector on a computer to which a serial device is attached. Serial devices include modems, mice, and certain printers.

Serial ATA A standard for interfacing computers to storage devices such as hard drives and DVD drives. SATA version 1 is capable of 1.5 Gbps, however the standard is scalable to 2x (3 Gbps) and 4x (6 Gbps). Current ATA interfaces transfer data in parallel, requiring wide, flat cables. SATA uses thinner cables and smaller connectors, which can improve air circulation inside computer cases and potentially allow the use of smaller cases. Abbreviated as SATA.

serial communications The transmission of information between devices one bit at a time over a single line. Serial communications can be synchronous (controlled by a clock or timing device) or asynchronous (managed by control signals that accompany the information). For modern machines, nearly all serial communication is asynchronous.

server A computer or other device that manages a component of a network. A *file server* holds shared files; a *print server* manages printers, and a *network server* controls communication functions of the network.

settle time A measurement of how long it takes the heads to begin reading the hard disk once the specified track is found. *See also* seek time.

setup A program used to store hardware configuration information in the CMOS chip of a modern machine.

SGRAM Synchronous Graphics RAM. A variant of SDRAM optimized for video processing. SGRAM is single-ported, so the processor cannot write to memory while an image is being refreshed.

shadowing A method to improve performance of a computer by copying some or all of the contents of ROM to faster RAM.

signal-to-noise ratio The relationship of a meaningful audio or video signal to background noise or interference; the greater the difference (the higher the ratio) the better the quality of the resulting output.

SIMM Single Inline Memory Modules are units that can hold a group of individual memory chips — typically eight or nine — in a single unit that plugs into a socket. A common current design is the 72-pin SIMM, which can hold from 1 to 64MB, delivered in a single 32-bit data path.

single user An operating system that allows only one user to use the computer at a time.

single user, multitask A version of single user that allows only one user to perform multiple tasks simultaneously. Examples include OS/2, Windows 3.1, and VM/386. *See* single user.

single user, single task A version of single user that allows only one user at a time to do one task at a time. DOS is an example.

SIP Single Inline Package. A design for holding an electronic component in which all connectors emerge from one side of the package. *See also* DIP.

slave A secondary device in a chain or other connection; the primary device is the *master*.

Slot A The attachment device for older AMD Athlon and Thunderbird CPUs, physically identical to but electrically incompatible with Slot 1, which was used for Intel microprocessors.

Smart Media A form of flash memory used in digital cameras and audio devices; it appears to the operating system as if it were a hard drive. Smart Media was first known as *SSFDC (solid state floppy disk card)*. Smart Media cards can be installed in readers attached to PCs for the download of information and can also be mounted in special PC Cards for the same purpose. *See also* CompactFlash.

software interrupt A request for service generated by a program.

SOHO Small Office/Home Office. A designation used by some computer manufacturers to identify a class of devices intended for small businesses.

south bridge An I/O controller hub that is part of a modern PC's chipset. The processor bus connects through the PCI bus to the south bridge, which controls the IDE bus that transports data to and from storage devices. Other elements of the south bridge include the USB serial subsystem, a bridge from PCI to the older ISA bus still used by some devices, the keyboard/mouse controller, power management, and various other features, including support for Plug-and-Play technology. *See also* North Bridge.

SRAM Static Random Access Memory chips that do not require refresh as long as they are powered. They are quick, but expensive, and, therefore, are usually not made to hold as much information as a DRAM chip. SRAMs are often used as cache memory.

stack A scratch pad for the microprocessor. When the microprocessor is interrupted in the middle of a task by a more urgent task, it saves notes to itself about the contents of registers, and so on. These notes are essential if the microprocessor is to resume the first task where it left off.

start/stop bits Signaling bits that are part of a communications frame, attached to the beginning and end of a character before it is transmitted by a modem.

state Condition, as in On-Off, High-Low, or Zero-One. In computers, this means the particular way that all memory locations, registers, and logic gates are set. State is also used casually to indicate the particular condition and status of the computer.

step rate On a floppy disk drive, the amount of time required for the read/write head to move from one track to another.

ST412/ST506 The names of the original hard drives in microcomputers. The drives are no longer made, but the interface Seagate developed for them is still used. This interface is used on inexpensive XT and AT drives and controllers. *See also* MFM and RLL.

surface mount A circuit-board design in which chips are directly attached to the board instead of being soldered in pin holes or attached through sockets. In theory, a surface mount design is less susceptible to problems caused by bad connections. However, a failed chip often requires replacement of the entire circuit board.

surge protector A device to protect electrical components from damage caused by overvoltage (surges). A more sophisticated *uninterruptible power supply (UPS)* also protects against undervoltage (brownouts) and a short power outage.

SVGA (Super VGA) The most common graphics standard for modern machines, an enhancement of VGA.

system The memory in the computer that DOS (or the chosen operating system) can use for the OS, applications, and data. On most DOS computers, this is also called conventional memory, and it has a maximum memory of 640K. DOS 5.0 and later versions, and DR DOS 6.0 can also use high memory (the first 64K of extended memory), so these operating systems have an effective system memory of 704K.

system boot parameters Many BIOS chips permit the user to specify a number of options at boot. These include bus speed, whether the Num Lock function is on or off, and boot sequence, which establishes whether the PC boots from the A: or B: floppy drive, or from the C: drive.

system files The hidden files necessary to boot the operating system.

SYSTEM.INI A Windows file that contains information about the hardware environment. *See* WIN.INI.

tape drive A data storage device that records data on a moving tape, like an audio tape recorder in concept. Tape drives are used for data backup.

target A SCSI device — including both peripherals and the SCSI host adapter — that performs an operation requested by an initiator.

task The job (usually an application program) that the computer does. A task is not the same as what the computer is doing. One person can simultaneously perform multiple tasks on a single computer. *See* multitasking.

TCP/IP Transmission Control Protocol/Internet Protocol. The underlying specification for identification of devices and packets of information on the Internet.

terabyte A trillion bytes; for RAM, 1,024 gigabytes — or more precisely, 1,099,511,627,776 bytes. Abbreviated as *TB*.

termination The first and last device on a SCSI bus must have a resistor pack that indicates it is the end of the line.

texels Pixels with a third layer of information defining the pixel's texture.

text mode A display mode in which the adapter converts ASCII character data directly into display information.

timeout The operating system or BIOS is usually instructed to end a process when a predetermined amount of time passes without response.

token ring A configuration for a network that places each device at a point on a continuous circle. The network carries tokens — special sequences of bits — and devices attach blocks of data to them for a circuit around the circle to the intended recipient.

tower An upright case for a computer.

tpi Tracks per inch, a measurement of the *track density* of recorded data on a rotating media such as a hard disk drive or CD.

track A magnetic ring of information on a disk drive, somewhat like a groove on an old vinyl record. On a sequential data storage device, such as a tape drive, tracks run parallel to the edge of the medium. *See also* sector.

track density *See* tpi.

track skew factor When a read/write head reaches the end of a track, and if information is sequential from one track to the next, the head must move to the next track in order to continue. If the next track starts at the sector where the preceding track ends, the disk drive must wait until the disk nearly completes spinning around before it can begin reading new information. Instead, most disk drives skew the starting point of each track from the other track by a few sectors so that information can be read and written in a nearly continuous stream.

track-to-track access time How long it takes for the heads of a drive to move from one track to another. This number determines much of the speed with which data is read from a drive.

transfer rate The amount of data, measured in bytes per second, that a computer can read from or write to a device, such as a hard disk, a modem, or a network.

transient response In a power supply, this is the time needed for the output voltage to return to the normal range following a major change load. The faster the transient response the lower the risk of read/write errors during access.

true color A term applied to display adapters or monitors capable of displaying 24-bit color, which is about 16.8 million (technically, 16,777,216) colors.

TSR Terminate and Stay Resident. A DOS program that pops back into use when a hot key sequence is pressed. Sidekick is an example. TSRs sometimes present problems when they clash with each other or programs loaded after them, and they cause symptoms that you might think are hardware related.

TWAIN An industry interface that works between image-editing software and scanners or other capture devices. One explanation for the name is that it is an acronym for Technology Without An Interesting Name.

twisted pair A cabling design that uses two thin unshielded wires twisted around each other to somewhat reduce interference. Twisted-pair cables are used for telephones and basic Ethernet local area networks. More sophisticated systems use coaxial or fiber optic cables, which are more expensive and difficult to install.

UART The Universal Asynchronous Receiver Transmitter chip set manages communications through a serial port. The original PC used an 8250A UART, which proved incapable of handling high-speed data transfer. Modern machines use the 16550 UART. Many older machines can be upgraded to use the new chip either through a direct swap of chips or by disabling the existing serial port and installing a new serial card in the expansion bus.

Ultra ATA *See* ATA/33, ATA/66, ATA/100, and ATA/133.

Ultra DMA *See* ATA/33, ATA/66, ATA/100, and ATA/133.

UMA The Upper Memory Area is PC memory with addresses between 640K and 1,024K (1MB).

UMB Upper Memory Blocks are ranges of memory located within the UMA.

uninterruptible power supply A device that combines a surge protector, a large battery, and electronic circuitry to shield a PC or other system from surges, undervoltages, and short power outages.

Unix An operating system developed by AT&T in the early 1970s to run its computerized phone switching system on PDP-11s. This operating system is known for low overhead with easy connecting of different tasks. Unlike DOS, Unix is a true multiuser, multitasking system.

upper memory Memory located between 640K and 1,024K (1MB). Divided into blocks (upper memory blocks), modern machines can use upper memory for the system BIOS, video BIOS, video memory, shadowing, adapter ROM, additional device drivers, and TSRs. It is sometimes also called reserved memory or high DOS memory. This usage disappeared when programmers discovered they could address the first 64K of extended memory and Microsoft created a driver called HIMEM.SYS.

URL Uniform Resource Locator. The global address system for files and resources attached to the World Wide Web, otherwise known as the Internet.

USB Universal Serial Bus. The high-speed external bus that allows easy connection and removal of devices while a computer is running. The original specifications of USB 1.0 and USB 1.1 have been supplanted by the considerably faster USB 2.0 model.

USRT Universal Synchronous Receiver-Transmitter. A synchronous equivalent of the UART, it is only used on PCs that have been adapted for use in synchronous communication applications.

VBI Vertical blanking interval. A short piece of a video field originally intended to account for the time an old television required to return the electron beam from the lower right corner to the upper right to trace a new frame. Today, the VBI is used to carry information including frame numbers and captions.

VGA Video Graphics Array. An advanced analog display standard capable of displaying as many as 256K colors at 640-×-480-pixel resolution. The Super VGA standard has superseded it in the market.

virtual address An alias address used to reference memory locations. In shadowing, it enables calls to a particular BIOS address to instead call the shadowed copy that resides in faster RAM at a different physical address. When using expanded memory, the memory management unit translates the virtual address to a physical address.

virtual memory A means to enable a system to work with a larger memory than it is permitted to use or with a memory that is larger than the memory that actually exists. Paged memory is one type of virtual memory. *See* EMS.

virtual mode A special protected mode of the 80386 and later CPUs that enables them to run multiple virtual real-mode segments. This is the mode Windows 3.1 uses for DOS windows.

virus A piece of code that corrupts your PC without your permission or knowledge.

VL-bus The VL-bus or VESA local bus is a high-speed data connection between the CPU and peripheral devices, developed by the Video Electronics Standards Association. It has been largely replaced in modern machines by the PCI bus.

VoIP Voice over Internet Protocol or Voice over IP. The technology that allows use of the Internet or other IP networks for telephone and other voice applications.

voltage spike An electrical geyser.

voltage surge A big electrical wave.

VRAM A special type of display adapter memory that enables simultaneous read and write operations.

Vx Modem communications standard.

WAN Wide area network. A physically connected network spread over a large area.

wait state A pause programmed into the operations of a microprocessor so that the CPU will wait for memory to catch up with it. The faster the memory, the fewer wait states necessary.

warm boot Restarting a computer without turning off the power or pressing the hardware reset button; that is, using the Ctrl + Alt + Delete combination. *See also* cold boot.

Weitek processor A dinosaur-era non-Intel math coprocessor that can be used with some systems by some applications.

WIN.INI A file containing configuration information about Windows applications and the user environment, such as fonts, colors, and general appearance. Used in versions through Windows 3.1.

word Depending on the processor design, the standard size for a chunk of data manipulated by the CPU. For 16-bit computers, a word is made up of two bytes. For 32-bit computers, a word is made up of four bytes.

WORM drive Write Once, Read Many. A WORM data storage device can be written to once and then read from as needed; the definition is now part of CD-R.

write precompensation As the head on a hard disk starts to write on the smaller inner tracks, data errors can occur if the data is recorded exactly as it was on the larger, outer tracks. Write precompensation boosts write current on the innermost tracks, providing clean, clear data storage.

Xenix A version of Unix developed for microcomputers that is not commonly used today.

XMS Extended Memory Specification. *See* EMS.

XT class A relic PC based on the 8088 or 8086 processor.

yottabyte 1,000,000,000,000,000,000,000,000 bytes, or 1,024 zettabytes. Abbreviated as *YB*.

z-buffering Used by advanced graphics cards to speed up the display of 3-D scenes. Z-buffering keeps track of each pixel's depth so that the graphics card can replace the color of that pixel if a 3-D object of less depth moves into that screen position. Hidden surface removal also helps speed up 3-D scenes because it minimizes the object pixels whose depths must be compared for z-buffering.

zettabyte 1,000,000,000,000,000,000,000 bytes, or 1,024 exabytes. Abbreviated as *ZB*.

ZIF socket A Zero Insertion Force socket is used on many modern motherboards to enable easy removal and replacement of certain computer chips, including the CPU.

Zip drive A popular design for a large-capacity removable storage device, holding 100 or 250MB on a platter about the size of a floppy disk.

Notes

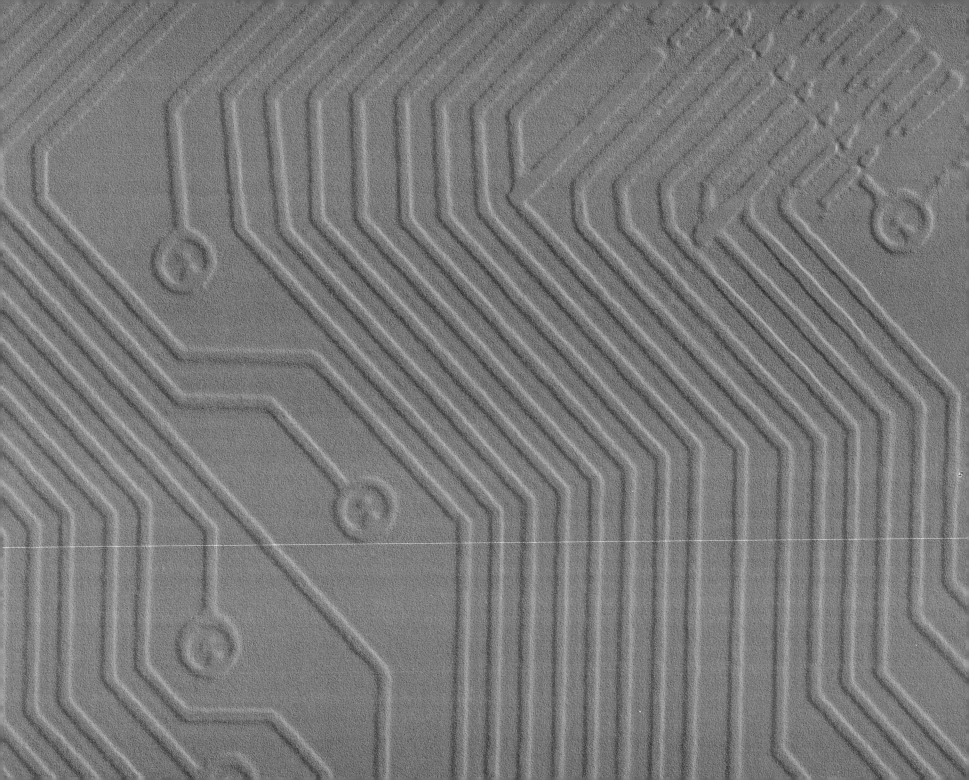

Index

Continued

Continued

Continued

Continued

Continued

Continued

Continued

Wiley Publishing, Inc. End-User License Agreement

5. Limited Warranty.

  (a) WPI warrants that the Software and Software Media are free from defects in materials and workmanship under normal use for a period of sixty (60) days from the date of purchase of this Book. If WPI receives notification within the warranty period of defects in materials or workmanship, WPI will replace the defective Software Media.

  (b) WPI AND THE AUTHOR(S) OF THE BOOK DISCLAIM ALL OTHER WARRANTIES, EXPRESS OR IMPLIED, INCLUDING WITHOUT LIMITATION IMPLIED WARRANTIES OF MERCHANTABILITY AND FITNESS FOR A PARTICULAR PURPOSE, WITH RESPECT TO THE SOFTWARE, THE PROGRAMS, THE SOURCE CODE CONTAINED THEREIN, AND/OR THE TECHNIQUES DESCRIBED IN THIS BOOK. WPI DOES NOT WARRANT THAT THE FUNCTIONS CONTAINED IN THE SOFTWARE WILL MEET YOUR REQUIREMENTS OR THAT THE OPERATION OF THE SOFTWARE WILL BE ERROR FREE.

  (c) This limited warranty gives you specific legal rights, and you may have other rights that vary from jurisdiction to jurisdiction.

6. Remedies.

  (a) WPI's entire liability and your exclusive remedy for defects in materials and workmanship shall be limited to replacement of the Software Media, which may be returned to WPI with a copy of your receipt at the following address: Software Media Fulfillment Department, Attn.: Fix Your Own PC, Eighth Edition, Wiley Publishing, Inc., 10475 Crosspoint Blvd., Indianapolis, IN 46256, or call 1-800-762-2974. Please allow four to six weeks for delivery. This Limited Warranty is void if failure of the Software Media has resulted from accident, abuse, or misapplication. Any replacement Software Media will be warranted for the remainder of the original warranty period or thirty (30) days, whichever is longer.

  (b) In no event shall WPI or the author be liable for any damages whatsoever (including without limitation damages for loss of business profits, business interruption, loss of business information, or any other pecuniary loss) arising from the use of or inability to use the Book or the Software, even if WPI has been advised of the possibility of such damages.

  (c) Because some jurisdictions do not allow the exclusion or limitation of liability for consequential or incidental damages, the above limitation or exclusion may not apply to you.

7. U.S. Government Restricted Rights. Use, duplication, or disclosure of the Software for or on behalf of the United States of America, its agencies and/or instrumentalities "U.S. Government" is subject to restrictions as stated in paragraph (c)(1)(ii) of the Rights in Technical Data and Computer Software clause of DFARS 252.227-7013, or subparagraphs (c) (1) and (2) of the Commercial Computer Software - Restricted Rights clause at FAR 52.227-19, and in similar clauses in the NASA FAR supplement, as applicable.

8. General. This Agreement constitutes the entire understanding of the parties and revokes and supersedes all prior agreements, oral or written, between them and may not be modified or amended except in a writing signed by both parties hereto that specifically refers to this Agreement. This Agreement shall take precedence over any other documents that may be in conflict herewith. If any one or more provisions contained in this Agreement are held by any court or tribunal to be invalid, illegal, or otherwise unenforceable, each and every other provision shall remain in full force and effect.

CD Installation Instructions

What's on the CD-ROM?

Here you find information on the contents of the CD that accompanies this book. For the latest and greatest information, please refer to the ReadMe file located at the root of the CD. Here is what you will find:

- System Requirements
- Using the CD with Windows
- What's on the CD
- Troubleshooting

System Requirements

Make sure that your computer meets the minimum system requirements listed in this section. If your computer doesn't match up to most of these requirements, you may have a problem using the contents of the CD.

For Windows 9x, Windows 2000, Windows NT4 (with SP 4 or later), Windows Me, Windows XP, or Windows Vista:

- PC with a Pentium processor running at 120 Mhz or faster
- At least 32 MB of total RAM installed on your computer; for best performance, we recommend at least 64 MB
- Ethernet network interface card (NIC) or modem with a speed of at least 28,800 bps
- A CD-ROM drive

Using the CD with Windows

To view the contents of the CD, follow these steps:

1. Insert the CD into your computer's CD-ROM drive. The license agreement appears.

   Note to Windows users: The interface won't launch if you have Autorun disabled. In that case, click Start➪Run. (For Windows Vista, click Start➪All Programs➪Accessories➪Run). In the dialog box that appears, type **D:\start.exe**. (Replace D with the proper letter if your CD drive uses a different letter. If you don't know which letter to use, check to see which letter your CD drive is associated with when you click the My Computer icon.) Click OK.

2. Read through the license agreement; then click the Accept button if you want to use the CD.

   The CD interface appears. The interface allows you to view the video clips and bonus content with just a click of a button or two.

What's on the CD

The following sections provide a summary of the software and other materials you'll find on the CD.

Videos

You have, at your disposal, nearly ten videos for reference. The CD shows you hot to set up and prepare for working on your PC, as well as how to add memory, clean your machine, and replace a hard drive. You can also view clips on replacing the power supply and adding an internal audio CD or DVD drive. If you don't yet feel comfortable opening your machine, you can sit back and watch the innards tour.

Appendixes

The appendixes contain references to some of the essential — and arcane — communications that you receive from a PC in distress, a listing of hardware and software suppliers and manufacturers, and an encyclopedia of cable connectors.

Also, let your fingers do the walking though 11 flowcharts that help you figure out the source of problems in your system.

The charts begin with diagnosing a dead machine and move on to specific problems with floppy disks, hard disk drives, parallel ports, serial ports, multimedia devices, and video quality. And finally, there's a guide to decisionmaking after an electrical disaster.

Each of the charts includes a cross-reference to the appropriate chapter of this book for details on troubleshooting, repair, and replacement.

Appendixes on the CD:

- Appendix A: Troubleshooting Charts
- Appendix B: Encyclopedia of Cables and Connectors
- Appendix C: Hardware and Software Toolkit
- Appendix D: Modern Machine Diagnostic Codes
- Appendix E: Senior-Citizen and Dinosaur Diagnostic Codes
- Appendix F: IRQ, DMA, and Memory Assignments

Bonus chapters

Some people have a hard time letting go. The bonus chapters are for you if your machine qualifies as a senior citizen (Pentium III processors, Pentium II chips, the original Intel Pentium series as well as the Intel 486 family, in DX, DX-2, and DX-4 versions) or a dinosaur (8088, 8086, 80286, 386, and 486SX microprocessors — including IBM PCs, PC-XTs, and PC-ATs, and clone machines using the same chips). On the CD you can find senior-citizen and dinosaur data that picks up where the book's Chapters 5–15, and 18–20 leave off.

eBook version of *Fix Your Own PC,* Eighth Edition

The complete text of this book is on the CD in Adobe's Portable Document Format (PDF). You can read and search through the file with the Adobe Acrobat Reader (also included on the CD).

Troubleshooting

If you have difficulty installing or using any of the materials on the companion CD, try the following solutions:

- **Turn off any anti-virus software that you may have running.** Installers sometimes mimic virus activity and can make your computer incorrectly believe that it is being infected by a virus. (Be sure to turn the anti-virus software back on later.)
- **Close all running programs.** The more programs you're running, the less memory is available to other programs. Installers also typically update files and programs; if you keep other programs running, installation may not work properly.
- **Reference the ReadMe:** Please refer to the ReadMe file located at the root of the CD-ROM for the latest product information at the time of publication.

Customer Care

If you have trouble with the CD-ROM, please call the Wiley Product Technical Support phone number at (800) 762-2974. Outside the United States, call 1(317) 572-3994. You can also contact Wiley Product Technical Support at **http://support.wiley.com**. John Wiley & Sons will provide technical support only for installation and other general quality control items. For technical support on the applications themselves, consult the program's vendor or author.

To place additional orders or to request information about other Wiley products, please call (877) 762-2974.

For more PC know-how and electronics expertise, try these.

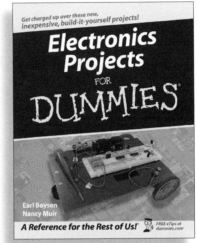
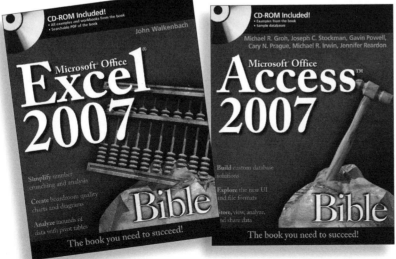
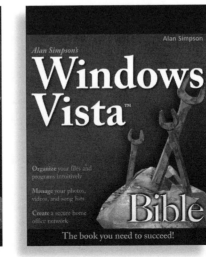

And check out these other books by Corey Sandler.